Conformity, Resistance,
and Self-Determination

Conformity, Resistance, and Self-Determination:
The Individual and Authority

Richard Flacks

University of California
Santa Barbara

LITTLE, BROWN AND COMPANY   Boston

Library of Congress Catalog Card No. 73-9119

First Printing

Published simultaneously in Canada by Little, Brown & Company (Canada) Limited

Printed in the United States of America

PREFACE

When I began working on this book several years ago, I was designing it as a general introduction to the field of social psychology. During these years, however, my own teaching of introductory social psychology as well as my conception of this book changed quite fundamentally. I came to feel that I was less interested in introducing an academic discipline than I was in examining some of the root moral and political problems which gave rise to the discipline in the first place. In particular, I found that the problem of authority was perhaps the central theme in the social psychology which most interested me—and it was certainly the central issue in social relations in the real world, as far as I could tell. The result is a book which is more idiosyncratic, and yet more broadly relevant, than originally planned.

Many of the specific intellectual influences that have shaped my thinking about authority are embodied in the pieces I have selected for inclusion in this volume. Perhaps some will find me guilty of an eclecticism gone wild, but I cannot help but feel that writers as disparate as Mills, Asch, Freud, Goffman, Erikson, Boulding, and Bookchin have each made fundamental contributions to understanding the problem of authority and the individual in the modern age—contributions which must be taken into account, and which may ultimately be synthesized, by a theoretically coherent social psychology of freedom.

This book reflects my way of teaching the first course in social psychology to undergraduates, and it is my hope that others who teach social psychology, either as psychologists or sociologists, may find it of use. But problems of conformity, resistance, and self-determination are, I hope, treated in other courses in sociology, psychology, and political science. I would welcome responses from individuals showing how they use this book and how it might be improved as a tool for treating the issues it raises.

Despite its idiosyncratic character, many people helped me bring this reader into being. Tom Crawford taught social psychology with me at Chicago and planned initially to collaborate with me, until circumstances got in the way. He made many useful criticisms and suggestions at the early stages. I also benefited from a brief teaching collaboration with Charlen Nemeth at Chicago. My understanding of many of the issues treated in this book was shaped by the opportunity of working with Herbert Kelman and Daniel Katz. Working together, politically and intellectually, with Paul Lauter and Florence Howe helped me to focus many of my concerns. I have also benefited greatly from opportunities to read the works of, and to interact with, Stanley Milgram, Kenneth Keniston, Paul Goodman, Marc Pilisuk, and John Seeley.

I am very grateful that Joanne Frankfurt was willing to devote many hours to the details of bringing this book into being. I'm grateful, too, for the kind encouragement and tolerance of editors Al Browne and Milton Johnson at Little Brown. I owe a special debt of thanks to Ian Nielsen of Little Brown without whose help I might never have delivered the manuscript, and to Ken Burke who is an extraordinarily sensitive editor.

This book is dedicated to all Americans who refuse to serve.

September, 1973   RICHARD FLACKS
Santa Barbara, California

CONTENTS

3

GETTING TO KNOW ONE'S PLACE:
Situational Determinants of Compliance   **121**

4

MOVING TOWARD LIBERTY:
Situational Conditions for Disaffection,
Delegitimation, and Resistance   **191**

5

RESPONSES OF AUTHORITIES TO THREAT:
Processes of Deliberate Social Control   **247**

6

ALTERNATIVES TO OBEDIENCE:
Some Conditions for Self-Determination   **281**

Conformity, Resistance,
and Self-Determination:

Under what conditions do men come to want to be free and capable of acting freely? Under what conditions are they willing and able to bear the burdens freedom does impose and to see them less as burdens than as gladly undertaken self-transformations? And on the negative side: Can men be made to want to become cheerful robots?

C. WRIGHT MILLS

If X tells Y to hurt Z, under what conditions will Y carry out the command of X and under what conditions will he refuse?

STANLEY MILGRAM

To be independent is to assert the authentic value of one's own experience; to yield is to deny the evidence of one's senses, to permit oneself to be confused about one's experience, to suppress evidence that cannot be assimilated—to renounce a condition upon which one's capacity to function depends in an essential way. What may be the reasons for these strikingly different reactions?

SOLOMON ASCH

Chapter 1

THE SPECTER OF THE CHEERFUL ROBOT:

The Problem of Authority in Modern Life

Consensus, regulation, and organization are absolutely essential to the survival of the human species. Without agreement on the nature of reality, human beings would be incapable of communication and cooperation. Without rules and the means of their enforcement there could be no trust or safety. Without differentiated allocation of tasks in pursuit of definite goals, the means of survival could not be obtained.

Thus every human settlement has been characterized by collectively held beliefs and values, by a pattern of forms and sanctions, by a structure of roles. Much of this culture, organization, and order arises out of the needs of individuals interacting in daily life. Much of the regulation of daily social life is thus experienced as "natural" (if it is experienced at all). Such constraints do not make us uncomfortable—indeed, we are distressed when they are erased.

The social order, however, is not completely open, nor fluidly responsive, to the needs and experiences of all its members. Fundamental aspects of consensus, regulation, and organization are *imposed* by some members on others. Virtually every social relationship involves some degree of inequality, hierarchy, or stratification in the participants' abilities to regulate terms and outcomes.

In the myriad encounters of daily life, there is a multiplicity of means by which individuals can impose upon others. Indeed, all individuals are at times advantaged and at times disadvantaged; sometimes relatively powerful, sometimes powerless; sometimes dominant and sometimes subordinate.

On the other hand, "civilization" has entailed the *concentration* of advantage, power, and domination. Some members of society are mostly imposed upon, while others have gained great scope for imposition. As the nation-state has arisen, a relatively tiny number of individuals have moved into positions which permit them to regulate the activities of tens of millions of others and to impose death on hundreds of millions. Opposite this tiny dominant minority, there have been, since the dawn of civilization, varying proportions of the populace whose survival depended almost completely upon accepting the regulations imposed upon them. It goes without saying, such profound inequality in exercising control is associated with a similar inequality in enjoying the goods of society.

A remarkable fact about human history is that minorities have been able to dominate majorities for prolonged periods. If, as Marx said, history is the history of class struggle, it is also true, and perhaps more evident, that history is the history of class rule. One of the reasons class rule has been so possible is undoubtedly the capacity and willingness of rulers to use force to quell resistance. But, obviously, neither actual force nor the threat of force sufficiently account for the innumerable instances of stable domination that are presented to us by history and contemporary life. Nor can acquiescence be explained by the additional fact that rulers are able to bestow specific material benefits on those who obey. The truly significant feature of stable domination is that the powerful very often have the capacity to command people to sacrifice their lives and material well-being, while such commands are accepted as "right" by those who suffer death or pain as a result of their obedience.

Throughout history most men have had much of their lives regulated by rulers who were largely unresponsive to their subjects' needs and experiences. And through much of this history, the underlying populations have worshipped, honored, respected, or resigned themselves to these same rulers. These phenomena point to the fact that the stability of the rulers' position depends upon the legitimacy of their power—its "rightness" in the eyes of those subject to it. Throughout history, most men have regarded their own subordination as right and their particular king, emperor, lord, or master as legitimate—even when he was quite unresponsive to their interests.

Thinkers who have analyzed power distinguish between two forms of domination: One form is based upon punishing resistance and rewarding compliance; another is based upon the rulers' claims to "rightness." No social order could last if its structure of control rested solely upon reward and punishment. For one thing, surveillance under such a structure would have to be total, if the individual subjects were to be kept performing the many onerous tasks necessary for collective survival. Second, such a social order would be characterized by continuous fickleness, betrayal, deceit, and competitive struggle, since its members would feel no need to maintain loyalty to those in power.

For a hierarchical structure of control and privilege to persist, those in power must be able to claim justification for their positions and actions. They must claim that their right to control is derived from a source external to themselves; they must deny having arrogated power to themselves and claim to have received it; they must insist that the order they establish and maintain is not arbitrary but validly derived from some set of ideas, principles, traditions, or values. Insofar as the members of a given culture share a common view of the appropriate sources of the right to govern, they will tend to accept claims made in the name of such sources. Power exercised in terms of culturally validated rights to govern, control, or lead is usually called *authority*. To exercise authority is to exercise *legitimate* power. When an individual respects and obeys authority, he may act against his will or against his personal interest, but he does so quite apart from possible punishments or rewards he may receive for resisting or obeying.

This is not to deny that authorities make use of reward and punishment; in the modern state, violence may be legitimately used only by officially constituted authority. But the use of force to maintain the established order is significantly incompatible with the exercise of authority. The more frequently those with power resort to coercion, the more likely it is that their legitimacy is eroding. Authority is at its apex when people speak enthusiastically of their duty, make willing sacrifices, and respond with delight to the sight of their leaders.

Cultures have differed widely in their notions of the appropriate sources of authority; but as Max Weber demonstrated several decades ago, it is possible to identify three broad types of authority based upon varying sources of legitimacy. One broad type Weber called *traditional:* The right to rule in many cultures is accorded to particular family lineages or is otherwise a birthright. The source of such rights is typically divine or supernatural. Legitimacy comes into question only when the lines of descent have become problematical. If the ruler establishes a legitimate claim to being the rightful ruler, there is no question. Thus, no actions of the ruler—no matter how arbitrary, stupid, or atrocious— can negate his right to rule.

A second type of authority Weber called *rational-legal:* The right to rule in some cultures is accorded to those who demonstrate some competence to do so. The actions of authority are definitely circumscribed and limited by constitutions, laws, and norms; legitimacy depends upon adherence to the constitution. The right to rule can therefore be negated when the ruler acts outside the law, exceeds his authority, or becomes incompetent. Succession to authority is regulated legally, and some process of selection usually occurs.

Finally Weber distinguished a third type of authority, called the *charismatic:* The right to rule is given to one who embodies the most deeply held values and aspirations of a people; his legitimacy depends on his continuing ability to be such an embodiment, to represent salvation or fulfillment for those who follow him. Charismatic authority tends to arise at moments of crisis—when tradition has been exhausted and laws are inadequate. It demands from its adherents a kind of commitment which is incompatible with mundane, daily life—intense devotion, sacrifice, and collective mobilization. According to Weber, such authority is therefore bound eventually to be "routinized"—that is, to be succeeded by a new tradition or a new legal structure as the basis for stable authority.

Weber's types of legitimacy are ideal or "pure." Any concrete case is likely to be a mixture of rational, traditional, and charismatic sources of legitimation. The American president, for example, derives his authority from his constitutionally established office and preserves his legitimacy only insofar as he acts according to law. However, the president is not selected by objective criteria of competence but by popular election, and that process depends in part on the ability to win a popular following on the basis of personal qualities. Moreover, presidents have been able to add to their authority because of their personal qualities—that is, because they have been able to achieve charismatic legitimation.

Because the particular criteria of legitimacy are likely to be deeply intertwined with the central values, patterns, and institutions of a culture, legitimated power has the capacity to elicit forms of obedience more complete, more reliable, more intense, and more durable than any other form of domination, control, or influence. In fact, no other human relationship has the capacity to bring about more complete self-sacrifice and self-abnegation, more wholehearted deference and submission, than the relationship between legitimate ruler and his subjects.

Ultimately, however, particular states and their forms of legitimacy decline. Every structure of authority has ultimately been confronted by disaffection, resistance, and challenge. Many structures have been overthrown by once enthusiastically obedient subjects; others have lost the capacity to defend themselves against external attack; still others have had to undergo fundamental self-transformation. Particular structures of authority are destroyed; but the idea of authority survives, and old forms are replaced by new ones. Political theorists, from Aristotle on, have tried to account for this pervasive need for authority and obedience. Essentially, they have agreed that human beings must band together for survival and fulfillment; in so doing they must simultaneously defend themselves against assault from without and from within their group. Internal conflict is inevitable, and it must be managed so that the group can be maintained while the needs of all members receive consideration. The needs for security and order seem to be the minimum requirements for the rise of authority and the consequent obligations to obey.

One type of theory (perhaps best represented by Hobbes) takes order and security as irreducible values; accordingly, any state which protects these values deserves obedience, since the possibility of total civil strife is a very likely outcome of disobedience. This theory apparently has its exponents in American public life even today, but it has not been the motif of most political thought in the modern era.

AUTHORITY IN MODERN SOCIETY

The central idea of the modern era is that authority cannot claim legitimacy on the traditional grounds of God-given right, natural law, or inheritance. Instead, authority must base its legitimacy on reason. This means that the performance of those in authority can and should be judged according to rational criteria, and that obedience to authority can only be expected when the criteria are reasonably satisfied.

The purpose of the state is to serve the needs for safety, security, and order, and those who govern the state are accountable to their subjects with respect to the performance of their duties. Furthermore, the purposes of government go beyond mere physical protection and the management of conflict; other goals involve providing a variety of goods and services that promote the general welfare of the people. The administration of order and the distribution of services cannot be done arbitrarily—the acts of government must be carried out with justice. Indeed, a central purpose of government is to promote justice.

In short, the modern idea holds that the legitimacy of authority depends upon the subjects' evaluation of how it is performed. In other words, legitimacy flows from the consent of the governed. The most influential subspecies of this view of authority, moreover, is the idea of democracy. Democratic theorists are perhaps able to concede that popular consent might be given to an elite; they may agree that, in theory, it is possible for a small group of men to govern rationally. But democratic theorists since Aristotle have strongly doubted the likelihood that such an elite could be created. Instead, the theorists have argued that legitimacy depends not only on the consent of the governed but on their systematic participation in government. Democratic authority is likely to be the most rational system because only through the regular participation of citizens can those in authority know what is required of them. The idea of democracy furthermore embodies the assumption that human beings are perfectible—capable of an ever-increasing talent for rational judgment and action. But such growth of individuals and collectivities depends upon their ability to practice self-government. The more men depend upon the decisions of rulers, the less likely they are to develop their own potentialities and reason.

To these fundamental precepts of liberal-rational-democratic theory, we can add one more. Authority, under the above principles, is to be strictly limited in scope. The point of government is to free men to act in behalf of their private interests. Such liberty requires that government protect order, provide security, and allocate resources. The actions of government can be prescribed by laws enacted by majority rule with due concern for the rights of minorities. Men must form a political community; but it must be a limited one, and its ultimate aim is to permit each member the maximum degree of individual freedom. In daily life, men are mostly strangers pitted against each other in competitive struggle; yet that competition, properly regulated, is the most rational way to secure the welfare of all.

According to the liberal-rational idea, authority is grounded in each individual. Ultimately only the individual knows what is right for him, understands his own interests, and can determine the meaning of his existence. Individual fulfillment depends upon association with other individuals, and therefore a governing authority is necessary. But that authority is accountable to and must be responsive to the individuals who are governed by it. Furthermore, it is to be continuously scrutinized with skepticism and mistrust to prevent it from encroaching upon that which is most authentic and precious—the freedom of each individual to develop his potentialities and pursue his interests.

This theory of authority is, of course, a normative one—a vision of the good society. But in many respects, it is intended to be factual. Liberalism embodied the crucial insight that authority always ultimately depends upon consent, no matter how sacred its claimed origins or how divinely inspired its commands purport to be. Despotic or corrupted regimes have never been eternal and have never been able perpetually to secure enthusiastic loyalty or willing obedience from the subjects who suffered under them. One intended paradox of liberal theory is that the authority based on its precepts would be the strongest of all, despite the fact that the theory also legitimated harsh criticism of authority. Authority grounded in democratic consent would be the most fully legitimated in history; not only would it be intimately bound up with popular support, but it would also be strengthened rather than undermined by open criticism.

Liberalism advocated a society based on rationalism and individualism and recognized that such a society was coming into existence. Western culture, once grounded in religious and traditional belief, was in fact being replaced by a culture grounded in scientific and technical practice. Communal and kinship ties were being broken by industrialization and urbanization, and a society of strangers was, in fact, being created. In short, a total transformation of Western civilization was going on, requiring a transformation of authority—and the theorists of liberalism in the eighteenth and nineteenth centuries attempted both to diagnose and prescribe for this situation.

Two centuries later, we inhabit a world that is the outcome of this transformation. The rationalist temper and the democratic vision, coupled with vast technological development and social upheaval, have been quite successful in eradicating the traditional, sacred, absolutist modes of authority. Everywhere in the world the Old Regime has toppled; few new regimes can claim authority without claiming to be rational and responsive. In societies newly liberated from traditional authority, nationalist aspirations replace religion as the source of communal identity. In these societies, enthusiastic devotion to self-sacrificing national duty is evident, and the people look to the national leader as a source of personal meaning and collective definition. Modern-day leaders—Mao, Ho, Fidel, for example—unlike past rulers of great personal power, claim that their authority derives from the people. They follow simple life-styles, present themselves as selflessly dedicated to serving the people, and as the enemies of privilege and injustice. The degree of selflessness and dutifulness present in China or North Vietnam is a constant source of wonderment to the Western visitor. In the West, we have become used to viewing those in authority with profound suspicion; we expect them to lie regularly, to be substantially ignorant of the needs and feelings of ordinary men, to be largely incapable of solving fundamental problems, and to articulate platitudes rather than insights concerning the human condition. In other words, in the fully developed industrial societies, legitimacy of authority is based on very minimal expectations of competence and legality and is highly tenuous. In these societies, social trust is quite generally low. On the whole, men rely upon themselves and their immediate social circles for self-definition. They conceive of their own private interests as more fundamental and real than the common interests advocated by the state. They have come to view selfless obedience to national authority as dangerous, unhealthy, and quite possibly fraudulent. One of the evident accomplishments of liberalism, then, has been the creation of profound suspicion and questioning of the claims of authority. The price of this situation is a very high degree of moral incoherence, social fragmentation, and political privatism; yet the liberal can claim that one of the great benefits of the situation is that mobilizing the masses for destructive (as well as constructive) ends becomes very difficult. Never has the willingness and freedom to criticize or defy authority been so high.

The erosion of authority is, in part, a result of the liberal-rational-democratic vision. And yet, it would be extremely hard to claim that the essence of that vision is now embodied in a society like the United States of America. This nation can hardly be said to consist of free and equal citizens actively engaged in the process of self-government. Alongside the sense that authority is eroding grows the sense that the power of those who possess authority is increasing—both in scope and concentration. Our time is said to be characterized by a loss of respect for authority and by a decline in collective responsibility and shared meanings; at the same time, the claim is also made that our time is characterized by the increasing inability of ordinary people to control their fate and influence the decisions that affect them.

Our everyday images of authority have been profoundly affected by the following kinds of situations.

—A national leadership can issue directives for the annihilation of all available members of several ethnic groups. As a result of these directives, technicians search for the most efficient means of mass annihilation, which are then put to use by thousands of officials assigned to the task. Some ten million human beings are in this way killed in a four-year period. Those engaged in this task later justify their actions by declaring that they were "only following orders."

—A national leadership can issue directives to eliminate the war-making potential of an enemy country during war, while minimizing cost to itself. The preferred technique for doing this is the use of aircraft to drop explosives, chemicals, and other devices. Scientists search for the most effective means of destruction and for the most efficient means of detecting desirable targets. The result is the calculated and accidental killing of tens of thousands of noncombat-ant civilians, the destruction of thousands of acres of crops and fertile lands, homes, and settlements. Millions of persons are made homeless and miserable refugees. Most of these consequences are officially denied by those in authority, who feel they are not obligated to justify their actions. Those engaged in aerial bombardment justify their participation by saying that they were "just doing their job."

—Two human beings, who happen to be the heads of state of the two most technologically developed nations, can issue directives which will lead to the obliteration of all human life within minutes. Scientists, technicians, and others are actively engaged in efforts to make this destructive capability increasingly reliable. The decision to place all civilian life in total jeopardy was made in the interest of "national security." Steps are taken to ensure that if the order to launch this holocaust is given it will be carried out.

Those persons who are in authority in the major nation-states today have a degree of power never before available in human history. Because of technological development, they virtually have total power over life and death and can expect their commands to be efficiently and reliably implemented as no previous authorities could. Because of the development of military and governmental bureaucracy and other modern organizational processes, authorities can deploy men and resources on a scale and with a smoothness never before possible. A further novel element is that men can order and implement massive destruction without unusual feeling. Such acts are made in the name of rational policy. They are not done out of anger, hate, moral fervor, greed, sadism, or a desire for glory. As Hannah Arendt suggested in her study of Adolf Eichmann, the men who are responsible for modern warfare and genocide are by and large emotionally indistinguishable from other men; the feelings they have when performing such acts are everyday feelings.

These circumstances suggest that, although authority has been desanctified for modern man, it has an increased capacity to shape man's life, and it has not lost its ability to exact obedience.

OBEDIENCE

Masses of human beings participate in a process involving the destruction of their fellow men, not because they each personally seek such an end, but primarily because they are authoritatively commanded to participate. This situation was relatively understandable when men believed that such orders came from the deity or when they believed that submission was a law of nature. It is much harder to comprehend their participation, however, in a culture which highly values rational evaluation of authority by those subject to it.

One critical reason why authority remains a fundamental social problem is the enormous destructive power now held by those in authoritative positions—a power which has grown despite the general spread of critical attitudes toward authorities. Liberal theory is therefore seriously challenged by the concentration of power to make war and command violence—and by the continued willingness of liberally socialized and educated men to participate in and support this situation. The persistence, and the increasingly frightening implications, of *destructive obedience* calls into question the assumption that popular sovereignty is a sufficient condition for the rule of reason.

Liberalism is challenged by the continued readiness of men to accept orders to destroy other men, and it is equally challenged by the fact that human beings continue to acquiesce to authority that is destructive to themselves. Our time has witnessed an unprecedented degree of mass incarceration. Millions have been herded into concentration camps, where a remarkable passivity was pervasive, despite instances of resistance. Thousands of Americans are kept in prisons and mental institutions in which they are deprived almost totally of the freedoms taken for granted in civilian life. Millions submit to military conscription, under which they are ordered not only to kill others but to be killed as well.

Such total institutions represent extreme forms of subjugation and unfreedom. They are not hangovers from traditional, preliberal society but, in certain respects, new patterns of authority and subordination. The classical liberal-democratic vision exalted citizenship and rights with respect to *state authority;* it did not, on the whole, consider that rights of citizenship were applicable to authority exercised in nongovernmental spheres. Thus, authority in such crucial institutional settings as the factory, the office, and the school does not depend for its legitimation upon principles of consent, participation, and self-government. An increasingly central issue of our time has been whether democracy can in fact exist if central spheres of life remain undemocratically organized. Can people be psychologically capable of self-government if most of their daily lives are spent in situations of submissive subordination, and most of the authority they encounter is not legitimately accountable to them?

Finally, liberal theory is challenged by the fact that fundamental principles of social equality and political liberty have not been extended to significant portions of the population. At the beginning, the vision of citizenship in this country was not intended to apply to black slaves and Indians. It was not intended to apply to women. Only in the last fifty years has the franchise been extended to females; and only in the last decade have voting restrictions on blacks been substantially removed.

The fundamental inequalities that result from the deprivation of full citizenship rights to these groups still pervade the society. The United States is not a society based on the association of free and equal citizens engaged in self-government, in large measure because of the continued pervasiveness of racism and sexism in our political and social institutions. Not only do racial and sexual inequalities deny full citizenship to women and oppressed ethnic minorities, they also have a profoundly deleterious effect on the capacity of white males to engage in a rational encounter with authority.

My point so far is this. After centuries of regarding political domination as a law of God and/or nature, men began to see it as man-made and therefore subject to human consent and evaluation. This perception marks the beginning of the modern age; the first time men universally came to believe that they were obliged to obey only that political authority whose actions they could guide and whose purposes matched their own needs. This democratic vision has been universally liberating. Nevertheless, in societies like our own, where the democratic vision has been most fully institutionalized, we do not yet see a structure based on full citizenship, full equality, rational leadership, and rational obedience. Why have the expectations of eighteenth and nineteenth century liberal-rationalist theorists not been fulfilled for the United States? Among other things, these theorists could not have taken into account the impact of a global empire based on technologized militarism; they did not consider the results of bureaucratized work, total institutions, racism, or sexism. Indeed, all of these factors have diminished considerably the chances of a democratic society.

As a consequence, we have a situation in which authority is largely desanctified, prosaic, and vulnerable; yet a high degree of mass obedience and acquiescence, and precious little self-government, can be found. We have neither social peace nor democracy, and there is widespread fear that the future will bring either total order or total chaos.

WHAT THIS BOOK TRIES TO DO

This book explores the social psychology of freedom in contemporary industrial society. The best way to see the point of the book is to read the quotations at the beginning of this chapter, and the subsequent selections by C. Wright Mills, Stanley Milgram, and Solomon Asch. These first three selections were crucial in my own intellectual and moral development. I first read Asch's study on group pressure as an undergraduate; it struck me as a brilliant demonstration of one of the critical problems of everyday social relations—the problem of reconciling personal integrity with the need for social acceptance. Asch showed that when individuals are confronted with a disparity between the evidences of their senses and the opinions of a unanimous majority they become enormously distressed. Many individuals yield to majority opinion; many others refuse to yield. What Asch does not provide is a detailed explanation of this variation. What factors prompt some individuals to yield? What factors enable others to overcome their anxieties and maintain their own perspectives? I first encountered Asch's study in his book *Social Psychology.* At that time, it seemed to me that if social psychology was a discipline which offered some means for confronting such basic questions about the human potentiality for integrity, then perhaps this was the vocation for which I had been searching.

Early in my graduate career, I read the chapter entitled "On Reason and Freedom" in C. Wright Mills' book *The Sociological Imagination.* It seemed that Mills was validating and enlarging the issue that Asch's work had presented. The problem of preserving individuality and integrity was posed not only by group pressures in face-to-face relations but, more fundamentally, by the rise of large-scale bureaucratic organization of work, education, and government, and by the rise of extremely sophisticated means of mass persuasion. It was not only that men's judgments of reality could be distorted by the pressures of others, but also that judgment itself could be made impossible as the result of the complexity, the specialization, the fragmentation, and the manipulation of contemporary life. Mills raised the spectre of the Cheerful Robot—a person who has lost all capacity for judgment and choice and who contentedly accepts his psychological dependence and subordination. He asks whether such a human type is on the increase—and also what conditions stand against it.

The idea of this book was finally crystallized for me by Stanley Milgram's experimental studies of obedience. Milgram created a laboratory paradigm of the problem of authority in its contemporary form. A figure of authority directs a subject to administer injurious punishment to another person. The subject is neither rewarded for compliance nor punished for refusal. The instructions are justified in vague terms as being necessary for the purposes of a scientific investigation; in other words, the subject is not given any emotionally significant ground for hurting the other. Nevertheless, despite the absence of any personally rooted motivation to do violence, and indeed despite the presence of strongly felt negative feelings about doing so, a large majority of subjects do what they are told to do. Milgram's most dramatic finding was the difficulty in getting substantial numbers of subjects to *disobey* such instructions. This finding is particularly stunning in the context of Mills' argument—for the behavior of Milgram's subjects suggests that the day of the Cheerful Robot may have already arrived.

At the same time, it is crucial to note that Milgram's experimental situation elicited a *range* of responses. Within each experimental variation, some subjects refused to cooperate; moreover, the experimental variations differed markedly in the degree to which they elicited obedience.

Some fundamental assumptions of eighteenth-century liberal-rationalism were that rationality was a product of individual intellectual activity; that applying science to nature and human problems would improve each individual's potential for rational action; and that scientific activity would be a powerful antidote to blind obedience to authority. All three of the following selections compel us to make a fundamental reexamination of these liberal-rational assumptions.

The Asch experiment demonstrates that individual human judgment is inextricably dependent, not only on each individual's perception of physical reality, but also on his perception of the perceptions of others. Individual comprehension of the physical world depends fundamentally on the concepts, categories, symbols, information, and validation we derive from interaction with others. Without a cultural framework, without language, without social interaction, perception, understanding, and rationality would be impossible. The cognitive interdependence of human organisms permits them to transcend immediate experience, to remember, predict, evaluate, and plan. But this same interdependence largely explains why group consensus is so powerful in molding individual belief and opinion. Asch's subjects were distressed when their private perceptions diverged from those of the group; their usual experience in everyday life confirmed that group consensus validates and supports everyday perceptions such as the relative lengths of lines. Indeed, such mutual validation of common experience is absolutely critical; without it, routine social relations and communication itself would become deeply problematic. Finding oneself at odds with a unanimous consensus over apparently unambiguous physical facts is threatening because it seems to call into question the very foundations of everyday existence. In addition, many of Asch's subjects felt threatened because they believed that dissent from the majority threatened their status in the eyes of the others. To be stubbornly insistent on one's point of view against the unanimous views of others opens one up to embarrassment, ridicule, and rejection. The strong association between conformity and group approval is a powerful mechanism supporting cohesiveness, smooth communication, sociability, and trust in intragroup relations. It is also a weapon which undermines the capacity of individuals to make and express their own judgments. Such propositions about the interdependence of individual judgments are the fundamental assumptions of social psychology. Quite obviously, these propositions are opposed to liberal-rationalist philosophy, which supposed that the maximization of individual independence was both possible and necessary for individual freedom.

Asch's study should not be read as a demonstration of some conformism inherent in human nature. On the contrary, Asch demonstrates that rational judgment and action are *contingent*. Thus, the fundamental question is not whether men can be free and rational. Rather, the question is: Under what *conditions* can men be free and rational? What conditions limit or undermine such capacities?

Mills' essay, "On Reason and Freedom," challenges rationalist assumptions in a different way. What if rationality is distributed unequally, so that an elite group comes to control the fruits of science, technology, and rationalized social organization? Under these conditions, a small group of men become capable of turning the masses of people into instruments of their will. Again, however, Mills should not be read simply as a prophet of technological doom. Men seem to be drifting toward robotization, but Mills asks whether they have points of resistance or capacities to reverse this drift.

The classic rationalists believed that science would undermine blind obedience to authority; in Milgram's situation, science becomes authority—and blind obedience is the result. Milgram's study can be interpreted as a demonstration of the degree to which ordinary people have come to trust the scientist; the white coat has become a very important legitimating symbol. Presumably, his subjects cooperated in part because they believed they were serving the interests of science and also because they believed that the men who gave them instructions knew what they were doing. The result of such trust is frighteningly reminiscent of Eichmann and his subordinates; scores of subjects administered push-button torture to screaming victims. Many have read Milgram's study as a demonstration of the prevalence of Eichmannism. Once again, such an interpretation would be too simple, for the study also demonstrates that such behavior is contingent and not inevitable.

The three selections that follow should be seen as fundamental challenges to the eighteenth-century rationalist creed—a creed which still pervades the political and academic rhetoric of our time. Asch's and Milgram's experiments are classic empirical demonstrations of the limitations of rationalism as a mode of explaining human action. Mills' essay is less directly grounded in data, but it is an eloquent summation of both the direct experience and the current intellectual temper concerning freedom in advanced industrial societies.

These selections do not endorse the facile (and rather fashionable) antidemocratic assumptions that men are fated to be sheep, that they are incapable of self-government, or that moral progress is an absurd illusion. Nor do the following three essays endorse the related assumption (equally facile and fashionable) that freedom equals the triumph of the irrational.

Instead, each piece calls for a social psychology of freedom—a serious effort to discover the conditions under which men obey and disobey, conform and resist, yield and refuse.

My reading of these three essays persuaded me that the core problem for contemporary social psychology was to clarify the conditions of individual self-determination. It seemed to me that, as Mills suggests, the central intellectual issue for our epoch is to understand why the eighteenth-century vision of the liberated individual had not been fulfilled, even though the democratic and socialist revolutions spawned by that vision have come to pass. Furthermore, as Mills suggests, the question is not only how to understand this failure, but also how to transcend it—how to find the terms of freedom in a post-modern, advanced industrial society. The task of the macro social studies—history, sociology, economics, political science—is to clarify the structure and development of society and its institutions in the modern era. The particular concern of social psychology is to try to comprehend the impact of the society and its institutions upon individuals, and to understand the subsequent responses of individuals to the conditions they experience. The problem of freedom involves the fact that men are bound and restrained by the social structures they are forced to inhabit. They are also bound by their own motivational and cognitive structures. One part of the promise of freedom, however, involves the fact that even when freedom seems to be most thoroughly denied by external social structures, men struggle to loosen their bonds. One way into the problem, therefore, might be to examine the variety of individual responses to authority structures and the conditions which seemingly determine such responses.

Social psychologists might not wish to organize their discipline in terms of such issues; it seems to me, however, that responses to authority is an excellent central theme around which to organize the *teaching* of social psychology to undergraduates. I have been trying to teach introductory social psychology for nearly a decade and have grown increasingly unhappy with the conventional format of such courses. Usually, an attempt is made to introduce students to the discipline as practiced by professionals engaged in social psychological re- search. As an academic discipline, social psychology opted very early for a conception of itself as a behavioral science—a type of discipline that tries to understand, predict, and control human behavior in social settings. Social psy- chologists are overwhelmingly engaged in efforts to test, empirically and quanti- tatively, an endless array of hypotheses. In most cases, the behavior studied in this way is simple, trivial, and microscopic. A large proportion of the work of social psychologists is devoted to the formalization of theories or to the elabora- tion of techniques of measurement, experimental manipulation, and data analy- sis. No wonder many undergraduates, who expect to find an opportunity to address fundamental problems concerning the individual and society, come to view the discipline as incoherent, irrelevant, or a complicated means to demon- strate the obvious. At least privately, many practitioners are prepared to agree with these criticisms. My own conclusion, after several years of teaching a rather conventional survey course, was that the educational process and the health of the discipline require that social psychology be taught as a set of core philosoph- ical and moral problems—not as academically practiced by professionals. This approach presents itself as the best way to teach and as the only way to be true to the intellectual promise and origins of the discipline.

There are several core issues which a philosophically and morally rooted social psychology might confront: the limits and potentialities of human reason; the social origins and implications of individuality; determinants and conse- quences of conflict, competition, exchange, and love; and so forth. To a very great extent the empirical work of present-day social psychologists derives from long intellectual traditions concerned with such issues. The trouble is that most practitioners, in their preoccupation with "scientism," have ceased to be aware of these philosophical moorings. A tremendously creative task might be to try to recapture the profundity of this field by showing how the mass of data and technique accumulated over the past three decades can be reorganized and reinterpreted in light of such age-old human concerns. Such a task is well beyond anything I might be able to do. What I have tried to do lately as a teacher, and now in this reader, is to select *one* of these core issues—the problem of the individual and authority—and to begin to bring it into focus as a problem for social psychological research and analysis. I've selected this issue primarily because I see it as the most urgent issue in our society at this time. Here, I am not trying to provide validated answers so much as I am attempting to formulate the questions raised by the issue as presented to us in contemporary life.

It should be obvious by now that this book embodies a point of view. That "bias" can be stated as follows: The human capacity for rational self-determination and self-government ought to be maximized. This implies minimizing the circumstances under which human beings are exploited and dominated— the circumstances under which human beings permit themselves to become instruments in transactions that contradict their interests. The particular emphasis of a social psychological examination of this issue should be on the activity of those who are subordinated. The range of response by those who are subordinated is extraordinarily extensive and complex: One can observe enthusiastic submission, dutiful acceptance, passive conformity, patterned evasion, covert resistance, overt defiance, collective protest, or effective overthrow. Can we understand the determinants of these various types of response? This appears to be a crucial question, because ultimately the maximization of human self-determination depends upon the *capacity* and *readiness* of human beings to be self-determining, and upon the degree to which constraining structures permit them to be free.

The organization of this book can best be understood by returning to Milgram's study. I have considered his experimental situation as a paradigm of the relations between the individual and authority. His study suggests that there are two broad types of determinants of obedience and disobedience. Milgram observed variation among the individuals within each experimental situation. These variations involved differences in willingness to follow orders, in the reaction time (or hesitation time) of subjects to the orders, and in the duration or intensity of the shock subjects were likely to give the victim. These variations were correlated with measures of difference in certain character traits. The findings suggested that one broad class of determinants of the response to authority involves *individual capacities or dispositions.*

Milgram also found variation *across* situations. In some situations almost all individuals obeyed (and individual differences in character or disposition were largely irrelevant). By varying certain elements of the situation, Milgram could substantially increase the rates of disobedience. These findings suggest that a second broad class of determinants of response to authority has to do with the structural and situational context. There are certain patterns of authority and organization which generate quite complete acquiescence; there are other circumstances which allow a far greater range of response; and there are still other situations in which forms of disobedience seem highly predictable.

Chapter 2 of this book focuses on individual character as a determinant of responses to authority. All of the readings start with the assumption that the responses of fully grown human beings to authority are partly the result of childhood experiences with authority. Action in the present is a function of what one has learned to do, feel, or want in the past.

Chapters 3 and 4 focus on how immediate action is shaped by the situation as it presents itself. Chapter 3 emphasizes how a variety of contemporary institutional and cultural situations generate various forms of obedience, acquiescence, and submissiveness. Chapter 4 suggests the conditions under which many of these types of settings can also generate forms of disobedience, resistance, and protest.

Chapter 5 shifts the focus from the reactions of subordinates to how those in authority respond to expressions of discontent and threat from below.

In Chapter 6 we try to leap beyond the present to examine some of the conditions which might be alternatives to domination—the conditions that·lie beyond the cycle of domination-resistance-domination which has so far characterized social life. We shall search for the conditions under which obedience and disobedience would be replaced by self-government.

A final caveat: The readings in each selection do not provide us with a coherent theory or set of propositions enabling us to solve the problems posed. The whole point of this book is to stimulate thought and discussion, study and observation. My main hope is that these readings lead you—as they have led me—to see certain familiar situations and relationships in a somewhat new light. Hopefully, these selections will make the taken-for-granted and the inevitable seem less so and will encourage the feeling that what is, does not necessarily have to be.

SOME SUGGESTED READING

The forms of order achieved in everyday life are brilliantly elucidated in Erving Goffman's recent book, *Relations in Public* (New York: Basic Books, 1971). Fundamental treatments of authority from the perspective of political philosophy and social science are available in the following: C. J. Friedrich, ed., *Authority* (Cambridge, Mass: Harvard University Press, 1958), and J. R. Pennock and J. W. Chapman, eds., *Political and Legal Obligation* (New York: Atherton, 1970). For Weber's analysis of legitimacy, see M. Weber, *The Theory of Economic and Social Organization* (Glencoe, Ill.: Free Press, 1947). An illuminating recent discussion of legitimacy is J. H. Schaar, "Legitimacy in the Modern State," in P. Green and S. Levinson, eds., *Power and Community: Dissenting Essays in Political Science* (New York: Vintage, 1970). A recent critique of liberal theory relevant to contemporary conditions is R. P. Wolff, *The Poverty of Liberalism* (Boston: Beacon Press, 1968). Essential readings for one's understanding of the purposes of social science are: C. Wright Mills, *Sociological Imagination* (New York: Oxford, 1959), and Solomon Asch, *Social Psychology* (New York: Prentice-Hall, 1952).

ON REASON AND FREEDOM

C. Wright Mills

The climax of the social scientist's concern with history is the idea he comes to hold of the epoch in which he lives. The climax of his concern with biography is the idea he comes to hold of man's basic nature, and of the limits it may set to the transformation of man by the course of history.

All classic social scientists have been concerned with the salient characteristics of their time—and the problem of how history is being made within it; with 'the nature of human nature'—and the variety of individuals that come to prevail within their periods. Marx and Sombart and Weber, Comte and Spencer, Durkheim and Veblen, Mannheim, Schumpeter, and Michels—each in his own way has confronted these problems. In our immediate times, however, many social scientists have not. Yet it is precisely now, in the second half of the twentieth century, that these concerns become urgent as issues, persistent as troubles, and vital for the cultural orientation of our human studies.

Nowadays men everywhere seek to know where they stand, where they may be going, and what—if anything—they can do about the present as history and the future as responsibility. Such questions as these no one can answer once and for all. Every period provides its own answers. But just now, for us, there is a difficulty. We are now at the ending of an epoch, and we have got to work out our own answers.

We are at the ending of what is called The Modern Age. Just as Antiquity was followed by several centuries of Oriental ascendancy, which Westerners provincially call The Dark Ages, so now The Modern Age is being succeeded by a post-modern period. Perhaps we may call it: The Fourth Epoch.

The ending of one epoch and the beginning of another is, to be sure, a matter of definition. But

definitions, like everything social, are historically specific. And now our basic definitions of society and of self are being overtaken by new realities. I do not mean merely that never before within the limits of a single generation have men been so fully exposed at so fast a rate to such earthquakes of change. I do not mean merely that we feel we are in an epochal kind of transition, and that we struggle to grasp the outline of the new epoch we suppose ourselves to be entering. I mean that when we try to orient ourselves—if we do try—we find that too many of our old expectations and images are, after all, tied down historically: that too many of our standard categories of thought and of feeling as often disorient us as help to explain what is happening around us; that too many of our explanations are derived from the great historical transition from the Medieval to the Modern Age; and that when they are generalized for use today, they become unwieldy, irrelevant, not convincing. I also mean that our major orientations—liberalism and socialism—have virtually collapsed as adequate explanations of the world and of ourselves.

These two ideologies came out of The Enlightenment, and they have had in common many assumptions and values. In both, increased rationality is held to be the prime condition of increased freedom. The liberating notion of progress by reason, the faith in science as an unmixed good, the demand for popular education and the faith in its political meaning for democracy—all these ideals of The Enlightenment have rested upon the happy assumption of the inherent relation of reason and freedom. Those thinkers who have done the most to shape our ways of thinking have proceeded under this assumption. It lies under every movement and nuance of the work of Freud: To be free, the individual must become more rationally aware; therapy is an aid to giving reason its chance to work freely in the course of an individual's life. The same assumption underpins the main line of marxist work: Men, caught in the irrational anarchy of production, must become rationally aware of their position in society; they must become 'class conscious'—the marxian meaning of which is as rationalistic as any term set forth by Bentham.

Liberalism has been concerned with freedom and reason as supreme facts about the individual; marxism, as supreme facts about man's role in the political making of history. The liberals and the radicals of The Modern Period have generally been men who believed in the rational making of history and of his own biography by the free individual.

But what has been happening in the world makes evident, I believe, why the ideas of freedom and of reason now so often seem so ambiguous in both the new capitalist and the communist societies of our time: why marxism has so often become a dreary rhetoric of bureaucratic defense and abuse; and liberalism, a trivial and irrelevant way of masking social reality. The major developments of our time, I believe, can be correctly understood neither in terms of the liberal nor the marxian interpretation of politics and culture. These ways of thought arose as guidelines to reflection about types of society which do not now exist. John Stuart Mill never examined the kinds of political economy now arising in the capitalist world. Karl Marx never analyzed the kinds of society now arising in the Communist bloc. And neither of them ever thought through the problems of the so-called underdeveloped countries in which seven out of ten men are trying to exist today. Now we confront new kinds of social structure which, in terms of 'modern' ideals, resist analysis in the liberal and in the socialist terms we have inherited.

The ideological mark of The Fourth Epoch—that which sets it off from The Modern Age—is that the ideas of freedom and of reason have become moot; that increased rationality may not be assumed to make for increased freedom.

The role of reason in human affairs and the idea of the free individual as the seat of reason are the most important themes inherited by twentieth century social scientists from the philosophers of the Enlightenment. If they are to remain the key values in terms of which troubles are specified and issues focused, then the ideals of reason and of freedom must now be restated as problems in more precise and solvable ways than have been available to earlier thinkers and investigators. For in our time

these two values, reason and freedom, are in obvious yet subtle peril.

The underlying trends are well known. Great and rational organizations—in brief, bureaucracies—have indeed increased, but the substantive reason of the individual at large has not. Caught in the limited milieux of their everyday lives, ordinary men often cannot reason about the great structures —rational and irrational—of which their milieux are subordinate parts. Accordingly, they often carry out series of apparently rational actions without any ideas of the ends they serve, and there is the increasing suspicion that those at the top as well—like Tolstoy's generals—only pretend they know. The growth of such organizations, within an increasing division of labor, sets up more and more spheres of life, work, and leisure, in which reasoning is difficult or impossible. The soldier, for example, "carries out an entire series of functionally rational actions accurately without having any idea as to the ultimate end of this action" or the function of each act within the whole. Even men of technically supreme intelligence may efficiently perform their assigned work and yet not know that it is to result in the first atom bomb.

Science, it turns out, is not a technological Second Coming. That its techniques and its rationality are given a central place in a society does not mean that men live reasonably and without myth, fraud, and superstition. Universal education may lead to technological idiocy and nationalist provinciality— rather than to the informed and independent intelligence. The mass distribution of historic culture may not lift the level of cultural sensibility, but rather, merely banalize it—and compete mightily with the chance for creative innovation. A high level of bureacratic rationality and of technology does not mean a high level of either individual or social intelligence. From the first you cannot infer the second. For social, technological, or bureaucratic rationality is not merely a grand summation of the individual will and capacity to reason. The very chance to acquire that will and that capacity seems in fact often to be decreased by it. Rationally organized social arrangements are not necessarily a means of increased freedom—for the individual or for the society. In fact, often they are a means of tyranny and manipulation, a means of expropriating the very chance to reason, the very capacity to act as a free man.

Only from a few commanding positions or—as the case may be, merely vantage points—in the rationalized structure is it readily possible to understand the structural forces at work in the whole which thus affect each limited part of which ordinary men are aware.

The forces that shape these milieux do not originate within them, nor are they controllable by those sunk in them. Moreover, these milieux are themselves increasingly rationalized. Families as well as factories, leisure as well as work, neighborhoods as well as states—they, too, tend to become parts of a functionally rational totality—or they are subject to uncontrolled and irrational forces.

The increasing rationalization of society, the contradiction between such rationality and reason, the collapse of the assumed coincidence of reason and freedom—these developments lie back of the rise into view of the man who is 'with' rationality but without reason, who is increasingly self-rationalized and also increasingly uneasy. It is in terms of this type of man that the contemporary problem of freedom is best stated. Yet such trends and suspicions are often not formulated as problems, and they are certainly not widely acknowledged as issues or felt as a set of troubles. Indeed, it is the fact of its unrecognized character, its lack of formulation, that is the most important feature of the contemporary problem of freedom and reason.

From the individual's standpoint, much that happens seems the result of manipulation, of management, of blind drift; authority is often not explicit; those with power often feel no need to make it explicit and to justify it. That is one reason why ordinary men, when they are in trouble or when they sense that they are up against issues, cannot get clear targets for thought and for action; they cannot determine what it is that imperils the values they vaguely discern as theirs.

Given these effects of the ascendant trend of rationalization, the individual "does the best he can." He gears his aspirations and his work to the situation he is in, and from which he can find no way out. In due course, he does not seek a way out: he adapts. That part of his life which is left over from work, he uses to play, to consume, 'to have fun.' Yet this sphere of consumption is also being rationalized. Alienated from production, from work, he is also alienated from consumption, from genuine leisure. This adaptation of the individual and its effects upon his milieux and self results not only in the loss of his chance, and in due course, of his capacity and will to reason; it also affects his chances and his capacity to act as a free man. Indeed, neither the value of freedom nor of reason, it would seem, are known to him.

Such adapted men are not necessarily unintelligent, even after they have lived and worked and played in such circumstances for quite some time. Karl Mannheim has made the point in a clear way by speaking of "self rationalization," which refers to the way in which an individual, caught in the limited segments of great, rational organizations, comes systematically to regulate his impulses and his aspirations, his manner of life and his ways of thought, in rather strict accordance with "the rules and regulations of the organization." The rational organization is thus an alienating organization: the guiding principles of conduct and reflection, and in due course of emotion as well, are not seated in the individual conscience of the Reformation man, or in the independent reason of the Cartesian man. The guiding principles, in fact, are alien to and in contradiction with all that has been historically understood as individuality. It is not too much to say that in the extreme development the chance to reason of most men is destroyed, as rationality increases and its locus, its control, is moved from the individual to the big-scale organization. There is then rationality without reason. Such rationality is not commensurate with freedom but the destroyer of it. It is no wonder that the ideal of individuality has become moot: in our time, what is at issue is the very nature of man, the image we have of his limits and possibilities as man. History is not yet done with its exploration of the limits and meanings of "human nature." We do not know how profound man's psychological transformation from the Modern Age to the contemporary epoch may be. But we must now raise the question in an ultimate form: Among contemporary men will there come to prevail, or even to flourish, what may be called The Cheerful Robot?

We know of course that man can be turned into a robot, by chemical and psychiatric means, by steady coercion and by controlled environment; but also by random pressures and unplanned sequences of circumstances. But can he be made to want to become a cheerful and willing robot? Can he be happy in this condition, and what are the qualities and the meanings of such happiness? It will no longer do merely to assume, as a metaphysic of human nature, that down deep in man-as-man there is an urge for freedom and a will to reason. Now we must ask: What in man's nature, what in the human condition today, what in each of the varieties of social structure makes for the ascendancy of the cheerful robot? And what stands against it?

The advent of the alienated man and all the themes which lie behind his advent now affect the whole of our serious intellectual life and cause our immediate intellectual malaise. It is a major theme of the human condition in the contemporary epoch and of all studies worthy of the name. I know of no idea, no theme, no problem, that is so deep in the classic tradition—and so much involved in the possible default of contemporary social science.

It is what Karl Marx so brilliantly discerned in his earlier essays on "alienation"; it is the chief concern of Georg Simmel in his justly famous essay on "The Metropolis"; Graham Wallas was aware of it in his work on The Great Society. It lies behind Fromm's conception of the "automaton." The fear that such a type of man will become ascendant underlies many of the more recent uses of such classic sociological conceptions as "status and contract," "community and society." It is the hard meaning of such notions as Riesman's "other-directed" and Whyte's "social ethic." And of course, most popularly, the triumph—if it may be called that—of such a man is the key meaning of George Orwell's *1984*.

On the positive side—a rather wistful side nowadays—the larger meanings of Freud's "id," Marx's "Freiheit," George Mead's "I," Karen Horney's "spontaneity," lie in the use of such conceptions against the triumph of the alienated man. They are trying to find some center in man-as-man which would enable them to believe that in the end he cannot be made into, that he cannot finally become, such an alien creature—alien to nature, to society, to self. The cry for "community" is an attempt, a mistaken one I believe, to assert the conditions that would eliminate the probability of such a man, and it is because many humanist thinkers have come to believe that many psychiatrists

by their practice produce such alienated and self-rationalized men that they reject these adaptive endeavors. Back of all this—and much more of traditional and current worrying and thinking among serious and sensible students of man—there lies the simple and decisive fact that the alienated man is the antithesis of the Western image of the free man. The society in which this man, this cheerful robot, flourishes is the antithesis of the free society—or in the literal and plain meaning of the word, of a democratic society. The advent of this man points to freedom as trouble, as issue, and —let us hope—as problem for social scientists. Put as a trouble of the individual—of the terms and values of which he is uneasily unaware—it is the trouble called "alienation." As an issue for publics —to the terms and values of which they are mainly indifferent—it is no less than the issue of democratic society, as fact and as aspiration.

It is just because this issue and this trouble are not now widely recognized, and so do not in fact exist as explicit troubles and issues, that the uneasiness and the indifference that betoken them are so deep and so wide in meaning and in effect. That is a major part of the problem of freedom today, seen in its political context, and it is a major part of the intellectual challenge which the formulation of the problem of freedom offers to contemporary social scientists.

It is not merely paradoxical to say that the values of freedom and reason are back of the absence of troubles, back of the uneasy feeling of malaise and alienation. In a similar manner, the issue to which modern threats to freedom and reason most typically lead is, above all, the absence of explicit issues—to apathy rather than to issues explicitly defined as such.

The issues and troubles have not been clarified because the chief capacities and qualities of man required to clarify them are the very freedom and reason that are threatened and dwindling. Neither the troubles nor the issues have been seriously formulated as the problems of the kinds of social science I have been criticizing in this book. The promise of classic social science, in considerable part, is that they will be.

The troubles and issues raised up by the crises of reason and freedom cannot of course be formulated as one grand problem, but neither can they be confronted, much less solved, by handling each of them microscopically as a series of small-scale issues, or of troubles confined to a scatter of milieux. They are structural problems, and to state them requires that we work in the classic terms of human biography and of ephocal history. Only in such terms can the connections of structure and milieux that effect these values today be traced and casual analysis be conducted. The crisis of individuality and the crisis of history making; the role of reason in the free individual life and in the making of history—in the restatement and clarification of these problems lies the promise of the social sciences.

The moral and the intellectual promise of social science is that freedom and reason will remain cherished values, that they will be used seriously and consistently and imaginatively in the formulation of problems. But this is also the political promise of what is loosely called Western culture. Within the social sciences, political crises and intellectual crises of our time coincide: Serious work in either sphere is also work in the other. The political traditions of classic liberalism and of classic socialism together exhaust our major political traditions. The collapse of these traditions as ideologies has had to do with the decline of free individuality and the decline of reason in human affairs. Any contemporary political restatement of liberal and socialist goals must include as central the idea of a society in which all men would become men of substantive reason, whose independent reasoning would have structural consequences for their societies, its history, and thus for their own life fates.

The interest of the social scientist in social structure is not due to any view that the future is structurally determined. We study the structural limits of human decision in an attempt to find points of effective intervention, in order to know what can and what must be structurally changed if the role of explicit decision in history making is to be enlarged. Our interest in history is not owing to any view that the future is inevitable, that the future is bounded by the past. That men have lived in certain kinds of society in the past does not set exact or absolute limits to the kinds of society they may create in the future. We study history to discern the alternatives within which human reason and human freedom can now make history. We study historical social structures, in brief, in order to find within them the ways in which they are and can be controlled. For only in this way can we come to know the limits and the meaning of human freedom.

Freedom is not merely the chance to do as one pleases; neither is it merely the opportunity to choose between set alternatives. Freedom is, first of all, the chance to formulate the available choices, to argue over them—and then, the opportunity to choose. That is why freedom cannot exist without an enlarged role of human reason in human affairs. Within an individual's biography and within a society's history, the social task of reason is to formulate choices, to enlarge the scope of human decisions in the making of history. The future of human affairs is not merely some set of variables to be predicted. The future is what is to be decided—within the limits, to be sure, of historical possibility. But this possibility is not fixed; in our time the limits seem very broad indeed.

Beyond this, the problem of freedom is the problem of how decisions about the future of human affairs are to be made and who is to make them. Organizationally, it is the problem of a just machinery of decision. Morally, it is the problem of political responsibility. Intellectually, it is the problem of what are now the possible futures of human affairs. But the larger aspects of the problem of freedom today concern not only the nature of history and the structural chance for explicit decisions to make a difference in its course; they concern also the nature of man and the fact that the value of freedom cannot be based upon "man's basic nature." The ultimate problem of freedom is the problem of the cheerful robot, and it arises in this form today because today it has become evident to us that *all* men do *not* naturally *want* to be free; that all men are not willing or not able, as the case may be, to exert themselves to acquire the reason that freedom requires.

Under what conditions do men come to *want* to be free and capable of acting freely? Under what conditions are they willing and able to bear the burdens freedom does impose and to see these less as burdens than as gladly undertaken self-transformations? And on the negative side: Can men be made to want to become *cheerful* robots?

In our time, must we not face the possibility that the human mind as a social fact might be deteriorating in quality and cultural level, and yet not many would notice it because of the overwhelming accumulation of technological gadgets? Is not that one meaning of rationality without reason? Of human alienation? Of the absence of any free role for reason in human affairs? The accumulation of gadgets hides these meanings: Those who use these devices do not understand them; those who invent them do not understand much else. That is why we may *not,* without great ambiguity, use technological abundance as the index of human quality and cultural progress.

To formulate any problem requires that we state the values involved and the threat to those values. For it is the felt threat to cherished values—such as those of freedom and reason—that is the necessary moral substance of all significant problems of social inquiry, and as well of all public issues and private troubles.

The values involved in the cultural problem of individuality are conveniently embodied in all that is suggested by the ideal of The Renaissance Man. The threat to that ideal is the ascendancy among us of The Cheerful Robot.

The values involved in the political problem of history making are embodied in the Promethean ideal of its human making. The threat to that ideal is twofold: On the one hand, history making may well go by default, men may continue to abdicate its willful making, and so merely drift. On the other hand, history may indeed be made—but by narrow elite circles without effective responsibility to those who must try to survive the consequences of their decisions and of their defaults.

I do not know the answer to the question of political irresponsibility in our time or to the cultural and political question of The Cheerful Robot. But is it not clear that no answers will be found unless these problems are at least confronted? Is it not obvious that the ones to confront them, above all others, are the social scientists of the rich societies? That many of them do not now do so is surely the greatest human default being committed by privileged men in our times.

SOME CONDITIONS OF OBEDIENCE AND DISOBEDIENCE TO AUTHORITY

Stanley Milgram

The situation in which one agent commands another to hurt a third turns up time and again as a significant theme in human relations. It is powerfully expressed in the story of Abraham, who is commanded by God to kill his son. It is no accident that Kierkegaard, seeking to orient his thought to the central themes of human experience, chose Abraham's conflict as the springboard to his philosophy.

War too moves forward on the triad of an authority which commands a person to destroy the enemy, and perhaps all organized hostility may be viewed as a theme and variation on the three elements of authority, executant, and victim.[1] We describe an experimental program, recently concluded at Yale University, in which a particular expression of this conflict is studied by experimental means.

In its most general form the problem may be defined thus: if X tells Y to hurt Z, under what conditions will Y carry out the command of X and under what conditions will he refuse. In the more limited form possible in laboratory research, the question becomes: If an experimenter tells a subject to hurt another person, under what conditions will the subject go along with this instruction, and under what conditions will he refuse to obey? The laboratory problem is not so much a dilution of the general statement as one concrete expression of the many particular forms this question may assume.

From The International Journal of Psychiatry, *Vol. 6, No. 4 (October 1968). Reprinted by permission of* The International Journal of Psychiatry *and the author. Footnotes and references have been edited.*

One aim of the research was to study behavior in a strong situation of deep consequence to the participants, for the psychological forces operative in powerful and lifelike forms of the conflict may not be brought into play under diluted conditions.

This approach meant, first, that we had a special obligation to protect the welfare and dignity of the persons who took part in the study; subjects were, of necessity, placed in a difficult predicament, and steps had to be taken to ensure their well-being before they were discharged from the laboratory. Toward this end, a careful, post-experimental treatment was devised and has been carried through for subjects in all conditions.[2]

TERMINOLOGY

If Y follows the command of X we shall say that he has obeyed X; if he fails to carry out the command of X, we shall say that he has disobeyed X. The terms *to obey* and *to disobey,* as used here, refer to the subject's overt action only, and carry no implication for the motive or experiential states accompanying the action.[3]

To be sure, the everyday use of the word *obedience* is not entirely free from complexities. It refers to action within widely varying situations, and connotes diverse motives within those situations: A child's obedience differs from a soldier's obedience, or the love, honor, and *obey* of the marriage vow. However, a consistent behavioral relationship is indicated in most uses of the term: In the act of obeying, a person does what another person tells him to do. Y obeys X if he carries out the prescription for action which X has addressed to him; the term suggests, moreover, that some form of dominance-subordination, or hierarchical element, is part of the situation in which the transaction between X and Y occurs.

A subject who complies with the entire series of experimental commands will be termed an *obedient* subject; one who at any point in the command series defies the experimenter will be called a *disobedient* or *defiant* subject. As used in this report, the terms refer only to the subject's performance in the experiment, and do not necessarily imply a general personality disposition to submit to or reject authority.

SUBJECT POPULATION

The subjects used in all experimental conditions were male adults, residing in the greater New Haven and Bridgeport areas, aged 20 to 50 years, and engaged in a wide variety of occupations. Each experimental condition described in this report employed 40 fresh subjects and was carefully balanced for age and occupational types. The occupational composition for each experiment was: workers, skilled and unskilled: 40 per cent; white collar, sales, business: 40 per cent; professionals: 20 per cent. The occupations were intersected with three age categories (subjects in 20s, 30s, and 40s, assigned to each condition in the proportions of 20, 40, and 40 per cent respectively).

THE GENERAL LABORATORY PROCEDURE

The focus of the study concerns the amount of electric shock a subject is willing to administer to another person when ordered by an experimenter to give the "victim" increasingly more severe punishment. The act of administering shock is set in the context of a learning experiment, ostensibly designed to study the effect of punishment on memory. Aside from the experimenter, one naive subject and one accomplice perform in each session. On arrival each subject is paid $4.50. After a general talk by the experimenter, telling how little scientists know about the effect of punishment on memory, subjects are informed that one member

of the pair will serve as teacher and one as learner. A rigged drawing is held so that the naive subject is always the teacher, and the accomplice becomes the learner. The learner is taken to an adjacent room and strapped into an "electric chair."[4]

The naive subject is told that it is his task to teach the learner a list of paired associates, to test him on the list, and to administer punishment whenever the learner errs in the test. Punishment takes the form of electric shock, delivered to the learner by means of a shock generator controlled by the naive subject. The teacher is instructed to increase the intensity of electric shock one step on the generator on each error. The learner, according to plan, provides many wrong answers, so that before long the naive subject must give him the strongest shock on the generator. Increases in shock level are met by increasingly insistent demands from the learner that the experiment be stopped because of the growing discomfort to him. However, in clear terms the experimenter orders the teacher to continue with the procedure in disregard of the learner's protests. *Thus, the naive subject must resolve a conflict between two mutually incompatible demands from the social field. He may continue to follow the orders of the experimenter and shock the learner with increasing severity, or he may refuse to follow the orders of the experimenter and heed the learner's pleas. The experimenter's authority operates not in a free field, but against ever-mounting countervailing pressures from the person being punished.*

A few technical points need to be considered before the findings of the study are described. For the purpose of delivering shock, a simulated shock generator is used, with 30 clearly marked voltage levels that range from 15 to 450 volts (and each activated by one of 30 individual lever switches set in a horizontal line). The naive subject is given a sample shock of 45 volts to convince him of the authenticity of the instrument. The generator bears verbal designations that range from "Slight Shock" to "Danger: Severe Shock."

The responses of the victim are standardized on tape, and each protest is coordinated to a particular voltage level on the shock generator. Starting with 75 volts the learner begins to grunt and moan. At 150 volts he demands to be let out of the experiment. At 180 volts he cries out that he can no longer stand the pain. At 300 volts he refuses to provide any more answers to the memory test, insisting that he is no longer a participant in the experiment and must be freed. In response to this last tactic, the experimenter instructs the naive subject to treat the absence of an answer as equivalent to a wrong answer, and to follow the usual shock procedure. The experimenter reinforces his demand with the statement: "You have no other choice, you must go on!" (This imperative is used whenever the naive subject tries to break off the experiment.) If the subject refuses to give the next higher level of shock, the experiment is considered at an end. A quantitative value is assigned to the subject's performance based on the maximum intensity shock he administered before breaking off. Thus any subject's score may range from zero (for a subject unwilling to administer the first shock level) to 30 (for a subject who proceeds to the highest voltage level on the board). For any particular subject and for any particular experimental condition the degree to which participants have followed the experimenter's orders may be specified with a numerical value, corresponding to the metric number on the shock generator.

This laboratory situation gives us a framework in which to study the subject's reactions to the principal conflict of the experiment. Again, this conflict is between the experimenter's demands that he continue to administer the electric shock, and the learner's demands, which become increasingly more insistent, that the experiment be stopped. The crux of the study is to vary systematically the factors believed to alter the degree of obedience to the experimental commands, to learn under what conditions submission to authority is most probable, and under what conditions defiance is brought to the fore.

PILOT STUDIES

Pilot studies for the present research were completed in the winter of 1960; they differed from the regular experiments in a few details: for one, the victim was placed behind a silvered glass, with the light balance on the glass such that the victim could be dimly perceived by the subject.[5]

Though essentially qualitative in treatment, these studies pointed to several significant features of the experimental situation. At first no vocal feedback was used from the victim. It was thought that the verbal and voltage designations on the control panel would create sufficient pressure to curtail the subject's obedience. However, this was not the case. In the absence of protests from the learner, virtually all subjects, once commanded, went blithely to the end of the board, seemingly indifferent to the verbal designations ("Extreme Shock" and "Danger: Severe Shock"). This deprived us of an adequate basis for scaling obedient tendencies. A force had to be introduced that would strengthen the subject's resistance to the experimenter's commands, and reveal individual differences in terms of a distribution of break-off points.

This force took the form of protests from the victim. Initially, mild protests were used, but proved inadequate. Subsequently, more vehement protests were inserted into the experimental procedure. To our consternation, even the strongest protests from the victim did not prevent all subjects from administering the harshest punishment ordered by the experimenter; but the protests did lower the mean maximum shock somewhat and created some spread in the subject's performance; therefore, the victim's cries were standardized on tape and incorporated into the regular experimental procedure.

The situation did more than highlight the technical difficulties of finding a workable experimental procedure: it indicated that subjects would obey authority to a greater extent than we had supposed. It also pointed to the importance of feedback from the victim in controlling the subject's behavior.

One further aspect of the pilot study was that subjects frequently averted their eyes from the person they were shocking, often turning their heads in an awkward and conspicuous manner. One subject explained: "I didn't want to see the consequences of what I had done." Observers wrote:

. . . subjects showed a reluctance to look at the victim, whom they could see through the glass in front of them. When this fact was brought to their attention they indicated that it caused them discomfort to see the victim in agony. We note, however, that although the subject refuses to look at the victim, he continues to administer shocks.

This suggested that the salience of the victim may have, in some degree, regulated the subject's performance. If, in obeying the experimenter, the subject found it necessary to avoid scrutiny of the victim, would the converse be true? If the victim were rendered increasingly more salient to the subject, would obedience diminish? The first set of regular experiments was designed to answer this question.

IMMEDIACY OF THE VICTIM

This series consisted of four experimental conditions. In each condition the victim was brought "psychologically" closer to the subject giving him shocks.

In the first condition (Remote Feedback) the victim was placed in another room and could not be heard or seen by the subject, except that, at 300 volts, he pounded on the wall in protest. After 315 volts he no longer answered or was heard from.

The second condition (Voice Feedback) was identical to the first except that voice protests were introduced. As in the first condition the victim was placed in an adjacent room, but his complaints could be heard clearly through a door left slightly ajar, and through the walls of the laboratory.[6]

The third experimental condition (Proximity) was similar to the second, except that the victim was now placed in the same room as the subject, and one and a half feet from him. Thus he was visible as well as audible, and voice cues were provided.

The fourth, and final, condition of this series (Touch-Proximity) was identical to the third, with this exception: The victim received a shock only when his hand rested on a shockplate. At the 150-volt level the victim again demanded to be let free and, in this condition, refused to place his hand on the shockplate. The experimenter ordered the naive subject to force the victim's hand onto the plate. Thus obedience in this condition required that the subject have physical contact with the victim in order to give him punishment beyond the 150-volt level.

Forty adult subjects were studied in each condition. The data revealed that obedience was significantly reduced as the victim was rendered more immediate to the subject. The mean maximum shock for the conditions is shown in Figure 1.

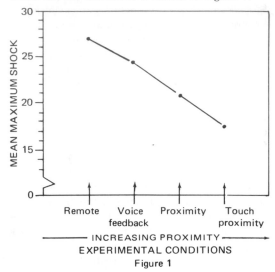

INCREASING PROXIMITY
EXPERIMENTAL CONDITIONS
Figure 1

Expressed in terms of the proportion of obedient to defiant subjects, the findings are that 34 per cent of the subjects defied the experimenter in the Remote condition, 37.5 per cent in Voice Feedback, 60 per cent in Proximity, and 70 per cent in Touch-Proximity.

How are we to account for this effect? A first conjecture might be that as the victim was brought closer the subject became more aware of the intensity of his suffering and regulated his behavior accordingly. This makes sense, but our evidence does not support the interpretation. There are no consistent differences in the attributed level of pain across the four conditions (i.e. the amount of pain experienced by the victim as estimated by the subject and expressed on a 14-point scale). But it is easy to speculate about alternative mechanisms:

Empathic Cues

In the Remote and to a lesser extent the Voice Feedback condition, the victim's suffering possesses an abstract, remote quality for the subject. He is aware, but only in a conceptual sense, that his actions cause pain to another person; the fact is apprehended, but not felt. The phenomenon is common enough. The bombardier can reasonably suppose that his weapons will inflict suffering and death, yet this knowledge is divested of affect, and does not move him to a felt, emotional response to the suffering resulting from his actions. Similar observations have been made in wartime. It is possible that the visual cues associated with the victim's suffering trigger empathic responses in the subject and provide him with a more complete grasp of the victim's experience. Or it is possible that the empathic responses are themselves unpleasant, possessing drive properties which cause the subject to terminate the arousal situation. Diminishing obedience, then, would be explained by the enrichment of empathic cues in the successive experimental conditions.

Denial and Narrowing of the Cognitive Field

The Remote condition allows a narrowing of the cognitive field so that the victim is put out of mind. The subject no longer considers the act of depressing a lever relevant to moral judgment, for it is no longer associated with the victim's suffering. When the victim is close it is more difficult to exclude him phenomenologically. He necessarily intrudes on the subject's awareness since he is continuously visible. In the Remote conditions his existence and reactions are made known only after the shock has been administered. The auditory feedback is sporadic and discontinuous. In the Proximity conditions his inclusion in the immediate visual field renders him a continuously salient element for the subject. The mechanism of denial can no longer be brought into play. One subject in the Remote condition said: "It's funny how you really begin to forget that there's a guy out there, even though you can hear him. For a long time I just concentrated on pressing the switches and reading the words."

Reciprocal Fields

If in the Proximity condition the subject is in an improved position to observe the victim, the reverse is also true. The actions of the subject now come under proximal scrutiny by the victim. Possibly, it is easier to harm a person when he is unable to observe our actions than when he can see what we are doing. His surveillance of the action directed against him may give rise to shame, or guilt, which may then serve to curtail the action. Many expressions of language refer to the discomfort or inhibitions that arise in face-to-face confrontation.

It is often said that it is easier to criticize a man "behind his back" than to "attack him to his face." If we are in the process of lying to a person it is reputedly difficult to "stare him in the eye." We "turn away from others in shame" or in "embarrassment" and this action serves to reduce our discomfort. The manifest function of allowing the victim of a firing squad to be blindfolded is to make the occasion less stressful for him, but it may also serve a latent function of reducing the stress of the executioner. In short, in the Proximity conditions, the subject may sense that he has become more salient in the victim's field of awareness. Possibly he becomes more self-conscious, embarrassed, and inhibited in his punishment of the victim.

Phenomenal Unity of Act

In the Remote conditions it is more difficult for the subject to gain a sense of *relatedness* between his own actions and the consequences of these actions for the victim. There is a physical and spatial separation of the act and its consequences. The subject depresses a lever in one room, and protests and cries are heard from another. The two events are in correlation, yet they lack a compelling phenomenological unity. The structure of a meaningful act—*I am hurting a man*—breaks down because of the spatial arrangements, in a manner somewhat analogous to the disappearance of phi phenomena when the blinking lights are spaced too far apart. The unity is more fully achieved in the Proximity conditions as the victim is brought closer to the action that causes him pain. It is rendered complete in Touch-Proximity.

Incipient Group Formation

Placing the victim in another room not only takes him further from the subject, but the subject and the experimenter are drawn relatively closer. There is incipient group formation between the experimenter and the subject, from which the victim is excluded. The wall between the victim and the others deprives him of an intimacy which the experimenter and subject feel. In the Remote condition, the victim is truly an outsider, who stands alone, physically and psychologically.

When the victim is placed close to the subject, it becomes easier to form an alliance with him against the experimenter. Subjects no longer have to face the experimenter alone. They have an ally who is close at hand and eager to collaborate in a revolt against the experimenter. Thus, the changing set of spatial relations leads to a potentially shifting set of alliances over the several experimental conditions.

Acquired Behavior Dispositions

It is commonly observed that laboratory mice will rarely fight with their litter mates. Scott[7] explains this in terms of passive inhibition. He writes: "By doing nothing under . . . circumstances [the animal] learns to do nothing, and this may be spoken of as passive inhibition . . . this principle has great importance in teaching an individual to be peaceful, for it means that he can learn not to fight simply by not fighting." Similarly, we may learn not to harm others simply by not harming them in everyday life. Yet this learning occurs in a context of proximal relations with others, and may not be generalized to that situation in which the person is physically removed from us. Or possibly, in the past, aggressive actions against others who were physically close resulted in retaliatory punishment which extinguished the original form of response. In contrast, aggression against others at a distance may have only sporadically led to retaliation. Thus the organism learns that it is safer to be aggressive toward others at a distance, and precarious to be so when the parties are within arm's reach. Through a pattern of rewards and punishments, he acquires a disposition to avoid aggression at close quarters, a disposition which does not extend to harming others at a distance. And this may account for experimental findings in the remote and proximal experiments.

Proximity as a variable in psychological research has received far less attention than it deserves. If men were sessile it would be easy to understand this neglect. But we move about; our spatial relations shift from one situation to the next, and the fact that we are near or remote may have a powerful effect on the psychological processes that mediate our behavior toward others. In the present situation, as the victim is brought closer to the man ordered to give him shocks, increasing numbers of subjects break off the experiment, refusing to obey.

The concrete, visible, and proximal presence of the victim acts in an important way to counteract the experimenter's power and to generate disobedience.[8]

CLOSENESS OF AUTHORITY

If the spatial relationship of the subject and victim is relevant to the degree of obedience, would not the relationship of subject to experimenter also play a part?

There are reasons to feel that, on arrival, the subject is oriented primarily to the experimenter rather than to the victim. He has come to the laboratory to fit into the structure that the experimenter —not the victim—would provide. He has come less to understand his behavior than to *reveal* that behavior to a competent scientist, and he is willing to display himself as the scientist's purposes require. Most subjects seem quite concerned about the appearance they are making before the experimenter, and one could argue that this preoccupation in a relatively new and strange setting makes the subject somewhat insensitive to the triadic nature of the social situation. In other words, the subject is so concerned about the show he is putting on for the experimenter that influences from other parts of the social field do not receive as much weight as they ordinarily would. This overdetermined orientation to the experimenter would account for the relative insensitivity of the subject to the victim, and would also lead us to believe that alterations in the relationship between subject and experimenter would have important consequences for obedience.

In a series of experiments we varied the physical closeness and degree of surveillance of the experimenter. In one condition the experimenter sat just a few feet away from the subject. In a second condition, after giving initial instructions, the experimenter left the laboratory and gave his orders by telephone; in still a third condition the experimenter was never seen, providing instructions by means of a tape recording activated when the subjects entered the laboratory.

Obedience dropped sharply as the experimenter was physically removed from the laboratory. The number of obedient subjects in the first condition (Experimenter Present) was almost three times as great as in the second, where the experimenter gave his orders by telephone. Twenty-six subjects were fully obedient in the first condition, and only 9 in the second (Chi square obedient *vs.* defiant in the two conditions, 1 d.f.$=14.7$; $p<.001$). Subjects seemed able to take a far stronger stand against the experimenter when they did not have to encounter him face to face, and the experimenter's power over the subject was severely curtailed.[9]

Moreover, when the experimenter was absent, subjects displayed an interesting form of behavior that had not occurred under his surveillance. Though continuing with the experiment, several subjects administered lower shocks than were required and never informed the experimenter of their deviation from the correct procedure. (Unknown to the subjects, shock levels were automatically recorded by an Esterline-Angus event recorder wired directly into the shock generator; the instrument provided us with an objective record of the subjects' performance.) Indeed, in telephone conversations some subjects specifically assured the experimenter that they were raising the shock level according to instruction, whereas in fact they were repeatedly using the lowest shock on the board. This form of behavior is particularly interesting: although these subjects acted in a way that clearly undermined the avowed purposes of the experiment, they found it easier to handle the conflict in this manner than to precipitate an open break with authority.

Other conditions were completed in which the experimenter was absent during the first segment of the experiment, but reappeared at the point that the subject definitely refused to give higher shocks when commanded by telephone. Although he had exhausted his power via telephone, the experimenter could frequently force further obedience when he reappeared in the laboratory.

Experiments in this series show that the physical *presence* of an authority is an important force contributing to the subject's obedience or defiance. Taken together with the first experimental series on the proximity of the victim, it would appear that something akin to fields of force, diminishing in effectiveness with increasing psychological distance from their source, have a controlling effect on the subject's performance. As the victim is brought closer, the subject finds it harder to administer shocks to him. When the victim's position is held constant relative to the subject, and the authority is made more remote, the subject finds it easier to break off the experiment. This effect is substantial in both cases, but manipulation of the experimenter's position yielded the more powerful results. Obedience to destructive commands is highly dependent on the proximal relations between authority and subject.

TENSIONS

The description of final scores does not fully convey the character of the subjects' performance, and it would be useful to interrupt our reporting of quantitative relationships to remark on the subjects' general reaction to the situation.

One might suppose that a subject would simply break off or continue as his conscience and temperament dictated. Yet this is very far from what happened. There were powerful reactions of tension and emotional strain in a substantial proportion of the participants. Persons were observed to sweat, tremble, stutter, bite their lips, and groan as they found themselves increasingly implicated in the experimental conflict. Some sense of the subjects' mood can be gotten from a transcript of their remarks at break-off point. Here are the remarks of two defiant subjects:

Is he banging? . . . Is he hurt out there? Well, I don't want to be responsible for anything that happens to him. No, I can't go on with it. I don't know whether he's all right or not. I mean he may have a heart condition or something; I wouldn't feel right doing it. He's banging for help. He's evidently in trouble or he wouldn't bang . . . I don't see any sense to this—to knocking him out or something. I just can't see it.

(Subject refuses to administer shocks)

[Subject 0108]

The man is banging. He wants to get out . . . I'm sorry. If the man wants to get out I'd just as soon stop . . . I don't want to administer any more [extremely excited] . . . I will gladly refund the check, but I will not harm this man ... I'm sorry, I will not give him any more if he obviously wants to get out. There is no money in the world that will make me hurt another individual.

[Subject 010X]

And here is a transcript from an obedient subject. He began the experiment calmly, but became increasingly tense as the experiment proceeded. After administering the 150-volt shock, he began to address the experimenter in agitated tones:

150 volts delivered. *You want me to keep going?*
165 volts delivered. *That guy is hollering in there. There's a lot of them here. He's liable to have a heart condition. You want me to go on?*
180 volts delivered. *He can't stand it! I'm not going to kill that man in there! You hear him hollering? He's hollering. He can't stand it. What if something happens to him? ... I'm not going to get that man sick in there. He's hollering in there. You know what I mean? I mean I refuse to take responsibility. He's getting hurt in there. He's in there hollering. Too many left here. Geez, if he gets them wrong. There's too many of them left. I mean who is going to take responsibility if anything happens to that gentleman?*
[The experimenter accepts responsibility.]
All right.
195 volts delivered. *You see he's hollering. Hear that. Gee, I don't know.* [The experimenter says: "The experiment requires that you go on."]—*I know it does, sir, but I mean—hugh—he don't know what he's in for. He's up to 195 volts.*
210 volts delivered.
225 volts delivered.
240 volts delivered. *Aw, no. You mean I've got to keep going up with the scale? No sir. I'm not going to kill that man! I'm not going to give him 450 volts!* [The experimenter says: "The experiment requires that you go on."]—*I know it does, but that man is hollering in there, sir ...*

Despite his numerous, agitated objections, which were constant accompaniments to his actions, the subject unfailingly obeyed the experimenter, proceeding to the highest shock level on the generator. He displayed a curious dissociation between word and action. Although at the verbal level he had resolved not to go on, his actions were fully in accord with the experimenter's commands. This subject did not want to shock the victim, and he found it an extremely disagreeable task, but he was unable to invent a response that would free him from *E's* authority. Many subjects cannot find the specific verbal formula that would enable them

to reject the role assigned to them by the experimenter. Perhaps our culture does not provide adequate models for disobedience.

One puzzling sign of tension was the regular occurrence of nervous laughing fits. In the first four conditions 71 of the 160 subjects showed definite signs of nervous laughter and smiling. The laughter seemed entirely out of place, even bizarre. Full-blown uncontrollable seizures were observed for 15 of these subjects. On one occasion we observed a seizure so violently convulsive that it was necessary to call a halt to the experiment. In the post-experimental interviews subjects took pains to point out that they were not sadistic types and that the laughter did not mean they enjoyed shocking the victim.

In the interview following the experiment subjects were asked to indicate on a 14-point scale just how nervous or tense they felt at the point of maximum tension (Figure 2). The scale ranged from "Not at all tense and nervous" to "Extremely tense and nervous." Self-reports of this sort are of limited precision, and at best provide only a rough indication of the subject's emotional response. Still, tak-

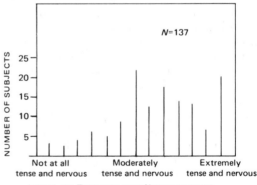

Figure 2

The figure shows the self-reports on "tension and nervousness" for 137 subjects in the Proximity experiments. Subjects were given a scale with 11 values ranging from "Not at all tense and nervous" to "Extremely tense and nervous." They were instructed: "Thinking back to that point in the experiment when you felt the most tense and nervous, indicate just how you felt by placing an X at the appropriate point on the scale." The results are shown in terms of midpoint values.

ing the reports for what they are worth, it can be seen that the distribution of responses spans the entire range of the scale, with the majority of subjects concentrated at the center and upper extreme. A further breakdown showed that obedient subjects reported themselves as having been slightly more tense and nervous than the defiant subjects at the point of maximum tension.

How is the occurrence of tension to be interpreted? First, it points to the presence of conflict. If a tendency to comply with authority were the only psychological force operating in the situation, all subjects would have continued to the end and there would have been no tension. Tension, it is assumed, results from the simultaneous presence of two or more incompatible response tendencies.[10] If sympathetic concern for the victim were the exclusive force, all subjects would have calmly defied the experimenter. Instead, there were both obedient and defiant outcomes, frequently accompanied by extreme tension. A conflict develops between the deeply ingrained disposition not to harm others and the equally compelling tendency to obey others who are in authority. The subject is quickly drawn into a dilemma of a deeply dynamic character, and the presence of high tension points to the considerable strength of each of the antagonistic vectors.

Moreover, tension defines the strength of the aversive state from which the subject is unable to escape through disobedience. When a person is uncomfortable, tense, or stressed, he tries to take some action that will allow him to terminate this unpleasant state. Thus tension may serve as a drive that leads to escape behavior. But in the present situation, even where tension is extreme, many subjects are unable to perform the response that will bring about relief. Therefore there must be a competing drive, tendency, or inhibition that precludes activation of the disobedient response. The strength of this inhibiting factor must be of greater magnitude than the stress experienced, else the terminating act would occur. Every evidence of extreme tension is at the same time an indication of the strength of the forces that keep the subject in the situation.

Finally, tension may be taken as evidence of the reality of the situations for the subjects. Normal subjects do not tremble and sweat unless they are implicated in a deep and genuinely felt predicament.

BACKGROUND AUTHORITY

In psychophysics, animal learning, and other branches of psychology, the fact that measures are obtained at one institution rather than another is irrelevant to the interpretation of the findings, so long as the technical facilities for measurement are adequate and the operations are carried out with competence.

But it cannot be assumed that this holds true for the present study. The effectiveness of the experimenter's commands may depend in an important way on the larger institutional context in which they are issued. The experiments described thus far were conducted at Yale University, an organization which most subjects regarded with respect and sometimes awe. In post-experimental interviews several participants remarked that the locale and sponsorship of the study gave them confidence in the integrity, competence, and benign purposes of the personnel; many indicated that they would not have shocked the learner if the experiments had been done elsewhere.

This issue of background authority seemed to us important for an interpretation of the results that had been obtained thus far; moreover it is highly relevant to any comprehensive theory of human obedience. Consider, for example, how closely our compliance with the imperatives of others is tied to particular institutions and locales in our day-to-day activities. On request, we expose our throats to a man with a razor blade in the barber shop, but would not do so in a shoe store; in the latter setting we willingly follow the clerk's request to stand in our stockinged feet, but resist the command in a bank. In the laboratory of a great university, subjects may comply with a set of commands that would be resisted if given elsewhere. *One must always question the relationship of obedience to a person's sense of the context in which he is operating.*

To explore the problem we moved our apparatus to an office building in industrial Bridgeport and replicated experimental conditions, without any visible tie to the university.

Bridgeport subjects were invited to the experiment through a mail circular similar to the one used in the Yale study, with appropriate changes in letterhead, etc. As in the earlier study, subjects were paid $4.50 for coming to the laboratory. The same age and occupational distributions used at Yale, and the identical personnel, were employed.

The purpose in relocating in Bridgeport was to assure a complete dissociation from Yale, and in this regard we were fully successful. On the surface, the study appeared to be conducted by Research Associates of Bridgeport, an organization of unknown character. (The title had been concocted exclusively for use in this study.)

The experiments were conducted in a three-room office suite in a somewhat run-down commercial building located in the downtown shopping area. The laboratory was sparsely furnished, though clean, and marginally respectable in appearance. When subjects inquired about professional affiliations, they were informed only that we were a private firm conducting research for industry.

Some subjects displayed skepticism concerning the motives of the Bridgeport experimenter. One gentleman gave us a written account of the thoughts he experienced at the control board:

... Should I quit this damn test? Maybe he passed out? What dopes we were not to check up on this deal. How do we know that these guys are legit? No furniture, bare walls, no telephone. We could of called the Police up or the Better Business Bureau. I learned a lesson tonight. How do I know that Mr. Williams [the experimenter] is telling the truth ... I wish I knew how many volts a person could take before lapsing into unconsciousness.
[Subject 2414]

Another subject stated:

I questioned on my arrival my own judgment [about coming]. I had doubts as to the legitimacy of the operation and the consequences of participation. I felt it was a heartless way to conduct memory or learning processes on human beings and certainly dangerous without the presence of a medical doctor.
[Subject 2440]

There was no noticeable reduction in tension for the Bridgeport subjects. And the subjects' estimation of the amount of pain felt by the victim was slightly, though not significantly, higher than in the Yale study.

A failure to obtain complete obedience in Bridgeport would indicate that the extreme compliance found in New Haven subjects was tied closely to the background authority of Yale University; if a large proportion of the subjects remained fully obedient, very different conclusions would be called for.

As it turned out, the level of obedience in Bridgeport, although somewhat reduced, was not significantly lower than that obtained at Yale. A large proportion of the Bridgeport subjects were fully obedient to the experimenter's commands (48 per cent of the Bridgeport subjects delivered the maximum shock *vs.* 65 per cent in the corresponding condition at Yale).

How are these findings to be interpreted? It is possible that if commands of a potentially harmful or destructive sort are to be perceived as legitimate they must occur within some sort of institutional structure. But it is clear from the study that it need not be a particularly reputable or distinguished institution. The Bridgeport experiments were conducted by an unimpressive firm lacking any credentials; the laboratory was set up in a respectable office building with title listed in the building directory. Beyond that, there was no evidence of benevolence or competence. It is possible that the *category* of institution, judged according to its professed function, rather than its qualitative position within that category, wins our compliance. Persons deposit money in elegant, but also in seedy looking banks, without giving much thought to the differences in security they offer. Similarly, our subjects may consider one laboratory to be as competent as another, so long as it *is* a scientific laboratory.

It would be valuable to study the subjects' performance in other contexts which go even further than the Bridgeport study in denying institutional support to the experimenter. It is possible that, beyond a certain point, obedience disappears completely. But that point had not been reached in the Bridgeport office: almost half the subjects obeyed the experimenter fully.

FURTHER EXPERIMENTS

We may mention briefly some additional experiments undertaken at the Yale series. A considerable amount of obedience and defiance in everyday life occurs in connection with groups. And we had reason to feel in the light of many group studies already done in psychology that group forces would have a profound effect on reactions to authority. A series of experiments was run to examine these effects. In all cases only one naive subject was studied per hour, but he performed in the midst of actors who, unknown to him, were employed by the experimenter. In one experiment (Groups for Disobedience) two actors broke off in the middle of the experiment. When this happened 90 per cent of the subjects followed suit and defied the experimenter. In another condition the actors followed the orders obediently; this strengthened the experimenter's power only slightly. In still a third experiment the job of pushing the switch to shock the learner was given to one of the actors, while the naive subject performed a subsidiary act. We wanted to see how the teacher would respond if he were involved in the situation but did not actually give the shocks. In this situation only three subjects out of forty broke off. In a final group experiment the subjects themselves determined the shock level they were going to use. Two actors suggested higher and higher shock levels; some subjects insisted, despite group pressure, that the shock level be kept low; others followed along with the group.

Further experiments were completed using women as subjects, as well as a set dealing with the effects of dual, unsanctioned, and conflicting authority. A final experiment concerned the personal relationship between victim and subject. These will have to be described elsewhere, lest the present report be extended to monographic length.

It goes without saying that future research can proceed in many different directions. What kinds of response from the victim are most effective in causing disobedience in the subject? Perhaps passive resistance is more effective than vehement protest. What conditions of entry into an authority system lead to greater or lesser obedience? What is the effect of anonymity and masking on the subject's behavior? What conditions lead to the subject's perception of responsibility for his own actions? Each of these could be a major research topic in itself, and can readily be incorporated into the general experimental procedure described here.

LEVELS OF OBEDIENCE AND DEFIANCE

One general finding that merits attention is the high level of obedience manifested in the experi-

mental situation. Subjects often expressed deep disapproval of shocking a man in the face of his objections, and others denounced it as senseless and stupid. Yet many subjects complied even while they protested. The proportion of obedient subjects greatly exceeded the expectations of the experimenter and his colleagues. At the outset, we had conjectured that subjects would not, in general, go above the level of "Strong Shock." In practice, many subjects were willing to administer the most extreme shocks available when commanded by the experimenter. For some subjects the experiment provides an occasion for aggressive release. And for others it demonstrates the extent to which obedient dispositions are deeply ingrained, and are engaged irrespective of their consequences for others. Yet this is not the whole story. Somehow, the subject becomes implicated in a situation from which he cannot disengage himself.

The departure of the experimental results from intelligent expectation, to some extent, has been formalized. The procedure was to describe the experimental situation in concrete detail to a group of competent persons, and to ask them to predict the performance of 100 hypothetical subjects. For purposes of indicating the distribution of break-off points judges were provided with a diagram of the shock generator, and recorded their predictions before being informed of the actual results. Judges typically underestimated the amount of obedience demonstrated by subjects.

In Figure 3, we compare the predictions of forty psychiatrists at a leading medical school with the actual performance of subjects in the experiment. The psychiatrists predicted that most subjects would not go beyond the tenth shock level (150 volts; at this point the victim makes his first explicit demand to be freed). They further predicted that by the twentieth shock level (300 volts; the victim refuses to answer) 3.73 per cent of the subjects would still be obedient; and that only a little over one-tenth of one per cent of the subjects would administer the highest shock on the board. But, as the graph indicates, the obtained behavior was very different. Sixty-two per cent of the subjects obeyed the experimenter's commands fully. Between expectation and occurrence there is a whopping discrepancy.

Why did the psychiatrists underestimate the level of obedience? Possibly because their predic-

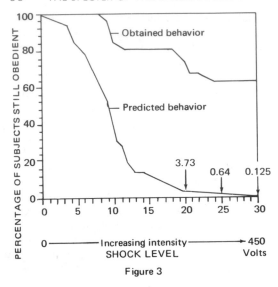

Figure 3

tions were based on an inadequate conception of the determinants of human action, a conception that focuses on motives *in vacuo*. This orientation may be entirely adequate for the repair of bruised impulses as revealed on the psychiatrist's couch, but as soon as our interest turns to action in larger settings, attention must be paid to the situations in which motives are expressed. A situation exerts an important press on the individual. It exercises constraints and may provide push. In certain circumstances it is not so much the kind of person a man is, as the kind of situation in which he is placed, that determines his actions.

Many people, not knowing much about the experiment, claim that subjects who go to the end of the board are sadistic. Nothing could be more foolish as an overall characterization of these persons. It is like saying that a person thrown into a swiftly flowing stream is necessarily a fast swimmer, or that he has great stamina because he moves so rapidly relative to the bank. The context of action must always be considered. The individual, upon entering the laboratory, becomes integrated into a situation that carries its own momentum. The subject's problem then is how to become disengaged from a situation which is moving in an altogether ugly direction.

The fact that disengagement is so difficult testifies to the potency of the forces that keep the subject at the control board. Are these forces to be conceptualized as individual motives and expressed in the language of personality dynamics, or are they to be seen as the effects of social structure and pressures arising from the situational field?

A full understanding of the subject's action will, I feel, require that both perspectives be adopted. The person brings to the laboratory enduring dispositions toward authority and aggression, and at the same time he becomes enmeshed in a social structure that is no less an objective fact of the case. From the standpoint of personality theory one may ask: What mechanisms of personality enable a person to transfer responsibility to authority? What are the motives underlying obedient and disobedient performance? Does orientation to authority lead to a short-circuiting of the shame-guilt system? What cognitive and emotional defenses are brought into play in the case of obedient and defiant subjects?

The present experiments are not, however, directed toward an exploration of the motives engaged when the subject obeys the experimenter's commands. Instead, they examine the situational variables responsible for the elicitation of obedience. Elsewhere, we have attempted to spell out some of the structural properties of the experimental situation that account for high obedience, and this analysis need not be repeated here.[11] The experimental variations themselves represent our attempt to probe that structure, by systematically changing it and noting the consequences for behavior. It is clear that some situations produce greater compliance with the experimenter's commands than others. However, this does not necessarily imply an increase or decrease in the strength of any single definable motive. Situations producing the greatest obedience could do so by triggering the most powerful, yet perhaps the most idiosyncratic, of motives in each subject confronted by the setting. Or they may simply recruit a greater number and variety of motives in their service. But whatever the motives involved—and it is far from certain that they can ever be known —action may be studied as a direct function of the situation in which it occurs. This has been the approach of the present study, where we sought to plot behavioral irregularities against manipulated properties of the social field. Ultimately, social psychology would like to have a compelling *theory of situations* which will, first, present a language in terms of which situations can be defined; proceed to a typology of situations; and then point to the manner in which definable properties of situations are transformed into psychological forces in the individual.[12]

Postscript. Almost a thousand adults were individually studied in the obedience research, and there were many specific conclusions regarding the variables that control obedience and disobedience to authority. Some of these have been discussed briefly in the preceding sections, and more detailed reports will be released subsequently.

There are now some other generalizations I should like to make, which do not derive in any strictly logical fashion from the experiments as carried out, but which, I feel, ought to be made. They are formulations of an intuitive sort that have been forced on me by observation of many subjects responding to the pressures of authority. The assertions represent a painful alteration in my own thinking; and since they were acquired only under the repeated impact of direct observation, I have no illusion that they will be generally accepted by persons who have not had the same experience.

With numbing regularity good people were seen to knuckle under to the demands of authority and to perform actions that were callous and severe. Men who are in everyday life responsible and decent were seduced by the trappings of authority, by the control of their perceptions, and by the uncritical acceptance of the experimenter's definition of the situation, into performing harsh acts.

What is the limit of such obedience? At many points we attempted to establish a boundary. Cries from the victim were inserted; not good enough. The victim claimed heart trouble; subjects still shocked him on command. The victim pleaded that he be let free, and his answers no longer registered on the signal box; subjects continued to shock him. At the outset we had not conceived that such drastic procedures would be needed to generate disobedience, and each step was added only as the ineffectiveness of the earlier techniques became clear. The final effort to establish a limit was the Touch-Proximity condition. But the very first subject in this condition subdued the victim on

command, and proceeded to the highest shock level. A quarter of the subjects in this condition performed similarly.

The results, as seen and felt in the laboratory, are to this author disturbing. They raise the possibility that human nature, or—more specifically—the kind of character produced in American democratic society, cannot be counted on to insulate its citizens from brutality and inhumane treatment at the direction of malevolent authority. A substantial proportion of people do what they are told to do, irrespective of the content of the act and without limitations of conscience, so long as they perceive that the command comes from a legitimate authority. If in this study an anonymous experimenter could successfully command adults to subdue a fifty-year-old man, and force on him painful electric shocks against his protests, one can only wonder what government, with its vastly greater authority and prestige, can command of its subjects. There is, of course, the extremely important question of whether malevolent political institutions could or would arise in American society. The present research contributes nothing to this issue.

In an article entitled "The Dangers of Obedience," Harold J. Laski wrote:

. . . civilization means, above all, an unwillingness to inflict unnecessary pain. Within the ambit of the definition, those of us who heedlessly accept the commands of authority cannot yet claim to be civilized men.
. . . Our business, if we desire to live a life not utterly devoid of meaning and significance, is to accept nothing which contradicts our basic experience merely because it comes to us from tradition or convention or authority. It may well be that we shall be wrong; but our self-expression is thwarted at the root unless the certainties we are asked to accept coincide with the certainties we experience. That is why the condition of freedom in any state is always a widespread and consistent skepticism of the canons upon which power insists.[13]

NOTES

[1]Consider, for example, J. P. Scott's analysis of war in his monograph on aggression: ". . . while the actions of key individuals in a war may be explained in terms of direct stimulation to aggression, vast numbers of other people are involved simply by being part of an organized

society." . . . Slightly rearranged from J. P. Scott, *Aggression,* Chicago: University of Chicago Press, 1958, p. 103.

[2]It consisted of an extended discussion with the experimenter and, of equal importance, a friendly reconciliation with the victim. It is made clear that the victim did not receive painful electric shocks. . . .

[3] . . . In the final analysis, the linguistic symbol representing the subject's action must take its meaning from the concrete context in which that action occurs; and there is probably no word in everyday language that covers the experimental situation exactly, without omissions or irrelevant connotations. It is partly for convenience, therefore, that the terms *obey* and *disobey* are used to describe the subject's actions. At the same time, our use of the words is highly congruent with dictionary meaning.

[4]A more detailed account of the laboratory procedure can be found in S. Milgram, "Behavioral Study of Obedience," *Journal of Abnormal Social Psychology,* **67:** 371–8, 1963. A similar and independently evolved experimental procedure, employing a shock generator, victim, and learning task, was reported by Arnold Buss, *The Psychology of Aggression,* New York: Wiley, 1961. . . .

[5]Stanley Milgram, "Dynamics of Obedience: Experiments in Social Psychology," mimeographed, *National Science Foundation,* January 25, 1961.

[6]It is difficult to convey on the printed page the full tenor of the victim's responses, for we have no adequate notation for vocal intensity, timing, and general qualities of delivery. Yet these features are crucial to producing the effect of an increasingly severe reaction to mounting voltage levels. (They can be communicated fully only by sending interested parties the recorded tapes.) In general terms, however, the victim indicates no discomfort until the 75-volt shock is administered, at which time there is a light grunt in response to the punishment. Similar reactions follow the 90- and 105-volt shocks, and at 120 volts the victim shouts to the experimenter that the shocks are becoming painful. Painful groans are heard on administration of the 135-volt shock, and at 150 volts the victim cries out, "Experimenter, get me out of here! I won't be in the experiment any more! I refuse to go on!" Cries of this type continue with generally rising intensity, so that at 180 volts the victim cries out, "I can't stand the pain," and by 270 volts his response to the shock is definitely an agonized scream. Throughout, he insists that he be let out of the experiment. At 300 volts the victim shouts in desperation that he will no longer provide answers to the memory test; and at 315 volts, after a violent scream, he reaffirms with vehemence that he is no longer a participant. From this point on, he provides no answers, but shrieks in agony whenever a shock is administered; this continues through 450 volts. Of course, many subjects will have broken off before this point. . . .

[7]J. P. Scott, *Aggression.*

[8]Admittedly, the terms *proximity, immediacy, closeness,* and *salience-of-the-victim* are used in a loose sense, and the experiments themselves represent a very coarse treatment of the variable. Further experiments are needed to refine the notion and tease out such diverse factors as spatial distance, visibility, audibility, barrier interposition, and so on. . . .

[9]The third condition also led to significantly lower obedience than this first situation, in which the experimenter was present, but it contains technical difficulties that require extensive discussion.

[10]N. E. Miller, "Experimental Studies in Conflict," in J. McV. Hunt (ed.), *Personality and the Behavior Disorders,* New York: Ronald Press, 1944.

[11]Stanley Milgram, "Behavioral Study of Obedience."

[12]My thanks to Professor Howard Leventhal of Yale for strengthening the writing in this paragraph.

[13]Harold J. Laski, "The Dangers of Obedience," *Harper's Monthly Magazine,* **159:** June 1–10, 1929.

A more thoroughgoing analysis of the experiments described in this article may be found in S. Milgram, *Obedience to Authority,* published by Harper and Row, 1973.

GROUP FORCES IN THE MODIFICATION AND DISTORTION OF JUDGMENTS

Solomon E. Asch

It has been a theme of this work that in society we become dependent on others for understanding, feeling, and the extension of the sense of reality. But this relation places a particular demand upon the participants in social action. If our dependence and trust are to have a solid ground, if we are to reach valid consensus, each must contribute out of his understanding and feeling. Often this condition is not fulfilled. The story of the emperor's new clothes is one example of baseless consensus produced by the failure of each to make his proper contribution. At other times social forces violently prevent the person from giving expression to his insights and purposes. Then the individual must take measures of defense; he may struggle to assert his individuality; he may restrict himself by submitting or resigning himself; he may even make common cause with those who oppress him. We are appalled by the spectacle of the pitiful women of the Middle Ages who, accused of being witches by authorities they never questioned, confessed in bewilderment to unthought-of crimes. But in a lesser measure we have each faced denials of our feelings and needs. What we did in response to these had much to do with what we are now and with our relations to others and to ourselves.

A theory of social influences must take into account the pressures upon persons to act contrary to their beliefs and values. They are likely to bring to the fore powerful forces that arise from the social milieu; at the same time they may reveal forces, perhaps no less powerful, that individuals can mobilize to resist coercion and threats to their integrity. . . .

From Solomon E. Asch, Social Psychology, © 1952. Reprinted by permission of Prentice-Hall, Inc., Englewood Cliffs, New Jersey. Some footnotes and references have been omitted.

In this chapter I shall report the first steps of an investigation the object of which was to study some conditions that induce individuals to remain independent or to yield to group pressures when these are *contrary to fact*. The issues related to this question are important both for theory and for their human implications. Whether a group will resist or submit to given pressures may be decisive for its future. It is an equally decisive fact about a person whether he has the freedom to act according to his beliefs or whether he has failed to develop (or has lost) the possibility of independence. Current thinking has stressed the power of social conditions to induce psychological changes arbitrarily. It has taken slavish submission to group forces as the general fact and has neglected or implicitly denied the capacities of men for independence, for rising under certain conditions above group passion and prejudice. Our present task is to observe directly the interaction between individuals and groups when the paramount issue is that of remaining independent or submitting to social pressure.

A MINORITY OF ONE VS. A UNANIMOUS MAJORITY

The Experimental Procedure

To this end an experimental technique was designed as the basis for a series of studies. A group of seven to nine individuals, all college students, are gathered in a classroom. The experimenter explains that they will be shown lines differing in length and that their task will be to match lines of equal length. The setting is that of a perceptual test. The experimenter places on the blackboard in front of the room two white cardboards on which are pasted vertical black lines. On the card at the left is a single line, the standard. The card at the right has three lines differing in length, one of which is equal to the standard line at the left. The task is to select from among the three lines the one equal in length to the standard line. [See Figure 1.]

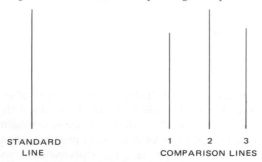

STANDARD
LINE

1   2   3
COMPARISON LINES

Figure 1 A Sample Comparison.

The cards on which the lines appeared were 17 1/2" x 6". The lines had a standard width of 3/8"; their lower ends were 2 1/2" from the lower edge of the cards. Standard lines appeared in the center of the card, while comparison lines were separated by a distance of 1 3/4". The numbering of the lines was done with black gum figures 3/4" long, which were placed 1/2" below the base of each line and directly underneath it.

The instructions to the subjects are as follows:

This is a task which involves the discrimination of lengths of lines. You see the pair of white cards in front. On the left is a single line; on the right are three lines differing in length; they are numbered 1, 2, and 3 in order. One of the three lines at the right is equal to the standard line at the left—you will decide in each case which is the equal line. You will state your judgment in terms of the corresponding number. There will be twelve such comparisons. As the number of lines is few and the group small, I shall call upon each of you in turn to announce your judgment, which I shall record here on a prepared form. Please be as accurate as possible. Suppose we start at the right and proceed to the left.

The lines are vertical and their lower ends are at the same level. The comparison lines are numbered 1, 2, 3. Correctly matched lines are always at a distance of forty inches. In giving his judgment each subject calls out, in accordance with the instruction, the number of the comparison line ("one," "two," "three") that he judges to be equal to the standards. When all the subjects have stated their judgments, the two cards are removed and replaced by a new pair of cards with new

standard and comparison lines. There are twelve sets of standard and comparison lines in all.

The differences to be discriminated are considerable; most unequal comparison lines are clearly longer or shorter than the standard. Table 1 shows the lengths of lines and the order in which they appeared. The comparison lines differ from the standard by varying amounts and no attempt was made to maintain a constant ratio between them. On successive trials the equal line appears in different positions, in random order. The two unequal comparison lines vary in their relation to the standard in the different trials: both are longer, or both are shorter, or one is longer and the other shorter than the standard.

The experiment proceeds normally during the first two trials. The discriminations are simple; each individual monotonously calls out the same judgment. Suddenly this harmony is disturbed at the third trial. While all other subjects call the middle of the three lines equal to the standard line, a single member of the group, seated toward the end, claims the first line to be the correct one. As the experiment progresses, this incident is repeated a number of times. From time to time the same individual continues to disagree with the group. On certain other trials there is complete unanimity.

An outsider, observing the experimental situation, would, after the first few trials, begin to single out this individual as somehow different from the rest of the group and this impression would grow stronger as the experiment proceeded. After the first one or two disagreements he would note certain changes in the manner and posture of this person. He would see a look of perplexity and bewilderment come over this subject's face at the contradicting judgments of the entire group. Often he becomes more active; he fidgets in his seat and changes the position of his head to look at the lines from different angles. He may turn around and whisper to his neighbor seriously or smile sheepishly. He may suddenly stand up to look more closely at the card. At other times he may become especially quiet and immobile.

What is the reason for this peculiar behavior? The answer lies in a crucial feature of the situation that we have not yet mentioned. The subject whose reactions we have been describing is the only member of the group who is reacting to the situation as it has been described. All the others

TABLE I   MAJORITY RESPONSES TO STANDARD AND COMPARISON
LINES ON SUCCESSIVE TRIALS

Trials	Length of Standard Line (in inches)	Length of Comparison Lines (in inches)			Majority Error (in inches)
		1	2	3	
1[a]	7 1/2	5	5 3/4	7 1/2	0
2[a]	5	6 1/2	7	5	0
3	8	8	7	6	1
4	3 1/2	3 3/4	5	3 1/2	1/4
5[a]	9	7	9	11	0
6	6 1/2	6 1/2	5 1/4	7 1/2	1
7	5 1/2	4 1/2	5 1/2	4	1
8[a]	1 3/4	2 3/4	3 1/4	1 3/4	0
9	2 1/2	4	2 1/2	3 3/8	7/8
10	8 1/2	8 1/2	10 1/4	11	1 3/4
11[a]	1	3	1	2 1/4	0
12	4 1/2	4 1/2	3 1/2	5 1/2	1

[a]These designate "neutral" trials, i.e., trials to which the majority responded correctly. All other trials were "critical," i.e., the majority responded incorrectly.
Underlined figures designate the incorrect majority responses.

are, without his knowledge, cooperating with the experimenter by giving at certain times unanimously wrong judgments, by calling two clearly unequal lines equal. The deviations of the group estimate from the correct values are considerable, ranging from 1/4" to 1¾". (The majority responses are underlined in Table 1.) Actually the group consists of two parts: the instructed subjects, whom we shall call the *majority,* and one naive person, whom we shall call the *critical subject,* and who is in the position of a *minority of one.* The instructed majority has met with the experimenter before the experimental sessions. During discussions the aim of the experiment was fully explained and their role in the experiment was carefully rehearsed. Their instructions were to act in a natural, confident way, to give the impression that they were new to the experiment, and to present a united front in defending their judgments when necessary. The group was instructed to be friendly but firm. As far as possible, the same cooperating group met with successive critical subjects. New members of the cooperating group were often obtained from ex-critical subjects.

The critical subjects were recruited by the members of the cooperating group from among their acquaintances. They were told that an experiment in psychology was being performed for which additional subjects were required. When the naive

subject arrived with his acquaintance, he found the others in the corridor or in the room, evidently waiting for the experimenter to appear. Shortly thereafter the experimenter entered and invited the group to be seated. It was also decided in advance that the critical subject was to occupy a seat near the end, usually one seat from the end. The members of the group simply took the available seats, leaving the designated seat for the critical subject. This procedure insured that the critical subject received during each trial the full impact of the majority trend before uttering his judgment. A majority of seven to nine seemed desirable for the purpose. Smaller groups, we feared, would lack the requisite "group volume," and larger groups are difficult to form and maintain.

1. *Responses of the cooperating group.* Altogether there were twelve judgments to be made. To seven of these the majority responded with wrong estimates. (See Table 1.) The first two responses were correct in order to establish a natural starting point. All responses of the majority were unanimous. The responses of the group were recorded by the experimenter on previously prepared forms. In addition, the experimenter and his assistant made independent records of the appearance, manner, and comments of the critical subject.

2.   *The group discussion.*   The experiment did not come to an end with the completion of the comparisons. To bring out more clearly the reactions of the critical subject it was decided to engage him, after the exposure of the cards, in a brief, informal discussion. The experimenter opened by saying that he had noticed disagreement at certain points and asked whether there were any remarks. Although the statement was not directed at any one in particular, the critical subject usually responded. At this point the members of the group joined in. They put their questions apparently out of curiosity and interest. At first the discussion centered on how to account for the disagreement that had developed. As the critical subject began increasingly to occupy the center of the scene, he was asked to indicate who, in his opinion, was right —the group or himself. He was asked whether it was likely that the entire group was in error and he alone right, how much confidence he placed in his judgments under the circumstances, and so on. The following questions were always included: "Who do you suppose was right?" If the subject replied that his judgments were correct he was asked: "Do you suppose that the entire group was wrong and that you alone were right?" "How confident of your judgments are you?" "If something important depended on your answer, if this were a matter of practical consequence, how would you act?" "What would you say to all this if you were an outsider?" The questions were asked in the order in which they are listed; any member of the group was free to raise the questions as the occasion warranted.

3.   *Interview and disclosure of the experimental purpose.*   At the conclusion of the discussion, which lasted approximately five minutes, the experimenter dismissed the group and asked to see the critical subject. During the interview the questions that were raised earlier were followed up, the object being to find out in greater detail the subject's reaction to the experimental situation. Toward the end of the interview the experimenter explained fully the object of the experiment and the structure of the experimental situation; this procedure was followed with all subjects. It did not seem advisable or justified to allow the subject to leave without full knowledge of what had happened. We may anticipate and say that nearly all subjects expressed interest and most were glad of the opportunity to have experienced a striking social situation from which they felt they had learned a lesson.

Finally, we may mention that in performing this experiment certain precautions must be taken for the sake of the critical individual. No subject should be allowed to leave without having the purport of the procedure fully explained. The subjects do not resent the temporary imposition practiced upon them provided they understand the purpose of the investigation. Many feel that the experiment has been an experience of some value. It brings home to them directly, and in a way that mere reading or discussions fail to do, the meaning of group opposition and the real possibility of an individual being right even if he has a unanimous public opinion against him. The critical subjects usually left with the feeling that they had witnessed a situation that touched upon a significant human problem.

This, then, was the object and the design of the experiments to be described. An individual was in the midst of a group of equals all of whom were judging in public a simple perceptual relation. By means of the procedure outlined a disagreement developed between the group and one of its members. Two opposing forces acted upon the single subject: one from a clearly perceived relation and another from a compact majority. Having placed the individual in conflict with a unanimous majority we proceeded to observe its effect upon him. There was a total of 31 male critical subjects in the present experiment, which we will call Experiment 1.

Quantitative Results

How did the critical subjects respond to the unanimous opposition of the majority? Did they remain independent and repudiate the wrong trend of the group? Or did they show a tendency to yield to the majority, and if so, to what extent? We shall attempt to answer these questions first in terms of the quantitative results.

Table 2 contains the frequency of correct and incorrect responses in the group of 31 critical subjects. We find that two-thirds of the responses were correct and independent of the majority trend; the remaining one-third were errors identical with those of the majority. In contrast, the errors obtained in a control group of 25 subjects,

TABLE 2 ESTIMATES OF EXPERIMENTAL AND CONTROL GROUPS

Experiment	N	Total Number of Estimates	Correct Estimates F	Per Cent	Pro-Majority Errors F	Per Cent
1: Minority of one vs. a unanimous majority	31	217	145	66.8	72	33.2
Control	25	175	162	92.6	13	7.4

who reported their judgments privately in writing, were 7.4 per cent of the total. The mean number of errors in the experimental group was 2.3; in the control group 0.5. From this we may draw two conclusions. First, the preponderance of estimates was, under the given conditions, correct and independent. Second, there occurred at the same time a pronounced movement toward the majority; their erroneous announcements contaminated one-third of the estimates of the critical subjects.

The errors were not however equally distributed among the critical subjects; indeed there is evidence of extreme individual differences, as Table 3 will show. The responses of the critical group cover the entire range; there were subjects who remained completely independent, and at the other extremes were some who went with the majority without exception. One-fifth of the subjects were entirely independent; if we include those who erred only once, which may be considered within the control range, we have 42 per cent of the group whose estimates were not appreciably affected by the experimental conditions. The range of errors in the control group was sharply curtailed, no subject erring more than twice. . . .

TABLE 3 DISTRIBUTION OF CRITICAL ERRORS IN EXPERIMENTAL AND CONTROL GROUPS

Number of Errors	Control Group	Experimental Group
0	14	6
1	9	7
2	2	6
3	0	4
4	0	4
5	0	1
6	0	1
7	0	2
N	25	31
Mean	0.5	2.3

In conclusion: The experimental condition significantly distorted the reported estimates. There were extreme individual differences in response to majority pressure, ranging from complete independence to complete yielding. . . .

Reactions to the Experimental Situation

How did the critical individuals face the situation, and what was its effect upon them? . . . We shall now attempt an account of what happened, based on the observations of the subjects and of their reactions in the post-experimental interview. . . .

EFFORT AT REESTABLISHING EQUILIBRIUM. The immediate reaction of most critical subjects is one of varying degrees of puzzlement or confusion. A few stop the proceedings at the first or second disagreement to inquire if they have understood the instructions correctly; others less bold make similar inquiries of their immediate neighbors. None are prepared for the fundamental disagreement; instead they look for a more obvious source of misunderstanding. The subjects are not yet fully in the conflict; they are in fact resisting it as a real possibility by searching for a simpler explanation. They hope that the early disagreements were episodic and that they will give way to solid unanimity. As the disagreements persist, they can no longer cling to this hope. They now believe that they are perceiving in one way, the group in another.

LOCALIZATION OF THE DIFFICULTY IN THE CRITICAL SUBJECT. Most subjects see a disturbance created, not by the majority, but by themselves. They do not call upon the majority to justify its judgments; most simply try to defend the validity of their own reactions. The subject assumes the burden of proof. He, not the majority, becomes the center of the trouble; it is he who is disrupting the consistent trend. Nearly all speak in terms of "the group contradicts what I see," not in terms of "I contradict what the group sees." In the same direction is the reluctance of many subjects to assert definitely that the majority is in error. It is noteworthy that the experimenter, too, despite full knowledge of the situation, at times perceives things in the same way, with the subject as the creator and center of disturbance.

ATTEMPTS AT SOLUTION.   Once the realization has taken hold that there is a basic disagreement, the subject makes an effort to overcome the difficulty by explaining it somehow. The doubts and tensions that the disagreements engender are conditions that support the flourishing of hypotheses, all designed to bridge the inexplicable gap. Some actually help to diminish the tension. Subjects may feel that the other members of the majority are conformists, following the first subject who for some reason is inaccurate. Others may mention that some in the group are wearing glasses. Most hypotheses are, however, *ad hoc* and half-hearted. Quite frequently a subject will say that the disagreements are the result of the different positions of the observers, overlooking the inconsistency of this proposal. Still others vaguely refer to psychological illusions, or propose that the group was judging on the basis of criteria other than length. As a rule, the subjects do not take their hypotheses, which fluctuate considerably, too seriously.

Many who have heard of these experiments express surprise at the fact that few suspect the genuineness of the majority. The surprise is understandable; during the first steps of this investigation the writer himself had considerable doubts that the episode could be sustained. We may add that the effect is not the result of unusual dramatic qualities in the majority; quite tepid groups have been sufficient to produce the experimental effect. A specific factor preventing a solution is the narrowing of the subject's mental field. As soon as he becomes concerned to know why *he* is wrong and as soon as he begins to respond to the urgencies of the situation, he becomes less free to look at it with a detached eye and to arrive at a solution that to an outsider seems relatively simple.

CENTERING ON THE OBJECT OF JUDGMENT.   In their eagerness to locate the source of the difficulty the subjects now look with greater care and become more attentive and scrupulous in observing and comparing. They act to increase the clearness of their perceptions and judgments. The more the subject is out of step with the group the more anxiously does he turn to the situation itself. That one effect of group opposition is to direct the person back to the situation and to induce a heightened objectivity is a trite observation. It has, however, been neglected in psychological discussion. A particularly interesting example of this tendency is the desire expressed by a few of the more spontaneous subjects to see the lines again and to measure them. Some suddenly jump up and approach the cards. It is as if these subjects were trying to eliminate the last possibility of indirectness involved in viewing the lines from a distance. A few, indeed, asserted that they would stick to their view until they were able to measure the lines. It is probable that in a less formal situation many more might have insisted on a close-up view of the cards or on the most direct test of superposition. In this behavior these subjects are showing that they are not accepting the group as the final arbiter in the matter.

GROWTH OF SELF-DOUBT.   Despite all efforts the disagreement persists. The subjects search for a principle of explanation, but they are deprived of the possibility of finding it. Nothing can be clearer or more certain than that the materials contain the relations perceived. There is something wrong, but they cannot say what it is. At this point doubt sets in for many. Some begin to fear that their senses may be deceiving them, and their consternation deepens. It is to this factor that we trace the poignancy of many reactions. Some of the most confident and independent subjects become shaken. One of these reported developing the feeling that he was either very right or very wrong. Another declared: "To me it seems I'm right, but my reason tells me I'm wrong, because I doubt that so many people could be wrong and I alone right." The responses of many others go in the same direction: "I would follow my own view, though part of my reason would tell me that I might be wrong." "From what I saw I thought I was right, but apparently I must be wrong. I began to doubt that my vision was right." "What I said appeared to me to be right, but I don't know who is right." "Now the whole class is disagreeing with me and it is possible that I may have been wrong." Some of the staunchest subjects admitted to feelings of doubt. "A little doubt came into my mind, but it was before my eyes, and I was determined to say what I saw. Even though in your mind you know you are right, you wonder why everybody else thinks differently. I was doubting myself and was puzzled."

Now differences in steadfastness between subjects emerge. Some continue firmly to defend their judgments, despite their perplexity. The following statements are representative: "I will believe that they were wrong until you show me who was right." This subject attributed the differences to his better perception. "I wouldn't believe I am wrong until I measure the lines." But others are more ready to yield to the possibility that the voice of the group is right. The following is an example: "I'd probably take that of the people here (if this were a practical situation). I'd figure my judgment was faulty. I feel puzzled . . . in all the years I've lived I haven't had any trouble like that." Still others concede even more to the majority.

Yet the subjects cannot rest in doubt. They might be relieved to find that they were wrong and the group right, provided they could understand the disagreement. But they are not permitted to resolve the difficulty in this way. No matter how shaken they may be they cannot get away from the compelling evidence of their senses. As a result the attitudes of many fluctuate rapidly during the experiment. An illustrative reaction is the following: "Probably I'm wrong . . . no, I don't mean that. If everyone saw it the other way, I guess I am wrong. But I still think I'm right." Some may suddenly begin to doubt their correctness and try to "improve" their judgment; and because they cannot succeed—the material clearly asserting its relationships—their healthy, usually taken-for-granted faith in their perceptions will suddenly reassert itself strongly. They then throw off the yoke of doubt energetically, only to have the burden of the opposition from the majority settle again on them and force them to reconsider. Lending strength to the dilemma is the sense of irreconcilability of the disagreement, the realization that two vectors that should be identical are starkly contradictory.

LONGING TO BE IN AGREEMENT WITH THE GROUP
Most subjects miss the feeling of being at one with the group. In addition, there is frequent reference to the concern they feel that they might appear strange and absurd to the majority. One of the strongest subjects reported: "Despite everything there was a lurking fear that in some way I did not understand I might be wrong; fear of exposing myself as inferior in some way. It is more pleasant if one is really in agreement." Another subject asserted: "I don't deny that at times I had the feeling 'To heck with it, I'll go along with the rest.' " Or: "I felt awfully funny, everything was going against me." "I felt disturbed, puzzled, separated, like an outcast from the rest. Every time I disagreed I was beginning to wonder if I wasn't beginning to look funny."

Introducing a Partner

The basic experiment had one major condition: The majority was *unanimous* in opposition to the minority. In what way will the situation change if the critical subject finds within the group one other person who sides with him? Will he draw strength from this support? Will he be more independent and face the opposition with greater steadiness? Can the presence of one supporting individual nullify the effect of the majority? How will the critical subject become aware of the presence of the partner?

One member of the cooperating group of 7 to 9 persons was instructed to give correct responses throughout. The partner was seated in the third position, thus preceding the critical subject at all times. He was instructed to answer in a firm manner, not to obtrude himself in the discussion, but to allow the critical subject to occupy the center. By this procedure we introduced another member who reported the discriminations the critical subject perceived and who was the first to contradict the majority. There were 18 subjects, consisting of 10 women and 8 men. All other conditions were identical with those of the first experiment.

The majority effect was markedly weakened under these conditions. There were sixteen majority errors (out of a total of 126 estimates), or 13 per cent of the number of estimates. Not only was the amount of yielding reduced, but also the degree to which any single subject yielded diminished strikingly; no one exceeded three errors. For the group as a whole the frequency of errors does not differ significantly from that obtained in the control group. However, the majority effect was not abolished in all instances. In appraising the results it is necessary to realize that an error under these conditions may have considerable significance, since it signalizes not only a movement toward the majority but also an abandonment of the partner.

In general, this condition reduced markedly the severity of tension. Three subjects insisted that they were not at all affected, and two others admitted to only a slight concern, a result strikingly different from that obtained with unanimous majorities. Although we possess no way of stating exactly the psychological tension engendered in the subjects, both our observations and the comments of the subjects point in the same direction. There was a less oppressive and tense attitude, and the quality of the disturbance was more complacent.

The sole condition differentiating this from the first experiment is the introduction of an additional subject who reports correct judgments. We were therefore particularly interested to establish how the critical subject perceived this condition. Nearly every one became immediately aware of the partner. Subject 1, with one majority response, looked constantly at the partner, was aware of him from the very beginning, and knew that there was only one partner. Subject 2, also with one majority error, made frequent attempts to contact the partner by looking his way. She subsequently stated that he gave her moral support: "I wonder how it would have been if I had sat where he sat." Those who were most affected noticed the partner least and apparently lost sight of him as they became increasingly occupied with their own problems. One became so overwrought that she failed to notice the partner. "Was there another one who agreed with me?" she replied to a direct question. "I heard the different answers but they didn't register; I didn't realize I was giving the same answers as the other girl." Many subjects felt that the partner made the situation more supportable, but few realized the full extent of the partner's help. This statement by one subject is representative of many: "I was not always aware of the other girl, but I knew about her." It was our impression that at the very outset nearly all subjects noticed the partner and that this realization served to mitigate from the start the worst difficulties produced in the main experiment. That the subjects were not fully aware of the

support they were receiving is understandable; they had no standard for comparison. The presence of a single voice pointing to the true state of affairs had an unmistakable liberating effect. With one person at their side most subjects were able to face the majority with independence and the weakest were spared the extremes of yielding. To understand this result we need to keep in mind the partner's double function: He provided support and at the same time broke the unanimity of the majority. By his action he loosened the compactness of the majority and demonstrated to the critical subject that his alternative had independent support. The finding points to a fundamental difference between the condition of being alone and having some source of human support. It is also clear that the effects obtained cannot be interpreted as a summation of influences proceeding from each member of the majority. The critical subjects were able to oppose a majority of seven when they could join forces with one other person.

INDEPENDENCE, CONFORMITY, AND CONSENSUS

The observations reported in the preceding pages, in particular those pertaining to the opposition between a minority of one and a unanimous group, describe an effect of a majority in a specially contrived experimental situation. What can it teach us about the operation of group forces? It may seem that the results were quite obvious, at least in outline. Two contradictory directions were simultaneously acting on a person: his direct experience and the indirectly known experiences of others. The divergence of the two posed a problem that individuals resolved in one way or another, all of them quite understandable. If, however, we divest the observations of their self-evidence, they pose questions that touch upon central issues in human relations.

The Social Significance of Independence and Yielding

The investigation under discussion has brought into relief a requirement of shared action that if violated exposes the social process to hazard.

We may first consider what the preceding observations signify for the effects that group conditions can exert on individuals in their midst. One point merits attention despite its obviousness. The distortions that we have found in action, judgment, and, to some extent, perception were a consequence of pressures from the social sphere, not of tendencies whose source is in the individual himself. The individuals who succumbed to the majority would have acted in an entirely sensible way had they been spared the warping influence of the group. The effects we have observed had their start in a prior contamination of the social field—evidence of the profound difference, from the standpoint of the individual, between being in a group that possesses an adequate view and being in a group whose view is distorted.

Let us now consider the import of the observations for the role of individuals in the social process. Social existence presupposes, we have seen, the achievement of consensus; but consensus, if it is not to be an empty or treacherous gesture, must have validity. The meaning of consensus collapses when individuals act like mirrors that reflect each other. Precisely because we live in an environment that is in a powerful way mediated by the psychological processes of others does the integrity of the individual's contribution play an indispensable role. If reliance upon mutual understanding and purpose is to have meaning, each must rely in an ultimate way upon his own understanding and purpose. The need for consensus demands that individuals should be able to refuse agreement when they see no way of reaching it. When individuals abrogate their capacity to think and judge in their own way, when they cease to relate themselves independently to things and persons, when they surrender initiative and delegate it to others, they are altering the social process and introducing into it a radical arbitrariness. The act of independence is productive from the social point of view, since it is the only way to correct errors and to steer the social process in accordance with felt requirements. On the other hand, the act of yielding is anti-social because it spreads error and confusion. Sharing itself is not enough; it can produce the spectacle of millions marching under the banner of a frightful Weltanschauung. Shared action that rests on the voluntary or involuntary suppression of individual experience is a malignant sociological process. By the same token, group action must have a wholly different dynamics and power when

its purposes and ideas rest on the insight of its human members.

We have implied above that independence and its failures in social life are in some respects significantly similar to what was observed under the experimental conditions described here. This inference needs to be justified, since the experimental situation was quite special and in many ways not representative of ordinary or even unusual social circumstances. For example, many social influences are possible because the facts are remote and complex, because they are not directly given and crystal clear. This is but one of the special conditions the experimental situation contains. In the absence of further evidence we cannot rigorously justify the relevance of the present observations to the conditions that persons generally face, but it seems fruitful to assume that there is a relation. There can be no doubt that personal independence and the lack of it are facts crucial for social life. There are times when one must choose between stark alternatives that have very much to do with the question of independence. Germans who lived near concentration camps could not escape the choice of breaking with their social order or of forcibly suppressing a range of facts and refusing to bring them into relation with their daily experience. But one also observes the relevance of these processes under less stringent conditions. Those who strive to think independently and not merely to repeat current slogans are playing a role in the social process quite different from those who veer away from ideas because they are threatening or who deny all reason to a side when it is out of favor. It is probably incorrect to suppose that states and tyrants achieve insidious aims entirely by giving a plausible account of themselves. What happens often is that people partly meet those who manipulate them. The threat of unpleasant consequences makes them more amenable to the tyrant's kind of "reason," which they allow to soften the edge of their scrupulousness by adopting a "dignified" alternative to autonomy. Social and political life would be far healthier if the yielder in most of us were less active and adroit.

The Personal Significance of Independence and Yielding

Independence and yielding are at the same time social events and actions having deep personal significance; rarely can one see more clearly the intimate unity of the personal and social. We shall be concerned here with their import for an understanding of personal functioning.

There is an obvious personal difference between the reactions of independence and yielding. To be independent is to assert the authentic value of one's own experience; to yield is to deny the evidence of one's senses, to permit oneself to become confused about one's experience, to suppress evidence that cannot be assimilated—to renounce a condition upon which one's capacity to function depends in an essential way. What may be the reasons for these strikingly different modes of reaction? For this purpose let us briefly return to the main experimental condition. An individual had the choice of adhering to the primary relation between himself and the object of judgment, or he could abandon the latter in favor of the presumed relation between the group and the external situation. We are observing how in a given situation an individual handles the data of individual and social experience when these are in contradiction. How the contradiction will be resolved will depend on a number of conditions. We have seen that it varies with the quality of the social evidence (e.g., its unanimity); we may be certain that it is also a function of the quality of the external conditions (e.g., their clarity). At present we are concerned with its dependence on the individual himself, on his personal qualities.

It should be stated at once that a definitive answer concerning the personal conditions responsible for independence and yielding awaits further investigation; the remarks that follow are therefore only tentative. The sheer difference between the contrasted reactions justifies the presumption that the behavior of the individuals was a function of certain relatively enduring characteristics. The path of independence required self-assertion in the face of an inexplicable dilemma; that of yielding involved the renunciation of the testimony of one's senses. There is, of course, the possibility that the reactions observed were the result of momentary circumstances and that the individual who was independent under the given conditions might have acted quite differently under other conditions or even in a similar situation at a later time. Because the technical difficulties are considerable, it has not been possible experimentally to establish the consistency of individual reactions to different forms of group pressure. Although a factor of contingency was doubtless at work in some instances, observations of the subjects and often their own comments support the assumption that other, more stable personal characteristics also exerted a pronounced effect. The situation was one fraught with seriousness for a considerable number; it often seemed clear that they responded in a way characteristic of them. There appear to be important differences between persons in the ease with which they can be shaken off their course by the actions of others.

The task of investigation is first to describe the properties of those who are socially independent and of those who cannot maintain a stand under opposition and then to inquire into the conditions responsible for modes of action so different. The differences we have observed concern the ability of the person to relate himself independently to things or his steadiness in relation to reality under social opposition. Some were able to accept a surprising stress and to endure social opposition without undue anxiety; others were quickly overwhelmed and became narrowed in perception and feeling. Observation suggests at this point a broad hypothesis: that individual immunity to distortion by group pressure is a function of the person's relation to himself and others. Independence always requires some assertion of the self; at the least it needs the ability to acknowledge a shortcoming without loss of self-respect or ability to accept criticism without feeling rejected. It is therefore an expression of a certain confidence about the self and its relation to others. Yielding on the other hand is a sign of a lack of stability or confidence in these relations. It marks an inability to resist or reject others by an open assertion of one's dissident personal judgment. The independent person possesses certain sources of strength within himself that enable him to bear a brief ordeal, whereas the yielding person can find safety only by merging anonymously with the group. It would however be wrong to conclude that those who are not independent feel more deeply the need of close contact with others; the manner in which they are willing to achieve this closeness casts doubt on this assumption. These formulations are of course general, and will need to be replaced by more specific propositions.

If we reject, as I think we should, the assumption

that the differences in question are constitutional, we shall want to inquire into the social and personal experiences that are responsible for them. Such an inquiry should center on the outstanding forms of relation persons establish in the course of growth to the human element in the surroundings and to themselves. In particular, it would be necessary to examine what social relations and demands further personal autonomy and what conditions hamper its development. The search for clarification will have, it seems to me, to start with the proposition of this chapter that social life makes a double demand upon us: to rely upon others with trust and to become individuals who can assert our own reality. The primary striving of humans in society is toward both trust and independence; this is the relation that all strive to achieve. On this basis they permit themselves to grow into the social fabric. We may suppose that this aim can be achieved under favorable conditions, but even then not without a struggle. At the least one has to face demands and opposition. But there are conditions less favorable for development which, while encouraging the need to live in a wider and richer world than the individual can encompass alone, also injure and undermine him. This happens when social circumstances stifle the individual's impulses and deny them expression. Many find such restrictions too taxing. Since in the early years the individual is particularly dependent on consensus, he may come to define his self in terms of the evaluations others have of him and find a measure of safety in this procedure. To live up to the demands of others he may find it necessary to blunt his experiences, to develop a self that is shadowy, and to become superficial about the character of others. Such conditions impair the ability to trust; at the same time they injure one's capacity to do without support on those occasions that demand it. Those who yield act at times as if they had entered a compact which will guarantee them a minimum of safety at the cost of self-restriction. It is probable that self-limitation is achieved by a restriction of awareness and that the course of the process is largely unknown to its actors.

The present discussion converges on a difficult and intriguing problem: the relation between character and social action. Is there a describable relation between the event considered in its dependence on the individual and its social function?

When extended beyond the present confines the question becomes one of the relation between the social import of action and its psychological foundations in the individual or of the relation between ideology and character. In considering this problem students have followed the most diverse directions. There are those who hold that social values are merely a way of satisfying strictly personal needs. For example, radicalism or conservatism in politics at a given time are not, it is asserted, decided in their own terms and in the light of actual problems; the choice of the individual is a way of projecting purely personal needs, which themselves have nothing to do with the content of the issues. Freudian thinkers have inclined to this mode of thinking. Others reverse this position, asserting that personal factors may be ignored when one considers social values, that the latter are directly determined by current concerns and social position, and that the same social values are held by those who differ deeply in personal ways. This view implies that the attempt to introduce a relation between social values and personal factors is to lose one's way in a morass of irrelevant psychological facts. This is the view one often encounters in Marxist thought. The reader will doubtless be able to think of instances that lend validity to each of these positions. There are instances in which social values are little more than an oblique expression of personal needs. On the other hand, it is obvious that the same social movement can attract the most varied personalities. Yet it is difficult to escape the conviction that the specific role a person plays in the social field cannot be divorced from his individual qualities. At this difficult and indecisive stage of thought it is important not to restrict oneself to already stated alternatives. There is, it seems to me, another possibility. Social and personal values, although they do not coincide, may be related. Each is determined by conditions in many respects too different to encourage the expectation of a unique relation between them, yet they touch at crucial points. The nub of the difficulty concerns the razor-like cleavage that is often introduced between the categories of social and personal. Too often we overlook the fact that personal values have an intrinsic social content and that the qualities a person expresses in his immediate human relations have an intrinsic relevance to wider concerns.

Civilization . . . obtains mastery over the individual's dangerous desire for aggression by weakening and disarming it and setting up an agency within him to watch over it, like a garrison in a conquered city.

SIGMUND FREUD

We find that the small child sees a vision of holiness when he chances to glance in the direction of government—a sanctity and rightness of the demigoddess who dispenses the milk of human kindness.

DAVID EASTON AND
JACK DENNIS

I learned early that crying out in protest could accomplish things.

MALCOLM X

Faced with a father who made questionable use of his brute superiority; a father who had at his disposal the techniques of making others feel morally inferior without being quite able to justify his own moral superiority; a father to whom he could not get close and from whom he could not get away—faced with such a father, how was he going to submit without being emasculated, or rebel without emasculating his father?

ERIK ERIKSON ON MARTIN LUTHER

Chapter 2

RESPONSES TO
AUTHORITY AS
A FUNCTION OF
INDIVIDUAL CHARACTER

Both the Asch and Milgram studies demonstrate that there are striking differences among individuals in how they respond to pressures to conform or comply. Some individuals readily submit to group consensus or authoritative orders. Others comply but provide visible evidence of reluctance and distress. Still others obey "part of the way." Finally, there are those who refuse—who insist on the validity of their own judgments or who question the validity of authoritative orders.

The responses obtained in these experiments may be situation specific. It is possible that a yielder in the Asch situation could be disobedient in a Milgram situation, or that the responses given by an individual on one particular day might be quite different from the responses he would give at some other time. But on the basis of our experience in everyday life, we are led to assume something quite different—namely, that the responses of subjects in a particular experimental situation are likely to be *symptomatic* of more general response tendencies of that individual. A plausible hypothesis would be that the highly compliant subject in Milgram's experiment tends to be a person who generally accepts orders from authoritative persons; that the defiant subject is likely to be more generally resistant, skeptical, and nonconforming.

That individuals tend to have such broad predispositions is suggested by ordinary speech. We tend to describe some people as submissive, docile, cooperative, conventional, and others are labelled as rebellious, argumentative, troublesome, self-confident, courageous. But intuitions spawned by everyday experience are not the only grounds for hypothesizing such general tendencies in individuals. For example, the very conditions of these experimental situations suggest the possibility that the subjects bring something to the situation that helps account for their behavior. First, both the Asch and Milgram situations present the subjects with a sharp discrepancy between their personal inclinations and perceptions and the external demands and judgments directed toward them. Although all subjects find this discrepancy disturbing, some tend to give greater weight to their own internal promptings, while others tend to accept and follow the external ones. Yielding and obedience in these situations would not present much explanatory difficulty if the external pressures were accompanied by *sanctions.* We could then say that subjects ignored their personal inclinations because they were rewarded for obedience, or punished for disobedience. But this was not the case in these situations. These experiments are challenging in large part because they produced subjects who overcame their personal inclinations and accepted external direction—despite the fact that they received no significant return for so doing. Why would you give greater weight to someone else's judgments than to your own when you don't have to? Perhaps part of the answer lies in a general tendency in individuals to doubt one's own judgments and downgrade one's own wishes.

The idea that a person's actions in a situation are determined not only by features of the situation but also by more enduring attributes of the person is central to that field of psychology known as the study of personality. There are innumerable theories of personality, but all tend to agree that persons respond to given situations in characteristic ways that differentiate them from one another. Many theorists argue that human beings strive for consistent, integrated perspectives on the world. A crucial point of integration has to do with the relationship between ideas and feelings. In a situation which has a range of possible intellectual perspectives, a person tends to adopt that perspective which most "resonates" with his feelings. If, for instance, a person is emotionally expressive, if he feels deeply and expresses his feelings openly, then he is likely to be committed to idea systems that elicit such expressiveness. If, on the other hand, a person is emotionally controlled, he is likely to be committed to ideologies that support control, restraint, and order.

In keeping with this, some persons are apparently predisposed to obey, while others are predisposed to avoid or refuse obedience—and both patterns are linked to deep tendencies in individual character. In my own view, these responses to authority constitute a core element in both intrapersonal and interpersonal relations. The question is, how do dispositions to resist or obey authority get established in the individual in the first place?

The most coherent and most influential attempt to answer such questions was undertaken by Sigmund Freud and has been carried on by his followers and critics within the psychoanalytic tradition. Freud's key proposition was that the central dispositions of adults have their origin in the experiences of early childhood. This explanation was particularly well worked out in the area of adult attitudes and responses to authority. The family is, among other things, an authority structure. One of the primary facts about childhood experience is that the child is totally dependent upon his parents—figures of awesome authority. Parents are authorities in their own right; in addition, they are consciously and unconsciously agents of the authoritative structure of society at large, actively preparing their offspring to confront the demands that the structure imposes.

For Freud, being raised in a family is the primary experience with authority. It is primary because it is first, and because it is the crucial determinant of how one is likely to act in all future relationships involving superordination. In relating to his parents, the child forms lasting expectations about how authorities ought to act and treat him; and he forms durable impressions of his own rights and capacities with respect to authority. He develops toward his parents feelings of love and respect, fear and hatred—some of which he is aware and some of which he is unaware. All future relations with authority cannot help but elicit these expectations, impressions, and feelings. They cannot help but become occasions in which the persons involved attempt to relive, replay, and rework the unfinished scenes and unresolved issues between themselves and their parents.

Freud formulated an extremely detailed conception of the means by which childhood experience became instituted as adult character. He started with the assumption that the unsocialized, "natural" organism seeks to deploy its psychic energy solely to maximize pleasure and avoid pain. He assumed further that the unlimited pursuit of pleasure was fundamentally incompatible with the requirements of the survival of civilization. Human beings must band together to preserve themselves, but the perpetuation of civilization requires that energy be devoted to painful and unpleasurable work, that pleasure be foregone and postponed, scarcity and deprivation tolerated. Moreover, Freud argued that the natural organism contained powerful aggressive drives, and that civilization required the control of such destructive tendencies in the interest of cooperation and harmony.

Childhood socialization was the principle means by which the natural organism's inappropriate pleasure-seeking and aggressive tendencies were brought under control, repressed, and rechanneled in the interest of civilization. According to Freud, since the parents are the principle agents of socialization, family life is inherently an arena of tension and conflict between parental demands and the natural inclinations of the child. At first, the child complies in order to maintain the parents' love, win their approval, and avoid punishment. But successful socialization requires something more than the capacity to respond to external rewards and punishments; the child must develop the capacity to guide his own behavior in appropriate ways, without direct parental supervision. He must also handle the frightening feelings of anger and hatred he experiences toward his parents because of their efforts to control his behavior and thwart his impulses. It is at this point that Freud introduces one of his most stunning conjectures: the child eventually sees that the way to secure parental love and approval is to strive to *become* them. By striving to be like the father the boy-child wins his father's approval and also comes closer to the possibility of eventually possessing the power, privilege, and independence that the father now has. This process, which Freud called *identification,* has its price, however; something must be done about the hatred and antagonism inevitably generated in the child. In the "normal" course of development, Freud proposed that this anger is turned inward against the "bad" parts of the self. The successfully socialized child is therefore one who has developed a superego—a component of his personality which represents internalized authority. The superego impels the ego to live up to the demands and standards of (parental) authority and converts feelings of anger and rebellion into feelings of guilt about those parts of the self that fail to meet internalized social standards.

For Freud, then, the process of civilizing young children inevitably results in predispositions to identify with and submit to authority. This identification and submission prevents the dissipation of energy in noninstrumental pleasure seeking by channeling energy into useful work and the achievement of high standards. Further, aggressive drives are diverted from destructive purposes and put into the service of morality and conscience. But the inevitable cost of such a civilization is high: the more productive and moral men become, the more docile and obedient they are. And the possibility for happiness becomes increasingly corroded by a sense of guilt.

If the normal man, according to Freud, is fated to submit to guilt and authoritarian rule, the rebel against authority fares no better. To Freud, the rebel is not someone possessing altruism and courage, nor someone striving for freedom. Rather, Freud regards the rebel as a person who was unable to successfully resolve his "Oedipal" crisis; the rebel is unable to fully identify with his father or appropriately handle his infantile hostilities toward authority; he is a person fated to challenge and resist authority obsessively, rather than accept it. Moreover, the more successful he is, the more likely the rebel is to experience guilt and remorse because of his "parricidal" activity. Rebellion for Freud can never escape the inexorable psychic limitations imposed by guilt—and thus it is fated to end in failure, self-destruction, or in the restoration of the very authoritarianism it sought to overthrow.

Those who wish to improve the human capacity for freedom will find little consolation in the writings of Freud. Increasing the ability of individuals to respond to authority rationally was Freud's only hope. That is to say, people could strive to understand the degree to which their obedience and guilt were rooted in *infantile, immature* perceptions of feelings about their parents. Such rational self-understanding could not be achieved easily, however; Freud thought that it required a long, painstaking, profound analysis of the self under professional guidance. And in the end, the cured patient still would not be liberated from the need for guilt and self-restraint; rather, he would be more capable of rational compliance and rational self-assertion.

Despite its profound pessimism, psychoanalysis does recognize human capabilities for rational exercise and acceptance of authority. It is doubtful that psychoanalysts regard the rise of Nazism in Germany as the inevitable expression of human nature. Nor do many believe that the only cure for mass subservience to authority is individual psychotherapy.

The phenomenon of Nazism forced the psychoanalytic movement to a still deeper examination of the problem of authority. Here was a case in which obedience and guilt unleashed aggression on a scale that was previously unimaginable. Many in the psychoanalytic mode were not unduly puzzled by the behavior of Hitler and other Nazi leaders—that could be understood in orthodox terms. Rather, it was the readiness of the German masses to submit to Hitler's rule which was so profoundly disturbing. Suddenly, extreme irrationality was not expressed merely by a minority of abnormally socialized persons, but apparently by an entire population of normal, well-socialized people.

Out of this experience came the idea that societies differ markedly in the degree to which they foster character types which are disposed to submission, on the one hand, or capable of independence, on the other. From this point of view, the value of psychoanalysis lay not only in comprehending the roots of individual pathology but, more fundamentally, in diagnosing the sources of irrationality rooted in culture and in prescribing "cures" for societies as a whole. Largely because of the German experience, the focus of the new social psychoanalysis was the problem of irrational submission. Works such as Wilhelm Reich's *Mass Psychology of Fascism* and Erich Fromm's *Escape from Freedom* contained brilliant suggestions as to how psychoanalytic concepts could be applied to understanding and combatting such mass tendencies. A central thesis of such works was that a highly repressive, paternalistic family structure could generate strong dispositions toward authoritarian obedience. At the same time, a harsh parental regime generates strong feelings of hostility which cannot be directed at the source of frustration and which are only partially rechannelled as guilt. The result of these intertwined tendencies to submit and to attack is a character type strongly disposed to obey a higher authority, while simultaneously seeking to aggress against those who are weak and subordinate. Such conjectures seemed particularly appropriate to the German situation, given the paternalistic, rigid character of the German family and the peculiar mixture of total submission and violent hatred which characterized the Nazi movement.

One outcome of this effort to link cultural and psychological factors in an explanation of the "proto-fascist character" was an ambitious empirical study conducted by a group of German refugee social scientists who had emigrated to Berkeley. This study, finally published as *The Authoritarian Personality* in 1950 and reviewed by F. I. Greenstein in the article reprinted here, attempted to test psychoanalytic hypotheses about the links between authoritarian submissiveness, racist attitudes, and early childhood experience with authority. Samples of American subjects were used, rather than Germans. This research, despite many substantial weaknesses, was extraordinarily influential, partly because it supplied a means to quantitatively measure "authoritarian" dispositions. It also persuasively established that such dispositions do indeed exist and that they can be linked to early experiences in the family.

The psychoanalytic tradition has taught us to regard family structure and methods of child rearing as crucial determinants of later attitudes and responses to authority. But common sense suggests that an additional aspect of early experience is important and deserves intensive research. Parents and other adults not only *act* authoritatively toward children, but they also carry on explicit conversations with children about the nature of government and politics. Freudians tend to downplay such overt attempts to teach attitudes; still, it makes sense that the early images children acquire of government are likely to establish a durable framework that influences adult feelings and actions.

A representative example of research on children's feelings about government (not reprinted here) is an article by David Easton and Jack Dennis entitled "The Child's Image of Government." These two authors argue that the legitimacy of political authority partly depends upon the degree to which positive feelings about the beneficence of government are established in childhood. Presumably, a corollary notion is that children who do not establish such positive feelings become less willing supporters of established authority in adulthood.

The selections in the second portion of this chapter are case studies. The emphasis of theory and research has been to account for the submission to and acceptance of authority. The case studies I have selected, however, illustrate various forms of rebellion against authority. Each illustrates that childhood experiences are relevant to an explanation of one's capacities to resist.

Erik Erikson is one of the truly great inheritors of the psychoanalytic tradition. His books on Martin Luther and Mahatma Gandhi are complex efforts to account for the greatness of these two rebels whose influence transformed history. Erikson takes great pains to transcend the conventional psychoanalytic approach of depicting rebels as persons who merely project Oedipal problems into the political arena. His work, moreover, is largely directed at overcoming the reductionist and individualistic biases of psychoanalytic theory; Erikson traces the links between the early family experiences of Luther and Gandhi and the broader historical and cultural contexts which shaped and gave meaning to those experiences. The selections reprinted here focus on apparently crucial moments in the relationship between each of these men and their parents—especially their fathers. Each selection offers rich suggestions about the Oedipal problems of these subjects and how these problems may have set the stage for future rebellion. But the reader would be profoundly misled if he believed that Erikson restricts his explanation of these men to such a formula.

Indeed, the contrast between Luther and Gandhi's Oedipal crises is dramatic and startling. Luther was apparently raised in a virtually prototypic authoritarian environment; yet he did not develop a submissive, docile character. A simple-minded application of psychoanalytic reasoning would perhaps conclude that Luther's rebellion against the Papacy could be reduced to his projection of repressed rebellion against his own father.

But then how account for Gandhi's rebellion? His childhood experience was quite the opposite of an authoritarian one; indeed, at an early age Gandhi found himself caring for an ailing father rather than submitting to paternal domination.

I do not want to pre-empt your own analysis of how adult rebellion can have origins in two such radically divergent early experiences. Let me, however, suggest one point for discussion. According to Freud, a crucial limitation on the capacity for effective nonconformity is the problem of guilt. Both Luther and Gandhi had particularly strong reservoirs of guilt—but for different reasons. Luther's guilt was rooted in fear of a dominating, brutal (and yet caring) father. How rebel in the face of terrible retribution? Gandhi's guilt had a different source—his sense that he had betrayed the father who needed his nurturance. Erikson suggests a major reason both Luther and Gandhi eventually had the capacity to rebel was that both found enormously creative ways to overcome and reinterpret their guilts. Luther, for example, interpreted his rebellion, not as a rejection of authority, but as a *higher obedience* (directly to God). Luther freed himself for rebellion by binding himself more totally to a truer, purer Authority. Gandhi interpreted his rebellion, not as a destructive betrayal of authority, but as an act of therapy, a way of *caring for* the opposed authority. By insisting on a revolution rooted in a nonviolent quest for truth rather than power, Gandhi found a way to disobey without betrayal and in good conscience. Moreover, the "cures" for guilt that these men created for themselves became relevant to the comparable problems of the millions who followed them. Erikson's work suggests that the capacity for rebellion is not rooted in individual pathology but rather in creative formulation of ideology—a new way of looking at social relations that legitimates the expression of resentment, that makes rebellion rather than submission an act of absolution.

In contrast to these two studies of great revolutionary leaders, I urge you to read *The Autobiography of Malcolm X*. Malcolm's account of his own childhood supplies little evidence that Oedipal rebellion played a crucial role in generating his later capacities for revolutionary leadership.

Instead, one gets the sense of still another dynamic—the possibility that revolutionary impulses can be rooted in identification with a father who was himself a rebel. In this case, moreover, the father was apparently destroyed because of his rebellion. One feels that the son would be wracked with guilt, unless he could carry on his father's work of overt resistance. We may assume, in addition, that Malcolm grew up with very little sense of the legitimacy of established, white political authority. He could hardly have had much trust for it after directly experiencing the corrupt representatives of that authority and the treatment they gave his family.

Similar, though milder, patterns of guilt (as related to conformity) and anti-authoritarianism (as related to expressions of identification with parents) were exhibited in the families of student protesters I studied in the early phases of the student revolt. These students were markedly departing from the political conservatism and apathy of their age-mates. Their capacity to do so was apparently strongly related to the fact that their families expected and encouraged skeptical attitudes toward conventional political beliefs and cultural values. Many of these parents felt guilt because of their own privilege and political quiescence. In a sense, they expected their sons and daughters to absolve them of that guilt by practicing what they as parents had only preached. The children of these parents had considerably more skeptical attitudes toward the government than did the "average" kids studied by Easton and Dennis.

Kenneth Keniston, the author of one other article reprinted here, has brilliantly attempted to make use of Erikson's lead in developing psychohistorical analysis. Keniston's study of the young man called "Inburn" uncovered an emergent character type in American society, the attributes and significance of which had not previously been noted. The young man who rejects conventional culture and is alienated from conventional adult roles was hardly noticed during the fifties when Keniston's study was conducted. The prevalent pattern among young people at that time was one which emphasized bland conformism and "making it." During the sixties, however, alienated youth were decisive in transforming the world view of their generation. In studying this type, Keniston fastened on still another way in which capacities for antiauthoritarianism can be developed in early childhood socialization—namely, the situation in which the male child identifies more strongly with his mother than with his father. Such a pattern can lead to antiauthoritarianism in a culture where authority is defined as masculine and linked to competitive achievement, and where the legitimacy of a life oriented toward aesthetic experience, sensuousness, and contemplation is denied in favor of self-denial and striving. Suburban migration, the exclusion of educated women from self-fulfilling careers, and the bureaucratization of adult work have had profound impacts on the family and the treatment of children —and it turns out that Inburn's experience has been duplicated in one way or another by millions of other relatively advantaged young people. The result has been a tremendous degree of alienation and anomie—but also the creation of new character types receptive to new cultural meanings and new types of relations with authority.

With these comments, I have only scratched the surface of possible discussion and reflection upon the readings that follow. I have deliberately left many points of comparison and contrast open. I have also left open the question of the usefulness of character analysis for understanding responses to authority. There are a variety of very fundamental criticisms to be made of such analysis, and of psychoanalytic theory. Aspects of such criticism will become evident in later sections of this book. Others I leave unstated here, hoping you will be stimulated enough to discover them for yourself.

SOME SUGGESTED READING

A good approach to the Freudian perspective on character and authority would be to read the following works by Freud: *Outline of Psychoanalysis, The Ego and the Id, Group Psychology and the Analysis of the Ego,* and *Civilization and Its Discontents;* all are published by W. W. Norton. Freud's position is critically analyzed and transformed in H. Marcuse, *Eros and Civilization* (New York: Vintage, 1962); N. Brown, *Life Against Death* (Middletown: Wesleyan University Press, 1959); and R. V. Sampson, *The Psychology of Power* (New York: Vintage, 1965). Seminal psychoanalytically rooted analyses of the Nazi phenomenon are: W. Reich, *The Mass Psychology of Fascism* (New York: Farrar, Strauss, Giroux, 1970); and E. Fromm, *Escape from Freedom* (New York: Farrar and Rinehart, 1941). The authoritarian personality research is reported in T. W. Adorno, *et al., The Authoritarian Personality* (New York: Harper, 1950). Erikson's books on Gandhi and Luther should be read in their entirety, along with his *Childhood and Society* (New York: Norton, 1950), and *Youth Identity and Crisis* (New York: Norton, 1968). Keniston's study of Inburn is a summary of his book entitled *The Uncommitted* (New York: Harcourt, 1965). This book, along with his *Young Radicals* (New York: Harcourt, 1968) constitute essential works for characterological understanding of contemporary youth revolt. A related effort with a more sociological emphasis is R. Flacks, *Youth and Social Change* (Chicago: Markham, 1971). A good overview on the links between character and political action is F. Greenstein and M. Lerner, *A Sourcebook on Personality and Politics* (Chicago: Markham, 1971). Two authors who have researched children's feelings about government are David Easton and Jack Dennis, in "The Child's Image of Government," *The Annals of the American Academy of Political and Social Science,* Vol. 361 (September, 1965). The limits and strengths of the characterological approach can be suggested by attempting to apply it to a book like the *Autobiography of Malcolm X* (New York: Grove, 1964).

CIVILIZATION AND ITS DISCONTENTS

Sigmund Freud

These interrelations are so complicated and at the same time so important that, at the risk of repeating myself, I shall approach them from yet another angle. The chronological sequence, then, would be as follows. First comes renunciation of instinct owing to fear of aggression by the *external* authority. (This is, of course, what fear of the loss of love amounts to, for love is a protection against this punitive aggression.) After that comes the erection of an *internal* authority, and renunciation of instinct owing to fear of it—owing to fear of conscience. In this second situation bad intentions are equated with bad actions, and hence come a sense of guilt and a need for punishment. The aggressiveness of conscience keeps up the aggressiveness of the authority. So far things have no doubt been made clear; but where does this leave room for the reinforcing influence of misfortune (of renunciation imposed from without), and for the extraordinary severity of conscience in the best and most tractable people? We have already explained both these peculiarities of conscience, but we probably still have an impression that those explanations do not go to the bottom of the matter, and leave a residue still unexplained. And here at last an idea comes in which belongs entirely to psychoanalysis and which is foreign to people's ordinary way of thinking. This idea is of a sort which enables us to understand why the subject-matter was bound to seem so confused and obscure to us. For it tells us that conscience (or more correctly, the anxiety which later becomes conscience) is indeed the cause of instinctual renunciation to begin with, but that later the relationship is reversed. Every renunciation of

instinct now becomes a dynamic source of conscience and every fresh renunciation increases the latter's severity and intolerance. If we could only bring it better into harmony with what we already know about the history of the origin of conscience, we should be tempted to defend the paradoxical statement that conscience is the result of instinctual renunciation, or that instinctual renunciation (imposed on us from without) creates conscience, which then demands further instinctual renunciation.

The contradiction between this statement and what we have previously said about the genesis of conscience is in point of fact not so very great, and we see a way of further reducing it. In order to make our exposition easier, let us take as our example the aggressive instinct, and let us assume that the renunciation in question is always a renunciation of aggression. (This, of course, is only to be taken as a temporary assumption.) The effect of instinctual renunciation on the conscience then is that every piece of aggression whose satisfaction the subject gives up is taken over by the superego and increases the latter's aggressiveness (against the ego). This does not harmonize well with the view that the original aggressiveness of conscience is a continuance of the severity of the external authority and therefore has nothing to do with renunciation. But the discrepancy is removed if we postulate a different derivation for this first installment of the superego's aggressivity. A considerable amount of aggressiveness must be developed in the child against the authority which prevents him from having his first, but nonetheless his most important, satisfactions, whatever the kind of instinctual deprivation that is demanded of him may be; but he is obliged to renounce the satisfaction of this revengeful aggressiveness. He finds his way out of this economically difficult situation with the help of familiar mechanisms. By means of identification he takes the unattackable authority into himself. The authority now turns into his superego and enters into possession of all the aggressiveness which a child would have liked to exercise against it. The child's ego has to content itself with the unhappy role of the authority—the father—who has been thus degraded. Here, as so often, the [real] situation is reversed: "If I were the father and you were the child, I should treat you badly." The relationship between the superego and the ego is a return, distorted by a wish, of the real relationship between the ego, as yet undivided, and an external object. That is typical, too. But the essential difference is that the original severity of the superego does not—or does not so much—represent the severity which one has experienced from it [the object], or which one attributes to it; it represents rather one's own aggressiveness towards it. If this is correct, we may assert truly that in the beginning conscience arises through the suppression of an aggressive impulse, and that it is subsequently reinforced by fresh suppressions of the same kind.

PERSONALITY AND POLITICAL SOCIALIZATION: THE THEORIES OF AUTHORITARIAN AND DEMOCRATIC CHARACTER

Fred I. Greenstein

The socialization experiences which culminate in adult citizenship can be divided into two rough categories: that learning which is specifically about government and politics, and nonpolitical personal development which affects political behavior. My concern here is with a particularly controversial, but intriguing, portion of the topics arising in the second category—the notions of "authoritarian" and "democratic" character. In addition to reviewing theory and research on these character types, I will discuss briefly several of the problems involved in untangling the complex connections among personal character, political beliefs, political action, and the functioning of political and other social institutions. This is an extensive and extraordinarily craggy intellectual terrain. In a brief essay I can only hope, as it were, to engage in high-altitude aerial reconnaissance—that is, to construct a rather abstract and quite selective map of the phenomena which interest us, illustrating rather than demonstrating my assertions.

Put bluntly, the questions which concern us are: "Can we distinguish types of individuals whose personal make-up—apart from their specifically political beliefs—disposes them to act in a democratic or an authoritarian manner?" "What social-

Reprinted from The Annals of The American Academy of Political and Social Sciences, Vol. 361 (September 1965). Reprinted by permission of The Annals and the author. Footnotes have been edited.

ization practices produce such individuals?" "What can be said about the circumstances under which the actual behavior of such individuals will be democratic or authoritarian, and about the aggregate effects which individuals with democratic or authoritarian dispositions may have on the functioning of political institutions?"

THE STUDY OF AUTHORITARIAN AND DEMOCRATIC CHARACTER

There is, by far, more literature on authoritarian than on democratic character. One of the wonders of recent social science scholarship has been the profusion of "authoritarianism" research in the past decade and a half. An admittedly selective review of writings on the topic through 1956 contained 260 bibliographical references.[1] Today, anything but the most sparse systematic discussion of the relevant research would require a monograph. Even as interest in this matter begins to fall off, it is rare to find an issue of a journal dealing with personality and attitude research that contains no reference to authoritarianism and no use of the various techniques designed to measure it.

The main immediate stimulus for this explosion of research was the publication in 1950 of a 990-page volume by T. W. Adorno, Else Frenkel-Brunswik, Nevitt Sanford, and Daniel J. Levinson, entitled *The Authoritarian Personality,*[2] which reported the fruits of several years of investigation into the psychology of anti-Semitism. On the basis of a rich but bewilderingly varied and uneven assortment of research procedures, the authors of this work reached a striking conclusion about the psychology of hostility to Jews and other minority groups. Such prejudiced attitudes, they argued, were not simply beliefs which people happened to have acquired. Rather, one could identify what might be called a "bigot personality,"[3] a type of individual with deepseated psychological needs which manifested themselves in a variety of ways over and beyond ethnic prejudice. *The Authoritarian Personality* is a book dealing more with prejudice than with the problem suggested by its title—psychological dispositions toward authority. "The title," as one of the authors points out, "was not thought of until the writing was virtually

finished."[4] But it was the title phrase which came to provide the heading under which subsequent investigation proceeded, and, in general, ethnic prejudice has become a secondary issue in research on authoritarianism.

The term "authoritarian" has at least two shortcomings as an analytic tool. First, it is applicable not only to individual psychological dispositions (our concern here), but also to the content of political belief and to the structure of political systems. Because of this we may easily gloss over the possibility that "authoritarianism" at any one of these levels is not necessarily accompanied by authoritarianism at the other levels. For example, democratic beliefs may be imposed in an authoritarian manner. And, within an authoritarian movement, the leadership may include individuals of nonauthoritarian dispositions, and may even conduct its own deliberations in a democratic fashion.

Secondly, the term seems almost inevitably to be a pejorative. In a liberal democracy "authoritarian" equals "bad." The evaluative connotations of the term interfere with our efforts to use it as a neutral instrument for denoting an empirical phenomenon. A historical note on the work of the Nazi psychologist E. R. Jaensch may help to remind us that the term can have meaning independent of its negative connotations. In 1938 Jaensch described a psychological type with remarkable similarities to the typology presented in *The Authoritarian Personality.* But his evaluation of the type was not at all negative. Rather, he saw it as exemplifying the best virtues of National Socialist manhood.[5]

There is, of course, nothing new in the awareness that some people are more deferential toward authority than others and that the same people often are harsh to their subordinates. The fawning underling is a stock character in fiction, as is the tyrannical superior. It is a safe assumption that the readers of Fielding's *Tom Jones* (1747) had no difficulty recognizing the character of Deborah Wilkins, who "seldom opened her lips either to her master or his sister till she had first sounded their inclinations, with which her sentiments were always strictly consonant," and of whom Fielding says:

It is the nature of such persons . . . to insult and tyrannize over little people. This being indeed the means which they use to recompense to themselves their extreme servility and condescension to their superiors; for nothing can be more reasonable than that slaves and flatterers should exact the same taxes on all below them which they themselves pay to all above them.[6]

What *is* new in the twentieth-century literature on authoritarianism is the specification of a constellation of psychological correlates of this tendency and the elaboration of a theory of its psychodynamics and genesis. This theory (which I shall shortly summarize) was woven from a number of strands of contemporary social psychological thought. Some of the formulations in *The Authoritarian Personality* were presaged by research in the 1930's and 1940's into "fascist attitudes."[7] Others can be found in the World War II and cold-war national-character literature, particularly the efforts to diagnose German, Japanese, and Russian character.[8] The discussion of "authoritarian character" in Erich Fromm's widely discussed *Escape from Freedom*[9] seems to have been particularly influential, as were the various efforts in the 1930's by Fromm and others connected with the Institut für Sozialforschung to blend Freud and Marx in an analysis of the role of the family "in maintaining authority in modern society."[10] Underlying all of these discussions was what still is probably the most revolutionary facet of twentieth-century social science—psychoanalysis—and, particularly, several overlapping elements in Freud's thought: the notion of the anal character, his analyses of obsessional neuroses and of paranoia, and his delineation of the mechanism of projection. (The dependence of the conception of authoritarianism upon a personality theory that places such a great emphasis on the significance of childhood experience makes authoritarianism a particularly strong candidate for discussion in a symposium on political socialization.)

The Authoritarian Personality, therefore, served to focus attention on hypotheses which had been in the air for some time, rather than to suggest completely new hypotheses. But it did something more—and this seems to have been especially important in spurring the subsequent research. The section of the book devoted to "measurement of ideological trends" provided a number of "ready-made tests that had already been taken through many of the technical procedures of validation which every [psychological] test must pass,"[11] the most notable and widely used of these being the F-(fascism) scale. The ready-made tests were very conveniently available to subsequent investigators, whereas the fascinating body of theory which guided the research was "in no single place in the volume"[12] conveniently stated. In the long run, this emphasis on certain restricted measurement techniques proved to be most unfortunate, since the authoritarian literature became progressively bogged in what in many respects was a comedy of methodological errors, and a number of the original insights in *The Authoritarian Personality* never received careful attention.[13]

In contrast to the several paragraphs required simply to make peremptory reference to the intellectual history of authoritarian personality study, the state of investigation into democratic personality can be briefly stated. There has been some theorizing on this topic and virtually no research. No one, to my knowledge, has attempted to devise and use a D- (democratic) scale. Our consideration of democratic character, therefore, has far less to go upon. I shall concentrate mainly on what seems to me to be an especially interesting discussion of the topic, an essay by Harold Lasswell which, I think, has not received the attention it merits.[14]

A number of commentators—including the authors of *The Authoritarian Personality*—have expressed skepticism over whether a concept such as "democratic character" corresponds sufficiently to anything found in the "real world" to be worth using.[15] The test of usefulness of a typology—or, in currently fashionable jargon, model—is, however, not merely its correspondence with presently available data. Typologies clarify thinking and guide research. They may serve to summarize aspects of what has already been observed, they may suggest hypotheses for future observations, and they may simply be vehicles for reasoning. What is important is that a typology make sufficient and appropriate distinctions for the purpose at hand.

AUTHORITARIAN CHARACTER

Three general distinctions appropriate for setting forth a typology of personality are: phenomenology, dynamics, and genesis. In other words, first we may take note of all of the psychological characteristics composing the type which, with a minimum of inferential interpretation, are readily observable. Then we summarize our hypotheses about the processes underlying the observables. How are the observed features related to each other? What ties them together? Finally, we assemble the hypotheses which are most relevant to the present essay: What accounts for the development of this type of individual? How does he arise in the socialization process?

These distinctions provide us, in effect, with a logical reconstruction of the process of inquiry: We observe that, although each individual we encounter is in many respects unique, individuals resemble some of their fellows more than they do others. If the pattern of resemblances is particularly striking, we begin to reflect on what makes such a type of individual work, on his inner dynamics. Then we endeavor to find out what made him the way he is. The distinctions also often reflect the state of knowledge. Agreement on matters of phenomenology is relatively easy to come by, even among scholars with quite different intellectual orientations. Interpretations of underlying dynamics are more controversial. Given the paucity of good longitudinal research—that is, studies of the same individuals over a period of time—reliable evidence of genesis may be especially rare.

Phenomenology of the Authoritarian

Some of the dozen or so traits appearing in the various conceptualizations of the authoritarian type are of immediate interest to the student of politics since they assume a form which directly parallels activities commonly performed in the political arena. Others would seem to be of more remote interest. Most central for our purposes is the pair of traits labeled "authoritarian aggression" and "authoritarian submission"—the dominance-submissiveness tendencies of the authoritarian. Such an individual, like Fielding's Mrs. Wilkins, abases himself before those who stand above him hierarchically, or whom he perceives to be powerful, and lords it over whoever seems to be weak, subordinate, or inferior. "German folklore," Adorno relates, "has a drastic symbol for this"— bicyclist's personality (*Radfahrernaturen*): "Above they bow, below they kick."[16]

Also politically relevant is the tendency of such individuals to *think* in power terms, to be acutely sensitive to questions of who dominates whom. Only at a slightly further remove from politics is the pervasive rigidity in the authoritarian's manner of confronting the world. He is, in Else Frenkel-Brunswik's phrase, "intolerant of ambiguity."[17] He likes order and is made uncomfortable by disorder; where the phenomena he is exposed to are complex and subtle, he imposes his own tight categories upon them, ignoring their nuances. His thinking therefore makes more than the usual use of stereotypes. Another of the traits composing the character type is "conventionalism." The authoritarian, much like Riesman's "radar-controlled" other-directed personality,[18] is described as being particularly sensitive to "external agencies" and, especially, to the prevailing standards of his own social group.

The foregoing authoritarian traits, all of which can be seen to have some rather immediate potential bearing on behavior in the political arena, hang together in a fashion which puts little strain on our common sense: dominance of subordinates; deference toward superiors; sensitivity to power relationships; need to perceive the world in a highly structured fashion; excessive use of stereotypes; and adherence to whatever values are conventional in one's setting. We can easily visualize an individual with these complementary attributes. But what is perhaps most intriguing about the authoritarian syndrome is that several further, less obvious, traits are found as a part of the presenting symptoms.

These rather exotic additional concomitants lead us beyond phenomenology to the psychoanalytically based theory of dynamics. For example, the authoritarian is described as being superstitious. (One of the items of the F-scale is: "Although many people may scoff, it may yet be shown that astrology can explain a lot of things.") He is preoccupied with virility, tending toward "exaggerated assertion of strength and toughness." (While this trait might be juxtaposed with the authoritarian's interest in power, there is the added element here of being hard-boiled and rugged. The equivalent trait in the less well-developed typology of female authoritarianism is "pseudo-femininity"—a preoccupation with being "feminine and soft.") The authoritarian's assumptions about human nature are generally pessimistic, and he tends to be cynical about the motives of others. He is disposed to believe that "wild and dangerous things go on in the world"—that "the world is a jungle." He shows a puritanical preoccupation with sex—a "concern with sexual 'goings on' " and "a strong inclination to punish violators of sex mores." And, finally, he shows a trait of which much is made in the theoretical explanation of this pattern—"anti-intraception." This is "an attitude of impatience with and opposition to the subjective and the tender-minded." One of its more conspicuous forms is an inability to introspect, to acknowledge one's own feelings and fantasies.

The authoritarian typology, like Freud's famous juxtaposition of orderliness, parsimoniousness, and obstinacy in the anal personality type, may well have the merit of being less obvious to common sense than most of the formulations with which social scientists work. But what is its basis in reality? Are individuals to be found who exhibit these characteristics, or a sufficient proportion of them, to make the notion of "authoritarian personality" more than an intriguing exercise in reasoning? The answer, I think, is yes, but I cannot even begin to refer to the elements in the tangled body of authoritarian research on which such a conclusion might be based. It can, at any rate, be seen that the question *is* potentially answerable, and much more readily so than the questions arising at the dynamic and genetic levels.[19]

Dynamics of Authoritarianism

While the typology of dynamics which has been proposed to account for this pattern of traits also can be elaborated in considerable detail, we must content ourselves here simply with suggesting its major themes. The authoritarian, it is argued, is an individual with strong, but ambivalent, dispositions toward figures of authority. Denial of the negative side of these feelings is central to such an individual's functioning. The authoritarian is able to conceal from himself his rage toward those in authority only by the massive defense procedure of reaction formation, involving a total repression of critical and other unacceptable impulses toward authority and a bending over backwards in excessive praise of it.[20] But repression has its costs and side-effects, and repressed impulses seek alternative outlets.

Hostility not only is rechanneled toward whoever is perceived as weak and unauthoritative, but also has a more diffuse effect on the authoritarian's generally negative views of man and his works, as well as contributing to his need to scan his environment for signs of authority relationships, his tendency (via projection) to see the world as full of dangerous things and people, and his desire to punish others, for example, sex offenders, who have surrendered to their impulses. Feelings of personal weakness are covered by a façade of toughness. A side-effect of channeling enormous energy into repression and reaction formation is that the authoritarian's emotional capacities and even certain of his cognitive capacities are stunted. He is unable to face the prospect of canvassing his own psyche—for fear of what such introspection may yield—and therefore becomes highly dependent upon external sources of guidance.[21]

This general thesis about authoritarian dynamics might be called the ego-defensive theory of authoritarianism. After the fashion of classical psychoanalysis, the theory places great emphasis on irrationality—on how the self, in seeking to maintain inner equilibrium (that is, to defend against impulses and conscience), is flawed in its perception of and response to the environment. Since the empirical standing of psychoanalysis continues to be controversial, it is not difficult to understand why this aspect of authoritarian theory is less settled than the question of phenomenology.[22]

It is quite possible to accept the phenomenological typology of authoritarianism and reject the ego-defensive thesis of its dynamics. This, in effect, has been done by several commentators who present what might be called a *cognitive* theory of authoritarianism. The cognitive theory holds that the patterns of expression and behavior that have been characterized as authoritarian are based upon simple learning of the conceptions of reality prevalent in one's culture or subculture, and that these patterns also may to some extent be accurate reflections of the actual conditions of adult life faced by some individuals, rather than having the labyrinthine roots in reaction formation suggested by the ego-defensive theory.[23] Recent research suggests that there is some merit in both the cognitive and the ego-defensive formulations. Much of what has been called "working-class authoritarianism" does seem to have its roots in simple cognitive learning, whereas, at the higher socioeconomic levels, authoritarian orientations seem more often to tap less accessible motivational sources.[24]

The Genesis of Authoritarianism

Adorno and his associates, in fact, anticipated the thesis of cognitive authoritarianism by acknowledging that the personality manifestations they were studying could in some instances merely reflect "surface resentment" with a "more or less rational" basis in learning. Subsequent extensions of the cognitive explanation, for example, by Hyman and Sheatsley, have stressed the lack of information available in lower-class subcultures and the lack of opportunity of lower-class individuals to acquire the desire and capacity to manipulate symbols—or, at least, the symbols with which public discourse is conducted—with any degree of sophistication. Such social settings, it is suggested, produce individuals who respond to the F-scale in much the same fashion as would be predicted by the ego-defensive theory of authoritarianism, but who do not show the pathology described in the theory. Furthermore, the lower-class world may, in many respects, really *be* a jungle. Under such circumstances "authoritarianism" reflects little more than learning from one's exemplars and realistic attempts to characterize one's environment.

The Authoritarian Personality, however, concentrates on elucidating the childhood antecedents of ego-defensive authoritarianism. The typical early determinants of this pattern come as no surprise in the light of the theory of underlying dynamics.

When we consider the childhood situation . . . we find reports of a tendency toward rigid discipline on the part of the parents, with affection which is conditional rather than unconditional, i.e., dependent upon approved behavior on the part of the child. Related to this is a tendency . . . to base [family] interrelationships in rather clearly defined roles of dominance and submission. . . . Forced into a surface submission to parental authority, the child develops hostility and aggression which are poorly channelized. The displacement of a repressed antagonism toward authority may be one of the sources, and perhaps the principal source, of his antagonism toward outgroups.[25]

The authors derived these and similar conclusions about how ego-defensive authoritarianism

arises in the socialization process partly from their subjects' retrospective reports of childhood experiences, but also from direct studies by Frenkel-Brunswik of ethnically prejudiced and unprejudiced children. The studies of children suggested that "warmer, closer and more affectionate interpersonal relationships prevail in the homes of the unprejudiced children" and that prejudice was associated with "strictness, rigidity, punitiveness, rejection vs. acceptance of the child."

In the home with the orientation toward rigid conformity . . . maintenance of discipline is often based upon the expectation of external rigid and superficial rules which are bound to be beyond the comprehension of the child. Family relationships are characterized by fearful subservience to the demands of the parents and by an early suppression of impulses not acceptable to the adults.

Since the moral requirements in such a home must appear to the child as overwhelming and at the same time unintelligible, and the rewards meager, submission to them must be reinforced by fear of and pressure from external agencies. Due to the lack of a genuine identification with the parents, the fearfully conforming child does not make the important developmental step from mere social anxiety to real conscience.[26]

I have earlier noted that the authoritarian personality research grew out of an intellectual tradition which drew on both Freudian psychology and Marxian sociology. It is the Freudian emphasis on early childhood socialization that occupies most of the discussion in *The Authoritarian Personality* of how authoritarianism is socialized. But occasionally a Marxian explanation of the genesis of authoritarianism appears, as in the final paragraph of the volume where the authors remark that "people are continuously molded from above because they must be molded if the overall economic pattern is to be maintained." The point being made here is evidently that of Fromm, who in *Escape from Freedom* develops, *inter alia,* a conception of "social character" as that which "internalizes external necessities and thus harnesses human energy for the task of a given economic and social system"; a conception of the authoritarian character as the energy source in the development of Western capitalism (in contrast to Weber's Protestant Ethic); and a conception of the family as, in effect, mainly a transmission belt providing the system with the type of personality it "requires." Apart from whatever merit there may be in Fromm's specific historical argument, we have here a further class of explanatory factors—overlapping the references to culture in the cognitive model—which may be introduced to explain the genesis of authoritarianism, namely, social structure and social role requirements.[27]

FROM CHARACTER STRUCTURE TO POLITICAL STRUCTURE

The field of culture and personality research, into which the authoritarian literature falls, is not in especially good repute. Particularly suspect are the attempts—perhaps most marked in the wartime national-character literature—to reason from (often imperfect) evidence about early socialization and personality development, rapidly and effortlessly, to explanations of broad social and historical phenomena, such as the rise of Nazism, Japanese militarism, and so forth. The disparaging label "psychologism" has come to be attached to such inferential leaps. These exercises in reducing politics and sociology to psychology often impress no one less than the psychoanalysts themselves. "Shortly after Pearl Harbor," an analyst relates:

a small group of noted social scientists, intent on studying the cultural roots of German National Socialism, invited a number of refugee scholars and interviewed them about their experiences and ideas on this subject. I was among those invited. I remember that I mentioned among the factors which seemed to me to have disposed the German people for a nationalistic dictatorship, the failure of German nineteenth century liberalism, and the subsequent success of Prussian militarism, in bringing about the much desired unification of Germany; this experience, I argued, had conditioned the German people to distrust the democratic process and to put their faith in strong-arm methods. I also mentioned the impact of rapid industrialization upon a society still almost feudal in its caste structure, without interceding commercialism and without a strong commercial class such as was already established in Anglo-Saxon countries at the outset of industrialization; such a situation seemed to make people more alert to the possibilities of power, rather than the potentialities of welfare, inherent in industry. I was then interrupted by my host, a noted anthropologist; this was not what I had

been expected to contribute. As a psychoanalyst I should point out how Nazism had developed from the German form of child rearing. I replied that I did not think that there was any such relationship; in fact, political opinion did not seem to be determined in early childhood at all. This view was not accepted and I was told that the way the German mother holds her baby must be different from that of mothers in democracies. When we parted, it was clear that my hosts felt that they had wasted their time.[28]

Although there are numerous statements by *Authoritarian Personality* contributors acknowledging that personality factors are neither "the major [n]or exclusive determinants of political or social movements," it is difficult to gainsay the critics who argue that the work is shot through with psychologism. For example, by labeling the personality trends we have been discussing "prefascist" and "potentially fascist," they tended to resolve by definition the complex empirical question of how deeper personality trends articulate with specifically political belief and with actual behavior. And their references to the "great . . . fascist potential" in American society seemed to reflect equally naïve assumptions about the relationship between the distribution of psychological dispositions in a society and its over-all political structure. By very briefly indicating some of the many factors which intervene between character structure and political structure, we can touch upon some of the further questions that have arisen in connection with the study of authoritarianism.

Personality and Belief System

As is often pointed out, persons with similar deep psychological characteristics may entertain different political beliefs, and persons with similar beliefs may differ in personality. This is so because there normally are a variety of alternative channels which can express underlying psychic needs, and also because, given the inattentiveness to politics of most citizens, political orientations often are acquired haphazardly, without engaging deeper personality sources. The original authoritarian personality research was influenced not only by the intellectual traditions to which I referred above, but also by the political climate of the 1930's and 1940's and, in particular, the grim history of German National Socialism and the presence in the United States of nativistic radical-right movements. This seems to have been one of the reasons for the insensitivity in the original research to the possibility—which subsequently received a good bit of attention—that authoritarian character traits may be manifested in other than rightist political beliefs.[29] Related to this was a tendency in the original reports to discuss the ethnically prejudiced and politically conservative attitudes of many authoritarians as if these were part of the defining characteristics of the syndrome itself. For some purposes it may be desirable to treat opinions as "an integral part of personality," but in studying personality and politics we can see that it often is essential to distinguish analytically between character and belief, lest the question of the connections between them be settled in our definitions rather than our research. The research, of course, may well show that authoritarian personality characteristics are associated with authoritarian beliefs, and that these personality characteristics *do* "fit" best with right-wing ideology. But, at best, the relationship is likely to be imperfect.

Effects of Personality and Belief System on Action

The individual with a "potentially fascist" character structure, then, does not necessarily hold "fascist" beliefs. Furthermore, the connections of character structure *and* belief content with action are not necessarily as straightforward as the usage "potential fascist" implies. Action results from the situations in which people find themselves, including the formal and informal roles they are called upon to perform, as well as from their psychological predispositions. The lack of "one-to-one correlation" between psychological dispositions and action is often pointed out. It may be less well appreciated that the correlation can even be negative; in some circumstances an individual's behavior may actually be the *reverse* of what would have been expected if only his predispositions were taken into account. An example of this is to be found in work by Katz and Benjamin on behavior of Northern white college undergraduates toward Negro co-workers. Presumably racially prejudiced "authoritarians were actually more deferential with Negroes than were nonauthoritari-

ans," a finding which the investigators felt was "due to the authoritarian's fear of revealing anti-Negro attitudes in a potentially punitive environment."[30] Still further insight into the subtleties of personality-role relationships might have been obtained if the investigators had also looked into whether authoritarians felt more strain in such situations than did nonauthoritarians, or how each group would have responded if sufficient tension and frustration had been introduced to challenge the authoritarians' "inner controls" of "their hostile impulses."[31] The point is that we must employ analytic distinctions which attune us to the possible subtleties of our subject.

Aggregate Effects of Individual Predispositions and Actions

So much more than simple addition is involved in moving from the distribution of individual characteristics in a society—for example, its proportion of authoritarians—to questions about over-all political structure that some social scientists are led to a kind of vulgar Durkheimianism, which denies on methodological grounds the relevance of psychology to sociology and political science. At the very least, the addition of personal characteristics is a matter of weighted rather than simple sums.[32] It takes a good many authoritarian voters to equal one authoritarian President of the United States. Moreover, "more than one set of personality characteristics" is needed "to make a political movement. . . . Movements and institutions, even if they are authoritarian, require both more and less than authoritarian personality structures," and even "a liberal democratic society itself could probably not function satisfactorily with only 'democratic liberal personalities' to fill all its roles."[33] Here again, the point is not to deny the significance of the sequelae of socialization (personality and political belief), but to suggest the care necessary to make inferences about the matter.

DEMOCRATIC CHARACTER

Lasswell's essay "Democratic Character," like the discussion which has just preceded, is essentially typological. In effect, he elaborates a hypothetical construct, in part from the existing research on the antidemocratic character, in part by deductions from an analysis of the role requirements of democratic society. The main general features of the psychological typology are a "self-system" (the individual's conscious orientations, which consist of his cognitive assumptions, his preferences, and his identifications), an "energy-system" (roughly equivalent to the Freudian unconscious, composed of conscience, ego ideals, and drives), and a special definition of the term "character," as "the self-system of the person, together with the degree of support, opposition, or non-support received from the unconscious parts of the personality." "Character" therefore acquires the dimension of strength and weakness, much as in lay usage. "When we say that a man is of steadfast character it is implied that he has sufficient command of the resources of the whole personality to maintain the self-system despite environing conditions which are adverse."[34]

At the cognitive level, the democratic character believes in the benevolent potentialities of mankind, rejecting the authoritarian's more Hobbesian conception of human nature. The democrat's preferences are consistent with the role requirements in the model of the democratic social system—that is, he *wants* to behave in the ways he should behave, if the functioning of the democratic system is to be successful. Furthermore, he is a "multivalued" moderate who can weigh alternative goals against each other, rather than an absolutist in pursuit of a single value who, because of his inability to compromise, might endanger the stability of the system. And it is especially important that the democratic character be free of the pursuit of power as a single end-in-itself. In addition, the democrat's identifications are broad and comprehensive—Lasswell speaks of the "open ego"—unlike the good guys-bad guys pattern of the authoritarian.

This pattern of conscious perspectives, Lasswell points out, might well be found among individuals who at the unconscious level had antidemocratic inclinations and, particularly, destructive, power-seeking, or self-punishing tendencies. Referring, in effect, to the curiously labeled "rigid low scorer" of the authoritarian studies, Lasswell acknowledges that

democratic responses often arise from motivations which are incompatible with ... [democracy], and

signify that the individual has achieved part of his democratic outlook by 'reaction formation' against tendencies of an opposite kind. Many democrats appear to develop in opposition to anti-democratic parents, for example.

While he grants that "the destructive energies of a person may be directed against enemies of the democratic community," he nevertheless excludes the democrat-by-reaction formation from his typology, since "from the point of view of modern personality research, the characters which are achieved by a complex process of balanced defense are viewed as constituting less enduring formations than those which evolve more directly." On the matter of socialization, Lasswell comments that "there is reason to believe that in some cultures the possibility of developing an outgoing democratic character is excluded at an early period. The prevailing patterns of child care appear to induce early despair that profound gratifications can emanate from other human beings." The concluding sections of the essay are directly addressed to the problem of how to socialize democratic characters.

There is a lapidary quality to Lasswell's essay—his formulation, overly condensed in this review, is itself quite elliptically stated. The formulation does, however, offer promising suggestions for expanding the scope of research on personality and political socialization. And the novel conception of character strength he introduces—the capacity to withstand environmental pressure adverse to one's values—raises interesting possibilities for bringing together two hitherto largely unconnected strands in the literature on prerequisites of democracy: the psychological writings we have been discussing here and the currently expanding work on the structural features of democracies and the typical belief systems to be found in them.

SUMMARY AND CONCLUSIONS

In comtemporary anthropology the distinction has occasionally been made between the old culture-and-personality literature, which was especially concerned with early childhood socialization and its effects on personality formation, and the new culture-and-personality literature, which focuses on systematic exploration of people's cognitive maps of their environment.[35] I have reviewed what might be called the old political socialization literature—itself a strand of the early culture-and-personality movement—in contrast to the recently burgeoning research on the development of specifically political orientations.

At base, these divisions between old and new are an artifact of the history of research. Human beings, at whatever stage of the lifelong socialization process, are not divided into self-contained compartments of personality versus cognitions, "specifically political" versus "non-political but politically relevant" development. What has been adventitiously separated needs to be pulled together. But in the present instance this will call for a good bit of careful conceptualization. We need sets of distinctions which "carve at the joints" for thinking about what intervenes between personality socialization and political systems.

Some of the distinctions suggested in this essay can be summarized in the following statements: Personality formation may be along ego-defensive or more cognitive lines; the connections between personality and political belief need to be examined rather than assumed; both personality and beliefs must be examined *in situations* in order to understand behavior; the ways in which individual predispositions and actions aggregate and affect the political and social system need to be explicated. And, to turn the circle, it is the political and social systems which provide the socializing environment for "political" and "politically relevant" personal development and the situations within which political action takes place. In a new-fangled way, this is to suggest no more than was evident to Plato: that politics needs to be understood (and undertaken) in the light of human nature and human development.

NOTES

[1]Richard Christie and Peggy Cook, "A Guide to Published Literature Relating to the Authoritarian Personality through 1956," *Journal of Psychology,* **45** (April 1958), 171–199.

[2]T. W. Adorno *et. al., The Authoritarian Personality,* New York: Harper, 1950, hereafter cited as the *AP.*

[3]A phrase used in a prepublication report of the study

to the general public: Jerome Himelhoch, "Is There a Bigot Personality?" *Commentary,* **3** (March 1947), 277–284.

[4]Nevitt Sanford, "The Approach of The Authoritarian Personality," in J. L. McCary (ed.), *Psychology of Personality,* New York: Grove Press, 1959, p. 256.

[5]E. R. Jaensch, "Der Gegentypus," *Beiheft zur Zeistschrift für angewandte Psychologie und Charakterkunde,* Beiheft 75 (1938). Just as the *AP* was mainly concerned with the type of individual whose dispositions are antithetical to democracy, Jaensch was most concerned with the "antitype," whose dispositions were incongruent with National Socialism.

[6]Henry Fielding, *Tom Jones,* Book I, Chaps. 6 and 8.

[7]For example, Ross Stagner, "Fascist Attitudes: Their Determining Conditions," *Journal of Social Psychology,* **7** (November 1936), 438–454; Allen L. Edwards, "Unlabeled Fascist Attitudes," *Journal of Abnormal and Social Psychology,* **36** (October 1941), 575–582.

[8]For example, Ruth F. Benedict, *The Chrysanthemum and the Sword,* Boston: Houghton Mifflin, 1946; Henry V. Dicks, "Personality Traits and National Socialist Ideology," *Human Relations,* **3** (1950), 111–154; and the same author's "Observations on Contemporary Russian Behavior," *ibid.,* **5** (1952), 111–175.

[9]Erich Fromm, *Escape from Freedom,* New York: Holt, Rinehart & Winston, 1941. The authors also acknowledged their indebtedness to A. H. Maslow's essay "The Authoritarian Character Structure," *Journal of Social Psychology,* **18** (1943), 401–411.

[10]Max Horkheimer (ed.), *Studien über Autorität und Familie,* Paris, 1936, p. 902.

[11]Nathan Glazer, "New Light on The Authoritarian Personality," *Commentary,* **17** (March 1954), 290.

[12]M. Brewster Smith, Review of *The Authoritarian Personality,* in *Journal of Abnormal and Social Psychology,* **45** (October 1950), 775.

[13]A variety of telling methodological criticisms of *The Authoritarian Personality* appear in the essays of Herbert H. Hyman and Paul B. Sheatsley and of Richard Christie, in Richard Christie and Marie Jahoda (eds.), *Studies in the Scope and Method of The Authoritarian Personality,* Glencoe, Ill.: Free Press, 1954; hereafter cited as *SSMAP.* . . . Somewhat after the publication of *SSMAP,* an extensive series of papers on "response set" in authoritarian research was published, adding further to the methodologically gnarled quality of the literature. . . . Some of the more interesting of these papers are conveniently reprinted in Chapter 6 of Martha T. Mednick and Sarnoff A. Mednick, *Research in Personality,* New York: Holt, Rinehart & Winston, 1963.

[14]Harold D. Lasswell, "Democratic Character," in *The Political Writings of Harold D. Lasswell,* Glencoe, Ill.: Free Press, 1951, pp. 465–525; hereafter cited as *DC.*

[15]*AP,* p. 1, but see pp. 781–783 for the authors' subtype "the genuine liberal." For a criticism of both the democratic and the authoritarian character typologies in

the context of what I take to be the argument that typologies are useless since no individual ever is a pure instance of a type, see David Spitz, "Power and Personality: The Appeal to the 'Right Man' in Democratic States," *American Political Science Review,* **52** (March 1958), 88–89.

[16]T. W. Adorno, "Freudian Theory and the Pattern of Fascist Propaganda," in Géza Roheim (ed.), *Psychoanalysis and the Social Sciences,* VII, New York: 1951, p. 291.

[17]Else Frenkel-Brunswik, "Intolerance of Ambiguity as an Emotional and Perceptual Personality Variable," *Journal of Personality,* **18** (September 1949), 108–143.

[18]David Riesman, with Nathan Glazer and Reuel Denney, *The Lonely Crowd,* New Haven: Yale University Press, 1950.

[19]Christie makes the following statement at the conclusion of an extensive, rigorous review of authoritarianism research: "Both the strength and weakness of *The Authoritarian Personality* lie in its basic assumptions which are rooted in psychoanalytic theory. Such an orientation has led to the uncovering of a host of data which in all likelihood would not have been discovered by investigators with differing theoretical viewpoints. Despite some methodological weaknesses in the original research, subsequent findings have been predominantly confirmatory," *SSMAP,* pp. 195–196.

[20]The authoritarian type is described as having repressed sexual as well as hostile impulses, but the significance of repressed sexuality in authoritarianism does not seem to have been fully explicated. . . .

[21]Dependence upon external guidance provides the common element in several of the surface manifestations of authoritarianism, which at first glance seem not to be related to each other: conventionality (accepting the prevailing values in one's environment); stereotypy (accepting the prevailing descriptive categories); superstition (belief that we are controlled from without by mysterious agencies); intolerance of ambiguity and use of rigid categories (discomfort when the environment provides few guideposts for thought and action).

[22]For two recent discussions designed to reduce polemics and seek empirical clarification of the issues underlying the controversial status of psychoanalysis, see B. A. Farrell, "The Status of Psychoanalytic Theory," *Inquiry,* **7** (Spring 1964), 104–123; and Peter Madison, *Freud's Concept of Repression and Defense: Its Theoretical and Observational Language,* Minneapolis: University of Minnesota Press, 1961.

[23]. . . I take the ego-defensive versus cognitive distinction from the recent literature on the functions served by opinions for the personality: M. Brewster Smith *et al., Opinions and Personality,* New York: John Wiley & Sons, 1956, Chap. 3; Daniel Katz, "The Functional Approach to the Study of Attitudes," *Public Opinion Quarterly,* **24** (Summer 1960), 163–204.

[24]See, for example, Angus Campbell *et al., The American Voter,* New York: John Wiley & Sons, 1960, pp. 512–515. Also the very interesting attempt by Thomas F. Pettigrew to demonstrate that the amount of personality-based (that is, ego-defensive) prejudice toward Negroes is the same in the American North, the American South, and in South Africa, and that the higher level of anti-Negro sentiment in the latter two areas is due to the cognitive learning which occurs in cultures where race prejudice is prevalent. "Personality and Sociocultural Factors in Intergroup Attitudes: A Cross-National Comparison," *Journal of Conflict Resolution,* **2** (March 1958), 29–42. . . .

[25] *The Authoritarian Personality,* pp. 482–83.

[26]Else Frenkel-Brunswik, "Further Explorations by a Contributor to *The Authoritarian Personality,*" in *SSMAP,* pp. 236–237.

[27]There is, of course, nothing incompatible between explanations of authoritarianism in terms of family socialization and explanations in terms of social structure. Nor need the latter be exclusively in economic terms. Evidence of the effects of the socioeconomic organization of a society on its members' personality characteristics is now becoming available from a study of personality differences between farmers and herders in four East African tribes. Two preliminary reports are Walter Goldschmidt, "Theory and Strategy in the Study of Cultural Adaptability," *American Anthropologist,* **67** (April 1965), 402–408, and Robert B. Edgerton, " 'Cultural' vs. 'Ecological' Factors in the Expression of Values, Attitudes, and Personality Characteristics," *ibid.,* pp. 442–447.

[28]Robert Waelder, *Basic Theory of Psychoanalysis,* New York: International Universities Press, 1960, pp. 53–54.

[29]See Shils' discussion of "left authoritarianism" in *SSMAP.* Also see . . . Milton Rokeach, "Political and Religious Dogmatism: An Alternative to the Authoritarian Personality," *Psychological Monographs,* No. 425 (1956) and *The Open and Closed Mind,* New York: Basic Books, 1960. One might say that the Marxian heritage of the original authoritarian research (by discouraging attention to authoritarianism on the left) hinders awareness of the diversity of belief consistent with common psychological characteristics, whereas the Freudian heritage (by pointing to ego-defensive rather than cognitive explanations) hinders awareness of the diversity of psychological characteristics consistent with common beliefs. For a discussion in *The Authoritarian Personality* of a personality subtype quite like Shils' notion of left-wing authoritarianism, see the treatment of the "rigid low scorer" on pp. 771–773.

[30]Irwin Katz and Lawrence Benjamin, "Effects of White Authoritarianism in Biracial Work Groups," *Journal of Abnormal and Social Psychology,* **61** (November 1960), 448–456.

[31]See David Riesman and Nathan Glazer, "*The Lonely Crowd:* A Reconsideration in 1960," in Seymour M. Lipset and Leo Lowenthal (eds.), *Culture and Social Character: The Work of David Riesman Reviewed,* New York: Free Press, 1961, p. 438. . . .

[32]A point made by Herbert Hyman in Bjorn Christiansen et al. (eds.), Cross-National Social Research, Oslo: Institute for Social Research; mimeographed, 1951, p. 31. . . .

[33]Shils, in SSMAP, p. 45 and p. 48.

[34]Lasswell, "Democratic Character," p. 428.

[35]Anthony F. C. Wallace, "The New Culture-and-Personality," Anthropology and Human Behavior, Washington, D.C.: The Anthropological Society of Washington, 1962, pp. 1–12.

OBEDIENCE TO WHOM?

Erik Erikson

I have so far mentioned two trends in the relationship between Hans and Martin: (1) the father's driving economic ambition, which was threatened by something (maybe even murder) done in the past, and by a feeling close to murder which he always carried inside; and (2) the concentration of the father's ambition on his oldest son, whom he treated with alternate periods of violent harshness and of habituating the son to himself in a manner which may well have been somewhat sentimental —a deadly combination.

I would add to these trends the father's display of righteousness. Hans seems to have considered himself the very conception, the Inbegriff, of justice. After all, he did not spare himself, and fought his own nature as ruthlessly as those of his children. But parents are dangerous who thus take revenge on their child for what circumstances and inner compulsion have done to them; who misuse one of the strongest forces in life—true indignation in the service of vital values—to justify their own small selves. Martin, however, seems to have sensed on more than one occasion that the father, behind his disciplined public identity, was possessed by an angry, and often alcoholic, impulsive-

ness which he loosed against his family (and would dare loose only against his family) under the pretense of being a hard taskmaster and righteous judge.

The fear of the father's anger, described as constant by some biographers, included the absolute injunction against any back-talk, any Widerrede. Here again the fact that only much later, and only after an attempt to screw down the lid with the rules of monastic silence, did Martin become one of the biggest and most effective back-talkers in history, forces us to ask what kept him silent for so long. But this was Martin: in Latin school he was caned for using the German language—and later he used that language with a vengeance! We can deduce from what burst forth later that which must have been forced to lie dormant in childhood; this may well have included some communality of experience with the mother, whose spontaneity and imagination are said to have suffered at the side of Hans Luder.

This much, I think, one can say about the paternal side of Martin's childhood dilemma. Faced with a father who made questionable use of his brute superiority; a father who had at his disposal the techniques of making others feel morally inferior without being quite able to justify his own moral superiority; a father to whom he could not get close and from whom he could not get away —faced with such a father, how was he going to submit without being emasculated, or rebel without emasculating the father?

Millions of boys face these problems and solve them in some way or another—they live, as Captain Ahab says, with half of their heart and with only one of their lungs, and the world is the worse for it. Now and again, however, an individual is called upon (called by *whom,* only the theologians claim to know, and by *what,* only bad psychologists) to lift his individual patienthood to the level of a universal one and to try to solve for all what he could not solve for himself alone.

Luther's statement of the maltreatment received at the hands of his mother is more specific; however, whatever resentment he felt against her was never expressed as dramatically as was his father-hate, which took the form of a burning doubt of divine righteousness. The Madonna was more or less gently pushed out of the way. What lack in Martin and what void in religion were thus created, we will discuss later.

To return to the statement quoted, it says that the mother beat him "until the blood came"; that this was for "one nut" which he presumably stole; and that such discipline "drove him into the monastery." Actually, the German text of this statement does not say "into the monastery"—and, indeed, Luther never relinquished the conviction that it was God who made him go into the monastery. *In die Moencherei* literally means "into monkery," into the monk-business, so to speak, and refers to his exaggeration of the ascetic and the scrupulous. He implies strongly, then, that such treatment was responsible for the excessive, the neurotic side of the religionism of his early twenties. "Such discipline," however, also refers to the general disciplinary methods of his time, not just to those of his mother; while "for one nut" may well cover, although we must not make too much of it, a complaint with many ramifications: it is one of a whole series of incidents which he cited even into old age to support a certain undertone of grievance in his self-justification.

We may add that if he was being punished for a breach of property rights, he may well have found the severity puzzling. Many children through the ages, like the juvenile delinquents of today, have found incomprehensible the absolutism of an adult conscience that insists that a little theft, if not pounced upon with the whole weight of society's wrath, will breed many big ones. Criminals are thus often made; since the world treats such small matters as a sure sign of potential criminality, the children may feel confirmed in one of those negative identity fragments which under adverse circumstances can become the dominant identity element. Luther all his life felt like some sort of criminal, and had to keep on justifying himself even after his revelation of the universal justification through faith had led him to strength, peace, and leadership.

"Until the blood came" (often translated as "flowed") has become a biographical stereotype which, in reading, one passes over as lightly as news about a widespread famine in China, or the casualties of an air raid. However, in regard to these larger news items, one would, if one stopped to think, detect some subliminal horror in oneself; but in regard to the blood thus exacted from children there seems to exist a widespread ambivalence. Some readers feel a slight revulsion in reading about it, others (and so the users of the stereotype seem to know), suspect it of being one of those factors which *made* the victim a sturdy personality worthy of a biography. Actually, in Martin's case, the German text only says that "afterwards there was blood," which at least takes out of the story that element of determined bloodthirstiness which the stereotype implies by the intentional "until." This whole disciplinary issue calls for a more general discussion before we send Martin to school and to further beatings.

The caning and whipping of children was as typical of Martin's time as the public torture of criminals. But since we are not making a zoological survey of human behavior, we are not obliged to accept what everybody does as natural. Nor do we have to agree with those hardy souls who, looking us straight in the eye, assure us that a good caning never did them any harm, quite the contrary. Since they could not escape the punishment when they were children, and can not undo it now, their statement only indicates their capacity to make the best of what cannot be helped. Whether or not it did them any harm is another question, to answer which may call for more information about the role they have come to play in adult human affairs.

It is well to remember that the majority of men have never invented the device of beating children into submission. Some of the American Plains Indian tribes were (as I had an opportunity to relate and to discuss twenty years ago) deeply shocked when they first saw white people beat their children. In their bewilderment they could not explain such behavior as part of an over-all missionary scheme—an explanation also supported by the white people's method of letting their babies cry themselves blue in the face. It all must mean, so they thought, a well-calculated wish to impress white children with the idea that this world is not a good place to linger in, and that it is better to look to the other world where perfect happiness is to be had at the price of having sacrificed this world. This is an ideological interpretation, and a shrewd one: it interprets a single typical act not on the basis of its being a possible cause of a limited effect, but as part of a world view. And indeed, we now beat our children less, but we are still harrying them through this imperfect world, not so much to get them to the next one as to make them hurry from one good moment to better ones, to climb, improve, advance, progress.

It takes a particular view of man's place on this earth, and of the place of childhood within man's total scheme, to invent devices for terrifying children into submission, either by magic, or by mental and corporeal terror. When these terrors are associated with collective and ritual observances, they can be assumed to contain some inner corrective which keeps the individual child from facing life all by himself; they may even offer some compensation of belongingness and identification. Special concepts of property (including the idea that a man can ruin his own property if he wishes) underlie the idea that it is entirely up to the discretion of an individual father when he should raise the morality of his children by beating their bodies. It is clear that the concept of children as property opens the door to those misalliances of impulsivity and compulsivity, or arbitrariness and moral logic, of brutality and haughtiness, which make men crueler and more licentious than creatures not fired with the divine spark. The device of beating children down —by superior force, by contrived logic, or by vicious sweetness—makes it unnecessary for the adult to become adult. He need not develop that true inner superiority which is naturally persuasive. Instead, he is authorized to remain significantly inconsistent and arbitrary, or in other words, childish, while beating into the child the desirability of growing up. The child, forced out of fear to pretend that he is better when seen than when unseen, is left to anticipate the day when he will have the brute power to make others more moral than he ever intends to be himself.

Historically, the increasing relevance of the Roman concepts of law in Luder's time helped to extend the concept of property so that fatherhood took on the connotation of an ownership of wife and children. The double role of the mother as one of the powerless victims of the father's brutality and also as one of his dutiful assistants in meting out punishment to the children may well account for a peculiar split in the mother image. The mother was perhaps cruel only because she had to be, but the father because he wanted to be. From the ideology inherent in such an arrangement there is —as we will see in Luther's punitive turn against the peasant rebels—only one psychological and a few political steps to those large-scale misalliances among righteousness, logic, and brutality that we find in inquisitions, concentration camps, and punitive wars.

The question, then, whether Martin's fears of the judgment day and his doubts in the justice then to be administered were caused by his father's great viciousness, or by his own greater sensitivity, or both, pales before the general problem of man's exploitability in childhood, which makes him the victim not only of overt cruelty, but also of all kinds of covert emotional relief, of devious vengefulness, or sensual self-indulgence, and of sly righteousness —all on the part of those on whom he is physically and morally dependent. Some day, maybe, there will exist a well-informed, well-considered, and yet fervent public conviction that the most deadly of all possible sins is the mutilation of a child's spirit; for such mutilation undercuts the life principle of trust, without which every human act, may it feel ever so good and seem ever so right, is prone to perversion by destructive forms of conscientiousness.

For the sake of the instructive illustration with which Luther's life may provide us, it is necessary to keep away from all-too-simple causal alternatives such as whether or not, in Luther's case, a brutal father beat a sickly or unstable son into such a state of anxiety and rebellion that God and even Christ became for him revengers only—*Stockmeister und Henker*—and not redeemers. As Luther puts it: "From childhood on, I knew I had to turn pale and be terror-stricken when I heard the name of Christ; for I was taught only to perceive him as a strict and wrathful judge." The psychiatrist and the priest—each for reasons of his own approach—consider this statement the quirk of an excessively gifted but unstable individual; and they bolster their contention with references to dozens of theologians of the time, none of whom exclusively emphasizes Christ's role as a revenger. And it is obvious that Luther's statement is most personal, influenced as it was by his upbringing and by his later decision to tackle that aspect of the disciplinary and religious atmosphere of his day which had almost crushed him, and which he felt was enslaving, not, of course, the professional religionists, but the common people of whom God had made so many.

We will hear more about the father; we have now all but exhausted the available references to the mother. We had better prepare ourselves, right here, for an almost exclusively masculine story: Kierkegaard's comment that Luther invented a religion for the adult man states the limitation as well as the true extent of Luther's theological creation. Luther provided new elements for the Western male's identity, and created for him new roles; but he contributed only one new feminine identity, the parson's wife—and this solely perhaps because his wife, Katherine of Bora, created it with the same determined unself-consciousness with which she made the great Doktor marry her. Otherwise, the Lutheran revolution only created ideals for women who wanted to be like parsons if they couldn't be like parsons' wives.

And in spite of Katherine and her children, wherever Luther's influence was felt, the Mother of God (that focus of women's natural religion-by-being-and-letting-be) was dethroned. Luther refers to her almost sneeringly as one of the female saints who might induce a man to "hang on their necks," or "hold on to their skirts": "And because we could never do enough penance and holy works, and in

spite of it all remained full of fear and terror of [God's] anger, they told us to look to the saints in heaven who should be the mediators between Christ and us; and they taught us to pray to the dear mother of Christ and reminded us of the breasts which she had given to her son so that she might ask him to go easy with his wrath toward us, and make sure of his grace." The sneer, it is true, is not for Mary but for those who suggested that he speak through her to Him to whom he "wanted to speak directly."

All of this comes to mind as one scans the thousands of pages of the literature on Luther; one comes to ask, over and over again, didn't the man have a mother?

Obviously, not much to speak of. The books repeat: of Luther's mother we know little. Didn't she stand between the father and the son whom she had suckled? Whose agent was she when she beat him "for one nut"? Did she disavow him on her own when he became a monk—a disavowal responsible for her one rather sandwiched mention in the *Documents of Luther's Development:* "I became a monk," Luther is quoted as saying, "against the wishes of my father, my mother, of God, and of the Devil." And what did she feel when she bore and lost so many children that their number and their names are forgotten? Luther does mention that some of her children "cried themselves to death," which may have been one of his after-dinner exaggerations; and at any rate, what he was talking about then was only that his mother had considered these children to have been bewitched by a neighbor woman. And yet, a friend of Luther's who visited her in her old age reported that Luther was her "spit and image."

The father seems to have been standoffish and suspicious toward the universe; the mother, it is said, was more interested in the imaginative aspects of superstition. It may well be, then, that from his mother Luther received a more pleasurable and more sensual attitude toward nature, and a more simply integrated kind of mysticism, such as he later found described by certain mystics. It has been surmised that the mother suffered under the father's personality, and gradually became embittered; and there is also a suggestion that a certain sad isolation which characterized young Luther was to be found also in his mother, who is said to have sung to him a ditty: "For me and you nobody cares. That is our common fault."

A big gap exists here, which only conjecture could fill. But instead of conjecturing half-heartedly, I will state, as a clinician's judgment, that nobody could speak and sing as Luther later did if his mother's voice had not sung to him of some heaven; that nobody could be as torn between his masculine and feminine sides, nor have such a range of both, who did not at one time feel that he was like his mother; but also, that nobody would discuss women and marriage in the way he often did who had not been deeply disappointed by his mother—and had become loath to succumb the way she did to the father, to fate. And if the soul is man's most bisexual part, then we will be prepared to find in Luther both some horror of mystic succumbing and some spiritual search for it, and to recognize in this alternative some emotional and spiritual derivatives of little Martin's "pre-historic" relation to his mother.

Preserved Smith (not a psychoanalyst) introduced the Oedipus complex into the literature on Luther. The psychiatrist picks it up, not without (quite figuratively speaking) crossing himself before the clinical world: "Maybe an orthodox psychoanalyst will phantasy into Luther's life the trivial outline of a deep and firmly anchored Oedipus complex which was aroused by a forceful and libidinal attachment to the vivacious and, as far as we know, gifted and imaginative mother, and accentuated by the sinister harshness of the father toward him, toward the siblings and maybe also to the mother." To this, we would reply that most certainly we would ascribe to Luther an Oedipus complex, and not a trivial one at that. We would not wish to see any boy—much less an imaginative and forceful one—face the struggles of his youth and manhood without having experienced as a child the love and the hate which are encompassed in this complex: love for the maternal person who awakens his senses and his sensuality with her ministrations, and deep and angry rivalry with the male possessor of this maternal person. We would also wish him with their help to succeed, in his boyhood, in turning resolutely away from the protection of women to assume the fearless initiative of men.

Only a boy with a precocious, sensitive, and intense conscience would *care* about pleasing his father as much as Martin did, or would subject himself to a scrupulous and relentless form of self-criticism instead of balancing the outer pressure with inventive deviousness and defiance. Martin's reactions to his father's pressure are the beginnings of Luther's preoccupation with matters of individual conscience, a preoccupation which went far beyond the requirements of religion as then practiced and formulated. Martin took unto himself the ideological structure of his parents' consciences: he incorporated his father's suspicious severity, his mother's fear of sorcery, and their mutual concern about catastrophes to be avoided and high goals to be met. Later he rebelled: first against his father, to join the monastery; then against the Church, to found his own church—at which point, he succumbed to many of his father's original values. We can only surmise to what extent this outcome was prepared for in childhood by a cumulative rebelliousness and by an ever-so-clandestine hate (for our conscience, like the medieval God, knows everything and registers and counts everything).

This biographical problem overlaps an historical one: Did Luther have a right to claim that his own fear, and his feeling of being oppressed by the image of an avenging God, were shared by others? Was his attitude representative of a pervasive religious atmosphere, at least in his corner of Christendom? The psychiatrist and the priest answer definitely not; the professor can dispense with this historical discussion altogether, since for him, God chose the moment of his word to Martin.

These questions can only be answered by a survey like the one Huizinga made of the waning Middle Ages in France and the Netherlands, in which he described the disintegration of the medieval identity and the emergence of the new burgher identity on evidence derived from literature and documentary art. In a general way, Huizinga's description must also apply to Martin's time and place:

At the close of the Middle Ages, a sombre melancholy weighs on people's souls. Whether we read a chronicle, a poem, a sermon, a legal document even, the same impression of immense sadness is produced by them all.

It would sometimes seem as if this period had been particularly unhappy, as if it had left behind only the memory of violence, of covetousness and mortal hatred, as if it had known no other enjoyment but that of intemperance, of pride and of cruelty.

In the records of all periods misfortune has left more traces than happiness. Great evils form the groundwork of history. We are perhaps inclined to assume without much evidence that, roughly speaking, and notwithstanding all calamities, the sum of happiness can have hardly changed from one period to another. But in the fifteenth century, as in the epoch of romanticism, it was, so to say, bad form to praise the world and life openly. It was fashionable to see only its suffering and misery, to discover everywhere signs of decadence and of the near end—in short, to condemn the times or to despise them.

No other epoch has laid so much stress as the expiring Middle Ages on the thought of death. An everlasting call of memento mori resounds through life.

*In earlier times, too, religion had insisted on the constant thought of death, but the pious treatises of these ages only reached those who had already turned away from the world. Since the thirteenth century, the popular preaching of the mendicant orders had made the eternal admonition to remember death swell into a sombre chorus ringing throughout the world. Towards the fifteenth century, a new means of inculcating the awful thought into all minds was added to the words of the preacher, namely the popular woodcut. Now these two means of expression, sermons and woodcuts, both addressing themselves to the multitude and limited to crude effects, could only represent death in a simple and striking form.**

In the evaluation of the dominant moods of any historical period it is important to hold fast to the fact that there are always islands of self-sufficient order—on farms and in castles, in homes, studies, and cloisters—where sensible people manage to live relatively lusty and decent lives: as moral as they must be, as free as they may be, and as masterly as they can be. If we only knew it, this elusive arrangement *is* happiness. But men, especially in periods of change, are swayed by alternating world moods which seem to be artificially created by the monopolists and manipulators of an era's opinions, and yet could not exist without the highly exploita-

From Johan Huizinga, The Waning of the Middle Ages, *pp. 76-77. Published in England by Edward Arnold Publishers, Ltd.; published in the U.S. by St. Martin's Press. Reprinted by permission.*

ble mood cycles inherent in man's psychological structure. The two most basic alternating moods are those of carnival and atonement: The first gives license and leeway to sensual enjoyment, to relief and release at all cost; the second surrenders to the negative conscience which constricts, depresses, and enjoins man for what he has left unsolved, uncared for, unatoned. Especially in a seemingly rational and informed period like our own, it is obvious how blithely such moods overshadow universally available sets of information, finding support for luxurious thoughtlessness at one time, panicky self-criticism at another. Thus we may say that beside and beyond a period's verifiable facts and official doctrines, the world image "breathes." It tends to expand and to contract in its perspectives, and to gain or lose solidity and coherence. In each careless period latent panic only waits for catastrophe—famines, pests and depressions, overpopulation and migration, sudden shifts in technology or in leadership—to cause a shrinkage in the world image, a kind of chill attacking the sense of identity of large masses.

We briefly outlined above the expansion of earthly space in Luther's times. But every expanding opens frontiers, every conquest exposes flanks. Gunpowder and the printing press could be used against their users; voyages revealed a world of disquieting cultural relativities; wider social contacts increased the chances of ideological contamination and of further inroads of plague and syphilis. The impact of all these Pyrrhic victories, and of the spiritual decline of the papacy and the fragmentation of the empire, produced both a shrinkage of that official perspective which was oriented toward eventual salvation, and an increase in the crudity and cruelty of the means employed to defend what remained of the Church's power of persuasion. Thus it is probable that in Martin's childhood and youth there lurked in the ideological perspective of his world, perhaps just because the great theologians were so engrossed in scholasticism, a world image of man as inescapably sinful, with a soul incapable of finding any true identity in its perishable body. This world-image implied only one hope: at an uncertain (and maybe immediately impending) moment, an end would come which might guarantee an individual the chance (to be denied to millions of others) of finding pity before the only true Identity, the only true Reality, which was Divine Wrath.

Among the increasing upper urban classes, among the patricians, merchants, and masters who were the town fathers of the ever more important cities, the reaction was developing which eventually became the northern Renaissance. These upper classes no more wanted to be the emperor's then growing economic proletariat than they wished to end on the day of judgment as God's proletariat who (as they could see in the paintings which they commissioned) were to be herded into oblivion by fiery angels, mostly of Italian extraction. This attitude reflected the discrepancy between the era of unlimited initiative then dawning and the era coming to an end which subordinated man's identity on earth to a super-identity in heaven. But these two eras, all too simply set off against each other as the Renaissance and the Middle Ages, corresponded, in fact, to two inner world moods; their very conflictedness corresponded to man's conflicted inner structure.

We are far ahead of ourselves. Yet, we must face the fact that when little Martin left the house of his parents, he was heavily weighed down by an overweening superego, which would give him the leeway of a sense of identity only in the obedient employment of his superior gifts, and only as long as he was more Martin than Luther, more son than man, more follower than leader.

Hans Luder in all his more basic characteristics belonged to the narrow, suspicious, primitive-religious, catastrophe-minded people. He was determined to join the growing class of burghers, masters, and town fathers—but there is always a lag in education. Hans beat into Martin what was characteristic of his own past, even while he meant to prepare him for a future better than his own present. This conflictedness of Martin's early education, which was *in* and *behind* him when he entered the world of school and college, corresponded to the conflicts inherent in the ideological-historical universe which lay *around* and *ahead* of him. The theological problems which he tackled as a young adult of course reflected the peculiarly tenacious problem of the domestic relationship to his own father; but this was true to a large extent because both problems, the domestic and the universal, were part of one ideological crisis: a crisis about the theory and practice, the power and responsibility, of the moral authority invested in fathers: on earth and in heaven; at home, in the market-place, and in politics; in the castles, the capitals, and in Rome. But it undoubtedly took a father and a son of tenacious sincerity and almost criminal egotism to make the most of this crisis, and to initiate a struggle in which were combined elements of the drama of King Oedipus and the passion of Golgotha, with an admixture of cussedness made in Saxony.

THE CURSE

Erik Erikson

The first and only childhood item reprinted in Gandhi's *Collected Works* is a letter which he wrote at the age of fifteen in order to confess to his unsuspecting father the fact that he "had removed a bit of gold from his brother's armlet to clear a small debt of the latter." According to his sister's account (as told to Pyarelal when she was ninety), he first confessed to his mother, who said: "Go and tell your father." "Would father thrash me for this?" he asked. "He won't," the mother replied, "why should he? Has he ever done so?" This, if correctly remembered, at least confirms that the otherwise short-tempered father never laid hands on *this* boy. Gandhi himself continues:

I decided at last to write out the confession, to submit it to my father, and to ask his forgiveness. I wrote it on a slip of paper and handed it to him myself. In this note not only did I confess my guilt, but I asked adequate punishment for it, and closed with a request to him not to punish himself [not to take the punishment on himself] for my offense. I also pledged myself never to steal in future.

I was [my hand was] trembling as I handed the confession to my father. He was then suffering from a fistula and was confined to bed. His bed was a plain wooden plank. I handed him the note and sat opposite the plank.

He read it through, and pearl drops trickled down his cheeks, wetting the paper. For a moment he closed his eyes in thought and then tore up the note. He had sat up to read it. He again lay down. I also cried. I could see my father's agony. If I were a painter, I could draw a picture of the whole scene today. [Even today] it is still so vivid in my mind.

[The love arrow of] those pearl drops of love cleansed [pierced] my heart and washed my sin away—[I became pure]. Only he who has experienced such love can

Reprinted from Gandhi's Truth, On the Origins of Militant Nonviolence, by Erik H. Erikson. By permission of W. W. Norton and Company, Inc. Copyright © 1969 by W. W. Norton and Company, Inc. Footnotes have been omitted.

know what it is. As the hymn says: "Only he who is smitten with the arrows of love [Rama] knows its power."

This was, for me, an object-lesson in Ahimsa. Then I could read *[see] in it nothing more than a father's love, but today I know that it was pure Ahimsa. When such Ahimsa becomes all-embracing, it transforms everything it touches. There is no limit to its power. [It is hard to measure this power.]*

This sort of sublime forgiveness was not natural [basically unnatural] to my father. I had thought that he would be angry, say hard things, and [probably] strike his forehead. But he was so wonderfully peaceful, and I believe this was due to my clean confession.

A clean confession, combined with a promise never to commit the sin again, when offered before one who has the right to receive it, is the purest type of repentance. I know that my confession made my father feel absolutely safe about me and increased his affection for me beyond measure.

My italics mark those passages in which the son, at the age of fifteen, is exquisitely aware of his power to induce in his father an extraordinary state of mind. If such "sublime forgiveness" was "basically unnatural" to his father and if the whole matter nevertheless turns out to be "an object-lesson in Ahimsa," then it is the son who with the spiritual will embodied in his "clean confession" purified the father. For old Kaba did not hit his son (something he seems to have done quite "naturally" to others), nor did he "take the punishment upon himself" by hitting himself on the forehead—an Indian custom which can be most resounding and utterly disconcerting to all within earshot. Instead, there was peace. All of which is emphasized here not only for its intrinsic importance in the development of Gandhi's sense of a superior destiny but also because the story has a certain "typical ring" —a resonance with the lives of other leading individuals with a premature conscience development and an early assumption of moral responsibility for a parent—a responsibility which they subsequently extended to mankind itself.

It seems fitting here to digress in the service of one of the dimensions of biographic interpretation. Even an item as idiosyncratic as Mohan's confession can be fruitfully compared with analogous items in the lives of comparable figures of world history, thus revealing a "typical" experience at least among those who write autobiographies. Let me offer for consideration two items from widely different settings.

Here is a famous passage from Kierkegaard:

Once upon a time there lived a father and a son. Both were very gifted, both witty, particularly the father. . . . *On one rare occasion, when the father looking upon his son saw that he was deeply troubled, he stood before him and said: Poor child, you go about in silent despair. (But he never questioned more closely, alas he could not, for he himself was in silent despair.) Otherwise, they never exchanged a word on the subject. Both father and son were, perhaps,* two of the most melancholy men *in the history of man.*

And the father believed that he was the cause of the son's melancholy, and the son believed that he was the cause of the father's melancholy, and so they never discussed it. . . . And what is the meaning of this? The point precisely is that he made me unhappy—*but out of love. His error did not consist in lack of love but in* mistaking a child for an old man.*

Again, I have italicized the phrases which illustrate what I have in mind, namely, that such encounter is possible only where the father-son relationship has assumed a very special peculiarity. In a patriarchal era a son with a precocious conscience and a deep sense of superior mission could, while still a child, feel spiritually equal to—nay responsible for—a father who, by his own desperate neediness, made it impossible for the boy to hate him. I would venture to suggest that certain kinds of greatness have as an early corollary a sense that a parent must be redeemed by the superior character of the child, and we shall see presently what "sin" it was that Mohandas felt he had to redeem in his father.

But in order to indicate the whole range of this problem, we will shift the scene radically to the autobiography of a woman and modern American and a bearer of a quite different kind of greatness. In Eleanor Roosevelt's life the overweening theme of owing maternal care to all of mankind, as well

as to special groups and individuals, manifested itself most decisively and most proudly in the support which she, a previously most undecisive young woman, determined to bestow on her stricken husband. Here is the account of Eleanor's last meeting with her father.

. . . I remember going down into the high-ceilinged dim library on the first floor of the house in West 37th Street. He sat in a big chair. He was dressed all in black, looking very sad. He held out his arms and gathered me to him. In a little while he began to talk, to explain to me that my mother was gone, that she had been all the world to him, and now he only had my brothers and myself, that my brothers were very young, and that he and I must keep close together. Some day I would make a home for him again; we would travel together and do many things which he painted as interesting and pleasant to be looked forward to in the future together.

Somehow it was always he and I. I did not understand whether my brothers were to be our children or whether he felt that they would be at school and college and later independent.

There started that day a feeling which never left me —that he and I were very close together, and some day would have a life of our own together. He told me to write to him often, to be a good girl, not to give any trouble, to study hard, to grow up into a woman he could be proud of, and he would come to see me whenever it was possible.

When he left, I was all alone to keep our secret of mutual understanding and to adjust myself to my new existence.

On August 14, 1894, just before I was ten years old, word came that my father had died. My aunts told me, but I simply refused to believe it, and while I wept long and went to bed still weeping, I finally went to sleep and began the next day living in my dream world as usual.

My grandmother decided that we children should not go to the funeral, and so I had no tangible thing to make death real to me. From that time on I knew in my mind that my father was dead, and yet I lived with him more closely, probably, than I had when he was alive.

Here it must be added that her father was an alcoholic and had been put away for years in a sanitarium. He was, in fact, permitted to see his daughter only on singular occasions—such as that of the mother's death. Yet here too the image of the guilty and suffering parent becomes an indelible secret possession and a source of a lifelong and

---

* *The Journals of Søren Kierkegaarde, A Selection,* ed. & trans. by Alexander Dru.

* *The Autobiography of Eleanor Roosevelt.*

very special strength. In a biographic study Joan Erikson makes a convincing case of it that Eleanor, as the wife of FDR, suddenly lost all her shy undecisiveness when she realized that her husband, then crippled by infantile paralysis, was to be put away, as her father had been at a time when she had been too young to prevent it. Thus Eleanor became great as a president's nurse, companion, and helper and later as a principle trustee of his spiritual-political estate and a co-author of the UN charter of human rights.

In the case of a maternal son, the element of ambivalence looms, of course, very much larger wherever the son is fanatically preoccupied with the care (physical or spiritual) of the father. And, indeed, at the very beginning of his Autobiography, Gandhi refers to his father not only as short-tempered (and we have seen how the son cured him of that) but also as possibly "given to carnal pleasures." For the father's marriage to his mother had been his fourth: and he had married the eighteen-year-old girl when he was already forty. Gandhi records that his father had lost all previous wives by death, but this does not seem to be correct: his third wife was, in fact, still alive, although hopelessly invalid, when Gandhi's father married Putali Ba—a not altogether negligible circumstance in a gossipy community's view of a prime minister's life. It may, in fact, have weighed heavily on Putali Ba. At any rate, that Gandhi, the master of *Brahma charya,* on the first page of his Autobiography refers to his father as possibly oversexed, and this because he married his mother and fathered him, is a rather fundamental statement of the generational dilemma. For it contains, I believe, the further accusation that the father, by insisting on the son's early marriage, had cursed the son with his own carnal weakness—certainly a powerful ontogenetic argument for the Augustinian stigma of primal sin. Kaba, by exposing his son to sexuality so early, also made him a father before the son could know what he was doing. Kierkegaard, like many a man devoted to the problem of existence as such, thanked God for the fact that He had saved him from becoming a father. If the Mahatma's eldest son would eventually take exquisite revenge on his father by dying a destitute's death, we recognize in Gandhi's life a son-father and father-son theme of biblical dimensions.

This will prepare us for the second, final, and fatal encounter with the father which the Mahatma recorded with such devastating vividness in his Autobiography. It has been quoted so often and overinterpreted so much that I cannot bring myself to reprint it yet again in full. Enough: One night his sick father was fast sinking; but the young son left the nursing care to the father's favorite brother and went to his bedroom to join his (then pregnant) wife. After a while, however, somebody came to fetch him. Rushing to the sickroom, he found that his father had died in the uncle's arms—"a blot," Gandhi writes, "which I have never been able to efface or to forget." A few weeks later his wife aborted.

This experience represents in Gandhi's life what, following Kierkegaard, I have come to call "the curse" in the lives of spiritual innovators with a similarly precocious and relentless conscience. It is indicative of an aspect of childhood or youth which comes to represent an account that can never be settled and remains an existential debt all the rest of a lifetime. But it must be clear that one single episode cannot be the *cause* of such a curse; rather, the curse is what we clinicians call a "cover memory," that is, a condensation and projection of a pervasive childhood conflict on one dramatized scene. In individual cases this may seem to be the cause in childhood of a set of dangerous and pathogenic developments in later life; but we may do well to ask what the propensity for such dramatization may mean in phylogenetic development. A dark preoccupation with the death of the old seems unavoidable in a species which must live through a period of infantile dependence unequaled in length elsewhere in nature, which develops a sensitive self-awareness in the very years of immaturity, and which becomes aware of the inexorable succession of generations at a stage of childhood when it also develops the propensity for intense and irrational guilt. To better the parent thus means to replace him; to survive him means to kill him; to usurp his domain means to appropriate the mother, the "house," the "throne." If such guilt is, as religions claim, of the very essence of revelation, it is still a fateful fact that mankind's Maker is necessarily first experienced in the infantile image of each man's maker.

This curse, clinical theory would suggest, must

be heir to the Oedipus conflict. In Gandhi's case the "feminine" service to his father would have served to deny the boyish wish to replace the (aging) father in the possession of the (young) mother and the youthful intention to outdo him as a leader in later life. Thus the pattern would be set for a style of leadership which can defeat a superior adversary only nonviolently and with the express intent of saving him as well as those whom he oppressed. Some of this interpretation, in fact, corresponds to what the Mahatma would have unhesitatingly acknowledged as his conscious intention.

It is of little help, then, to submit Gandhi's confession to such pseudo-clinical formulations as that "Gandhi in his inner being was quite the reverse of the filial model he defends in his Autobiography." This is too nonspecific an assertion to explain the magnitude of his confessed conflict— and what he did with it. It purports to unmask something which Gandhi, in fact, was aware of to a fault. The question is, rather, why certain men of genius can do no less than take upon themselves an evolutionary and existential curse shared by all, and why other men will be only too eager to ascribe to such a man a god-given greatness surpassing that of all others.

The question is a threefold one: how does the child and the youth come to develop the capacity to take on such a fate, and the man, the determination to honor it; what motivation makes the multitudes wait for such a man, eager to consider him holy; and how does he learn to make their motivation and his converge in events which release creative, as well as destructive, energies of great magnitude?

While Gandhi's Autobiography pictures him as a child and as a youth totally obsessed with matters of guilt and purity and as a failure in the ways of the world, he, of course, "somehow" acquired at the same time superior powers of observation as well as an indomitable determination. But I believe that just because Mohandas was early (if only darkly) aware of the unlimited horizon of his aspiration, his failure to preside mercifully over his father's death and thus to receive a lasting sanction for his superior gifts was, indeed, the curse of his life. But this, as we saw, is (typically) a shared curse, for if "carnal weakness" was to blame, it was the father's weakness which had become the son's.

The ontogenetic version of this childhood curse remains fateful. The theme of nursing a stricken (and ambivalently loved) superior adversary reappears in Gandhi's later life both literally and symbolically. We shall meet it in the role of one who twice, although an adversary of British policy, recruits for an ambulance corps in support of British war efforts when the Empire was in danger. And we shall find it in the conviction of the Satyagrahi that in fighting nonviolently, he is really taking care of his adversary's soul and its latent "truth."

Yet this theme of nursing a stricken father, too, must and can be seen in historical perspective. One would not wish to overdo the parallel, but it is thought-provoking that in Freud's reported dreams the conviction of having been of medical assistance to his dying father looms large as a dream-wish counteracting his guilt over his medical ambitions.

In order to illustrate this, again, with an analogous scene from a different background, let me turn to the writer Lu Hsün, who is often quoted with veneration by Mao as the founding father of modern China's revolutionary literature. His famous short story, "Diary of a Madman" (1918), the first literary work written in vernacular Chinese, is a masterpiece not only (we are told) in the power of its style but (as we can see) as a very modern combination of a precise psychiatric description of paranoia (Lu Hsün had studied medicine in Japan) and a nightmarish allegory of the fiercer aspects of traditional and revolutionary China. In an essay entitled "Father's Illness," Lu Hsün combines a historical theme—namely, the discrepancy between Western and Confucian concepts concerning a man's last moments—with the ambivalent emotions of a son. He had spent much of his adolescent years, he reports, searching for herbs that might cure his ailing father. But now death was near.

Sometimes an idea would flash like lightning into my mind: better to end the gasping faster . . . and immediately I knew that the idea was improper; it was like committing a crime. But at the same time I thought this idea rather proper, for I loved my father. Even now, I still think so.

This is the Western doctor speaking; but at the time a Mrs. Yen, a kind of midwife for the departing soul, had suggested the application of some traditional magic actions and had urged the son to scream into his father's ear so that he would not stop breathing.

"Father! Father!"
His face, which had quieted down, suddenly became tense. He opened his eyes slightly as if he felt something bitter and painful.
"Yell! Yell! Quick!"
"Father!"
"What?... don't shout... don't..." he said in a low tone. Then he gasped frantically for breath. After a while, he returned to normal and calmed down.
"Father!" I kept calling him until he stopped breathing. Now I can still hear my own voice at that time. Whenever I hear it, I feel that this is the gravest wrong I have done to my father.

Lu Hsün was fifteen at the time (to Gandhi's sixteen). His forebears, like Gandhi's, had been high officials whose fortunes were on the decline during the son's adolescence. At any rate, his story clearly suggests that in his life, too, a desperate clinging to the dying father and a mistake made at the very last moment represented a curse overshadowing both past memory and future redemption.

It is not enough, however, to reduce such a curse to the "Oedipus Complex" reconstructed in thousands of case histories as the primal complex. The Oedipal crisis, too, must be evaluated as part of man's over-all development. In its habitual connotations it is only the infantile and often only the neurotic core of an existential dilemma which (less mythologically) may be called the *generational complex,* for it derives from the fact that man experiences life and death—and past and future—as a matter of the turnover of generations. Yet, this human crisis is obviously shared by all men, and to highlight it retrospectively in the case of an uncommon man would seem to be a rather minor triumph of ingenuity, if one cannot clarify what makes the man and his complex uncommon.

It is, in fact, rather probable that a highly uncommon man experiences filial conflicts with such mortal intensity just because he already senses in himself early in childhood some kind of originality that seems to point beyond competition with the personal father. Often, also, an especially early and exacting conscience development makes him feel

(and appear) old while still young and maybe even older in single-mindedness than his conformist parents, who in turn may treat him somehow as their potential redeemer. Thus he grows up almost with an obligation, beset with guilt, to surpass and to create at all cost. In adolescence this may prolong his identity confusion because he must find the one way in which he (and he alone!) can re-enact the past and create a new future in the right medium at the right moment on a sufficiently large scale. His prolonged identity crisis, in turn, may invoke a premature generativity crisis that makes him accept as his concern a whole communal body or mankind itself and embrace as his dependents those weak in power, poor in possessions, and seemingly simple in heart. Such a deflection in life plan, in fact, may crowd out his chances for the enjoyment of intimacy, sexual and other, wherefore the "great" are often mateless, friendless, and childless in the midst of veneration and confound further the human dilemma of combining the responsibilities of procreation with those of individual existence.

But not all highly uncommon men are chosen; and the psychohistorical question is not only how such men come to experience the inescapability of an existential curse, but how it comes about that they have the pertinacity and the giftedness to re-enact it in a medium communicable to their fellow men and meaningful in their stage of history. The emphasis here is on the word *re-enactment,* which in such cases goes far beyond the dictates of that "repetition compulsion" which characterizes symptoms and irrational acts. For the mark of a creative re-enactment of a curse (and here we may recall King Oedipus on the stage) is that its communal experience becomes a liberating event for each member of an awe-stricken audience. Some dim awareness of this idea must be the reason why the wielders of power in different periods of history appreciate and support the efforts of creative men to re-enact the universal conflicts of mankind in the garb of the historical day, as the great dramatists have done and as the great autobiographers do. A political leader like Mao, then, may recognize a writer like Lu Hsün not for any ideological oratory, but for his precise and ruthless presentation of the inner conflicts that must accompany the emergence of a revolutionary mind in a society as bound to filial piety as China. In a man like Gandhi the autobiographer and the leader are united in one person but remain distinct in the differentiation between re-enactments in writing and re-enactments in action. In all re-enactment, however, only the transcendence of an infantile curse by an adult deed marks the man. But as we trace the curse through the stages which prepare the deed, we remind ourselves of that great fact in human life which bridges infantile guilt and adult action: playful enactments in childhood. Seasoned playfulness is long in developing, and I think that in Gandhi's life it can be shown to have alleviated his moral precocity and to have added a significant dimension to his evolving personal and political style. It even seems to be an essential ingredient in nonviolence.

INBURN: AN AMERICAN ISHMAEL

Kenneth Keniston

Inburn's appearance in no way set him apart from other undergraduates. Tall, with blue eyes and sandy hair, he wore the uniform of his classmates: baggy corduroys, a button-down shirt, horn-rimmed glasses, and a tie more often than not slid down from the collar. He walked with something of a slouch, hands deep in his pockets, his eyes mostly fixed on the pavement as if he were deep in some private thought. From the cafeterias he frequented, one versed in the ways of the college might have surmised that he was of literary bent, and from the fact that he so often ate breakfast in one particular cafeteria at 11:00 A.M. (having overslept the dining hall's more Spartan hours), that he was given neither to regular hours nor to impeccable attendance at lectures. But these qualities in no way distinguished him from a goodly proportion of his fellow sophomores.

Nor did he create an unusual impression on others. The opinion of a woman of fifty who knew him

casually can perhaps stand as typical: "I rather liked him. He is thin and pleasant—perhaps not a decisive, strong-willed person, but always agreeable, never obviously depressed, perhaps a little shy, as talkative as most men his age." A psychologist who knew him slightly commented, "He is a nice-looking fellow, with a deep voice that might go over well on the stage. He speaks hesitantly but well, despite pauses and hesitations—more like written prose than ordinary speech." His manner was polite, reserved, and even detached, which implied to some that he was proud and condescending, and to others that he tended to brood. Though he seldom looked directly at the person to whom he was speaking, occasionally, when caught up in a topic, he would gaze deeply and intently into his interlocutor's eyes, suggesting deeper feelings than his outward manner expressed.

On the surface, his background and interests were also altogether unextraordinary. Like many of his classmates, he came from a middle-class family outside of New England, and he had gone to a good high school where he had graduated near the top of his class and been editor of the school paper.

Even his outstanding intelligence, however, did not distinguish him from his classmates, also of high talent; and although his grades in his freshman year were slightly uneven, they adequately reflected his ability, and he made dean's list. His father was an executive in a large Detroit corporation; and his mother, for a time a schoolteacher, had early abandoned her career for domesticity. Inburn himself had been undecided for a time as to his major, but had finally settled on English literature as a field in which he could combine his interest in writing and his superior high-school training in literature. Like other students with artistic interests, he had tried his hand at student dramatics and at writing, a career he sometimes thought of following. He was a student who was in good standing with the college authorities, who had caused no one any trouble, and who would not easily be picked out in a crowd.

In the most public sides of Inburn's personality, then, there was little to suggest what was the case: that he was deeply dissatisfied with society, the world, and himself; that he almost completely rejected the institutional forms within which he was living; that he would spend his first reading period for exams in platonic partnership with a call girl whose memoirs he was ostensibly recording for future use; and that, though he passed his exams, he would withdraw from the college at midyear, never to return, heading instead on a motorcycle across the country to live with an "irredeemably dissolute" high-school friend in San Francisco. Despite his conventional surface, indeed because of it, Inburn can stand as a prototypically alienated young man, separated partly by his own volition from the people, institutions, and beliefs which sustain most young men at his age in America; rejecting the forms by which most American men and women live; and condemned, like the Biblical Ishmael by his past and like Melville's Ishmael by his own temper, to live on the outskirts of society. We do not know what has become of Inburn in the years since he volunteered to be studied in a clinical research project, whether his alienation persisted or dissolved with time and benign experience—though he himself implied in one Thematic Apperception Test story that the best resolution of his estrangement would be its incorporation in the role of a writer. In Inburn we see alienation—the

rejection of the roles and values and institutions he sees as typical of adult American life—in unusually pure form; and the themes of his life can stand as introduction to and summary of comparable themes in the lives of others like him.

AN ENDLESS AND FEATURELESS COUNTRYSIDE

Like seventy other volunteers for a psychological research project, Inburn took a battery of paper-and-pencil tests, many of which were designed to measure alienated outlooks.[1] He first came to our attention even before the questionnaires were scored, because of his mordant marginal comments on items which he considered stupid or irrelevant. He made among the highest scores on every index we then had of alienation—on distrust, pessimism, resentment, anxiety, egocentricity, the sense of being an outsider, the rejection of conventional values, rejection of happiness as a goal, and a feeling of distance from others. And, had other subsequently developed measures of alienation been available, it is clear he would have scored high on them—on subspection (the desire to look beneath appearances), self-contempt, interpersonal alienation, dislike of conventional social groups, rejection of American culture, and the view of the universe as an unstructured and meaningless chaos. But even more revealing than test scores are some of the individual statements which he marked "strongly agree," often with exclamation points added; taken together, they constitute a kind of credo of disaffiliation: "The idea of trying to adjust to society as now constituted fills me with horror"; "There are sad and depressing times when the whole world strikes the eye as a huge, heartless, impersonal machine, almost devoid of understanding, sympathy, and mercy"; "I sometimes feel that I am the plaything of forces beyond my control"; "I feel strongly how different I am even from some of my closest friends"; "I have very little in common with most of the people I meet"; "I don't think I'll ever find a woman who really understands me"; "I have very little self-confidence"; "I usually try to keep my thoughts to myself"; "I sometimes wish I were a child again."

Soon after, when Inburn was asked to write a statement of his philosophy of life, he was unique among twenty-five students chosen for intensive clinical study in that he wrote an allegory instead of a formal statement:

A group of men are motoring through an endless and featureless countryside in a tightly closed car, with all the windows rolled up. They reach a city, emerge from their vehicle, stretch their legs, and look around. They have a two-week stay ahead of them; after that they must move on into the wastes on the other side of the town, the same as before they arrived.

"Well," I ask (being one of them), "what shall we do?" To all our surprises, each wants to spend his time differently. . . . "Personally," say I, "I would like to see the sights of this place."

In this rather naive allegory lies the ideal of my philosophy of life. If human (i.e., my) existence is looked on as a short time spent on a physical world with an inscrutable void on either side, it seems that the time can be most profitably spent in accumulating the most varied, the most valuable, and the most significant set of sense experiences it is possible to take in. . . .

One must not see the same sights over-frequently. What experiences are most valuable to fill this sixty-to-seventy-year interlude are those that bring one into the closest contact with reality, with the ground, the bedrock of sheer existence. This, of course, involves living close to nature, outside of (or rather beneath) the superstructure of tin and shit and kite-paper man has built up to live in.

Rather obviously, I am not practicing what I preach to any extent at all now. I wouldn't be in this room writing this little essay if I were. So far, all I do is insult myself by saying it's a fine idea, in fact, it's the only idea in the universe, but you don't have the guts to put it into practice.

Inburn's statement is as noteworthy for what it excludes as for what it says. Unlike many other students, whose philosophies of life stress the importance of other people, Inburn mentions others only once, and then to state that he is different from them. Also unlike many of his classmates, he explicitly rejects the "superstructure" of society and seeks above all the accumulation of sense experience, defined as that which will bring him into contact with "the bedrock of sheer existence."

Inburn's generally distrustful view of people was amplified when he was asked what harms and benefits he chiefly anticipated from his fellow men. He listed only "hostility, injustice, hypocrisy, slander, abuse." Asked whom he admired, he said: "I never thought about it. Alexander maybe. Hemingway in Paris. Chopin." But asked whom he disliked, he responded with a catalogue which begins, "Nearly everything, and everyone that's complacently middle-class"; enumerates many specific examples; and concludes, "I hate officious, supercilious, imperious, pompous, stupid, contented, or bigoted persons. I especially dislike opportunists." And asked what his chief satisfactions and ambitions were, he said, "I don't think I'll ever have a main source of satisfaction. Only to live so that I may have the truest picture of the world possible when I die. You mean vaulting ambition? Nobody strives for ideas any more. It's hard enough just to strive." And asked how he would reform the world if he could, he said, "This is an unfair question. I guess I'd like to have us all go back to the womb."

Here, then, is a young man whose every attitude fits an alienated pattern. Full of distrust, he expects only harm from his fellow men; he has few admired figures, but many he dislikes; he sees life as a meaningless interlude whose chief object is the accumulation of varied sense experiences. He rejects society and conventional institutions; though he has no plans for his life, he clearly wants something different from the conventional life which draws most of his classmates; he denies all ambition; and his facetious Utopia is the womb.

MORE THAN A MERE MOTHER-AND-ONLY-CHILD

Inburn's autobiography, written for the research project for which he had volunteered, begins to provide some clues as to the development of his alienation. Like one or two of the more literarily ambitious research subjects, he began his autobiography in the third person:

He came screaming and red-faced into the world on a December night in 1938, loath to leave his insensible sanctuary. . . . It was in a hospital in St. Louis; his mother was a small, young woman and she never had a child again. His parents were both schoolteachers and poor, after the ravages of the depression. His mother was particularly good-looking when she was young—black

hair, a good nose, striking dark eyes, a sensuous lip, and
a delicate yet hard, vibrant, vivacious body.

Inburn goes on to describe his mother's Greek immigrant parents, her mother "a simple, exuberant, and cruel woman," and her father, who ran a small restaurant, "a strong man, and strong-willed, tireless, too tireless."

His further description of his mother is extremely detailed. Despite her immigrant parents, "she made herself socially to nearly every family in St. Louis" [*sic*]. "Her petite and much-in-demand bottom was between two worlds. . . . She dropped her restaurant-owner's daughter's bad manners and grossness and made herself, completely, at the cost of great emotional and psychological complexity." She was ambitious; she taught herself to play the piano beautifully (she even gave recitals). "She *would* read poetry (though she never wrote it), she *would* paint, she *would* play tennis on the bank president's private court, and with his son." Despite her parents' lack of sympathy with her educational goals, she worked her way through high school and college, finishing each in three years. Elsewhere, Inburn notes that his mother is at the extreme end of the temperament scale: "volatile, passionate, typically Mediterranean"; and he adds that she "has a delicate constitution and has been warned against severe mental as well as physical strains."

In contrast to his full description of his mother, Inburn has far less to say of his father. His father's family originally came from a farm in the Midwest, and Inburn's grandfather married his own brother's pregnant and cast-off girl friend, became a milkman in St. Louis, and was thereafter dominated by his wife, a "scolding, officious hypochondriac." The father's ancestry was primarily Welsh, with a mixture of German and Irish. Inburn's father showed early signs of intelligence and musical talent and worked his way through high school and college, where he met his future wife. As a child, he seems to have been dominated by his mother, the "scolding, officious hypochondriac," who forced him to work in the evenings for the family landlord, "an idea he has recalled with bitterness at times." Awarded a scholarship to an Eastern college, Inburn's father was unable to accept it because he had to help support his parents—a re-

sponsibility which included helping to pay his older half-brother's debts. Inburn describes his father now as a "phlegmatic, deliberate, steady-minded Welshman," noting the extreme contrast with his mother. "Father is pretty much of a failure in his own eyes," he comments, adding: "He's done pretty well as far as the world is concerned, though." Elsewhere he calls his father "a pillar in the community," adding parenthetically, "Small pillar. Small community." He describes "a great distance" between himself and his father, noting rather unenthusiastically, "We are friendly, though, except when my Greek side is up and I become disgusted with him and he annoyed at me."

His parents were married immediately after graduating from college, and both worked as high-school teachers, his father occasionally holding two jobs to supplement the family income. Inburn's account continues:

This, then, is the situation (one might say predicament) Inburn was born into. By 1938 his parents had saved enough money to have a house of their own . . . they hired an architect and had the place built just as they wanted. The father is acquiescent and the mother has excellent taste, and it came out beautifully.

The first memories Inburn has are of this house—door knobs, the carpeting, the bright yellow and white kitchen, the apple tree in the back yard, the plum trees in the field beyond. It was in a fairly undeveloped suburban section, staunchly middle class.

He was pretty as a child, a little plump, with his mother's eyes and grace and quite curly blond hair. Mama tells me proudly how people often stopped her on the street and exclaimed about him. The closest friend he had in preschool days was a girl his own age. . . . He had nearly no male companionship until he entered school in the first grade, a year early, and he was somewhat precocious (not alarmingly so). He seems to have been quite well adjusted, pretty well liked by everyone, quite well liked by his teachers.

Although he showed some intelligence, he was not remarkable. He liked his dog, his home, radio programs, soccer ball, brick walls, the janitor at school, trees, mornings, green lawns, walking, playing with toys, having imaginary adventures with the boy across the street in the orchard behind his house.

But as with most children his age, the Second World War profoundly affected Inburn:

When he was five years old, his father went into the war; he was gone for four years. In these four years he and his mother had the most intimate of relationships. They were one. Every thought, every action of one could be anticipated by the other. Somehow it seemed more than a mere mother-and-only-child relationship. We were in complete spiritual and mental and physical harmony with each other. Sometimes she was even shy with me. It was a strange relationship.

This description is as remarkable for the element of fantasy it contains as it is for the undeniable facts it must refer to. Inburn emphasizes the fusion of mother and child, the completeness of their understanding, their total anticipation of each other's thoughts and actions, their oneness. But in fact, such oneness and fusion can seldom occur after the first year of life; thereafter, mother and child assume an increasing separateness which usually eventuates in the child's independence as an adult. That Inburn so describes his relationship with his mother at ages five to nine suggests a strong element of wish, perhaps on the mother's part, but certainly on Inburn's, that all separateness between him and her be obliterated.

The end of the war brought a double dislocation for Inburn: first, his father returned; and, second, immediately thereafter he left teaching and moved with his family to a more lucrative and more bureaucratic position in a Detroit corporation, where he is now, in his son's words, "a kind of minor official." Inburn himself makes little of either of these facts; but without noting the connection, he dates several changes in his behavior from the age of nine or ten. Of his state of mind, he writes, "From about nine or ten on, he got to be very moody, thinking too much or reading the wrong kind of books. The moodiness was always well within himself, though, and he was seldom snappish, perverse, or irritable." Elsewhere, he dates the beginning of intermittent constipation from the same age. And in a supplement to his autobiography, when recounting his sexual development, he writes:

I was disturbed when I was finally convinced that children came out of women. I didn't want to believe it. It seemed base and carnal at the time. . . . I thought that if people wished for children strongly enough they would just come. I was first enlightened by some slightly

older boys [9–10?]; later and more clear-headedly by my parents, though sketchily [14].

After the move to Detroit, Inburn's family continued to travel during summer vacations, which he recalls with pleasure. But he also notes: "But the summers away made it impossible for Inburn to play baseball. In that red-blooded American community baseball was a big thing. I was a little estranged from my fellows because of this."

Expanding on his subsequent relationships with his peers, he says:

I was accepted, but made people indignant toward me because they felt I was not only superior to them but scornful of them. All but one friendship pretty casual, red-blooded. Few quarrels. It didn't matter that much. Frequent periods of extreme moodiness and solitariness. Disenchantment—estrangement.

In sum, his father's return and the family move to Detroit seems to have been a turning point in Inburn's life, marking the beginning of his moodiness, his constipation, his estrangement, and even coinciding with his disgust at the "base and carnal" nature of birth. But all of this is our surmise, and Inburn himself does not note the coincidence of dates.

When he was fourteen, Inburn first became interested in girls, describing himself as "struck dumb" by a girl "with eyes as blue as his, and deeper, framed in a simple kerchief, staring into his face in an autumn dusk." He continues:

Not long later sex reared its ugly head. He fell in with some of his male contemporaries. And boys can be dirty. They can be vile. A hundred times we talked about the girls at school, describing with great vigor their proportions, or lack of them. Girls with breasts the size of five-cent ice cream cones. . . .

He reports "excessive masturbation," accompanied by "great clouds of guilt," and characterizes his major current feelings about sex as "anxiety, shame, disgust." Not surprisingly, he has never had intercourse.

No further events of outward importance occurred in Inburn's life until he was a junior in high school, when he met Hal, who played a major role in the development of his outlook:

Hal was, and is, a cynical young man. Cynical, profound, skeptical, sarcastic, highly intelligent, casual in his manner, yet intense in his questioning. And he always questioned. His cynicism infected me; he became my very good, my best friend, the best and closest I ever had. What were we cynical about? You, for one thing, and ourselves, our teachers, our world—cynical about the very act of existence. Or rather, the fact of existence, for with us it was a passive experience. We let time and values and actions pass over us like a wash, like a coating of wax. We both had been raised as agnostics, but it was a mild sort of agnosticism, an unthought-about agnosticism. First of all we turned everybody's religion upside down and we shouted. We were roundly condemned, but Hal more, since he shouted more, and louder. They went by the board and we began on our contemporaries and on our society. We attacked everything, every person, every institution, with a bitter tooth. Our long secret conversations were rank with contempt. We were full of a magnificent disdain, and we fed it with all the knowledge we could get (and what wouldn't fit we disregarded)—Kafka, D. H. Lawrence, Hume, Rousseau, Voltaire, Shaw, Jung, Freud, Marx. We read voraciously, but not the right things, and not enough.

Hal is gone now. He went to college in Berkeley for a while, but now he is apparently irredeemably dissolute. . . . And he just doesn't give a damn. There was a great rift between us when I went to the college. He thinks that it will ruin me and now calls me a coward for not "finding out some things" on my own.

Maybe he's right. If he means I'm becoming more complacent, I must plead guilty. As far as I can see, we both want knowledge; we want to know about the underpinnings of existence. I'm trying to do it through the institutions of my society, the college, for example. Hal is trying to "find out some things" on his own.

And on this inconclusive note, Inburn ends his autobiography.

In what he tells us about his life, certain themes and facts stand out. First is the marked contrast between his two parents. His mother emerges from his account as "Mediterranean," ambitious, energetic, high-strung, driving, volatile, passionate, and, in her son's eyes, sensual and physically attractive. Even her family is characterized as strong, tireless, simple, exuberant, and cruel. But he suggests that she has paid a high price in "complexity" and in a "delicate" constitution and psychology for her efforts in "making herself." Inburn's father, in contrast, comes from Celtic stock and from a long line of men who were dominated by their women. Recall how his chances for a better education were limited by having to pay his half-brother's debts. And consider his move from his first love, teaching, to a more lucrative job, where he now considers himself a failure despite contrary community judgment. Without fully stating it, Inburn clearly implies his father's weakness vis-à-vis his mother's drive ("My father is acquiescent and my mother has excellent taste"). Further, it is clear that Inburn finds his mother's vivid sensuousness far more interesting than his father's phlegmatic and taciturn nature. All of this makes Inburn's father a man difficult to emulate; and we would anticipate that this fact, coupled with Inburn's unusual past relationship with his mother, would cause him difficulty.

In addition, several events stand out as having crucial importance in Inburn's life. One is his romanticized idyll with his mother during the war. The absence of any child's father for three or four years would be important to his development; but for Inburn, its importance must have been accentuated by his "unique, more than a mere mother-and-only-child relationship" with her. His friendship with Hal, too, was crucial. Until Hal, Inburn's life seems little different on the surface than that of most young men his age, "with his moodiness . . . always well within himself": Hal acted as a catalyst for Inburn's alienation. Inburn's initial unwillingness to accept the fact of birth, his inability to work through his not unusual first reactions to sex, and his current anxious attitudes are also worth underlining. Although many a young man in our society has difficulty in reconciling himself to the "facts of life," it is remarkable at the age of nineteen to list "anxiety, shame, and disgust" as the only three emotions which sex evokes. And finally, Inburn's relations with his peers follow a familiar pattern for an alienated young man. He was not good at the games which mattered in his "red-blooded" community, his fellows felt that he was scornful of them, and he felt "frequent periods of estrangement." Even when he became editor of the school paper, with his friend Hal, the two of them "managed to ruin it in three months."

But so far, we know only as much about Inburn as he himself knows and is willing to tell us. To understand the underlying dynamics of his alienation, we must turn to his stories in the Thematic

Apperception Test, for in these he gives us a deeper and less conscious picture of the way he views the world.

THE CAT THAT SWALLOWED THE CANARY

Inburn's image of older women in the T.A.T. adds several new elements to the description of his mother in his autobiography. Confronted with a picture of a young man, a woman, and a girl with books in her hand (Card 2), he is reminded of D. H. Lawrence's book, *"Sons and Mothers"* [sic]. The older woman is described as "a rather possessive person," "obviously a strong figure," who feels "not quite like the cat that swallowed the canary but rather supercilious towards the girl and proud of her victories since the girl has . . . gone back to the family." Reminding himself of the play, *The Silver Cord,* he cannot decide whether the girl will be "finally engulfed by the mother at the end" or whether she will escape the mother's clutches. Or on Card 5, which shows an older woman peering around a half-opened door, he describes a woman spying on a boy. He says several times that the woman is "some kind of odd member of the household," that there is an

. . . odd relationship between her and the boy. . . . There's something between them so they can't get close to each other. I said that there was something between them, but I didn't mean that, I mean there's no relationship between them because there's something blocking their getting closer to each other. She suspects on the part of the boy some monstrous and horrible act of some kind . . . something insidious and disgusting. Maybe it's some sexual act with himself, or maybe it's not that at all.

In the end, the boy, who, Inburn tells us, is not doing anything wrong at all, begins "to wonder whether there's something monstrous that *she* commits. . . . The boy would seriously consider looking in on her [in her room] sometime to find out. . . . But he never does . . . nothing comes of it."

Another story (Card 10) again involves a similar bond between a man and a woman.

The girl . . . is a rather unstable character. . . . She is violently in love with the boy and has more or less thrown herself at him. The boy has been sort of disturbed at this . . . and finally decided to play along . . . it wouldn't hurt—why not? . . . He would be just about to make a proposal that they go to bed with each other. She will undoubtedly agree, and if he can close his eyes just a little more and block out that rather unpleasant nose of hers, he'll be delighted because well, why not? And she'll be delighted because she thinks . . . this particular device will certainly bind him to her more strongly. . . . Afterwards . . . the boy again feels wretched. . . . he feels that it was something that shouldn't have been done . . . for he has no real affection for her other than a kind of—not a man-to-man relationship exactly, but just a kind of friendly, somewhat intellectual relationship. . . . Other than that he has no real desire for her, although he thinks she is a desirable girl . . . , but then maybe he has known her from too early an age or something, but she's just grown up with the wrong relationship with him and nothing would ever be successful in that way. . . .

Here the woman is dominant and initiating, seeking with sex to bind the man to her, while he feels that "maybe he has known her from too early an age" for there to be anything but a platonic and "intellectual" friendship.

In another story (Card 7), he tells of a man who has committed a minor transgression and who returns home to face his accusing mother.

It's not important to anyone with any reasonable perspective on the situation. But both he and his mother have a funny perspective on the situation. Maybe something silly. . . . He will probably continue to do these things wrong again in the future and his mother will continue to rail at him until he's fifty years old, I imagine.

And, significantly, in yet another story, when he is trying to imagine an especially unpleasant treatment for one of his characters, he recalls the scene in *East of Eden* where one brother takes the other and "pushes him . . . onto his mother, not in a sexual position but just makes them both fall to the floor and rub against each other, which is somehow an incredibly vile and loathsome thing to happen. . . ."

In all of these references to women, Inburn intertwines two related themes: the fear of domination and the fear of sexual closeness. His heroes are caught in "odd relationships" with their mothers or other women who dominate and control them, although at the same time the heroes remain bound because of their "unreasonable perspective on the situation." Mothers are seen as "possessive" and "not quite like the cat that swallowed the canary, but. . . ." Parallel with this is the "peculiar" nature of relationships between men and women, a "strangeness" which appears related to the ambivalent fear of sexual intimacy. Thus, the strange woman who spies on the boy suspects him among other things of some "monstrous" sexual act with himself; but in the end, the boy, instead of proclaiming his innocence or leaving, considers spying on the older woman as well. Throughout these stories there is "something between" men and women which prevents them from either intimacy or satisfactory sex, "something" related to their having known each other "from too early an age," perhaps something like the fear of the "most incredibly vile and loathsome thing," incest. Unconsciously, then, Inburn sees himself as bound to a possessive and even predatory mother, unable to break away from her, and at the same time both tantalized and horrified by the sexual connotations of closeness to her.

THE FATHER, BEING ABSENT . . .

Just as he says less of his father than of his mother in his autobiography, so in his T.A.T. stories Inburn has less to say of older men than of women. Characteristic of all his stories is his reference to the father of the girl with the possessive mother (Card 2), of whom he notes, "The father, being absent, sort of leaves him out of my mind. . . . He was rather inconsequential." And when he does tell stories involving older men, his tales are usually facetious or cynical. Thus, he tells a caustic story about heaven (Card 15) in which it turns out that "Jehovah Himself is an incredibly ugly figure. . . . Regrettably the situation up there has been a little deceptively colored . . . sold a little better than it is by the angelic ad men and the established church." Or again, to a picture of an older man who outstretches his hand over a prone figure (Card 12), he tells of an "evil German-doctor type"

who gets boys under his mystical spell and eats them: "He's just an evil fellow through and through." And perhaps closest to his conscious image of potentially helpful older men is a story of a kindly teacher who understands and wants to help the hero (Card 7). The young man

thinks [the teacher] is a fine person and that there should be more like him. And yet somehow he is repelled by the picture of himself being like this, and he realizes that that's how it must be if he is to go along and follow along, drop in line, follow suit and so forth. . . . [The young man thinks of Marlowe and musical geniuses who died young, or] a man who lives with such vigor and strength and intensity that in twenty-five or thirty years he's burned himself out and drops dead because he hasn't anything else to do. . . . He wonders whether an intenser life like that wouldn't be a better thing than just fobbing along course by course and day by day, the way the venerable and openly respectable [teacher] has done.

Inburn's anger at older males breaks through fully in only one story (Card 18). He starts a facetious account of the president of Harvard College, who on a pretext sneaks away from his wife to buy a pizza pie at a nearby tavern. The president is, however, set upon by a three-armed man who has been installing sewer connections, and "this dreadful three-armed man with a dirty sleeve on each arm of his jacket" rubs against him in that "incredibly vile and loathsome way" which, as we have seen earlier, Inburn associates with a son in sexual position with his mother. When Inburn fully expresses aggression at a paternal figure, he does it in what he makes clear is the most disgusting and degrading way possible. But though this is the most direct instance, Inburn always sees to it that older men, when not omitted from the action, are debased, defiled, or ridiculed. Paternal figures are not what they seem: the doctor is an evil hypnotist; Jehovah has been oversold by the heavenly ad men; the president must sneak pizza pies and is vilely humiliated by a three-armed man from the sewer; and even the venerable teacher, for all of his understanding, turns out to be dull and pedestrian. But most important is Inburn's comment that "the father, being absent, sort of leaves him out of my mind."

EXISTENTIAL PESSIMISM

Many of Inburn's stories imply a kind of pessimistic, existential world view, stressing the futility of endeavor, the intensification of life, the emptiness of love, and the desirable role of detached observer and commentator. In one story (Card 14), the hero, after a long and arduous climb up the inside of a dark tower, at last pushes open the windows:

He looks out on the surrounding country and somehow he doesn't like the view very much. He doesn't think it's much of an accomplishment after all. He thought he would really get something out of it, but the country just looks farther away from the way it was on the ground. And there's no change in it; there's nothing he can see farther from his vantage point. So I'll just leave him standing looking out of the window. . . .

The arduous effort has proved futile: the view is merely more distant.

In the story of the kindly teacher, Inburn has wondered whether it would not be better to "burn himself out" in twenty-five or thirty years rather than lead a dull, plodding life. To Card 17, showing a man climbing a rope, he tells a story of a hero who actually does die an early death: he is a circus acrobat in a land where there is

. . . nothing but side shows and other circuses. [The hero] is in the springtime of life, as many have undoubtedly said, free and free-limbed. He is strong and not only strong but proficient in acrobatics and light, not a clumsy kind of strength but not delicate exactly either. He's refined his talents which are nearly entirely bodily. . . . There is no such thing as intellectualism in this delightful land. He is free from any foreboding thoughts but . . . here he is just before his death. After doing a stupendous trick from which he gets a great roar from the crowd . . . he falls off the rope, not meaning to . . . falls a long way down and kills himself with a smile on his face . . . with no regrets on the way down. . . . Afterwards the crowd . . . does not gasp, is not horrified. . . . There is no great tension. . . . Things just go on as usual. They don't take him away at all. [The crowd envies him] because here is a man in the prime of youth, who is in tune with life, who can get up in the morning and sing and fall asleep at night without a wrinkle on his brow and has done this all his life—he's never known death or old age. And his life has been made more perfect by

annihilation. . . . He will never know the infirmities of old age in all their various forms—in the mind, in the darkening sight, and the creaking body. . . . And then the show is over, and people pour out into the little streets and passageways that a carnival has. And then things go on as usual.

Here Inburn extols a purely unreflective and physical existence and returns to his earlier value of dying in the height of life.

Another story stresses the same value in another way. Inburn tells of a pious boy who self-righteously keeps himself apart from the grossness, murderousness, and sensuality of the world (Card 8):

But the boy has refined himself away to nothing, kept out of any sort of relations with people . . . and for this reason he has got so far away from everything that he indeed is not living life as much as the people who are murdering. . . . It's better to murder, which is just an act, than to make no acts at all. . . . It seems more desirable right now, if one must choose, to choose the part of those horrid old men in the background cutting up other horrid old men than to be the snotty over-refined, completely ineffectual boy who is, in fact, wasting his life much more than the men in the background are.

The gratuitous act, even if it be murder, is better than no action at all.

Even the most optimistic and forward-looking of Inburn's stories has something of the same "existential" quality. His hero in one story (Card 9) is said to be in some way "different" from his bum-companions:

Maybe some day he will be a kind of spokesman for this group of people. Maybe he'll write a book about them, or maybe he will try to portray them on the stage, or maybe he'll try to paint them. . . . He's different because he's not only a complete product of his times and his society, and so forth, but he's a man that doesn't come along very often . . . a man who can understand the society that he's in—which is probably the greatest trick in the book—who can look at himself in context and can understand completely what's going on, get it in the right perspective . . . understand why he is there, not in the great metaphysical and religious sense, but why the social forces have put him where he is. . . . At least he has this latent in him, the power to bring this out and put it down for others to understand. . . . And

he will write a book . . . it'll be a good book, I imagine.
. . . It's not a social criticism, it's not that he'll be making
a plea. . . . He's not unhappy that these people don't
have the best food in the world, that they have to sleep
on the ground like that. It's not a matter of that; it's a
judgmentless kind of interpretation and explanation
rather than an emotional and sentimental Uncle Tom's
Cabin *business.*

Here Inburn doubtless speaks of himself and his own best potential; and this story has an affirmation and hope lacking in all the other nineteen. But even here he rejects "judgment," "social criticism," "making a plea," and any "emotional and sentimental *Uncle Tom's Cabin* business." In other words, morality has no conscious place in his scheme of things.

Consonant with the lack of any inherent meaning or values in life is Inburn's image of love. Long-range intimacy between two people is never mentioned, and the act of sex is empty. In one story (Card 13) the hero is walking down a New York street:

It is late in the afternoon, and in the afternoon those
brownstones take on a particularly remarkably intense
russet color. It seems to stand out and glow, almost. . . .
He notices a girl . . . looking out the window on the
second floor of one of the brownstones. . . . She hap-
pens to look at him, and he glances up at her and, just
by chance, their eyes meet naturally. And he stands
there a long minute, just looking up, oddly. And she
doesn't divert her eyes, and it's a kind of a very long
instant that stays in one's mind. . . . There's something
about the whole scene that entrances them both. . . .
He keeps staring at the window. And in a few moments
she appears below, behind the door, which has got a
kind of curtain in front of it and an iron grill. And then
she opens the door, and after a moment he crosses the
street and goes up the steps . . . the polished white
steps. She's rather thin and not good looking—drab hair
and a very cheap dress. . . . And without a word but
"with eyes on the double string," or whatever that
quote is from Donne, they go up the stairs to a . . . kind
of single room. The shade is pulled down and there's a
very warm color on the window shade, even from the
inside. . . .

Finally, after all, they fall asleep. And he's awakened
when it's dark at night by the window shade flapping,
with some wind and some rain coming in, and the cold
air wakes him up. It doesn't wake her. Now there's a
light in the window shade, too, which is the street light

from outside shining in, which is rather bright. . . . He
gets up and dresses and doesn't do anything. Leave a
note? It would seem a little ludicrous. He puts on his tie
and coat and leaves. The hero eventually finds his way
into a church, and the story ends.

In this *nouvelle vague* story, Inburn makes the lovers silent, neither is described except in externals; they have no relationship; the man leaves the woman without saying good-bye; and throughout, the narrator is more interested in eyes, lights, architectural details, and colors than in the man and woman.

All of these stories entail the same denial of meaning in life apart from unreflective action, perception, and sensation. At worst, Inburn's heroes are Raskolnikovs who would rather murder than do nothing; intermediately, existential acrobats who die happy at the acme of their flight, strangers who love and depart without speaking, or strivers whose efforts are futile; and at best, mere observers of their world who firmly refuse to judge, influence, or change it. All of this is an elaboration in fantasy of Inburn's earlier more intellectual assertion that as a stranger in a foreign city, his best plan is to "see the sights" and to accumulate "the most varied, the most valuable, and most significant set of sense experiences it is possible to take in."

THE RAGE TO RE-ENTER

Inburn's autobiography begins with a description of him as "screaming and red-faced, loath to leave his insensible sanctuary." Here he states unequivocally what is the major theme of his life and the dominant motif of his T.A.T. stories: his longing to return to that first claustrum of security; his rage and desolation at being expelled; his continual sense thereafter of being a stranger in a foreign city. More than half of Inburn's stories contain some variant on the theme of being inside or outside, beginning with the first card, where he tells of a son of professional musicians who smashes his violin as a "violent rebellion." The father is restrained from "throwing him out in the street" because of "certain ties that he has—certain obligations to the family and the community"; but the boy will thereafter be "an estranged member" of the family, and "he'll probably leave his family at an early age and won't be associated with them any more." In his second story, too, the central conflict is about leaving the girl's home and getting away from the mother who is "not quite like the cat that swallowed the canary, but. . . ."

Having as it were introduced his main theme, in a variation whereby the hero *chooses* rebellion and estrangement, Inburn states it in almost pure form in the third story. Here he tells of a student walking down the street at night on his way home from the library, where he had read a book which disturbed him. He stopped in front of

. . . an old gray house, one of those turn-of-the-century jobs with a slate roof on it and this phony Greek revival business with all the pillars and the stuff in wood on the porch. He stops on the steps of the house. . . . He noticed one of the windows on either side of the door. The door was in the middle and there was a large window on either side. It was dark inside the little hallway. . . . He stood there looking at the window for ten or fifteen minutes, with this unusual, indescribable ding-batty he has in his hand. . . . It could be any kind of odd piece of iron that he somehow picked up. And he stood there a long time, sort of standing there contemplating smashing the window. And if he could have just smashed it and gone away, throwing the thing through, or just smashed it holding it in his hand, it would have been all right. . . . He would have got whatever it was inside out of him. But he could not force himself to smash the damn thing. He stood there, as I say, for a long time, standing there very "still and stiff" with his arms down at his side and finally walked away, walked down the steps. . . . I remember in Herodotus the story of tying the woman's legs together just when she's beginning to be pregnant and then letting things go on as they did . . . probably the most exquisite torture that could be devised. Maybe this is the same sort of idea that he's got something enormous, monstrous inside of him, but he can't get it out. He could have got it out by smashing the window but he still got it in him. . . .

In contrast to the two previous stories, in which his heroes sought to escape home and mother, here the hero tries to break his way back into a house. Unable to force an opening with the "ding-batty" in his hand, he is left with "something enormous, monstrous inside of him," which he associates

with a child within his mother's womb. (Recall his facetious remark, "I guess I'd have us all go back to the womb.") Note, too, the detail with which Inburn describes the architecture of the house, emphasizing the central door and the windows, which mirror the hero's preoccupation with looking.

From this story alone we would have grounds for surmising that Inburn's "violent rebellion" and self-imposed estrangement overlays a deeper wish to re-enter his "insensible sanctuary" and that his "estrangement" was not only chosen by him, but first forced upon him by a closed house which he cannot re-enter. In the primitive logic of fantasies and dreams, houses, wombs, maternal warmth, and women's bodies can stand for each other; and the regular symmetry of the face parallels the configurations of the house façade: the windows are for seeing from and into, the door is the mouth of entry. In such equations, to look into a window, to gaze into the eyes, to enter the door of the house, or to re-enter the surrounding warmth of a mother's arms become equivalent. These interpretations are supported in other stories. Through them all runs the same preoccupation with seeing, gazing, and looking—especially with a kind of obsessive standing and staring into the eyes of another or the windows of a house. (Recall his first girlfriend, "with eyes as blue as his, and deeper . . . staring into his face in an autumn dusk.") In the previously discussed story of the silent lovers, the descriptions of the facade of the house, of looking into the window and gazing into the girl's eyes, the account of the light that comes in the window—these narratively extraneous elements overpower the ostensibly central theme of the relation of man and woman. And in the end of that story, the hero again stands looking, "much longer than he stood looking at the window," at the church which he finally enters. In this story, it is as if Inburn's seeking could finally be solaced neither by sex nor by looking, but only by entering a church, whose secure walls signify asylum. And even with Inburn's writer-hero the highest form of perception is looking at the world around him and understanding it.

As counterpoint to these stories in which the hero is outside an enclosure looking in, Inburn tells three in which the hero manages to get inside and look out. In one previously mentioned (Card 14), he is inside a

*... tower that goes very far up with a turret on it. ...
He enters through the door and finds darkness is
throughout the place. It's a vertical maze: it goes up
instead of spreading out. The tower, incidentally, has no
windows except one toward the very top, on the other
side of the building from the door he entered by, so that
he doesn't know it's there. He goes up and all is in
darkness, and he is feeling his way around. Finally, he
works his way all through the day and the next night
and gets to the top, gets into a final room where there
is a casement window, but he can't see it. It's closed,
and there's no light coming through. ... [He] finally
comes to the window, which he feels out and finally
gets the handle of. ... He's tired and hungry and exhausted and covered with sweat. With his last bit of
force, he pushes open the two windows one with each
hand, and the bright light of the early morning streams
in on him. ... The window is facing the east, and he's
blinded for a few minutes. ... The feeling he has on his
skin and on his silk shirt is like climbing up—how many
flights it is up that circular thing?—the Statue of Liberty,
and finally looking out her head, out of one of those
windows and usually getting a cold from it. He looks out
on the surrounding country and doesn't like the view
very much. He doesn't think it's much of an accomplishment after all. ...*

Here the identification of the inside of a building
and the inside of a woman's body is explicit, although, at the same time, Inburn seems to wonder
if his obsessive search for a way back in is doomed
to failure—perhaps the view from within is really
no better than the view outside. The scene calls to
mind a small child's wonder at his mother's height,
his curiosity about whether what she sees is different from what he sees, and his fantasy that perhaps
he could enter her body and see through her eyes.

But in two other stories, the view from within is
unqualifiedly good. One story (Card 18) tells of

*... a cheerful presentation of Noah's Ark ... the two
little windows, sort of homey portholes with curtains.
There are two comical little animals—in a pair, of
course—looking out ... animals who have got a nice
berth on the ark and they're enjoying the view. ... [He
wonders why there is a smokestack in the picture.] The
clouds would be all sorts of fantastic colors—purple. ...
The water, of course, would be blue and the ship would
be all sorts of colors. The animals would be brown, I
imagine. They've been sailing for a long time. And I
suppose the most remarkable thing is that they just keep
sailing. They don't land anywhere. The water never
recedes; that's the most pleasant part about it.*

Inburn's "cheerful presentation" here has "comical little animals" looking out on never-receding
waters in a childhood idyll and happy because
there is no landing, no receding waters to break up
the happy communion of son and mother. With its
bright colors and "comical" animals, the story is
reminiscent of a childhood fairy tale, covertly expressing the child's wish to sail away forever inside
the life-filled ark, which represents the secure
warmth of his mother's surrounding presence.

But perhaps the most remarkable portrayal of a
full return to claustral security, coupled with gazing
out, is found in Card 16, in which Inburn manufac-
tures both picture and story:

*Well, the scene is rather dark, streaked with light. It's
under water, very warm water, although it's apparently
a sea. ... This missile most resembles a one-man submarine. It's propelled by a very unbulky kind of machinery.
It's just very simple, cigar-shaped, I suppose. ... It's
angling down toward the bottom right-hand corner of
the card. ... The water is uniformly dark ... since the
surface is at this time considerably far above the top of
the card.*

*And inside this thing is a face which you can see. In
a kind of window in front, a man is stretched out. Well,
the thing is small. It's only about eight feet long, perhaps
even shorter than that. He's on a cushion inside, a long
cushion. His hands are at his sides. He's on his stomach,
with his chin not resting on anything, looking forward,
looking out into the water. And although we can see
the thing, it's very dark to him. He can see, oh, perhaps
some of those small fish that glow, but that's about all.
That's the only thing that lights up, that lights up the
scene. As I said, the water is very warm. This is hard to
illustrate, but it's that, and heavy. ... This thing was
custom-built for him, fitted for his size and height. And
he does have controls. ... He can go up and down and
to the left and to the right, though there's no change in
speed.*

*This is the fulfillment of something this young man
has always inanely wanted to do since he was a very
little boy. In fact, he pictured himself doing just this
when he was perhaps seven or eight or nine or ten years
old. ... The idea occurred to him once when he was in
his bedroom stretched out on his bed in this kind of
position with his elbows up supporting him, and it was
dark and very hot in the room. The room had grown
slowly dark—he didn't notice the absence of light from
the windows until it was all gone. And then this idea
occurred to him, that of slipping through these heavy,
silent, liquid seas in a very warm and utterly comfort-*

able state. And he was eating some crackers out of a box. . . . This was a very pleasurable sort of thing.

As a matter of fact, in the picture the young man is . . . eating crackers from a small box and falling down into the ocean. He didn't direct his life toward doing this, but circumstances just sort of permitted it. He remembered his urge and had enough resources, enough leisure time to do this thing. He's probably not going to surface, just go down, down, and down. Somehow once he got into the water, it became not the Atlantic Ocean or the Mediterranean, but it was just a sea, the sea, with nothing on the surface, with no continents to go back to . . . and the place not being there from which he set off anymore. . . . This is the kind of extended moment which he wouldn't mind going on with forever —which he probably will, just continuing down into the dark water. . . .

If Inburn were consciously searching for an analogy on the intrauterine condition, on the symbiosis of mother and child, he would be hard pressed to find a better one. Even the age at which this fantasy first occurred to the hero is significant, for it was at "seven or eight or nine or ten" that his father returned to break the oneness of mother and son, and inevitably to awaken a powerful wish for this unity to be restored. And how better restore it than by re-entering the sanctuary from which, as Inburn had recently learned with revulsion, he had been born?

Thus, the central and unifying themes in Inburn's fantasy life center on the rage to re-enter the "insensible" sanctuary he had with his mother. So intense is this wish that it surpasses the desire for a more adult intimacy with her or any other woman, and it is expressed symbolically as a craving to re-enter the body of the woman who bore and nurtured him. That the re-entry and fusion are to be accomplished through the eyes, through looking, through the communion of a gaze, and through an often obstructing window is doubly understandable. The infant first perceives his mother when he gazes into her eyes while nursing; and thereafter, for most people, to "look deeply into someone's eyes" remains a symbol of that communion which anticipates and forever thereafter surpasses all mere speech. But also, for Inburn, the eyes are the organ of the body farthest from that "base and carnal" place from which infants truly emerge; and for a young man who can identify himself with a "man from the sewer" and who

feels only "anxiety, shame, and disgust" about sex, communion through the eyes is far less "vile" than that other communion which adult men and women can know and by which men regain at least temporary sanctuary in women. Indeed, the story of the Greek revival house with the hero's "indescribable ding-batty" in his hand, the tale of silent lovers in which the empty act of sex is followed by entering a church, the intrusive smokestack on Noah's ark, and the cigar-shaped submarine suggest that Inburn's sexuality is at times an irrelevant intrusion on his central fantasies about women.

THE OUTSIDER WHO WOULD BE INSIDE

We now have learned enough of the central themes in Inburn's life to enable us to try to reconstruct the origins and current functions of his alienation. In any such reconstruction it is well to keep in mind that the principle of parsimony seldom applies in explaining individual lives; rather, only when we have begun to understand the subtle interweaving of themes, the "overdetermination" of any single act, belief, or fantasy, and the multiple functions that every dream, wish, behavior, and philosophy serves, do we begin to understand something of an individual. Thus, even with the best of intentions, the psychologist must continually oversimplify, and by singling out one set of alienated beliefs and outlooks for special explanation, I here oversimplify Inburn the more.

To begin with, the outward circumstances of Inburn's life provided a setting within which his alienation became more than casually possible. As an only child, he was destined to experience and feel more intensely about his parents than would a child who had siblings or an extended family to dissipate the concentration of his affections and angers. Further, his father's absence for the four crucial years of the war must inevitably have intensified his pre-existing feelings about his mother. And then, too, an American son of a third-generation Greek mother and a father of northern European stock is very likely to note a sharp temperamental contrast between his two parents and their families. But these assured facts only provide a setting for the more central psychological events and fantasies which underlie Inburn's estrangement.

For further explanations, we must assume that Inburn's account of his parents is in many ways correct, at least as it describes their impact on him. His mother, as we have noted, emerges as a possessive, ambitious, driving woman, who, however, once she stopped teaching, devoted herself exclusively to domestic life. And at the same time, Inburn describes her as moody, passionate, highly sensual, and physically attractive. The T.A.T. story in which a woman seeks to bind an unwilling man to her through sex again suggests that Inburn sees his mother as not only possessive, but as emotionally seductive, seeking from her son a kind of emotional fulfillment he could not provide and perhaps unconsciously attempting to use her attractiveness to bind him to her. Thus, even as a small child, Inburn probably felt torn between his dependency on his mother and his enjoyment of their extraordinary closeness, on the one hand, and, on the other, her possessiveness and her unconscious needs that he be more to her than a son.

With a strong and vital husband, a possessive and seductive mother's effects on her son are usually limited; indeed, with such a husband, a woman is less likely in the first place to seek excessive fulfillment in her relationship with her children. But Inburn's father, at least as Inburn perceives him, was neither strong nor vital. "Taciturn," "phlegmatic," and "acquiescent," he had probably been better prepared by his own childhood for the role of the dominated than the dominant. Inburn also suggests that his father was disappointed with his own life, perhaps partly because he "acquiesced" by leaving his original vocation for a better-paying, if less idealistic, job. And, finally, one can only wonder how the father felt about being denied an excellent education, about struggling in the Depression, or about the war which took him away from his family, work, and country for four years. In short, Inburn gives us little ground for believing that his father had the zestful qualities to offset the mother's drive and sensuousness.

Even without Inburn's father's long absence during the war, such parents would have made for a rivalrous family triangle of singular intensity and dubious outcome. More often than we generally

acknowledge, husbands must struggle with their children for their wives' affections, especially with only sons, who may draw the full force of excessive maternal devotion. And if the wife should come to find her husband dull or a failure in life, then the outcome is especially difficult. But in Inburn's case, the wish to supplant his father must have been overwhelmingly reinforced by the latter's sudden departure for the war. Few five-year-olds could resist the temptation unconsciously to consider such a four-year absence a token of their own triumph. We know something of the ensuing relationship from Inburn's idyllic account of his "unique" understanding with his mother; and we learn more from his T.A.T. stories in which the central relationships are peculiar intimacies between young men and women, with fathers and older men either absent or somehow debased and scorned out of significant existence.

I have already noted the component of fantasy in Inburn's recollections of this idyll, which he endows with qualities more like those of an infant-mother symbiosis than those of the relationship of a five-year-old child with his mother. In part, this symbiotic relationship must have been real, perhaps encouraged by his mother's increased need of and responsiveness to him in her husband's absence. But some of it was clearly a fantasy, and time alone would have probably sufficed to break the illusion of perfect understanding and oneness. But his father's sudden return exacerbated, underlined, and made more traumatic Inburn's probably dawning awareness that he was less and less his mother's pretty little child and more and more a separate person, alone in crucial ways. It is from the age of nine or ten that he dates a variety of new feelings of moodiness and estrangement, and it is to about the same age that his submarining hero traces his wish to slip forever downward in the deep warm sea. Repeatedly, Inburn, as a college sophomore, expresses or symbolizes this overpowering wish for fusion with the maternal, for a blissful state without consciousness, for an "insensible sanctuary"—the wish, in the last analysis, to be like a tiny infant in his mother's arms, who by gazing into her eyes enters her enveloping protection. What time and his increasing age had not accomplished in destroying the possibility of asylum, his father's return completed.

For most children, such a loss—which is after all universal—can be assimilated without excessive backward yearning because there are active pulls into a future seen as better than what must be abandoned. For a boy, such forces are usually embodied in his father, who by the mere fact of an admired existence implicitly teaches his son that it is worthwhile to grow up to be a man. When there is no such father, when the mother's excessive devotion to her son undermines her mate's relative worth in the son's eyes, or when the father considers himself a failure and thus implicitly denies that the son should become a man like him—then the son's incentives to leave gracefully his ties with his mother are diminished, and physiological growth goes unmatched by psychological readiness.

For Inburn, then, there was an especially great deal to lose and especially little reason to give it up. Once he had been the apple of his mother's eye, fused at least in fantasy to her answering gaze, the child with whom she had been so strangely intimate as to be shy. In his desire to retain his claustral estate, however, he had, without wishing it, lost it and was left instead with a possessive and sensuous mother and no father. Small wonder that his father's return brought moodiness, brooding, and constipation and that when, during the same year, he learned the facts of birth, they seemed "base and carnal" compared with his own developing fantasies of regaining his former sanctuary. Henceforth, Inburn was to consider himself an outcast, dreaming of an Eden from which he perhaps dimly recalled he came, forever comparing his exiled realities of a dominating, seductive mother and a taciturn, psychologically absent father with the cozy cabin in Noah's Ark and the down-slipping submarine in the warm sea.

But so far, his inner feelings of estrangement were "always well within himself," and he was "seldom snappish, perverse, or irritable." In the development of a more overt alienation, two further facts are crucial. The first is Inburn's sexual maturation and its accompanying psychological changes, which he describes in his scornful account of "sex's ugly head" and the "dirtiness" and "vileness" of adolescent boys. Few boys in our culture, however enlightened by their parentage, can pass through adolescence without further reassessing their closeness with their mother; and for many the acute fear of any sexual intimacy with anyone like her continues throughout life. But such fears, normally a part of development in American society, can reach panic proportions in a youth who brings into adolescence an unresolved need to enter a woman not as a man but as a child seeking shelter. When coupled with a prior notion that sex and birth are base and carnal (undoubtedly transmitted in part by parents), deep anxieties about sex can last long into adulthood. And finally, if, as for Inburn, the prospect of becoming a man like one's father is deeply disconcerting and implicitly discouraged by mother and father alike, then the advent of manhood is even more disruptive. Adolescence must have further complicated Inburn's already tortuous relationship with his mother, adding to her possessiveness the new threat of that "most loathesome thing," incest.

In all young men and women the advent of adulthood releases immense new energies and potentials, which in most are greatly involved in establishing new intimacies with the opposite sex. Such new learning is seldom smooth; but when it is severely blocked by unresolved needs and frustrations from the past, it takes only a slight catalyst —or sometimes no catalyst at all—to transform these energies into rage, scorn, and aggression, often symbolically directed against those who have stood in the way of full adulthood. It was Hal, then, who provided the second crucial fact, the catalyst and vehicle for the transformation of Inburn's inward moodiness into an open and scornful alienation. From Hal, or with his help and encouragement, he learned cynicism, disdain, scorn, and contempt for the "superstructure of tin and shit and kite-paper" which represented society to them. Hal became for Inburn a kind of anti-social superego, so much so that Inburn put his discontents with college into Hal's mouth, and when he finally left college, it was not to return to his parents, but to live with Hal and demonstrate that he had not, in fact, become "complacent." Further, with Hal he learned the vocabulary and logic of his instincts, culling from the works of the most alienated writers of the last two alienated centuries the diction of estrangement. The sense of alienation and exile, the rage and frustration which might have found outlet in delinquency in a youth of less intelligence, perceptiveness, and articulateness, in Inburn were aimed at targets sanctioned by usage and made meaningful by their personal symbolism and thus found expression within a historical tradition. What had been contained was now released, and Inburn became overtly alienated.

Inburn's alienation in word and deed thus serves multiple purposes. Most centrally, it rationalizes his felt condition as an outcast from his first sanctuary: The feeling of exile is generalized, universalized into the human condition, as in his tale of travelers in the endless and featureless countryside. Furthermore, by condemning the society and the forms of society from which he himself came, Inburn states the partial truth that there is no sanctuary and that he does not wish to return. And by attacking society and all its authoritative concomitants, Inburn indirectly criticizes his father and all he stands for: conventionality, being a "small pillar in a small community," being "complacently middle-class," perhaps even being a "failure in his own eyes." Inburn's grievance against his father is a double one: his father disrupted the idyll with his mother, and—probably more important—he was not strong enough to offer anything better than the mother-son intimacy that he disrupted. Inburn has accounts to render, and render them he does in his alienation.

MAJOR THEMES OF THE ALIENATED

In Inburn we see most of the features common to other alienated Ss, but in exacerbated form, writ large, as the dominant, even obsessive concerns of his life. It is rare to find a subject about whom we have said so much when we have said that he is alienated; in many other young men themes of alienation take their place, sometimes a secondary place, alongside unrelated motifs of equal or greater importance. But with Inburn alienation forms the core of his personality; and estrangement, exclusion, disaffection, and the rage to return are the nuclear themes of his life. Thus, in summarizing his main themes, we can at the same time state schematically a number of the leitmotivs of alienation in other young Americans.

Expulsion from Early Oral Paradise

The fantasies of alienated young men abound in idyllic references to earliest childhood or the modes of experience most typical of them. And at the same time stories of starvation, separation from the sources of supply, and the disaster which follows such separation are equally frequent. Unconsciously, the alienated look back to early infancy as the model for all later satisfactions and implicitly find all later relationships wanting insofar as they lack the passivity, claustral security, and effortless gratification of infancy.

Fixation on Childhood Modes of Experience

Paralleling the fantasy of an interrupted infantile idyll is a fixation on childhood modes of perception, apperception, and experience in general. Concretely this involves an effort to cut through conventional schemata of apperception to a mode of experience more direct, immediate, and "whole" than normal adult experience. Alienated subjects find Schachtel's concept of "allocentricity" appealing when familiar with it and seek means of heightening sensation to allow a breakthrough to less categorized awareness of their surroundings.[2]

Pyrrhic Oedipal Victory

Like Inburn, many alienated young men show signs of having partially supplanted their fathers in their mothers' affections. The consequence, however, is usually highly unsatisfactory for the subject, in that he is left with a debased image of his father, a mother whose demands he is incapable of meeting, and an excessive fear of his own aggression (which he believes proved so effective). Since the mother is usually perceived as the more powerful of the parents, these young men tend to identify in part with her and strongly to resist identification with the father.

Discontinuous Parental Images

As a result of this inverse resolution of Oedipal rivalries, most alienated subjects have sharply discontinuous images of parental figures. Women are ambivalently seen either as nurturing, supplying, bountiful providers, who shelter and solace, or else as binding, restrictive, limiting, emasculating controllers, who bar the way to full masculinity. Paternal figures are portrayed either as archaic, pre-Oedipal fathers, destructive and unassailable, or, more often, as weak, debased, defeated, dependent, and passive creatures, with whom the subject resolutely refuses to identify. One of the dangers about relationships with either men or women is that one can have little confidence that they will remain unchanged; hence, alienated subjects often see nurturant women as becoming possessive and controlling or apparently strong men as being basically weak and fraudulent.

Distrust

Given a world in which initial images of the crucial male and female figures had to be drastically revised, the alienated subject has an implicitly and usually explicitly distrustful view of the world. All appearances are suspect, and not until he has shown the underlying sham, hypocrisy, deceit, self-interest, egocentricity, and resentment in others does he rest content that he has struck bottom. "Reductionism" and "subspection," coupled with an anxious probing for flaws and underlying chicaneries, characterize his intellectual style.

Existential Pessimism

Usually arrived at spontaneously, but sometimes reinforced by reading, the alienated subject's world view resembles that of the most pessimistic existentialists. The universe is inherently chaotic and unpredictable, as are human relations, which are based on mutual exploitation and appropriation. Men live in a Hobbesian state of nature, restrained from exploitative egocentricity only by their fear of punishment. The future looks gloomy, and the state of the world is itself ample ground for acute anxiety—the lot of all men honest enough to face things as they are. Intimacy is impossible, as men are separated by their self-centeredness and their inability to understand each other. Religion, conventional values, social institutions, culture itself—all are arbitrary games played by the conventional and fearful in order to blind themselves to the deeper absurdity of the world.

Exacerbated Identity Crisis

One way of characterizing the late adolescence of alienated young men is in terms of Erikson's discussion of the pathology of identity crisis.[3] They show many of the symptoms mentioned by Erikson: a diffusion of time and inability to work at assigned tasks; a "rock-bottom" attitude combining the search for a viable foundation for identity with the desire to regress to the states of early childhood; role diffusion; the choice of a negative identity (becoming all that they have been warned not to become); the coupling of intense repudiation with an inability to repudiate selectively; ideological "totalism" in the form of a refusal to allow any possible validity to outlooks different from their own; and an all-or-nothing attitude, especially with regard to participation in conventional society. In a highly selected college population, alienation is perhaps the most likely form for an exacerbated identity crisis to take.

Confusions of Sexual Identification

As might be expected from their family background, virtually all alienated subjects show signs of confused sexual identification, with the central conflict usually centering on the simultaneous desire for passivity (being done to) and masculine sexuality. Thus, the preferred heterosexual fantasies of alienated subjects tend to have a strong passive component; and some subjects are unusually drawn to homosexuality or to relationships with children which do not require active masculinity.

The Failure of Repression

Alienated subjects do not and often cannot repress unacceptable feelings, fantasies, and impulses. On the contrary, they are keenly aware of their socially unconventional and taboo instincts, and they make it a matter of policy to admit them. Thus on personality tests, as in conversation, they defiantly admit neurotic symptoms; and in interpersonal situations they report more unpleasant feelings than they demonstrate in behavior. Creative ability and a capacity for artistic control enable some subjects to cope with the flood of disturbing feelings; but in most others the flood is threatening, only partly controlled, and it sometimes leads to feelings of unreality, to a sensation of being the plaything of irrational forces and fantasies, and to bizarre ideation and unsublimated primary process thinking. These alienated subjects suggest strongly how much repression, ego restriction, and conventional schematization of experience is necessary in our culture (and perhaps in any) for "normal" functioning. At the same time, however, alienated subjects differ from more self-punitive neurotics by virtue of their outward projection of blame, by universalizing their own into the human condition, and by sharp rejection of those who see the world in more conventional terms.

Alienation: The Rejection of Conventional Adult Commitments

The unifying characteristic of all alienated subjects is their rejection, more or less complete, of adult values, groups, institutions, and roles as conventionally defined in America. These are students who think of themselves as deliberately choosing a deviant outlook; and although they are usually deeply and openly unhappy, they aver that others would be unhappy, too, if they but saw the same things with the same honesty. This alienation fulfills many simultaneous functions: unconsciously, it is often a description of their own felt condition as outcasts from Eden; it provides an ideology for attacking apparently authoritative ideas, constitutions, and principles which might prove untrustworthy; it reflects a fear of commitment to an adult male role which, as instanced by their own fathers, has often proved inadequate and inconsistent; and, finally, in important respects, it contains major truths, though often overstated, about life in America.

THE ROOTS OF ALIENATION

A young man like Inburn would be of limited interest if he spoke for only a small number of overprivileged and overintellectual young men. But these notes on his sophomore year, I think, illustrate the extreme of a trend which exists in more moderate degree in a great many men and women, young and old. Insofar as this is true, we must search for the roots of alienation not only in the individual case histories and fantasies of alienated lives but in the common social, generational, and ideological backgrounds of these lives.

Even a partial delineation of this background would be impossible here, but the mention of a few of the broad historical forces underlying alienation may correct that individualistic bias which occurs if one studies lives in a social and historical vacuum.

Most immediately, Inburn himself notes the impact of the "ravages of the Depression" on his parents' initial poverty and perhaps even on the fact that they had but one child. Further, the Second World War took his father away from the family for four crucial years and thus facilitated the development of that "more than a mere mother-and-only-child relationship" of such vital importance in his life. And lastly, when Inburn's father was lured away from his first love, teaching, by the higher salary scales of Detroit's burgeoning bureaucracies, he followed another national social trend and added to his son's scorn for him as a man who is "a failure in his own eyes." In all these respects, the press of history on Inburn's life was immediate, direct, and shared by countless others.

But behind these concrete impingements of social history are other developments less tangible but no less important. For one, consider the contrast, repeated a million times over, between the Greek restaurant-keepers and the midwestern farmers, who were Inburn's grandparents, and Inburn's own life as a disaffected college student. The world in these three generations has changed so vastly as to be unrecognizable to his grandparents; and, more important to Inburn, it has altered so vastly that even the world in which his parents were formed in the twenties is now of chiefly historical interest to him, lacking value as a signpost for his own life. The upward mobility of his parents is but a part of that collective social mobility which has characterized Americans as a nation, bringing shifts in values, technologies, and patterns of life, the like of which have rarely if ever occurred in so short a time. The effects of such changes on individuals are unsettling, in that they suggest to many youths that there *are* no values, institutions, or ways of life that withstand the tests of time. If such is one's conviction, then perhaps the search for "the most valuable and the most significant set of sense experiences it is possible to take in" is the only quest that is left.

Or consider another characteristic of our changing social scene: the consolidation of the isolated nuclear family, or what the French, with greater historical sense, call *la famille réduite*. Such a family, limited to mother, father, and immediate offspring, produces an extreme intensification of emotional ties, especially between mother and child—usually at the very same time that the wider society insists on more impersonal and unemotional relationships in the sphere of work. This intensity of mother-child ties is further exaggerated by the increasing absence of the father at work, leaving the mother (even without wars) to develop further her central role as the primary educative agent. Thus, an ambitious woman like Inburn's mother, condemned whether by fate or modernity to a small family, often finds it hard *not* to feel frustrated, *not* to rejoice in and magnify her control over her domestic realm, and *not* to try to find in her children the satisfactions that her absent husband might have provided in another era. In sum, the family ambiance that we infer in exaggerated form in Inburn's life is far from unique; and a similar if less extreme constellation sets the stage for a life-long contrast in almost every American between the immediacy, intimacy, and dependency of childhood and the impersonal bureaucracies in which he will spend much of his adult life. To be sure, most still find in adulthood sufficient compensation to cancel the backward pull of indistinct and often romanticized childhood recall; but the tension exists for all.

But perhaps most important, a considerable amount of alienation is fully justified, I think, in America in the 1960's; and, even when not justified, an even greater amount is actively reinforced and supported by our society and our world. Our vocabularies brim over with synonyms for alienation—estrangement, neutralism, noninvolvement, apartheid, apathy, disengagement, withdrawal, anomie, detachment, segregation, indifference—and we lack words for the opposite which remain untainted by sentimentalism. In many cases the facts justify such attitudes, for ours is a society in which commercialism and marketing, whether of personalities or of unnecessary goods, have too often replaced value, worth, and merit. And even more than the facts warrant, we are fascinated by the corrupt, the unethical, and the sordid. The prevailing images of our television screens, our newspapers, and our magazines are either those of

commercially exploited sentimentality or of violence, depravity, and suspicion. As Nevitt Sanford writes in *The American College:*

> One of the hardest things about growing up in contemporary America is that at just the time when a young person most needs models of private and public virtue he is likely to become aware of corruption in high places, of organized immorality in some of our major institutions, of the inconsistencies in our economic system and in our sexual mores, and of meanness in people close at hand whom he thought he could admire. . . . He courts a new danger: that he will reject the existing order out of hand, and become totally alienated from the society and value system represented by his parents and his community.[4]

Fortunately, most young Americans still develop a capacity for selective blindness to these aspects of society or respond to them only in some dissociated corner of their psyches—though this blindness or learned incapacity often generalizes to prevent response to the beautiful, the genuine, the moving, and the decent as well. But for those who insist on seeing everything, a large modicum of alienation seems justified.

Consider, too, the international situation, with its two superpowers, each deeply distrustful of the other, each unwilling to compromise lest it appear to expose its own feared weaknesses, each poised to annihilate the other on a few hours' (soon, a few minutes') notice. This is a projection of distrust on so large a scale that had it been anticipated in the fantasies of some undergraduate two decades ago he would surely have been deemed borderline, if not paranoid, by assessing psychologists. The world of Melville's *Confidence Man*, with its motto of "No Trust," has been realized on a scale so vast as to be beyond the capacity of even Melville's colossal (and deeply alienated) imagination. Thus it cannot surprise us that individuals sometimes greet their fellows with distrust or view the world as the arena of anxiety and pessimism, no matter how much we may also understand of the individual roots of this alienation.

In sum, in this superficially quite ordinary sophomore there occurs a confluence of individual and historical forces, some of them unique to Inburn's life, some of them congruent with archetypal themes of outcastness from mother, tribe, and Eden, and some which are the reflections on a selectively predisposed individual of social and historical forces, whose impact we seldom know how to fathom. Henry Murray writes:

It seems to me that the major determinant of alienation is the nature of Western culture and society. The alienating features of it are first perceived by the variant or underprivileged (with ideals or without ideals), who are hurt by it, and by the overprivileged with ideals. . . . The increase in freedom has gone hand in hand with the increase in alienation. [5]

But for all that Inburn is enmeshed in his own, in his generation's, and in mankind's history—most of all when he seeks to deny the fact—I think it likely that from among the Inburns of the world will be recruited those who may eventually learn to relieve the lesser alienations of the rest of us. For the alienated—though they pay a high price in unhappiness, in distortions of personal growth, and in indiscriminate rejection—more often than most retain and insist on an openness to experience, a detachment, and a critical spirit, which are the positive side of estrangement.

NOTES

[1] The bulk of the research reported here was done at the Annex to the Center for Research in Personality and was partly supported by grant number M-1287 of the National Institute of Mental Health, Dr. Henry A. Murray, project director. I am especially indebted to Dr. Murray for his help and guidance and to Erik H. Erikson and David Riesman for their insight into the close interweaving of personality development and social setting.

[2] Ernest J. Schachtel, *Metamorphosis,* New York: Basic Books, 1959, Chap. 5.

[3] Erik H. Erikson, "Identity and the Life Cycle," *Psychological Issues,* **1** (1959), 122–146.

[4] Nevitt Sanford, ed., *The American College,* New York: John Wiley, 1962, p. 262.

[5] Personal communication.

THE LIBERATED GENERATION: AN EXPLORATION OF THE ROOTS OF STUDENT PROTEST[1]

Richard Flacks

As all of us are by now aware, there has emerged, during the past five years, an increasingly self-conscious student movement in the United States. This movement began primarily as a response to the efforts by southern Negro students to break the barriers of legal segregation in public accommodations—scores of northern white students engaged in sympathy demonstrations and related activities as early as 1960. But as we all know, the scope of the student concern expanded rapidly to include such issues as nuclear testing and the arms race, attacks on civil liberties, the problems of the poor in urban slum ghettoes, democracy and educational quality in universities, the war in Vietnam, conscription.

This movement represents a social phenomenon of considerable significance. In the first place, it is having an important direct and indirect impact on the larger society. But secondly it is significant because it is a phenomenon which was unexpected—unexpected, in particular, by those social scientists who are professionally responsible for locating and understanding such phenomena. Because it is an unanticipated event, the attempt to understand and explain the sources of the student movement may lead to fresh interpretations of some important trends in our society.

From The Journal of Social Issues, Vol. 23, No. 3 (July 1967). Reprinted by permission of The Journal of Social Issues.

RADICALISM AND THE YOUNG INTELLIGENTSIA

In one sense, the existence of a radical student movement should not be unexpected. After all, the young intelligentsia seem almost always to be in revolt. Yet if we examine the case a bit more closely I think we will find that movements of active disaffection among intellectuals and students tend to be concentrated at particular moments in history. Not every generation produces an organized oppositional movement.

In particular, students and young intellectuals seem to have become active agents of opposition and change under two sets of interrelated conditions:

When they have been marginal in the labor market because their numbers exceed the opportunities for employment commensurate with their abilities and training. This has most typically been the case in colonial or underdeveloped societies; it also seems to account, in part, for the radicalization of European Jewish intellectuals and American college-educated women at the turn of the century (Coser, 1965; Shils, 1960; Veblen, 1963).

When they found that the values with which they were closely connected by virtue of their upbringing no longer were appropriate to the developing social reality. This has been the case most typically at the point where traditional authority has broken down due to the

impact of Westernization, industrialization, moderniza-
tion. Under these conditions, the intellectuals, and par-
ticularly the youth, felt called upon to assert new
values, new modes of legitimation, new styles of life.
Although the case of breakdown of traditional authority
is most typically the point at which youth movements
have emerged, there seems, historically, to have been
a second point in time—in Western Europe and the
United States—when intellectuals were radicalized.
This was, roughly, at the turn of the century, when
values such as gentility, laissez-faire, naive optimism,
naive rationalism and naive nationalism seemed in-
creasingly inappropriate due to the impact of large-
scale industrial organization, intensifying class conflict,
economic crisis and the emergence of total war. Vari-
ants of radicalism waxed and waned in their influence
among American intellectuals and students during the
first four decades of the twentieth century (Aaron,
1965; Eisenstadt, 1956; Lasch, 1965).

If these conditions have historically been those
which produced revolts among the young intelligentsia, then I think it is easy to understand why a
relatively superficial observer would find the new
wave of radicalism on the campus fairly mysterious.

In the first place, the current student generation
can look forward, not to occupational insecurity or
marginality, but to an unexampled opening up of
opportunity for occupational advance in situations
in which their skills will be maximally demanded
and the prestige of their roles unprecedentedly
high.

In the second place, there is no evident erosion
of the legitimacy of established authority; we do
not seem, at least on the surface, to be in a period
of rapid disintegration of traditional values—at
least no more so than a decade ago when sociologists were observing the *exhaustion* of opportunity
for radical social movements in America (Bell,
1962; Lipset, 1960).

In fact, during the fifties sociologists and social
psychologists emphasized the decline in political
commitment, particularly among the young, and
the rise of a bland, security-oriented conformism
throughout the population, but most particularly
among college students. The variety of studies conducted then reported students as overwhelmingly
unconcerned with value questions, highly complacent, status-oriented, privatized, uncommitted

(Jacob, 1957; Goldsen, *et al,* 1960). Most of us
interpreted this situation as one to be expected
given the opportunities newly opened to educated
youth, and given the emergence of liberal pluralism
and affluence as the characteristic features of postwar America. Several observers predicted an
intensification of the pattern of middle-class conformism, declining individualism, and growing
"other-directedness" based on the changing styles
of child-rearing prevalent in the middle class. The
democratic and "permissive" family would produce young men who knew how to cooperate in
bureaucratic settings, but who lacked a strongly
rooted ego-ideal and inner control (Miller and
Swanson, 1958; Bronfenbrenner, 1961; Erikson,
1963). Although some observers reported that
some students were searching for "meaning" and
"self-expression," and others reported the existence of "subcultures" of alienation and bohemianism on some campuses (Keniston, 1965a; Trow,
1962; Newcomb and Flacks, 1963), not a single
observer of the campus scene as late as 1959 anticipated the emergence of the organized disaffection, protest, and activism which was to take shape
early in the sixties.

In short, the very occurrence of a student movement in the present American context is surprising
because it seems to contradict our prior understanding of the determinants of disaffection among
the young intelligentsia.

A REVOLT OF THE ADVANTAGED

The student movement is, I think, surprising for
another set of reasons. These have to do with its
social composition and the kinds of ideological
themes which characterize it.

The current group of student activists is predominantly upper middle class, and frequently these
students are of elite origins. This fact is evident as
soon as one begins to learn the personal histories
of activist leaders. Consider the following scene at
a convention of Students for a Democratic Society
a few years ago. Toward the end of several days of
deliberation, someone decided that a quick way of
raising funds for the organization would be to appeal to the several hundred students assembled at

the convention to dig down deep into their pockets on the spot. To this end, one of the leadership, skilled at mimicry, stood on a chair, and in the style of a Southern Baptist preacher, appealed to the students to come forward, confess their sins and be saved by contributing to SDS. The students did come forward, and in each case the sin confessed was the social class or occupation of their fathers. "My father is the editor of a Hearst newspaper, I give $25!" "My father is Assistant Director of the _____ Bureau, I give $40." "My father is dean of a law school, here's $50!"

These impressions of the social composition of the student movement are supported and refined by more systematic sources of data. For example, when a random sample of students who participated in the anti-Selective Service sit-in at the University of Chicago Administration Building was compared with a sample composed of nonprotesters and students hostile to the protest, the protesters disproportionately reported their social class to be "upper middle," their family incomes to be disproportionately high, their parents' education to be disproportionately advanced. In addition, the protesters' fathers' occupations were primarily upper professional (doctors, college faculty, lawyers) rather than business, white collar, or working class. These findings parallel those of other investigators (Braungart, 1966). Thus, the student movement represents the disaffection not of an underprivileged stratum of the student population but of *the most advantaged* sector of the students.

One hypothesis to explain disaffection among socially advantaged youth would suggest that, although such students come from advantaged backgrounds, their academic performance leads them to anticipate downward mobility or failure. Stinchcombe, for example, found high rates of quasi-delinquent rebelliousness among middle-class high school youth with poor academic records (Stinchcombe, 1964). This hypothesis is not tenable with respect to college student protest, however. Our own data with respect to the antidraft protest at Chicago indicate that the grade point average of the protesters was around B-B+ (with 75% of them reporting a B- or better average). This was slightly higher than the grade point average of our sample of nonprotesters. Other data from our own research indicate that student activists tend to be

at the top of their high school class; in general, data from our own and other studies support the view that many activists are academically superior, and that very few activists are recruited from among low academic achievers. Thus, in terms of *both* the status of their families of origins *and* their own scholastic performance, student protest movements are predominantly composed of students who have been born to high social advantage and who are in a position to experience the career and status opportunities of the society without significant limitations.

THEMES OF THE PROTEST

The positive correlation between disaffection and status among college students suggested by these observations is, I think, made even more paradoxical when one examines closely the main value themes which characterize the student movement. I want to describe these in an impressionistic way here; a more systematic depiction awaits further analysis of our data.

Romanticism

There is a strong stress among many Movement participants on a quest for self-expression, often articulated in terms of leading a "free" life—i.e., one not bound by conventional restraints on feeling, experience, communication, expression. This is often coupled with aesthetic interests and a strong rejection of scientific and other highly rational pursuits. Students often express the classic romantic aspiration of "knowing" or "experiencing" "everything."

Anti-authoritarianism

A strong antipathy toward arbitrary rule, centralized decision-making, "manipulation." The anti-authoritarian sentiment is fundamental to the widespread campus protests during the past few years; in most cases, the protests were precipitated by an administrative act which was interpreted as arbitrary, and received impetus when college administrators continued to act unilaterally, coercively, or secretively. Anti-authoritarianisn is manifested further by the styles and internal processes within activist organizations; for example, both SDS and SNCC have attempted to decentralize their operations quite radically and members are strongly critical of leadership within the organization when it is too assertive.

Egalitarianism, populism

A belief that all men are capable of political participation, that political power should be widely dispersed, that the locus of value in society lies with the people and not elites. This is a stress on something more than equality of opportunity or equal legal treatment; the students stress instead the notion of "participatory democracy"—direct participation in the making of decisions by those affected by them. Two common slogans—"One man, one vote"; "Let the people decide."

Anti-dogmatism

A strong reaction against doctrinaire ideological interpretations of events. Many of the students are quite restless when presented with formulated models of the social order, and specific programs for social change. This underlies much of their antagonism to the varieties of "old left" politics and is one meaning of the oft-quoted (if not seriously used) phrase: "You can't trust anyone over thirty."

Moral purity

A strong antipathy to self-interested behavior, particularly when overlaid by claims of disinterestedness. A major criticism of the society is that it is "hypocritical." Another meaning of the criticism of the older generation has to do with the perception that (a) the older generation "sold out" the values it espouses; (b) to assume conventional adult roles usually leads to increasing self-interestedness, hence selling-out, or "phoniness." A particularly important criticism students make of the university is that it fails to live up to its professed ideals; there is an expectation that the institution ought to be moral—that is, not compromise its official values for the sake of institutional survival or aggrandizement.

Community

A strong emphasis on a desire for "human" relationships, for a full expression of emotions, for the breaking down of interpersonal barriers and the refusal to accept conventional norms concerning interpersonal contact (e.g., norms respecting sex, status, race, age, etc.). A central positive theme in the campus revolts has been the expression of the desire for a campus "community," for the breaking down of aspects of impersonality on the campus, for more direct contact between students and faculty. There is a frequent counterposing of bureaucratic norms to communal norms; a testing of the former against the latter. Many of the students involved in slum projects have experimented with attempts to achieve a "kibbutz"-like community amongst themselves, entailing communal living and a strong stress on achieving intimacy and resolving tensions within the group.

Anti-institutionalism

A strong distrust of involvement with conventional institutional roles. This is most importantly expressed in the almost universal desire among the highly involved to avoid institutionalized careers. Our data suggest that few student activists look toward careers in the professions, the sciences, industry, or politics. Many of the most committed expect to continue to work full time in the "movement" or, alternatively, to become free-lance writers, artists, intellectuals. A high proportion are oriented toward academic careers—at least so far the academic career seems still to have a reputation among many student activists for permitting "freedom."

Several of these themes, it should be noted, are not unique to student activists. In particular, the value we have described as "romanticism"—a quest for self-expression—has been found by observers, for example Kenneth Keniston (1965b), to be a central feature of the ideology of "alienated" or "bohemian" students. . . . Perhaps more important, the disaffection of student activists with conventional careers, their low valuation of careers as important in their personal aspirations, their quest for careers outside the institutionalized sphere—these attitudes toward careers seem to be characteristic of other groups of students as well. It is certainly typical of youth involved in "bohemian" and aesthetic subcultures; it also characterizes students who volunteer for participation in such programs as the Peace Corps, Vista, and other full-time commitments oriented toward service. In fact, it is our view that the dissatisfaction of socially advantaged youth with conventional career opportunities is a significant social trend, the most important single indicator of restlessness among sectors of the youth population. One expression of this restlessness is the student movement, but it is not the only one. One reason why it seems important to investigate the student movement in detail, despite the fact that it represents a small minority of the student population, is that it is a symptom of social and psychological strains experienced by a larger segment of the youth—strains not well understood or anticipated heretofore by social science.

If some of the themes listed above are not unique to student activists, several of them may characterize only a portion of the activist group itself. In particular, some of the more explicitly political values are likely to be articulated mainly by activists who are involved in radical organizations, particularly Students for a Democratic Society, and the Student Nonviolent Coordinating Committee. This would be true particularly for such notions as "participatory democracy" and deep commitments to populist-like orientations. These orientations have been formulated within SDS and SNCC as these organizations have sought to develop a coherent strategy and a framework for establishing priorities. It is an empirical question whether students not directly involved in such organizations articulate similar attitudes. The impressions we have from a preliminary examination of our data suggest that they frequently do not. It is more likely that the student movement is very heterogeneous politically at this point. Most participants share a set of broad orientations, but differ greatly in the degree to which they are oriented toward ideology in general or to particular political positions. The degree of politicization of student activists is probably very much a function of the kinds of peer group and organizational relationships they have had; the underlying disaffection and tendency toward activism, however, is perhaps best understood as being based on more enduring, pre-established values, attitudes, and needs.

SOCIAL-PSYCHOLOGICAL ROOTS OF STUDENT PROTEST: SOME HYPOTHESES

How, then, can we account for the emergence of an obviously dynamic and attractive radical movement among American students in this period? Why should this movement be particularly appealing to youth from upper-status, highly educated families? Why should such youth be particularly concerned with problems of authority, of vocation, of equality, of moral consistency? Why should students in the most advantaged sector of the youth population be disaffected with their own privilege?

It should be stressed that the privileged status of the student protesters and the themes they express in their protest are not *in themselves* unique or surprising. Student movements in developing nations—e.g., Russia, Japan and Latin America—typically recruit people of elite background; moreover, many of the themes of the "new left" are reminiscent of similar expressions in other student movements (Lipset, 1966). What is unexpected is that these should emerge in the American context at this time.

Earlier theoretical formulations about the social and psychological sources of strain for youth, for example the work of Parsons (1965), Eisenstadt (1956), and Erikson (1959), are important for understanding the emergence of self-conscious oppositional youth cultures and movements. At first glance, these theorists, who tend to see American youth as relatively well integrated into the larger society, would seem to be unhelpful in providing a framework for explaining the emergence of a radical student movement at the present moment. Nevertheless, in developing our own hypotheses we have drawn freely on their work. What I want to do here is to sketch the notions which have guided our research; a more systematic and detailed exposition will be developed in future publications.

What we have done is to accept the main lines of the argument made by Parsons and Eisenstadt about the social functions of youth cultures and movements. The kernel of their argument is that self-conscious subcultures and movements among adolescents tend to develop when there is a sharp disjunction between the values and expectations embodied in the traditional families in a society and the values and expectations prevailing in the occupational sphere. The greater the disjunction, the more self-conscious and oppositional will be the youth culture (as for example in the situation of rapid transition from a traditional-ascriptive to a bureaucratic-achievement social system).

In modern industrial society, such a disjunction exists as a matter of course, since families are, by definition, particularistic, ascriptive, diffuse, and the occupational sphere is universalistic, impersonal, achievement-oriented, functionally specific. But Parsons, and many others, have suggested that over time the American middle-class family has developed a structure and style which tends to articulate with the occupational sphere; thus, whatever youth culture does emerge in American society is likely to be fairly well integrated with conventional values, not particularly self-conscious, not rebellious (Parsons, 1965).

The emergence of the student movement, and other expressions of estrangement among youth, leads us to ask whether, in fact, there may be families in the middle class which embody values and expectations which do *not* articulate with those prevailing in the occupational sphere, to look for previously unremarked incompatibilities between trends in the larger social system and trends in family life and early socialization.

The argument we have developed may be sketched as follows: First, on the macro-structural level we assume that two related trends are of importance: one, the increasing rationalization of student life in high schools and universities, symbolized by the "multiversity," which entails a high degree of impersonality, competitiveness, and an increasingly explicit and direct relationship between the university and corporate and governmental bureaucracies; two, the increasing unavailability of coherent careers independent of bureaucratic organizations.

Second, these trends converge, in time, with a particular trend in the development of the family; namely, the emergence of a pattern of familial rela-

tions, located most typically in upper middle-class, professional homes, having the following elements: (a) a strong emphasis on democratic, egalitarian interpersonal relations; (b) a high degree of permissiveness with respect to self-regulation; (c) an emphasis on values *other than achievement;* in particular, a stress on the intrinsic worth of living up to intellectual, aesthetic, political, or religious ideals.

Third, young people raised in this kind of family setting, contrary to the expectations of some observers, find it difficult to accommodate to institutional expectations requiring submissiveness to adult authority, respect for established status distinctions, a high degree of competition, and firm regulation of sexual and expressive impulses. They are likely to be particularly sensitized to acts of arbitrary authority, to unexamined expressions of allegiance to conventional values, to instances of institutional practices which conflict with professed ideals. Further, the values embodied in their families are likely to be reinforced by other socializing experiences—for example, summer vacations at progressive children's camps, attendance at experimental private schools, growing up in a community with a high proportion of friends from similar backgrounds. Paralleling these experiences of positive reinforcement, there are likely to be experiences which reinforce a sense of estrangement from peers or conventional society. For instance, many of these young people experience a strong sense of being "different" or "isolated" in school; this sense of distance is often based on the relative uniqueness of their interests and values, their inability to accept conventional norms about appropriate sex-role behavior, and the like. An additional source of strain is generated when these young people perceive a fundamental discrepancy between the values espoused by their parents and the style of life actually practiced by them. This discrepancy is experienced as a feeling of "guilt" over "being middle class" and a perception of "hypocrisy" on the part of parents who express liberal or intellectual values while appearing to their children as acquisitive or self-interested.

Fourth, the incentives operative in the occupational sphere are of limited efficacy for these young people—achievement of status or material advantage is relatively ineffective for an individual who already has high status and affluence by virtue of his family origins. This means, on the one hand, that these students are less oriented toward occupational achievement; on the other hand, the operative sanctions within the school and the larger society are less effective in enforcing conformity.

It seems plausible that this is the first generation in which a substantial number of youth have both the impulse to free themselves from conventional status concerns *and can afford to do so.* In this sense they are a "liberated" generation; affluence has freed them, at least for a period of time, from some of the anxieties and preoccupations which have been the defining features of American middle-class social character.

Fifth, the emergence of the student movement is to be understood in large part as a consequence of opportunities for prolonged interaction available in the university environment. The kinds of personality structures produced by the socializing experiences outlined above need not necessarily have generated a collective response. In fact, Kenneth Keniston's recently published work on alienated students at Harvard suggests that students with similar characteristics to those described here were identifiable on college campuses in the fifties. But Keniston makes clear that his highly alienated subjects were rarely involved in extensive peer relationships, and that few opportunities for collective expressions of alienation were then available. The result was that each of his subjects attempted to work out a value system and a mode of operation on his own (Keniston, 1965b).

What seems to have happened was that during the fifties, there began to emerge an "alienated" student culture, as students with alienated predispositions became visible to each other and began to interact. There was some tendency for these students to identify with the "beat" style and related forms of bohemianism. Since this involved a high degree of disaffiliation, "cool" noncommitment, and social withdrawal, observers tended to interpret this subculture as but a variant of the prevailing privatism of the fifties. However, a series of precipitating events, most particularly the southern student sit-ins, the revolutionary successes of students in Cuba, Korea, and Turkey, and the suppression of student demonstrations against the House Un-American Activities Committee in San Fran-

cisco, suggested to groups of students that direct action was a plausible means for expressing their grievances. These first stirrings out of apathy were soon enmeshed in a variety of organizations and publicized in several student-organized underground journals—thus enabling the movement to grow and become increasingly institutionalized. The story of the emergence and growth of the movement cannot be developed here; my main point now is that many of its characteristics cannot be understood solely as consequences of the structural and personality variables outlined earlier—in addition, a full understanding of the dynamics of the movement requires a "collective behavior" perspective.

Sixth, organized expressions of youth disaffection are likely to be an increasingly visible and established feature of our society. In important ways, the "new radicalism" is *not* new, but rather a more widespread version of certain subcultural phenomena with a considerable history. During the late nineteenth and early twentieth century a considerable number of young people began to move out of their provincial environments as a consequence of university education; many of these people gathered in such locales as Greenwich Village and created the first visible bohemian subculture in the United States. The Village bohemians and associated young intellectuals shared a common concern with radical politics and, influenced by Freud, Dewey, etc., with the reform of the process of socialization in America—i.e., a restructuring of family and educational institutions (Lasch, 1965; Coser, 1965). Although many of the reforms advocated by this group were only partially realized in a formal sense, it seems to be the case that the values and style of life which they advocated have become strongly rooted in American life. This has occurred in at least two ways: first, the subcultures created by the early intellectuals took root, have grown and been emulated in various parts of the country. Second, many of the *ideas* of the early twentieth century intellectuals, particularly their critique of the bourgeois family and Victorian sensibility, spread rapidly; it now seems that an important defining characteristic of the college-educated mother is her willingness to adopt child-centered techniques of rearing, and of the college-educated couple that they create a family which is democratic and egalitarian in style. In this way, the values that an earlier generation espoused in an abstract way have become embodied as *personality traits* in the new generation. The rootedness of the bohemian and quasi-bohemian subcultures, and the spread of their ideas with the rapid increase in the number of college graduates, suggests that there will be a steadily increasing number of families raising their children with considerable ambivalence about dominant values, incentives, and expectations in the society. In this sense, the students who engage in protest or who participate in "alienated" styles of life are often not "converts" to a "deviant" adaptation, but people who have been socialized into a developing cultural tradition. Rising levels of affluence and education are drying up the traditional sources of alienation and radical politics; what we are now becoming aware of, however, is that this same situation is creating new sources of alienation and idealism, and new constituencies for radicalism.

THE YOUTH AND SOCIAL CHANGE PROJECT

These hypotheses have been the basis for two studies we have undertaken. Study One, begun in the Summer of 1965, involved extensive interviews with samples of student activists and nonactivists and their parents. Study Two, conducted in the Spring of 1966, involved interviews with samples of participants, nonparticipants and opponents of the tumultuous "anti-ranking" sit-in at the University of Chicago.

Study One—The Socialization of Student Activists

For Study One, fifty students were selected from mailing lists of various peace, civil rights, and student movement organizations in the Chicago area. An additional fifty students, matched for sex, neighborhood of parents' residence, and type of college attended, were drawn from student directories of Chicago-area colleges. In each case, an attempt was made to interview both parents of the student respondent, as well as the student himself. We were able to interview both parents of 82 of the students; there were two cases in which no parents were available for the interview; in the remaining 16 cases, one parent was interviewed. The interviews with both students and parents averaged about three hours in length, were closely parallel in content and covered such matters as: political attitudes and participation; attitudes toward the student movement and "youth"; "values," broadly defined; family life, child-rearing, family conflict, and other aspects of socialization. Rating scales and "projective" questions were used to assess family members' perceptions of parent-child relationships.

It was clear to us that our sampling procedures were prone to a certain degree of error in the classification of students as "activists" and "nonactivists." Some students who appeared on mailing lists of activist organizations had no substantial involvement in the student movement, while some of our "control" students had a considerable history of such involvement. Thus the data to be reported here are based on an index of Activism constructed from interview responses to questions about participation in seven kinds of activity: attendance at rallies, picketing, canvassing, working on a project to help the disadvantaged, being jailed for civil disobedience, working full time for a social action organization, serving as an officer in such organizations.

Study Two—The "Anti-Ranking" Sit-in

In May, 1966, about five hundred students sat in at the Administration Building on the campus of the University of Chicago, barring the building to official use for two and a half days. The focal issue of the protest, emulated on a number of other campuses in the succeeding days, was the demand by the students that the University not cooperate with the Selective Service System in supplying class standings for the purpose of assigning student deferments. The students who sat in formed an organization called "Students Against the Rank" (SAR). During the sit-in, another group of students, calling themselves "Students for a Free Choice" (SFC), circulated a petition opposing the sit-in and supporting the University Administration's view that each student had a right to submit (or withhold) his class standings—the University could not withhold the "rank" of students who requested it. This petition was signed by several hundred students.

Beginning about ten days after the end of the sit-in, we undertook to interview three samples of students: a random sample of 65 supporters of SAR (the protesters); a random sample of 35 signers of the SFC petition (the antiprotesters); approximately 60 students who constituted the total population of two randomly selected floors in the student dormitories. Of about 160 students thus selected, 117 were finally either interviewed or returned mailed questionnaires. The interview schedule was based largely on items used in the original study; it also included some additional items relevant to the sit-in and the "ranking" controversy.

Some Preliminary Findings

At this writing, our data analysis is at an early stage. In general, however, it is clear that the framework of hypotheses with which we began is substantially supported, and in interesting ways, refined, by the data. Our principal findings thus far include the following.[2]

ACTIVISTS TEND TO COME FROM UPPER-STATUS FAMILIES.

As indicated earlier, our study of the Chicago sit-in suggests that such actions attract students predominantly from upper-status backgrounds. When compared with students who did not sit in, and with students who signed the anti-sit-in petition, the sit-in participants reported higher family incomes, higher levels of education for both fathers and mothers, and overwhelmingly perceived themselves to be "upper middle-class." One illustrative finding: in our dormitory sample, of 24 students reporting family incomes of above $15,000, half participated in the sit-in. Of 23 students reporting family incomes below $15,000, only two sat in.

Certain kinds of occupations are particularly characteristic of the parents of sit-in participants. In particular, their fathers tend to be professionals (college faculty, lawyers, doctors) rather than businessmen, white-collar employees, or blue-collar workers. Moreover, somewhat unexpectedly, activists' mothers are likely to be employed, and are more likely to have "career" types of employment, than are the mothers of nonactivists.

Also of significance, although not particularly surprising, is the fact that activists are more likely to be Jewish than are nonactivists. (For example, 45 percent of our SAR sample reported that they were Jewish; only about one-fourth of the nonparticipants were Jewish.) Furthermore, a very high proportion of both Jewish and non-Jewish activists report no religious preference for themselves and their parents. Associated with the Jewish ethnicity of a large proportion of our activist samples is the fact the great majority of activists' grandparents were foreign born. Yet, despite this, data from Study One show that the grandparents of activists tended to be relatively highly educated as compared to the grandparents of nonactivists. Most of the grandparents of nonactivists had not completed high school; nearly half of the grandparents of activists had at least a high school education and fully one-fourth of their maternal grandmothers had attended college. These data suggest that relatively high status characterized the families of activists over several generations; this conclusion is supported by data showing that, unlike nonactivist grandfathers, the grandfathers of activists tended to have white-collar, professional, and entrepreneurial occupations rather than blue-collar jobs.

In sum, our data suggest that, at least at major northern colleges, students involved in protest activity are characteristically from families which are urban, highly educated, Jewish or irreligious, professional, and affluent. It is perhaps particularly interesting that many of their mothers are uniquely well educated and involved in careers, and that high status and education has characterized these families over at least two generations.

ACTIVISTS ARE MORE "RADICAL" THAN THEIR PARENTS; BUT ACTIVISTS' PARENTS ARE DECIDEDLY MORE LIBERAL THAN OTHERS OF THEIR STATUS. The demographic data reported above suggests that activists come from high-status families, but the occupational, religious, and educational characteristics of these families are unique in several important ways. The distinctiveness of these families is especially clear when we examine data from Study One on the political attitudes of students and their parents. In this study, it should be remembered, activist and nonactivist families were roughly equivalent in status, income, and education because of our sampling procedures. Our data quite clearly demonstrate that the fathers of activists are disproportionately liberal. For example, whereas 40 per cent of the nonactivists' fathers said that they were Republcan, only 13 per cent of the activists' fathers were Republicans. Only 6 per cent of nonactivists' fathers were willing to describe themselves as "highly liberal" or "socialist," whereas 60 per cent of the activists' fathers accepted such designations. Forty per cent of the nonactivists' fathers described themselves as conservative; none of the activists' fathers endorsed that position.[3]

In general, differences in the political preferences of the students paralleled these parental differences. The nonactivist sample is only slightly less conservative and Republican than their fathers; all of the activist students with Republican fathers report their own party preferences as either Democrat or independent. Thirty-two per cent of the activists regard themselves as "socialist" as compared with 16 per cent of their fathers. In general, both nonactivists and their fathers are typically "moderate" in their politics; activists and their fathers tend to be at least "liberal," but a substantial proportion of the activists prefer a more "radical" designation.

A somewhat more detailed picture of comparative political positions emerges when we examine responses of students and their fathers to a series of 6-point scales on which respondents rated their attitudes on such issues as: U.S. bombing of North Vietnam, U.S. troops in the Dominican Republic, student participation in protest demonstrations, civil rights protests involving civil disobedience, Lyndon Johnson, Barry Goldwater, congressional

investigations of "un-American activities," full socialization of all industries, socialization of the medical profession.

Table 1 presents data on activists and non-activists and their fathers with respect to these items. This table suggests, first, wide divergence between the two groups of fathers on most issues, with activist fathers typically critical of current policies. Although activists' fathers are overwhelmingly "liberal" in their responses, for the most part, activist students tend to endorse "left-wing" positions more strongly and consistently than do their fathers. The items showing strongest divergence between activists and their fathers are interesting. Whereas activists overwhelmingly endorse civil disobedience, nearly half of their fathers do not. Whereas fathers of both activists and nonactivists tend to approve of Lyndon Johnson, activist students tend to disapprove of him. Whereas activists' fathers tend to disapprove of "full socialization of industry," this item is endorsed by the majority of activists (although fewer gave an extremely radical response on this item than on any other); whereas the vast majority of activists approve of socialized medicine, the majority of their fathers do not. This table provides further support for the view that activists, though more "radical" than their fathers, come predominantly from very liberal homes. The attitudes of nonactivists and their fathers are conventional and supportive of current policies; there is a slight tendency on some items for nonactivist

TABLE 1 STUDENTS' AND FATHERS' ATTITUDES ON CURRENT ISSUES

Issue	Activists		Nonactivists	
	Students	Fathers	Students	Fathers
Percent who approve:				
Bombing of North Vietnam	9	27	73	80
American troops in Dominican Republic	6	33	65	50
Student participation in protest				
demonstrations	100	80	61	37
Civil disobedience in civil rights protests	97	57	28	23
Congressional investigations of				
"un-American activities"	3	7	73	57
Lyndon Johnson	35	77	81	83
Barry Goldwater	0	7	35	20
Full socialization of industry	62	23	5	10
Socialization of the medical profession	94	43	30	27
N	34	30	37	30

students to endorse more conservative positions than their fathers.

It seems fair to conclude, then, that most students who are involved in the movement (at least those one finds in a city like Chicago) are involved in neither "conversion" from nor "rebellion" against the political perspectives of their fathers. A more supportable view suggests that the great majority of these students are attempting to fulfill and renew the political traditions of their families. However, data from our research which have not yet been analyzed as of this writing will permit a more systematic analysis of the political orientations of the two generations.

ACTIVISM IS RELATED TO A COMPLEX OF VALUES, NOT OSTENSIBLY POLITICAL, SHARED BY BOTH THE STUDENTS AND THEIR PARENTS. Data which we have just begun to analyze suggest that the political perspectives which differentiate the families of activists from other families at the same socioeconomic level are part of a more general clustering of values and orientations. Our findings and impressions on this point may be briefly summarized by saying that, whereas nonactivists and their parents tend to express conventional orientations toward achievement, material success, sexual morality, and religion, the activists and their parents tend to place greater stress on involvement in intellectual and esthetic pursuits, humanitarian concerns, opportunity for self-expression, and tend to de-emphasize or positively disvalue personal achievement, conventional morality, and conventional religiosity.

When asked to rank order a list of "areas of life," nonactivist students and their parents typically indicate that marriage, career and religion are most important. Activists, on the other hand, typically rank these lower than the "world of ideas, art, and music" and "work for national and international betterment"—and so, on the whole, do their parents.

When asked to indicate their vocational aspirations, nonactivist students are typically firmly decided on a career and typically mention orientations toward the professions, science, and business. Activists, on the other hand, are very frequently undecided on a career; and most typically those who have decided mention college teaching, the arts, or social work as aspirations.

These kinds of responses suggest, somewhat crudely, that student activists identify with life goals which are intellectual and "humanitarian" and that they reject conventional and "privatized" goals more frequently than do nonactivist students.

FOUR VALUE PATTERNS

More detailed analyses which we are just beginning to undertake support the view that the value patterns expressed by activists are highly correlated with those of their parents. This analysis has involved the isolation of a number of value patterns which emerged in the interview material, the development of systems of code categories related to each of these patterns, and the blind coding of all the interviews with respect to these categories. The kinds of data we are obtaining in this way may be illustrated by describing four of the value patterns we have observed.

Romanticism: Esthetic and Emotional Sensitivity

This variable is defined as: "Sensitivity to beauty and art—appreciation of painting, literature and music, creativity in art forms—concern with esthetic experience and the development of capacities for esthetic expression—concern with emotions deriving from perception of beauty—attachment of great significance to esthetic experience. More broadly, it can be conceived of as involving explicit concern with experience as such, with feeling and passion, with immediate and inner experience; a concern for the realm of feeling rather than the rational, technological or instrumental side of life; preference for the realm of experience as against that of activity, doing or achieving." Thirteen items were coded in these terms: For each item a score of zero signified no mention of "romanticist" concerns; a score of one signified that such a concern appeared. Table 2 indicates the relationship between "romanticism" and activism. Very few activists received scores on romanticism which placed them as "low"; conversely, there were very few high "romantics" among the nonactivists.

TABLE 2 SCORES ON SELECTED VALUES BY ACTIVISM
(PERCENTAGES)

		Activists	Nonactivists
(a)	*Romanticism*		
	High	35	11
	Medium	47	49
	Low	18	40
(b)	*Intellectualism*		
	High	32	3
	Medium	65	57
	Low	3	40
(c)	*Humanitarianism*		
	High	35	0
	Medium	47	22
	Low	18	78
(d)	*Moralism*		
	High	6	54
	Medium	53	35
	Low	41	11
	N	34	37

Intellectualism

This variable is defined as: "Concern with ideas —desire to realize intellectual capacities—high valuation of intellectual creativities—appreciation of theory and knowledge—participation in intellectual activity (e.g., reading, studying, teaching, writing)—broad intellectual concerns." Ten items were scored for "intellectualism." Almost no activists are low on this variable; almost no nonactivists received a high score.

Humanitarianism

This variable is defined as: "Concern with plight of others in society; desire to help others—value on compassion and sympathy—desire to alleviate suffering; value on egalitarianism in the sense of opposing privilege based on social and economic distinction; particular sensitivity to the deprived position of the disadvantaged." This variable was coded for ten items; an attempt was made to exclude from this index all items referring directly to participation in social action. As might be expected, "humanitarianism" is strongly related to activism, as evidenced in Table 2.

Moralism and Self-Control

This variable is defined as: "Concern about the importance of strictly controlling personal impulses —opposition to impulsive or spontaneous behav-

ior—value on keeping tight control over emotions —adherence to conventional authority; adherence to conventional morality—a high degree of moralism about sex, drugs, alcohol, etc.—reliance on a set of external and inflexible rules to govern moral behavior; emphasis on importance of hard work; concern with determination, 'stick-to-itiveness'; antagonism toward idleness—value on diligence, entrepreneurship, task orientation, ambition." Twelve items were scored for this variable. As Table 2 suggests, "moralism" is also strongly related to activism; very few activists score high on this variable, while the majority of nonactivists are high scorers.

These values are strongly related to activism. They are also highly intercorrelated, and, most important, parent and student scores on these variables are strongly correlated.

These and other value patterns will be used as the basis for studying value transmission in families, generational similarities and differences, and several other problems. Our data with respect to them provide further support for the view that the unconventionality of activists flows out of and is supported by their family traditions.

ACTIVISTS' PARENTS ARE MORE "PERMISSIVE" THAN PARENTS OF NONACTIVISTS. We have just begun to get some findings bearing on our hypothesis that parents of activists will tend to have been more "permissive" in their child-rearing practices than parents of equivalent status whose children are not oriented toward activism.

One measure of parental permissiveness we have been using is a series of rating scales completed by each member of the family. A series of seven-point bipolar scales was presented in a format similar to that of the "Semantic Differential." Students were asked to indicate "how my mother (father) treated me as a child" on such scales as "warm-cold," "stern-mild," "hard-soft"—ten scales in all. Each parent, using the same scales, rated "how my child thinks I treated him."

that their child was living with a member of the opposite sex. Responses to this item were coded as "strongly intervene, mildly intervene, not intervene." Data for this item for fathers appears in Table 5. Both tables show that fathers of activists report themselves to be much less interventionist than fathers of nonactivists. Similar results were obtained with mothers, and for other hypothetical situations.

Clearly both types of measures just reported provide support for our hypothesis about the relationship between parental permissiveness and activism. We expect these relationships to be

TABLE 3 SONS' AND DAUGHTERS' RATINGS OF PARENTS BY
ACTIVISM (PERCENTAGES)

| | Males | | Females | |
Trait of parent	Hi Act	Lo Act	Hi Act	Lo Act
Mild-Stern				
Per cent rating mother "mild"	63	44	59	47
Per cent rating father "mild"	48	33	48	32
Soft-Hard				
Per cent rating mother "soft"	69	61	60	57
Per cent rating father "soft"	50	50	62	51
Lenient-Severe				
Per cent rating mother "lenient"	94	61	66	63
Per cent rating father "lenient"	60	44	47	42
Easy-Strict				
Per cent rating mother "easy"	75	50	77	52
Per cent rating father "easy"	69	44	47	37
N	23	24	27	26

Table 3 presents data on how sons and daughters rated each of their parents on each of four scales: "mild-stern," "soft-hard," "lenient-severe," and "easy-strict." In general, this table shows that activist sons and daughters tend to rate their parents as "milder," "more lenient," and "less severe" than do nonactivists. Similar data were obtained using the parents' ratings of themselves.

A different measure of permissiveness is based on the parents' response to a series of "hypothetical situations." Parents were asked, for example, what they would do if their son (daughter) "decided to drop out of school and doesn't know what he really wants to do." Responses to this open-ended question were coded as indicating "high intervention" or "low intervention." Data for fathers on this item are reported in Table 4. Another hypothetical situation presented to the parents was

strengthened if "activism" is combined with certain of the value patterns described earlier.

A CONCLUDING NOTE

The data reported here constitute a small but representative sampling of the material we have collected in our studies of the student movement. In general, they provide support for the impressions and expectations we had when we undertook this work. Our view of the student movement as an expression of deep discontent felt by certain types of high-status youth as they confront the incongruities between the values represented by the authority and occupational structure of the larger society and the values inculcated by their families and peer culture seems to fit well with the data we have obtained.

TABLE 4 FATHER'S INTERVENTION—"IF CHILD DROPPED OUT OF SCHOOL"
(PERCENTAGES)

Degree of Intervention	Activism of Child	
	High	Low
Low	56	37
High	44	63
N	30	30

TABLE 5 FATHER'S INTERVENTION—"IF CHILD WERE LIVING WITH MEMBER
OF OPPOSITE SEX" (PERCENTAGES)

Degree of Intervention	Activism of Child	
	High	Low
None	20	14
Mild	50	28
Strong	30	58
N	30	30

A variety of questions remain which, we hope, can be answered, at least in part, by further analyses of our data. Although it is clear that value differences between parents of activists and nonactivists are centrally relevant for understanding value, attitudinal, and behavioral cleavages among types of students on the campus, it remains to be determined whether differences in family status, on the one hand, and child-rearing practices, on the other, make an independent contribution to the variance. A second issue has to do with political ideology. First impressions of our data suggest that activists vary considerably with respect to their degree of politicization and their concern with ideological issues. The problem of isolating the key determinants of this variation is one we will be paying close attention to in further analysis of our interview material. Two factors are likely to be of importance here—first, the degree to which the student participates in radical student organizations; second, the political history of his parents.

At least two major issues are not confronted by the research we have been doing. First, we have not examined in any detail the role of campus conditions as a determinant of student discontent. The research reported here emphasizes family socialization and other antecedent experiences as determinants of student protest, and leads to the prediction that students experiencing other patterns of early socialization will be unlikely to be in revolt. This view needs to be counterbalanced by recalling instances of active student unrest on campuses where very few students are likely to have the backgrounds suggested here as critical. Is it possible that there are two components to the student protest movement—one generated to a great extent by early socialization, the second by grievances indigenous to the campus? At any rate, the interrelationships between personal dispositions and campus conditions need further detailed elucidation.

A second set of questions unanswerable by our research has to do with the future—what lies ahead for the movement as a whole and for the individual young people who participate in it? One direction for the student movement is toward institutionalization as an expression of youth discontent. This outcome, very typical of student movements in many countries, would represent a narrowing of the movement's political and social impact, a way of functionally integrating it into an otherwise stable society. Individual participants would be expected to pass through the movement on their way to eventual absorption, often at an elite level, into the established institutional order. An alternative direction would be toward the development of a full fledged political "left," with the student movement serving, at least initially, as a nucleus. The potential for this latter development is apparent in recent events. It was the student movement which catalyzed professors and other adults into protest with respect to the Vietnam war. Students for a Democratic Society, the main organizational expression of the student movement, has had, for several years, a program for "community organizing," in which students and ex-students work full time at the mobilization of constituencies for independent radical political and social action. This SDS program began in poverty areas; it is now beginning to spread to "middle-class" communities. These efforts, and others like them, from Berkeley to New Haven, became particularly visible during the 1966 congressional elections, as a wave of "new left" candidates emerged across the country, often supported by large and sophisticated political organizations. Moreover, in addition to attempts at political organizations, SDS, through its "Radical Education Project," has begun to seek the involvement of faculty members, professionals, and other intellectuals for a program of research and education designed to lay the foundations for an intellectually substantial and ideologically developed "new left."

At its convention in September, 1966, SDS approached, but did not finally decide, the question of whether to continue to maintain its character as a campus-based, student organization or to transform itself into a "Movement for a Democratic Society." Characteristically, the young people there assembled amended the organization's constitution so that anyone regardless of status or age could join, while simultaneously they affirmed the student character of the group by projecting a more vigorous program to organize uncommitted students.

The historical significance of the student movement of the sixties remains to be determined. Its impact on the campus and on the larger society has already been substantial. It is clearly a product of deep discontent in certain significant and rapidly growing segments of the youth population. Whether it becomes an expression of generational discontent, or the forerunner of major political realignments—or simply disintegrates—cannot really be predicted by detached social scientists. The ultimate personal and political meaning of the student movement remains a matter to be determined by those who are involved with it—as participants, as allies, as critics, as enemies.

REFERENCES

Aaron, Daniel, *Writers on the Left,* New York: Avon, 1965.

Bell, Daniel, *The End of Ideology,* New York: Free Press, 1962.

Braungart, R. G., Social Stratification and Political Attitudes, unpublished manuscript, Pennsylvania State University, 1966.

Bronfenbrenner, U., "The Changing American Child: A Speculative Analysis," *Merrill-Palmer Quarterly,* **7** (1961), 73–85.

Coser, Lewis, *Men of Ideas,* New York: Free Press, 1965.

Erikson, Erik, "Identity and the Life-Cycle," *Psychological Issues,* **1** (1959), 1–171.

Erikson, Erik, *Childhood and Society.* New York: Norton, 1963, pp. 306–325.

Eisenstadt, Shmuel N., *From Generation to Generation,* Glencoe: Free Press, 1956.

Flacks, R., "The Liberated Generation," University of Chicago, 1966 (mimeographed).

Goldsen, Rose; Rosenberg, Morris; Williams, Robin; and Suchman, Edward, *What College Students Think,* Princeton: Van Nostrand, 1960.

Jacob, Philip, *Changing Values in College,* New York: Harper, 1957.

Keniston, Kenneth, *The Uncommitted,* New York: Harcourt Brace, 1965a.

Keniston, Kenneth, "Social Change and Youth in America," in E. Erikson (ed.), *The Challenge of Youth,* Garden City: Doubleday Anchor, 1965b.

Lasch, Christopher, *The New Radicalism in America,* New York: Knopf, 1965.

Lipset, Seymour, *Political Man, the Social Bases of Politics,* Garden City: Doubleday Anchor, 1960.

Lipset, Seymour, "University Students and Politics in Underdeveloped Countries," *Comparative Education Review,* **10** (1966a), 132–162.

Lipset, Seymour, and Altbach, P., "Student Politics and Higher Education in the United States," *Comparative Education Review,* **10** (1966b), 320–349.

Miller, Daniel, and Swanson, G. E., *The Changing American Parent,* New York: Wiley, 1958.

Newcomb, Theodore, and Flacks, R., *Deviant Subcultures on a College Campus,* U.S. Office of Education, 1963.

Parsons, Talcott, "Youth in the Context of American Society," in E. Erikson (ed.), *The Challenge of Youth,* Garden City: Doubleday Anchor, 1965.

Shils, Edward, "The Intellectuals in the Political Development of New States," *World Politics,* **12** (1960), 329–368.

Stinchcombe, Arthur, *Rebellion in a High School,* Chicago: Quadrangle, 1964.

Trow, Martin, "Student Cultures and Administrative Action," in R. Sutherland, *et al.* (eds.), *Personality Factors on the College Campus,* Austin: Hogg Foundation for Mental Health, 1962.

Veblen, Thorstein, "The Intellectual Pre-eminence of Jews in Modern Europe," in B. Rosenberg (ed.), *Thorstein Veblen,* New York: Crowell, 1963.

NOTES

[1] The research reported here stemmed from a coalescence of interests of the author and of Professor Bernice Neugarten of the Committee on Human Development of the University of Chicago. . . . I wish to thank Professor Neugarten, Charles Derber and Patricia Schedler for their help in preparing this manuscript; its flaws are entirely my own responsibility.

[2] A more detailed report of the procedures and findings of these studies is available in Flacks (1966).

[3] For the purposes of this report, "activists" are those students who were in the top third on our activism index; "nonactivists" are those students who were in the bottom third—this latter group reported virtually no participation in any activity associated with the student movement. The "activists" on the other hand had taken part in at least one activity indicating high commitment to the movement (e.g., going to jail, working full time, serving in a leadership capacity).

A study of human behavior requires, first and foremost, a study of the social contexts within which people move, the expectations as to how they will behave, and the authority which tells them who they are and what they are supposed to do.

N. WEISSTEIN

Free societies depend on their members to learn early and thoroughly that public authority is not *like that of the family.*

E. FRIEDENBERG

How is policy maintained, despite the fact that it often contravenes journalistic norms, that staffers often personally disagree with it, and that executives cannot legitimately command that it be followed?

W. BREED

The streetcorner man is under continuous assault by his job experiences and his job fears. His experiences and fears feed on one another. The kind of job he can get—and frequently only after fighting for it, if then—steadily confirms his fears, depresses his self-confidence and self-esteem until finally, terrified of an opportunity even if one presents itself, he stands defeated by his experiences, his belief in his own self-worth destroyed and his fears a confirmed reality.

ELLIOT LIEBOW

Chapter 3

GETTING TO KNOW ONE'S PLACE:

Situational Determinants of Compliance

In Milgram's study on obedience and disobedience to authority, individuals differed in their readiness to obey within each experimental situation. In the previous section, we observed how such individual variations can be accounted for in terms of differences in character and disposition—differences rooted in early childhood experience with authority. But the most dramatic differences in readiness to obey in Milgram's studies occurred not among individuals in each situation, but across the range of situations. Compliance with destructive orders is far more likely when the victim is remote and unseen than when his pain and protest can be directly observed. Individuals tend to avoid compliance when their behavior can be shielded from the continuous scrutiny of authority. Individuals are very likely to disobey when fellow subordinates do. These findings suggest that, on the average, the situational context in which compliance is expected is a more significant determinant of obedience than the personal characteristics of the participants in that situation. The forces that operate on an individual in the present are more likely to account for his actions than the residue of the individual's past.

There are several different senses in which the above argument has validity. First, and most obvious, is the fact that characterological dispositions can only be acted out in terms of particular situations. A person with authoritarian tendencies, for example, does not inevitably become a participant in racial genocide. This would only become likely if genocidal institutions were created in a society, and authoritarian types were then recruited. The case of Martin Luther demonstrates how an individual with an authoritarian disposition can become a rebel against authority. In Luther's case, the situational context permitted him to define rebellion against the church as a more authentic form of obedience to God. Persons with different character structures may define situations in divergent ways; still no one's action can be understood or predicted unless it is understood in the context of the immediate situation. This particular line of argument does not fundamentally challenge the psychoanalytic mode of explanation. Freud himself would not have disagreed with it. One of Erikson's special contributions, however, was to demonstrate the necessity for taking full account of the cultural and historical situation which the actor confronts.

A second reason for emphasizing the immediate situation as a prime determinant of action does depart from the psychoanalytic perspective. Although most social theorists now accept the psychoanalytic insight into the importance of childhood experience in forming relations with authority, they argue that the process of socialization does not end in childhood. Rather, they recognize that institutional settings beyond the family may be crucial in establishing individual patterns of response to authority. The school, the workplace, the mass communications media, the "correctional institution" are all designed to socialize and instill attitudes toward authority; it would be illogical to deny the possibility that experiences with such institutions fundamentally affect the ways that individuals respond to authority. It seems more useful to argue that we now need to extend Freud's illumination of the profound impact of family structure on individuals to an understanding of the similarly profound impact of institutions other than the family.

A third reason for emphasizing situational determinants is that characterological differences among people do not explain very much. Characterological factors seem most useful in accounting for the action of exceptional individuals —for instance, the person who refuses to obey when all those around him are going along, or, conversely, the person who enthusiastically does his duty when everyone else is demonstrating their discontent. But if we are interested in the behavior of people in general, if we want to predict the most likely response in a particular situation, or understand regularly observed differences in the proportion of people who obey in different situations, then a strategy of explanation focusing on the structure of the situation may be more fruitful.

A final ground for questioning exclusive dependence on the psychoanalytic mode of explanation is that it tends to see social relations as arising from the motives, needs, and values of individuals. There is certainly truth in such a view, but it may be particularly misleading when accounting for responses to authority in our present-day society. Indeed, one of the chief characteristics of the institutions of advanced industrial society is that they are organized to ensure that the behavior of the individuals within their scope is reliable, predictable, and standardized. Huge corporations dependent upon the actions of millions of consumers for their survival and growth cannot remain at the mercy of individualized needs—they must exercise reliable control over the ways those needs are expressed. These same corporations must coordinate huge work forces that reliably perform standardized work in a predictable way. Schools, mental hospitals, prisons, and amusement parks must maintain order among large crowds of people who are potentially unruly and not necessarily inclined to be docile. Millions who are impoverished and disadvantaged in a society of abundance must be treated in such a way that they do not threaten the established distribution of privilege. All of these situations require a standardization of behavior so that prediction and control can be efficiently achieved. Character structures rooted in family socialization are insufficiently standardized; thus, our form of society introduces new modes of socialization and control that render the individuality of the person in the family irrelevant to the operation of "secondary" institutions.

C. Wright Mills once suggested that "the next step forward in psychoanalytic studies is to do fully for other institutional areas what Freud began to do so magnificently for kinship institutions of a selected type." We have no Freud of the factory, school, office, or prison—no coherent, fully developed social psychology of these institutional frameworks. Nevertheless, there is a rich supply of social psychological studies which attempt to trace the impact of institutionalized social relations upon the individual. In this chapter, I present a sampling of such studies. Each piece describes a way in which compliant or conforming behavior is a function of a particular social situation. Many of these pieces suggest ways in which such situations are organized to make impulses rooted in individual character irrelevant. Other articles suggest ways in which such impulses are rechanneled by institutional arrangements so that reliable compliance becomes more likely than defiance. Still others suggest processes of "resocialization," in which individual characterological tendencies are altered in the interests of institutional functioning.

Each of the following selections describes aspects of the process by which people come to know and accept their subordinate place in an institutional or societal scheme. The means of accomplishing this process are quite varied. The most obvious and straightforward means of ensuring compliant behavior is to use threats and rewards. Persons are likely to stay in line if they believe that deviations will result in the loss of a valued job or an undermining of their status. They are likely to accept and even endorse demands for conformity (or otherwise come to identify with those in authority), if conformity is seen as substantially instrumental in improving one's status, receiving approval, or otherwise attaining valued objects. Warren Breed's essay on the acceptance by "liberal" newsmen of the "conservative" policies of their publishers nicely illustrates how a mixture of reward and threat are important components of an institutional strategy for producing standardized behavior.

But external rewards and punishments are often insufficient. Institutions, like parents, hope that subordinates will be self-disciplined, that they will internalize the demands imposed upon them, and accept the demands as legitimate. An important element in such legitimation, as suggested by many of the following selections, is an explicitly articulated and inculcated ideology. For instance, as Edgar Litt shows, high schools explicitly inculcate passive images of citizenship into working-class students, while teaching upper-status youths that their active political participation can be effective. Edgar Friedenberg suggests how an ideology of *in loco parentis* is utilized by high school authorities to legitimate arbitrary control over students' personal habits and private lives. Naomi Weisstein's essay is a brilliant critique of the way in which "scientific" theory in psychology (especially psychoanalysis) is used as an ideology to legitimate the subordination of women. An ideology with "scientific" support is especially powerful as a tool of legitimation in a culture like ours, which so values objective and rational grounds for action.

Ideologies are especially influential in making people accept their place when social arrangements are, in Marcuse's phrase, "one-dimensional." When those who are subordinated have access to alternatives, when conflicting ideas are abroad, ideologies which justify subordination and deprivation begin to lose their force. Several of the following selections illustrate how institutional set-ups can be organized one-dimensionally so that access to alternative possibilities becomes highly unlikely.

A pure instance of the one-dimensional life occurs in the "total institution" as defined by Erving Goffman. In total institutions, those in charge expend great effort and imagination to screen inmates from external society, including even the selves which they brought with them from outside. High schools are not total institutions, since pupils do have an outside life after school hours; but Friedenberg's description of the physical and organizational structure of the school bears a striking resemblance to Goffman's depiction of prisons and asylums. Friedenberg, in particular, stresses the way one-dimensionality is achieved by preventing pupils from having any time or place which is free for self-initiated activity. One-dimensionality thus involves not only a pattern of insulation from alternative and critical ideas, but also a pattern which prevents subordinates from testing their capacities for initiative, independence, and self-regulation.

People accept their subordinate place as right to the extent that they lack confidence in their worth as human beings and in their capacity for independent, competent judgment and action. One way to deprive people of such confidence is to deprive them of the opportunity to learn about their capacities, as Friedenberg suggests. A more fundamental and pervasive means is to attack self-esteem directly. In our culture, the central means of proving one's worth is through successful achievement in work. A man is worthless if he cannot provide security for himself and his family through steady work; an inability to do so is interpreted, in our culture, as a failure of the person in the competitive struggle, rather than as a failure of the economic system. Elliot Liebow provides a striking close-up of the personal effects of competitive achievement on workers. Liebow demonstrates how ghetto men are trapped in a cycle which requires failure and which consequently destroys self-esteem and breeds resignation.

Our culture appears to value independence; but the fact that independence is so tightly linked with competitive achievement, material success, and occupational status means that the quest for it often ironically leads individuals toward submission, dependence, and conformity. This theme is present in most of the selections which follow. It is evident not only in the selection by Liebow, but also in Breed's study of how newsmen are led to sacrifice their integrity, and in William Westley's study of how policemen are led to commit illegal violence as a means of protecting or enhancing their status. Westley's study of the police is interesting in the context of individual responses to authoritarianism. Presumably, many men are attracted to police work because of authoritarian tendencies in their character structures. But Westley shows how authoritarian patterns of behavior can be generated by situational, rather than characterological, factors. The role of the policeman in our society, the "culture" of the police force, and the experiences and pressures of police work combine to create men who act as if they *are* authoritarians, irrespective of their upbringing or scores on the F-scale.

The situations described in these selections suggest that everyday life in our society is characterized by a very substantial degree of authoritarian domination and submission. Men and women at work, at school, and at home are regularly required to sacrifice their well-being, their aspirations, and their principles in the interest of institutional authority and private profit. These situations are arranged so that such sacrifices, if not made willingly, are at least regarded as legitimate by those who make them. I have tried in these introductory remarks to sketch some of the ways this happens. There are many others you may be able to discover in reading these selections and in your own experience.

But everyday authority relations in our society are not absolute, nor fully one-dimensional. One way to see this is to study Goffman's depiction of "total institutions." These are situations in which authority is, or tries to be, virtually absolute. In the excerpt reprinted here, Goffman describes some of the measures which totalistic authority must employ to achieve compliance and acceptance of its legitimacy. These institutions are part of our society. Many of their arrangements are continuous with practices of everyday civilian life. But the mortification of self carried out in total institutions goes well beyond the boundaries of legitimate authoritative action which would be accepted by adults in institutions that are not total. Many are now coming to question the legitimacy of total institutions in a democratic society; at the same time, there is considerable fear that our society as a whole is becoming more totalistic. In any case, the handling of inmates in total institutions is a dramatic illustration of how the situation can supersede and obliterate character in the determination of behavior.

SOME SUGGESTED READINGS

In addition to all of the books which have been excerpted here, I would suggest the following as fundamental to an understanding of situational determinants of compliance: K. Mannheim, *Man and Society in an Age of Reconstruction* (New York: Harcourt, 1950); R. Merton, *Social Theory and Social Structure* (New York: Free Press, 1969); C. W. Mills, *White Collar* (New York: Oxford, 1950); D. Riesman *et al., The Lonely Crowd* (New Haven: Yale, 1950); H. Marcuse, *One-Dimensional Man* (Boston: Beacon, 1965); A. Memmi, *Dominated Man* (Boston: Beacon, 1970) and *The Colonizers and the Colonized* (New York: Orion Press, 1965); J. I. Galbraith, *The New Industrial State* (Boston: Houghton Mifflin, 1967); S. Elkins, *Slavery* (Chicago: University of Chicago, 1969); V. Gornick and B. Moran, *Woman in Sexist Society* (New York: Basic Books, 1971); A. Etzioni, *The Active Society* (New York: Free Press, 1968); N. Sanford and C. Comstock, eds., *Sanctions for Evil* (San Francisco: Jossey-Bass, 1971); H. Swados, *On the Line* (Boston: Little, Brown, 1957); B. Friedan, *The Feminine Mystique* (New York: W. W. Norton, 1963).

THE CRADLE OF LIBERTY

Edgar Z. Friedenberg

Not far from Los Angeles, though rather nearer to Boston, may be located the town of Milgrim, in which Milgrim High School is clearly the most costly and impressive structure. Milgrim is not a suburb though it is only fifty miles from a large and dishonorable city and a part of its conurbation. Comparatively few Milgrimites commute to the city for work. Milgrim is an agricultural village which has outgrown its nervous system; its accustomed modes of social integration have never even begun to relate its present, recently acquired inhabitants to one another. So, though it is not a suburb, Milgrim is not a community either.

Milgrim's recent, fulminating growth is largely attributable to the extremely rapid development of light industry in the outer suburbs, with a resulting demand for skilled labor. But recent demographic changes in the area have produced a steady demand for labor that is not so skilled. In an area not distinguished for racial tolerance or political liberalism, Milgrim has acquired, through no wish of its own, a sizable Negro and Puerto Rican minority. On the shabby outskirts of town, a number of groceries label themselves Spanish-American. The advanced class in Spanish at Milgrim High School makes a joyful noise—about the only one to be heard.

Estimates of the proportion of the student body at Milgrim who are, in the ethnocentric language of demography, non-White, vary enormously. Some students who are clearly middle-class and of pinkish-gray color speak as if they were besieged. But responsible staff members estimate from 12 to 30 percent. Observations in the corridors and lunchrooms favor the lower figure. They also establish that the non-Whites are orderly and well behaved, though somewhat more forceful in their movements and manner of speech than their light-skinned colleagues.

What is Milgrim High like? It is a big, expensive building, on spacious but barren grounds. Every door is at the end of a corridor; there is no reception area, no public space in which one can adjust to the transition from the outside world. Between class periods the corridors are tumultuously crowded; during them they are empty; but they are always guarded with teachers and students on patrol duty. Patrol duty does not consist primarily in the policing of congested throngs of moving students, though it includes this, or the guarding of property from damage. Its principle function is the checking of corridor passes. Between classes, no student may walk down the corridor without a form, signed by a teacher, telling where he is coming from, where he is going, and the time, to the minute, at which the pass is valid. A student caught in the corridor without such a pass is taken to the office where a detention slip is made out against him, and he is required to remain at school for two or three hours after the close of the school day. He may do his homework during this time, but he may not leave his seat or talk.

There is no physical freedom whatever at Milgrim. That is, there is no time at which, or place in which, a student may simply go about his business. Privacy is strictly forbidden. Except during class breaks, the toilets are kept locked, so that a student must not only obtain a pass but find the custodian and induce him to unlock the facility. My mother, who had a certain humor about these matters unusual in her generation, had a favorite story about a golfer who, in a moment of extreme need, asked his caddy to direct him to the nearest convenience. The poor boy, unfortunately, stuttered; and the desperate golfer finally interrupted him, sadly, saying, "Never mind, now, son; I've made other arrangements." How often this occurs at Milgrim I do not know, but when it does, the victim is undoubtedly sent for detention.

Milgrim High's most memorable arrangements are its corridor passes and its johns; they dominate social interaction. "Good morning, Mr. Smith," an attractive girl will say pleasantly to one of her teachers in the corridor. "Linda, do you have a pass to be in your locker after the bell rings?" is his greeting in reply. There are more different kinds of washrooms than there must have been in the Confederate Navy. The common sort, marked just "Boys" and "Girls," are generally locked. Then, there are some marked "Teachers, Men" and "Teachers, Women," unlocked. Near the auditorium are two others marked simply "Men" and "Women," intended primarily for the public when the auditorium is being used for some function. During the school day a cardboard sign saying "Adults only" is added to the legend on these washrooms; this is removed at the close of the school day. Girding up my maturity, I used this men's room during my stay at Milgrim. Usually it was empty; but once, as soon as the door clicked behind me, a teacher who had been concealed in the cubicle began jumping up and down to peer over his partition and verify my adulthood.

He was not a voyeur; he was checking on smoking. At most public high schools students are forbidden to smoke, and this is probably the most common source of friction with authority. It focuses, naturally, on the washrooms, which are the only places students can go where teachers are not supposed to be. Milgrim, last year, was more liberal than most; its administration designated an area behind the school where seniors might smoke during their lunch period. Since, as a number of students explained to me during interviews, some of these students had "abused the privilege" by lighting up before they got into the area, the privilege had been withdrawn. No student, however, questioned that smoking *was* a privilege rather than a right.

The concept of privilege is important at Milgrim. Teachers go to the head of the chow line at lunch; whenever I would attempt quietly to stand in line the teacher on hall duty would remonstrate with me. He was right, probably; I was fouling up an entire informal social system by my ostentation. Students on hall patrol also, when relieved from duty, were privileged to come bouncing up to the head of the line; so did seniors. Much of the be-

havior Milgrim depends on to keep it going is motivated by the reward of getting a government-surplus peanut butter or tunafish sandwich without standing in line for it.

The lunchroom itself is a major learning experience which must make quite an impression over four years' time. There are two large cafeterias which are used as study halls during the periods before and after the middle of the day—the middle three or four are lunch shifts. The food, by and large, is more tempting than the menu; it tastes better than it sounds. The atmosphere is not quite that of a prison, because the students are permitted to talk quietly, under the frowning scrutiny of teachers standing around on duty, during their meal—they are not supposed to talk while standing in line, though this rule is only sporadically enforced. Standing in line takes about a third of their lunch period, and leaves plenty of time for them to eat what is provided them. They may not, in any case, leave the room when they have finished, any more than they may leave class in the middle. Toward the end of the period, a steel gate is swung down across the corridor, dividing the wing holding the cafeterias, guidance offices, administrative offices, and auditorium from the rest of the building where the library and classrooms are. Then the first buzzer sounds, and the students sweep out of the cafeteria and press silently forward to the gate. A few minutes later a second buzzer sounds, the gate is opened, and the students file on to their classrooms.

During the meal itself the atmosphere varies in response to chance events and the personality of the teachers assigned supervisory duty, especially in the corridor where the next sitting is standing in line. The norm is a not unpleasant chatter; but about one teacher in four is an embittered martinet, snarling, whining, continually ordering the students to stand closer to the wall and threatening them with detention or suspension for real or fancied insolence. On other occasions, verbal altercations break out between students in the cafeteria or in line and the *student* hall patrolmen. In one of these that I witnessed, the accused student, a handsome, aggressive-looking young man, defended himself in the informal but explicit language of working-class hostility. This roused the teacher on duty, who walked over toward the boy and, silently but with a glare of contempt, beckoned him from the room with a crooked and waggling finger and led him along the corridor to the administrative office: the tall boy rigid in silent protest; the teacher, balding and duck-bottomed in a wrinkled suit, shambling ahead of him. The youth, I later learned, was suspended for a day. At some lunch periods all this is drowned out by Mantovani-type pop records played over the public address system.

What adults generally, I think, fail to grasp even though they may actually know it, is that there is no refuge or respite from this; no coffee break, no taking ten for a smoke; no room like the teachers' room, however poor, where the youngsters can get away from adults. High schools don't have club rooms; they have organized gym and recreation. A student cannot go to the library when he wants a book; on certain days his schedule provides a forty-five-minute library period. "Don't let anybody leave early," a guidance counselor urged during a group testing session at Hartsburgh, an apparently more permissive school in our sample. "There really isn't any place for them to go." Most of us are as nervous by the age of five as we will ever be, and adolescence adds to the strain; but one thing a high school student learns is that he can expect no provision for his need to give in to his feelings, or to swing out in his own style, or to creep off and pull himself together.

The little things shock most. High school students—and not just, or even particularly, at Milgrim—have a prisoner's sense of time. They don't know what time it is outside. The research which occasioned my presence at Milgrim, Hartsburgh, and the other schools in the study required me to interview each of twenty-five to thirty students at each school three times. Just before each interview, the student was given a longish description of an episode at a fictitious high school to read as a basis for our subsequent discussion, and I tried to arrange to be interviewing his predecessor while he was reading the descriptive passage. My first appointment with each student was set up by the guidance counselor; I would make the next appointment directly with the student and issue him the passes he needed to keep it. The student has no *open* time at his own disposal; he has to select the period he can miss with least loss to himself. Stu-

dents well adapted to the school usually pick study halls; poorer or more troublesome students pick the times of their most disagreeable classes; both avoid cutting classes in which the teacher is likely to respond vindictively to their absence. Most students, when asked when they would like to come for their next interview, replied, "I can come any time." When I pointed out to them that there must, after all, be some times that would be more convenient for them than others, they would say, "Well, tomorrow, fourth period," or whatever. *But hardly anyone knew when this would be in clock time.* High school classes emphasize the importance of punctuality by beginning at regular but uneven times like 10:43 and 11:27, which are, indeed, hard to remember; and the students did not know when this was.

How typical is all this? The elements of the composition—the passes, the tight scheduling, the reliance on threats of detention or suspension as modes of social control—are nearly universal. The complete usurpation of any possible *area* of student initiative, physical or mental, is about as universal. Milgrim forbids boys to wear trousers that end more than six inches above the floor, and has personnel fully capable of measuring them. But most high schools have some kind of dress regulation; I know of none that accepts and relies on the tastes of its students. There are differences, to be sure, in tone; and these matter. They greatly affect the impact of the place on students.

Take, for comparison and contrast, Hartsburgh. Not fifteen miles from Milgrim, it is an utterly different community. It is larger; the school district is more compact and more suburban, more of a place. First impressions of Hartsburgh High are almost bound to be favorable. The building, like Milgrim, is new; unlike Milgrim, it is handsome. External walls are mostly glass which gives a feeling of light, air, and space. There is none of the snarling, overt hostility that taints the atmosphere at Milgrim. There are no raucous buzzers, no bells of any kind. Instead, there are little blinker lights arranged like the Italian flag. The green light blinks and the period is over; the white light signals a warning; when the red light blinks it is time to be in your classroom. Dress regulations exist but are less rigorous than at Milgrim. Every Wednesday, however, is dress-up day; boys are expected to wear ties and jackets; the girls, dresses rather than skirts and sweaters. On Wednesday the school day ends with an extra hour of required assembly and, the students explain, there are often outside visitors for whom they are expected to look their best.

Students at Hartsburgh seem much more relaxed than at Milgrim. In the grounds outside the main entrance, during lunch period, there is occasional horseplay. For ten minutes during one noon hour I watched three boys enacting a mutual fantasy. One was the audience who only sat and laughed, one the aggressor, and the third—a pleasant, inarticulate varsity basketball player—was the self-appointed victim. The two participants were portraying in pantomime old, silent-movie-type fights in slow motion. The boy I did not know would slowly swing at Paul, who would sink twisting to the ground with grimaces of anguish; then the whole sequence would be repeated with variations, though the two boys never switched roles. In my interviews with Paul I had never solved the problems arising from the fact that he was eloquent only with his arms and torso movements, which were lost on the tape recorder, and it was a real pleasure to watch him in his own medium. This was a pleasure Milgrim would never have afforded me. Similarly, in the corridors at Hartsburgh I would occasionally come upon couples holding hands or occasionally rather more, though it distressed me that they always broke guiltily apart as they saw me or any other adult. One of my subjects, who had completed the preliminary readings for his interview and was waiting outside for me to finish with the previous subject, was dancing a little jig by himself in the corridor when I got to him. This is all rather reassuring.

It is also contrary to policy. There is a regulation against couples holding hands and they are punished if caught by the kind of teacher who hates sexuality in the young. The air and space also, subtly, turn out to be illusions if you try to use them. Hartsburgh High is built around a large landscaped courtyard with little walks and benches. I made the mistake of trying to conduct an interview on one of these benches. When it was over we could not get back into the building except by disturbing a class; the doors onto this inviting oasis can only be opened from the inside, so nobody ever goes there. Since the courtyard is completely enclosed

by the high school building this affords no additional protection from intruders; but it does sequester a possible place of informal refuge. The beautiful glass windows do not open enough to permit a body to squirm through and consequently do not open enough to ventilate the rooms, in which there are no individual controls for the fiercely effective radiators. Room temperature, at Hartsburgh, is a matter of high policy.

Teachers do not hide in the washrooms at Hartsburgh, but the principal recently issued to all students a letter warning that any student caught in the vicinity of the school with "tobacco products" on him would be subject to suspension; students were directed to have their parents sign the letter as written acknowledgment that they were aware of the regulation and return it to school. Staff, of course, are permitted to smoke.

A former teacher, promoted to assistant principal, is now a full-time disciplinarian, but students are not dragged to his office by infuriated teachers as sometimes happens at Milgrim. Instead, during the first period, two students from the school Citizenship Corps go quietly from classroom to classroom with a list, handing out summonses. The air at Hartsburgh is less rancorous and choleric than at Milgrim, and there seem to be more teachers there who like teaching and like kids. But the fundamental pattern is still one of control, distrust, and punishment.

The observable differences—and they are striking—are the result almost entirely, I believe, of structural and demographic factors and occur despite very similar administrative purposes. Neither principal respected adolescents at all or his staff very much. Both were preoccupied with good public relations as they understood them. Both were inflexible. But their situations are different.

At Milgrim there is a strong and imaginative district superintendent who takes cognizance of educational problems. He likes to have projects going on that place the district in the national eye, particularly in research and guidance. Guidance officers report through their chairman directly to him, not to the building principal; and the guidance staff is competent, tough, and completely professional. When wrangles occur over the welfare of a student they are likely to be open, with the principal and the guidance director as antagonists; both avoid such encounters if possible, and neither can count on the support of the district office; but when an outside force—like an outraged parent—precipitates a conflict, it is fought out. At Hartsburgh, the district superintendent is primarily interested in keeping a taut ship with no problems. To this end, he backs the authority of the building principal whenever this might be challenged. The guidance office is rudimentary and concerned primarily with college placement and public relations in the sense of inducing students to behave in socially acceptable ways with a minimum of fuss.

In these quite different contexts, demographic differences in the student bodies have crucial consequences. At Milgrim, the working-class students are not dominant—they have not got quite enough self-confidence or nearly enough social savvy to be —but they are close enough to it to be a real threat to the nice, college-bound youngsters who used to set the tone of the place in their old elementary or junior high school and who expect to go on dominating the high school. The working-class influx has left many middle-class students feeling engulfed by the rising wave of lower-status students, as they see it; while the lower-status students, many of whom are recent migrants and even high school transfers from the city, can remember schools in which they felt more at home.

The result is both to split and to polarize student feeling about the school, its administration, and other students. Nobody likes Milgrim High. But the middle-class students feel that what has ruined it is the lower-class students and that the punitive constraint with which the school is run is necessary to keep them in line. In some cases these middle-class students approach paranoia; thus, one girl, in commenting on the mythical high school described in our research instrument, said, "Well, it says here that the majority of the students are Negro—about a third!" (The actual statement is "about a fifth.")

The working-class students are hard-pressed, but being hard-pressed they are often fairly realistic about their position. If the Citizenship Corps that functions so smoothly at Hartsburgh went about its duties as smugly at Milgrim, actually turning people in and getting them in trouble, they would pretty certainly receive some after-school instruction in the way social classes differ in values and in the propensity for nonverbal self-expression. At Milgrim, the working-class kids know where they stand, and stand there. They are exceptionally easy to interview, for example, because it isn't necessary to be compulsively nondirective. Once they sense that they are respected, they respond enthusiastically and with great courtesy, but they do not alter their position to give the interviewer what they think he wants, or become notably anxious at disagreeing with him. They are very concrete in handling experience, not given to generalization. Most of them seem to have liked their elementary school and they share the general American respect for education down to the last cliché—then one will add, as an afterthought, not bothering even to be contemptuous, "Of course, you can't respect *this* school." They deal with the situation it presents them with in correspondingly concrete terms. Both schools had student courts last year, for example, and Hartsburgh still does, though few students not in the Citizenship Corps pay much attention to it. Student traffic corpsmen give out tickets for corridor offenses, and the culprits are brought before an elected student judge with an administrative official of the school present as adviser. But Milgrim had a student court last year that quickly became notorious. The "hoody element" got control of it, and since most of the defendants were their buddies, they were either acquitted or discharged on pleas of insanity. The court was disbanded.

The struggle at Milgrim is therefore pretty open; though none of the protagonists see it as a struggle for freedom, or could define its issues in terms of principle. The higher-status students merely assent to the way the school is run, much as middle-class white Southerners assent to what the sheriff's office does, while the lower-status students move, or get pushed, from one embroilment to the next without ever quite realizing that what is happening to them is part of a general social pattern. At Hartsburgh there aren't very many lower-status students, and those that there are can easily be dismissed by their middle-class compeers, who set the tone, as a "hoody element." There are not enough of these and they are not sufficiently aggressive to threaten the middle-class youngsters or their folkways, but, for that same reason, they do not force the middle-class youngsters to common cause with the administration. The administration, like forces of law and order generally in the United States, is accepted without deference, as a part of the way things work. In America, one doesn't expect authority to be either intelligent or forthright; it looks out for its own interests as best it can. Reformers and troublemakers can only make it nervous and therefore worse; the best thing is to take advantage of it when it can help you and at other times to go on living your own life and let it try to stop you.

This is what the Hartsburgh students usually do and, on the whole, the results are pleasant. The youngsters, being to some degree Ivy, do not constantly remind the teachers, as the Milgrim students do, that their jobs have no connection with academic scholarship. Many of the teachers, for their part, act and sound like college instructors, do as competent a job, and enjoy some of the same satisfactions. The whole operation moves smoothly. Both Milgrim and Hartsburgh high schools are valid examples—though of very different aspects—of American democracy in action. And in neither could a student learn as much about civil liberty as a Missouri mule knows at birth.

What is learned in high school, or for that matter anywhere at all, depends far less on what is taught than on what one actually experiences in the place. The quality of instruction in high school varies from sheer rot to imaginative and highly skilled teaching; but classroom content is often handled at a creditable level and is not in itself the source of much difficulty. Generally speaking, both at Milgrim and Hartsburgh, for example, the students felt that they were receiving competent instruction and that this was an undertaking the school tried seriously to handle. Throughout our sample of nine schools— though not necessarily in each of them—more than four-fifths of our pretest sample, aggregating nearly one thousand students, agreed that the following statements applied to their school:

There are teachers here who, when they tell you your work is well done, you know it is good.

Many of the teachers know a great deal about things other than what they cover in their subject in class.

Some teachers surprise you by getting you interested in subjects you'd never really thought of before.

But important as it is to note that students generally recognize academic quality in the schools, and particularly the contributions of exceptional teachers, serious questions remain as to how the school affects the students' conception of either academic mastery or of themselves. For more than 80 percent also agree that:

You have to be concerned about marks here; that is, if you are going to get anywhere and be anything.

The school doesn't expect students to wear expensive clothes, but they do have to be neat and clean. Clothes that are too sporty or sexy are "out."

The student newspaper here is pretty careful not to report things in such a way that they might make trouble for the school with other people.

Keeping everybody quiet when they're in the library is a regular cause with the librarians here.

A girl who went too far here and got into trouble would be suspended or expelled.

In my judgment, the kind of tutelage and status that the high school assigns students affects their lives and subsequent development far more crucially than the content and quality of formal instruction. What is learned most thoroughly by attendance at Milgrim or Hartsburgh is certain core assumptions that govern the conditions of life of most adolescents in this country and train them to operate as adult, if not as mature, Americans. The first of these is the assumption that the state has the right to compel adolescents to spend six or seven hours a day, five days a week, thirty-six or so weeks a year, in a specific place, under the charge of a particular group of persons in whose selection they have no voice, performing tasks about which they have no choice, without remuneration and subject to specialized regulations and sanctions that are applicable to no one else in the community nor to them except in this place. So accustomed are we to assuming that education is a *service* to the young that this statement must seem flagrantly biased. But it is a simple statement of what the law provides. Whether this provision is a service or a burden to the young—and, indeed, it is both, in varying degrees—is another issue altogether. Compulsory school attendance functions as a bill of attainder against a particular age group, so the first thing the young learn in school is that there are certain sanctions and restrictions that apply only to them, that they do not participate fully in the freedoms guaranteed by the state, and that, *therefore, these freedoms do not really partake of the character of inalienable rights.*

When services are to be provided to an individual whom the law respects as it does the agency providing the services, the normal legal instrument is, of course, a contract, which defines the rights and obligations of both parties and provides each with legal remedies against the contract's breach.

Compulsory school attendance, however, is provided by a law which recognizes no obligation of the school that the student can enforce. He cannot petition to withdraw if the school is inferior, does not maintain standards, or treats him brutally. There are other laws, certainly, that set standards for school construction and maintenance, the licensing of teachers, technics of discipline, and so forth; and proceedings under these may be invoked if the school does not abide by them. But they do not abate the student's obligation to attend the school and accept its services. His position is purely that of a conscript who is protected by certain regulations but in no case permitted to use their breach as a cause for terminating his obligation.

Of course not. The school, as schools continually stress, acts *in loco parentis;* and children may not leave home because their parents are unsatisfactory. What I have pointed out is no more than a special consequence of the fact that students are minors, and minors do not, indeed, share all the rights and privileges—and responsibilities—of citizenship. Very well. However one puts it, we are still discussing the same issue. The high school, then, is where you really learn what it means to be a minor.

For a high school is not a parent. Parents may love their children, hate them, or like most parents, do both in a complex mixture. But they must, nevertheless, permit a certain intimacy and respond to their children as persons. Homes are not run by regulations, though the parents may think they are, but by a process of continuous and almost entirely unconscious emotional homeostasis, in which each member affects and accommodates to the needs, feelings, fantasy life, and character structure of the others. This may be, and often is, a terribly destructive process; I intend no defense of the family as a social institution. Salmon, actually, are much nicer than people: more dedicated, more energetic, less easily daunted by the long upstream

struggle and less prudish and reticent about their reproductive functions, though inclined to be rather cold-blooded. But children grow up in homes or the remnants of homes, are in physical fact dependent on parents, and are too intimately related to them to permit their area of freedom to be precisely defined. This is not because they have no rights or are entitled to less respect than adults, but because intimacy conditions freedom and growth in ways too subtle and continuous to be defined as overt acts.

Free societies depend on their members to learn early and thoroughly that public authority is *not* like that of the family; that it cannot be expected —or trusted—to respond with sensitivity and intimate perception to the needs of individuals but must rely basically, though as humanely as possible, on the impartial application of general formulae. This means that it must be kept functional, specialized, and limited to matters of public policy; the meshes of the law are too coarse to be worn close to the skin. Especially in an open society, where people of very different backgrounds and value systems must function together, it would seem obvious that each must understand that he may not push others further than their common undertaking demands or impose upon them a manner of life that they feel to be alien.

After the family, the school is the first social institution an individual must deal with—the place in which he learns to handle himself with strangers. The school establishes the pattern of his subsequent assumptions as to which relations between the individual and society are appropriate and which constitute invasions of privacy and constraints on his spirit—what the British, with exquisite precision, call "taking a liberty." But the American public school evolved as a melting pot, under the assumption that it had not merely the right but the duty to impose a common standard of genteel decency on a polyglot body of immigrants' children and thus insure their assimilation into the better life of the American dream. It accepted, also, the tacit assumption that genteel decency was as far as it could go. If America has generally been governed by the practical man's impatience with other individuals' rights, it has also accepted the practical man's respect for property and determination to protect it from the assaults of public servants. With its contempt for personal privacy and individual autonomy, the school combines a con-siderable measure of Galbraith's "public squalor." The plant may be expensive—for this is capital goods; but nothing is provided graciously, liberally, simply as an amenity, either to teachers or stu-dents, though administrative offices have begun to assume an executive look. In the schools I know, the teachers' lounges are invariably filled with shabby furniture and vending machines. Teachers do not have offices with assigned clerical assis-tance and business equipment that would be considered satisfactory for, say, a small-town, small-time insurance agency. They have desks in staffrooms, without telephones.

To justify this shabbiness as essential economy and established custom begs the question; the level of support and working conditions customarily provided simply defines the status of the occupa-tion and the value the community in fact places on it. An important consequence, I believe, is to help keep teachers timid and passive by reminding them, against the contrasting patterns of commer-cial affluence, of their relative ineffectiveness; and to divert against students their hostilities and their demands for status. Both teachers and students, each at their respective levels, learn to regard the ordinary amenities and freedoms of middle-class life as privileges. But the teacher has a few more of them. He hasn't a telephone, but he may make calls from a phone in the general office, while, in some schools, the public pay phone in the hallway has a lock on it and the student must get a key from the office before he can dial his call. Where a hotel or motel, for example, provides in its budget for normal wear and tear and a reasonable level of theft of linens and equipment and quietly covers itself with liability insurance, the school—though it may actually do the same thing—pompously in-doctrinates its students with "respect for public property," "good health habits," and so forth be-fore it lets them near the swimming pool. In a large city, the pool may have been struck out of the architect's plans before construction began, on the grounds that it would be unfair to provide students in a newer school with a costly facility that students in older schools do not have.

If the first thing the student learns, then, is that he, as a minor, is subject to peculiar restraints, the second is that these restraints are general, and are not limited to the manifest and specific functions of education. High school administrators are not pro-fessional educators in the sense that a physician, an attorney, or a tax accountant are professionals. They are not practitioners of a specialized *instruc-tional* craft, who derive their authority from its requirements. They are specialists in keeping an essentially political enterprise from being strangled by conflicting community attitudes and pressures. They are problem-oriented, and the feelings and needs for growth of their captive and disfranchised clientele are the least of their problems; for the status of the "teenager" in the community is so low that even if he rebels the school is not blamed for the conditions against which he is rebelling. He is simply a truant or juvenile delinquent; at worst the school has "failed to reach him." What high school personnel become specialists in, ultimately, is the *control* of large groups of students even at catastrophic expense to their opportunity to learn. These controls are not exercised primarily to facili-tate instruction, and, particularly, they are in no way limited to matters bearing on instruction. At several schools in our sample boys had, for exam-ple, been ordered by the assistant principal—sometimes on the complaint of teachers—to shave off beards. One of these boys, who had played football for the school all season, was told that, while the school had no legal authority to require this, he would be barred from the banquet honor-ing the team unless he complied. Dress regulations are another case in point.

Of course these are petty restrictions, enforced by petty penalties. American high schools are not concentration camps; and I am not complaining about their severity but about what they teach their students concerning the proper relationship of the individual to society. The fact that the restrictions and penalties are petty and unimportant in them-selves in one way makes matters worse. Gross in-vasions are more easily recognized for what they are; petty restrictions are only resisted by "trou-blemakers." What matters in the end, however, is that the school does not take its own business of education seriously enough to mind it.

The effects on the students of the school's diffuse willingness to mind everybody's business but its own are manifold. The concepts of dignity and privacy, notably deficient in American adult folkways, are not permitted to develop here. The high school, certainly, is not the material cause of this deficiency, which is deeply rooted in our social institutions and values. But the high school does more than transmit these values—it exploits them to keep students in line and develop them into the kinds of people who fit the community that supports it.

A corollary of the school's assumption of custodial control of students is that power and authority become indistinguishable. If the school's authority is not limited to matters pertaining to education, it cannot be derived from educational responsibilities. It is a naked, empirical fact, to be accepted or controverted according to the possibilities of the moment. In this world power counts more than legitimacy; if you don't have power it is naive to think you have rights that must be respected; wise up. High school students experience regulation only as control, not as protection; they know, for example, that the principal will generally uphold the teacher in any conflict with a student, regardless of the merits of the case. Translated into the high school idiom, *suaviter in modo, fortiter in re* becomes "If you get caught, it's just your ass."

Students, I find, do not resent this; that is the tragedy. All weakness tends to corrupt, and impotence corrupts absolutely. Identifying, as the weak must, with the more powerful and frustrating of the forces that impinge upon them, they accept the school as the way life is and close their minds against the anxiety of perceiving alternatives. Many students like high school; others loathe and fear it. But even these do not object to it on principle; the school effectively obstructs their learning of the principles on which objection might be based; though these are among the principles that, we boast, distinguish us from totalitarian societies.

Yet, finally, the consequence of submitting throughout adolescence to diffuse authority that is not derived from the task at hand—as a doctor's orders, or the training regulations of an athletic coach, for example, usually are—is more serious than political incompetence or weakness of character. There is a general arrest of development. An essential part of growing up is learning that, though differences of power among men lead to brutal consequences, all men are peers; none is omnipotent, none derives his potency from magic but only from his specific competence and function. The policeman represents the majesty of the State, but this does not mean that he can put you in jail; it means, precisely, that he cannot—at least not for long. Any person or agency responsible for handling throngs of young people—especially if it does not like them or is afraid of them—is tempted to claim diffuse authority and snare the youngster in the trailing remnants of childhood emotion, which always remain to trip him. Schools are permitted to infantilize adolescence and control pupils by reinvoking the sensations of childhood punishment, effective because it was designed, with great unconscious guile, to dramatize the child's weakness in the face of authority. In fact, they are strongly encouraged to do so by the hostility to "teenagers" and the anxiety about their conduct that abound in our society.

In the process, the school affects society in two complementary ways. It alters individuals: their values, their sense of personal worth, their patterns of anxiety and sense of mastery and ease in the world on which so much of what we think of as our fate depends. But it also performs a Darwinian function. The school endorses and supports the values and patterns of behavior of certain segments of the population, providing their members with the credentials and shibboleths needed for the next stages of their journey, while instilling in others a sense of inferiority and warning the rest of society against them as troublesome and untrustworthy. In this way, the school contributes simultaneously to social mobility and social stratification. It helps to see to it that the kinds of people who get ahead are those who will support the social system it represents; while those who might, through intent or merely by their being, subvert it are left behind as a salutary moral lesson.

CIVIC EDUCATION, COMMUNITY NORMS, AND POLITICAL INDOCTRINATION

Edgar Litt

All national educational systems, observes V. O. Key, Jr., "indoctrinate the coming generation with the basic outlooks and values of the political order."[1] But this indoctrination is not uniform. Do different socioeconomic communities, for instance, differ in the kinds of textbooks they employ in civic education? Do differing political attitudes and norms in these communities affect the process of indoctrination? To answer these questions, we analyzed textual material in civic education programs, attitudes of leaders in the school's political and educational milieu, and changes in political attitudes accompanying participation in civic education classes.

PROCEDURE

The study was conducted in the major secondary school in each of three communities in the Boston metropolitan area (to be referred to as Alpha, Beta, and Gamma).[2] The three communities differ in socioeconomic and political characteristics: Alpha is an upper middle-class community with much political activity; Beta is a lower middle-class community with moderate political activity; and Gamma is a working-class community with little political activity (Table 1).

A content analysis, described in the Appendix, was made of all textbooks used in the civic education programs in Alpha, Beta, and Gamma schools over the past five years (ten texts were investigated in Alpha, eight in Beta, and seven in Gamma). A

From the American Sociological Review, Vol. 28, No. 1 (February 1963). Reprinted by permission of The American Sociological Association. Footnotes have been edited.

TABLE 1 SOCIOECONOMIC AND POLITICAL CHARACTERISTICS OF ALPHA, BETA, AND GAMMA

Characteristic	Alpha	Beta	Gamma
Percent of working force in professions	38%	15%	7%
Median family income	$5,900	$4,250	$3,620
Median voting turnout for five gubernatorial elections	67.8%	43.8%	32.1%

Source: U.S. Bureau of the Census, General Characteristics of the Population, Massachusetts, Washington: Government Printing Office, 1960; and Secretary of State, Compilation of Massachusetts Election Statistics: Public Document 43, Boston: Commonwealth of Massachusetts, 1950–1960.

random sample of paragraphs was selected in each text and classified, where applicable, along one of the following five dimensions:[3]

1. Emphasis on citizen political participation—references to voting, norms of civic duty, political activity, and the effectiveness of citizen action in influencing the behavior of public officials.

2. Political chauvinism—references to the unique and nationalistic character of "democracy" or "good government" as an American monopoly, and glorified treatment of American political institutions, procedures, and public figures.

3. The democratic creed—references to the rights of citizens and minorities to attempt to influence governmental policy through non-tyrannical procedures.

4. Emphasis on political process—references to politics as an arena involving the actions of politicians, public officials, and the use of power and

influence, contrasted with references to government as a mechanistic set of institutions allocating services to citizens with a minimum of intervention by political actors.

5. Emphasis on politics as the resolution of group conflict—references to political conflicts among economic, social, and ethno-religious groupings resolved within an agreed-upon framework of political rules of the game.

A second measure of civic education norms consisted of a series of interviews with a pool of "potential civic and educational influentials" in each of the three communities.[4] The interviews included a sample of all school administrators who were responsible for the school's civic education program; all teachers of civic education; the president and vice-president of each school's Parent and Teachers Association or Home and School Association over the past five years; and the current and most recent presidents and vice-presidents of ten major civic groups in each community. Interviewees included leaders of business, fraternal, labor, patriotic, religious, and civic betterment associations, and the chairmen of the local Republican and Democratic party organizations. A total of 66 leaders were interviewed in Alpha, 57 in Beta, and 63 in Gamma.[5]

The interview schedule was designed to tap the intensity of the respondent's attitudes toward the proper orientation of the community school's civic education program in each of the five political dimensions.

A third measure involved the effects of exposure to a formal course in civic education. A civic education class in each community was matched with a control group in age, academic attainment, parental social class, parental political affiliation, and ethno-religious affiliation. The control group, which did not take a course in civic education, was used to measure the changes in attitudes along the five political dimensions.

These dimensions were adapted for a questionnaire given to the three civic education classes, and their corresponding control groups, before and after a semester's exposure to the course. Thus we can compare attitudinal changes attributable to the school's "official version" of political phenomena,

TABLE 2 REFERENCES ON SALIENT POLITICAL DIMENSIONS IN CIVICS TEXTBOOKS

Political Dimension	Alpha	Beta	Gamma
Emphasis on democratic creed	56%	52%	47%
Chauvinistic references to American political institutions	3%	6%	2%
Emphasis on political activity, citizen's duty, efficacy	17%	13%	5%
Emphasis on political process, politicians, and power	11%	2%	1%
Emphasis on group conflict-resolving political function	10%	1%	2%
Other	3%	26%	43%
(Totals)	100%	100%	100%
Number of paragraphs	(501)	(367)	(467)

and the differential effects of the course in each community.

FINDINGS

The content analysis of textbooks in the civic education programs of Alpha, Beta, and Gamma schools revealed no substantial differences in references to elements of the democratic creed, or in chauvinistic treatment of American political procedures and institutions. Few references in the material employed by the three schools connoted an insular view of American politics; the isolationist and jingoist orientation of civic education texts observed in Pierce's pioneer study were absent in this sampling.[6] Nor does the textual material differ in references endorsing the political rights of minorities and political procedures available to them. Indeed, the endorsement of the democratic creed far exceeds the other political dimensions. The blandness of the Gamma texts should be noted; they contain a large number of descriptive references (dates of major political events, anatomical presentations of political procedure) that could not be classified along one of the five political dimensions (see Table 2).

Differences do exist in the formal exposure to norms supporting political participation, in the view of politics as process, and in the functions of the political system. Unlike Alpha and Beta texts, Gamma texts contain only a few references to norms that encourage voting, feelings of political effectiveness, and a sense of civic duty. References to the political process as a conduit involving political actors and the use of political power—rather than the workings of an invisible hand of governmental institutions—are also sparse in the Gamma texts.

Both Beta and Gamma texts are short on references to politics as a mechanism for settling competing group demands. Table 2 reveals that only Alpha schools indicate to some degree a political process in which politicians and power are the main ingredients, and through which a political group struggle is periodically ameliorated.

How do the norms of civic education that prevail among the potential civic and educational influentials of each community compare with the formal classroom material designed to shape student political attitudes? Are salient themes in the curriculum reinforced, opposed, or ignored by community norms?

Potential community influentials do support the inculcation of basic democratic principles (the democratic creed) and the avoidance of chauvinistic references to American political institutions—attitudes that were stressed in the texts. They also support material encouraging political activity and competence in young citizens, an attitude that is less reinforced in the Gamma school texts.

Table 3 indicates, however, that the potential influentials in the three milieux differ about the presentation of politics as a process involving the resources of politicians and power, and the conflict-alleviating goal of politics. Alpha leaders endorse these "realistic" political themes; and attempts to impart elements of political reality are present only in the Alpha civic education program. In Beta and Gamma the low level of support for these themes reinforces the contextual material of their school programs which ignores or avoids these perspectives on political phenomena.

It would be useless to talk about the effects of civic education programs without considering changes in political attitudes as functions of differ-

ent textual emphasis and norms of community leaders. Comparisons of attitude changes in the schools do not uncover any reversal of beliefs along the five political dimensions that can be attributed to the school's indoctrination.

Several patterns, however, relate the effects of the civic education program on student attitudes to its material and the community's potential political support. Based on the "before" and "after" questionnaires administered to the three classes and matched control groups, the data in Table 4 reveal that students in the civic education classes were more likely to endorse aspects of the democratic creed and less likely to hold chauvinistic political sentiments than students not exposed to the program. But none of the three "exposed" classes was more likely to favor political participation than their control group. And only in Alpha were perceptions of politics as group conflict involving politicians and political power strengthened through exposure to civic education.

In Alpha, Beta, and Gamma, we observe (Table 4) that exposure to the course strengthened support for democratic processes and negated chauvinistic sentiment, thus reinforcing the material presented in the civic education program and supporting attitudes of community leaders. The result is to level the sociopolitical differences among the three communities and their school populations. Training in the tenets of democratic fair play and

TABLE 3   COMMUNITY 'LEADERS' SUPPORT OF POLITICAL THEMES IN CIVIC EDUCATION PROGRAM

Community Leaders	Democratic Creed	Political Chauvinism	Political Participation
Alpha (66)[a]	87%[b]	7%	89%
Beta (57)	82%	16%	89%
Gamma (63)	78%	21%	87%

	Politics As Process, Power	Politics As Group Conflict
Alpha	72%	68%
Beta	32%	34%
Gamma	24%	21%

[a]Denotes number of cases.
[b]Percent of sample strongly agreeing that theme should be taught in civic education program.

tolerance is sustained by civic education courses within a supporting educational and political milieu.

But civic education does not affect the varying positive attitudes toward citizen political participation manifested by the school population of the three communities. Despite the positive references of civic education material in Alpha and Beta, and the supporting community norms in all three communities, different attitudes—based on sociopolitical cleavages—remain about the citizen's role in public affairs. Apparently attitudes toward political activity are so strongly channeled through other agencies in each community that the civic education program's efforts have little independent effect.

Attitudes toward political process and function are related to other variables in the classroom and community climate. In Alpha, where community attitudes and texts are supportive, a positive change in views of political process and function occurs among students in civic education. In Beta and Gamma, where attitudes and texts are relatively nonsupportive, little change in such views occurs; politics is treated and learned as a formal, mechanistic set of governmental institutions with emphasis on its harmonious and legitimate nature, rather than as a vehicle for group struggle and change.

CONCLUSIONS

The civic education program does not simply reinforce the prevailing sentiments and political climate of the community. Nor are attitudes about political participation and varying levels of political activity affected by courses in civic education. Even a combination of numerous textual references and support from community leaders fails to result in attitude changes about the role of the citizen in public life.

Nevertheless, without some degree of reinforcement from its material and the political environment, the school system's effort at political indoctrination also fails. The materials, support, and effects of civic education differ in the three communities, and it is the nature of these differ-

ences that are crucial in evaluating the political role of citizenship training.

All three classes are instructed in the equalitarian ground rules of democracy. Agreement with the maxims of the democratic creed and rejection of political chauvinism are increased in the civic education programs of all three communities. But the

TABLE 4 EFFECT OF SEMESTER COURSE IN CIVIC EDUCATION ON POLITICAL ATTITUDES IN THREE COMMUNITIES (IN PERCENTAGES)

	Alpha			
	Class		Control	
Political Attitude	Before	After	Before	After
Support of democratic creed	62[a]	89	57	61
Political chauvinism	23	8	19	18
Support of political participation	70	72	79	76
Politics as process of power, politicians	59	72	53	58
Function of politics to resolve group conflict	32	59	39	34
Number of cases	(38)		(44)	

	Beta			
	Class		Control	
Political Attitude	Before	After	Before	After
Democratic creed	56	74	53	50
Political chauvinism	31	19	29	27
Political participation	55	56	54	49
Political process	23	21	27	26
Political group conflict	17	21	19	17
Number of cases	(51)		(46)	

	Gamma			
	Class		Control	
Political Attitude	Before	After	Before	After
Democratic creed	47	59	38	44
Political chauvinism	29	10	33	38
Political participation	32	29	31	33
Political process	12	15	16	14
Political group conflict	9	12	8	6
Number of cases	(59)		(63)	

[a]Denotes percent of sample strongly holding political attitude.

material and effects of the working-class community, Gamma, and its civic education program, do not encourage a belief in the citizen's ability to influence government action through political participation. And only the texts and community support of Alpha are related through its civic education course to a developed awareness of political processes and functions.

In sum, then, students in the three communities are being trained to play different political roles, and to respond to political phenomena in different ways. In the working-class community, where political involvement is low, the arena of civic education offers training in the basic democratic procedures without stressing political participation or the citizen's view of conflict and disagreement as indigenous to the political system. Politics is conducted by formal governmental institutions working in harmony for the benefit of citizens.

In the lower middle-class school system of Beta —a community with moderately active political life—training in the elements of democratic government is supplemented by an emphasis on the responsibilities of citizenship, not on the dynamics of public decision-making.

Only in the affluent and politically vibrant community (Alpha) are insights into political processes and functions of politics passed on to those who, judging from their socioeconomic and political environment, will likely man those positions that involve them in influencing or making political decisions.

APPENDIX

The content analysis of the 27 civic education textbooks was conducted in the following manner. A random sample of paragraphs, as the content unit, was selected from each text. The text was entered by use of a random table of numbers to select page and paragraph. Every twentieth paragraph was read and classified by the writer and two other judges. The criteria of classification are noted in the text. In case of disagreement among the judges, a paragraph was classified in the "other" category. Dominant emphasis, based on sentence counts within paragraphs, was determining when a paragraph contained more than one politically relevant theme. In this manner, 1,235 paragraphs were classified.

Five indices were used in the questionnaire administered to the student populations, and the interview with community leaders. Responses ran across a five-point scale from "agree strongly" to "disagree strongly." Unlike the students, the community leaders were asked whether or not each statement should be included in the civic education program. The content, reliability, and source of the political indices follow.

1. *The Democratic Creed* (coefficient of reliability =.911):
    Every citizen should have an equal chance to influence government policy.
    Democracy is the best form of government.
    The minority should be free to criticize government decisions.
    People in the minority should be free to try to win majority support for their opinions.
    (Adapted from James W. Prothro and Charles M. Grigg, "Fundamental Principles of Democracy: Bases of Agreement and Disagreement," *The Journal of Politics,* **22** (1960), 276–294).

2. *Political Chauvinism* (cr=.932):
    The American political system is a model that foreigners would do well to copy.
    The founding fathers created a blessed and unique republic when they gave us the Constitution.
    Americans are more democratic than any other people.
    American political institutions are the best in the world.
    (Index constructed for this study.)

3. *Political Activity* (cr=.847):
    It is not very important to vote in local elections.
    It is very important to vote even when so many other people vote in an election.
    Public officials do care what people like me think.
    Given the complexity of issues and political organizations, there is little an individual can do to make effective changes in the political system.
    People like me do not have any say about what the government does.
    Politics is often corrupt and the interests of the underworld are looked after by some public officials.
    (Adapted from the civic duty and sense of political effectiveness measures of the Michigan Survey Research Center, and Agger's index of political

E

DGAR LITT 141

cynicism. See Angus Campbell, Gerald Gurin, and Warren E. Miller, *The Voter Decides,* Evanston: Row-Peterson, 1954, pp. 187–204; and Robert E. Agger, Marshall N. Goldstein, and Stanley A. Pearl, "Political Cynicism: Measurement and Meaning," *The Journal of Politics,* **23** (1961), 477–506.)

4. *Political Process* (cr=.873):
    The use of political power is crucial in public affairs.
    Many political decisions are made by a minority of political activists who seek to secure the agreement of the majority to the decisions.
    Politics is basically a conflict in which groups and individuals compete for things of value.
    Differences of race, class, and income are important considerations in many political issues.
    Governmental institutions cannot operate without politicians.
    (Index constructed for this study.)

5. *Political Function* (cr=.919):
    Politics should settle social and other disagreements as its major function.
    Since different groups seek favorable treatment, politics is the vehicle for bargaining among these competing claims.
    Politics is not a means of insuring complete harmony, but a way of arriving at temporary agreements about policies within agreed-upon rules.
    The politician is the key broker among competing claims made within society.
    (Index constructed for this study.)

NOTES

[1] V. O. Key, Jr., *Public Opinion and American Democracy,* New York: Knopf, 1961, p. 316.

[2] Course titles of civic education instruction vary in the three communities. A control group was available in the same schools of Alpha and Gamma where the civic education course was not required. For Beta, a control group was selected from a school in an adjoining, and comparable, community.

[3] Based on procedures developed in Bernard B. Berelson, *Content Analysis in Communications Research,* Glencoe: Free Press, 1952; and Lloyd Marcus, *The Treatment of Minorities in Secondary School Textbooks,* New York: B'nai B'rith Anti-Defamation League, 1961.

[4] The designation "potential civic and educational leaders or influentials" is used because we have no data on overt attempts to influence the school's civic education program. Our immediate concern is with their attitudes toward the political themes in the program. This distinction between manifested and imputed political influence is drawn in Raymond Wolfinger, "Republic and Reality in the Study of Community Power," *American Sociological Review,* **25** (October, 1960), 636–644.

[5] Wherever possible, civic leaders were selected from comparable organizations in each community, such as the Chamber of Commerce and political party organizations. Differences in social structure made complete matching impossible. For example, labor union leaders were included in the Gamma sample, but not in the Alpha or Beta pools. There were 8 nonrespondents or 12 percent of the sample in Alpha, 7 (13 percent) in Beta, and 11 (18 percent) in Gamma.

[6] Bessie L. Pierce, *Civic Attitudes in American Schools,* Chicago: University of Chicago Press, 1930.

MEN AND JOBS

Elliot Liebow

A pickup truck drives slowly down the street. The truck stops as it comes abreast of a man sitting on a cast-iron porch and the white driver calls out, asking if the man wants a day's work. The man shakes his head and the truck moves on up the block, stopping again whenever idling men come within calling distance of the driver. At the Carry-out corner, five men debate the question briefly and shake their heads no to the truck. The truck turns the corner and repeats the same performance up the next street. In the distance, one can see one man, then another, climb into the back of the truck and sit down. In starts and stops, the truck finally disappears.

What is it we have witnessed here? A labor scavenger rebuffed by his would-be prey? Lazy, irresponsible men turning down an honest day's pay for an honest day's work? Or a more complex phenomenon marking the intersection of economic forces, social values and individual states of mind and body?

Let us look again at the driver of the truck. He has been able to recruit only two or three men from each twenty or fifty he contacts. To him, it is clear that the others simply do not choose to work. Singly or in groups, belly-empty or belly-full, sullen or gregarious, drunk or sober, they confirm what he has read, heard, and knows from his own experience: these men wouldn't take a job if it were handed to them on a platter.

Quite apart from the question of whether or not this is true of some of the men he sees on the street, it is clearly not true of all of them. If it were, he would not have come here in the first place; or having come, he would have left with an empty truck. It is not even true of most of them, for most of the men he sees on the street this weekday morning do, in fact, have jobs. But since, at the

moment, they are neither working nor sleeping, and since they hate the depressing room or apartment they live in, or because there is nothing to do there, or because they want to get away from their wives or anyone else living there, they are out on the street, indistinguishable from those who do not have jobs or do not want them. Some, like Boley, a member of a trash-collection crew in a suburban housing development, work Saturdays and are off on this weekday. Some, like Sweets, work nights cleaning up middle-class trash, dirt, dishes, and garbage, and mopping the floors of the office buildings, hotels, restaurants, toilets, and other public places dirtied during the day. Some men work for retail businesses such as liquor stores which do not begin the day until ten o'clock. Some laborers, like Tally, have already come back from the job because the ground was too wet for pick and shovel or because the weather was too cold for pouring concrete. Other employed men stayed off the job today for personal reasons: Clarence to go to a funeral at eleven this morning and Sea Cat to answer a subpoena as a witness in a criminal proceeding.

Also on the street, unwitting contributors to the impression taken away by the truck driver, are the halt and the lame. The man on the cast-iron steps strokes one gnarled arthritic hand with the other and says he doesn't know whether or not he'll live long enough to be eligible for Social Security. He pauses, then adds matter-of-factly, "Most times, I don't care whether I do or don't." Stoopy's left leg was polio-withered in childhood. Raymond, who looks as if he could tear out a fire hydrant, coughs up blood if he bends or moves suddenly. The quiet man who hangs out in front of the Saratoga apartments has a steel hook strapped onto his left elbow. And had the man in the truck been able to look into the wine-clouded eyes of the man in the green cap, he would have realized that the man did not even understand he was being offered a day's work.

Others, having had jobs and been laid off, are drawing unemployment compensation (up to $44 per week) and have nothing to gain by accepting work which pays little more than this and frequently less.

Still others, like Bumdoodle the numbers man, are working hard at illegal ways of making money, hustlers who are on the street to turn a dollar any way they can: buying and selling sex, liquor, narcotics, stolen goods, or anything else that turns up.

Only a handful remains unaccounted for. There is Tonk, who cannot bring himself to take a job away from the corner, because, according to the other men, he suspects his wife will be unfaithful if given the opportunity. There is Stanton, who has not reported to work for four days now, not since Bernice disappeared. He bought a brand new knife against her return. She had done this twice before, he said, but not for so long and not without warning, and he had forgiven her. But this time, "I ain't got it in me to forgive her again." His rage and shame are there for all to see as he paces the Carry-out and the corner, day and night, hoping to catch a glimpse of her.

And finally, there are those like Arthur, able-bodied men who have no visible means of support, legal or illegal, who neither have jobs nor want them. The truck driver, among others, believes the Arthurs to be representative of all the men he sees idling on the street during his own working hours. They are not, but they cannot be dismissed simply because they are a small minority. It is not enough to explain them away as being lazy or irresponsible or both because an able-bodied man with responsibilities who refuses work is, by the truck driver's definition, lazy and irresponsible. Such an answer begs the question. It is descriptive of the facts; it does not explain them.

Moreover, despite their small numbers, the don't-work-and-don't-want-to-work minority is especially significant because they represent the strongest and clearest expression of those values and attitudes associated with making a living which, to varying degrees, are found throughout the streetcorner world. These men differ from the others in degree rather than in kind, the principal difference being that they are carrying out the implications of their values and experiences to their logical, inevitable conclusions. In this sense, the others have yet to come to terms with themselves and the world they live in.

Putting aside, for the moment, what the men say and feel, and looking at what they actually do and the choices they make, getting a job, keeping a job, and doing well at it is clearly of low priority. Arthur will not take a job at all. Leroy is supposed to be on his job at 4:00 P.M. but it is already 4:10 and he still cannot bring himself to leave the free games he has accumulated on the pinball machine in the Carry-out. Tonk started a construction job on Wednesday, worked Thursday and Friday, then didn't go back again. On the same kind of job, Sea Cat quit in the second week. Sweets had been working three months as a busboy in a restaurant, then quit without notice, not sure himself why he did so. A real estate agent, saying he was more interested in getting a job done than in the cost, asked Richard to give him an estimate on repairing and painting the inside of a house, but Richard, after looking over the job, somehow never got around to submitting an estimate. During one period, Tonk would not leave the corner to take a job because his wife might prove unfaithful; Stanton would not take a job because his woman had been unfaithful.

Thus, the man-job relationship is a tenuous one. At any given moment, a job may occupy a relatively low position on the streetcorner scale of real values. Getting a job may be subordinated to relations with women or to other non-job considerations; the commitment to a job one already has is frequently shallow and tentative.

The reasons are many. Some are objective and reside principally in the job; some are subjective and reside principally in the man. The line between them, however, is not a clear one. Behind the man's refusal to take a job or his decision to quit one is not a simple impulse or value choice but a complex combination of assessments of objective reality on the one hand, and values, attitudes and beliefs drawn from different levels of his experience on the other.

Objective economic considerations are frequently a controlling factor in a man's refusal to take a job. How much the job pays is a crucial question but seldom asked. He knows how much it pays. Working as a stock clerk, a delivery boy, or even behind the counter of liquor stores, drug stores and other retail businesses pays one dollar an hour. So, too, do most busboy, car-wash, janitorial and other jobs available to him. Some jobs, such as dishwasher, may dip as low as eighty cents an hour and others, such as elevator operator or work in a junk yard, may offer $1.15 or $1.25. Take-home pay for jobs such as these ranges from $35 to $50 a week, but a take-home pay of over $45 for a five-day week is the exception rather than the rule.

One of the principal advantages of these kinds of jobs is that they offer fairly regular work. Most of them involve essential services and are therefore somewhat less responsive to business conditions than are some higher paying, less menial jobs. Most of them are also inside jobs not dependent on the weather, as are construction jobs and other higher paying outside work.

Another seemingly important advantage of working in hotels, restaurants, office and apartment buildings and retail establishments is that they frequently offer an opportunity for stealing on the job. But stealing can be a two-edged sword. Apart from increasing the cost of the goods or services to the general public, a less obvious result is that the practice usually acts as a depressant on the employee's own wage level. Owners of small retail establishments and other employers frequently anticipate employee stealing and adjust the wage rate accordingly. Tonk's employer explained why he was paying Tonk $35 for a 55–60 hour workweek. These men will all steal, he said. Although he keeps close watch on Tonk, he estimates that Tonk steals from $35 to $40 a week.[1] What he steals, when added to his regular earnings, brings his take-home pay to $70 or $75 per week. The employer said he did not mind this because Tonk is worth that much to the business. But if he were to pay Tonk outright the full value of his labor, Tonk would still be stealing $35–$40 per week and this, he said, the business simple would not support.

This wage arrangement, with stealing built-in, was satisfactory to both parties, with each one independently expressing his satisfaction. Such a wage-theft system, however, is not as balanced and equitable as it appears. Since the wage level rests on the premise that the employee will steal the unpaid value of his labor, the man who does not steal on the job is penalized. And furthermore,

even if he does not steal, no one would believe him; the employer and others believe he steals because the system presumes it.

Nor is the man who steals, as he is expected to, as well off as he believes himself to be. The employer may occasionally close his eyes to the worker's stealing, but not often and not for long. He is, after all, a businessman and cannot always find it within himself to let a man steal from him, even if the man is stealing his own wages. Moreover, it is only by keeping close watch on the worker that the employer can control how much is stolen and thereby protect himself against the employee's stealing more than he is worth. From this viewpoint, then, the employer is not in wage-theft collusion with the employee. In the case of Tonk, for instance, the employer was not actively abetting the theft. His estimate of how much Tonk was stealing was based on what he thought Tonk was able to steal despite his own best efforts to prevent him from stealing anything at all. Were he to have caught Tonk in the act of stealing, he would, of course, have fired him from the job and perhaps called the police as well. Thus, in an actual if not in a legal sense, all the elements of entrapment are present. The employer knowingly provides the conditions which entice (force) the employee to steal the unpaid value of his labor, but at the same time he punishes him for theft if he catches him doing so.

Other consequences of the wage-theft system are even more damaging to the employee. Let us, for argument's sake, say that Tonk is in no danger of entrapment; that his employer is willing to wink at the stealing and that Tonk, for his part, is perfectly willing to earn a little, steal a little. Let us say, too, that he is paid $35 a week and allowed to steal $35. His money income—as measured by the goods and services he can purchase with it—is, of course, $70. But not all of his income is available to him for all purposes. He cannot draw on what he steals to build his self-respect or to measure his self-worth. For this, he can draw only on his earnings—the amount given him publicly and voluntarily in exchange for his labor. His "respect" and "self-worth" income remains at $35—only half that of the man who also receives $70 but all of it in the form of wages. His earnings publicly measure the worth of his labor to his employer, and they are important to others and to himself in taking the measure of his worth as a man.[2]

With or without stealing, and quite apart from any interior processes going on in the man who refuses such a job or quits it casually and without apparent reason, the objective fact is that menial jobs in retailing or in the service trades simply do not pay enough to support a man and his family. This is not to say that the worker is underpaid; this may or may not be true. Whether he is or not, the plain fact is that, in such a job, he cannot make a living. Nor can he take much comfort in the fact that these jobs tend to offer more regular, steadier work. If he cannot live on the $45 or $50 he makes in one week, the longer he works, the longer he cannot live on what he makes.

Construction work, even for unskilled laborers, usually pays better, with the hourly rate ranging from $1.50 to $2.60 an hour.[3] Importantly, too, good references, a good driving record, a tenth grade (or any high school) education, previous experience, the ability to "bring police clearance with you" are not normally required of laborers as they frequently are for some of the jobs in retailing or in the service trades.

Construction work, however, has its own objective disadvantages. It is, first of all, seasonal work for the great bulk of the laborers, beginning early in the spring and tapering off as winter weather sets in.[4] And even during the season the work is frequently irregular. Early or late in the season, snow or temperatures too low for concrete frequently sends the laborers back home, and during late spring or summer, a heavy rain on Tuesday or Wednesday, leaving a lot of water and mud behind it, can mean a two or three day work-week for the pick-and-shovel men and other unskilled laborers.[5]

The elements are not the only hazard. As the project moves from one construction stage to another, laborers—usually without warning—are laid off, sometimes permanently or sometimes for weeks at a time. The more fortunate or the better workers are told periodically to "take a walk for two, three days."

Both getting the construction job and getting to it are also relatively more difficult than is the case for the menial jobs in retailing and the service trades. Job competition is always fierce. In the city, the large construction projects are unionized. One has to have ready cash to get into the union to become eligible to work on these projects and, being eligible, one has to find an opening. Unless one "knows somebody," say a foreman or a laborer who knows the day before that they are going to take on new men in the morning, this can be a difficult and disheartening search.

Many of the nonunion jobs are in suburban Maryland or Virginia. The newspaper ads say, "Report ready to work to the trailer at the intersection of Rte. 11 and Old Bridge Rd., Bunston, Virginia (or Maryland)," but this location may be ten, fifteen, or even twenty-five miles from the Carry-out. Public transportation would require two or more hours to get there, if it services the area at all. Without access to a car or to a car-pool arrangement, it is not worthwhile reading the ad. So the men do not. Jobs such as these are usually filled by word of mouth information, beginning with someone who knows someone or who is himself working there and looking for a paying rider. Furthermore, nonunion jobs in outlying areas tend to be smaller projects of relatively short duration and to pay somewhat less than scale.

Still another objective factor is the work itself. For some men, whether the job be digging, mixing mortar, pushing a wheelbarrow, unloading materials, carrying and placing steel rods for reinforcing concrete, or building or laying concrete forms, the work is simply too hard. Men such as Tally and Wee Tom can make such work look like child's play; some of the older work-hardened men, such as Budder and Stanton, can do it too, although not without showing unmistakable signs of strain and weariness at the end of the workday. But those who lack the robustness of a Tally or the time-inured immunity of a Budder must either forego jobs such as these or pay a heavy toll to keep them. For Leroy, in his early twenties, almost six feet tall but weighing under 140 pounds, it would be as difficult to push a loaded wheelbarrow, or to unload and stack 96-pound bags of cement all day long, as it would be for Stoopy with his withered leg.

Heavy, backbreaking labor of the kind that used to be regularly associated with bull gangs or concrete gangs is no longer characteristic of laboring jobs, especially those with the larger, well-equipped construction companies. Brute strength is still required from time to time, as on smaller jobs where it is not economical to bring in heavy equipment or where the small, undercapitalized contractor has none to bring in. In many cases, however, the conveyor belt has replaced the wheelbarrow or the Georgia buggy, mechanized forklifts have eliminated heavy, manual lifting, and a variety of digging machines have replaced the pick and shovel. The result is fewer jobs for unskilled laborers and, in many cases, a work speed-up for those who do have jobs. Machines now set the pace formerly set by men. Formerly, a laborer pushed a wheelbarrow of wet cement to a particular spot, dumped it, and returned for another load. Another laborer, in hip boots, pushed the wet concrete around with a shovel or a hoe, getting it roughly level in preparation for the skilled finishers. He had relatively small loads to contend with and had only to keep up with the men pushing the wheelbarrows. Now, the job for the man pushing the wheelbarrow is gone and the wet concrete comes rushing down a chute at the man in the hip boots who must "spread it quick or drown."

Men who have been running an elevator, washing dishes, or "pulling trash" cannot easily move into laboring jobs. They lack the basic skills for "unskilled" construction labor, familiarity with tools and materials, and tricks of the trade without which hard jobs are made harder. Previously unused or untrained muscles rebel in pain against the new and insistent demands made upon them, seriously compromising the man's performance and testing his willingness to see the job through.

A healthy, sturdy, active man of good intelligence requires from two to four weeks to break in on a construction job.[6] Even if he is willing somehow to bull his way through the first few weeks, it frequently happens that his foreman or the craftsman he services with materials and general assistance is not willing to wait that long for him to get into condition or to learn at a glance the difference in size between a rough 2" X 8" and a finished 2" X 10". The foreman and the craftsman are themselves "under the gun" and cannot "carry" the man when other men, who are already used to the work and who know the tools and materials, are lined up to take the job.

Sea Cat was "healthy, sturdy, active and of good intelligence." When a judge gave him six weeks in which to pay his wife $200 in back child-support payments, he left his grocery-store job in order to take a higher-paying job as a laborer, arranged for him by a foreman friend. During the first week the weather was bad and he worked only Wednesday and Friday, cursing the elements all the while for cheating him out of the money he could have made. The second week, the weather was fair but he quit at the end of the fourth day, saying frankly that the work was too hard for him. He went back to his job at the grocery store and took a second job working nights as a dishwasher in a restaurant,[7] earning little if any more at the two jobs than he would have earned as a laborer, and keeping at both of them until he had paid off his debts.

Tonk did not last as long as Sea Cat. No one made any predictions when he got a job in a parking lot, but when the men on the corner learned he was to start on a road construction job, estimates of how long he would last ranged from one to three weeks. Wednesday was his first day. He spent that evening and night at home. He did the same on Thursday. He worked Friday and spent Friday evening and part of Saturday draped over the mailbox on the corner. Sunday afternoon, Tonk decided he was not going to report on the job the next morning. He explained that after working three days, he knew enough about the job to know that it was too hard for him. He knew he wouldn't be able to keep up and he'd just as soon quit now as get fired later.

Logan was a tall, two-hundred-pound man in his late twenties. His back used to hurt him only on the job, he said, but now he can't straighten up for increasingly longer periods of time. He said he had traced this to the awkward walk he was forced to adopt by the loaded wheelbarrows which pull him down into a half-stoop. He's going to quit, he said, as soon as he can find another job. If he can't find one real soon, he guesses he'll quit anyway. It's not worth it, having to walk bent over and leaning to one side.

Sometimes, the strain and effort is greater than the man is willing to admit, even to himself. In the early summer of 1963, Richard was rooming at Nancy's place. His wife and children were "in the country" (his grandmother's home in Carolina), waiting for him to save up enough money so that he could bring them back to Washington and start over again after a disastrous attempt to "make it" in Philadelphia. Richard had gotten a job with a fence company in Virginia. It paid $1.60 an hour. The first few evenings, when he came home from work, he looked ill from exhaustion and the heat. Stanton said Richard would have to quit, "he's too small [thin] for that kind of work." Richard said he was doing O.K. and would stick with the job.

At Nancy's one night, when Richard had been working about two weeks, Nancy and three or four others were sitting around talking, drinking, and listening to music. Someone asked Nancy when was Richard going to bring his wife and children up from the country. Nancy said she didn't know, but it probably depended on how long it would take him to save up enough money. She said she didn't think he could stay with the fence job much longer. This morning, she said, the man Richard rode to work with knocked on the door and Richard didn't answer. She looked in his room. Richard was still asleep. Nancy tried to shake him awake. "No more digging!" Richard cried out. "No more digging! I can't do no more God-damn digging!" When Nancy finally managed to wake him, he dressed quickly and went to work.

Richard stayed on the job two more weeks, then suddenly quit, ostensibly because his paycheck was three dollars less than what he thought it should have been.

In summary of objective job considerations, then, the most important fact is that a man who is able and willing to work cannot earn enough money to support himself, his wife, and one or more children. A man's chances for working regularly are good only if he is willing to work for less than he can live on, and sometimes not even then. On some jobs, the wage rate is deceptively higher than on others, but the higher the wage rate, the more difficult it is to get the job, and the less the job security. Higher paying construction work tends to be seasonal and, during the season, the amount of work available is highly sensitive to business and weather conditions and to the changing requirements of individual projects.[8] Moreover, high-paying construction jobs are frequently beyond the physical capacity of some of the men, and some of the low-paying jobs are scaled down even lower in accordance with the self-fulfilling assumption that the man will steal part of his wages on the job.[9]

Bernard assesses the objective job situation dispassionately over a cup of coffee, sometimes poking at the coffee with his spoon, sometimes staring at it as if, like a crystal ball, it holds tomorrow's secrets. He is twenty-seven years old. He and the woman with whom he lives have a baby son, and she has another child by another man. Bernard does odd jobs—mostly painting—but here it is the end of January, and his last job was with the Post Office during the Christmas mail rush. He would like postal work as a steady job, he says. It pays well (about $2.00 an hour), but he has twice failed the Post Office examination (he graduated from a Washington high school) and has given up the idea as an impractical one. He is supposed to see a man tonight about a job as a parking attendant for a large apartment house. The man told him to bring his birth certificate and driver's license, but his license was suspended because of a backlog of unpaid traffic fines. A friend promised to lend him some money this evening. If he gets it, he will pay the fines tomorrow morning and have his license reinstated. He hopes the man with the job will wait till tomorrow night.

A "security job" is what he really wants, he said. He would like to save up money for a taxicab. (But having twice failed the postal examination and having a bad driving record as well, it is highly doubtful that he could meet the qualifications or pass the written test.) That would be "a good life." He can always get a job in a restaurant or as a clerk in a drugstore but they don't pay enough, he said. He needs to take home at least $50 to $55 a week. He thinks he can get that much driving a truck somewhere. . . . Sometimes he wishes he had stayed in the army. . . . A security job, that's what he wants most of all, a real security job. . . .

When we look at what the men bring to the job rather than at what the job offers the men, it is essential to keep in mind that we are not looking at men who come to the job fresh, just out of school perhaps, and newly prepared to undertake the task of making a living, or from another job where they earned a living and are prepared to do the same on this job. Each man comes to the job with a long job history characterized by his not being able to support himself and his family. Each man carries this knowledge, born of his experience, with him. He comes to the job flat and stale, wearied by the sameness of it all, convinced of his own incompetence, terrified of responsibility—of being tested still again and found wanting. Possible exceptions are the younger men not yet, or just, married. They suspect all this but have yet to have it confirmed by repeated personal experience over time. But those who are or have been married know it well. It is the experience of the individual and the group; of their fathers and probably their sons. Convinced of their inadequacies, not only do they not seek out those few better-paying jobs which test their resources, but they actively avoid them, gravitating in a mass to the menial, routine jobs which offer no challenge—and therefore pose no threat—to the already diminished images they have of themselves.

Thus Richard does not follow through on the real estate agent's offer. He is afraid to do on his own —minor plastering, replacing broken windows, other minor repairs and painting—exactly what he had been doing for months on a piecework basis under someone else (and which provided him with a solid base from which to derive a cost estimate).

Richard once offered an important clue to what may have gone on in his mind when the job offer was made. We were in the Carry-out, at a time when he was looking for work. He was talking about the kind of jobs available to him.

I graduated from high school [Baltimore] but I don't know anything. I'm dumb. Most of the time I don't even say I graduated, 'cause then somebody asks me a question and I can't answer it, and they think I was lying about graduating. . . . They graduated me but I didn't know anything. I had lousy grades but I guess they wanted to get rid of me.

I was at Margaret's house the other night and her little sister asked me to help her with her homework. She showed me some fractions and I knew right away I couldn't do them. I was ashamed so I told her I had to go to the bathroom.

And so it must have been, surely, with the real estate agent's offer. Convinced that "I'm dumb . . . I don't know anything," he "knew right away" he couldn't do it, despite the fact that he had been doing just this sort of work all along.

Thus, the man's low self-esteem generates a fear of being tested and prevents him from accepting a job with responsibilities or, once on a job, from staying with it if responsibilities are thrust on him, even if the wages are commensurately higher. Richard refuses such a job, Leroy leaves one, and another man, given more responsibility and more pay, knows he will fail and proceeds to do so, proving he was right about himself all along. The self-fulfilling prophecy is everywhere at work. In a hallway, Stanton, Tonk, and Boley are passing a bottle around. Stanton recalls the time he was in the service. Everything was fine until he attained the rank of corporal. He worried about everything he did then. Was he doing the right thing? Was he doing it well? When would they discover their mistake and take his stripes (and extra pay) away? When he finally lost his stripes, everything was all right again.

Lethargy, disinterest, and general apathy on the job, so often reported by employers, has its street-corner counterpart. The men do not ordinarily talk about their jobs or ask one another about them.[10] Although most of the men know who is or is not working at any given time, they may or may not know what particular job an individual man has. There is no overt interest in job specifics as they relate to this or that person, in large part perhaps because the specifics are not especially relevant. To know that a man is working is to know approximately how much he makes and to know as much as one needs or wants to know about how he makes it. After all, how much difference does it make to know whether a man is pushing a mop and pulling trash in an apartment house, a restaurant, or an office building, or delivering groceries, drugs, or liquor, or, if he's a laborer, whether he's pushing a wheelbarrow, mixing mortar, or digging a hole. So much does one job look like every other that there is little to choose between them. In large part, the job market consists of a narrow range of non-descript chores calling for nondistinctive, un-differentiated, unskilled labor. "A job is a job."

A crucial factor in the streetcorner man's lack of job commitment is the overall value he places on the job. *For his part, the streetcorner man puts no lower value on the job than does the larger society around him.* He knows the social value of the job by the amount of money the employer is willing to pay him for doing it. In a real sense, every payday, he counts in dollars and cents the value placed on the job by society at large. He is no more (and frequently less) ready to quit and look for another job than his employer is ready to fire him and look for another man. Neither the streetcorner man who performs these jobs nor the society which requires him to perform them assesses the job as one "worth doing and worth doing well." Both employee and employer are contemptuous of the job. The employee shows his contempt by his reluctance to accept it or keep it, the employer by paying less than is required to support a family.[11] Nor does the low-wage job offer prestige, respect, interesting work, opportunity for learning or advancement, or any other compensation. With few exceptions, jobs filled by the streetcorner men are at the bottom of the employment ladder in every respect, from wage level to prestige. Typically, they are hard, dirty, uninteresting, and underpaid. The rest of society (whatever its ideal values regarding the dignity of labor) holds the job of the dishwasher or janitor or unskilled laborer in low esteem if not outright contempt.[12] So does the streetcorner man. He cannot do otherwise. He cannot draw from a job those social values which other people do not put into it.

Only occasionally does spontaneous conversation touch on these matters directly. Talk about jobs is usually limited to isolated statements of intention, such as "I think I'll get me another gig [job]," "I'm going to look for a construction job when the weather breaks," or "I'm going to quit. I can't take no more of his shit." Job assessments typically consist of nothing more than a noncommittal shrug and "It's O.K." or "It's a job."

One reason for the relative absence of talk about one's job is, as suggested earlier, that the sameness of job experiences does not bear reiteration. Another and more important reason is the emptiness of the job experience itself. The man sees middle-class occupations as a primary source of prestige, pride, and self-respect; his own job affords him none of these. To think about his job is to see himself as others see him, to remind him of just where he stands in this society. And because society's criteria for placement are generally the same as his own, to talk about his job can trigger a flush of shame and a deep, almost physical ache to change places with someone, almost anyone, else. The desire to be a person in his own right, to be

noticed by the world he lives in, is shared by each of the men on the streetcorner. Whether they articulate this desire (as Tally does below) or not, one can see them position themselves to catch the attention of their fellows in much the same way as plants bend or stretch to catch the sunlight.[13]

Tally and I were in the Carry-out. It was summer, Tally's peak earning season as a cement finisher, a semiskilled job a cut or so above that of the unskilled laborer. His take-home pay during these weeks was well over a hundred dollars—"a lot of bread." But for Tally, who no longer had a family to support, bread was not enough.

"You know that boy came in last night? That Black Moozlem? That's what I ought to be doing. I ought to be in his place."

"What do you mean?"

"Dressed nice, going to [night] school, got a good job."

"He's no better off than you, Tally. You make more than he does."

"It's not the money. [Pause] It's position, I guess. He's got position. When he finish school he gonna be a supervisor. People respect him. . . . Thinking about people with position and education gives me a feeling right here [pressing his fingers into the pit of his stomach]."

"You're educated, too. You have a skill, a trade. You're a cement finisher. You can make a building, pour a sidewalk."

"That's different. Look, can anybody do what you're doing? Can anybody just come up and do your job? Well, in one week I can teach you cement finishing. You won't be as good as me 'cause you won't have the experience but you'll be a cement finisher. That's what I mean. Anybody can do what I'm doing and that's what gives me this feeling. [Long pause] Suppose I like this girl. I go over to her house and I meet her father. He starts talking about what he done today. He talks about operating on somebody and sewing them up and about surgery. I know he's a doctor 'cause of the way he talks. Then she starts talking about what she did. Maybe she's a boss or a supervisor. Maybe she's a lawyer and her father says to me, 'And what do you do, Mr. Jackson?' [Pause] You remember at the courthouse, Lonny's trial? You and the lawyer was talking in the hall? You remember? I just stood there listening. I didn't say a word. You know why? 'Cause I didn't even know what you was talking about. That's happened to me a lot."

"Hell, you're nothing special. That happens to everybody. Nobody knows everything. One man is a doctor, so he talks about surgery. Another man is a teacher, so *he talks about books. But doctors and teachers don't know anything about concrete. You're a cement finisher and that's your specialty."*

"Maybe so, but when was the last time you saw anybody standing around talking about concrete?"

The streetcorner man wants to be a person in his own right, to be noticed, to be taken account of, but in this respect, as well as in meeting his money needs, his job fails him. The job and the man are even. The job fails the man and the man fails the job.

Furthermore, the man does not have any reasonable expectation that, however bad it is, his job will lead to better things. Menial jobs are not, by and large, the starting point of a track system which leads to even better jobs for those who are able and willing to do them. The busboy or dishwasher in a restaurant is not on a job track which, if negotiated skillfully, leads to chef or manager of the restaurant. The busboy or dishwasher who works hard becomes, simply, a hard-working busboy or dishwasher. Neither hard work nor perseverance can conceivably carry the janitor to a sit-down job in the office building he cleans up. And it is the apprentice who becomes the journeyman electrician, plumber, steamfitter, or bricklayer, not the common unskilled Negro laborer.

Thus, the job is not a steppingstone to something better. It is a dead end. It promises to deliver no more tomorrow, next month, or next year than it does today.

Delivering little, and promising no more, the job is "no big thing." The man appears to treat the job in a cavalier fashion, working and not working as the spirit moves him, as if all that matters is the immediate satisfaction of his present appetites, the surrender to present moods, and the indulgence of whims with no thought for the cost, the consequences, the future. To the middle-class observer, this behavior reflects a "present-time orientation" —an "inability to defer gratification." It is this "present-time" orientation—as against the "future orientation" of the middle-class person—that "explains" to the outsider why Leroy chooses to spend the day at the Carry-out rather than report to work; why Richard, who was paid Friday, was drunk Saturday and Sunday and penniless Monday; why Sweets quit his job today because the boss looked at him "funny" yesterday.

But from the inside looking out, what appears as a "present-time" orientation to the outside observer is, to the man experiencing it, as much a future orientation as that of his middle-class counterpart. The difference between the two men lies not so much in their different orientations to time as in their different orientations to future time or, more specifically, to their different futures.

The future orientation of the middle-class person presumes, among other things, a surplus of resources to be invested in the future and a belief that the future will be sufficiently stable both to justify his investment (money in a bank, time and effort in a job, investment of himself in marriage and family, etc.) and to permit the consumption of his investment at a time, place, and manner of his own choosing and to his greater satisfaction. But the streetcorner man lives in a sea of want. He does not, as a rule, have a surplus of resources, either economic or psychological. Gratification of hunger and the desire for simple creature comforts cannot be long deferred. Neither can support for one's flagging self-esteem. Living on the edge of both economic and psychological subsistence, the streetcorner man is obliged to expend all his resources on maintaining himself from moment to moment.[14]

As for the future, the young streetcorner man has a fairly good picture of it. In Richard or Sea Cat or Arthur he can see himself in his middle twenties; he can look at Tally to see himself at thirty, at Wee Tom to see himself in his middle thirties, and at Budder and Stanton to see himself in his forties. It is a future in which everything is uncertain except the ultimate destruction of his hopes and the eventual realization of his fears. The most he can reasonably look forward to is that these things do not come too soon. Thus, when Richard squanders a week's pay in two days it is not because, like an animal or a child, he is "present-time oriented," unaware of, or unconcerned with his future. He does so precisely because he is aware of the future and the hopelessness of it all.

Sometimes this kind of response appears as a conscious, explicit choice. Richard had had a violent argument with his wife. He said he was going to leave her and the children, that he had had enough of everything and could not take any more, and he chased her out of the house. His chest still heaving, he leaned back against the wall in the hallway of his basement apartment.

"I've been scuffling for five years," he said. "I've been scuffling for five years from morning till night. And my kids still don't have anything, my wife don't have anything, and I don't have anything.

"There," he said, gesturing down the hall to a bed, a sofa, a couple of chairs and a television set, all shabby, some broken. "There's everything I have and I'm having trouble holding onto that."

Leroy came in, presumably to petition Richard on behalf of Richard's wife, who was sitting outside on the steps, afraid to come in. Leroy started to say something but Richard cut him short.

"Look, Leroy, don't give me any of that action. You and me are entirely different people. Maybe I look like a boy and maybe I act like a boy sometimes but I got a man's mind. You and me don't want the same things out of life. Maybe some of the same, but you don't care how long you have to wait for yours and I—want—mine—right—now." [15]

Thus, apparent present-time concerns with consumption and indulgences—material and emotional—reflect a future-time orientation. "I want mine right now" is ultimately a cry of despair, a direct response to the future as he sees it. [16]

In many instances, it is precisely the streetcorner man's orientation to the future—but to a future loaded with "trouble"—which not only leads to a greater emphasis on present concerns ("I want mine right now") but also contributes importantly to the instability of employment, family and friend relationships, and to the general transient quality of daily life.

Let me give some concrete examples. One day, after Tally had gotten paid, he gave me four twenty-dollar bills and asked me to keep them for him. Three days later he asked me for the money. I returned it and asked why he did not put his money in a bank. He said that the banks close at two o'clock. I argued that there were four or more banks within a two-block radius of where he was working at the time and that he could easily get to any one of them on his lunch hour. "No, man," he said, "you don't understand. They close at two o'clock and they closed Saturday and Sunday. Suppose I get into trouble and I got to make it [leave]. Me get out of town, and everything I got in the world layin' up in that bank? No good! No good!"

In another instance, Leroy and his girlfriend were discussing "trouble." Leroy was trying to decide how best to go about getting his hands on some "long green" (a lot of money), and his girlfriend cautioned him about "trouble." Leroy sneered at this, saying he had had "trouble" all his life and wasn't afraid of a little more. "Anyway," he said, "I'm famous for leaving town." [17]

Thus, the constant awareness of a future loaded with "trouble" results in a constant readiness to leave, to "make it," to "get out of town," and discourages the man from sinking roots into the world he lives in. Just as it discourages him from putting money in the bank, so it discourages him from committing himself to a job, especially one whose payoff lies in the promise of future rewards rather than in the present. In the same way, it discourages him from deep and lasting commitments to family and friends or to any other persons, places or things, since such commitments could hold him hostage, limiting his freedom of movement, and thereby compromising his security which lies in that freedom.

What lies behind the response to the driver of the pickup truck, then, is a complex combination of attitudes and assessments. The streetcorner man is under continuous assault by his job experiences and job fears. His experiences and fears feed on one another. The kind of job he can get—and frequently only after fighting for it, if then—steadily confirms his fears, depresses his self-confidence and self-esteem until finally, terrified of an opportunity even if one presents itself, he stands defeated by his experiences, his belief in his own self-worth destroyed and his fears a confirmed reality.

NOTES

[1] Exactly the same estimate as the one made by Tonk himself. On the basis of personal knowledge of the stealing routine employed by Tonk, however, I suspect the actual amount is considerably smaller.

[2] Some public credit may accrue to the clever thief, but not respect.

[3] The higher amount is 1962 union scale for building laborers. According to the Wage Agreement Contract for

Heavy Construction Laborers (Washington, D.C., and vicinity) covering the period from May 1, 1963 to April 30, 1966, minimum hourly wage for heavy construction laborers was to go from $2.75 (May 1963) by annual increments to $2.92, effective November 1, 1965.

[4]"Open-sky" work, such as building overpasses, highways, etc., in which the workers and materials are directly exposed to the elements, traditionally begins in March and ends around Thanksgiving. The same is true for much of the street repair work and the laying of sewer, electric, gas, and telephone lines by the city and public utilities, all important employers of laborers. Between Thanksgiving and March, they retain only skeleton crews selected from their best, most reliable men.

[5]In a recent year, the crime rate in Washington for the month of August jumped 18 percent over the preceding month. A veteran police officer explained the increase to David L. Bazelon, Chief Judge, U.S. Court of Appeals for the District of Columbia. "It's quite simple. . . . You see, August was a very wet month. . . . These people wait on the street corner each morning around 6:00 or 6:30 for a truck to pick them up and take them to a construction site. If it's raining, that truck doesn't come, and the men are going to be idle that day. If the bad weather keeps up for three days . . . we know we are going to have trouble on our hands—and sure enough, there invariably follows a rash of purse-snatchings, house-breakings and the like. . . . These people have to eat like the rest of us, you know." David L. Bazelon, Address to the Federal Bar Association, p. 3.

[6]Estimate of Mr. Francis Greenfield, President of the International Hod Carriers, Building and Common Laborers' District Council of Washington, D.C., and Vicinity. I am indebted to Mr. Greenfield for several points in these paragraphs dealing with construction laborers.

[7]Not a sinecure, even by streetcorner standards.

[8]The overall result is that, in the long run, a Negro laborer's earnings are not substantially greater—and may be less—than those of the busboy, janitor, or stock clerk. . . .

[9]For an excellent discussion of the self-fulfilling assumption (or prophecy) as a social force, see "The Self-Fulfilling Prophecy," Chap. 11, in Robert K. Merton's Social Theory and Social Structure.

[10]This stands in dramatic contrast to the leisure-time conversation of stable, working-class men. For the coal miners (of Ashton, England), for example, "the topic [of conversation] which surpasses all others in frequency is work—the difficulties which have been encountered in the day's shift, the way in which a particular task was accomplished, and so on." Josephine Klein, Samples from English Cultures, Vol. I.

[11]It is important to remember that the employer is not entirely a free agent. Subject to the constraints of the larger society, he acts for the larger society as well as for himself. Child labor laws, safety, and sanitation regulations, minimum wage scales in some employment areas, and other constraints, are already on the books; other control mechanisms, such as a guaranteed annual wage, are to be had for the voting.

[12]See, for example, the U.S. Bureau of the Census, Methodology and Scores of Socioeconomic Status. The assignment of the lowest SES ratings to men who hold such jobs is not peculiar to our own society. A low SES rating for "the shoeshine boy or garbage man . . . seems to be true for all [industrial] countries."

[13]Sea Cat cuts his pants legs off at the calf and puts a fringe on the raggedy edges. Tonk breaks his "shades" and continues to wear the horn-rimmed frames minus the lenses. Richard cultivates a distinctive manner of speech. Lonny gives himself a birthday party. And so on.

[14]And if, for the moment, he does sometimes have more money than he chooses to spend or more food than he wants to eat, he is pressed to spend the money and eat the food anyway since his friends, neighbors, kinsmen, or acquaintances will beg or borrow whatever surplus he has or, failing this, they may steal it.

[15]This was no simple rationalization for irresponsibility. Richard had indeed "been scuffling for five years" trying to keep his family going. Until shortly after this episode, Richard was known and respected as one of the hardest-working men on the street. . . . At the time of this episode, Leroy was just starting marriage and raising a family. He and Richard were not, as Richard thought, "entirely different people." Leroy had just not learned, by personal experience over time, what Richard had learned. But within two years Leroy's marriage had broken up and he was talking and acting like Richard. "He just let go completely," said one of the men on the street.

[16]There is no mystically intrinsic connection between "present-time" orientation and lower-class persons. Whenever people of whatever class have been uncertain, skeptical, or downright pessimistic about the future, "I want mine right now" has been one of the characteristic responses. . . . It seems that future-time orientation tends to collapse toward the present when persons are in pain or under stress. The point is that, the label notwithstanding, (what passes for) present-time orientation appears to be a situation-specific phenomenon rather than a part of the standard psychic equipment of Cognitive Lower-Class Man.

[17]And proceeded to do just that the following year when "trouble"—in this case, a grand jury indictment, a pile of debts, and a violent separation from his wife and children—appeared again.

SOCIAL CONTROL IN THE NEWSROOM: A FUNCTIONAL ANALYSIS

Warren Breed

Top leaders in formal organizations are makers of policy, but they must also secure and maintain conformity to that policy at lower levels. The situation of the newspaper publisher is a case in point. As owner or representative of ownership, he has the nominal right to set the paper's policy and see that staff activities are coordinated so that the policy is enforced. In actuality the problem of control is less simple, as the literature of "human relations" and informal group studies and of the professions[1] suggests.

Ideally, there would be no problem of either "control" or "policy" on the newspaper in a full democracy. The only controls would be the nature of the event and the reporter's effective ability to describe it. In practice, we find the publisher does set news policy, and this policy is usually followed by members of his staff. Conformity is *not* automatic, however, for three reasons: (1) the existence of ethical journalistic norms; (2) the fact that staff subordinates (reporters, etc.) tend to have more "liberal" attitudes (and therefore perceptions) than the publisher and could invoke the norms to justify antipolicy writing; and (3) the ethical taboo preventing the publisher from commanding subordinates to follow policy. How policy comes to be maintained, and where it is bypassed, is the subject of this paper.

Several definitions are required at this point. As to personnel, "newsmen" can be divided into two main categories. "Executives" include the publisher and his editors. "Staffers" are reporters, rewrite men, copy readers, etc. In between there may be occasional city editors or wire editors who

occupy an interstitial status. "Policy" may be defined as the more or less consistent orientation shown by a paper, not only in its editorials but in its news columns and headlines as well, concerning selected issues and events. "Slanting" almost never means prevarication. Rather, it involves omission, differential selection, and preferential placement, such as "featuring" a propolicy item, "burying" an antipolicy story in an inside page, etc. "Professional norms" are of two types: technical norms deal with the operations of efficient news gathering, writing, and editing; ethical norms embrace the newsman's obligation to his readers and to his craft and include such ideals as responsibility, impartiality, accuracy, fair play, and objectivity.[2]

Every newspaper has a policy, admitted or not.[3] One paper's policy may be pro-Republican, cool to labor, antagonistic to the school board, etc. The principal areas of policy are politics, business, and labor; much of it stems from considerations of class. Policy is manifested in "slanting." Just what determines any publisher's policy is a large question and will not be discussed here. Certainly, however, the publisher has much say (often in veto form) in both long-term and immediate policy decisions (which party to support, whether to feature or bury a story of imminent labor trouble, how much free space to give "news" of advertisers' doings, etc.). Finally, policy is covert, due to the existence of ethical norms of journalism; policy often contravenes these norms. No executive is willing to risk embarrassment by being accused of open commands to slant a news story.

While policy is set by the executives, it is clear that they cannot personally gather and write the news by themselves. They must delegate these tasks to staffers, and at this point the attitudes or

From Social Forces, *Vol. 33 (1955). Reprinted by permission of* Social Forces, *University of North Carolina Press. Footnotes have been edited.*

interests of staffers may—and often do—conflict with those of the executives. Of 72 staffers interviewed, 42 showed that they held more liberal views than those contained in their publisher's policy; 27 held similar views, and only 3 were more conservative. Similarly, only 17 of 61 staffers said they were Republicans. The discrepancy is more acute when age (and therefore years of newspaper experience) is held constant. Of the 46 staffers under 35 years of age, 34 showed more liberal orientations; older men had apparently "mellowed." It should be noted that data as to intensity of attitudes are lacking. Some staffers may disagree with policy so mildly that they conform and feel no strain. The present essay is pertinent only insofar as dissident newsmen are forced to make decisions from time to time about their relationship to policy.[4]

We will now examine more closely the workings of the newspaper staff. The central question will be: How is policy maintained, despite the fact that it often contravenes journalistic norms, that staffers often personally disagree with it, and that executives cannot legitimately command that it be followed? The frame of reference will be that of functional analysis, as embodied in Merton's paradigm.[5]

The present data come from the writer's newspaper experience and from intensive interviews with some 120 newsmen, mostly in the northeastern quarter of the country. The sample was not random and no claim is made for representativeness, but on the other hand no paper was selected or omitted purposely and in no case did a newsman refuse the request that he be interviewed. The newspapers were chosen to fit a "middle-sized" group, defined as those with 10,000 to 100,000 daily circulation. Interviews averaged well over an hour in duration.

There is an "action" element inherent in the present subject—the practical democratic need for "a free and responsible press" to inform citizens about current issues. Much of the criticism of the press stems from the slanting induced by the bias of the publisher's policy.[6] This criticism is often directed at flagrant cases such as the Hearst press, the *Chicago Tribune,* and New York tabloids, but also applies, in lesser degree, to the more conventional press. The description of mechanisms of policy maintenance may suggest why this criticism is often fruitless, at least in the short-run sense.

HOW THE STAFFER LEARNS POLICY

The first mechanism promoting conformity is the "socialization" of the staffer with regard to the norms of his job. When the new reporter starts work he is not told what policy is. Nor is he ever told. This may appear strange, but interview after interview confirmed the condition. The standard remark was "Never, in my ___ years on this paper, have I ever been told how to slant a story." No paper in the survey had a "training" program for its new men; some issue a "style" book, but this deals with literary style, not policy. Further, newsmen are busy and have little time for recruit training. Yet all but the newest staffers know what policy is. On being asked, they say they learn it "by osmosis." Sociologically, this means they become socialized and "learn the ropes" like a neophyte in any subculture. Basically, the learning of policy is a process by which the recruit discovers and internalizes the rights and obligations of his status and its norms and values. He learns to anticipate what is expected of him so as to win rewards and avoid punishments. Policy is an important element of the newsroom norms, and he learns it in much the following way.

The staffer reads his own paper every day; some papers *require* this. It is simple to diagnose the paper's characteristics. Unless the staffer is naive or unusually independent, he tends to fashion his own stories after others he sees in the paper. This is particularly true of the newcomer. The news columns and editorials are a guide to the local norms. Thus a southern reporter notes that Republicans are treated in a "different" way in his paper's news columns than Democrats. The news about whites and Negroes is also of a distinct sort. Should he then write about one of these groups, his story will tend to reflect what he has come to define as standard procedure.

Certain editorial actions taken by editors and

older staffers also serve as controlling guides. "If things are blue-penciled consistently," one reporter said, "you learn he [the editor] has a prejudice in that regard."[7] Similarly an executive may occasionally reprimand a staffer for policy violation. From our evidence, the reprimand is frequently oblique, due to the covert nature of policy, but learning occurs nevertheless. One staffer learned much through a series of incidents:

I heard [a union] was going out on strike, so I kept on it; then the boss said something about it, and well—I took the hint and we had less coverage of the strike forming. It was easier that way. We lost the story, but what can you do?

We used a yarn on a firm that was coming to town, and I got dragged out of bed for that. The boss is interested in this industrial stuff—we have to clear it all through him. He's an official in the Chamber. So . . . after a few times, it's irritating, so I get fed up. I try to figure out what will work best. I learn to try and guess what the boss will want.

In fairness it should be noted that this particular publisher was one of the most dictatorial encountered in the study. The pattern of control through reprimand, however, was found consistently. Another staffer wrote, on his own initiative, a series about discrimination against Jews at hotel resorts.

It was the old "Gentlemen's Agreement" stuff, documented locally. The boss called me in . . . didn't like the stuff . . . the series never appeared. You start to get the idea. . . .

Note that the boss does not "command"; the direction is more subtle. Also, it seems that most policy indications from executives are negative. They veto by a nod of the head, as if to say, "Please don't rock the boat." Exceptions occur in the "campaign" story, which will be discussed later. It is also to be noted that punishment is implied if policy is not followed.

Staffers also obtain guidance from their knowledge of the characteristics, interests, and affiliations of their executives. This knowledge can be gained in several ways. One is gossip. A reporter said:

Do we gossip about the editors? Several of us used to meet—somewhere off the beaten path—over a beer—and talk for an hour. We'd rake 'em over the coals.

Another point of contact with executives is the news conference (which on middle-sized papers is seldom *called* a news conference), wherein the staffer outlines his findings and executives discuss how to shape the story. The typical conference consists of two persons, the reporter and the city editor, and can amount to no more than a few words. (Reporter: "One hurt in auto accident uptown." City editor: "Okay, keep it short.") If policy is at stake, the conference may involve several executives and require hours of consideration. From such meetings, the staffer can gain insight through what is said and what is not said by executives. It is important to say here that policy is not stated explicitly in the news conference nor elsewhere, with few exceptions. The news conference actually deals mostly with journalistic matters, such as reliability of information, newsworthiness, possible "angles," and other news tactics.

Three other channels for learning about executives are house organs (printed for the staff by syndicates and larger papers), observing the executive as he meets various leaders, and hearing him voice an opinion. One staffer could not help but gain an enduring impression of his publisher's attitudes in this incident:

I can remember [him] saying on election night [1948], when it looked like we had a Democratic majority in both houses, "My God, this means we'll have a labor government." (Q: How did he say it?) He had a real note of alarm in his voice; you couldn't miss the point that he'd prefer the Republicans.

It will be noted that in speaking of "how" the staffer learns policy, there are indications also as to "why" he follows it.

REASONS FOR CONFORMING TO POLICY

There is no one factor which creates conformity-mindedness, unless we resort to a summary term such as "institutionalized statuses" or "structural roles." Particular factors must be sought in particular cases. The staffer must be seen in terms of his status and aspirations, the structure of the newsroom organization and of the larger society. He also must be viewed with reference to the operations he performs through his workday, and their consequences for him. The following six reasons appear to stay the potentially intransigent staffer from acts of deviance—often, if not always.[8]

Institutional Authority and Sanctions

The publisher ordinarily owns the paper and from a purely business standpoint has the right to expect obedience of his employees. He has the power to fire or demote for transgressions. This power, however, is diminished markedly in actuality by three facts. First, the newspaper is not conceived as a purely business enterprise, due to the protection of the First Amendment and a tradition of professional public service. Secondly, firing is a rare phenomenon on newspapers. For example, one editor said he had fired two men in 12 years; another could recall four firings in his 15 years on that paper. Thirdly, there are severance pay clauses in contracts with the American Newspaper Guild (CIO). The only effective causes for firing are excessive drunkenness, sexual dalliance, etc. Most newspaper unemployment apparently comes from occasional economy drives on large papers and from total suspensions of publication. Likewise, only one case of demotion was found in the survey. It is true, however, that staffers still fear punishment; the myth has the errant star reporter taken off murders and put on obituaries—"the Chinese torture chamber" of the newsroom. Fear of sanctions, rather than their invocation, is a reason for conformity, but not as potent a one as would seem at first glance.

Editors, for their part, can simply ignore stories which might create deviant actions, and when this is impossible, can assign the story to a "safe" staffer. In the infrequent case that an antipolicy story reaches the city desk, the story is changed; extraneous reasons, such as the pressure of time and space, are given for the change.[9] Finally, the editor may contribute to the durability of policy by insulating the publisher from policy discussions. He may reason that the publisher would be embarrassed to hear of conflict over policy and the resulting bias, and spare him the resulting uneasiness; thus the policy remains not only covert but undiscussed and therefore unchanged.[10]

Feelings of Obligation and Esteem for Superiors

The staffer may feel obliged to the paper for having hired him. Respect, admiration, and gratitude may be felt for certain editors who have perhaps schooled him, "stood up for him," or supplied favors of a more paternalistic sort. Older staffers who have served as models for newcomers or who have otherwise given aid and comfort are due return courtesies. Such obligations and warm personal sentiments toward superiors play a strategic role in the pull to conformity.

Mobility Aspirations

In response to a question about ambition, all the younger staffers showed wishes for status achievement. There was agreement that bucking policy constituted a serious bar to this goal. In practice, several respondents noted that a good tactic toward advancement was to get "big" stories on Page One; this automatically means no tampering with policy. Further, some staffers see newspapering as a "steppingstone" job to more lucrative work: public relations, advertising, free-lancing, etc. The reputation for troublemaking would inhibit such climbing.

A word is in order here about chances for upward mobility. Of 51 newsmen aged 35 or more, 32 were executives. Of 50 younger men, 6 had reached executive posts and others were on their way up with such jobs as wire editors, political reporters, etc. All but five of these young men were college graduates, as against just half of their elders. Thus there is no evidence of a "break in the skill hierarchy" among newsmen.

Absence of Conflicting Group Allegiance

The largest formal organization of staffers is the American Newspaper Guild. The Guild, much as it might wish to, has not interfered with internal matters such as policy. It has stressed business unionism and political interests external to the newsroom. As for informal groups, there is no evidence available that a group of staffers has ever "ganged up" on policy.

The Pleasant Nature of the Activity

IN-GROUPNESS IN THE NEWSROOM.   The staffer has a low formal status vis-à-vis executives, but he is not treated as a "worker." Rather, he is a co-worker with executives; the entire staff cooperates congenially on a job they all like and respect: getting the news. The newsroom is a friendly, first-namish place. Staffers discuss stories with editors on a give-and-take basis. Top executives with their own offices sometimes come out and sit in on newsroom discussions.[11]

REQUIRED OPERATIONS ARE INTERESTING.   Newsmen like their work. Few voiced complaints when given the opportunity to gripe during interviews. The operations required—witnessing, interviewing, briefly mulling the meanings of events, checking facts, writing—are not onerous.

NONFINANCIAL PERQUISITES.   These are numerous: the variety of experience, eye-witnessing significant and interesting events, being the first to know, getting "the inside dope" denied laymen, meeting and sometimes befriending notables and celebrities (who are well-advised to treat newsmen with deference). Newsmen are close to big decisions without having to make them; they touch power without being responsible for its use. From talking with newsmen and reading their books, one gets the impression that they are proud of being newsmen. There are tendencies to exclusiveness within news ranks, and intimations that such near outgroups as radio newsmen are entertainers, not real newsmen. Finally, there is the satisfaction of being a member of a live-wire organization dealing with important matters. The newspaper is an "institution" in the community. People talk about it and quote it; its big trucks whiz through town; its columns carry the tidings from big and faraway places, with pictures.

Thus, despite his relatively low pay, the staffer feels, for all these reasons, an integral part of a going concern. His job morale is high. Many newsmen could qualify for jobs paying more money in advertising and public relations, but they remain with the newspaper.

News Becomes a Value

Newsmen define their job as producing a certain quantity of what is called "news" every 24 hours. This is to be produced *even though nothing much has happened.* News is a continuous challenge, and meeting this challenge is the newsman's job. He is rewarded for fulfilling this, his manifest function. A consequence of this focus on news as a central value is the shelving of a strong interest in objectivity at the point of policy conflict. Instead of mobilizing their efforts to establish objectivity over policy as the criterion for performance, their energies are channeled into getting more news. The demands of competition (in cities where there are two or more papers) and speed enhance this focus. Newsmen do talk about ethics, objectivity, and the relative worth of various papers, but not when there is news to get. News comes first, and there is always news to get.[12] They are not rewarded for analyzing the social structure, but for getting news. It would seem that this instrumental orientation diminishes their moral potential. A further consequence of this pattern is that the harmony between staffers and executives is cemented by their common interest in news. Any potential conflict between the two groups, such as slowdowns occurring among informal work groups in industry, would be dissipated to the extent that news is a positive value. The newsroom solidarity is thus reinforced.

The six factors promote policy conformity. To state more exactly how policy is maintained would be difficult in view of the many variables contained in the system. The process may be somewhat better understood, however, with the introduction of one further concept—the reference group. The staffer, especially the new staffer, identifies himself through the existence of these six factors with the executives and veteran staffers. Although not yet one of them, he shares their norms, and thus his performance comes to resemble theirs. He conforms to the norms of policy rather than to whatever personal beliefs he brought to the job, or to ethical ideals. All six of these factors function to encourage reference group formation. Where the allegiance is directed toward legitimate authority, that authority has only to maintain the equilibrium within limits by the prudent distribution of rewards and punishments. The reference group itself, which has as its "magnet" element the elite of executives and old staffers, is unable to change policy to a marked degree because first, it is the group charged with carrying out policy, and second, because the policy maker, the publisher, is often insulated on the delicate issue of policy.

In its own way, each of the six factors contributes to the formation of reference group behavior. There is almost no firing, hence a steady expectation of continued employment. Subordinates tend to esteem their bosses, so a convenient model group is present. Mobility aspirations (when held within limits) are an obvious promoter of inter-status bonds as is the absence of conflicting group loyalties with their potential harvest of cross pressures. The newsroom atmosphere is charged with the related factors of in-groupness and pleasing nature of the work. Finally, the agreement among newsmen that their job is to fasten upon the news, seeing it as a value in itself, forges a bond across status lines.

As to the six factors, five appear to be relatively constant, occurring on all papers studied. The varying factor is the second: obligation and esteem held by staffers for executives and older staffers. On some papers, this obligation-esteem entity was found to be larger than on others. Where it was large, the paper appeared to have two characteristics pertinent to this discussion. First, it did a good conventional job of news-getting and news-publishing, and second, it had little difficulty over policy. With staffers drawn toward both the membership and the reference groups, organization was efficient. Most papers are like this. On the few smaller papers where executives and older staffers are not respected, morale is spotty; staffers withhold enthusiasm from their stories, they cover their beats perfunctorily, they wish for a job on a better paper, and they are apathetic and sometimes hostile to policy. Thus the obligation-esteem factor seems to be the active variable in determining not only policy conformity, but morale and good news performance as well.

SITUATIONS PERMITTING DEVIATION

Thus far it would seem that the staffer enjoys little "freedom of the press." To show that this is an oversimplification, and more important, to suggest a kind of test for our hypothesis about the strength of policy, let us ask: "What happens when a staffer *does* submit an antipolicy story?" We know that this happens infrequently, but what follows in these cases?

The process of learning policy crystallizes into a process of social control, in which deviations are punished (usually gently) by reprimand, cutting one's story, the withholding of friendly comment by an executive, etc. For example, it is punishment for a staffer when the city editor waves a piece of his copy at him and says, "Joe, don't *do* that when you're writing about the mayor." In an actual case, a staffer acting as wire editor was demoted when he neglected to feature a story about a "sacred cow" politician on his paper. What can be concluded is that when an executive sees a clearly antipolicy item, he blue-pencils it, and this constitutes a lesson for the staffer. Rarely does the staffer persist in violating policy; no such case appeared in all the interviews. Indeed, the best-known cases of firing for policy reasons—Ted O. Thackrey and Leo Huberman—occurred on liberal New York City dailies, and Thackrey was an editor, not a staffer.

Now and then cases arise in which a staffer finds his antipolicy stories printed. There seems to be no consistent explanation for this, except to introduce two more specific subjects dealing first, with the staffer's career line, and second, with particular empirical conditions associated with the career line. We can distinguish three stages through which the staffer progresses. First, there is the cub stage, the first few months or years in which the new man learns techniques and policy. He writes short, non-policy stories, such as minor accidents, meeting activity, the weather, etc. The second, or "wiring-in" stage, sees the staffer continuing to assimilate the newsroom values and to cement informal relationships. Finally there is the "star" or "veteran" stage, in which the staffer typically defines himself as a full, responsible member of the group, sees its goals as his, and can be counted on to handle policy sympathetically.[13]

To further specify the conformity-deviation problem, it must be understood that newspapering is a relatively complex activity. The newsman is responsible for a range of skills and judgments which are matched only in the professional and entrepreneurial fields. Oversimplifications about policy rigidity can be avoided if we ask, *"Under what conditions* can the staffer defy or by-pass policy?"* We have already seen that staffers are free to argue news decisions with executives in brief "news conferences," but the arguments generally revolve around points of "newsiness," rather than policy as such. Five factors appear significant in the area of the reporter's power to by-pass policy.

1. The norms of policy are not always entirely clear, just as many norms are vague and unstructured. Policy is covert by nature and has large scope. The paper may be Republican, but standing only lukewarm for Republican Candidate A who may be too "liberal" or no friend of the publisher. Policy, if worked out explicitly, would have to include motivations, reasons, alternatives, historical developments, and other complicating material. Thus a twilight zone permitting a range of deviation appears.[14]

2. Executives may be ignorant of particular facts, and staffers who do the leg (and telephone) work to gather news can use their superior knowledge to subvert policy. On grounds of both personal belief and professional codes, the staffer has the option of selection at many points. He can decide whom to interview and whom to ignore, what questions to ask, which quotations to note, and on writing the story which items to feature (with an eye toward the headline), which to bury, and in general what tone to give the several possible elements of the story.

3. In addition to the "squeeze" tactic exploiting executives' ignorance of minute facts, the "plant" may be employed. Although a paper's policy may proscribe a certain issue from becoming featured, a staffer, on getting a good story about that issue, may "plant" it in another paper or wire service through a friendly staffer and submit it to his own editor, pleading the story is now too big to ignore.

4. It is possible to classify news into four types on the basis of source of origination. These are: the policy or campaign story, the assigned story, the beat story, and the story initiated by the staffer.

The staffer's autonomy is larger with the latter than the former types. With the campaign story (build new hospital, throw rascals out, etc.), the staffer is working directly under executives and has little leeway. An assigned story is handed out by the city editor and thus will rarely hit policy head on, although the staffer has some leverage of selection. When we come to the beat story, however, it is clear that the function of the reporter changes. No editor comes between him and his beat (police department, city hall, etc.); thus the reporter gains the "editor" function. It is he who, to a marked degree, can select which stories to pursue, which to ignore. Several cases developed in interviews of beat men who smothered stories they knew would provide fuel for policy—policy they personally disliked or thought injurious to the professional code. The cooperation of would-be competing reporters is essential, of course. The fourth type of story is simply one which the staffer originates, independent of assignment or beat. All respondents, executives, and staffers averred that any employee was free to initiate stories. But equally regularly, they acknowledged that the opportunity was not often assumed. Staffers were already overloaded with beats, assignments, and routine coverage, and besides, rewards for initiated stories were meager or nonexistent unless the initiated story confirmed policy. Yet this area promises much, should staffers pursue their advantage. The outstanding case in the present study concerned a well-educated, enthusiastic reporter on a conventional daily just north of the Mason-Dixon line. Entirely on his own, he consistently initiated stories about Negroes and Negro-white relations, "making" policy where only void had existed. He worked overtime to document and polish the stories; his boss said he didn't agree with the idea but insisted on the reporter's right to publish them.

5. Staffers with "star" status can transgress policy more easily than cubs. This differential privilege of status was encountered on several papers. An example would be Walter Winchell during the Roosevelt administration, who regularly praised the president while the policy of his boss, Mr. Hearst, was strongly critical of the regime. A *New York Times* staffer said he doubted that any copy reader on the paper would dare change a word of the copy of Meyer Berger, the star feature writer.

These five factors indicate that given certain conditions, the controls making for policy conformity can be bypassed. These conditions exist not only within the newsroom and the news situation but within the staffer as well; they will be exploited only if the staffer's attitudes permit. There are some limitations, then, on the strength of the publisher's policy.

NOTES

[1] See, for instance, F. J. Roethlisberger and William J. Dickson, *Management and the Worker,* Cambridge: Harvard University Press, 1947; and Logan Wilson, *The Academic Man,* New York: Oxford University Press, 1942.

[2] The best-known formal code is The Canons of Journalism, of the American Society of Newspaper Editors. See Wilbur Schramm (ed.), *Mass Communications,* Urbana: University of Illinois Press, 1949, pp. 236–238.

[3] It is extremely difficult to measure the extent of objectivity or bias. One recent attempt is reported in Nathan B. Blumberg, *One-Party Press?* Lincoln: University of Nebraska Press, 1954. . . . It should be noted, too, that there are different areas of policy depending on local conditions. The chief difference occurs in the deep South, where frequently there is no "Republican" problem and no "union" problem over which the staff can be divided. Color becomes the focus of policy.

[4] It is not being argued that "liberalism" and objectivity are synonymous. A liberal paper can be biased too, but it is clear that few liberal papers exist among the many conservative ones. It should also be stressed that much news is not concerned with policy and is therefore probably unbiased.

[5] Robert K. Merton, *Social Theory and Social Structure,* Glencoe: Free Press, 1949, esp. pp. 49–61. Merton's elements will not be explicitly referred to but his principal requirements are discussed at various points.

[6] For a summary description of this criticism, see Commission on the Freedom of the Press, *A Free and Responsible Press,* Chicago: University of Chicago Press, 1947, Chap. 4.

[7] While the concept of policy is crucial to this analysis, it is not to be assumed that newsmen discuss it fully. Some do not even use the word in discussing how their paper is run. To this extent, policy is a latent phenomenon; either the staffer has no reason to contemplate policy or he chooses to avoid so doing. It may be that one strength of policy is that it has become no more manifest to the staffers who follow it.

Note that such executives' actions as blue-pencilling play not only the manifest function of preparing the story for publication but also the latent one of steering the future action of the staffer.

[8] Two cautions are in order here. First, it will be recalled that we are discussing not all news, but only policy news. Secondly, we are discussing only staffers who are potential nonconformers. Some agree with policy; some have no views on policy matters; others do not write policy stories. Furthermore, there are strong forces in American society which cause many individuals to choose harmonious adjustment (conformity) in any situation, regardless of the imperatives. See Erich Fromm, *Escape From Freedom,* New York: Farrar and Rinehart, 1941; and David Riesman, *The Lonely Crowd,* New Haven: Yale, 1950.

[9] Excellent illustration of this tactic is given in the novel by an experienced newspaperwoman: Margaret Long, *Affair of the Heart,* New York: Random House, 1953, Chap. 10. This chapter describes the framing of a Negro for murder in a middle-sized southern city, and the attempt of a reporter to tell the story objectively.

[10] The insulation of one individual or group from another is a good example of social (as distinguished from psychological) mechanisms to reduce the likelihood of conflict. Most of the factors inducing conformity could likewise be viewed as social mechanisms. See Talcott Parsons and Edward A. Shils, "Values, Motives and Systems of Action," in Parsons and Shils (eds.), *Toward A General Theory of Action,* Cambridge: Harvard University Press, 1951, pp. 223–230.

[11] Further indication that the staffer-executive relationship is harmonious came from answers to the question, "Why do you think newspapermen are thought to be cynical?" Staffers regularly said that newsmen are cynical because they get close enough to stark reality to see the ills of their society, and the imperfections of its leaders and officials. Only 2, of 40 staffers, took the occasion to criticize their executives and the enforcement of policy. This displacement, or lack of strong feelings against executives, can be interpreted to bolster the hypothesis of staff solidarity.

[12] This is a variant of the process of "displacement of goals," newsmen turning to "getting news" rather than to seeking data which will enlighten and inform their readers. The dysfunction is implied in the nation's need not for more news but for better news—quality rather than quantity. See Merton, *op. cit.,* pp. 154–155.

[13] Does the new staffer, fresh from the ideals of college, really "change his attitudes"? It would seem that attitudes about socioeconomic affairs need not be fixed, but are capable of shifting with the situation. There are arguments for and against any opinion; in the atmosphere of the newsroom the arguments "for" policy decisions are made to sound adequate, especially as these are evoked by the significant others in the system.

[14] Related to the fact that policy is vague is the more general postulate that executives seek to avoid formal issues and the possibly damaging disputes arising therefrom. See Chester I. Barnard, *Functions of the Executive,* Cambridge: Harvard University Press, 1947.

VIOLENCE AND THE POLICE

William A. Westley

Brutality and the third degree have been identified with the municipal police of the United States since their inauguration in 1844. These aspects of police activity have been subject to exaggeration, repeated exposure, and virulent criticism. Since they are a breach of the law by the law-enforcement agents, they constitute a serious social, but intriguing sociological, problem. Yet there is little information about or understanding of the process through which such activity arises or of the purposes which it serves.

This paper is concerned with the genesis and function of the illegal use of violence by the police and presents an explanation based on an interpretative understanding of the experience of the police as an occupational group.[1] It shows that (a) the police accept and morally justify their illegal use of violence; (b) such acceptance and justification arise through their occupational experience; and (c) its use is functionally related to the collective occupational, as well as to the legal, ends of the police.

The analysis which follows offers both an occupational perspective on the use of violence by the police and an explanation of policing as an occupation, from the perspective of the illegal use of violence. Thus the meaning of this use of violence is derived by relating it to the general behavior of policemen as policemen, and occupations in general are illuminated through the delineation of the manner in which a particular occupation handles one aspect of its work.

The technical demands of a man's work tend to specify the kinds of social relationships in which he will be involved and to select the groups with whom these relationships are to be maintained. The social definition of the occupation invests its

From The American Journal of Sociology, *Vol. 59 (1953). Reprinted by permission of the University of Chicago Press. Footnotes have been edited.*

members with a common prestige position. Thus, a man's occupation is a major determining factor of his conduct and social identity. This being so, it involves more than man's work, and one must go beyond the technical in the explanation of work behavior. One must discover the occupationally derived definitions of self and conduct which arise in the involvements of technical demands, social relationships between colleagues and with the public, status, and self-conception. To understand these definitions, one must track them back to the occupational problems in which they have their genesis.[2]

The policeman finds his most pressing problems in his relationships to the public. His is a service occupation but of an incongruous kind, since he must discipline those whom he serves. He is regarded as corrupt and inefficient by, and meets with hostility and criticism from, the public. He regards the public as his enemy, feels his occupation to be in conflict with the community, and regards himself to be a pariah. The experience and the feeling give rise to a collective emphasis on secrecy, an attempt to coerce respect from the public, and a belief that almost any means are legitimate in completing an important arrest. These are for the policeman basic occupational values. They arise from his experience, take precedence over his legal responsibilities, are central to an understanding of his conduct, and form the occupational contexts within which violence gains its meaning. This then is the background for our analysis.

The materials which follow are drawn from a case study of a municipal police department in an industrial city of approximately one hundred and fifty thousand inhabitants. This study included participation in all types of police activities, ranging from walking the beat and cruising with policemen in a squad car to the observation of raids, interrogations and the police school. It included intensive interviews with over half the men in the department, who were representative as to rank, time in service, race, religion, and specific type of police job.

DUTY AND VIOLENCE

In the United States the use of violence by the police is both an occupational prerogative and a necessity. Police powers include the use of violence, for to them, within civil society, has been delegated the monopoly of the legitimate means of violence possessed by the state. Police are obliged by their duties to use violence as the only measure adequate to control and apprehend in the presence of counterviolence.

Violence in the form of the club and the gun is for the police a means of persuasion. Violence from the criminal, the drunk, the quarreling family, and the rioter arises in the course of police duty. The fighting drunk who is damaging property or assailing his fellows and who looks upon the policeman as a malicious intruder justifies for the policeman his use of force in restoring order. The armed criminal who has demonstrated a casual regard for the lives of others and a general hatred of the policeman forces the use of violence by the police in the pursuit of duty. Every policeman has some such experiences, and they proliferate in police lore. They constitute a common-sense and legal justification for the use of violence by the police and for training policemen in the skills of violence. Thus, from experience in the pursuit of their legally prescribed duties, the police develop a justification for the use of violence. They come to see it as good, as useful, and as their own. Furthermore, although legally their use of violence is limited to the requirements of the arrest and the protection of themselves and the community, the contingencies of their occupation lead them to enlarge the area in which violence may be used. Two kinds of experience—that with respect to the conviction of the felon and that with respect to the control of sexual conduct—will illustrate how and why the illegal use of violence arises.

The Conviction of the Felon

The apprehension and conviction of the felon is, for the policeman, the essence of police work. It is the source of prestige both within and outside police circles, it has career implications, and it is a major source of justification for the existence of the police before a critical and often hostile public. Out of these conditions a legitimation for the illegal use of violence is wrought.

The career and prestige implication of the "good pinch"[3] elevates it to a major end in the conduct of the policeman. It is an end which is justified both legally and through public opinion as one which should be of great concern to the police. Therefore it takes precedence over other duties and tends to justify strong means. Both trickery and violence are such means. The "third degree" has been criticized for many years, and extensive administrative controls have been devised in an effort to eliminate it. Police persistence in the face of that attitude suggests that the illegal use of violence is regarded as functional to their work. It also indicates a tendency to regard the third degree as a legitimate means for obtaining the conviction of the felon. However, to understand the strength of this legitimation, one must include other factors: the competition between patrolmen and detectives and the publicity value of convictions for the police department.

The patrolman has less access to cases that might result in the "good pinch" than the detective. Such cases are assigned to the detective, and for their solution he will reap the credit. Even where the patrolman first detects the crime, or actually apprehends the possible offender, the case is likely to be turned over to the detective. Therefore patrolmen are eager to obtain evidence and make the arrest before the arrival of the detectives. Intimidation and actual violence frequently come into play under these conditions. This is illustrated in the following case recounted by a young patrolman when he was questioned as to the situations in which he felt that the use of force was necessary:

One time Joe and I found three guys in a car, and we found that they had a gun down between the seats. We wanted to find out who owned that gun before the dicks arrived so that we could make a good pinch. They told us.

Patrolmen feel that little credit is forthcoming from a clean beat (a crimeless beat), while a number of good arrests really stands out on the record. To a great extent this is actually the case, since a good arrest results in good newspaper publicity, and the policeman who has made many "good pinches" has prestige among his colleagues.

A further justification for the illegal use of violence arises from the fact that almost every police department is under continuous criticism from the community, which tends to assign its own moral responsibilities to the police. The police are therefore faced with the task of justifying themselves to the public, both as individuals and as a group. They feel that the solution of major criminal cases serves this function. This is illustrated in the following statement:

There is a case I remember of four Negroes who held up a filling station. We got a description of them and picked them up. Then we took them down to the station and really worked them over. I guess that everybody that came into the station that night had a hand in it, and they were in pretty bad shape. Do you think that sounds cruel? Well, you know what we got out of it? We broke a big case in ————. There was a mob of twenty guys, burglars and stick-up men, and eighteen of them are in the pen now. Sometimes you have to get rough with them, see. The way I figure it is, if you can get a clue that a man is a pro and if he won't cooperate, tell you what you want to know, it is justified to rough him up a little, up to a point. You know how it is. You feel that the end justifies the means.

It is easier for the police to justify themselves to the community through the dramatic solution of big crimes than through orderly and responsible completion of their routine duties. Although they may be criticized for failures in routine areas, the criticism for the failure to solve big crimes is more intense and sets off a criticism of their work in noncriminal areas. The pressure to solve important cases therefore becomes strong. The following statement, made in reference to the use of violence in interrogations, demonstrates the point:

If it's a big case and there is a lot of pressure on you and they tell you you can't go home until the case is finished, then naturally you are going to lose patience.

The policeman's response to this pressure is to extend the use of violence to its illegal utilization in interrogations. The apprehension of the felon or the "good pinch" thus constitutes a basis for justifying the illegal use of violence.

Control of Sexual Conduct

The police are responsible for the enforcement of laws regulating sexual conduct. This includes the suppression of sexual deviation and the protection of the public from advances and attacks of persons of deviant sexual tendencies. Here the police face a difficult task. The victims of such deviants are notoriously unwilling to cooperate, since popular curiosity and gossip about sexual crimes and the sanctions against the open discussion of sexual activities make it embarrassing for the victim to admit or describe a deviant sexual advance or attack and cause him to feel that he gains a kind of guilt by association from such admissions. Thus the police find that frequently the victims will refuse to identify or testify against the deviant.

These difficulties are intensified by the fact that, once the community becomes aware of sexual depredations, the reports of such activity multiply well beyond reasonable expectations. Since the bulk of these reports will be false, they add to the confusion of the police and consequently to the elusiveness of the offender.

The difficulties of the police are further aggravated by extreme public demand for the apprehension of the offender. The hysteria and alarm generated by reports of a peeping Tom, a rapist, or an exhibitionist result in great public pressure on the police; and, should the activities continue, the public becomes violently critical of police efficiency. The police, who feel insecure in their relationship to the public, are extremely sensitive to this criticism and feel that they must act in response to the demands made by the political and moral leaders of the community.

Thus the police find themselves caught in a dilemma. Apprehension is extremely difficult because of the confusion created by public hysteria and the scarcity of witnesses, but the police are compelled to action by extremely public demands. They dissolve this dilemma through the illegal utilization of violence.

A statement of this "misuse" of police powers is represented in the remarks of a patrolman:

Now in my own case when I catch a guy like that I just pick him up and take him into the woods and beat him until he can't crawl. I have had seventeen cases like that in the last couple of years. I tell that guy that if I catch him doing that again I will shoot him. I tell him that I carry a second gun on me just in case I find guys like him and that I will plant it in his hand and say that he tried to kill and that no jury will convict me.

This statement is extreme and is not representative of policemen in general. In many instances the policeman is likely to act in a different fashion. This is illustrated in the following statement of a rookie who described what happened when he and his partner investigated a parked car which had aroused their suspicions:

He [the partner] went up there and pretty soon he called me, and there were a couple of fellows in the car with their pants open. I couldn't understand it. I kept looking around for where the woman would be. They were both pretty plastered. One was a young kid about eighteen years old, and the other was an older man. We decided, with the kid so drunk, that bringing him in would only really ruin his reputation, and we told him to go home. Otherwise we would have pinched them. During the time we were talking to them they offered us twenty-eight dollars, and I was going to pinch them when they showed the money, but my partner said, "Never mind, let them go."

Nevertheless, most policemen would apply no sanctions against a colleague who took the more extreme view of the right to use violence and would openly support some milder form of illegal coercion. This is illustrated in the statement of another rookie:

They feel that its okay to rough a man up in the case of sex crimes. One of the older men advised me that if the courts didn't punish a man we should. He told me about a sex crime, the story about it, and then said that the law says the policeman has the right to use the amount of force necessary to make an arrest and that in that kind of a crime you can use just a little more force. They feel definitely, for example, in extreme cases like rape, that if a man was guilty he ought to be punished even if you could not get any evidence on him. My feeling is that all the men on the force feel that way, at least from what they have told me.

Furthermore, the police believe, and with some justification it seems, that the community supports their definition of the situation and that they are operating in terms of an implicit directive.

The point of this discussion is that the control of sexual conduct is so difficult and the demand for it so incessant that the police come to sanction the illegal use of violence in obtaining that control. This does not imply that all policemen treat all sex deviants brutally, for, as the above quotations indicate, such is not the case. Rather, it indicates that this use of violence is permitted and condoned by the police and that they come to think of it as a resource more extensive than is included in the legal definition.

LEGITIMATION OF VIOLENCE

The preceding discussion has indicated two ways in which the experience of the police encourages them to use violence as a general resource in the achievement of their occupational ends and thus to sanction its illegal use. The experience, thus, makes violence acceptable to the policeman as a generalized means. We now wish to indicate the particular basis on which this general resource is legitimated. In particular we wish to point out the extent to which the policeman tends to transfer violence from a legal resource to a personal resource, one which he uses to further his own ends.

Seventy-three policemen, drawn from all ranks and constituting approximately 50 per cent of the patrolmen, were asked, "When do you think a policeman is justified in roughing a man up?" The intent of the question was to get them to legitimate the use of violence. Their replies are summarized in Table 1.

An inspection of the types and distribution of the responses indicates (1) that violence is legitimated by illegal ends (A, C, E, F, G) in 69 per cent of the cases; (2) that violence is legitimated in terms of purely personal or group ends (A) in 37 per cent of the cases (this is important, since it is the largest single reason for the use of violence given); and (3) that legal ends are the bases for legitimation in 31 per cent of the cases (B and D). However, this probably represents a distortion of the true feelings of some of these men, since both the police chief and the community had been severely critical of the use of violence by the men, and the respondents had a tendency to be very cautious with the interviewer, whom some of them never fully trusted. Furthermore, since all the men were con-

TABLE 1[a] BASES FOR THE USE OF FORCE NAMED BY 73 POLICEMEN

	Type of Response	Fre-quency	Percent-age
(A)	Disrespect for police	27	37
(B)	When impossible to avoid	17	23
(C)	To obtain information	14	19
(D)	To make an arrest	6	8
(E)	For the hardened criminal	5	7
(F)	When you know man is guilty	2	3
(G)	For sex criminals	2	3
	Total	73	100

[a]Many respondents described more than one type of situation which they felt called for the use of violence. The "reason" which was either (a) given most heatedly and at greatest length and/or (b) given first was used to characterize the respondent's answer to the question. However, this table is exhaustive of the types of replies which were given.

scious of the chief's policy and of public criticism, it seems likely that those who did justify the use of violence for illegal and personal ends no longer recognized the illegality involved. They probably believed that such ends fully represented a moral legitimation for their use of violence.

The most significant finding is that at least 37 per cent of the men believed that it was legitimate to use violence to coerce respect. This suggests that policemen use the resource of violence to persuade their audience (the public) to respect their occupational status. In terms of the policeman's definition of the situation, the individual who lacks respect for the police, the "wise guy" who talks back, or any individual who acts or talks in a disrespectful way, deserves brutality. This idea is epitomized in admonitions given to the rookies such as "You gotta make them respect you" and "You gotta act tough." Examples of some of the responses to the preceding question that fall into the "disrespect for the police" category follow:

Well, there are cases. For example, when you stop a fellow for a routine questioning, say a wise guy, and he starts talking back to you and telling you you are no good and that sort of thing. You know you can take a man in on a disorderly conduct charge, but you can practically never make it stick. So what you do in a case like that is to egg the guy on until he makes a remark where you can justifiably slap him and, then, if he fights back, you can call it resisting arrest.

Well, it varies in different cases. Most of the police use punishment if the fellow gives them any trouble. Usually you can judge a man who will give you trouble though. If there is any slight resistance, you can go all out on him. You shouldn't do it in the street though. Wait until you are in the squad car, because, even if you are in the right and a guy takes a poke at you just when you are hitting back, somebody's just likely to come around the corner, and what he will say is that you are beating the guy with your club.

Well, a prisoner deserves to be hit when he goes to the point where he tries to put you below him.

You gotta get rough when a man's language becomes very bad, when he is trying to make a fool of you in front of everybody else. I think most policemen try to treat people in a nice way, but usually you have to talk pretty rough. That's the only way to set a man down, to make him show a little respect.

If a fellow called a policeman a filthy name, a slap in the mouth would be a good thing, especially if it was out in the public where calling a policeman a bad name would look bad for the police.

There was the incident of a fellow I picked up. I was on the beat, and I was taking him down to the station. There were people following us. He kept saying that I wasn't in the army. Well, he kept going on like that, and I finally had to bust him one. I had to do it. The people would have thought I was afraid otherwise.

These results suggest (1) that the police believe that these private or group ends constitute a moral legitimation for violence which is equal *or superior* to the legitimation derived from the law and (2) that the monopoly of violence delegated to the police, by the state, to enforce the ends of the state has been appropriated by the police as a personal resource to be used for personal and group ends.

THE USE OF VIOLENCE

The sanctions for the use of violence arising from occupational experience and the fact that policemen morally justify even its illegal use may suggest that violence is employed with great frequency and little provocation. Such an impression would be erroneous, for the actual use of violence is limited by other considerations, such as individual inclinations, the threat of detection, and a sensitivity to public reactions.

Individual policemen vary of course in psychological disposition and past experience. All have been drawn from the larger community which tends to condemn the use of violence and therefore have internalized with varying degrees of intensity this other definition of violence. Their experience as policemen creates a new dimension to their self-conceptions and gives them a new perspective on the use of violence. But individual men vary in the degree to which they assimilate this new conception of self. Therefore, the amount of violence which is used and the frequency with which it is employed will vary among policemen according to their individual propensities. However, policemen cannot and do not employ sanctions against their colleagues for using violence,[4] and individual men who personally condemn the use of violence and avoid it whenever possible[5] refuse openly to condemn acts of violence by other men on the force. Thus, the collective sanction for the use of violence permits those men who are inclined to its use to employ it without fear.

All policemen, however, are conscious of the dangers of the illegal use of violence. If detected, they may be subject to a lawsuit and possibly dismissal from the force. Therefore, they limit its use to what they think they can get away with. Thus, they recognize that, if a man is guilty of a serious crime, it is easy to "cover up" for their brutality by accusing him of resisting arrest, and the extent to which they believe a man is guilty tends to act as a precondition to the use of violence.[6]

The policeman, in common with members of other occupations, is sensitive to the evaluation of his occupation by the public. A man's work is an important aspect of his status, and to the extent that he is identified with his work (by himself and/or the community) he finds that his self-esteem requires the justification and social elevation of his work. Since policemen are low in the occupational prestige scale, subject to continuous criticism, and in constant contact with this criticizing and evaluating public, they are profoundly involved in justifying their work and its tactics to the public and to themselves. The way in which the police empha-

size the solution of big crimes and their violent solution to the problem of the control of sexual conduct illustrate this concern. However, different portions of the public have differing definitions of conduct and are of differential importance to the policeman, and the way in which the police define different portions of the public has an effect on whether or not they will use violence.

The police believe that certain groups of persons will respond only to fear and rough treatment. In the city studied they defined both Negroes and slum dwellers in this category. The following statements, each by a different man, typify the manner in which they discriminate the public:

In the good districts you appeal to people's judgment and explain the law to them. In the South Side the only way is to appear like you are the boss.

You can't ask them a question and get an answer that is not a lie. In the South Side the only way to walk into a tavern is to walk in swaggering as if you own the place and if somebody is standing in your way give him an elbow and push him aside.

The colored people understand one thing. The policeman is the law, and he is going to treat you rough and that's the way you have to treat them. Personally, I don't think the colored are trying to help themselves one bit. If you don't treat them rough, they will sit right on top of your head.

Discriminations with respect to the public are largely based on the political power of the group, the degree to which the police believe that the group is potentially criminal, and the type of treatment which the police believe will elicit respect from it.

Variations in the administration and community setting of the police will introduce variations in their use of violence. Thus, a thoroughly corrupt police department will use violence in supporting the ends of this corruption, while a carefully administrated nonpolitical department can go a long way toward reducing the illegal use of violence. However, wherever the basic conditions here described are present, it will be very difficult to eradicate the illegal use of violence.

Given these conditions, violence will be used when necessary to the pursuit of duty or when basic occupational values are threatened. Thus a threat to the respect with which the policeman believes his occupation should be regarded or the opportunity to make a "good pinch" will tend to evoke its use.

CONCLUSIONS

This paper sets forth an explanation of the illegal use of violence by the police based on an interpretative understanding of their occupational experience. Therefore, it contains a description and analysis of *their* interpretation of *their* experience.

The policeman uses violence illegally because such usage is seen as just, acceptable, and, at times, expected by his colleague group and because it constitutes an effective means for solving problems in obtaining status and self-esteem which policemen as policemen have in common. Since the ends for which violence is illegally used are conceived to be both just and important, they function to justify, to the policeman, the illegal use of violence as a general means. Since "brutality" is strongly criticized by the larger community, the policeman must devise a defense of his brutality to himself and the community, and the defense in turn gives a deeper and more lasting justification to the "misuse of violence." This process then results in a transfer in property from the state to the colleague group. The means of violence which were originally a property of the state, in loan to its law-enforcement agent, the police, are in a psychological sense confiscated by the police, to be conceived of as a personal property to be used at their discretion. This, then, is the explanation of the illegal use of violence by the police which results from viewing it in terms of the police as an occupational group.

The explanation of the illegal use of violence by the police offers an illuminating perspective on the social nature of their occupation. The analysis of their use of brutality in dealing with sexual deviants and felons shows that it is a result of their desire to defend and improve their social status in the absence of effective legal means. This desire in turn is directly related to and makes sense in terms of the low status of the police in the community, which results in a driving need on the part of policemen to assert and improve their status. Their general legitimation of the use of violence *primarily* in terms of coercing respect and making a "good pinch" clearly points out the existence of occupational goals, which are independent of and take precedence over their legal mandate. The existence of such goals and patterns of conduct indicates that the policeman has made of his occupation a preoccupation and invested in it a large aspect of his self.

NOTES

This paper presents part of a larger study of the police by the writer. For the complete study see William A. Westley, "The Police: A Sociological Study of Law, Custom, and Morality" (unpublished Ph.D. dissertation, University of Chicago, Department of Sociology, 1951).

[1] Interpretative understanding is here used as defined by Max Weber. See *The Theory of Social and Economic Organization,* New York: Oxford University Press, 1947, p. 88.

[2] The ideas are not original. I am indebted for many of them to Everett C. Hughes, although he is in no way responsible for their present formulation. See E. C. Hughes, "Work and the Self" in Rohrer and Sherif, *Social Psychology at the Crossroads,* New York: Harper & Bros., 1951.

[3] Policemen, in the case studied, use this term to mean an arrest which (a) is politically clear and (b) likely to bring them esteem. Generally it refers to felonies, but in the case of a "real" vice drive it may include the arrest and *conviction* of an important bookie.

[4] The emphasis on secrecy among the police prevents them from using legal sanctions against their colleagues.

[5] Many men who held jobs in the police station rather than on beats indicated to the interviewer that their reason for choosing a desk job was to avoid the use of violence.

[6] In addition, the policeman is aware that the courts are highly critical of confessions obtained by violence and that, if violence is detected, it will "spoil his case."

KINDE, KUCHE, KIRCHE AS SCIENTIFIC LAW: PSYCHOLOGY CONSTRUCTS THE FEMALE

Naomi Weisstein

It is an implicit assumption that the area of psychology which concerns itself with personality has the onerous but necessary task of describing the limits of human possibility. Thus when we are about to consider the liberation of women, we naturally look to psychology to tell us what 'true' liberation would mean: what would give women the freedom to fulfill their own intrinsic natures.

Psychologists have set about describing the true natures of women with an enthusiasm and absolute certainty which is rather disquieting. Bruno Bettelheim, of the University of Chicago, tells us (1965) that "We must start with the realization that, as much as women want to be good scientists or engineers, they want first and foremost to be womanly companions of men and to be mothers." Erik Erikson of Harvard University (1964), upon noting that young women often ask whether they can "have an identity before they know whom they will marry, and for whom they will make a home," explains somewhat elegiacally that "Much of a young woman's identity is already defined in her kind of attractiveness and in the selectivity of her search for the man (or men) by whom she wishes to be sought. . . ." Mature womanly fulfillment, for Erikson, rests on the fact that a woman's ". . . somatic design harbors an 'inner space' destined to bear the offspring of chosen men, and with it, a biological, psychological, and ethical commitment to take care of human infancy."

Some psychiatrists even see the acceptance of woman's role by women as a solution to societal problems. "Woman is nurturance . . .," writes Jo-

seph Rheingold (1964), a psychiatrist at Harvard Medical School; "anatomy decrees the life of a woman. . . . When women grow up without dread of their biological functions and without subversion by feminist doctrine, and therefore enter upon motherhood with a sense of fulfillment and altruistic sentiment, we shall attain the goal of a good life and a secure world in which to live it."

These views from men of high prestige reflect a fairly general consensus: Liberation for women will consist first in their attractiveness, so that second, they may obtain the kinds of homes, and the kinds of men, which will allow joyful altruism and nurturance.

Business does not disagree. If views such as Bettelheim's and Erikson's do indeed have something to do with real liberation for women, then seldom in human history has so much money and effort been spent on helping a group of people realize their true potential. Clothing, cosmetics, home furnishings, are multimillion-dollar businesses: if you don't like investing in firms that make weaponry and flaming gasoline, then there's a lot of cash in "inner space." Sheet and pillowcase manufacturers are somewhat concerned on how to fill this inner space:

Mother, for a while this morning, I thought I wasn't cut out for married life. Hank was late for work and forgot his apricot juice and walked out without kissing me, and when I was all alone I started crying. But then the postman came with the sheets and towels you sent, that look like big bandanna handkerchiefs, and you know what I thought? That those big red and blue handkerchiefs are for girls like me to dry their tears on so they can get busy and do what a housewife has to do. Throw open the windows and start getting the house ready, and the dinner, maybe clean the silver and put new geraniums in the box. Everything to be ready for him when he walks through that door. *(Fieldcrest, 1966; emphasis added)*

It is an interesting but limited exercise to show that psychologists' ideas of women's nature fit so remarkably the common prejudice and serve industry and commerce so well. Just because it's good for business doesn't mean it's wrong. What we will show is that it *is wrong;* that there isn't the tiniest shred of evidence that these fantasies of servitude and childish dependence have anything to do with women's true potential; that the idea of the nature of human possibility which rests on the accidents of individual development of genitalia, on what is possible today because of what happened yesterday, on the fundamentalist myth of sex organ causality, has strangled and deflected psychology so that it is relatively useless in describing, explaining, or predicting humans and their behavior. It then goes without saying that present psychology is less than worthless in contributing to a vision which could truly liberate—men as well as women.

The central argument of my paper, then, is this. Psychology has nothing to say about what women are really like, what they need and what they want, essentially, because psychology does not know. I want to stress that this failure is not limited to women; rather, the kind of psychology which has addressed itself to how people act and who they are has failed to understand, in the first place, why people act the way they do, and certainly failed to understand what might make them act differently.

The kind of psychology which has addressed itself to these questions is in large part clinical psychology and psychiatry, which in America means endless commentary on and refinement of Freudian theory. Here, the causes of failure are obvious and appalling: Freudians and neo-Freudians, and clinicians and psychiatrists in general, have simply refused to look at the evidence against their theory and their practice, and have used as evidence for their theory and their practice stuff so flimsy and transparently biased as to have absolutely no standing as empirical evidence. But even psychology which conforms to rigorous methodology has gone about looking at people in such a way

as to have limited usefulness. This is because it has been a central assumption for most psychologists of human personality that human behavior rests primarily on an individual and inner dynamic, perhaps fixed in infancy, perhaps fixed by genitalia, perhaps simply arranged in a rather immovable cognitive network. But this assumption is rapidly losing ground as personality psychologists fail again and again to get consistency in the assumed personalities of their subjects (Block, 1968) and as the evidence collects that what a person does and who he believes himself to be, will in general be a function of what people around him expect him to be, and what the overall situation in which he is acting implies that he is. Compared to the influence of the social context within which a person lives, his or her history and traits, as well as biological makeup, may simply be random variations, noise superimposed on the true signal which can predict behavior. To summarize: The first reason for psychology's failure to understand what people are and how they act, is that clinicians and psychiatrists, who are generally the theoreticians on these matters, have essentially made up myths without any evidence to support them; the second reason for psychology's failure is that personality theory has looked for inner traits when it should have been looking for social context.

THEORY WITHOUT EVIDENCE

Let us turn to the first cause of failure: the acceptance by psychiatrists and clinical psychologists of theory without evidence. If we inspect the literature of personality, it is immediately obvious that the bulk of it is written by clinicians and psychiatrists, and that the major support for their theories is "years of intensive clinical experience." This is a tradition started by Freud. His "insights" occurred during the course of his work with his patients. Now there is nothing wrong with such an approach to theory *formulation;* a person is free to make up theories with any inspiration which works: divine revelation, intensive clinical practice, a random numbers table. But he is not free to claim any validity for his theory until it has been tested and confirmed. But theories are treated in no such tentative way in ordinary clinical practice. Consider Freud. What he thought constituted evidence violated the most minimal conditions of scientific rigor. In *The Sexual Enlightenment of Children* (1963), the classic document which is supposed to demonstrate empirically the existence of a castration complex and its connection to a phobia, Freud based his analysis on the reports of the father of the little boy, himself in therapy, and a devotee of Freudian theory. I really don't have to comment further on the contamination in this kind of evidence. It is remarkable that only recently has Freud's classic theory on the sexuality of women—the notion of the double orgasm—been actually tested physiologically and found just plain wrong. Now those who claim that fifty years of psychoanalytic experience constitutes evidence enough of the essential truths of Freud's theory should ponder the robust health of the double orgasm. Did women, until Masters and Johnson (1966), believe they were having two different kinds of orgasm? Did their psychiatrists cow them into reporting something that was not true? If so, were there other things they reported that were also not true? Did psychiatrists ever learn anything different than their theories had led them to believe? If clinical experience means anything at all, surely we should have been done with the double orgasm myth long before the Masters and Johnson studies.

But certainly, you may object, "years of intensive clinical experience" is the only reliable measure in a discipline which rests for its findings on insight, sensitivity, and intuition. The problem with insight, sensitivity, and intuition is that they can confirm for all time the biases that one started out with. People used to be absolutely convinced of their ability to tell which of their number were engaging in witchcraft. All it required was some sensitivity to the workings of the devil.

Years of intensive clinical experience is not the same thing as empirical evidence. The first thing an experimenter learns in any kind of experiment which involves humans is the concept of the "double blind." The term is taken from medical experiments, where one group is given a drug which is presumably supposed to change behavior in a certain way, and a control group is given a placebo.

If the observers or the subjects know which group took which drug, the result invariably comes out on the positive side for the new drug. Only when it is not known which subject took which pill is validity remotely approximated. In addition, with judgments of human behavior, it is so difficult to precisely tie down just what behavior is going on, let alone what behavior should be expected, that one must test again and again the reliability of judgments. How many judges, blind, will agree in their observations? Can they replicate their own judgments at some later time? When, in actual practice, these judgment criteria are tested for clinical judgments, then we find that the judges cannot judge reliably, nor can they judge consistently: they do no better than chance in identifying which of a certain set of stories were written by men and which by women; which of a whole battery of clinical test results are the products of homosexuals and which are the products of heterosexuals (Hooker, 1957), and which of a battery of clinical test results *and* interviews (where questions are asked such as "Do you have delusions?" Little and Schneidman, 1959) are products of psychotics, neurotics, psychosomatics, or normals. Lest this summary escape your notice, let me stress the implications of these findings. The ability of judges, chosen for their clinical expertise, to distinguish male heterosexuals from male homosexuals on the basis of three widely used clinical projective tests —the Rorschach, the TAT, and the MAP—was *no better than chance.* The reason this is such devastating news, of course, is that sexuality is of fundamental importance in the deep dynamic of personality; if what is considered gross sexual deviance cannot be caught, then what are psychologists talking about when they, for example, claim that at the basis of paranoid psychosis is "latent homosexual panic"? They can't even identify what homosexual anything is, let alone "latent homosexual panic." More frightening, expert clinicians cannot be consistent on what diagnostic category to assign to a person, again on the basis of both tests and interviews; a number of normals in the Little and Schneidman study were described as psychotic, in such categories as "schizophrenic with homosexual tendencies" or "schizoid character with depressive trends." But most disheartening, when the judges were asked to rejudge the test protocols some weeks later, their diagnosis of the same subjects, on the basis of the same protocols, differed markedly from their initial judgments. It is obvious that even simple descriptive conventions in clinical psychology cannot be consistently applied; that these descriptive conventions have any explanatory significance is therefore, of course, out of the question.

As a student in a graduate class at Harvard some years ago, I was a member of a seminar which was asked to identify which of two piles of a clinical test, the TAT, had been written by males and which by females. Only four students out of twenty identified the piles correctly, and this was after one and a half months of intensively studying the differences between men and women. Since this result is below chance—that is, this result would occur by chance about four out of a thousand times—we may conclude that there *is* finally a consistency here; students are judging knowledgeably within the context of psychological teaching about the differences between men and women; the teachings themselves are simply erroneous.

Ah, you may argue, the theory may be scientifically "unsound" but at least it cures people. There is no evidence that it does. In 1952, Eysenck reported the results of what is called an "outcome of therapy" study of neurotics which showed that of the patients who received psychoanalysis the improvement rate was 44 percent; of the patients who received psychotherapy the improvement rate was 64 percent; and of the patients who received no treatment at all the improvement rate was 72 percent. These findings have never been refuted; subsequently, later studies have confirmed the negative results of the Eysenck study. (Barron and Leary, 1955; Bergin, 1963; Cartwright and Vogel, 1960; Truax, 1963; Powers and Witmer, 1951). How can clinicians and psychiatrists, then, in all good conscience, continue to practice? Largely by ignoring these results and being careful not to do outcome-of-therapy studies. The attitude is nicely summarized by Rotter (1960, quoted in Astin, 1961): "Research studies in psychotherapy tend to be concerned more with some aspects of the psychotherapeutic procedure and less with outcome. . . . To some extent, it reflects an interest

in the psychotherapy situation as a kind of personality laboratory." Some laboratory.

THE SOCIAL CONTEXT

Thus, we can conclude that since clinical experience and tools can be shown to be worse than useless when tested for consistency, efficacy, agreement, and reliability, we can safely conclude that theories of a clinical nature advanced about women are also worse than useless. I want to turn now to the second major point in my paper, which is that, even when psychological theory is constructed so that it may be tested, and rigorous standards of evidence are used, it has become increasingly clear that in order to understand why people do what they do, and certainly in order to change what people do, psychologists must turn away from the theory of the causal nature of the inner dynamic and look to the social context within which individuals live. Before examining the relevance of this approach for the question of women, let me first sketch the groundwork for this assertion.

In the first place, it is clear (Block, 1968) that personality tests never yield consistent predictions; a rigid authoritarian on one measure will be an unauthoritarian on the next. But the reason for this inconsistency is only now becoming clear, and it seems overwhelmingly to have much more to do with the social situation in which the subject finds himself than with the subject himself.

In a series of brilliant experiments, Rosenthal and his coworkers (Rosenthal and Jacobson, 1968; Rosenthal, 1966) have shown that if one group of experimenters has one hypothesis about what they expect to find, and another group of experimenters has the opposite hypothesis, both groups will obtain results in accord with their hypotheses. Thus, in a success rating task, where subjects were required to rate faces cut out from magazines on a twenty point scale from −10 (very unsuccessful) to +10 (highly successful), the group of subjects whose experimenters had been told they would rate the faces high had mean ratings, in every case, above the highest mean rating for the group of subjects whose experimenters expected the subjects to rate the faces low. In all, about 375 subjects were run; the results would have happened by chance about one in one thousand times. The experimenters were instructed to read the same set of instructions, and to say no more than was in the instructions; obviously, the cues which influenced subjects were nonverbal. Even with animals, in two separate studies (Rosenthal and Fode, 1960; Rosenthal and Lawson, 1961), those experimenters who were told that rats learning mazes had been especially bred for brightness obtained better learning from their rats than did experimenters believing their rats to have been bred for dullness. These results would have happened by chance one out of one hundred times. In a very recent study, Rosenthal and Jacobson (1968) extended their analysis to the natural classroom situation. Here, they found that when teachers expected randomly selected students to show great promise, these students' IQ's increased significantly from control group students, with the most dramatic increments in the area of reasoning ability.

Thus, even in carefully controlled experiments, and with no outward or conscious difference in behavior, the hypotheses we start with will influence enormously the behavior of another organism. These studies are extremely important when assessing the validity of psychological studies of women. Since it is fairly safe to say that most of us start with hypotheses as to the nature of men and women, the validity of a number of observations on sex differences is questionable, even when these observations have been taken under carefully controlled conditions. Second, and more importantly, the Rosenthal experiments point quite clearly to the influence of social expectation. In some extremely important ways, people are what you expect them to be or at least they behave as you expect them to behave. Thus, if women, according to Bruno Bettelheim, want first and foremost to be good wives and mothers, it is extremely likely that that is what Bruno Bettelheim, and the rest of society, want them to be.

There is another series of social psychological experiments which points to the inescapable overwhelming effect of social context in an extremely vivid way. These are the obedience experiments of Stanley Milgram (1965a), concerned with the extent to which subjects in psychological experiments will obey the orders of unknown experimenters, even when these orders carry with them the distinct possibility that the subject is killing somebody.

Briefly, a subject is made to administer electric shocks in ascending 15-volt increments to another person, whom the subject believes to be another subject but who is in fact a stooge. The voltages range from 15 to 450 volts; for each four consecutive voltages there are verbal descriptions such as "mild shock," "danger, severe shock," and finally, for the 435- and 450-volt switches, simply a red XXX marked over the switches. The stooge, as the voltage increases, begins to cry out against the pain; he then screams that he has a heart condition, begging the subject to stop, and finally he goes limp and stops responding altogether at a certain voltage. Since even at this point the subject is instructed to keep increasing the voltage, it is possible for the subjects to continue all the way up to the end switch—450 volts. The percentage of subjects who do so is quite high; all in all, about one thousand subjects were run, and about 65 percent go to the end switch in an average experiment. No tested individual differences between subjects predicted which of the subjects would continue to obey, and which would break off the experiment. In addition forty psychiatrists were asked to predict out of one hundred subjects how many would go to the end, and where subjects would break off the experiment. They were way below actual percentages, with an average prediction of 3 percent of the subjects obeying to the end switch. But even though psychiatrists have no idea of how people are going to behave in this situation (despite one of the central facts of the twentieth century, which is that people have been made to kill enormous numbers of other people), and even though individual differences do not predict which subjects are going to obey and which are not, it is very easy to predict when subjects will be obedient and when they will be defiant. All the experimenter has to do is change the social situation. In a variant of the experiment (Milgram, 1965b), when two other stooges who were also administering electric shocks refused to continue, only 10 percent of the subjects continued to the end switch. This is critical for personality theory, for it says that the lawful behavior is the behavior that can be predicted from the social situation, not from the individual history.

Finally, an ingenious experiment by Schachter and Singer (1962) showed that subjects injected with adrenalin, which produces a state of physiological arousal in all but minor respects identical to that which occurs when subjects are extremely afraid, became euphoric when they were in a room with a stooge who was acting euphoric, and became extremely angry when they were placed in a room with a stooge who was acting extremely angry.

To summarize: If subjects under quite innocuous and noncoercive social conditions can be made to kill other subjects and under other types of social conditions will positively refuse to do so; if subjects can react to a state of physiological fear by becoming euphoric because there is somebody else around who is euphoric, or angry because there is somebody else around who is angry; if students become intelligent because teachers expect them to be intelligent, and rats run mazes better because experimenters are told that the rats are bright, then it is obvious that a study of human behavior requires, first and foremost, a study of the social contexts within which people move, the expectations as to how they will behave, and the authority which tells them who they are and what they are supposed to do.

BIOLOGICALLY BASED THEORIES

Two theories of the nature of women, which come not from psychiatric and clinical tradition, but from biology, can be disposed of now with little difficulty. The first argument notices social interaction in primate groups, and observes that females are submissive and passive. Putting aside for a moment the serious problem of experimenter bias (for instance, Harlow (1962) of the University of Wisconsin, after observing differences between male and female rhesus monkeys, quotes Lawrence Sterne to the effect that women are silly and trivial, and concludes that "men and women have differed in the past and they will differ in the future"), the problem with the argument from primate groups is that the crucial experiment has not

been performed. The crucial experiment would manipulate or change the social organization of these groups, and watch the subsequent behavior. Until then, we must conclude that, since primates are at present too stupid to change their social conditions by themselves, the "innateness" and fixedness of their behavior is simply not known. As applied to humans, the argument becomes patently irrelevant, since the most salient feature of human social organization is its variety; and there are a number of cultures where there is at least a rough equality between men and women (Mead, 1949). Thus, primate arguments tell us very little.

The second theory of sex differences argues that since females and males differ in their sex hormones, and sex hormones enter the brain (Hamburg and Lunde in Maccoby, 1966), there must be innate differences in "nature." But the only thing this argument tells us is that there are differences in physiological state. The problem is whether these differences are at all relevant to behavior. Recall that Schachter and Singer (1962) have shown that a particular physiological state can itself lead to a multiplicity of felt emotional states, and outward behavior, depending on the social situation. In brief, the uselessness of present psychology with regard to women is simply a special case of the general conclusion: One must understand social expectations about women if one is going to characterize the behavior of women.

How are women characterized in our culture, and in psychology? They are inconsistent, emotionally unstable, lacking in a strong conscience or superego, weaker, nurturant rather than productive, intuitive rather than intelligent, and, if they are at all normal, suited to the home and the family. In short, the list adds up to a typical minority group stereotype of inferiority (Hacker, 1951): If they know their place, which is in the home, they are really quite lovable, happy, childlike, loving creatures. In a review of the intellectual differences between little boys and little girls, Eleanor Maccoby (1966) has shown that there are no intellectual differences until about high school, or, if there are, girls are slightly ahead of boys. At high school, girls begin to do worse on a few intellectual tasks, such as arithmetic reasoning, and beyond high school, the achievement of women now measured in terms of productivity and accomplishment drops off even more rapidly. There are a number of other, nonintellectual tests which show sex differences; I choose the intellectual differences since it is seen clearly that women start becoming inferior. It is no use to talk about women being different but equal; all of the tests I can think of have a "good" outcome and a "bad" outcome. Women usually end up at the "bad" outcome. In light of social expectations about women, what is surprising is not that women end up where society expects they will; what is surprising is that little girls don't get the message that they are supposed to be stupid until high school; and what is even more remarkable is that some women resist this message even after high school, college, and graduate school.

My paper began with remarks on the task of discovering the limits of human potential. Until psychologists realize that it is they who are limiting discovery of human potential, by their refusal to accept evidence, if they are clinical psychologists, or, if they are rigorous, by their assumption that people move in a context-free ether, with only their innate dispositions and their individual traits determining what they will do, then psychology will have nothing of substance to offer in this task. I don't know what immutable differences exist between men and women apart from differences in their genitals; perhaps there are some other unchangeable differences; probably there are a number of irrelevant differences. But it is clear that until social expectations for men and women are equal, until we provide equal respect for both men and women, our answers to this question will simply reflect our prejudices.

REFERENCES

Astin, A. W., "The Functional Autonomy of Psychotherapy," *American Psychologist,* **16** (1961), 75–78.

Barron, F., and Leary, T., "Changes in Psychoneurotic Patients with and without Psychotherapy," *Journal of Consulting Psychology,* **19** (1955), 239–245.

Bettelheim, B., "The Commitment Required of a Woman Entering a Scientific Profession in Present-Day American Society," *Woman and the Scientific Professions,* The MIT Symposium on American Women in Science and Engineering, 1965.

Block, J., "Some Reasons for the Apparent Inconsistency of Personality," *Psychological Bulletin,* **70** (1968), 210–212.

Bregin, A. E., "The Effects of Psychotherapy: Negative Results Revisited," *Journal of Consulting Psychology,* **10** (1963), 244–250.

Cartwright, R. D., and Vogel, J. L., "A Comparison of Changes in Psychoneurotic Patients during Matched Periods of Therapy and No-therapy," *Journal of Consulting Psychology,* **24** (1960), 121–127.

Erikson, E., "Inner and Outer Space: Reflections on Womanhood," *Daedalus,* **93** (1964), 582–606.

Eysenck, H. J., "The Effects of Psychotherapy: An Evaluation," *Journal of Consulting Psychology,* **16** (1952), 319–324.

Freud, S., *The Sexual Enlightenment of Children,* Collier Books Edition, 1963.

Goldstein, A. P., and Dean, S. J., *The Investigation of Psychotherapy: Commentaries and Readings,* New York: John Wiley & Sons, 1966.

Hacker, H. M., "Women as a Minority Group," *Social Forces,* **30** (1951), 60–69.

Hamburg, D. A., and Lunde, D. T., "Sex Hormones in the Development of Sex Differences in Human Behavior," in Maccoby, ed., *The Development of Sex Differences,* Stanford: Stanford University Press, 1966, pp. 1–24.

Harlow, H. F., The Heterosexual Affectional System in Monkeys," *American Psychologist,* **17** (1962), 1–9.

Hooker, E., "Male Homosexuality in the Rorschach," *Journal of Projective Techniques,* **21** (1957), 18–31.

Little, K. B., and Schneidman, E. S., "Congruences Among Interpretations of Psychological and Anamestic Data," *Psychological Monographs,* **73** (1959), 1–42.

Maccoby, Eleanor E., "Sex Differences in Intellectual Functioning," in Maccoby, ed., *The Development of Sex Differences,* Stanford: Stanford University Press, 1966, pp. 25–55.

Masters, W. H., and Johnson, V. E., *Human Sexual Response,* Boston: Little, Brown, 1966.

Mead, M., *Male and Female: A Study of the Sexes in a Changing World,* New York: William Morrow, 1949.

Milgram, S., "Some Conditions of Obedience and Disobedience to Authority," *Human Relations,* **18** (1965a), 57–76.

Milgram, S., "Liberating Effects of Group Pressure," *Journal of Personality and Social Psychology,* **1** (1965b), 127–134.

Powers, E., and Witmer, H., *An Experiment in the Prevention of Delinquency,* New York: Columbia University Press, 1951.

Rheingold, J., *The Fear of Being a Woman,* New York: Grune & Stratton, 1964.

Rosenthal, R., "On the Social Psychology of the Psychological Experiment: The Experimenter's Hypothesis as Unintended Determinant of Experimental Results," *American Scientist,* **51** (1963), 268–283.

Rosenthal, R., *Experimenter Effects in Behavioral Research,* New York: Appleton-Century-Crofts, 1966.

Rosenthal, R., and Fode, K. L., "The Effect of Experimenter Bias on the Performance of the Albino Rat," Unpublished Manuscript, Harvard University, 1960.

Rosenthal, R., and Jacobson, L., *Pygmalion in the Classroom: Teacher Expectation and Pupil's Intellectual Development,* New York: Holt, Rinehart & Winston, 1968.

Rosenthal, R., and Lawson, R., "A Longitudinal Study of the Effects of Experimenter Bias on the Operant Learning of Laboratory Rats," Unpublished Manuscript, Harvard University, 1961.

Rotter, J B., "Psychotherapy," *Annual Review of Psychology,* **11** (1960), 381–414.

Schachter, S., and Singer, J. E., "Cognitive, Social, and Physiological Determinants of Emotional State," *Psychological Review,* **69** (1962), 379–399.

Truax, C. B., "Effective Ingredients in Psychotherapy: An Approach to Unraveling the Patient-Therapist Interaction," *Journal of Counseling Psychology,* **10** (1963), 256–263.

THE MORTIFICATION OF SELF

Erving Goffman

The recruit comes into the establishment with a conception of himself made possible by certain stable social arrangements in his home world. Upon entrance, he is immediately stripped of the support provided by these arrangements. In the accurate language of some of our oldest total institutions, he begins a series of abasements, degradations, humiliations, and profanations of self. His self is systematically, if often unintentionally, mortified. He begins some radical shifts in his *moral career,* a career composed of the progressive changes that occur in the beliefs that he has concerning himself and significant others.

The processes by which a person's self is mortified are fairly standard in total institutions;[1] analysis of these processes can help us to see the arrangements that ordinary establishments must guarantee if members are to preserve their civilian selves.

The barrier that total institutions place between

From Erving Goffman, "The Characteristics of Total Institutions," in Donald R. Cressey, ed., The Prison: Studies in Institutional Organization and Change. © 1961 by Holt Rinehart and Winston, Inc. Reprinted by permission. Some footnotes have been omitted.

the inmate and the wider world marks the first curtailment of self. In civil life, the sequential scheduling of the individual's roles, both in the life cycle and in the repeated daily round, ensures that no one role he plays will block his performance and ties in another. In total institutions, in contrast, membership automatically disrupts role scheduling, since the inmate's separation from the wider world lasts around the clock and may continue for years. Role dispossession therefore occurs. In many total institutions the privilege of having visitors or of visiting away from the establishment is completely withheld at first, ensuring a deep initial break with past roles and an appreciation of role dispossession. A report on cadet life in a military academy provides an illustration:

This clean break with the past must be achieved in a relatively short period. For two months, therefore, the swab is not allowed to leave the base or to engage in social intercourse with non-cadets. This complete isolation helps to produce a unified group of swabs, rather than a heterogeneous collection of persons of high and low status. Uniforms are issued on the first day, and discussions of wealth and family background are taboo. Although the pay of the cadet is very low, he is not permitted to receive money from home. The role of the cadet must supersede other roles the individual has been accustomed to play. There are few clues left which will reveal social status in the outside world. [2]

I might add that when entrance is voluntary, the recruit has already partially withdrawn from his home world; what is cleanly severed by the institution is something that had already started to decay.

Although some roles can be re-established by the inmate if and when he returns to the world, it is plain that other losses are irrevocable and may be painfully experienced as such. It may not be possible to make up, at a later phase of the life cycle, the time not now spent in educational or job advancement, in courting, or in rearing one's children. A legal aspect of this permanent dispossession is found in the concept of "civil death": prison inmates may face not only a temporary loss of the rights to will money and write checks, to contest divorce or adoption proceedings, and to vote, but may have some of these rights permanently abrogated. [3]

The inmate, then, finds certain roles are lost to him by virtue of the barrier that separates him from the outside world. The process of entrance typically brings other kinds of loss and mortification as well. We very generally find staff employing what are called admission procedures, such as taking a life history, photographing, weighing, fingerprinting, assigning numbers, searching, listing personal possessions for storage, undressing, bathing, disinfecting, haircutting, issuing institutional clothing, instructing as to rules, and assigning to quarters. [4] Admission procedures might better be called "trimming" or "programming" because in thus being squared away the new arrival allows himself to be shaped and coded into an object that can be fed into the administrative machinery of the establishment, to be worked on smoothly by routine operations. Many of these procedures depend upon attributes such as weight or fingerprints that the individual possesses merely because he is a member of the largest and most abstract of social categories, that of human being. Action taken on the basis of such attributes necessarily ignores most of his previous bases of self-identification.

Because a total institution deals with so many aspects of its inmates' lives, with the consequent complex squaring away at admission, there is a special need to obtain initial cooperativeness from the recruit. Staff often feel that a recruit's readiness to be appropriately deferential in his initial face-to-face encounters with them is a sign that he will take the role of the routinely pliant inmate. The occasion on which staff members first tell the inmate of his deference obligations may be structured to challenge the inmate to balk or to hold his peace forever. Thus these initial moments of socialization may involve an "obedience test" and even a will-breaking contest: an inmate who shows defiance receives immediate visible punishment, which increases until he openly "cries uncle" and humbles himself.

An engaging illustration is provided by Brendan Behan in reviewing his contest with two warders upon his admission to Walton prison:

"And 'old up your 'ead, when I speak to you."

"'Old up your 'ead, when Mr. Whitbread speaks to you," said Mr. Holmes.

I looked round at Charlie. His eyes met mine and he quickly lowered them to the ground.

"What are you looking round at, Behan? Look at me."

I looked at Mr. Whitbread. "I am looking at you," I said.

"You are looking at Mr. Whitbread—what?" said Mr. Holmes.

"I am looking at Mr. Whitbread."

Mr. Holmes looked gravely at Mr. Whitbread, drew back his open hand, and struck me on the face, held me with his other hand and struck me again.

My head spun and burned and pained and I wondered would it happen again. I forgot and felt another smack, and forgot, and another, and moved, and was held by a steadying, almost kindly hand, and another, and my sight was a vision of red and white and pity-coloured flashes.

"You are looking at Mr. Whitbread—what, Behan?"

I gulped and got together my voice and tried again till I got it out. "I, sir, please, sir, I am looking at you, I mean, I am looking at Mr. Whitbread, sir." [5]

Admission procedures and obedience tests may be elaborated into a form of initiation that has been called "the welcome," where staff or inmates, or both, go out of their way to give the recruit a clear notion of his plight. [6] As part of this rite of passage he may be called by a term such as "fish" or "swab," which tells him that he is merely an inmate, and, what is more, that he has a special low status even in this low group.

The admission procedure can be characterized as a leaving off and a taking on, with the midpoint marked by physical nakedness. Leaving off of course entails a dispossession of property, important because persons invest self-feelings in their possessions. Perhaps the most significant of these possessions is not physical at all, one's full name; whatever one is thereafter called, loss of one's name can be a great curtailment of the self.[7]

Once the inmate is stripped of his possessions, at least some replacements must be made by the establishment, but these take the form of standard issue, uniform in character and uniformly distributed. These substitute possessions are clearly marked as really belonging to the institution and in some cases are recalled at regular intervals to be, as it were, disinfected of identifications. With objects that can be used up—for example, pencils the inmate may be required to return the remnants before obtaining a reissue. Failure to provide inmates with individual lockers and periodic searches and confiscations of accumulated personal property reinforce property dispossession. Religious orders have appreciated the implications for self of such separation from belongings. Inmates may be required to change their cells once a year so as not to become attached to them. The Benedictine Rule is explicit:

For their bedding let a mattress, a blanket, a coverlet, and a pillow suffice. These beds must be frequently inspected by the Abbot, because of private property which may be found therein. If anyone be discovered to have what he has not received from the Abbot, let him be most severely punished. And in order that this vice of private ownership may be completely rooted out, let all things that are necessary be supplied by the Abbot: that is, cowl, tunic, stockings, shoes, girdle, knife, pen, needle, handkerchief, and tablets; so that all plea of necessity may be taken away. And let the Abbot always consider that passage in the Acts of the Apostles: "Distribution was made to each according as anyone had need."

One set of the individual's possessions has a special relation to self. The individual ordinarily expects to exert some control over the guise in which he appears before others. For this he needs cosmetic and clothing supplies, tools for applying, arranging, and repairing them, and an accessible, secure place to store these supplies and tools—in short, the individual will need an "identity kit" for the management of his personal front. He will also need access to decoration specialists such as barbers and clothiers.

On admission to a total institution, however, the individual is likely to be stripped of his usual appearance and of the equipment and services by which he maintains it, thus suffering a personal defacement. Clothing, combs, needle and thread, cosmetics, towels, soap, shaving sets, bathing facilities—all these may be taken away or denied him, although some may be kept in inaccessible storage, to be returned if and when he leaves. In the words of St. Benedict's Holy Rule:

Then forthwith he shall, there in the oratory, be divested of his own garments with which he is clothed and be clad in those of the monastery. Those garments of which he is divested shall be placed in the wardrobe, there to be kept, so that if, perchance, he should ever be persuaded by the devil to leave the monastery (which God forbid), he may be stripped of the monastic habit and cast forth.

As suggested, the institutional issue provided as a substitute for what has been taken away is typically of a "coarse" variety, ill-suited, often old, and the same for large categories of inmates. The impact of this substitution is described in a report on imprisoned prostitutes:

First, there is the shower officer who forces them to undress, takes their own clothes away, sees to it that they take showers and get their prison clothes—one pair of black oxfords with cuban heels, two pairs of much-mended ankle socks, three cotton dresses, two cotton slips, two pairs of panties, and a couple of bras. Practically all the bras are flat and useless. No corsets or girdles are issued.

There is not a sadder sight than some of the obese prisoners who, if nothing else, have been managing to keep themselves looking decent on the outside, confronted by the first sight of themselves in prison issue.[8]

In addition to personal defacement that comes from being stripped of one's identity kit, there is personal disfigurement that comes from direct and permanent mutilations of the body such as brands or loss of limbs. Although this mortification of the self by way of the body is found in few total institutions, still, loss of a sense of personal safety is common and provides a basis for anxieties about disfigurement. Beatings, shock therapy, or, in mental hospitals, surgery—whatever the intent of staff in providing these services for some inmates—may lead many inmates to feel that they are in an environment that does not guarantee their physical integrity.

At admission, loss of identity equipment can prevent the individual from presenting his usual image of himself to others. After admission, the image of himself he presents is attacked in another way. Given the expressive idiom of a particular civil society, certain movements, postures, and stances will convey lowly images of the individual and be avoided as demeaning. Any regulation, command, or task that forces the individual to adopt these movements or postures may mortify his self. In total institutions, such physical indignities abound. In mental hospitals, for example, patients may be forced to eat all food with a spoon.[9] In military prisons, inmates may be required to stand at attention whenever an officer enters the compound.[10] In religious institutions, there are such classic gestures of penance as the kissing of feet,[11] and the posture recommended to an erring monk that he

. . . lie prostrate at the door of the oratory in silence; and thus, with his face to the ground and his body prone, let him cast himself at the feet of all as they go forth from the oratory.[12]

In some penal institutions we find the humiliation of bending over to receive a birching.

Just as the individual can be required to hold his body in a humiliating pose, so he may have to provide humiliating verbal responses. An important instance of this is the forced deference pattern of total institutions; inmates are often required to punctuate their social interaction with staff by verbal acts of deference, such as saying "sir." Another instance is the necessity to beg, importune, or humbly ask for little things such as a light for a cigarette, a drink of water, or permission to use the telephone.

Corresponding to the indignities of speech and action required of the inmate are the indignities of treatment others accord him. The standard examples here are verbal or gestural profanations: staff or fellow inmates call the individual obscene names, curse him, point out his negative attributes, tease him, or talk about him or his fellow inmates as if he were not present.

Whatever the form or the source of these various indignities, the individual has to engage in activity whose symbolic implications are incompatible with his conception of self. A more diffuse example of this kind of mortification occurs when the individual is required to undertake a daily round of life that he considers alien to him—to take on a disidentifying role. In prisons, denial of heterosexual opportunities can induce fear of losing one's masculinity. In military establishments, the patently useless make-work forced on fatigue details can make men feel their time and effort are worthless. In religious institutions there are special arrangements to ensure that all inmates take a turn performing the more menial aspects of the servant role. An extreme is the concentration-camp practice requiring prisoners to administer whippings to other prisoners.

There is another form of mortification in total institutions; beginning with admission a kind of contaminative exposure occurs. On the outside, the individual can hold objects of self-feeling—such as his body, his immediate actions, his thoughts, and some of his possessions—clear of contact with alien and contaminating things. But in total institutions these territories of the self are violated; the boundary that the individual places between his being and the environment is invaded and the embodiments of self profaned.

There is, first, a violation of one's informational preserve regarding self. During admission, facts about the inmate's social statuses and past behavior—especially discreditable facts—are collected and recorded in a dossier available to staff. Later, insofar as the establishment officially expects to alter the self-regulating inner tendencies of the inmate, there may be group or individual confession—psychiatric, political, military, or religious, according to the type of institution. On these occasions the inmate has to expose facts and feelings about self to new kinds of audiences. The most spectacular examples of such exposure come to us from Communist confession camps and from the *culpa* sessions that form part of the routine of Catholic religious institutions. The dynamics of the process have been explicitly considered by those engaged in so-called milieu therapy.

New audiences not only learn discreditable facts about oneself that are ordinarily concealed but are also in a position to perceive some of these facts directly. Prisoners and mental patients cannot prevent their visitors from seeing them in humiliating circumstances.[13] Another example is the shoulder patch of ethnic identification worn by concentration-camp inmates. Medical and security examinations often expose the inmate physically, sometimes to persons of both sexes; a similar exposure follows from collective sleeping arrangements and doorless toilets. An extreme here, perhaps, is the situation of a self-destructive mental patient who is stripped naked for what is felt to be his own protection and placed in a constantly lit seclusion room, into whose Judas window any person passing on the ward can peer. In general, of course, the inmate is never fully alone; he is always within sight and often earshot of someone, if only his fellow inmates. Prison cages with bars for walls fully realize such exposure.

Perhaps the most obvious type of contaminative exposure is the directly physical kind—the besmearing and defiling of the body or of other objects closely identified with the self. Sometimes this involves a breakdown of the usual environmental arrangements for insulating oneself from one's own source of contamination, as in having to empty one's own slops or having to subject one's evacuation to regimentation, as reported from Chinese political prisons:

An aspect of their isolation regimen which is especially onerous to Western prisoners is the arrangement for the elimination of urine and feces. The "slop jar" that is usually present in Russian cells is often absent in China. It is a Chinese custom to allow defecation and urination only at one or two specified times each day —usually in the morning after breakfast. The prisoner is hustled from his cell by a guard, double-timed down a long corridor, and given approximately two minutes to squat over an open Chinese latrine and attend to all his wants. The haste and the public scrutiny are especially difficult for women to tolerate. If the prisoners cannot complete their action in about two minutes, they are abruptly dragged away and back to their cells.[14]

A very common form of physical contamination is reflected in complaints about unclean food, messy quarters, soiled towels, shoes and clothing impregnated with previous users' sweat, toilets without seats, and dirty bath facilities. Orwell's comments on his boarding school may be taken as illustrative:

For example, there were the pewter bowls out of which we had our porridge. They had overhanging rims, and under the rims there were accumulations of sour porridge, which could be flaked off in long strips. The porridge itself, too, contained more lumps, hairs and unexplained black things than one would have thought possible, unless someone were putting them there on purpose. It was never safe to start on that porridge without investigating it first. And there was the slimy water of the plunge bath—it was twelve or fifteen feet long, the whole school was supposed to go into it every morning, and I doubt whether the water was changed at all frequently—and the always-damp towels with their cheesy smell: . . . And the sweaty smell of the changing-room with its greasy basins, and, giving on this, the row of filthy, dilapidated lavatories, which had no fastenings of any kind on the doors, so that whenever you were sitting there someone was sure to come crashing in. It is not easy for me to think of my school days without seeming to breathe in a whiff of something cold and evil-smelling—a sort of compound of sweaty stockings, dirty towels, fecal smells blowing along corridors, forks with old food between the prongs, neck-of-mutton stew, and the lunging doors of the lavatories and the echoing chamberpots in the dormitories.[15]

There are still other sources of physical contamination, as an interviewee suggests in describing a concentration-camp hospital:

We were lying two in each bed. And it was very unpleasant. For example, if a man died he would not be removed before twenty-four hours had elapsed because the block trusty wanted, of course, to get the bread ration and the soup which was allotted to this person. For this reason the dead person would be reported dead twenty-four hours later so that his ration would still be allotted. And so we had to lie all that time in bed together with the dead person.

We were on the middle level. And that was a very gruesome situation, especially at night. First of all, the dead men were badly emaciated and they looked terri-

ble. In most cases they would soil themselves at the moment of death and that was not a very esthetic event. I saw such cases very frequently in the lager, in the sick people's barracks. People who died from phlegmonous, suppurative wounds, with their beds overflowing with pus, would be lying together with somebody whose illness was possibly more benign, who had possibly just a small wound which now would become infected. [16]

The contamination of lying near the dying has also been cited in mental-hospital reports, and surgical contamination has been cited in prison documents:

Surgical instruments and bandages in the dressing-room lie exposed to the air and dust. George, attending for the treatment, by a medical orderly, of a boil on his neck, had it lanced with a scalpel that had been used a moment before on a man's foot, and had not been sterilized in the meantime. [17]

Finally, in some total institutions the inmate is obliged to take oral or intravenous medications, whether desired or not, and to eat his food, however unpalatable. When an inmate refuses to eat, there may be forcible contamination of his innards by "forced feeding."

I have suggested that the inmate undergoes mortification of the self by contaminative exposure of a physical kind, but this must be amplified: when the agency of contamination is another human being, the inmate is in addition contaminated by forced interpersonal contact and, in consequence, a forced social relationship. (Similarly, when the inmate loses control over who observes him in his predicament or knows about his past, he is being contaminated by a forced relationship to these people—for it is through such perception and knowledge that relations are expressed.)

The model for interpersonal contamination in our society is presumably rape; although sexual molestation certainly occurs in total institutions, there are many other less dramatic examples. Upon admission, one's on-person possessions are pawed and fingered by an official as he itemizes and prepares them for storage. The inmate himself may be frisked and searched to the extent—often reported in the literature—of a rectal examination. [18] Later in his stay he may be required to undergo searchings of his person and of his sleeping quarters, either routinely or when trouble arises. In all these cases it is the searcher as well as the search that penetrates the private reserve of the individual and violates the territories of his self. Even routine inspections can have this effect, as Lawrence suggests:

In the old days men had weekly to strip off boots and socks, and expose their feet for an officer's inspection. An ex-boy'd kick you in the mouth, as you bent down to look. So with the bath-rolls, a certificate from your N.C.O that you'd had a bath during the week. One bath! And with the kit inspections, and room inspections, and equipment inspections, all excuses for the dogmatists among the officers to blunder, and for the nosy-parkers to make beasts of themselves. Oh, you require the gentlest touch to interfere with a poor man's person, and not give offense.

Further, the practice of mixing age, ethnic, and racial groups in prisons and mental hospitals can lead an inmate to feel he is being contaminated by contact with undesirable fellow inmates. A public-school prisoner, describing his admission to prison, provides an example:

Another warder came up with a pair of handcuffs and coupled me to the little Jew, who moaned softly to himself in Yiddish.

Suddenly, the awful thought occurred to me that I might have to share a cell with the little Jew and I was seized with panic. The thought obsessed me to the exclusion of all else.

Obviously, group living will necessitate mutual contact and exposure among inmates. At the extreme, as in cells for Chinese political prisoners, mutual contact may be very great:

At some stage in his imprisonment the prisoner can expect to find himself placed in a cell with about eight other prisoners. If he was initially isolated and interrogated, this may be shortly after his first "confession" is accepted; but many prisoners are placed in group cells from the outset of their imprisonment. The cell is usually barren, and scarcely large enough to hold the group it contains. There may be a sleeping-platform, but all of the prisoners sleep on the floor; and when all lie down, every inch of floor space may be taken up. The atmosphere is extremely intimate. Privacy is entirely nonexistent. [19]

Lawrence provides a military illustration in discussing his difficulties in merging with fellow airmen in the barracks hut:

You see, I cannot play at anything with anyone: and a native shyness shuts me out from their free-masonry of ———— and blinding, pinching, borrowing, and talking dirty: this despite my sympathy for the abandon of functional frankness in which they wallow. Inevitably, in our crowded lodging, we must communicate just those physical modesties which polite life keeps veiled. Sexual activity's a naive boast, and any abnormalities of appetite or organ are curiously displayed. The Powers encourage this behaviour. All latrines in camp have lost their doors. "Make the little————sleep and ————————and eat together," grinned old Jock Mackay, senior instructor, "and we'll have 'em drilling together, naturally."

One routine instance of this contaminative contact is the naming system for inmates. Staff and fellow inmates automatically assume the right to employ an intimate form of address or a truncated formal one; for a middle-class person, at least, this denies the right to hold oneself off from others through a formal style of address. When the individual has to eat food he considers alien and polluted, this contamination sometimes derives from other persons' connection with the food, as is nicely illustrated in the penance of "begging soup" practiced in some nunneries:

. . . she placed her pottery bowl on the left of the Mother Superior, knelt, clasped her hands and waited until two spoonfuls of soup had been put into her beggar's bowl, then on to the next oldest and the next, until the bowl was filled. . . . When at last her bowl was filled, she returned to her place and swallowed the soup, as she knew she must, down to the last drop. She tried not to think how it had been tossed into her bowl from a dozen other bowls that had already been eaten from.[20]

Another kind of contaminative exposure brings an outsider into contact with the individual's close relationship to significant others. For example, an inmate may have his personal mail read and censored, and even made fun of to his face. Another example is the enforced public character of visits, as reports from prisons suggest:

But what a sadistic kind of arrangement they have for these visits! One hour a month—or two half-hours—in a big room with perhaps a score of other couples, with guards prowling about to make sure you exchange neither the plans nor the implements of escape! We met across a six-foot-wide table, down the middle of which a sort of bundling-board six inches high presumably prevents even our germs from intermingling. We were permitted one sanitary handshake at the beginning of the visit and one at the end; for the rest of the time we could only sit and look at each other while we called across that vast expanse![21]

Visits take place in a room by the main gate. There is a wooden table, at one side of which sits the prisoner and at the other side his visitors. The warder sits at the head; he hears every word that is spoken, watches every gesture and nuance of expression. There is no privacy at all—and this when a man is meeting his wife whom he may not have seen for years. Nor is any contact allowed between prisoner and visitor, and, of course, no articles are allowed to change hands.[22]

A more thoroughgoing version of this type of contaminative exposure occurs, as already implied, in institutionally arranged confessions. When a significant other must be denounced, and especially when this other is physically present, confession of the relationship to outsiders can mean an intense contamination of the relationship and, through this, of the self. A description of practices in a nunnery provides an illustration:

The bravest of the emotionally vulnerable were the sisters who stood up together in the culpa and proclaimed each other—for having gone out of their way to be near to one another, or perhaps for having talked together in recreation in a way that excluded others. Their tormented but clearly spoken disclosures of a nascent affinity gave it the coup de grace which they themselves might not have been able to do, for the entire community would henceforth see to it that these two would be kept far apart. The pair would be helped to detach themselves from one of those spontaneous personal attachments which often sprang to life in the body of the community as unexpectedly as wildflowers appeared, now and again, in the formal geometric patterns of the cloister gardens.

A parallel example can be found in mental hospitals devoted to intensive milieu therapy, where patient pairs conducting an affair may be obliged to discuss their relationship during group meetings.

In total institutions, exposure of one's relationships can occur in even more drastic forms, for there may be occasions when an individual witnesses a physical assault upon someone to whom he has ties and suffers the permanent mortification of having (and being known to have) taken no action. Thus we learn of a mental hospital:

This knowledge [of shock therapy] is based on the fact that some of the patients in Ward 30 have assisted the shock team in the administration of therapy to patients, holding them down, and helping to strap them in bed, or watching them after they have quieted. The administration of shock on the ward is often carried out in full sight of a group of interested onlookers. The patient's convulsions often resemble those of an accident victim in death agony and are accompanied by choking gasps and at times by a foaming overflow of saliva from the mouth. The patient slowly recovers without memory of the occurrence, but he has served the others as a frightful spectacle of what may be done to them.

Melville's report on flogging aboard a nineteenth-century man-of-war provides another example:

However much you may desire to absent yourself from the scene that ensues, yet behold it you must; or, at least, stand near it you must; for the regulations enjoin the attendance of almost the entire ship's company, from the corpulent captain himself to the smallest boy who strikes the bell.
And the inevitableness of his own presence at the scene: the strong arm that drags him in view of the scourge, and holds him there till all is over: forcing upon his loathing eye and soul the sufferings and groans of men who have familiarly consorted with him, eaten with him, battled out watches with him—men of his own type and badge—all this conveys a terrible hint of the omnipotent authority under which he lives.[23]

Lawrence offers a military example:

Tonight's crash of the stick on the hut door at roll call was terrific; and the door slammed back nearly off its hinges. Into the light strode Baker, V.C., a corporal who assumed great license in the camp because of his war decoration. He marched down my side of the hut, checking the beds. Little Nobby, taken by surprise, had one boot on and another off. Corporal Baker stopped. "What's the matter with YOU?" "I was knocking out a nail which hurts my foot." "Put your boot on at once. Your name?" He passed on to the end door and there whirled round, snorting, "Clarke." Nobby properly cried "Corporal" and limped down the alley at a run (we must always run when called) to bring up stiffly at attention before him. A pause, and then curtly, "Get back to your bed."

Still the Corporal waited and so must we, lined up by our beds. Again, sharply, "Clarke." The performance was repeated, over and over, while the four files of us looked on, bound fast by shame and discipline. We were men, and a man over there was degrading himself and his species, in degrading another. Baker was lusting for trouble and hoped to provoke one of us into some act or word on which to base a charge.

The extreme of this kind of experiential mortification is found, of course, in the concentration-camp literature:

A Jew from Breslau named Silbermann had to stand by idly as SS Sergeant Hoppe brutally tortured his brother to death. Silbermann went mad at the sight, and late at night he precipitated a panic with his frantic cries that the barracks was on fire.[24]

I have considered some of the more elementary and direct assaults upon the self—various forms of disfigurement and defilement through which the symbolic meaning of events in the inmate's immediate presence dramatically fails to corroborate his prior conception of self. I would now like to consider a source of mortification that is less direct in its effect, with a significance for the individual that is less easy to assess: a disruption of the usual relationship between the individual actor and his acts.

The first disruption to consider here is "looping": an agency that creates a defensive response on the part of the inmate takes this very response as the target of its next attack. The individual finds that his protective response to an assault upon self is collapsed into the situation; he cannot defend himself in the usual way by establishing distance between the mortifying situation and himself.

Deference patterns in total institutions provide one illustration of the looping effect. In civil society, when an individual must accept circumstances and commands that affront his conception of self, he is allowed a margin of face-saving reactive expression—sullenness, failure to offer usual signs of deference, *sotto voce* profaning asides, or fugitive expressions of contempt, irony, and derision. Compliance, then, is likely to be associated with an expressed attitude to it that is not itself subject to the same degree of pressure for compliance. Although such self-protective expressive response to humiliating demands does occur in total institutions, the staff may directly penalize inmates for such activity, citing sullenness or insolence explicitly as grounds for further punishment. Thus, in describing the contamination of self resulting from having to drink soup from the beggar's bowl, Kathryn Hulme says of her subject that she

. . . blanked out from her facial expression the revolt that rose up in her fastidious soul as she drank her dregs. One look of rebellion, she knew, would be enough to invite a repetition of the awful abasement which she was sure she could never go through again, not even for the sake of the Blessed Lord Himself

The desegregating process in total institutions creates other instances of looping. In the normal course of affairs in civil society, audience and role segregation keep one's avowals and implicit claims regarding self made in one physical scene of activity from being tested against conduct in other settings.[25] In total institutions spheres of life are desegregated, so that an inmate's conduct in one scene of activity is thrown up to him by staff as a comment and check upon his conduct in another context. A mental patient's effort to present himself in a well-oriented, unantagonistic manner during a diagnostic or treatment conference may be directly embarrassed by evidence introduced concerning his apathy during recreation or the bitter comments he made in a letter to a sibling—a letter which the recipient has forwarded to the hospital administrator, to be added to the patient's dossier and brought along to the conference.

Psychiatric establishments of the advanced type provide excellent illustrations of the looping process, since in them didactic feedback may be erected into a basic therapeutic doctrine. A "permissive" atmosphere is felt to encourage the inmate to "project" or "act out" his typical difficulties in living, which can then be brought to his attention during group-therapy sessions.[26]

Through the process of looping, then, the inmate's reaction to his own situation is collapsed back into this situation itself, and he is not allowed to retain the usual segregation of these phases of action. A second assault upon the inmate's status as an actor may now be cited, one that has been loosely described under the categories of regimentation and tyrannization.

In civil society, by the time the individual is an adult he has incorporated socially acceptable standards for the performance of most of his activity, so that the issue of the correctness of his action arises only at certain points, as when his productivity is judged.[27] He need not constantly look over his shoulder to see if criticism or other sanctions are coming. In addition, many actions will be defined as matters of personal taste, with choice from a range of possibilities specifically allowed. For much activity the judgment and action of authority are held off and one is on one's own. Under such circumstances, one can with over-all profit schedule one's activities to fit into one another—a kind of "personal economy of action," as when an individual postpones eating for a few minutes in order to finish a task, or lays aside a task a little early in order to join a friend for dinner. In a total institution, however, minute segments of a person's line of activity may be subjected to regulations and judgments by staff; the inmate's life is penetrated by constant sanctioning interaction from above, especially during the initial period of stay before the inmate accepts the regulations unthinkingly. Each specification robs the individual of an opportunity to balance his needs and objectives in a personally efficient way and opens up his line of action to sanctions. The autonomy of the act itself is violated.

Although this process of social control is in effect in all organized society, we tend to forget how detailed and closely restrictive it can become in total institutions. The routine reported for one jail for youthful offenders provides a striking example:

At 5:30 we were wakened and had to jump out of bed and stand at attention. When the guard shouted "One!" you removed your night shirt; at "Two!" you folded it; at "Three!" you made your bed. (Only two minutes to make the bed in a difficult and complicated

manner.) All the while three monitors would shout at us: "Hurry it up!" and "Make it snappy!"

We also dressed by numbers: shirts on at "One!"; pants at "Two!"; socks at "Three!"; shoes at "Four!" Any noise, like dropping a shoe or even scraping it along the floor, was enough to send you to the line. . . . Once downstairs everyone faced the wall at strict attention, hands at side, thumbs even with the trouser seams, head up, shoulders back, stomach in, heels together, eyes straight ahead, no scratching or putting hands to face or head, no moving even the fingers. [28]

A jail for adults provides another example:

The silence system was enforced. No talking outside the cell, at meals or at work.

No pictures were allowed in the cell. No gazing about at meals. Bread crusts were allowed to be left only on the left side of the plate. Inmates were required to stand at attention, cap in hand, until any official, visitor or guard moved beyond sight. [29]

And a concentration camp:

In the barracks a wealth of new and confusing impressions overwhelmed the prisoners. Making up beds was a particular source of SS chicanery. Shapeless and matted straw pallets had to be made as even as a board, the pattern of the sheets parallel to the edges, head bolsters set up at right angles. . . . The SS seized on the most trifling offenses as occasions for punishment: keeping hands in pockets in cold weather; turning up the coat collar in rain or wind; missing buttons; the tiniest tear or speck of dirt on the clothing; unshined shoes . . .; shoes that were too well shined—indicating that the wearer was shirking work; failure to salute, including so-called "sloppy posture"; . . . The slightest deviation in dressing ranks and files, or arranging the prisoners in the order of size, or any swaying, coughing, sneezing—any of these might provoke a savage outburst from the SS. [30]

From the military comes an example of the specifications possible in kit laying:

Now the tunic, so folded that the belt made it a straight edge. Covering it, the breeches, squared to the exact area of the tunic, with four concertina-folds facing forward. Towels were doubled once, twice, thrice, and flanked the blue tower. In front of the blue sat a rectangular cardigan. To each side a rolled puttee. Shirts were packed and laid in pairs like flannel bricks. Before

them, pants. Between them, neat balls of socks, wedged in. Our holdalls were stretched wide, with knife, fork, spoon, razor, comb, toothbrush, lather brush, button-stick, in that order, ranged across them. [31]

Similarly, an ex-nun is reported as having to learn to keep her hands still and hidden and to accept the fact that only six specified items were permitted in one's pockets. An ex-mental patient speaks of the humiliation of being doled out limited toilet paper at each request.

As suggested earlier, one of the most telling ways in which one's economy of action can be disrupted is the obligation to request permission or supplies for minor activities that one can execute on one's own on the outside, such as smoking, shaving, going to the toilet, telephoning, spending money, or mailing letters. This obligation not only puts the individual in a submissive or suppliant role "unnatural" for an adult but also opens up his line of action to interceptions by staff. Instead of having his request immediately and automatically granted, the inmate may be teased, denied, questioned at length, not noticed, or, as an ex-mental patient suggests, merely put off:

Probably anyone who has never been in a similarly helpless position cannot realize the humiliation to anyone able-bodied yet lacking authority to do the simplest offices for herself of having to beg repeatedly for even such small necessities as clean linen or a light for her cigarette from nurses who constantly brush her aside with "I'll give it to you in a minute, dear," and go off leaving her unsupplied. Even the canteen staff seemed to share the opinion that civility was wasted upon lunatics, and would keep a patient waiting indefinitely, while they gossiped with their friends. [32]

I have suggested that authority in total institutions is directed to a multitude of items of conduct —dress, deportment, manners—that constantly occur and constantly come up for judgment. The inmate cannot easily escape from the press of judgmental officials and from the enveloping tissue of constraint. A total institution is like a finishing school, but one that has many refinements and is little refined. I would like to comment on two aspects of this tendency toward a multiplication of actively enforced rulings.

First, these rulings are often geared in with an obligation to perform the regulated activity in unison with blocks of fellow inmates. This is what is sometimes called regimentation.

Second, these diffuse rulings occur in an authority system of the *echelon* kind: *any* member of the staff class has certain rights to discipline *any* member of the inmate class, thereby markedly increasing the probability of sanction. (This arrangement, it may be noted, is similar to the one that gives any adult in some small American towns certain rights to correct any child not in the immediate presence of his parents and to demand small services from him.) On the outside, the adult in our society is typically under the authority of a *single* immediate superior in connection with his work, or the authority of one spouse in connection with domestic duties; the only echelon authority he must face— the police—is typically not constantly or relevantly present, except perhaps in the case of traffic-law enforcement.

Given echelon authority and regulations that are diffuse, novel, and strictly enforced, we may expect inmates, especially new ones, to live with chronic anxiety about breaking the rules and the consequence of breaking them—physical injury or death in a concentration camp, being "washed out" in an officer's training school, or demotion in a mental hospital:

> Yet, even in the apparent liberty and friendliness of an "open" ward, I still found a background of threats that made me feel something between a prisoner and a pauper. The smallest offense, from a nervous symptom to displeasing a sister personally, was met by the suggestion of removing the offender to a closed ward. The idea of a return to "J" ward, if I did not eat my food, was brandished at me so constantly that it became an obsession and even such meals as I was able to swallow disagreed with me physically, while other patients were impelled to do unnecessary or uncongenial work by a similar fear. [33]

In total institutions staying out of trouble is likely to require persistent conscious effort. The inmate may forego certain levels of sociability with his fellows to avoid possible incidents.

In concluding this description of the processes of mortification, three general issues must be raised.

First, total institutions disrupt or defile precisely those actions that in civil society have the role of attesting to the actor and those in his presence that he has some command over his world—that he is a person with "adult" self-determination, autonomy, and freedom of action. A failure to retain this kind of adult executive competency, or at least the symbols of it, can produce in the inmate the terror of feeling radically demoted in the age-grading system.

A margin of self-selected expressive behavior— whether of antagonism, affection, or unconcern— is one symbol of self-determination. This evidence of one's autonomy is weakened by such specific obligations as having to write one letter home a week, or having to refrain from expressing sullenness. It is further weakened when this margin of behavior is used as evidence concerning the state of one's psychiatric, religious, or political conscience.

There are certain bodily comforts significant to the individual that tend to be lost upon entrance into a total institution—for example, a soft bed or quietness at night. Loss of this set of comforts is apt to reflect a loss of self-determination, too, for the individual tends to ensure these comforts the moment he has resources to expend. [34]

Loss of self-determination seems to have been ceremonialized in concentration camps; thus we have atrocity tales of prisoners being forced to roll in the mud, stand on their heads in the snow, work at ludicrously useless tasks, swear at themselves, or, in the case of Jewish prisoners, sing anti-Semitic songs. A milder version is found in mental hospitals where attendants have been reported forcing a patient who wanted a cigarette to say "pretty please" or jump up for it. In all such cases the inmate is made to display a giving up of his will. Less ceremonialized, but just as extreme, is the embarrassment to one's autonomy that comes from being locked in a ward, placed in a tight wet pack, or tied in a camisole, and thereby denied the liberty of making small adjustive movements.

Another clear-cut expression of personal inefficacy in total institutions is found in inmates' use of speech. One implication of using words to convey decisions about action is that the recipient of an order is seen as capable of receiving a message and acting under his own power to complete the suggestion or command. Executing the act himself, he can sustain some vestige of the notion that he is self-determining. Responding to the question in his own words, he can sustain the notion that he is somebody to be considered, however slightly. And since it is only words that pass between himself and the others, he succeeds in retaining at least physical distance from them, however unpalatable the command or statement.

The inmate in a total institution can find himself denied even this kind of protective distance and self-action. Especially in mental hospitals and political training prisons, the statements he makes may be discounted as mere symptoms, with staff giving attention to nonverbal aspects of his reply.[35] Often he is considered to be of insufficient ritual status to be given even minor greetings, let alone listened to. Or the inmate may find that a kind of rhetorical use of language occurs: questions such as "Have you washed yet?" or "Have you got both socks on?" may be accompanied by simultaneous searching by the staff which physically discloses the facts, making these verbal questions superfluous. And instead of being told to move in a particular direction at a particular rate, he may find himself pushed along by the guard, or pulled (in the case of over-alled mental patients), or frog-marched. And finally, as will be discussed later, the inmate may find that a dual language exists, with the disciplinary facts of his life given a translated ideal phrasing by the staff that mocks the normal use of language.

The second general consideration is the rationale that is employed for assaults upon the self. This issue tends to place total institutions and their inmates into three different groupings.

In religious institutions the implications environmental arrangements have for the self are explicitly recognized:

That is the meaning of the contemplative life, and the sense of all the apparently meaningless little rules and observances and fasts and obediences and penances and humiliations and labors that go to make up the routine of existence in a contemplative monastery: they all serve to remind us of what we are and Who God is —that we may get sick of the sight of ourselves and turn to Him: and in the end, we will find Him in ourselves, in our own purified natures which have become the mirror of His tremendous Goodness and of His endless love.[36]

The inmates, as well as the staff, actively seek out these curtailments of the self, so that mortification

is complemented by self-mortification, restrictions by renunciations, beatings by self-flagellations, inquisition by confession. Because religious establishments are explicitly concerned with the processes of mortification, they have a special value for the student.

In concentration camps and, to a lesser extent, prisons, some mortifications seem to be arranged solely or mainly for their mortifying power, as when a prisoner is urinated on, but here the inmate does not embrace and facilitate his own destruction of self.

In many of the remaining total institutions, mortifications are officially rationalized on other grounds, such as sanitation (in connection with latrine duty), responsibility for life (in connection with forced feeding), combat capacity (in connection with Army rules for personal appearance), "security" (in connection with restrictive prison regulations).

In total institutions of all three varieties, however, the various rationales for mortifying the self are very often merely rationalizations, generated by efforts to manage the daily activity of a large number of persons in a restricted space with a small expenditure of resources. Further, curtailments of the self occur in all three, even where the inmate is willing and the management has ideal concerns for his well-being.

Two issues have been considered: the inmate's sense of personal inefficacy and the relation of his own desires to the ideal interests of the establishment. The connection between these two issues is variable. Persons can voluntarily elect to enter a total institution and cease thereafter, to their regret, to be able to make such important decisions. In other cases, notably the religious, inmates may begin with and sustain a willful desire to be stripped and cleansed of personal will. Total institutions are fateful for the inmate's civilian self, although the attachment of the inmate to this civilian self can vary considerably.

The processes of mortification I have been considering have to do with the implications for self that persons oriented to a particular expressive idiom might draw from an individual's appearance, conduct, and general situation. In this context I want to consider a third and final issue: the relation between this symbolic-interaction framework for considering the fate of the self and the conventional psycho-physiological one centered around the concept of stress.

The basic facts about self in this report are phrased in a sociological perspective, always leading back to a description of the institutional arrangements which delineate the personal prerogatives of a member. Of course, a psychological assumption is also implied; cognitive processes are invariably involved, for the social arrangements must be "read" by the individual and others for the image of himself that they imply. But, as I have argued, the relation of this cognitive process to other psychological processes is quite variable; according to the general expressive idiom of our society, having one's head shaved is easily perceived as a curtailment of the self, but while this mortification may enrage a mental patient, it may please a monk.

Mortification or curtailment of the self is very likely to involve acute psychological stress for the individual, but for an individual sick with his world or guilt-ridden in it mortification may bring psychological relief. Further, the psychological stress often created by assaults on the self can also be produced by matters not perceived as related to the territories of the self—such as loss of sleep, insufficient food, or protracted decision-making. So, too, a high level of anxiety, or the unavailability of fantasy materials such as movies and books, may greatly increase the psychological effect of a violation of the self's boundaries, but in themselves these facilitating factors have nothing to do with the mortification of the self. Empirically, then, the study of stress and of encroachments on the self will often be tied together, but, analytically, two different frameworks are involved.

NOTES

[1] An example of the description of these processes may be found in Gresham M. Sykes, *The Society of Captives,* Princeton: Princeton University Press, 1958, pp. 63–83.

[2] Sanford M. Dornbusch, "The Military Academy as an Assimilating Institution," *Social Forces,* **33** (1955), p. 317. For an example of initial visiting restrictions in a mental hospital, see D. McI. Johnson and N. Dodds, eds., *The Plea for the Silent,* London: Christopher Johnson, 1957, p. 16. Compare the rule against having visitors

which has often bound domestic servants to their total institution. See J. Jean Hecht, *The Domestic Servant Class in Eighteenth-Century England,* London: Routledge and Kegan Paul, 1956, pp. 127–128.

[3] A useful review in the case of American prisons may be found in Paul W. Tappan, "The Legal Rights of Prisoners," *The Annals,* **293** (May 1954), 99–111.

[4] See, for example, J. Kerkhoff, *How Thin the Veil: A Newspaperman's Story of His Own Mental Crack-up and Recovery,* New York: Greenberg, 1952, p. 110; Elie A. Cohen, *Human Behaviour in the Concentration Camp,* London: Jonathan Cape, 1954, pp. 118–122; Eugen Kogon, *The Theory and Practice of Hell,* New York: Berkley Publishing Corp., n.d., pp. 63–68.

[5] Brendan Behan, *Borstal Boy,* London: Hutchinson, 1958, p. 40. See also Anthony Heckstall-Smith, *Eighteen Months,* London: Allan Wingate, 1954, p. 26.

[6] For a fictionalized treatment of the welcome in a girls' reformatory, see Sara Harris, *The Wayward Ones,* New York: New American Library, 1952, pp. 31–34. A prison version, less explicit, is found in George Dendrickson and Frederick Thomas, *The Truth About Dartmoor,* London: Gollancz, 1954, pp. 42–57.

[7] For example, Thomas Merton, *The Seven Storey Mountain,* New York: Harcourt, Brace, 1948, pp. 290–291.

[8] John M. Murtagh and Sara Harris, *Cast the First Stone,* New York: Pocket Books, 1958, pp. 239–240.

[9] For a prison version see Alfred Hassler, *Diary of a Self-Made Convict,* Chicago: Regnery, 1954, p. 33.

[10] L. D. Hankoff, "Interaction Patterns Among Military Prison Personnel," *U.S. Armed Forces Medical Journal,* **10** (1959), 1419.

[11] Kathryn Hulme, *The Nun's Story,* London: Muller, 1957, p. 52.

[12] *The Holy Rule of Saint Benedict,* Chap. 44.

[13] Wider communities in Western society, of course, have employed this technique too, in the form of public floggings and public hangings, the pillory and stocks. Functionally correlated with the public emphasis on mortifications in total institutions is the commonly found strict ruling that staff is not to be humiliated by staff in the presence of inmates.

[14] L. E. Hinkle, Jr., and H. G. Wolff, "Communist Interrogation and Indoctrination of 'Enemies of the State,'" *A.M.A. Archives of Neurology and Psychiatry,* **75** (1956), 153. An extremely useful report on the profanizing role of fecal matter, and the social necessity of personal as well as environmental control, is provided in C. E. Orbach, *et al.,* "Fears and Defensive Adaptations to the Loss of Anal Sphincter Control," *The Psychoanalytic Review,* **44** (1957), 121–175.

[15] George Orwell, "Such, Such Were the Joys," *Partisan Review,* **19** (September-October 1952), 523.

[16] David P. Boder, *I Did Not Interview the Dead,* Urbana: University of Illinois Press, 1949, p. 50.

[17]Dendrickson and Thomas, *The Truth about Dartmoor,* p. 122.

[18]For example, Lowell Naeve, *A Field of Broken Stones,* Glen Gardner, New Jersey: Libertarian Press, 1950, p. 17; and Holley Cantine and Dachine Rainer, *Prison Etiquette,* Bearsville, N.Y.: Retort Press, 1950, p. 46.

[19]Hinkle and Wolff, "Communist Interrogation . . .," p. 156.

[20]Hulme, *The Nun's Story,* pp. 52–53.

[21]Hassler, *Diary of a Self-Made Convict,* pp. 62–63.

[22]Dendrickson and Thomas, *The Truth about Dartmoor,* p. 175.

[23]Herman Melville, *White Jacket,* New York: Grove Press, n.d., p. 135.

[24]Kogon, *The Theory and Practice of Hell,* p. 160.

[25]In civil society, crimes and certain other forms of deviance affect the way in which the offender is received in all areas of life, but this breakdown of spheres applies mainly to offenders, not to the bulk of the population that does not offend in these ways or offends without being caught.

[26]A clear statement may be found in R. Rapoport and E. Skellern, "Some Therapeutic Functions of Administrative Disturbance," *Administrative Science Quarterly,* **2** (1957), 84–85.

[27]The span of time over which an employee works at his own discretion without supervision can in fact be taken as a measure of his pay and status in an organization. See Elliott Jaques, *The Measurement of Responsibility: A Study of Work, Payment, and Individual Capacity,* Cambridge: Harvard University Press, 1956. And just as "time-span of responsibility" is an index of position, so a long span of freedom from inspection is a reward of position.

[28]Hassler, *Diary of a Self-Made Convict,* p. 155, quoting Robert McCreery.

[29]T. E. Gaddis, *Birdman of Alcatraz,* New York: New American Library, 1958, p. 25. For a similar rule of silence in a British prison, see Frank Norman, *Bang to Rights,* London: Secker and Warburg, 1958, p. 27.

[30]Kogon, *The Theory and Practice of Hell,* p. 68, and pp. 99–100.

[31]Lawrence, p. 83. In this connection see the comments by M. Brewster Smith on the concept of "chicken," in Samuel Stouffer *et al., The American Soldier,* Princeton: Princeton University Press, 1949, Vol. I, p. 390.

[32]Johnson and Dodds, *The Plea for the Silent,* p. 39.

[33]*Ibid.,* p. 36.

[34]This is one source of mortification that civilians practice on themselves during camping vacations, perhaps on the assumption that a new sense of self can be obtained by voluntarily foregoing some of one's previous self-impregnated comforts.

[35]See Alfred H. Stanton and Morris S. Schwartz, *The Mental Hospital,* New York: Basic Books, 1954, pp. 200, 203, 205–206.

[36]Merton, *The Seven Storey Mountain,* p. 372.

Whenever we look at a social establishment . . . we find that participants decline in some way to accept the official view of what they should be putting into and getting out of the organization and, behind this, of what sort of self and world they are to accept for themselves. Where enthusiasm is expected, there will be apathy; where loyalty, there will be disaffection; where attendance, absenteeism; where robustness, some kind of illness; where deeds are to be done, varieties of inactivity. We find a multitude of homely little histories, each in its way a movement of liberty. Whenever worlds are laid on, underlives develop.

ERVING GOFFMAN

If I am correct in assuming that men resist danger and want freedom from all servitudes, then it follows that rebellion does not take place until it has become compulsory.

CARL OGLESBY

It is at the greatest extent and power of a regime, nation or empire that it often suddenly collapses through sheer loss of belief in it.

KENNETH BOULDING

Chapter 4

MOVING TOWARD LIBERTY

Situational Conditions for Disaffection, Delegitimation, and Resistance

We have seen that childhood experience and family structure instill dispositions which tend toward submission. We have seen how institutional authority makes use of such dispositions to ensure compliance, and how pockets of disobedience within the character can be liquidated or neutralized by authority structures through such methods as the manipulation of reward and threat, ideological justification, one-dimensional arrangements, and the undermining of self-confidence. To these means of authoritarian control, we ought to add an additional determinant of compliance: the fact, as we saw in the Asch experiment, that individuals seek to be in accord with each other over the nature of reality in order to maintain the possibility of human interaction. This tendency to seek and accept consensual validation of one's perceptions and feelings is a powerful undergirding for all forms of organized, stable domination.

It is tempting to assume (as most sociologists have tended to assume) that the combined weight of culture and social organization, of superego and external sanctions, of ideology and group pressure, creates a society in which most men do what they are expected to do most of the time, where resistance to expectations is a "deviation," symptomatic of "imperfect socialization" or a malfunctioning of the social system.

But as Goffman points out, in the selection reprinted below, such an assumption may not do justice to actual human experience. Most readers of Milgram's experiments are impressed with the degree to which his subjects were ready to do what they were told to do. But some subjects resisted. We have seen how the behavior of the disobedient in this experiment can be interpreted in characterological terms—they were socialized differently from the average, obedient subjects; in a statistical sense, they were not normal. Such an account is helpful, but it cannot be the whole story. Consider, first, that even the subjects who were most obedient tended to raise objections to their orders and exhibit signs of marked stress. Some part of themselves wished to hold back. More significantly, as soon as Milgram permitted space for disobedience (as when the experimenter left the room), as soon as social support for resistance was manifest, as soon as the "victim" was in direct contact with the subject—rates of disobedience markedly increased.

These findings support the position eloquently sketched by Goffman below. We should not assume that conformity and obedience are the most natural or fundamental tendencies of individuals. Perhaps equally powerful is a tendency to withhold the self from total commitment to any particular role, relationship, group, or institution. Social relations need to be viewed *dialectically,* as situations in which forces leading toward identification, commitment, and compliance are always in counterposition to forces generating opposition, withdrawal, and resistance.

What we are really talking about here are two different strategies for inquiry. The more conventional sociological perspective suggests that investigation ought to emphasize the ways in which control, order, and regularity are achieved in social life. The dialectical perspective asks us to search out the expressions of opposition and the tendencies toward disorder and breakdown which are also always present.

Goffman's study of the mental hospital as a total institution is an outstanding illustration of the value of the dialectical approach. As we saw, in the previous section, the total institution represents the most extreme form of authoritarian domination known to society. By definition, the total institution aims to control, not just a part of the behavior of its inmates, but the totality of their existence, including even the kind of character structures they are to have and the kind of persons they conceive themselves to be. Yet the dialectical strategy of analysis leads Goffman to observe not only compliance but also a rich variety of means of resistance on the part of patients.

In Goffman's terminology, activity whereby subordinates do what they are expected or authorized to do can be called "primary adjustment." But alongside primary adjustment, there flourishes "secondary adjustment"—activity which is unsanctioned, unauthorized, or otherwise meaningful as a deliberate departure from the officially laid down regimen. Secondary adjustments are not directed at changing or overthrowing authority; rather they may be seen as the most elementary form of resistance—the refusal to have one's self totally defined by the authority structure or to have one's needs totally dependent upon that structure for satisfaction. As Goffman makes clear, some secondary adjustments are straightforward attempts to satisfy needs which are unrecognized or frustrated by official arrangements. But there is a deeper meaning to secondary adjustments than simply the satisfaction of particular needs; these actions are also and more fundamentally efforts at self-assertion and autonomy—efforts to create a world for oneself independent of, and often at odds with, the world "laid on" by the institutional situation.

The underlife created by efforts at secondary adjustment is an extraordinarily varied one. It includes, most poignantly, acts of pretended obsequiousness and self-abnegation, such as those described by Carl Oglesby in the selection reprinted here or those immortalized in the character of the "Good Soldier Schweik." Superficially, such exemplary obedience seems like the ultimate triumph of authority, but underneath we detect elements of sarcasm and insult to the master. As Oglesby suggests, such pretense suggests that the enslaved is still capable of exercising a certain degree of choice.

But most forms of secondary adjustment are more assertive than acts of exaggerated obedience. There is an infinite variety of unauthorized means of satisfying officially unapproved wants. The procurement and trading of contraband in prisons is an example. In civilian society, it is plausible to label various forms of organized crime, bribery, graft, and embezzlement as secondary adjustment, as well as less clearly illegal means of going outside official channels.

In total institutions, and in everyday life outside these institutions, individuals are continuously involved in creating a world of their own, in little acts of expressive defiance. Escape, as Goffman suggests, can be accomplished by such means as overinvolvement in certain authorized activities, but it can involve more extended journeys with the aid of alcohol, drugs, or psychosis. Defiance or evasion of authority may be expressed in transitory gestures, or the individual may find a way to pattern his style of being so as to insulate part of himself from the full implications of official regimen.

But the most effective means of secondary adjustment are organized collectively rather than individually. Within all total institutions may be found inmate subcultures that enable unapproved wants to be fulfilled in unauthorized, but systematic, ways. These subcultures protect members against the full weight of official surveillance; they offer definitions of self and status differing markedly from those that are officially promulgated; and they provide possibilities for affection and fraternity officially denied by the institution. Inmate subcultures are paralleled by similar forms of collective secondary adjustment in all bureaucratic work organizations, in schools, and in urban communities—in short, wherever persons are governed by rules or laws which frustrate their felt needs and are not of their own making. Thus, bureaucratic, urbanized society has a richly proliferated underlife of subcultures; typical examples are informal factory groups which keep down production rates; teenage gangs; the gay life; the drug culture; religious cults; nudist colonies; bohemian quarters; communal families; and so on.

Secondary adjustments represent acts of resistance to authority, but it is crucial to recognize that, in themselves, they do not threaten the stability or challenge the fundamental legitimacy of the official authority structure. Indeed, in many cases, secondary adjustments strengthen a system of domination, inso-far as an otherwise intolerable situation becomes tolerable. An authority struc-ture can remain stable if it can maintain a delicate equilibrium between its own demands for conformity and the patterns of secondary adjustment which may emerge. At bottom, secondary adjustments are efforts by subordinates to fulfill their needs and maintain their identities without fundamentally disturbing the structure of power in the situation.

In order to understand how resistance becomes a direct challenge to author-ity, we should return to the dialectical perspective recommended by Goffman. Goffman urges us to define the individual as a "stance-taking entity" who adopts a position somewhere between identification with and opposition to authority; the individual is "ready at the slightest pressure to regain its balance by shifting its involvement in either direction." We have already seen (Chapter 2) how patterns of early socialization lead to individual differences in what we can now call the point of balance between obedience and resistance. Some persons are characterologically predisposed toward submission; others, toward opposition —but all, according to Goffman, are open to pressures in either direction. Secondary adjustment is the most straightforward way to resolve such tensions, but the equilibrium can break down, and overt protest or rebellion can break out for at least two fundamental reasons.

On the one hand, individuals may find that established modes of secondary adjustment are no longer satisfactory for defending their acquired sense of self or for satisfying their felt needs. On the other hand, the authority structure may force subordinates into overt opposition by actively repressing or undermining forms of secondary adjustment which had previously been overlooked or ig-nored. In the first type of situation, we find individuals developing a new sense of their own power, competence, rights, or moral obligation, and, therefore, finding that the established relationship with authority is no longer legitimate. In the second type of situation, we find individuals threatened, uprooted, or con-strained, and, therefore, finding that they can no longer accommodate. Instead they are forced to defend themselves against further encroachment on what they had considered their legitimate prerogatives.

Changing conceptions of the legitimacy of established authority may have complex origins. Some illustrations of this process are provided in the selections which follow. Agis Salpukas' article, for instance, shows how new attitudes toward work, arising in the "youth culture," and new conceptions of self, arising from higher levels of education, have had an impact on the readiness of young workers to accept the discipline of boring, repetitive, assembly-line work. The very youthfulness of the work force at Lordstown may make the workers there less prone to resignation than older workers.

Nathan Caplan suggests that rising levels of education have affected the self-conceptions and expectations of black youth in cities. The young generation of blacks have, in addition, been strongly influenced by public lip-service to the goals of equal rights and by liberation movements in Africa and in the United States. They feel that they are no longer obligated to accept oppressive conditions. A further source of change was undoubtedly federal programs which promised to end poverty and provide equal opportunity—programs which made the established situation illegitimate (since even the authorities declared it to be wrong) but which did not in fact achieve the promised goals.

Todd Gitlin and Nanci Hollander's description of the rise of a protest movement among white Southern migrant youth to Chicago suggests that an important source of new consciousness of rights can be the deliberate political organizer (in this case college students sent to the neighborhood by Students for a Democratic Society, and a minister sent by a liberal church organization). The organizer articulates new possibilities and suggests tactics. In this case, the organizers did not lead the young guys so much as suggest that new ways of acting were possible and morally right.

Finally, the case of Daniel Ellsberg suggests how an individual who is an accomplice of power can find his equilibrium disrupted—by the discovery that his sense of self and moral obligation is no longer consonant with the practices and goals of the authority structure he is supporting.

All of these cases illustrate the contagion of resistance. When one group, previously quiescent, begins to claim rights and to engage in protest, the act ripples out to affect other subordinated or accommodating groups and individuals. This is in part because of the new conceptions of rights and obligations which are thus set loose, but also because the methods employed give the subordinated a new sense of potential efficacy. Thus young workers acquire a new spirit of protest because of the student revolt; young Southern whites (raised as racists and authoritarians) learn the possibilities of protest from the black revolt.

But these cases of overt resistance did not occur simply because those involved acquired new ideas of legitimacy and their own efficacy. In each case, such ideas converged with the fact that the structure of authority was placing increased pressure on the patterns of previously established adjustment. The Lordstown workers were confronted with unprecedented speedup; young blacks with an unprecedented scarcity of jobs; young migrants with unprecedented harassment by police; Ellsberg by an unprecedented failure of military expertise. All revolts are thus complex combinations of self-assertion and self-defense, and our attempt to divide these into two clearly delimited sources of motivation cannot apply to any real case.

All of the illustrations of overt resistance I have so far discussed have involved for participants genuine experiences of release and rebellion, and they all represent fundamental challenges to the legitimacy of the situation in which they occurred. But the experience was momentary and the challenge was partial. As Kenneth Boulding argues, an established structure of authority can make use of such protest. In particular, authorities can relegitimate the structure by accommodating to the new expectations of subordinates, and by withdrawing its power from the encroachment on rights which has provoked revolt. We shall, in the next section, examine some of the ways authority structures can react to such challenges, but at this point let us at least be clear that a reestablishment of equilibrium is typically possible, and the result can well be a more stable, and more rational, system of rule.

Protests can be stifled, as well as adapted to. One of the truly original points made by Carl Oglesby is that there is no simple straight line from increased repression to effectively organized revolutionary overthrow of the structure of authority. Even when those in authority provide the dominated with no space for adjustment, a major leap is required from the stance of the radically disaffected to the committed revolutionary. For the latter stance may require a degree of selflessness even more total than thoroughgoing subjugation. I think Oglesby goes too far when he seems to argue that the overthrow of oppressive authority *requires* such total commitment. Mass insurrections have often occurred and often led to the downfall of regimes without participants undergoing the type of total transformation described by Oglesby. Moreover, he seems to suggest that revolutionaries act when death or total degradation are the only alternatives. It seems to me that revolutionary commitment can be rooted in material well-being as well as deprivation, and in experiences less directly related to physical oppression. Despite these reservations, however, I think that Oglesby's reflections are profoundly helpful in understanding how ordinary men and women can be impelled into revolutionary commitment—how fundamentally problematic such commitment is for one's individuality, yet how necessary such commitment may be for the realization of self. Goffman's description of secondary adjustment and Oglesby's description of revolutionary commitment represent the extreme poles of resistance; yet, when they are compared, one can see a dialectical unity between them.

SOME SUGGESTED READINGS

For illustrations of secondary adjustment, see G. Sykes, *Society of Captives* (Princeton: Princeton University Press, 1958); A. Cohen, *Delinquent Boys* (Glencoe: Free Press, 1955); B. Blau, *Dynamics of Bureaucracy* (Chicago: University of Chicago, 1955); J. S. Coleman, *The Adolescent Society* (New York: Free Press, 1961).
   Some useful sources on conditions giving rise to resistance and revolt:
   J. Davies, ed. *When Men Revolt and Why* (New York: Free Press, 1971); A. Kornhauser, R. Dubin, and A. Ross, eds., *Industrial Conflict* (New York: McGraw, 1954); F. Fanon, *The Wretched of the Earth* (New York: Grove, 1968); E. Hobsbawm, *Primitive Rebels* (New York: Norton, 1965); L. Edwards, *The Natural History of Revolution* (Chicago: University of Chicago, 1970); R. Rubenstein, *Rebels in Eden* (Boston: Little, Brown, 1970); and R. Ash, *Social Movements in America* (Chicago: Markham, 1972).

THE UNDERLIFE OF A PUBLIC INSTITUTION

Erving Goffman

In every social establishment, there are official expectations as to what the participant owes the establishment. Even in cases where there is no specific task, as in some night-watchman jobs, the organization will require some presence of mind, some awareness of the current situation, and some readiness for unanticipated events; as long as an establishment demands that its participants not sleep on the job, it asks them to be awake to certain matters. And where sleeping is part of the expectation, as in a home or a hotel, then there will be limits on where and when the sleeping is to occur, with whom, and with what bed manners.[1] And behind these claims on the individual, be they great or small, the managers of every establishment will have a widely embracing implicit conception of what the individual's character must be for these claims on him to be appropriate.

Whenever we look at a social establishment, we find a counter to this first theme: we find that participants decline in some way to accept the official view of what they should be putting into and getting out of the organization and, behind this, of what sort of self and world they are to accept for themselves. Where enthusiasm is expected, there will be apathy; where loyalty, there will be disaffection; where attendance, absenteeism; where robustness, some kind of illness; where deeds are to be done, varieties of inactivity. We find a multitude of homely little histories, each in its way a movement of liberty. Whenever worlds are laid on, underlives develop.

The study of underlife in restrictive total institutions has some special interest. When existence is cut to the bone, we can learn what people do to flesh out their lives. Stashes, means of transportation, free places, territories, supplies for economic and social exchange—these apparently are some of the minimal requirements for building up a life. Ordinarily these arrangements are taken for granted as part of one's primary adjustment; seeing them twisted out of official existence through bargains, wit, force, and cunning, we can see their significance anew. The study of total institutions also suggests that formal organizations have standard places of vulnerability, such as supply rooms, sick bays, kitchens, or scenes of highly technical labor. These are the damp corners where secondary adjustments breed and start to infest the establishment.

The mental hospital represents a peculiar instance of those establishments in which underlife is likely to proliferate. Mental patients are persons who caused the kind of trouble on the outside that led someone physically, if not socially, close to them to take psychiatric action against them. Often this trouble was associated with the "prepatient" having indulged in situational improprieties of some kind, conduct out of place in the setting. It is just such misconduct that conveys a moral rejection of the communities, establishments, and relationships that have a claim to one's attachment.

Stigmatization as mentally ill and involuntary hospitalization are the means by which we answer these offenses against propriety. The individual's persistence in manifesting symptoms after entering the hospital, and his tendency to develop additional symptoms during his initial response to the hospital, can now no longer serve him well as expressions of disaffection. From the patient's point of view, to decline to exchange a word with the staff or with his fellow patients may be ample evidence of rejecting the institution's view of what and who he is; yet higher management may construe this alienative expression as just the sort of

"The Underlife of a Public Institution" from Asylums *by Erving Goffman. Reprinted by permission of Doubleday and Company, Inc. Footnotes have been edited.*

symptomatology the institution was established to deal with and as the best kind of evidence that the patient properly belongs where he now finds himself. In short, mental hospitalization outmaneuvers the patient, tending to rob him of the common expressions through which people hold off the embrace of organizations—insolence, silence, *sotto voce* remarks, un-cooperativeness, malicious destruction of interior decorations, and so forth; these signs of disaffiliation are now read as signs of their maker's proper affiliation. Under these conditions all adjustments are primary.

Furthermore, there is a vicious-circle process at work. Persons who are lodged on "bad" wards find that very little equipment of any kind is given them—clothes may be taken from them each night, recreational materials may be withheld, and only heavy wooden chairs and benches provided for furniture. Acts of hostility against the institution have to rely on limited, ill-designed devices, such as banging a chair against the floor or striking a sheet of newspaper sharply so as to make an annoying explosive sound. And the more inadequate this equipment is to convey rejection of the hospital, the more the act appears as a psychotic symptom, and the more likely it is that management feels justified in assigning the patient to a bad ward. When a patient finds himself in seclusion, naked and without visible means of expression, he may have to rely on tearing up his mattress, if he can, or writing with feces on the wall—actions management takes to be in keeping with the kind of person who warrants seclusion.

We can also see this circular process at work in the small, illicit, talisman-like possessions that inmates use as symbolic devices for separating themselves from the position they are supposed to be in. What I think is a typical example may be cited from prison literature:

Prison clothing is anonymous. One's possessions are limited to toothbrush, comb, upper or lower cot, half the space upon a narrow table, a razor. As in jail, the urge to collect possessions is carried to preposterous extents. Rocks, string, knives—anything made by man and forbidden in man's institution—anything—a red comb, a different kind of toothbrush, a belt—these things are assiduously gathered, jealously hidden or triumphantly displayed. [2]

But when a patient, whose clothes are taken from him each night, fills his pockets with bits of string and rolled-up paper, and when he fights to keep these possessions in spite of the consequent inconvenience to those who must regularly go through his pockets, he is usually seen as engaging in symptomatic behavior befitting a very sick patient, not as someone who is attempting to stand apart from the place accorded him.

Official psychiatric doctrine tends to define alienative acts as psychotic ones—this view being reinforced by the circular processes that lead the patient to exhibit alienation in a more and more bizarre form—but the hospital cannot be run according to this doctrine. The hospital cannot decline to demand from its members exactly what other organizations must insist on; psychiatric doctrine is supple enough to do this, but institutions are not. Given the standards of the institution's environing society, there have to be at least the minimum routines connected with feeding, washing, dressing, bedding the patients, and protecting them from physical harm. Given these routines, there have to be inducements and exhortations to get patients to follow them. Demands must be made, and disappointment is shown when a patient does not live up to what is expected of him. Interest in seeing psychiatric "movement" or "improvement" after an initial stay on the wards leads the staff to encourage "proper" conduct and to express disappointment when a patient backslides into "psychosis." The patient is thus re-established as someone whom others are depending on, someone who ought to know enough to act correctly. Some improprieties, especially ones like muteness and apathy that do not obstruct and even ease ward routines, may continue to be perceived naturalistically as symptoms, but on the whole the hospital operates semi-officially on the assumption that the patient ought to act in a manageable way and be respectful of psychiatry, and that he who does will be rewarded by improvement in life conditions and he who doesn't will be punished by a reduction of amenities. Within this semi-official reinstatement of ordinary organizational practices, the patient finds that many of the traditional ways of taking leave of a place without moving from it have retained their validity; secondary adjustments are therefore possible.

Of the many different kinds of secondary adjustment, some are of particular interest because they bring into the clear the general theme of involvement and disaffection, characteristic of all these practices.

One of these special types of secondary adjustment is "removal activities" (or "kicks"), namely, undertakings that provide something for the individual to lose himself in, temporarily blotting out all sense of the environment which, and in which, he must abide. In total institutions a useful exemplary case is provided by Robert Stroud, the "Birdman," who, from watching birds out his cell window, through a spectacular career of finagling and make-do, fabricated a laboratory and became a leading ornithological contributor to medical literature, all from within prison. Language courses in prisoner-of-war camps and art courses in prisons can provide the same release.

Central Hospital provided several of these escape worlds for inmates.[3] One, for example, was sports. Some of the baseball players and a few tennis players seemed to become so caught up in their sport, and in the daily record of their efforts in competition, that at least for the summer months this became their overriding interest. In the case of baseball this was further strengthened by the fact that, within the hospital, parole patients could follow national baseball as readily as could many persons on the outside. For some young patients, who never failed to go, when allowed, to a dance held in their service or in the recreation building, it was possible to live for the chance of meeting someone "interesting" or remeeting someone interesting who had already been met—in much the same way that college students are able to survive their studies by looking forward to the new "dates" that may be found in extracurricular activities. The "marriage moratorium" in Central Hospital, effectively freeing a patient from his marital obligations to a non-patient, enhanced this removal activity. For a handful of patients, the semi-annual theatrical production was an extremely effective removal activity: tryouts, rehearsals, costuming, scenery-making, staging, writing and rewriting, performing—all these seemed as successful as on the outside in building a world apart for the participants. Another kick, important to some patients—and a worrisome concern for the hospital chaplains—was

the enthusiastic espousal of religion. Still another, for a few patients, was gambling.

Portable ways of getting away were much favored in Central Hospital, paper-back murder mysteries, cards, and even jigsaw puzzles being carried around on one's person. Not only could leave be taken of the ward and grounds be taken leave of through these means, but if one had to wait for an hour or so upon an official, or the serving of a meal, or the opening of the recreation building, the self-implication of this subordination could be dealt with by immediately bringing forth one's own world-making equipment.

Individual means of creating a world were striking. One depressed, suicidal alcoholic, apparently a good bridge player, disdained bridge with almost all other patient players, carrying around his own pocket bridge player and writing away occasionally for a new set of competition hands. Given a supply of his favorite gumdrops and his pocket radio, he could pull himself out of the hospital world at will, surrounding all his senses with pleasantness.

In considering removal activities we can again raise the issue of overcommitment to an establishment. In the hospital laundry, for example, there was a patient worker who had been on the job for several years. He had been given the job of unofficial foreman, and, unlike almost all other patient workers, he threw himself into his work with a capacity, devotion, and seriousness that were evident to many. Of him, the laundry charge attendant said: "That one there is my special helper. He works harder than all the rest put together. I would be lost without him."

In exchange for his effort, the attendant would bring from home something for his patient to eat almost every day. And yet there was something grotesque in his adjustment, for it was apparent that his deep voyage into the work world had a slightly make-believe character; after all, he was a patient, not a foreman, and he was clearly reminded of this off the job.

Obviously, as some of these illustrations imply, removal activities need not be in themselves illegitimate; it is the function that they come to serve for the inmate that leads us to consider them along with other secondary adjustments. An extreme here, perhaps, is individual psychotherapy in state mental hospitals; this privilege is so rare in these institutions,[4] and the resulting contact with a staff psychiatrist so unique in terms of hospital status structure, that an inmate can to some degree forget where he is as he pursues his psychotherapy. By actually receiving what the institution formally claims to offer, the patient can succeed in getting away from what the establishment actually provides. There is a general implication here. Perhaps every activity that an establishment obliges or permits its members to participate in is a potential threat to the organization, for it would seem that there is no activity in which the individual cannot become over-engrossed.

Another property is clearly evident in some undercover practices and possibly a factor in all of them: I refer to what Freudians sometimes call "overdetermination." Some illicit activities are pursued with a measure of spite, malice, glee, and triumph, and at a personal cost, that cannot be accounted for by the intrinsic pleasure of consuming the product. True, it is central to closed restrictive institutions that apparently minor satisfactions can come to be defined as great ones. But even correcting for this re-evaluation, something remains to be explained.

One aspect of the overdetermination of some secondary adjustments is the sense one gets of a practice being employed *merely* because it is forbidden.[5] Inmates in Central Hospital who had succeeded in some elaborate evasion of the rules often seemed to seek out a fellow inmate, even one who could not be entirely trusted, to display before him evidence of the evasion. A patient back from an overlate foray into the local town's night life would be full of stories of his exploits the next day; another would call aside his friends and show them where he had stashed the empty liquor bottle whose contents he had consumed the night before, or display the condoms in his wallet. Nor was it surprising to see the limits of safe concealment tested. I knew an extremely resourceful alcoholic who would smuggle in a pint of vodka, put some in a paper drinking cup, and sit on the most exposed part of the lawn he could find, slowly getting drunk; at such times he took pleasure in offering hospitality to persons of semi-staff status. Similarly, I knew an attendant who would park his car just outside the patient canteen—the social hub of the

patient universe—and there he and a friendly patient would discuss the most intimate qualifications of the passing females while resting a paper cup full of bourbon on the differential covering, just below the sight line of the crowd, drinking a toast, as it were, to their distance from the scene around them.

Another aspect of the overdeterminism of some secondary adjustments is that the very pursuit of them seems to be a source of satisfaction. As previously suggested in regard to courtship contacts, the institution can become defined as one's opponent in a serious game, the object being to score against the hospital. Thus I have heard cliques of patients pleasurably discuss the possibility that evening of "scoring" for coffee, accurately employing this larger term for a smaller activity.[6] The tendency of prison inmates to smuggle food and other comforts into the cell of someone suffering solitary confinement may be seen not only as an act of charity but also as a way of sharing by association the spirit of someone taking a stand against authority. Similarly, the time-consuming elaborate escape planning that patients, prisoners, and P.O.W. internees engage in can be seen not merely as a way of getting out but also as a way of giving meaning to being in.

I am suggesting that secondary adjustments are overdetermined, some of them especially so. These practices serve the practitioner in ways other than the most evident ones: whatever else they accomplish these practices seem to demonstrate—to the practitioner if no one else—that he has some selfhood and personal autonomy beyond the grasp of the organization.

If a function of secondary adjustments is to place a barrier between the individual and the social unit in which he is supposed to be participating, we should expect some secondary adjustments to be empty of intrinsic gain and to function solely to express unauthorized distance—a self-preserving "rejection of one's rejectors."[7] This seems to happen with the very common forms of ritual insubordination, for example, griping or bitching, where this behavior is not realistically expected to bring about change. Through direct insolence that does not meet with immediate correction, or remarks passed half out of hearing of authority, or gestures performed behind the back of authority, subordinates express some detachment from the place officially accorded them. An ex-inmate of the penitentiary at Lewisburg provides an illustration:

On the surface, life here appears to run almost placidly, but one needs to go only a very little beneath the surface to find the whirlpools and eddies of anger and frustration. The muttering of discontent and rebellion goes on constantly: the sotto voce sneer whenever we pass an official or a guard, the glare carefully calculated to express contempt without arousing overt retaliation.[8]

Brendan Behan provides a British prison illustration:

*The warder shouted at him.
"Right, sir," he shouted. "Be right along, sir," adding in a lower tone, "You shit-'ouse."*[9]

Some of these ways of openly but safely taking a stand outside the authorized one are beautiful, especially when carried out collectively. Again, prisons provide ready examples:

How to express contempt for authority? The manner of "obeying" orders is one way. . . . Negroes are especially apt at parody, sometimes breaking into a goose-step. They seat themselves at table 10 at a time, snatching off caps simultaneously and precisely.

When the sky pilot got up in the pulpit to give us our weekly pep talk each Sunday he would always make some feeble joke which we always laughed at as loud and as long as possible, although he must have known that we were sending him up. He still used to make some mildly funny remark and every time he did the whole church would be filled with rawcous [sic] laughter, even though only half the audience had heard what had been said.

Some acts of ritual insubordination rely on irony, found in the wider society in the form of gallows gallantry and in institutions in the construction of heavily meaningful mascots. A standard irony in total institutions is giving nicknames to especially threatening or unpleasant aspects of the environment. In concentration camps, turnips were sometimes called "German pineapples," fatigue drill, "Geography." In mental wards in Mount Sinai Hospital, brain-damage cases held for surgery would call the hospital "Mount Cyanide," and staff doctors were

typically misnamed, being referred to by such terms as "lawyer'" "white-collar worker," "chief of crew," "one of the presidents," "bartender," "supervisor of insurance" and "credit manager." One of us (E.A.W.) was called by such variations as "Weinberg," "Weingarten," "Weiner" and "Wiseman."[10]

In prison, the punishment block may be called the "tea-garden." In Central Hospital, one of the wards containing incontinent patients was sometimes felt to be the punishment ward for attendants, who called it "the rose garden." An ex-mental patient provides another illustration:

Back in the dayroom Virginia decided that her change of clothing represented Dressing Therapy. D.T. Today was my turn for D.T. This would have been rather amusing if you had had a good stiff drink. Of paraldehyde. The Juniper Cocktail, as we call it, we gay ladies of Juniper Hill. A martini, please, we more sophisticated ones say. And where, nurse, is the olive?[11]

It should be understood, of course, that the threatening world responded to with ironies need not be one sponsored by an alien human authority, but may be one that is self-imposed, or imposed by nature, as when dangerously ill persons joke about their situation.[12]

Beyond irony, however, there is an even more subtle and telling kind of ritual insubordination. There is a special stance that can be taken to alien authority; it combines stiffness, dignity, and coolness in a particular mixture that conveys insufficient insolence to call forth immediate punishment and yet expresses that one is entirely one's own man. Since this communication is made through the way in which the body and face are held, it can be constantly conveyed wherever the inmate finds himself. Illustrations can be found in prison society:

"Rightness" implies bravery, fearlessness, loyalty to peers, avoidance of exploitation, adamant refusal to concede the superiority of the official value system, and repudiation of the notion that the inmate is of a lower order. It consists principally in the reassertion of one's basic integrity, dignity, and worth in an essentially degrading situation, and the exhibition of these personal

qualities regardless of any show of force by the official system.[13]

Similarly, in Central Hospital, in the "tough" punishment wards of maximum security, where inmates had very little more to lose, fine examples could be found of patients not going out of their way to make trouble but by their very posture conveying unconcern and mild contempt for all levels of the staff, combined with utter self-possession.

It would be easy to account for the development of secondary adjustments by assuming that the individual possessed an array of needs, native or cultivated, and that when lodged in a milieu that denied these needs the individual simply responded by developing makeshift means of satisfaction. I think this explanation fails to do justice to the importance of these undercover adaptations for the structure of the self.

The practice of reserving something of oneself from the clutch of an institution is very visible in mental hospitals and prisons but can be found in more benign and less totalistic institutions, too. I want to argue that this recalcitrance is not an incidental mechanism of defense but rather an essential constituent of the self.

Sociologists have always had a vested interest in pointing to the ways in which the individual is formed by groups, identifies with groups, and wilts away unless he obtains emotional support from groups. But when we closely observe what goes on in a social role, a spate of sociable interaction, a social establishment—or in any other unit of social organization—embracement of the unit is not all that we see. We always find the individual employing methods to keep some distance, some elbow room, between himself and that with which others assume he should be identified. No doubt a state-type mental hospital provides an overly lush soil for the growth of these secondary adjustments, but in fact, like weeds, they spring up in any kind of social organization. If we find, then, that in all situations actually studied the participant has erected defenses against his social bondedness, why should we base our conception of the self upon how the individual would act were conditions "just right"?

The simplest sociological view of the individual and his self is that he is to himself what his place in an organization defines him to be. When

pressed, a sociologist modifies this model by granting certain complications: the self may be not yet formed or may exhibit conflicting dedications. Perhaps we should further complicate the construct by elevating these qualifications to a central place, initially defining the individual, for sociological purposes, as a stance-taking entity, a something that takes up a position somewhere between identification with an organization and opposition to it, and is ready at the slightest pressure to regain its balance by shifting its involvement in either direction. It is thus *against something* that the self can emerge. This has been appreciated by students of totalitarianism:

In short, Ketman means self-realization against something. He who practices Ketman suffers because of the obstacles he meets; but if these obstacles were suddenly to be removed, he would find himself in a void which might perhaps prove much more painful. Internal revolt is sometimes essential to spiritual health, and can create a particular form of happiness. What can be said openly is often much less interesting than the emotional magic of defending one's private sanctuary. [14]

I have argued the same case in regard to total institutions. May this not be the situation, however, in free society, too?

Without something to belong to, we have no stable self, and yet total commitment and attachment to any social unit implies a kind of selflessness. Our sense of being a person can come from being drawn into a wider social unit; our sense of selfhood can arise through the little ways in which we resist the pull. Our status is backed by the solid buildings of the world, while our sense of personal identity often resides in the cracks.

NOTES

[1]When stagecoach travelers in Europe in the fifteenth century might be required to share an inn bed with a stranger, courtesy books laid down codes of proper bed conduct. See Norbert Elias, *Über den Prozess Der Zivilisation,* Basel: Verlag Haus Zum Falken, 1934, Vol. II, pp. 219–221. On the sociology of sleep I am indebted to unpublished writings of Vilhelm Aubert and Kaspar Naegle.

[2] Cantine and Rainer, p. 78. Compare the things that small boys stash in their pockets; some of these items also seem to provide a wedge between the boy and the domestic establishment.

[3] Behind informal social typing and informal group formation in prisons there is often to be seen a removal activity. Caldwell, pp. 651–653, provides some interesting examples of prisoners on such kicks: those involved in security and using drugs; those focused on leatherwork for sale; and "Spartans," those involved in the glorification of their bodies, the prison locker room apparently serving as a muscle beach; the homosexuals; the gamblers, etc. The point about these activities is that each is world-building for the person caught up in it, thereby displacing the prison.

[4] Of approximately 7,000 patients in Central Hospital, I calculated at the time of the study that about 100 received some kind of individual psychotherapy in any one year.

[5] This theme is developed by Albert Cohen in *Delinquent Boys,* Glencoe, Ill.: The Free Press, 1955.

[6] Traditionally, the value of pursuit itself is considered relative to the wider society, as when drug addicts are defined as playing an intensely meaningful daily game against society in obtaining the daily fix, and hustlers, grifters, and delinquents are seen as working hard at the intriguing, honorable task of making money without being seen working for it.

[7] Lloyd W. McCorkle and Richard Korn, "Resocialization Within Walls," *The Annals,* **293** (1954), 88.

[8] Alfred Hassler, *Diary of a Self-made Convict,* Chicago: Regnery, 1954, pp. 70–71.

[9] B. Behan, *Borstal Boy,* London: Hutchinson, 1958, p. 45. Primary school children in American society very early learn how to cross their fingers, mutter contradictions, and grimace covertly—through all of these means expressing a margin of autonomy even while submitting to the teacher's verbal punishment.

[10] Edwin Weinstein and Robert Kahn, *Denial of Illness,* Springfield, Ill.: Charles Thomas, 1955, p. 61. See especially Chap. 6.

[11] Mary Jane Ward, *The Snake Pit,* New York: New American Library, 1955, p. 65.

[12] A useful report on ironies and other devices for dealing with life threat is provided by Renee Fox in *Experiment Perilous,* Glencoe, Ill.: The Free Press, 1959, pp. 170 ff.

[13] Richard Cloward, "Social Control in the Prison," S.S.R.C. Pamphlet No. 15, p. 40. Some minority groups have, relative to the society at large, a variant of this non-provoking but hands-off-me stance. Compare, for example, the "cool stud" complex among urban American Negroes.

[14] Czeslaw Milosz, *The Captive Mind,* New York: Vintage Books, 1955, p. 76.

YOUNG WORKERS DISRUPT KEY G.M. PLANT

Agis Salpukas

Production on the world's fastest assembly line, on which the General Motors Corporation has pinned its hopes of being able to meet foreign competition, has been seriously disrupted by mostly young workers who say they are being asked to work too hard and too fast to be able to turn out quality automobiles.

The outcome of the labor dispute, in which the youngest local of the United Automobile Workers is confronting one of General Motor's toughest management teams, could have wide repercussions for United States industry.

The struggle has raised a wider issue of how management can deal with a young worker who is determined to have a say as to how a job should be performed and is not as easily moved by management threats that there are plenty of others waiting in line if he does not want to do the job.

It also comes at a time when the Nixon Administration is stressing rising productivity as the way to stop inflation and the influx of foreign goods.

The costly dispute centers on whether management has eliminated jobs and distributed extra work to the remaining men to the extent that they are unable to keep up with the assembly line in the Lordstown plant.

General Motors estimates that it has lost the production of 12,000 Vega automobiles and about 4,000 Chevrolet trucks worth about $45 million. Management has had to close down the assembly line repeatedly since last month after workers slowed their work and allowed cars to move down the line without performing all operations.

A. B. Anderson, the plant manager, said in an interview, "We've had engine blocks pass 40 men without them doing their work."

Management has also accused workers of sabotage, such as breaking windshields, breaking off rear-view mirrors, slashing upholstery, bending signal levers, putting washers in carburetors and breaking off ignition keys.

In the last four weeks a lot that holds about 2,000 cars has often been filled with Vegas that had to be taken back into the plant for repair work before they could be shipped to dealers. Sales of Vegas in the last two weeks have been cut about in half.

The union, which concedes that there may have been some sabotage by a few angry workers, maintains that the bulk of the problems with the cars were a result of cutbacks in numbers of workers in a drive by management to increase efficiency and cut costs.

According to the union, the remaining workers have had to absorb the extra work and cannot keep up with the assembly line. The result, the union men say, is improperly assembled cars.

The dispute is taking place in one of the most modern and sophisticated assembly plants in the world, built in 1966 on a farm field near Lordstown, Ohio.

Through better design, a variety of new types of power tools and other automated devices, much of the heavy lifting and hard physical labor has been eliminated in the plant. Even the parking lots were planned in such a way that the long walk to one's car has been done away with.

LESS BENDING REQUIRED

Workers on the assembly line have easier access to the car body and do not have to do as much bending and crawling in and out as in the older plants in Detroit. The Vega also has 43 percent fewer parts than a full-size car, making the assembly easier.

The wages are good. Workers start out on the line at $4.37 an hour, get a 10-cent-an-hour increase within 30 days and another 10 cents after 90 days. Benefits come to $2.50 more an hour.

The plant sits almost in the center of the heavy industrial triangle made up of Youngstown, with its steel plants; Akron, with its rubber industry; and Cleveland, a major center for heavy manufacturing.

The plant, which produces all the Vegas made by General Motors, draws its 7,700 workers, whose average age is 24 years, from areas that have felt the sting of foreign competition and where unemployment and layoffs have been heavy.

Many of the fathers of the young auto workers are employed in steel and rubber and have watched their jobs dwindle because foreign products have undercut their industries.

But the threat of unemployment and pressure from mothers and fathers, from the local press and public officials, have so far had little effect on the militant young workers who began their struggle with General Motors last October.

It was then that General Motors Assembly Division, a management team that has developed the reputation for toughness in cutting costs and bettering productivity, took over the operation of the Fisher Body Plant and Chevrolet assembly plant here and began to consolidate the operations.

From the point of view of management, the two plants had not been operating at their peak efficiency.

A major reorganization of work began. According to management it consisted mostly of changing jobs to make them more efficient, although management conceded that about 300 jobs had been eliminated and some workers had been given additional work.

Mr. Anderson explained that changes had to be made to bring the assembly line, which can turn out 100 Vegas in an hour, up to the potential it was designed for.

"If we are to remain competitive, we will have to take advantage of those sections of the contract on making the work more efficient," he said.

But across the Ohio Turnpike, Gary Bryner, the 29-year-old president of Local 1112, in an interview in his office in a modern brick union hall, said that about 700 jobs had been eliminated and that much of the extra work had been shifted to men who had no time to do it.

"That's the fastest line in the world," Mr. Bryner said. "A guy has about 40 seconds to do his job. The company does some figuring and they say, 'Look, we only added one thing to his job.' On paper it looks like he's got time."

INCREASE IN GRIEVANCES

"But you've got 40 seconds to work with," he continued. "You add one more thing and it can kill you. The guy can't get the stuff done on time and a car goes by. The company then blames us for sabotage and shoddy work."

He said that before the new management team took over, there were about 100 grievances in the plant. Since then, he said, grievances have increased to 5,000—about 1,000 of which consist of protests of too much work added to a job.

Mr. Bryner, on whose desk sit a peace symbol and a little book of *Revolutionary Quotations by Great Americans,* said that a decision by the workers to work at their old pace to protest the changes had come from the rank and file and not from the union leadership.

"These guys have become tigers," he said. "They've got guts. You used to not see them at union meetings. Now we've got them in the cafeteria singing *Solidarity.*"

Both union and management concede that they were surprised by the depth of the resistance that has arisen among the work force, whose average age on some assembly lines is about 22.

Management has attempted conciliation and has instituted sensitivity sessions with groups of workers to find out what the complaints are.

But the over-all management strategy so far has been one of toughness of hoping for results from the smaller paychecks that are issued when workers are sent home early when there is a slowdown and from foremen's disciplining workers by sending them home without pay.

When the workers went into the plant yesterday they found on the bulletin boards a notice saying that not only would work slowdowns be dealt with through disciplinary measures but also that workers could be dismissed.

Many young workers said in interviews that, the tougher the company became, the more they would stiffen their resistance, even though other jobs were scarce and many of them had recently been married and had families.

Nick Schecodonic, Jr., 27, a repair spot welder, said, "In some of the other plants where they did the same thing, the workers were older. They took some of this. But I've got 25 years ahead of me in that plant."

Mr. Schecodonic, who is married and has children, added, "I actually saw a woman in the plant running along the line to keep up with the work. I'm not going to run for anybody. There ain't anyone in that plant that is going to tell me to run."

Another worker who is worried about keeping his job said that he decided to support the union rank-and-file when he saw a gap between the body of a car and the instrument panel and brought it to the attention of the foreman.

The worker, who has a job as an inspector, said the foreman told him, "To hell with it. Ship it to the dealer." He said that after he refused to approve the car, the foreman signed the paper himself.

Mr. Bryner said that, at one meeting with the company, a management official said that in November there were about 6,000 complaints from Chevrolet dealers about the quality of the Vegas shipped to them, more than the combined complaints from the other assembly plants.

Andrew O'Keefe, public relations director at the plant, denied that any defective cars had been shipped and said that any foreman passing on a defective car would be "fired on the spot."

Mr. Anderson attributed part of the dispute to the attitude of the young worker. But he also said much of the resistance was due to the fear that a worker's job would be changed. "We're getting problems in areas where we haven't changed a thing," he said.

He added that management faced a difficult task in getting workers "to take pride in our product—if a man drops a bolt and he doesn't pick it up and put it on, he's more apt to let it go the second time."

But many industrial engineers have recently been questioning whether the direction of management toward assembly line work can continue.

Most of the efforts, brought to a highly advanced state in the Lordstown plant, have been to make the job simpler and easier, but they have often resulted in removing the last traces of skill.

As the jobs become easier and simpler, the rate at which they can be done can be increased. Workers at the Lordstown plant, for example, take about 40 seconds to complete a task while workers in a regular plant take about a minute. Most assembly lines run at about 55 cars an hour.

Some of the industrial engineers are saying that perhaps it is not so much the physical nature of the work as its constant, repetitive unskilled nature that is being resisted by assembly line workers, who are more educated and have higher expectations.

THE NEW GHETTO MAN:
A REVIEW OF RECENT
EMPIRICAL STUDIES

Nathan Caplan

What clearly emerges from the recent research findings on Negroes is a picture of a new ghetto man: a black militant who is committed to the removal of traditional racial restraints by open confrontation and, if necessary, by violence; a ghetto man who is very different in his actions and sympathies from the Negro of the past and from the white ghetto dwellers of an earlier period in this country's history. He is a ghetto man whose characteristics are seldom recognized and understood by most white Americans. It is our purpose here to describe him based on existing empirical data—to determine what he is like as a person, how large a segment of the Negro community he represents, what he wants, and how he intends to get it.

PROFILE OF THE BLACK MILITANT

Political authorities tend to categorize militants who advocate social and economic change through open confrontations as "riffraff"—irresponsible deviants, criminals, unassimilated migrants, emotionally disturbed persons, or members of an underclass. The riffraff theory sees these militants as being peripheral to organized society, with no broad social or political concerns; it views the frustration that leads to rioting or other forms of militant confrontation as simply part of a long history of personal failure.

It is not difficult to understand why protesters are generally labelled in these terms. By attributing the causes of riots to individual deficiencies, the riffraff theory relieves white institutions of most of the blame. It suggests that individual militants should be changed through psychotherapy, social work,

From The Journal of Social Issues, *Vol. 26, No. 1 (Winter 1970). Reprinted by permission of the Society for the Psychological Study of Social Issues, a division of the American Psychological Association.*

or, if all else fails, prolonged confinement. If protesting militants can be publicly branded as unable to compete successfully because of personal reasons, then their demands for system changes can be declared illegitimate with impunity. Authorities would have the right to use punitive and coercive forms of control in place of working to ameliorate structural deficiencies and injustices.

The data show, however, that the militants are no more socially or personally deviant that their nonmilitant counterparts. In fact, there is good reason to believe that they are outstanding on some important measures of socioeconomic achievement. Tomlinson (1968) concludes from this study that the militants are "the cream of urban Negro youth in particular and urban Negro citizens in general" (p. 28).

THE EXTENT OF MILITANCY

The available data run counter to the commonly held belief that militancy is characteristic of only a small fraction of the Negro community. Militancy in pursuit of civil rights objectives represents a considerable force in the ghetto. Its support approaches normative proportions.

As shown in Table 1, in a group of studies using related criterion variables, about one-third to one-half of the ghetto residents surveyed express support for riots and militant civil rights positions. The proportion of persons reporting active participation in riots is less, but the data across studies are equally consistent if differences in methodology and data sources are taken into consideration. Based on random probability sampling of general population, survey data show the level of self-reported riot participation to be 15 percent for Watts (Sears and McConahay, 1970a), and 11 percent for Detroit (Caplan and Paige, 1968a). In Newark, where only males between the ages of fifteen and thirty-five were sampled, 45 percent of the respondents reported riot activity (Caplan and Paige, 1968a). The riot participation figure for males in the same age group from the general population sample surveyed in Detroit is practically identical with the Newark findings.

Interpolating from arrest records, Fogelson and Hill (1968) estimated that 20 percent of ghetto residents participated in riots that occurred in their cities. Finally, two studies involving surveys in a number of different cities report that 15 percent of the ghetto population advocate or express willingness to participate in riots (Brink and Harris, 1966; Campbell and Schuman, 1968).

In most of these studies, riot sympathy and riot participation related to age and sex. The militant, particularly the rioter, is usually young and most likely male. Insofar as it is possible to determine from the available literature, the differences between militants and nonmilitants to be discussed here hold up after age and sex are controlled.

INCOME—ABSOLUTE

According to one variety of the riffraff theory, the rioter is a member of a deprived underclass, part of the "hard core" unemployed—often out of work for long periods of time or chronically unemployable because he lacks skill or education. Having lost contact with the job market and all hope of finding work, he is economically at the very bottom of Negro society.

Data from the major research studies do not support this hypothesis. There is no significant difference in income between rioters and nonrioters. In fact, income and militancy are related only in the way Karl Marx predicted: In the main, the black *lumpenproletariat* is quiescent, not militant. The available data show that those in the lowest socioeconomic position are the least militant and the least likely to riot (Murphy and Watson, 1970; Caplan and Paige, 1968a; Darrow and Lowinger, 1967; Shulman, 1967).

The poorest of the poor are also low on those variables which show relationships with active pro-

TABLE 1 ATTITUDES EXPRESSED BY NEGROES RELATING TO RIOTS

Attitudes Expressed	Percent Study Sample	Locale and Source
A. *RIOT SYMPATHY*		
Do not view riots as "essentially bad"	50%	Nationwide, *Fortune,* 1967 (Beardwood, 1968)
In sympathy with rioters	54%	Fifteen American Cities (Campbell and Schuman, 1968)
Believe riots are helpful	30%	Houston, 1967 (McCord and Howard, 1968)
Believe riots are helpful	51%	Oakland, 1967 (McCord and Howard, 1968)
B. *RIOT PARTICIPATION*		
Active participation in Watts riot	15%	Watts (Sears and Mc-Conahay, 1970a)
Active participation in Detroit riot	11%	Detroit (Caplan and Paige, 1968a)
Active participation in Newark riot	45% (males, age 15-35)	Newark (Caplan and Paige, 1968a)
Active participation in riots	20%	Six major riot cities, 1967 (Fogelson and Hill, 1968)
Willingness to participate in riots	15%	Nationwide, *Newsweek* poll (Brink and Harris, 1966)
Advocated use of violence	15%	Fifteen American Cities (Campbell and Schuman, 1968)

test. Caplan and Paige (1968a) found that the lowest income group tends to score low on black pride and more readily accepts the traditional deprecating Negro stereotypes. Campbell and Schuman (1968) reported a surprising degree of job satisfaction among those who are the most economically disadvantaged. Brink and Harris (1966) found that approval of "Black Power" was lowest among those in the poorest group. Only 13 percent of their low-income respondents approved of the term, compared with 31 percent in the lower middle-income and 26 percent in the middle- and upper-income groups. Apparently, continued injustice and the severe withdrawal of resources increase a deprived group's dependency behavior and approval of those who control scarce resources. These findings argue strongly against an "underclass" or strictly economic interpretation of militancy and violent protest in the ghetto.

INCOME—RELATIVE

Objective poverty in the sense of destitution is not the only issue associated with economic standing which has drawn research attention. The subjective meaning of one's wealth, or the absence of it, in relation to what others have, may also be important in producing the frustration that leads to unrest and rioting.

The widening gap between income levels of whites and blacks often has been cited as a possible cause for the present social unrest. The assumption is that members of the black community are concerned not so much with what they have as with what they feel they deserve compared with the whites. Attention to the discrepancy arouses a sense of social injustice that generates the frustration leading to rioting.

In order to examine the relation of the racial economic gap to riot participation, Caplan and Paige (1968b) asked respondents whether they thought the income gap between Negroes and whites was increasing, remaining the same, or decreasing. They found that 45 percent of the rioters but 55 percent of the nonrioters said the gap was *increasing.* Although the difference between these groups is small, it is opposite in direction to what one would predict on the basis of a relative depri-

vation hypothesis. More important, when these respondents were questioned about the income gap between the wealthier and poorer Negroes, these percentages were reversed. Fifty-five percent of the rioters and 45 percent of the nonrioters said the gap between the very poor and the higher-income-level Negroes was increasing.

Thus the rioters are particularly sensitive to where they stand in relation to other Negroes, not to whites. If the "black capitalism" idea, as presently formulated, is carried out seriously as a remedial step to prevent further rioting, it is likely to increase this income gap among Negroes and thereby produce disturbing consequences.

EDUCATION

McCord and Howard (1968) found that educational attainment had no linear relationship to participation in civil rights activity although college-educated respondents in their study were the *least opposed* to the use of violence. Campbell and Schuman (1968) reported no relationship between education and expressed favorability toward riots. Conversely, Tomlinson (1970) found that militants in Watts had attained a higher level of formal education than their more conservative neighbors. Marx (1967) reported a linear relationship between education and militancy—the higher the respondent's education, the greater the likelihood that he would score high on militancy measures. Forty-two percent of the militants in his study had attended college.

There was a slight tendency for the Watts riot participants to be better educated than the nonparticipants but the difference is too small to be statistically reliable (Murphy and Watson, 1970). Finally, Caplan and Paige (1968a) reported that rioters in Detroit and Newark were significantly higher on an educational achievement scale than the nonrioters.

Thus, while the average rioter was likely to be a high school dropout, data show that the average nonrioter was more likely to be an elementary school dropout. There is a significant relationship between schooling, militancy, and riot activity, but it is the militants and rioters who are better educated.

EMPLOYMENT

A major difficulty arises in interpreting the relationships between employment and militancy because researchers use varying definitions of unemployment and different criteria for ranking occupational skill levels. It is clear from the available evidence, however, that the militants are not the hardcore unemployed. Rather, the militants, particularly the rioters, have greater job dissatisfaction since they are continually on the margin of the job market, often employed but never for long.

Murphy and Watson (1970) found a tendency for unemployment to be higher among those who were active during the Watts riot although there was no relationship between riot sympathy and employment. Fogelson and Hill (1968) reported a 25 percent unemployment rate among riot arrestees and pointed out that this is about the same level of unemployment as in comparable samples in the open community.

In Detroit, Caplan and Paige (1968a) found that the unemployment rate for rioters and nonrioters was practically identical, about 31 percent. But in Newark, where the respondents were all young males, unemployment was higher among rioters; 31 percent as compared to 19 percent. Further, in Newark the rioters held higher job aspirations than nonrioters and were also more likely to blame their employment failures on racial barriers rather than on personal deficiencies. The same study showed that the rioters were not chronically but only temporarily unemployed and were marginally related to the labor force, i.e., persons who tended to move in and out of the labor force several times throughout the year.

SOCIAL INTEGRATION AND VALUES

Political theories often emphasize that the militant is isolated or cut off from the rest of the community. More parochial views speculate that the militant is a social deviant who is alienated from the more responsible elements and forces in the social environment. The data from these studies, however, do not support such views. At least two of the major studies show that the Negro who is militant in the pursuit of civil rights objectives is more likely to be the person best integrated into the black community.

Marx (1967) found a positive relationship between militancy and the number of organizational memberships held. In Detroit and Newark, Caplan and Paige (1968a) reported a similar relationship and, in addition, found that rioters socialized with their neighbors and others in the community more frequently than nonrioters. Finally, Marx (1967) and Caplan and Paige (1968a) demonstrated that the militants were more strongly identified with Negro cultural values and civil rights objectives than those in the black community who neither support nor participate in militant activities.

Neither Murphy and Watson (1970) nor Caplan and Paige (1968a) found any relationship between church attendance and riot participation. Marx (1967), however, found that militancy and church attendance related negatively.

Several of the studies included questions intended to show whether or not militancy and rioting are related to differences in support for an important American value: belief in work and the Protestant ethic. Rioters and nonrioters were virtually identical in their responses to most of these questions (Caplan and Paige, 1968a). About 75 percent of both groups in this study expressed the belief that hard work rather than luck or dependence upon help from others was important for achieving a successful life. Similarly, about 65 percent of the sample studied by Marx (1967) agreed that Negroes could get ahead through hard work.

Fogelson and Hill (1968) found that the crime rate for the riot arrestees was similar to that of the community as a whole. They did, however, report a difference with respect to the types of past offenses. Rioters tended to have committed less serious crimes.

SOCIALIZATION

Several of the studies include information about some important elements of adjustment. The possibility that the frustrations of the militant may be caused by inadequate socialization because of family disorganization or migration has been investigated. Data on family background are available only in the study by Caplan and Paige (1968a), which found that there was essentially no difference between rioters and nonrioters in the presence of an adult male in the home during formative years.

Region of socialization has also been related to militancy in a number of different studies but the direction of the relationship is opposite to the riff-raff hypothesis that rioters are most likely to be found among recent migrants to the urban area. On the contrary: The militant is no parvenu to the city. Rather, he is the long-term resident who knows urban life best.

Watts respondents born in California were more favorable to the riot (Murphy and Watson, 1970) and more likely to participate in it (Sears and McConahay, 1970a) than those who migrated to the area. Rioters in Detroit and Newark were more likely than nonrioters to have been born and raised in the North (Caplan and Paige, 1968a). In Detroit, six out of ten of the rioters, in contrast to three out of ten of the nonrioters, were born in that city. The distinction between region of socialization and riot participation is even more clearly drawn in the Newark data from the same study. There almost half of the nonrioters but only a quarter of the rioters had been born and raised in the South.

The readiness of the long-term northern-born ghetto resident to participate in riot activity is even more clearly defined in Fogelson and Hill (1968). In addition to finding that the arrestees were more likely to be northern-born, they also discovered that the highest proportion of northern-born rioters and the lowest proportion of southern-born rioters were arrested on the first day of rioting. The arrestees on and after the third day represented the highest proportion of southern-born and lowest proportion of northern-born. Fogelson and Hill also noted a tendency for the southern-born to be involved in less flagrant aspects of the riot. They were least likely to have been charged with "assault" and most likely to have been arrested for looting.

Finally, in their study of the meaning of "Black Power" carried out in Detroit, Aberbach and Walker (1968) found that northern-born Negroes more frequently define this concept in militant, political terms. Southern-born Negroes were less likely to view the slogan favorably and less likely to interpret it in a militant context.

BLACK CONSCIOUSNESS

Possibly the characteristic of the new ghetto man which has the most etiological significance for understanding the rise of militancy is his Black Consciousness. Both the Detroit and the Newark studies indicate that rioters have strong feelings of racial pride and even racial superiority (Caplan and Paige, 1968a, 1968b). They not only have rejected the traditional stereotype of the Negro but also have created a positive stereotype.

In both cities, rioters were more likely to view their race more positively than nonrioters on racial comparison items involving dependability, smartness, courage, "niceness," etc. For example, about one-half of rioters but less than one-quarter of nonrioters felt Negroes were "more dependable" than whites. Responses in these studies reflect a higher level of black pride among rioters; those who attempted to quell the disturbance and control the level of destruction deviate in the opposite direction. When the sample was divided into rioters, the uninvolved, and counter-rioters, the rioters were highest and counter-rioters were lowest on several measures of racial pride. Furthermore, half of the rioters and only a third of the nonrioters preferred to be called "black" rather than "colored," "Negro," or "Afro-American." Similarly, Caplan and Paige (1968a, 1968b) found a tendency for rioters to be stronger in the belief that all Negroes should study Negro history and African languages in the high schools.

Marx (1967) reported that militants prefer Negro newspapers and magazines, are better able to identify Negro writers and civil rights leaders, and have a more positive appreciation of Negro culture than nonmilitants. Darrow and Lowinger (1967) also encountered feelings of a new, positive Negro self-image among the rioters they studied. Consequently, these authors argue against the psychoanalytic interpretations of rioting which hold that participants release aggression associated with self-hatred.

This positive affirmation of racial identity is found not only among the militants but is widespread throughout the Negro community (Campbell and Schuman, 1968). Ninety-six percent of the sample in this study agreed that "Negroes should take more pride in Negro history." Also, four out of ten of the respondents thought that "Negro school children should study an *African* language" (italics mine).

Thucydides said long ago that social revolution occurs when old terms take on new meanings. The wisdom of this statement is apparent in the dramatic, recent change of the meaning for the term "black"—a word that has become a badge of intense pride which borders on racial superiority: "Black is Beautiful."

ATTITUDES TOWARD WHITES

The fact that racial pride is so high in the black community and the suspicion that it may play a causal role in the rise of militancy raise questions about Negro attitudes toward whites. Do black pride and the desire for black self-development go hand-in-hand with white hatred? What is the overall attitude of the ghetto toward whites?

Although there are some slight inconsistencies in the findings, in general militancy does not appear associated with increased hostility toward whites; the black community as a whole is not markedly anti-white nor preoccupied by social cross-comparison with whites.

Marx (1967) found that militancy and antiwhite attitudes were inversely related. The variables which were most closely related to militancy—intellectual sophistication, high morale, and a positive self-image—correlated negatively with antiwhite sentiment. Marx concluded that "they don't hate (whites), but they don't like them either" (p. 179). In an earlier study, Noel (1964) also found that those lowest in antiwhite feelings were the most militant proponents of civil rights action. Although he presents no supporting data, Tomlinson (1970) also reported that the militants in the Watts study are not notably antiwhite.

Murphy and Watson (1970) reported a slight tendency for the economically better-off riot participants to be more hostile toward whites. Caplan and Paige (1968a) similarly found the rioters to be slightly more antiwhite, but equally hostile to more affluent Negroes. Also, it should be pointed out that several attempts to test if rioters are more likely to use whites as social comparative referents have found no support for this possibility.

When considered in the aggregate, the Negro community is probably far less antiwhite than most whites are prepared to believe. Campbell and Schuman (1968) found little evidence of antiwhite hostility in their study. Only 13 percent of their respondents wanted to live in an all black or mostly black neighborhood; only 6 percent believed that American Negroes should establish a separate black nation; and only 9 percent felt that Negroes should have as little as possible to do with whites. Furthermore, only 6 percent wanted Negro children to go to only Negro shcools and 5 percent preferred to have only Negro friends. On the basis of responses to these and a number of similar items, Campbell and Schuman concluded: "Negroes hold strongly, perhaps more strongly than any other element in the American population, to a belief in nondiscrimination and racial harmony" (p. 17).

In general, these findings are not different from the results of earlier studies. Noel and Pinkney (1964) found that 41 percent of Negroes sampled in four cities expressed no particular antipathy toward whites. Among the respondents in the nationwide survey by Brink and Harris (1966), 80 percent reported that they preferred to work with a racially mixed group; 68 percent preferred to live in an integrated neighborhood; 70 percent preferred to have their children attend school with white children; and only 5 percent supported Black Nationalism. Only about 4 percent of Marx's (1967) total sample supported pronationalistic statements.

In the Murphy and Watson (1970) and Caplan and Paige (1968b) studies, antiwhite sentiment was most intense among riot participants when associated with perceived discrimination practices which restricted social and economic mobility for Negroes. Neither social envy of whites nor material greed motivates men to riot, but rather anger over the conditions that produce—and the practices that sustain—barriers denying Negroes the same freedoms and opportunities available to whites.

POLITICAL ATTITUDES

Almost all recent studies of Negro communities have included political items in their interview schedules and, without exception, the data show that militants are politically more sensitive and better informed than nonmilitants. They are not, however, politically alienated. What they want is what is already guaranteed by law, not a new political system.

Tomlinson (1970) reported that, compared with nonmilitants, militants in Watts were politically more active, more likely to refer to the riot in "revolutionary" terms, and less distrustful of elected officials. Marx (1967) found that almost twice as many militants as nonmilitants voted during the 1960 presidential election (31 percent vs. 17 percent). Sears (1970) and Sears and McConahay (1970b) reported that Watts arrestees and riot participants expressed greater political discontent and were more cynical of the responsiveness of local political powers to Negro grievances than nonrioter samples.

Caplan and Paige (1968a) found that rioters were more familiar with the identification of political personalities, more distrustful of politicians, and more likely to cite anger at politicians as a cause of the riot. In Newark, 44 percent of the rioters and 34 percent of the nonrioters reported "almost never" when asked if local government could be trusted "to do what is right." In Detroit, 42 percent of the rioters but only 20 percent of the nonrioters cited "anger with politicians" as a major cause of the riot.

The kinds of discontents that are felt most intensely by the militants reflect feelings that are wisespread throughout the Negro community. Sears (1969) reported that 45 percent of the random sample of Watts residents said that "elected officials cannot generally be trusted" (p. 21); this figure compares with 17 percent of a comparable white sample. Despite these discontents with political representation and the domination of the political system by whites, there is no evidence of broad rejection of the political system itself. Brink and Harris (1966) found that 74 percent of the Negroes in their sample expressed the desire to attain civil rights objectives through existing political channels. Also, Campbell and Schuman (1968) found no evidence indicating that Negroes want a new form of political functioning.

FATE CONTROL

The final characteristic of the militant that must be given special emphasis can be called fate control or the power to maintain control over those environmental forces that affect one's destiny. Although none of the researchers conceptualize this variable as such, several findings imply its distinct character as well as its significance to the emergence of militancy in the ghetto.

For example, Marx (1967) identifies "intellectual sophistication" as one of the three variables most strongly related to militancy. He describes intellectual sophistication as greater knowledge of the world and a way of looking at the world. Two important related factors that make up this variable are a broad liberated world outlook and a great sensitivity to the way social factors shape human behavior. In essence, Marx stresses that the militant is more likely to be cognitively correct about the external forces that influence his behavior and how they impede his ability to effectuate personal goals.

Meyer (1968) concluded that Miami-area Negroes who scored high on militancy possess ". . . a strong feeling that they can and should shape their destinies" (p. 22). He based his interpretation on the association between the respondents' scores on militancy and their sense of personal and political efficacy. In a survey study of Los Angeles Negroes, Ransford (1968) found that "powerlessness," which he defines as "a low expectancy of control over events" (p. 583), was strongly related to the respondent's willingness to use violence. Those with the highest scores on powerlessness held the highest commitment to violence.

Crawford and Naditch (1968) reexamined Ransford's data along with data from two other survey studies. By combining powerlessness with Rotter's internal-external schema, they found that the more militant respondents were characterized by a high sense of personal efficacy and low control over external forces that affect the probability of achieving personal goals. Employing a similar analytical framework, Gurin et al. (1969) found a marked tendency for militancy among Negro students to be associated with the belief that they could not reach personal goals because of external or social systemic constraints. Finally, the blocked-opportunity theory which emphasizes environmental rather than personal factors as the cause of riots (Caplan and Paige, 1968b) is supported by the survey data from that study which found that rioters desire increased mastery over the distribution of resources rather than the mere acquisition of resources. For a more extensive discussion of this concept see the Forward and Williams (1970) article.

CONCLUSIONS

There is a surprising degree of empirical regularity and basic coherence to the findings discussed here, even though they come from studies carried out in several parts of the country by different investigators employing various methodological approaches. This agreement allows us to draw some important conclusions with reasonable comfort and confidence in their validity, conclusions which should help achieve a better understanding of the militant and a safer evaluation of his behavior.

1. Militancy in the pursuit of civil rights objectives represents a considerable force within the ghetto. Its support approaches normative proportions and is by no means limited to a deviant and irresponsible minority.

2. The militant is a viable creature in search of practical responses to arbitrary institutional constraints and preemptions which deny him the same freedom and conventional opportunities as the white majority. He is the better educated but underemployed, politically disaffected but not the politically alienated. He is willing to break laws for rights already guaranteed by law, but under ordinary circumstances he is no more likely to engage in crime than his nonmilitant neighbor. He is intensely proud of being black, but neither desires revenge from whites nor is socially envious of them. He has little freedom or resources to effectuate his personal goals, but strongly desires freedom and ownership of his own life. Indeed, this new man of the ghetto is also the man of paradox.

3. The characteristics of the militants together with the large proportion of ghetto blacks who share their views certainly indicate that the fight for civil rights will not end with the recent riots. Even though the time and place of their occurrence may not be predictable nor their instrumental value always clear, the riots are neither random events nor marginal, temporary phenomena. The militants

must be taken seriously and not simply treated as troublemakers.

4. With candor and a few frills, the Kerner Commission cited white racism as the major cause of ghetto riots. Undoubtedly, white racism is a root issue, but it has been present for over three hundred years and, therefore, is insufficient as a sole explanation of riots of such magnitude and intensity as occur at this point in time. The logic of scientific proof would require that we look for causal factors whose relationships are more contemporaneous.

The findings reviewed here suggest that Negroes who riot do so because their conception of their lives and their potential has changed without commensurate improvement in their chances for a better life. In the midst of squalor and despair, Negroes have abandoned the traditional stereotypes that made nonachievement and passive adaptation seem so natural. Rather, they have developed a sense of black consciousness and a desire for a way of life with which they can feel the same pride and sense of potency they now derive from being black. Without these changes in self-perception, the demands to be regarded and treated as an individual with the same liberties as white Americans would never have reached the intensity that they have today. If this interpretation of the research is correct, it could be argued that the riots and other forms of civil rights protest are caused by the self-discovery of the American Negro and his attempt to recreate himself socially in ways that are commensurate with this new image. This battle for greater personal rights can be expected to continue as long as the Negro's political, social, and economic efficacy is not aligned with his new and increasing sense of personal potency.

5. The limited data available at this time do not permit us to make fine-grain projections about the maturation pattern of riot activity, the future forms of other protest activity, or their outcome. Possibly the most that one can say at this time about the meaning of these outbreaks is: First, they are more similar to the early slaveship uprisings than they are to the white-initiated interracial riots that occurred after World Wars I and II. Ghetto-locked blacks are claiming ownership of their behavior and are de-

manding the freedom and opportunity necessary to control their destiny. They are interested in bettering their position in American society; they are not interested in "white blood" or the glorification of violence. Second, it seems safe to conclude that the riots represent an elementary form of political activity. But, it must be emphasized that the political objectives are conservative. The militants are not rebelling against the system itself but against the inequities and contradictions of the system.

If this nation is serious about the application of democratic principles to human affairs, then it must increase the power of the black man to improve his position beyond anything now possible in American society. The stereotype of the Negro —which for seven generations has been used to destroy his initiative, motivation, and hope—is a reality apart from what these studies show him to be. He emerges in these studies as more American than those who built the ghetto and those who now maintain it. Unless this nation acts now to redress the balance in social and economic distance between the races, we will probably have lost forever the ideal of the democratic prospect and, like other nations in the past, will resort to what C. P. Snow calls "hideous crimes in the name of obedience." It is clear that the Negro will not give up the struggle for a better life. Unlike the Negro in the past, the present ghetto dwellers have neither the psychological defenses nor the social supports that permit passive adaptation to barriers that prevent implementation of their potential capabilities. In a sense, they are the hearing children of deaf parents.

REFERENCES

Aberbach, D., and Walker, L., "The Meanings of Black Power: A Comparison of White and Black Interpretations of a Political Slogan," paper presented at the meeting of the American Political Science Association, Washington, D.C., 1968.

Beardwood, R., "The New Negro Mood," Fortune Magazine, 77 (1968), 146–152.

Brink, W., and Harris, L., Black and White, New York: Simon and Schuster, 1966.

Campbell, A., and Schuman, H., "Racial Attitudes in Fifteen American Cities," Supplement Studies for The National Advisory Commission on Civil Disorders, Government Printing Office, 1968.

Caplan, N. S., and Paige, J. M., In O. Kerner, et al., Report of The National Advisory Commission on Civil Disorders, New York: Bantam Press, 1968, 127–137. (a)

Caplan, N. S., and Paige, J. M., "A Study of Ghetto Rioters," Scientific American, 219:2 (August 1968), 15–21. (b)

Crawford, T. J., and Naditch, M., "Unattained and Unattainable Goals: Relative Deprivation, Powerlessness, and Racial Militancy," paper presented at the meeting of the American Psychological Association, San Francisco, California, 1968.

Darrow, C., and Lowinger, P., "The Detroit Uprising: A Psychosocial Study," paper presented at the meeting of the American Academy of Psychoanalysis, New York, 1967.

Fogelson, R. M., and Hill, R. B., "Who Riots? A Study of Participation in the 1967 riots," Supplement Studies for The National Advisory Commission on Civil Disorders, Government Printing Office, 1968.

Forward, J., and Williams, J., "Internal-External Control and Black Militancy," Journal of Social Issues, 26 (1970).

Gurin, P., Gurin, G., Lao, R., and Beattie, M., "Internal-External Control in the Motivational Dynamics of Negro Youth," Journal of Social Issues, 25 (1969), 29–53.

Marx, G. T., Protest and Prejudice: A Study of Belief in the Black Community, New York: Harper and Row, 1967.

McCord, W., and Howard, J., "Negro Opinions in Three Riot Cities," American Behavioral Scientist, 11 (March/April, 1968), 24–27.

Meyer, P., "Negro Militancy and Martin Luther King: The Aftermath of Martyrdom," Washington, D.C.: Knight Newspapers, 1968.

Murphy, R. J., and Watson, J. M., "The Structure of Discontent," in N. E. Cohen (ed.), The Los Angeles Riots: A Socio-Psychological Study, New York: Praeger, 1970.

Noel, D. L., "Group Identification Among Negroes: An Empirical Analysis," Journal of Social Issues, 20 (1964), 71–84.

Noel, D. L., and Pinkney, A., "Correlates of Prejudice: Some Racial Differences and Similarities," American Journal of Sociology, 69 (1964), 609–622.

Ransford, H. E., "Isolation, Powerlessness, and Violence: A Study of Attitudes and Participation in the Watts Riot," American Journal of Sociology, 73 (1968), 581–591.

Sears, D. O., "Political Attitudes of Los Angeles Negroes," in N. E. Cohen (ed.), The Los Angeles Riots: A Socio-Psychological Study, New York: Praeger, 1970.

Sears, D. O., and McConahay, J. B., "Riot Participation," in N. E. Cohen (ed.), The Los Angeles Riots: A Socio-Psychological Study, New York: Praeger, 1970. (a)

Sears, D. O., and McConahay, J. B., "The Politics of Discontent," in N. E. Cohen (ed.), *The Los Angeles Riots: A Socio-Psychological Study,* New York: Praeger, 1970. (b)

Shulman, J., "Ghetto Residence, Political Alienation and Riot Orientation," unpublished manuscript, Cornell University, 1967.

Tomlinson, T. M., "The Development of a Riot Ideology Among Urban Negroes," *American Behavioral Scientist,* **11** (March/April, 1968), 27–31.

Tomlinson, T. M., "Militance, Violence, and Poverty: Ideology and Foundation for Action," in N. E. Cohen (ed.), *The Los Angeles Riots: A Socio-Psychological Study,* New York: Praeger, 1970.

PEACEMAKERS, GOODFELLOWS, AND THE POLICE: SUMMER 1966

Todd Gitlin and Nanci Hollander

I started bummin around on Leland Avenue. That's where the fun begun. That's where I learned the life of Chicago. That restaurant there on the corner of Leland and Sheridan, they used to call the Hut, Dixie Hut—it's gone now—that's where we used to hang out, a bunch a boys there, all from the South. Mostly you'd meet em through girls. You'd talk to a girl or somethin, she'd invite you over, you'd meet guys, mess around with em. Usually when you'd first meet a bunch you gotta fight about half of em. I guess about twenty-five of us went around together for about eight, ten months. Then we decided we was gonna organize, gonna name the bunch. We had fun, we had parties and stuff like 'at. Wore our jackets like we were a gang. We were tryin to fight everybody. We just had our one place, we didn't want nobody else comin in and messin it up. . . .

We had the whole area, from Montrose to Lawrence, anywheres in between there, between Clark and the Lake. Nobody, north, south, east or west, came in

within it, startin trouble. . . . There's two things that you don't mess with in this neighborhood: that's a guy's woman or his car. Some don't care for anything else but them two. . . .

And that's where I learned about dope and fightin. Wish I'd left em alone. You know what a benny is? That's mostly what it was. And we used to really get hopped up on it. And lot of the guys took em to stay awake, cause we was up four or five, six days at a time without goin to bed, drinkin, runnin around. And I was workin, and then runnin around every night and stayin out all night and then goin to work the next mornin, I had to have somethin to keep me awake. . . .

We got in trouble with the cops, and they told us if we didn't bust up, we was all goin to jail. They were always comin around, searchin us, bustin up eight or ten guys. One mornin real early, about twelve, the cops come to the restaurant. There was two girls they wanted to see. Anyway, one of em said somethin, she said somethin back, he pushed her up against the wall and started chokin her. So this friend of mine, he didn't like it, so he told the cop to get his hands off of her. The cop wouldn't, so he smacked the cop, and they got him outside and about beat him to death. I still got the picture of it, it was in the paper. He got a year, in county, "resistin arrest." It's gonna be a lot wilder in about another week, when he gets outa jail. He's from Kentucky too, from up in the hills, the eastern part, Harlan County.

This friend, Charles Otis, had a fierce reputation and his return was awaited with a mixture of enthusiasm and fear. He would bring back good times, but the police would surely have it in for him: two of the arresting police had been heard threatening to kill him when he got out. In the meantime, most of the Peacemakers had gone straight, the name a memory, the jackets hung in closets. Gene, also eighteen and an ex-Peacemaker from Tennessee, said:

After we'd get through drinkin we might fuck a broad or either go out, get in a fight, shit like that, and we did like that for I guess six, seven months, just fuckin, fightin, screwin around. Then the cops got Charles Otis and guys stopped comin around a lot then. Cops had got us all afraid. Then some of em started gettin serious over the girls, girls they'd fucked with. And they'd take her and leave, or either get married, shit like that. They weren't actually tired, they just had other things to do. Maybe problems, you know, in their family and stuff. But some don't never come out of it, Charles Otis, for instance.

"I just quit runnin around," Clayton said for himself. "Started stayin home, workin, stayin home. George was my help."

George was the Reverend. He recruited not only Clayton and Tompkins, but Marvin Jackson and Gerald Akers, past president and vice-president of the Peacemakers, and put them to work running a pool hall and social club on Wilson Avenue. For the hard core of Tompkins, Jackson, and Akers, the Reverend was a mighty deliverer. Akers said he'd been popping pills, smoking marijuana, and contemplating suicide the day the Reverend had walked into the Dixie Hut. A few months later Akers and Tompkins had taken a public-speaking course, Akers was answering the phone with assurance, conducting the daily business of the club, and drawing a respectable salary from the Urban Progress Center.

Akers, from a coal-mining family of fourteen, was also studying the dictionary, hoping, by his own account, to be known all over Chicago as an

up-and-coming hillbilly. Some of his former friends came to see him as "high-eaved," highfalutin, and he moved into that uncomfortable no-man's-land reserved for the poor who climb alone and too fast: somewhat detached from their old peers but for a long time, maybe forever, faintly subsidiary in their new-chosen circles. Such people, pinched by their upwardly mobile guilt, become vulnerable to radical appeals to their undisposable pasts and identities—especially when couched in new and erudite accents. So it is with the black bourgeoisie, so it was with Gerald Akers, but Gerald took his new-found radicalism seriously, took care to maintain his old roots at the same time. He was reached first by a young non-Southern neighborhood man, a veteran of civil rights work in Mississippi who had returned from college to his own roots; and then by a JOIN organizer. Still studying the dictionary, Akers decided in April, 1966, to travel to the Citizens' Crusade Against Poverty conference in Washington, where organizers and poor people had been invited to talk about the war on poverty. The liberal financiers got more than they bargained for. War-on-poverty employees booed Sargent Shriver off the platform. Akers was among them, and as the only white he became something of a special hero to the radical student organizers.

He came back to Chicago fired up, confirmed in his new loyalties. He agreed promptly to speak to a student rally against the draft, where he revised his already fervent text with remarks like this: "They say people who're against the war, who demonstrate and agitate, are Commonists. Well, who ever heard of a hillbilly Commonist?" "My first fight is here," he said, "and the fight I'm fighting is the war-on-poverty fight. We been dying for the rich all our lives. Why should we defend them? The people we're fightin over there, they're poor and starvin too." After denouncing the student draft deferment and the Urban Progress Center, and reading Buddy Tompkins' "Wilson Avenue," he departed from his text once more: "What I've said today is what I feel. I ain't been brainwashed and I'm nobody's tool. I say what comes out of me, what I feel."

His old buddies had their doubts. When the soft-spoken uncitified Tennessean Marvin Jackson ribbed Akers one day, "You'd protest a piss-ant crawlin across the floor," after Akers defended some student antiwar sit-ins and Marvin thought they were "stupid," it was tempting for some organizers to assume that Marvin was the unenlightened one. But other organizers, with a finer feel for the neighborhood's texture, were spending more time with Marvin, Gene, and other ex-Peacemakers. At the same time, the Reverend closed Friendship House, deciding to work with elders but leaving the young guys no place of their own, and no more interesting hangout than JOIN. Then, in June, the Urban Progress Center fired Akers for "falsifying his time sheet," an administrative abbreviation for having hooted Sargent Shriver.

Though his supervisor, the Reverend, had in fact permitted Akers to go to Washington, and lobbied in his behalf, the ruling was final. The young guys got jumpier. Older loyalties revived in defense of Akers. Marvin said he was ready to sit in against the OEO director. No direct action beyond a picket was ever taken, Akers and the Reverend trying (without success) to arrange a quiet settlement, but Marvin and some others recoiled in further disgust from any middle-class intrusions into their neighborhood—war on poverty, ministers, radical ex-students, all of them.

As summer opened there were long, slow, sweet evenings on the beach, young guys and JOIN organizers—those relaxed and informal occasions in which lasting organizing linkages are always forged. Marvin, in a "sad lonesome mood," having just split up with his wife, would sing country-western songs about men in bars, men in prison, men on the road, and once in a while something gently chiding the organizers' college-folk tastes, like "Red is the color of my true love's eyes, in the morning." And this one he wrote:

IS IT ALL BECAUSE OF YOU?

I walk the streets at night
  With my head bowed low
I don't remember
  Who I see or where I go
I walk alone and cry
  Because I feel so blue
And I wonder
  Is it all because of you?
                              Chorus
Is it all because of you
  I'm feeling lonely

Is it all because of you
  I'm feeling blue
This old ache in my heart
  Is oh so painful
And I wonder
  Is it all because of you?

I go to movies
  And I think that I'll feel better
I set down alone
  The way I always do
Then she kisses him,
  I start to feeling lonely
And I wonder
  Is it all because of you?

I try to sleep at night
  But all I do is toss and turn
And recall the things
  You used to say and do
Then my eyes break down
  And cry until the morning comes
And I wonder
  Is it all because of you?

Marvin and some others came to JOIN meetings, listening, playing their minds over the JOIN rhetoric of community power, trying to puzzle it out. It sounded good, but then why did the ex-students dominate? Friendship with a few organizers left them no less estranged from the organization, with its highfalutin talk, its preoccupation with older people, its unfamiliar leadership. "Hell, man," Junior told a friend, "you don't wanna go to a students' party. We do the watusi and the frug, they do the sophisticated watusi and the sophisticated frug." They waited in the wings: until an occasion arose for their participation, they would continue to watch, to razz from the sidelines.

Then Uptown made the occasion the organizers couldn't. It began with a ratbite. The enraged father of the injured baby had seen the rent-strike picket of another building in the spring, remembered JOIN, met one of the Friendship House ex-cons, then chairman of the JOIN housing committee, and persuaded him to check out the building. It was appalling even by the standards of the neighborhood. In the words of the baby's mother: "Our bathroom ceiling is falling down, the insulation is peeling off the wiring. The windows—we've got our own private air-conditioning system because there's no putty in the windows. The linoleum's peeling off the floor, with dead bedbugs underneath. There isn't a faucet in our apartment that doesn't leak. No screens, paint's chipping, we asked for three days to get a toilet seat. He turned off our lights the day before our rent was due. The baby's milk is spoiling in the refrigerator and I don't know what we're going to do tonight, because the lights usually keep the rats away and if we don't have any light we're going to have fun. The landlord won't admit that there's any rats or roaches or bedbugs in the building. A hundred dollars a month, with our own furniture! He says, 'Well, I know welfare rent schedules and I can get a hundred dollars for this apartment.' He knows exactly what he can get, the highest he can charge in order to have welfare recipients in the building, so he takes advantage of it. He puts on a real smooth bit with the caseworker, you know really soft-soaps em.'' The disgusted manager volunteered her apartment for a tenants' meeting to discuss a rent strike. Half the tenants were there. They divided, but as if to clinch the matter the landlord burst in and fired the manager on the spot, replacing her a few days later with an upwardly mobile hustler who had made opportunistic feints toward JOIN and counseled a waiting-game. The tenants remained split, just the situation in which the weight of an organizer may throw the balance toward collective action.

The next meeting of JOIN's housing committee was unusually well attended. The ex-con asked backing for a rent strike. There was a long debate: Were the tenants ready? Since the landlord had gotten some tenants to threaten violence, was the risk too great? Should the new manager be alienated from JOIN? Most skeptical were two of the dominant ex-students, who hoped the new manager, representative of a more stable type in the neighborhood, would prove a more durable ally than the tenants. But the vote went six to five for proceeding: three ex-students and three community people for, five ex-students against. The two skeptical ex-students promptly called the decision "stupid." Since their work would count heavily in the next week's organizing, their opposition amounted to a veto.

Word spread to the young guys that the ex-con had been humiliated. The merits of the issue were beside the point; they cared little about the build-

ing. They saw only that a "community person" had been affronted by two ex-students; the power of the ex-students, always obvious, became illegitimate; it was no longer a mere nuisance, but a threat to their integrity. They had to intervene, probably would have intervened on some other ground had the building not become an issue. At the prompting of a friend-organizer, Bob, they called an emergency meeting for the next night, July 8. Everyone sensed impending crisis, maybe doom.

Marvin came late; rumor had it he was so angry he had talked of bringing a gun. But Tompkins, Akers, and the rest easily made the meeting theirs. Akers blasted the ex-students with their own rhetorical weapons. Who could believe the ex-students were committed to the community, when they could always slink back into middle-class comfort? Then why should they hold power in a poor people's organization? And if the poor could not rule there, where else could they? Some ex-students tried to defend themselves, almost pleading, but the insurgents had already seized the moral initiative. But now what did they want? Whatever it was, they had JOIN's permission, even JOIN's blessing, but they couldn't work in the shadow of the old history. The rent strike was not their affair. It was the inspiration of one organizer, Bob, to pull them away for a few minutes, and when they returned they had determined to have their own form, with their own issue, the issue that belonged distinctively to them: the police. Everyone felt vindicated; JOIN having attracted new energy and let it find its channels, the young guys having discovered their strength. Redemption and new beginnings, here as always, had required crisis.

The young guys met again the next night, alone, and decided their first task would be to find jobs for their friends. "You feel different walkin down the street if you have a job," said Gene. "You know the cops won't bother you." They prevailed upon Marvin to lead them, though his personal life was a shambles. Having come this far he could not turn back.

But Bob quickly convinced Marvin that many young guys with jobs still didn't feel protected. The way to reach them was to attack police brutality, frontally. They decided to collect affidavits on police brutality from their friends, for publicity and legal action; and to call a larger meeting. Needing a name to reserve a meeting room at the Urban Progress Center—for they would have to be clearly different from JOIN—they became the Uptown Goodfellows.

Bob suggested to Marvin a community patrol, patterned on one devised in Watts: Goodfellows would drive around the neighborhood, unarmed but for notebooks and cameras, to put the police on notice. The first night of Uptown's patrol, the police got the point: they would not submit to observation. Bob and Marvin spotted policemen beating a Mexican-American kid on Wilson Avenue; writing down badge numbers, Bob was rammed into the wall and arrested for disorderly conduct and assault. A few days later Marvin wrote this "Ballad to Michael":

It was late one night, the cops were riding round
Looking for someone to stomp into the ground
When just as they passed
A little boy threw a glass
They stopped but they didn't hear a sound.

They remembered Michael from some time ago.
He was fast asleep and so he didn't know.
Two policemen came inside
And turned on all the lights.
They grabbed him and then they said Let's go.

As they opened the door that led into the street
They shoved him and he fell to his feet.
And when he turned around
They knocked him to the ground.
They hit him till his head began to bleed.

By this time another policeman joined the fun.
He tried to get up but he was nearly done.
I could tell he was in pain
But they kicked him just the same.
Michael pleaded but they kept on with their fun.

Still they beat him with their clubs and fists
    and feet.
Michael was helpless as he lay there on the street.
Plenty people were on hand
But no one would give a hand
As poor Michael just lay there in the street.

I wonder what this world's becoming to.
You can't even trust the men in the blue.
I'm sure the man above

Didn't mean this to be love.
If he did then it's not right for me and you.

For Marvin, whose third song was to be a hymn, this was a considerable blasphemy.

The first big Goodfellows meeting drew more than twenty guys; the next, fifty. They were riotous and disorderly affairs, but the guys were beginning to come together again, a few signing up for patrols, some agreeing to collect affidavits. (By the end of the third meeting, more than fifty had been signed.) But the next step, whatever it was to be, needed the authority and energy of Charles Otis and his following. Charles had just been released from jail, but before Marvin could get very far with him he had been arrested again. He had been coming home from a party with a friend. The friend had gotten into a fight with a Puerto Rican. Later that night the police arrested Charles on a warrant sworn by the Puerto Rican, claiming he had stolen his wallet and sunglasses. Charles was charged with strong-arm robbery and locked up on $5,000 bond. Marvin investigated and found an eyewitness, a young Catholic priest who said Charles had done nothing. In fact the sunglasses had fallen on the street during the fight: the priest had them himself. He was prevailed upon to write a letter, cosigned by the Reverend and other respectables, asking the State's Attorney to drop charges, or at least let Charles out on his own recognizance. A week later the appeal was refused. A JOIN organizer raised the bail money.

On the way to pick him up at the jail, Marvin told one of us [Nanci Hollander] he was planning a white lie for the good of the Goodfellows. He had warned the organizers before not to broach the delicate question of race with Charles; Charles had once had his arm sliced by a black; "he's the meanest guy in Uptown" (half in admiration, half cautioning) "and he hates niggers"; there's a time for everything. But Marvin himself had been infected with the JOIN spirit, had learned "that Negroes are poor and we're poor, that the cops belt us around like they do to Negroes, especially that if we're ever gonna stop bein poor, it's gonna take Negroes and whites together to do it." Driving back from the jail, Marvin turned to Charles:

"Charles, this might break your heart, but some colored guys gave us the money to get you out. They're fighting the police too, and they really had to scrape to get this money, because their guys are in trouble too."

Charles was very cool. "I don't care, man," he said. "Those niggers are in it too, man. You know I used to run with some niggers, didn't I, Marvin? Good guys, too."

Charles Otis brought with him the untamed wing of the old Peacemakers, those who had never felt comfortable at Friendship House. When the Dixie Hut was demolished they had removed to Eva's, a nearby restaurant, where they made innocuous headquarters. They still affected Charles's peculiar swagger, a grinding motion of the shoulders and hanging of the arms that made them seem to lumber forward rather than walk. One of them, Jerry Smith, from Alabama, joined the nightly patrol, where he learned that the organizer Bob had marched through Mississippi in June in the wake of James Meredith. "Shit," said Jerry, "if the word ever gets back to Alabama that I've been goin around with a freedom rider, I'm through!" When Bob suggested they go over to the JOIN office to sing, Jerry said he'd sing anything but "We Shall Overcome." The baiting was friendly, the ordinarily volatile race issue succumbing to the larger, more proximate fact of organizing momentum. Jerry would confront organizers, announce that in Alabama "we don't serve niggers in restaurants," insist on getting an argument in rebuttal, and then brag, "Well, you know, Eva's serves niggers too."

Charles and Marvin wanted action, wanted to weld the young guys into a force against police abuses, rather than leave them by their separate devices exposed to the massed power of the law. Although the organizer, Bob, argued against them, they pushed through a proposal to march on the police station, demanding civilian review, an end to brutality, and the dismissal of one particular plainclothesman, Sam Joseph. Joseph was Charles's nemesis—it was he Charles had found mistreating the girls at the Dixie Hut—and without doubt the most feared cop in Uptown. One Goodfellow told Marvin, "If you ain't scared of him you're either a fool or crazy." "Well, I ain't scared," said Marvin, "so I must be a fool or crazy," but his bravado was showing. Joseph was

also Chicago's most decorated policeman; he seemed to court trouble as well as heroism, and he had important defenders. A year before he had made the mistake of beating a middle-class boy, who brought charges through the Police Department's Internal Investigation Division (IID). The case for brutality was so strong that the IID had recommended a thirty-day suspension, whereupon several aldermen had called for an investigation of the IID. "This is a foul day for Chicago," said one. "Officer Joseph has been a credit to the police department and a guardian of the peaceful elements of the community," said another. The Mayor asked Superintendent Wilson to take a "personal interest" in the case. Wilson did; he dismissed the charges. Joseph stayed in Uptown.

The march was set for August 11, ten days away. Buttons appeared [which read]: "People must control their police." Leaflets [read]: "Are they protecting you?" Goodfellows divided up the blocks and spread the word. The impending march moved to the center of the neighborhood grapevine.

And the police got the message too. Petty harassments became daily, and not so petty. A policeman asked Marvin one day, "How much education do you have?"

"Fifth grade."

"Then how are you going to control me?"

"See, you're doing what you always do, putting me down because of my education."

"You're never gonna control me."

A nearby camera kept his face jovial, but there was menace enough in his tone. Another time Sam Joseph told Bob, "We're gonna march all over your heads." Leafleteers were stopped, threatened with littering charges and dark appointments in an alley.

A few days before the march, one of the old JOIN corner guys unexpectedly said he would come along. Although at most times he saw himself as a member of a small, distinct grouping—*this* corner, *that* block—the march was an event that promised to overcome the most provincial impulses. I [Todd Gitlin] found him on the corner on the eve of the march. No, he couldn't go. (Not "don't want to," but "can't.") Some months before, he had been arrested for disorderly conduct (for standing on the corner); the arresting plainclothesman had withheld the warrant on him on the promise of $10 a week for ten weeks. The bribe was almost fully paid off, but the warrant was still outstanding. And moments before I arrived, the plainclothesman had appeared to say that if he was seen on the line of march, the warrant would be issued. The young guy, of course, had paid in cash; he would have no proof, either of blackmail or of betrayal. He didn't march.[1]

The police's main weapon was intimidating force; a close second was the support of Uptown's older, more settled people, who wanted a buffer between themselves and the unruly young. But in the heat of their rage, the police confused their weapons, and the Sunday before the march they treated the respectable citizens of a busy block to a full-dress verification of the worst horror story the Goodfellows could have told.

One witness to that Sunday's beating was Amelia Jenkins, a sharp-witted I've-seen-everything building manager. Chicago-born but married to a Southerner, she was a community leader in the strict sense—someone whose choices carry weight for definite others. She had befriended a JOIN organizer—he said from curiosity, she said from pity —but remained anchored to her private life, to the wry hope of getting by. In fact, on the subject of the August 11 march she would shed her usual playfulness for a diatribe against Charles Otis and his friends, whom she blamed for disturbing the peace of Leland Avenue: why did the otherwise quaint and even admirable JOIN have to sully itself with such hoodlums? "We have read your letters on police brutality," she and six others wrote to the Newsletter. "Most of us all said to ourselves, o.k. now, JOIN must be stretching it just a little. But after witnessing this incident last night, it has made a believer out of us." Let her speak at length for what she reveals of the teller—the flow of her respectability as it crashed against the police reality —as well as the tale:

Well, this man was givin em a struggle at first. I'll give him credit for that. He wasn't gonna go. . . . Everybody standin around said they had already started beatin im in the apartment, fore they took im outa the apartment. Now I didn't see that, I wouldn't say that they done it. But I seen em when they got im down in the hall and he set down—whether they threw im down or not I

don't know—but he was sittin up against the glass door and that's when another squad car come up then. And finally three more of em come up. And when they come out, they hit im, one, two, three, all three of em, boom, boom, boom, as soon as they got im outside in front. And that's what really started the rest of the crowd then. After that I never seen the man throw any more punches. I seen im one time when they pushed him, he kicked his leg, but now whether he was aimin at one a the police or not, I don't know. You can't hardly blame im for halfway tryin to defend himself, not gettin that kind a treatment. And he wasn't even treated like a white man. Treated more like a dog.

Now they said he was drunk, but he didn't act that drunk to me. Cause he was talkin too sensible to be drunk. And he was speakin with intelligence. He was sayin, "Well now, I want you to get a good look at what's happenin." He said, "Get an idea of how your police force acts." In fact the first thing I thought of was, maybe he was one of JOIN's members, you know, the way he was goin against the police brutality. But evidently he's a man that's probably just been pushed around so many times that he figured, Well, I'm gonna get whipped when I get down there so I may as well take it out here. . . .

When they come out, I turned away because I didn't wanna watch what was goin on. But I went across the street, they had throwed im down, they hit him with their billy clubs and they was jabbin im in the stomach. They got im down and had his face turned and pushed up against the curb. And then one cop took his knee and put it in the side of his head to hold him down. Three of em stood on his legs, just stood there. . . . He was already handcuffed when they come outa the building, but when they got him down, they handcuffed his feet together. And he kept screamin, you know, "This is injustice, I didn't do anything." Well, then they kept callin more and more and more cops. So finally they had eight squad cars there and eleven cops. And all those people they was screamin, "Turn him loose! What'd he do?" And there was this one cop stood right out in the middle of the street and he just dared em. Minute anybody screamed, he said, "Come on out here and you get a little bit of it! If you don't like what's goin on, you come out and get a little bit of it!" And showed em his fist or his billy club. So I happened to say, "Why don't they let the man up?" So the cop heard me, the one that was standin on his head, and he turned over and looked at me, said, "You don't like it, lady? Why don't you come over here and you help him up?" So I told him, I said, "I know who you are, you're the one that wouldn't come up after that Indian that was drunk up in our apartment." And he's the one that refused to get a drunken Indian out of my building. But he was brave when he had the other twelve behind him. They just kept it up. Every time he acted like he was just gonna move a little bit, to get a little air, they'd either kick him or poke him or hit him. Now when they'd ask what he'd done, they just kept sayin, "You all holler you want help, now this is our job, we're doin what we have to do." And the man he started beggin. He said, "If you let me up I'll get in, I won't give you no more trouble." They said they was gonna hold him until the paddy wagon come. And finally they got tired of standin on his leg and they just got down and kneeled on his leg. But he couldn't possibly move.

Now, just like I said, I'd read about it, and I know they do it when they get you to the station, but I never dreamt they'd do it out there, with that many witnesses watchin em. Cause that street was full. Oh my God, there were about a hundred people around, at least. Everybody was screamin. They were all yellin to the cops, "Turn im loose! Let im up! What'd he do?" And the rougher the people got, the smarter the cops got, and they kept takin it out on that man. They just kept kickin im. And the one cop said, "Get these kids away from here! Get these kids away from here!" That man yelled, he said, "No, let your children watch." He said, "Let em know what this is called justice, let them see what the police officers are supposed to serve and protect and do." And every time he'd open his mouth why they'd ram that knee right down in that head. Well, they had the side of his face bleedin from pushin it so hard. . . .

Now one man asked them, asked em all—he had a piece of paper and a pen. He said, "I want your badge numbers." Young fella in a checkered shirt. [Bill Carter. He and Amanda, who had just happened along, verified this account.] Well, the one cop, he said, "You want badge numbers? Here, here's mine." Oh, he was proud to give im his un. But when he tried to get the sergeant's badge number, the sergeant said, "You're not gettin my badge number. If you want it you come down to the station and get it."

And there was one woman, now I don't know who she was, but she was really readin em a verse. Oooh! Now she called them every name in the book, and she told em just what she thought. And he told her to shut up and go away before he put her in the paddy wagon too. And I believe if she'd a kept on they would have put her in, cause she was really callin em down in front a all them other people out there. And he said, "You wanna join him?" And that man turned around, "Yes, they wanna join me, yes, they want to." He was tryin to encourage everybody, you know, to get a little mob going there but nobody did. Lot of em said afterward they wished they had. . . .

Some a the cops didn't go over there, I'll say that.

Some of em just got out a the squad cars and watched. They didn't join in on it. But those that was doin the beatin was pretty proud that they was doin it. And the kids all standin around—that's nothin for children to see. And my daughter walked over and I led her away, I wouldn't let her look at it, because let's face it, we do try to teach the kids that the law is here to help us. And then they'll get a good view of that, and they'll say, "Well, why should I try to do the right thing if I'm gonna get this if I—" Oh no. Uh-uh. I didn't want her to see it, I just got her and made her go on away. . . .

Well, when the paddy wagon got there, they picked him up by his feet and by his hands and they threw him in the paddy wagon. Well, when they did, his legs was hangin out. And they just took the door and they just slammed it on him, full force. And it sprung back open again, they just took it, about three of em, and pushed it back again. Then the sergeant come back around and told that one guy that had been yellin, "Hero," said, "You too, buddy." Said, "Bigmouth, you come with us." So they took him then, put him in the paddy wagon. . . .

When it was all over there was thirteen cops there, cause I stood there and counted em.

People wanna do somethin, and yet they don't wanna do anything where they'll be publicized. They might sign a petition or somethin like that but there's too many people, just like when they work in a factory —they're willin to sit around and gripe about it in their apartment but they're not willin to go out and do anything about it. . . .

"Will you march with us?" we asked.

Yeah. I know there's gonna be one, two, three, four, five, six people in this building to go, and maybe seven, depending if the guy has to work nights. Cause I've done went and talked to everybody in the buildin, and most of em all said, "Well, not too crazy about goin, but if you and your old man go, we'll go right along with you."

Her husband added,

I've never seen anything like that, and I've been around this city a long time. A thing like that has to be stopped. Whether it's JOIN or O. W. Wilson, somebody's gotta stop it.[2]

August 11 the Carters marched, the Jenkinses didn't: political inclinations shrink before the mingled pressures of overtime work, children, fear. But there were 250 marchers over the "one and one-half" mile distance, half of them young Southerners. Passing by the black blocks, Jerry Smith, tickled by his new tolerance, smiled and said, "Let's march through Niggertown." "Yeah, let's do that," said an Arkansas friend, "cause all we need is to get one. You know how they are bout followin a sign." Fears of police violence dissolved in that spirit. Through Uptown the marchers, now integrated, were watched in apprehensive silence, but at the police station a mile away—in an adjoining working-class area of two-family homes, where many police live—several hundred jeerers gathered to appreciate their protectors. With them were members of an Uptown gang whom the police had promised free run of the beach for drag-racing in return for their appearance. (The police later reneged, and the gang turned toward the Goodfellows.) Bob, Marvin, Charles, another Goodfellow, and the young Catholic priest met with the Commander, who glanced at the dozens of affidavits presented to him, modestly disclaimed the power to discipline his police, and taped the meeting "for Superintendent Wilson," "He says he knows nothin about brutality," Charles said later. "He's gotta know, he's the boss here." The Commander in turn tried to discredit the march by waving a mug shot of Charles and displaying his arrest record. An officer told Charles as he was leaving the meeting, "We'll get you, Otis. We'll kill you." The press considered this hearsay.

News media were caught off guard by this unprecedented demonstration, the first in anyone's memory by whites against brutal police, and they moved to assimilate the new fact in their old stereotypes. Utterly apart from JOIN and Uptown, but in the same weeks, Martin Luther King had been leading open-housing marches into white enclaves in Chicago. On August 14, the liberal *Sun-Times* jammed the two facts together and libelously misquoted Marvin Jackson to produce a story that made sense to them, about a march "to the Summerdale station to protest police handling of 'counter-demonstrators' at open housing marches. . . . Jackson said that most of them had taken part in the abuse of the rights marchers." They need not have intended to slur, so fierce is the liberal prejudice against poor Southern whites, so bullheaded the need of the white moderate to occupy the moral center, manufacturing extremists careless of side. The reporters would not have un-

derstood the rage of Jerry Smith, who spurred us to arrange a meeting with the city editor. "There was niggers on our march! Mexcans and everything!" said Jerry, insisting no one he knew had attacked civil rights marchers. The editor apologized for the unexplained, "unfortunate" error. No retraction was published.

Retribution follows the just faster than justice. Marvin was abruptly fired by the suburban factory where he worked, with no explanation. Charles and his friends were stopped and frisked nightly, and Charles told Bob not to be surprised if some of the Goodfellows passed him without so much as a hello: "Police been tellin us if we're seen with you they'll bust us." Another Goodfellow backed him up: "Guys were told they would be busted and beaten if they had anything to do with JOIN." Even a wino said that when he had shown his JOIN card to the police as identification, they had taken him to the station and beaten him.

Pacification, in Uptown as in Vietnam, finally depends on the overwhelming might of the occupiers. The night of September 1, the JOIN office was raided by local police and state narcotics agents. About twenty laughing policemen tore down a wall, scattered files, broke chairs, smashed a mimeograph machine, opened a locked box containing membership cards and dues—"a reasonable search," they said. Two organizers who happened to be present were arrested for possession of marijuana and amphetamines and—if that was not enough—hypodermic needles. The police arrested the untouchable Reverend in a simultaneous raid on his office, and also took Marvin Jackson to the station, but released him there, perhaps to cast aspersions on his loyalty. (An organizer was later told by a newspaper reporter that his paper had received an anonymous tip that Marvin had informed on JOIN. If the police thought they could split the organization so clumsily, they were wrong.) "The light's shinin brighter on Wilson Avenue," said Marvin the next morning. "A lot more people are gonna come to JOIN because of this." Another Goodfellow thought JOIN would close up; when the office opened the next morning, he was impressed. But the raid cost JOIN a good deal of support, from people like Amelia Jenkins; the stakes of protest had climbed. The *American*'s page one headline read: "Nab Uptown Protestors in Dope Raid: pro-Viet Cong literature found." And the screaming innuendo taking the entire first page of the neighborhood paper was not rectified by their report on September 13 that 25 North Side clergymen had issued this statement: "Clergymen Protest Police Narcotics Raid." Nor was it mitigated by JOIN marches downtown, organized in large part by an energized Buddy Tompkins. Over months of court proceedings, the police testimony turned out to be so self-contradictory, the charges so embarrassingly absurd, they were ultimately dismissed, but the damage had been done. And that wasn't all.

Two nights after the raid, Ronnie Williams, brother of Goodfellow Kenny, was shot and killed by Task Force police on Wilson Avenue. Accounts varied. All agreed that Ronnie had quarreled with Kenny and shot him through the shoulder, that he had started to run through the parking lot under the el tracks when police arrived. Police said they ordered him to halt; he turned and shot at them; they returned his fire and found him dead. The medical examination had revealed two wounds.

A half-dozen witnesses with whom we spoke said Ronnie had never fired at the cops, indeed had dropped his gun; panicked, he kept running; the police kept shooting, scooping up Ronnie's gun as they ran by; hit, he fell against a parked car; from closer range, they fired again, spinning him off the car and onto the ground, where an officer put a bullet in his head point-blank. Another witness rushed up, asked the officer what had happened. "Just another dead hillbilly," was the reply.

The undertaker told one of us [Nanci Hollander] that he saw four bullet holes: two in the back, one in the head, one in the arm. Would he testify to that effect? No, the city would take away his license. The body was buried back home in Kentucky.

The six old men of the coroner's jury two weeks later returned a verdict of "justifiable homicide," though they never discredited the testimony of the witnesses, nor did they produce a civilian witness to corroborate the police story.

The mother of Ronnie and Kenny stopped by the JOIN office a few days later. "I told my husband I'd be gone for twenty minutes; but I've been walk-in around for hours. I'm not satisfied at home, I'm not satisfied out here on the streets, I'm not satisfied nowhere." She said Ronnie's widow "got

stopped by the cops yesterday, and they saw her JOIN button. You know I got her to JOIN. And they said, 'Why're you wearin that button?' And she said, 'To stop this goddamn police brutality!' They didn't like that! Boy, I was never so proud of her —I never did hear her cuss before. . . .

"I never thought the cops was good but I didn't used to feel the way I feel now. You wouldn't know how I feel 'less you lost one yourself. I just don't want to talk to em. Smitty, the colored cop, he used to walk on Wilson Avenue here, he's up on Argyle now. He'd always give everybody a break, and he was good to me. He'd say to me, 'You know the white Southerners and the Negroes is alone in the city, we got to stick together.' Smitty's good, he's real good, but now I see him on the street and I just can't talk to him."

Her neighbors and Ronnie's friends—he had many friends—were edgy but the young guys were unorganized. The march now seemed a failure: it had brought nothing but a dope raid and a murder. "Won't they learn," asked Kenny, "before somebody in their own families gets killed?" But the Goodfellows' leadership, always fragile, now lacked the cementing force of a timetable, the patrols ceased as young guys lost interest and crumbled. Bob went back to finish college.[3]

Marvin Jackson returned to his wife, who feared for him and insisted he work regularly and live in a better part of town. Not long afterward they separated again, but even after the Commander reportedly admitted that dozens of police (not including Sam Joseph) had been transferred as a result of the march, his resolve was shattered. Opposed to the war as he was, he joined the U.S. Army. He had been overorganized, coaxed too far too fast to catch his breath. But he was no "loss." Wounded in Vietnam, he began distributing an antiwar GI newspaper on his return to the States.

Buddy Tompkins, a good spokesman but never a Goodfellow organizer, realized he was a radical and decided his mission was to organize his countrymen back home in West Virginia. He left this poem behind him:

We hear the stories of the wisest men
But it's always the ones with money who wins
We know Black and White aren't strong enough to fight
And everyone judges these people with delight

Even those who knows what it means to vote
They also have the same hands around their throat
And a fool fighting for his citizen rights
So he can get them right this same night
There still stands this great mass of men
Who will have to fight to the end
For our words of small, or of a group
We are or should all become fighting troops
For no one knows this story so true
As the people who are fighting to see this through.

The general bitterness had been framed by Charles in an interview with *The Movement,* a San Francisco paper:

> I been here eleven years. When I first came out here the police would stop you and say, "OK, kids, get off the street." They was always nice about it. And every year it was a little bit worse. First they started pickin you up for nothin. Then they started to whuppin you. Now they framin you. Like I said, it's gettin worse. Now they kill you if they get a chance, and ain't gonna say nothin about it.
>
> I tell you, people are gonna get fed up with it. And they'll start pickin em off one by one. That's my opinion.

But Charles himself was lying low while his trial for strong-arm robbery was still pending. The witness-priest had cooled his affection for the young guys. (Another clergyman said the priest had yielded to pressure from the archdiocese.) One morning a drunken Charles rammed his car into another car, and, expecting doubled reprisals, he fled the city.

"Charles Otis was the leader," said one of the disenchanted Goodfellows. "Everyone would follow him. Now there's no leader. There are lots of groups and each is separate." They had never been involved fully in planning the march, discussing what would constitute success and what failure.

The principle of joint action had been asserted, true, but too many had expected to end police brutality with a march, if they expected anything at all. Now they would suffer reprisals for action, and saw no counter-balancing prospects. Groups returned to their separate street corners. Beaten, some muttered of Molotov cocktails.

New leaders would have to work more slowly, less flamboyantly, talking to young guys one by one, hanging out with them in bars and pool halls, plucking guitars with them, folding them into a more democratic structure. Whether there was time or not, time had to be taken. This was Gene's assessment. Made radical in that way himself in the course of the summer, Gene now came on the JOIN (later National Community Union) staff full-time, where he has worked two years at this writing. Late in September he brought in an old friend, Bobby Joe Wright. Gene and Bobby Joe began the steady work of rebuilding the Goodfellows, this time from the bottom up.

NOTES

[1] Three weeks later, he was picked up on the corner, thrown in a paddy wagon, taken into the alley, and beaten with billy clubs, and his wallet was stolen. After running the maze of police depositories he subsequently retrieved the wallet. The cash was gone.

[2] "In recent weeks there has been especially strict law enforcement in Uptown because of excesses in public drunkenness, damage to property, and threats to people in the area. Whether this strict enforcement of the law resulted in police brutality or not, I do not know. I personally have not been advised of any brutality by the police." Alderman O'Rourke, *Uptown News,* August 16, 1966.

[3] Finish he did, and then he returned to the Midwest, working in the National Organizing Committee with poor and working-class young whites in Cincinnati and other cities.

THE IMPACT OF THE DRAFT ON THE LEGITIMACY OF THE NATIONAL STATE

Kenneth E. Boulding

One of the most neglected aspects of the dynamics of society is the study of dynamic processes which underlie the rise and fall of legitimacy. This neglect reflects, in the United States at least, not merely a deficiency in social sciences and social thought; it reflects a grave deficiency in what might be called the popular image of the social system. We all tend to take legitimacy for granted. Thus, the economist hardly ever inquires into the legitimacy of exchange, even though this is the institution on which his science is built. The political scientist rarely inquires into the legitimacy of political institutions or of the institutions of organized threat, such as the police and the armed forces. Consequently we are much given to discussions of economic development as if this were a mechanical or quasi-automatic process without regard to the conditions of legitimacy of various activities and institutions. Similarly, in our discussions of the strategy of threat we rarely take account of the legitimacy of the institutions which either make the threats or provide their credibility. To put the matter simply, we tend to regard both wealth and power as self-justifying and this could well be a disastrous error.

The truth is that the dynamic of legitimacy, mysterious as it may seem, in fact governs to a remarkable extent all the other processes of social life. Without legitimacy no permanent relationship can be established, and if we lose legitimacy we lose everything. A naked threat, such as that of the bandit or the armed robber, may establish a temporary relationship. The victim hands over his money or even his person at the sword's point or the pistol's mouth. If we want to establish a permanent relationship, however, such as that of a land-

lord demanding rent or a government demanding taxes, the threat must be legitimized. The power both of the landlord and of the government depend in the last analysis upon the consent of the rentpayer or the taxpayer and this consent implies that the whole procedure has been legitimated and is accepted by everyone concerned as right and proper. Legitimacy may be defined as general acceptance by all those concerned in a certain institution, role, or pattern of behavior that it constitutes part of the regular moral or social order within which they live. Thus legitimacy is a wider concept than the formal concept of law, even though the law is a great legitimator. At times, however, law itself may become illegitimate, and when it does so its capacity to organize society is destroyed.

Legitimacy has at least two dimensions, which might be described as intensity and extent. Its intensity refers to the degree of identification or acceptance in the mind of a particular individual, and it may be measured roughly by the extent of sacrifice which he is prepared to make for an institution rather than deny it or abandon it. The extent of legitimacy refers to the proportion of the relevant population which regards the institution in question as legitimate. An overall measure of the legitimacy of any particular institution might be achieved by multiplying its intensity by its extent, but such a measure might easily obscure certain important characteristics of the system. A case in which an institution was regarded with intense allegiance by a small proportion of the people concerned would be very different from one in which there was a mild allegience from all the people; the former, indeed, would probably be less stable than the latter. In considering any particular case, therefore, it is always important that we consider both dimensions.

The creation, maintenance, and destruction of legitimacy of different institutions presents many difficult problems. Legitimacy is frequently created by the exercise of power, either economic power in the form of wealth or political power in the form of threat capability. Legitimacy, furthermore, frequently increases with age so that old wealth and old power are more legitimate than new. The nouveau riche may be looked upon askance but their grandchildren easily become aristocrats. The conqueror likewise is illegitimate at first, but if his conquest is successful and his empire lasts, it eventually acquires legitimacy. All these relationships, however, seem to be nonlinear, and reverse themselves beyond a certain point. Thus, the display of wealth tends to become obscene and damages the legitimacy of the wealthy. In order to retain legitimacy they often have to diminish their wealth by giving it away, establishing foundations, or at least by abstaining from ostentatious consumption. Similarly, political power often seems to lose its legitimacy when it is apparently at its very height. It is at the greatest extent and power of a regime, nation, or empire that it often suddenly collapses through sheer loss of belief in it. Even age does not always guarantee legitimacy. After a certain point an ancient person or institution simply becomes senile or old-fashioned and its legitimacy abruptly collapses.

There have been enough examples of collapse of legitimacy of apparently large, prosperous and invincible institutions to suggest that we have here a general, though not necessarily a universal, principle at work. It is perhaps an example of another much-neglected proposition, that nothing fails like success because we do not learn anything from it. Thus in Europe the institution of the absolute monarchy seemed to be most secure and invincible at the time of Louis XIV, yet only a few decades later it was in ruins. Similarly, in the early years of the twentieth century the concept of empire seemed invincible and unshakably legitimate, yet in another few decades it was discredited, illegitimate, and the empires themselves collapsed or had to be transformed.

It looks indeed as if there is some critical moment at which an institution must be transformed if it is to retain its legitimacy and transformed, furthermore, in the direction of abandonment of either its wealth or its power in some degree. Thus, after the eighteenth century the only way in which the institution of the monarchy could retain its legitimacy was to abandon its power and become constitutional. By abandoning his political power, that is, his threat capability, the monarch was able to become a symbol of the legitimacy of the state and hence was able to preserve his role in the society. Where the monarch did not make this transition, as for instance in France, Germany, and Russia, the incumbent frequently lost his head, the whole institution was destroyed, and the role simply abandoned. Similarly, in the twentieth century, if any semblance of empire was to be maintained, the political power had to be abandoned and the empire transformed into a commonwealth or community based on sentiment rather than on threat. Even the church in the twentieth century has largely had to abandon the fear of hell, that is, its spiritual threat system, as the prime motivation in attracting support. In most countries, furthermore, it has likewise had to abandon the support of the state and the secular arm, that is, the secular threat system, in an attempt to enforce conformity. Here again we see an example of the abandonment of power in the interests of retaining legitimacy.

THE NATIONAL STATE

At the present time by far the most wealthy, powerful, and legitimate type of institution is the national state. In the socialist countries the national state monopolizes virtually all the wealth and the threat capability of the society. Even in the capitalist world the national state usually commands about 25 per cent of the total economy and is a larger economic unit than any private corporation, society, or church. Thus the United States government alone wields economic power roughly equal to half the national income of the Soviet Union, which is the largest socialist state. Within the United States government the United States Department of Defense has a total budget larger than the national income of the Peoples Republic of China and can well claim to be second largest centrally planned economy in the world. It is true that the great corporations wield an economic power roughly equal to that of the smaller socialist states; there are, indeed, only about 11 countries with a gross national product larger than General Motors. Nevertheless, when it comes to legitimacy the national state is supreme. All other loyalties are expected to bow before it. A man may deny his parents, his wife and his friends, his God, or his profession and get away with it, but he cannot deny his country unless he finds another one. In our world a man without a country is regarded with pity and scorn. We are expected to make greater sacrifices for our country than we make for anything else. We are urged, "Ask not what your country can do for you, ask what you can do for your country," whereas nobody ever suggests that we should "Ask not what General Motors can do for you, ask what you can do for General Motors."

An institution of such monumental wealth, power, and legitimacy would seem to be invincible. The record of history suggests clearly, however, that it is precisely at this moment of apparent invincibility that an institution is in gravest danger. It may seem as absurd today to suggest that the national state might lose its legitimacy as it would have been to suggest the same thing of the monarchy in the days of *le Grand Monarque.* Nevertheless both monarchy and empire have lost their legitimacy and that at the moment of their greatest power and extent. If history teaches us anything, therefore, it should teach us at this moment to look at the national state with a quizzical eye. It may be an institution precisely filling the conditions which give rise to a sudden collapse of legitimacy, which will force the institution itself to transform itself by abandoning its power or will create conditions in which the institution cannot strive.

These conditions can be stated roughly as follows: An institution which demands sacrifices can frequently create legitimacy for itself because of a strong tendency in human beings to justify to themselves sacrifices which they have made. We cannot admit that sacrifices have been made in vain, for this would be too great a threat to our image of ourselves and our identity. As the institution for which sacrifices are made gains legitimacy, however, it can demand more sacrifices, which further increases legitimacy. At some point, however, the sacrifices suddenly seem to be too much. The terms of trade between its devotees and the institu-

tion become too adverse, and quite suddenly the legitimacy of the whole operation is questioned and ancient sacrifices are written off and the institution collapses. Thus men sacrificed enormously for the monarchy, and the king was able to say for centuries, "Ask not what I can do for you, ask only what you can do for me," until the point when suddenly people began to ask "What can the king do for me?" and the answer was "Nothing." At that moment the monarchy either died or had to be transformed.

We may be in a similar moment in the case of the national state. The real terms of trade between an individual and his country have been deteriorating markedly in the past decades. In the eighteenth century the national state made relatively few demands on its citizens, and provided some of them at least with fair security and satisfactory identity. As the nation has gathered legitimacy however from the bloodshed and treasure expended for it, it has become more and more demanding. It now demands ten to twenty per cent of our income, at least two years of our life—and it may demand the life itself—and it risks the destruction of our whole physical environment. As the cost rises, it eventually becomes not unreasonable to ask for what. If the payoffs are in fact low, the moment has arrived when the whole legitimacy of the institution may be threatened.

We must here distinguish the internal from the external payoffs of the national state. Internally the payoffs may still be quite high, though it is perhaps still a question whether governments today, like the medical profession a hundred years ago, really do more good than harm. In the external relations, however, there can be no doubt that the system of national states is enormously burdensome and costly. It is not only that the world-war industry is now about 140 billion dollars, which is about equal to the total income of the poorest half of the human race, it is that this enormous expenditure gives us no real security in the long run and it sets up a world in which there is a positive probability of almost total disaster. It is perfectly reasonable indeed to ask ourselves this question: After a nuclear war, if there is anybody left, are they going to set up again the institutions which produced the disaster? The answer would clearly seem to be "No," in which case we may say that as the present system contains a positive probability of nuclear war it is in fact bankrupt and should be changed *before* the nuclear war rather than afterward. It can be argued very cogently indeed that modern technology has made the national state obsolete as an instrument of unilateral national defense, just as gunpowder made the feudal baron obsolete, the development of the skills of organization and public administration made the monarchy obsolete, and economic development made empire obsolete. An institution, no matter how currently powerful and legitimate, which loses its function will also lose its legitimacy, and the national state in its external relations seems precisely in this position today. Either it must be transformed in the direction of abandoning its power and threat capability or it will be destroyed, like the absolute monarchy and the absolute church before it.

THE IMPACT OF THE DRAFT

What then is the role of the draft in this complex dynamic process? The draft may well be regarded as a symbol of a slow decline in the legitimacy of the national state (or of what perhaps we should call more exactly the warfare state, to distinguish it from the welfare state which may succeed it), that slow decline which may presage the approach of collapse. In the rise and decline of legitimacy, as we have seen, we find first a period in which sacrifices are made, voluntarily and gladly, in the interests of the legitimate institution, and, indeed, reinforce the legitimacy of the institution. As the institution becomes more and more pressing in its demands, however, voluntary sacrifices become replaced with forced sacrifices. The tithe becomes a tax, religious enthusiasm degenerates into compulsory chapel, and voluntary enlistment in the threat system of the state becomes a compulsory draft. The legitimacy of the draft, therefore, is in a sense a subtraction from the legitimacy of the state. It represents the threat system of the state turned in on its own citizens, however much the threat may be disguised by a fine language about service and "every young man fulfilling his obligation." The language of duty is not the language of love and it is a symptom of approaching delegitimation.

A marriage in which all the talk is of obligations rather than of love is on its way to the divorce court. The church in which all worship is obligatory is on its way to abandonment or reformation, and the state in which service has become a duty is in no better case. The draft therefore, which undoubtedly increases the threat capability of the national state, is a profound symptom of its decay and insofar as it demands a forced sacrifice it may hasten that decay and may hasten the day when people come to see that to ask "what can your country do for you" is a very sensible question.

The draft, furthermore, inevitably creates strong inequities. It discriminates against the poor, or at least against the moderately poor; the very poor, because of their poor educational equipment, may escape it just as the rich tend to escape it, and the main burden therefore falls on the lower end of the middle-income groups. As these groups also in our society bear the brunt of taxation—for a great deal of what is passed as "liberal" legislation in fact taxes the poor in order to subsidize the rich—an unjust distribution of sacrifice is created. Up to now it is true this strain has not been very apparent. It cannot indeed be expressed directly because of the enormous legitimacy of the national state, hence it tends to be expressed indirectly in alienation, crime, internal violence, race and group hatreds and also in an intensified xenophobia. This is the old familiar problem of displacement. We dare not vent our anger at frustrations upon their cause and we therefore have to find a legitimated outlet in the foreigner, or the communist, or whoever the enemy happens to be at the moment. What is worse, the frustrated adult frequently displaces his anger on his children who in turn perpetuate the whole miserable business of hatred and lovelessness.

Like compulsory chapel or church attendance, which is its closest equivalent, the draft has a further disadvantage in that while it may at best produce a grudging and hostile acquiescence in the methods of the society, it frequently closes the mind to any alternative or to any reorganization of information. The psychological strains which are produced by compulsory service of any kind naturally result in displaced aggressions rather than in any reform of the system which created them. Consequently the draft by the kind of indoctrination and hidden frustrations which it produces may be an important factor in preventing that reevaluation of the national policy and the national image which is so essential in the modern world if the national state itself is to survive. The draft therefore is likely to be an enemy of the survival of the very state in the interests of which it is supposedly involved. It produces not a true love of country based on a realistic appraisal of the present situation of human society but rather a hatred of the other which leads to political mental ill health, and an image of the world which may be as insulated from the messages which come through from reality as is the mind of a paranoid.

Perhaps the best thing that can be said in defense of the draft is that the alternative, namely, raising a voluntary armed force by offering sufficient financial inducements, or by persuasion and advertising, would involve even more the whipping up of hatred of the foreigner and the reinforcement of paranoid political attitudes. The draft by its very absurdities and inequities at least to some extent helps to make the whole operation faintly ridiculous, as we see it in comic strips like Beetle Bailey or in movies such as *Dr. Strangelove,* and hence makes the operation of national defense commonplace rather than charismatic. The draft certainly represents the institutionalization of the charisma of the national state, to use an idea from Max Weber, and this may be something on the credit side. Even this merit, however, is dubious. Insofar as the draft leads to widespread commonplace acceptance of mass murder and atrocities, and an attitude of mind which is blind to any but romantically violent solutions of conflict, its influence is wholly negative. Certainly the political wisdom of the American Legion is no advertisement for the political virtues of having passed through the Armed Forces.

It seems clear therefore that those of us who have a genuine affection for the institution of the national state and for our own country in particular should constantly attack the legitimacy of the draft, and the legitimacy of the whole system of unilateral national defense which supports it, in the interest of preserving the legitimacy of the national state itself. The draft, it is true, is merely a symbol or a symptom of a much deeper disease, the disease of unilateral national defense, and it is this concept which should be the prime focus of our attack. Nevertheless, cleaning up a symptom sometimes helps to cure the disease, otherwise the sales of aspirin would be much less, and a little aspirin of dissent applied to the headache of the draft might be an important step in the direction of the larger objective. Those of us, therefore, who are realistically concerned about the survival of our country should probably not waste too much time complaining about the inequities and absurdities of the draft or attempt the hopeless task of rectifying it when the plain fact is that the draft can only begin to approach "justice" in time of major war, and a peacetime draft has to be absurd and unjust by its very nature. The axe should be applied to the root of the tree, not to its branches. An attempt to pretty up the draft and make it more acceptable may actually prevent that radical reevaluation of the whole system of unilateral national defense which is now in order. We are very close to the moment when the only way to preserve the legitimacy of the national state will be to abandon most of its power. The draft is only a subplot in this much greater drama.

ELLSBERG AND THE NEW HEROISM

Todd Gitlin

Daniel Ellsberg won't like being called a hero any more than I like calling him one. We have had enough of heroes who abuse the privilege to make themselves into celebrities in order to define their distance from the rest of us—a difficult thing to avoid when mass media are relied upon for images of honorable prowess. Besides, Ellsberg only did "what he had to do." But everyone does precisely that, no more, no less.

Ellsberg became a hero because of both opportunity and irreducible will, because he was in a position to be a certain kind of hero and because he had the grace or audacity or pigheadedness to seize the occasion; most people have none of these, and many who don't have his opportunity, or his complicity, splatter their will in fruitless symbolic violence. The hero is socially defined; he does what he has to do and other people make a place for him in their socialized categories. He does something that is not expected of him, something outside his boundaries of class, career, race, sex, as people who live within those boundaries see it; and if enough people can identify with his experience and therefore his need, he thereby stretches the boundaries of the possible, and beckons followers.

Ellsberg is an authentic hero, but he is not unprecedented. The specific nature of his achievement emerges most sharply in contrast to other styles of radical and antiwar activity. Most public political actions, whatever their virtues and vices, however effective or moving, however they feel from the inside, are, when seen from the outside, necessarily rather inexpressive of the people who take part in them. In a picket line, a demonstration crowd, or a riotous confrontation, one is playing a role, "standing up to be counted," *literally* to be counted, to become a number in a police estimate. The act, like voting, is impersonal; it does not flow

From Commonweal, *Vol. 94, No. 19 (September 3, 1971). Copyright © 1971 by Todd Gitlin.*

from one's special experience, and does not express that experience except in a kind of muffled average. The act has no more or less significance whether X or Y is doing it, unless X happens to be Dr. Spock or Martin Luther King.

More expressive are actions which reveal both oppression and the self-affirming commitment of people to change the situation: sit-ins, freedom rides, strikes, occupations of buildings. Here the act is directly demonstrative of one's experience and demands: the black students assert their right to sit at a lunch counter by sitting at a lunch counter; people who live in slums assert their right to decent housing by squatting in unoccupied buildings. But both kinds of actions are joined by a sense of *innocence:* one knows one has been a victim, or at worst a passive bystander, but in any case one has been more acted upon than acting; one has not committed a concrete crime, nor has one been overtly rewarded for it; one is outraged at what has been done to Vietnam, or to oneself, by other people or forces or ideas; with the act one buttresses one's continuing innocence and forestalls any conceivable *future* complicity ("I don't want it said that I stood idly by. . . ."). This is why so many student demonstrators since Columbia have demanded amnesty; not only do they *feel* innocent, they want the authorities to recognize and validate that innocence. (This is diametrically opposed to the Gandhian idea that one who wants the society to change should himself suffer the social costs, that one should gladly accept the retaliation of one's enemies until they come to terms. But very few American activists have held fast to the logic of self-renunciation.) Conceivably, Freudians will argue, the demand for amnesty conceals a sense of (patricidal) guilt which can only be exorcised by the (paternal) authorities; one can dig endlessly for unconscious motives. But the point is that these activists *feel* innocent, and that measured by the standard of power, they *are* innocent if anyone is.

Of course there have been intermediate forms of

activity, and corresponding varieties of heroism. Draftcard burners destroyed the emblems of their bondage and refused to be accomplices in murder, but by any commonsense estimate they were certainly more innocent than complicit; the fact was that they killed no one, nor even advised anyone to kill; they had not been in a position to do either. But their activity was directly expressive of the stakes of their own freedom; and since most Americans felt exquisitely innocent at the time, the draftcard burners had to take extreme measures and make themselves vulnerable to express both the need and the risk of real innocence. Those who turned in draft cards, or refused to step forward at induction, were also heroes, but their acts did not ripple very far outward; they were necessarily lost in the whirl of what is taken to be news. Those who burned draft files went still further out of their way to reject the lingering possibility of their complicity in the war, but most of them were not of draft age themselves; however driven by a sense of political obligation, even Christian guilt, by the standards of *overt* and *concrete* guilt they must be judged innocents. The Weathermen were also driven by both guilt and innocence, yet if one carefully examines the guilt which is being cast off in their deeds —guilt over having been rich, guilt over standing by while the Vietnamese are murdered—it becomes abstract, farfetched, almost fantastic; they too act more from innocence than from complicity.

COMPLICITY

The new heroism begins in undeniable complicity. There is nothing abstract about the complicity of Ellsberg or a Vietnam vet, especially one who has committed war crimes or been in a position to try to prevent them; it is embedded in acts of commission, not omission; it is not conjured up; it requires no psychoanalysis to be uncovered. The new heroism consists in conspicuously throwing one's own complicity back in the face of power, and thereby struggling to free oneself of it; I say "struggling" because I doubt this liberation comes with a single act, however dramatic. The act is a direct, unmistakable rejection of one's past participation in evil. What is different about the new heroes is that they know they have been accomplices, not merely in the passive sense in which almost all of us find ways to go along and can fairly

be judged to be sanctioning the *status quo;* the new heroes can document the ways, they can explain them easily and plausibly to others. Ellsberg knows what advice he gave between 1964 and 1967, in the Pentagon and in Vietnam. The new heroism has a specific political location: it happens within the most potent institutions of social control.

I am thinking of the Vietnam Vets Against the War in Washington on April 23, each speaking a few words (no more were necessary) and hurling their medals at the Capitol: a clear message that the atonement and rebirth that was possible for them was possible for the Congress. As I watched the vets on TV I was moved as I had not been in a long time: I saw men reclaiming themselves, reliving both the monstrousness of what they had once found themselves doing and the passion of renewal. I am *not* thinking of the come-lately peaceniks, the Arthur Goldbergs and Townsend Hoopes' and Clark Cliffords, who exercise the luxury of last-minute conversions, making the relatively comfortable moves of election campaigns and books and speeches, without rejecting their previous roles or exposing their previous lies and barbarisms. They only take up the time-honored elite prerogative of deserting a sinking yacht: no regrets, no responsibility, faces turned photogenically to the wind, ascots carefully tucked into their blazers. If they atone at all it is within the conventions of their class; to probe their previous complicity too deeply in public would be to abandon their etiquette and their protection. One does not break the rules; indeed one follows them, for within the elite there is even a rule permitting, even encouraging, discreet resignation and judiciously worded critical books and speeches at important junctures —when done with Olympian detachment and especially when there is a different party in power. (Not surprisingly, the high officials whose departures from government policy and finally from government have been most outspoken—Henry Wallace and Walter Hickel—were both, by geography and training, marginal to the elite.)

No, the easy-going converts are not heroes, though their repentance is politically useful by a crass calculation. But the vets and Daniel Ellsberg have rejected not only their past practices but their very codes and manners and security, the gentlemen's agreements, even the rules by which information is monopolized on top—the very practical rewards of past complicity. In May, according to Noam Chomsky in *The New York Review of Books* (June 17), Ellsberg joined the anti-war rally in Boston, where he went to the aid of a demonstrator being clubbed by a cop, and was himself beaten. Although the vets threw back only the symbols of their status, turned the tokens of their achievement into trash, those tokens were their only real rewards; in fact the society accords them no other privilege, in many cases not even jobs. Since his power and knowledge—and therefore his complicity—had been so much greater, Ellsberg had more to give, and gave it. "I felt," he told Walter Cronkite on June 23, "that the knowledge [of the Pentagon papers] gave me a kind of responsibility that others didn't have." Accordingly, he may have to pay a much higher price.

Certainly the new heroes have predecessors. I think of the German generals' 1944 plot against Hitler; the similarity may seem farfetched, though grosser elite failures generate more extreme resistance at high levels, higher than Ellsberg's. But in recent American history I can only think of some of the Manhattan Project atomic scientists, whose complicity seems comparable to Ellsberg's. In Oppenheimer's words, they had "known sin," and after Hiroshima many of them moved to political action as atonement. (Ironically, their major victory, the creation of the Atomic Energy Commission to assert civilian control over the bomb, seems at this juncture utterly pyrrhic.) Few of them were interested in striking to stop bomb production, though such a proposal was floated in the government laboratories after the war. Individual actions were more comfortable and common: Many left the labs, and a few simply abandoned physics, certain that their work would end up destructive. One of these was Leo Szilard, whose later attempt at political action, a fund-raising lobby called the Council for a Livable World, did succeed in helping elect George McGovern to the Senate. The political atomic scientists were heroes in their way, for they broke an age-old stereotype of the scientist "on tap, not on top"; for them, setting up an office and lobbying was almost as outrageous and unprecedented as throwing back medals or making documents public, though certainly not as risky as the latter. But one could also argue that the scientists, operating under a much less repressive regime, could and should have done much more.

Jorge Luis Borges says that every literary innovator calls forth, even "invents," his own predecessors. So it is with heroes, and it would be interesting to scour American history for other men and women who converted atonement to political action. But such a search should not obscure the fact that the new heroes are creatures and makers of an uncommon political situation. To put it crudely, in all societies advanced enough to do great evil, the innocents—those lacking direct access to the tools of evil, or lacking the luxury of time and information to form a moral judgment and act on it—greatly outnumber the accomplices, who in turn outnumber the high criminals.

There is, of course, the tricky question of how innocent are the innocents, as Milton Mayer discovered when he asked postwar German townspeople whether they had known about the concentration camps; he ended up not knowing what "knowing" meant, but suspecting that the townspeople "could have known" if they had invested some energy. (His *They Thought They Were Free* needs a revival at this moment.) When some of the worst atrocities are daily paraded across the dinner-time TV screen, the standards for innocence must be reassessed. But against the vagaries of ignorance and innocence stands the hard, undeniable knowledge and complicity of the State's hired hands: from the highest decision-makers and weapon-makers, down through the ranks of administrative advice and consent, to the soldiers and the police. When the State is confident, successful (in its own terms) and coherent, it can count on its hired hands. However upset or opposed are the passive citizens, criminal power is intact as long as it holds the active loyalty of the accomplices, for the vast majority of citizens are marginal to the actual machinery of evil; the State can always resort to terror to passify discontent outside administrative ranks. But when the evil is unspeakable enough, when evil's rewards aren't high enough or its explanations not compelling enough, the accomplices begin to doubt too. And when a certain critical mass of doubt is reached, accomplices begin to fall out: discreetly at first, then noisily, finally with action that reverberates throughout the society.

America in 1971 has reached that point. Aside from the vets and the organized antiwar soldiers on virtually every base, one can be sure there are thousands of GIs involved in a range of opposition from "not fighting very hard" to "fragging" to mutiny. This is at the lowest level of complicity, where the opportunity for evil is most immediate and least willed; most GIs, especially draftees, had far fewer life-choices than Ellsberg or I or Robert McNamara or Richard Nixon. Yet also at the bottom of the pyramid of complicity, since disaffection is so widespread, there is some safety in numbers. In 1966, of course, when Green Beret Don Duncan quit the Army and published his denunciation of the war in *Ramparts,* he stood virtually alone; five years have made the difference between single hero and mass movement. Now it is Ellsberg who is isolated—but for how long?

At a congressional conference on war crimes last year, Ellsberg framed the special relationship between complicity and responsibility:

Notice that in the massacre at My Lai and in other such military incidents there were individuals who, despite apparent risk to their lives, did resist atrocities or at least failed to cooperate. It is a terrible shame—one that I share as a former official—that I know of no civilian official in the government who has acted comparably in any area of the Vietnam involvement.

He believed in "institutional and political changes," yet he was quick to add:

Yet even if these changes do occur, I believe that we cannot avoid much, much worse crimes and horrors than we have seen in the past unless many individuals within the government do assume greater risks and a greater sense of responsibility than has been shown in the past decade. (Los Angeles Times)

FIRST OF MANY

Perhaps Ellsberg will be the first in a new line of accomplices-turned-rebels; perhaps the *Times* will soon be deluged with documents expropriated from the expropriators. (It is delicious historical irony that the instrument of Ellsberg's act was that technological marvel, the Xerox machine, whose very built-in purpose, perverted by its cost and monopolization in hierarchical offices, is to explode private property in ideas and information.) Possibly the rebellion of accomplices would stir the higher past and present criminals to unease, and beyond unease to separation or even action. One could go so far as to imagine a series of public resignations and recantations, where disgust with the war is no longer whispered at dinner parties but proclaimed at press conferences, and specific lies are exposed. After all, it was as far back as 1964 and 1965, while he was working in the Pentagon, that Ellsberg first felt "while reading documents late at night that I was looking at future exhibits [in war crimes trials]" (*Los Angeles Times,* June 18). Plenty of other officials must have had the same sinking feeling. The new heroism might have great appeal for accomplices who could never fully identify with the flamboyant innocence of orthodox protests, but may recognize themselves in the public self-redemption of an Ellsberg. Certainly the vets and Ellsberg have spoken to younger people being trained to follow in their footsteps—and indeed to all of us, perched between innocence and complicity, who are from time to time clutched by the thought, "There but by the grace of class, age and education go I." No one gets a hearing like a repentant sinner, especially if he testifies vividly and even at cost to himself. Needless to say, the government will do everything possible to discourage emulation; Ellsberg must be made an object lesson.

The political effect of Ellsberg's action remains to be seen; Johnson ("close to treason") and McNamara ("the sensational way in which the documents were released is tragic") have been heard from, and of course the Administration. The *Times,* the *Post* and the *Globe* have become faintly heroic for daring—like most of the American people at this time—to proclaim that they are better judges of the national interest than the government: still another sign of the crisis of legitimacy throughout the society. (Ten years ago, the *Times* refused to report its knowledge of the upcoming Bay of Pigs invasion.) Praise where praise is due, high praise for daring to print the truth despite Mitchell, yet a sober look reveals that what replaces the government as the repository of wisdom is not the people or "the revolution" but the *Times.* Each of us with some part of himself is asked to file a private *amicus curiae* brief for that same *Times* whose distortions, biases and omissions are built into the very code of its objectivity.

The remarkable thing is that, according to the *Times'* and other papers' report of the Pentagon documents (I have not read the documents themselves), they seem to contain very little that has not been known, inferred, or deeply intuited by antiwar activists and scholars and by independent journalists like I. F. Stone, in hundreds of articles and books and speeches since 1965. The documents have only congealed the educated guess and sometime documentation of a minority into hard high-level information, sanctioned by a government seal. Will the *Times* now admit that it was tricked for six years and that the antiwar movement was not? Will Mr. Sulzberger reconsider his distaste for the Columbia students who in 1968 intuited and acted on the truth of the Pentagon study? Will he consider the proposition that there is something about the antiwar movement that better equips it to ask the right questions and to smell a rat than the *Times* itself with its vaunted objectivity? I don't imagine so, any more than he would concede and advertise the fact that *Liberation* and *Ramparts* and the Bertrand Russell War Crimes Tribunal uncovered American atrocities long before mass media were prepared to hear about My Lai. The continuing and saddening fact is that information becomes fit to print when the editors of the *New York Times* are willing to define it that way. They still make the news, they still compose our minds and dispense legitimacy like holy water.

And yet one cannot afford the luxury of a whole-hearted attack on the *Times*. What else was Ellsberg to do, Xerox a million copies of the documents and pass them out on the streets? Give them to the underground press? And then who would find the documents credible? That is precisely the point. "Indeed we live in the Dark Ages," when for truth one must rely on the very institution that has encouraged people not to believe what they discover elsewhere. Still—in the contest between Mitchell and Sulzberger I must certainly choose Sulzberger. Can I clap with one hand? I must root for the *Times,* all right, recognizing all the while that necessity seats me as only a spectator to this bare-fisted match between the powerful over the fate of millions. But my thoughts turn more to Ellsberg—it is most natural to root for him.

Ellsberg and the vets and many unorganized and anonymous new heroes have secularized redemption by converting private atonement into public political act. They justly accuse the top powers of having ordered their crimes, but they are not satisfied to stop there. The vets must tell their stories, even risking prosecution; Ellsberg must directly contest one of the State's most pernicious and hallowed prerogatives. At the end of his terrifying *New York Review* article about Nixon's Indochina strategy (March 11, 1971), Ellsberg wrote: "If we are ever to return to the soft quiet seasons—and we have not earned an easy passage—enough Americans must look past options, briefings, pros and cons, to see what is being done in their name, and to refuse to be accomplices." He is a man of his word, and so in this America he becomes a criminal.

THE REVOLTED

Carl Oglesby and Richard Shaull

Killing is evil. . . . All countries are different and progress should be achieved by peaceful means whenever possible.

—Che Guevara

The young men joining them [the NLF] have been attracted by the excitement of the guerrilla life.

—Robert S. McNamara

Everyone in the rich world has heard that there is another world out there, almost out of sight, where two-thirds of all of us are living, where misery and violence are routine, where Mozart has not been widely heard nor Plato and Shakespeare much studied.

There is a world, that is, which, according to the mainstream intuitions of mainstream middle-class America, must be somebody's exaggeration, a world which is fundamentally implausible. For the most part, we really believe in it, this poor world, only to the extent that we have it to blame for certain of our troubles. It is the "breeding ground," we say (a favorite term, packed with connotations of the plague), of those discontents which harass us. Most ordinary rich-world people would much prefer never even to have heard of Vietnam or Mozambique, not to mention the nearly thirty other states of the world where long-term insurgencies are under way.

The main fact about the revolutionary is that he demands total change. The corresponding fact about most Americans is that they are insulted by that demand. But what of that demand's moral force? When the statistics of world poverty reach us, as they now and then do, we can respond in several characteristic ways. Sometimes we cluck our tongues, shake our heads, and send a check off to CARE. Sometimes we tell tales about brave missionaries of either the Baptist or the AID persua-

sion. Someone might name the Alliance for Progress. And someone else might cough. When the statistics are voiced by the poor man's machine-gun fire, we are more decisive. While waiting for our bombers to warm up, we develop our poor-devils theory, according to which the wretched have been duped by Communist con men. It is a bad thing to be hungry; we can see that. But it is better to be hungry and patient than hungry and Red, for to be Red proves to us that all this hunger was really just a trick. It is probably the case that a Communist *has* no hunger.

In the land of remote-controlled adventure, the office-dwelling frontiersman, the automated pioneer—how can matters be seen otherwise?

Middle-class American is the nation to which the forthcoming obsolescence of the moral choice has been revealed.

Middle-class America is the condition of mind which supposes that a new, plastic Eden has been descried upon a calm sea, off our bow. A point here and there, a firm rudder, a smart following breeze, a bit of pluck, and we shall make port any time now in this "American Century."

Middle-class America regards itself as the Final Solution. Its most intense desire is not to be bothered by fools who disagree about that.

What must be difficult for any nation seems out of the question for us: To imagine that we may from time to time be the enemies of men who are just, smart, honest, courageous, and *correct*—Who could think such a thing? Since we love rose arbors and pretty girls, our enemies must be unjust, stupid, dishonest, craven, and *wrong*.

Such conceptions are sometimes shaken. After the 1965 battle of Plei Me, Special Forces Major Charles Beckwith described NLF guerrilla fighters as "the finest soldiers I have ever seen in the world except Americans. I wish we could recruit them." After the same battle, another American said of a captured Viet Cong, "We ought to put this guy on the north wall and throw out these Government troops. He could probably hold it alone. If we could get two more, we would have all the walls [of the triangular camp] taken care of." Major Beckwith was intrigued with the "high motivation" and "high dedication" of this enemy force and suggested an explanation: "I wish I knew what they were drugging them with to make them fight like that."

That curiosity, at least, is good. Why do men rebel? Let us try to find out what could possibly be so wrong with so many of the world's men and women that they should fight so hard to stay outside the Eden we think we are offering them.

I make three assumptions. First, everyone who is now a rebel *became* a rebel; he was once upon a time a child who spoke no politics. The rebel is someone who has changed.

Second, men do not imperil their own and others' lives for unimpressive reasons. They are sharp accountants on the subject of staying alive. When they do something dangerous, they have been convinced that not to do it was more dangerous. There are always a few who can evidently be persuaded by some combination of statistics and principles to put their lives on the line. Lenin, for example, did not materially *need* the Russian Revolution. His commitment was principled and it originated from a basic detachment. But I am not trying to describe the Lenins. I am after those nameless ones but for whom the Lenins would have remained only philosophers, those who (as Brecht put it) grasp revolution first in the hand and only later in the mind.

Third, I assume that the rebel is much like myself, someone whom I can understand. He is politically extraordinary. That does not mean that he is psychologically so. My assumption is that what would not move me to the act of rebellion would not move another man.

It is safe to say first that revolutionary potential exists only in societies where material human misery is the denominating term in most social relationships. No one thinks that bankers are going to make disturbances in the streets. Less obviously, this also implies that privation can be political only if it is not universal. The peasant who compares his poverty to someone else's richness is able to conceive that his poverty is special, a social identity. To say that hunger does not become a rebellious

sensation until it coexists with food is to say that rebellion has less to do with scarcity than with maldistribution. This states a central theme: revolutionary anger is not produced by privation, but by understood injustice.

But the self-recognized victim is not at once his own avenger. He is first of all a man who simply wants to reject his humiliation. He will therefore recreate his world via social pantomimes which transfigure or otherwise discharge that humiliation. "They whipped Him up the hill," sang the black slave, "and He never said a mumbling word." That divine reticence is clearly supposed to set an example. But it also does much more. In such a song, the slave plays the role of himself and thus avoids himself, puts his realities at the distance of a pretense which differs from the realities only to the extent that it *is* a pretense. The slave creates for the master's inspection an exact replica of himself, of that slave which he is; and even as the master looks, the slave escapes behind the image. It is not that he pretends to be other than a slave. Such an act would be quickly punished. He instead pretends to be what he knows himself to be, acts out the role of the suffering and humiliated, in order to place a psychic foil between himself and the eyes of others. The American Negro's older Steppinfetchit disguise, or the acutely ritualized violence of ghetto gangs: these are intentional lies which intentionally tell the truth. The victim-liar's inner reality, his demand for freedom, precludes telling the truth. His outer reality, his victimhood, precludes telling a lie. Therefore he *pretends* the truth, pretends to hold the truth in his hand and to pass judgment on it. And by choosing to enact what he *is* he disguises from himself the fact that he had no choice.

A crucial moment comes when something ruptures this thin membrane of pretense. What can do that? A glimpse of weakness in his master sometimes; sometimes the accidental discovery of some unsuspected strength in himself. More often it will be the master's heightened violence that confronts the slave with the incorrigible authenticity of his slave act. A black man sings blues about his powerlessness, his loneliness; he has taken refuge behind that perfect image of himself. The white master, for no reason, in mid-song, takes the guitar away, breaks it, awaits the slave's reaction. The slave is at that moment forced into his self-image space, is psychologically fused with this truth-telling pretense of his: He *is* powerless; he *is* lonely. He cannot now enact himself; he must *be* that man of whom he had tried to sing. This encounter strips life of its formality and returns it to pure, primitive substance. For the victim, there is no longer even the fragile, rare escape of the simultaneous re-enactment of reality. He lives wholly now in his victim space, without manners, not even allowed to mimic the horror of victimhood in the same gesture that expresses it. He is nothing now but the locus of injustice.

Grown less random, injustice becomes more coherent. Confronted at every instant by that coherence, the victim may find that it is no longer so easy to avoid the truth that his suffering is *caused,* that it is not just an accident that there are so many differences between his life and the life of the round, white-suited man in the big hillside house. He begins to feel singled out. He rediscovers the idea of the system of power.

And at that same moment he discovers that he also may accuse. When the victim sees that what had seemed universal is local, that what had seemed God-given is man-made, that what had seemed quality is mere condition—his permanent immobility permanently disappears. Being for the first time in possession of the stark idea that his life could be different were it not for others, he is for the first time someone who might move. His vision of change will at this point be narrow and mundane, his politics naive: Maybe he only wants a different landlord, a different mayor, a different sheriff. The important element is not the scope or complexity of his vision but the sheer existence of the idea that change can happen.

Then who is to be the agent of this change? Surely not the victim himself. He has already seen enough proof of his impotence, and knows better than anyone else that he is an unimportant person. What compels him to hope nevertheless is the vague notion that his tormentor is answerable to a higher and fairer authority. This sheriff's outrageous conduct, that is, belongs strictly to this particular sheriff, not to sheriffness. Further, this sheriff represents only a local derangement within a system which the victim barely perceives and certainly does not yet accuse, a hardship which High Authority did not intend to inflict, does not need,

and will not allow. (Once Robin Hood meets King Richard, the Sheriff of Nottingham is done for.)

We meet in this the politics of the appeal to higher power, which has led to some poignant moments in history. It is the same thing as prayer. Its prayerfulness remains basic even as it is elaborated into the seemingly more politically aggressive mass petition to the king, a main assumption of which is that the king is not bad, only uninformed. This way of thinking brought the peasants and priests to their massacre at Kremlin Square in 1905. It prompted to so-called Manifesto of the Eighteen which leading Vietnamese intellectuals published in 1960. It rationalized the 1963 March on Washington for Jobs and Freedom. The Freedom Rides, the nonviolent sit-ins, and the various Deep South marches were rooted in the same belief: that there was indeed a higher power which was responsive and decent. (What was new was the way these forms enlarged the concept of petition. Instead of merely writing down the tale of grievance, they reproduced the grievance itself in settings that forced everyone to behold it, tzar included, and to respond. The Vietnam war protest demonstrations are no different. The speeches they occasion may sometimes seem especially pugnacious. But inasmuch as the antiwar movement has never been able to dream up a threat which it might really make good, this fiercer face-making has remained basically a kind of entertainment. The main idea has always been to persuade higher authority—Congress, the UN, Bobby Kennedy—to do something. Far from calling higher authority into question, these wildly militant demonstrations actually dramatize and even exaggerate its power.)

Sometimes mass-based secular prayer has resulted in change. But more often it has only shown the victim-petitioners that the problem is graver and change harder to get than they had imagined. The bad sheriffs turn out to be everywhere; indeed, there seem to be no other kind. It turns out that the king is on their side, that the state's administrative and coercive-punitive machinery exists precisely to serve the landlords. It turns out that the powerful know perfectly well who their victims are and why there should be victims, and that they have no intention of changing anything. This recognition is momentous, no doubt the spiritual low point of the emergent revolutionary's education. He finds that the enemy is not a few men but a whole system whose agents saturate the society, occupying and fiercely protecting its control centers. He is diverted by a most realistic despair.

But this despair contains within itself the omen of that final shattering reconstitution of the spirit which will prepare the malcontent, the fighter, the wino, the criminal for the shift to insurgency, rebellion, revolution, He had entertained certain hopes about the powerful: They can tell justice from injustice, they support the first, they are open to change. He is now instructed that these hopes are whimsical. At the heart of his despair lies the new certainty that there will be no change which he does not produce by himself.

The man who belives that change can only come from his own initiative will be disinclined to believe that change can be less than total. Before he could see matters otherwise, he would have to accept on some terms, however revised, the power which he now opposes. The compromises which will actually be made will be arranged by his quietly "realistic" leaders and will be presented to him as a total victory. He himself is immoderate and unconciliatory. But the more important, more elusive feature of this immoderation is that he may be powerless to change it. He could only compromise with rebelled-against authority if he were in possession of specific "solutions" to those "problems" that finally drove him to revolt. Otherwise there is nothing to discuss. But the leap into revolution has left these "solutions" behind because it has collapsed and wholly redefined the "problems" to which they referred. The rebel is an incorrigible absolutist who has replaced all "problems" with the one grand claim that the entire system is an error, all "solutions" with the single irreducible demand that change shall be total, all diagnoses of disease with one final certificate of death. To him, total change means only that those who now have all power shall no longer have any, and that those who now have none—the people, the victimized—shall have all. Then what can it mean to speak of compromise? Compromise is whatever absolves and reprieves an enemy who has already been sentenced. It explicitly restores the legitimacy of the very authority which the rebel defines himself by repudiating. This repudiation being total, it leaves exactly no motive—again, not even the *motive*—

for creating that fund of specific proposals, that *conversation,* without which a compromise is not even *technically* possible.

"What do you want?" asks the worried, perhaps intimidated master. "What can I give you?" he inquires, hoping to have found in this rebel a responsible, realistic person, a man of the world like himself. But the rebel does not fail to see the real meaning of this word *give.* Therefore he answers, "I cannot be purchased." The answer is meant mainly to break off the conference. But at one level, it is a completely substantive comment, not at all just a bolt of pride. It informs the master that he no longer exists, not even in part.

At another level, however, this answer is nothing but an evasion. The master seems to have solicited the rebel's views on the revolutionaized, good society. The rebel would be embarrassed to confess the truth: that he has no such views. Industry? Agriculture? Foreign trade? It is not such matters that drive and preoccupy him. The victorious future is at the moment any society in which certain individuals no longer have power, no longer exist. The rebel fights for something that will not be like *this.* He cannot answer the question about the future because that is not his question. It is not the future that is victimizing him. It is the present. It is not an anticipated Utopia which moves him to risk his life. It is pain. "Turn it over!" he cries, because he can no longer bear it as it is. The revolutionary is not *by type* a Lenin, a Mao, a Castro, least of all a Brezhnev. He is neither an economist nor a politician nor a social philosopher. He may become these; ultimately he must. But his motivating vision of change is at root a vision of something absent— not of something that *will* be there, but of something that will be there *no longer.* His good future world is elementally described by its empty spaces: a missing landlord, a missing mine owner, a missing sheriff. Who or what will replace landlord, owner, sheriff? Never mind, says the revolutionary, glancing over his shoulder. Something better. If he is thereupon warned that this undefined "something" may turn out to make things worse than ever, his response is a plain one: "Then we should have to continue the revolution."

The fundamental revolutionary motive is not to construct a Paradise but to destroy an Inferno. In time, Utopian ideas will appear. Because the world now has a revolutionary past, it may seem that they appear at the same moment as destructive anger, or even that they precede and activate or even cause it. This is always an illusion produced by the predictive social analytic which revolutionist intellectuals claim to have borrowed from history. We may be sure that the people have not said: Here is a plan for a better life—socialism, Montes called it. He has proved to us that it is good. In its behalf, we shall throw everything to the wind and risk our necks. Rather, they have said: What we have here in the way of life cannot be put up with anymore. Therefore, we must defend ourselves.

It happens that at least the spirit of socialism will be implied by the inner dynamics of mass revolt: What was collectively won should be collectively owned. But it cannot be too much emphasized that the interest in developing other social forms, however acute it will become, follows, *does not precede,* the soul-basic explosion against injustice which is the one redemption of the damned. When Turcios takes his rebel band to a Guatemalan village for "armed propaganda," there is no need to talk of classless societies. Someone kneels in the center of the circle and begins to speak of his life, the few cents' pay for a hard day's labor, the high prices, the arrogance of the *patrón,* the coffins of the children. It is this talk—very old talk, unfortunately always new—which finally sets the circle ringing with the defiant cry, *"Si, es cierto!"* Yes, it is true. Something will have to be done.

Revolutionary consciousness exists for the first time when the victim elaborates his experience of injustice into an inclusive definition of the society in which he lives. *The rebel is someone for whom injustice and society are only different words for the same thing.* Nothing in the social world of the master is spared the contempt of this definition, which, as soon as it exists, absorbs everything in sight. No public door is marked overnight with a device that permits its survival. The loanshark's corner office and the Chase Manhattan Bank, Coney Island and Lincoln Center, look very much the same from 137th Street. They are all owned by someone else.

Everywhere he looks, the man-who-is-being-revolted sees something which is not his. The good land which the *campesino* works belongs to the *hacienda.* That belongs to the *patrón.* As often as

not, the *patrón* belongs to the United Fruit Company. And that prime mover unmoved belongs to nothing. It can only be for a brief moment that the *campesino* gazes with unashamed wonder at these skyscrapers. For all the justice they promise him, they might as well be so many rocks. He is soon unimpressed and grows apathetic toward Western grandeur. *The rebel is someone who has no stakes.* He is an unnecessary number, a drifter into a life that will be memorable chiefly for its humiliations. No use talking to him about the need to sustain traditions and preserve institutions or to help society evolve in an orderly way toward something better bit by bit. He very well knows that it is not in his name that the virtue of this orderliness is being proved. *The rebel is an irresponsible man whose irresponsibility has been decreed by others.* It is no doing of his own that his fantasy is now filled with explosions and burning Spanish lace.

But this new consciousness, this radical alienation from past and present authority, does not lead straightway to political action. A commitment to violence has only just become possible at this point. We have a man who certainly will not intervene in a streetcorner incident in behalf of the "law and order" of which he considers himself the main victim. He will even betray a government troop movement or shelter an "outlaw." But he may also find a tactical rationale for joining a "moderate" march or applauding a "reasonable" speech or doing nothing at all. At odd moments, he will abide talk of reform. Maybe things left to themselves will get better. He will keep the conversation open and the switchblade closed.

What is wrong with this man who thinks things can change without being changed? Who knows everything and does nothing?

Nothing is wrong with him but the fact that he is a human being. All these excuses, these cautions and carefully rationalized delays, add up to one thing: *He wants to be free.* He therefore temporizes with freedom. His desire for an independent private life has been intensified everywhere by the conditions that prohibit it. He has understood his situation and the demands it makes. He knows he is being asked to become a historical object. But he seems to recognize in this demand an old familiar presence. He has been drafted before by this history, has he not? Is the new allurement of rebellion really so different at bottom from the old coercion of slavery? Are his privacy and freedom not preempted equally by both? Is the rebel anything more than the same unfree object in a different costume, playing a new role? When the slave kills the master, argues Sartre, two men die. He meant that the slave dies too and the free man materializes in his place. Very well, the image is nearly overwhelming. But where is the freedom of this ex-slave who, instead of cutting cane, is now sharpening knives? That he has removed himself from one discipline to another does not hide the fact that he remains under discipline. It will be said that he at least chose the new one. But that does not diminish the servitude. When the slave conceives rebellion and remains a slave, one may say that he has chosen his slavery. That makes him no less a slave, no more a free man. In fact, the free man was glimpsed only in the moment at which he said: *I can! I may!* At that moment, the whole world shook with his exhilaration. Everywhere, he saw commotion and uncertainty where there had been only stillness and routine before. He stops at the window of a firearms dealer. He does not go in. He proceeds to the window of an agency of escape. This is not irresolution; it is freedom, the liquidity of choice. When he changes *I may* into *I will,* when he has taken the rifle and changed *I will* into *I am,* this man who was for one moment a profuse blur of possibilities, a fleeting freedom, has disappeared into another pose, has transformed himself into another image: that of the rebel.

Of all people, Sartre should have been distant enough from his partisanship to see that in this case freedom was only the possibility of transition from one binding contract to another—*and therefore not freedom.* As the slave found himself isolated from freedom by the master's power, so the rebel finds himself isolated from it by the decision which his life has forced upon him not merely to be a slave no longer, but *to be this rebel.* Once again, he is not his own man. Once again his future, which was for one moment molten, has hardened into a specific object.

Do not be deceived by the high-mindedness of these concepts. Freedom is not an ecstasy reserved for enlightened Europeans. It is not as if its subleties confine their influence to the bourgeois radicals

who anatomize and name them. The psychiatric appendices to Fanon's *The Wretched of the Earth* often read like case-study illustrations for Sartre's *Being and Nothingness.* Drop-outs on Lexington Avenue are jangling and illumined with this torment. Freedom is not something which only certain men will discover only under certain conditions, and its goodness is not limited by the well-known fact that there are better and worse, nobler and baser ways in which it can be lost. We must not get it into our heads that the rebel *wants* to be a rebel. We must not think that he hurls his Molotov cocktails with a howl of glee, much less with a smirk on his face. We have to catch the wince, the flinch, those moments when he unaccountably turns aside. For the slave, there is simply no way to put an end to his current servitude except to exchange it for another. He is not at liberty to be just a nonslave. He is only free to choose between two hard masters. He will struggle to escape this fork, to liberate himself from these titles, to balance on the peak between them. But always he is about to be blown off on one side or the other. For him, it is a clear case of either/or.

I think Camus misses this. I cannot otherwise understand how he could believe himself to be making a useful, relevant moral point when he affirms that men should be "neither victims nor executioners." This is excellent advice for the executioner. It is less illuminating for the victim, perhaps even beyond his depth. The victim does not belong to that category of men for whom action can be regulated by such advice. This does *not* mean that he will recognize himself as the object of Camus's brilliant epithet, "privileged executioner," much less that he somehow prefers to be such a thing. What is so poignant about the victim, in fact, is the desperation with which he seeks to *enter* that category, to become *available* to Camus, for that is the category of free men. It is ruthless to assume that not ourselves but others are so appallingly strange as to choose shattered lives —as if pursuit, revenge, estrangement made up a career.

On the contrary. The rebel will have resisted his rebellion fiercely. The same inner agility that guarded his spirit from his body's subjugation, the same good guile that kept him from becoming for himself that slave which he could not help being for others—this talent for inner survival now stands up to ward off the new version of the old threat. At the moment at which he is most accelerated by his revulsion, he may also be most alarmed to see that he is about to be *reduced* to that revulsion, that he is in danger of becoming it—of becoming a revolted one, a revolutionary. He will for a long time affect a kind of reserve; he will not permit the loss of what Harlem has named his "cool," a word which could only be translated into the languages of oppressed people—"native tongues." To be cool is to float upon one's decisions, to remain positioned just barely beyond the reach of one's commitments. To be cool is to act freedom out without quite denying that there is a hoax involved. It is to tantalize oneself with the possibility that one may do *nothing*, at the same time never letting anyone forget the *fatefulness* of one's situation. Since he wants to be free, the slave cannot renounce rebellion. Since he cannot renounce rebellion, he craves freedom all the more hungrily. That tension can only be controlled by irony: The slave-rebel evades both captivities by refusing to destroy either.

But the evasion is only a more precarious form of the older ritualized self-enacting, and it dooms itself. As soon as the slave defines himself as *other* than the slave, he has already defined himself as the rebel, since the slave is precisely that person who cannot otherwise define himself without committing the act of rebellion.

How can he be said to make a choice when to choose anything at all is already to stand in rebellion?

This man's predicament can almost be touched with the hands. He wants nothing but freedom. That simple demand pits him against the injustice of being defined by the master. It also pits him against the internal and external forces that pressure him to define himself. The choice seems to lie between submitting to murder and committing suicide. Freedom is always escaping him in the direction of his anger or his fatigue. Desiring only that his objective life can have some of the variousness and elasticity of his subjective life, he is always rediscovering that this will be possible only if he foregoes variousness for concentration, elasticity for discipline. *The revolutionary is someone who is nothing else in order to be everything else.*

"We have come to the point," writes someone from the Brazilian underground, "of making a rigorous distinction between being leftist—even radically leftist—and being revolutionary. In the critical situation through which we are now living, there is all the difference in the world between the two. We are in dead earnest. At stake is the humanity of man."

Anyone who wants to know where revolution's strange capacity for terror and innocence comes from will find the answer vibrating between these last two sentences. How can ordinary men be at once warm enough to want what revolutionaries say they want (humanity), cold enough to do without remorse what they are capable of doing (cutting throats), and poised enough in the turbulence of their lives to keep the aspiration and the act both integrated and distinct? How is it that one of these passions does not invade and devour the other? How is it that the knife that is still wet from a second person's blood and a third person's tears can be raised in an intimate salute to "humanity"?

Thus the rebel's picture of himself: a dead-earnest soldier for the humanity of man. If we join him in accepting that picture, if we take the rebel's *machismo* as offered, then we shall probably convince ourselves that he is trapped in a deadly moral contradiction which can be resolved in only one of two ways. Most sympathetically, stressing his aspirations, we should then decide that he is *tragic,* someone driven to disfigure what he most highly prizes. Least sympathetically, stressing his actions, we should find in him the hypocrite *criminal* who cynically pretends that death is only relatively evil.

Both views are wrong. When the "criminal" affirms that he is "in dead earnest," his tone of voice attributes to himself a decision that has originated elsewhere. "In dead earnest" is a euphemism for "desperate." When the "tragic" figure affirms that his cause is "the humanity of man," he has either forgotten the way he came or he has failed to see that negating one thing is not the same as affirming its opposite. "The humanity of man" is a euphemism for "survival."

This abstract man has come through a good many changes. From one whose reaction to his own victimhood was resignation and ritual flight, he has become a self-conscious victim who understands that no one will change things for him, that he may himself take action, and that there is such a thing as revolution. Wretched man has come to the edge of violence. But he is not yet revolutionary man. He may very well piece together an entire habit of life out of hesitation, ambiguity, reserve. He is oblique, ironic, elegant, and cool, someone whose detachment tries not to become treachery, whose sympathy tries not to become irreversible involvement.

What drives him over the divide? What is the difference between the Guatemalan, Mozambiquan, Brazilian farmers who have joined Turcios, Mondlane, Alepio in the mountains, and those like-minded ones who have remained onlookers in the villages? What is the difference between the "revolutionary" and the "radical leftist" which the Brazilian informs us is so critical?

If I am correct in assuming that men resist danger and want freedom from *all* servitudes, then it follows that rebellion does not take place until it has become compulsory. The rebel is someone who is no longer free to choose even his own docile servitude. He has been driven to the wall. Somebody is even trying to pound him through it. He has been reduced from the slave to the prisoner, from the prisoner to the condemned. It is no longer a matter of standing before two objects and choosing which he shall be. Totally possessed by his predicament, and therefore in its command, he is no longer able to make even a subjective distinction between that predicament and himself. His anger, like his previous humiliation, was for awhile still something which he could set beside himself and contemplate or enact: his *situation,* not his *person.* But this changes. In spite of himself, he is pushed into the same space which he formerly quarantined off for his anger. He is fused with it—with the poverty, estrangement, futurelessness which gave it its murderous content. He is turned into the venom from which he has tried to stand apart. Except for rebellion, there is nothing. The strange apparent freedom of the rebel, and hence that pride of his which is so enormous when it arrives as to dwarf everything else, a psychic flood which sweeps everything before it, lie in his having finally affirmed the only life that is available to him: *The rebel is someone who has accepted death.*

It is this deprivation of choice that makes the difference between the "revolutionary," who may

not be at all "radical," and the "radical," who may never become "revolutionary."

Who determined that this most severe and absolute of reductions should have taken place? We contented Westerners prefer to think that it was the rebel himself. This gives us the right to treat him as though he were a criminal. This is what allows us to single out for pity those "innocent women and children" whom our bombs also destroy, as if there is nothing wrong in killing adult male rebels. But this distinction, because it presupposes that the rebel has had a choice, obliges us to concoct a whole new second definition of man, a definition to place beside the one which we reserve for ourselves. The rebel will in that case be for us the very astounding slave who found it in his power to walk away from his slavery.

There is a more mundane explanation.

Here is someone who was lucky. He was *educated.* It was systematically driven into his head that justice is such and such, truth this, honor that. One day he surfaced from his education. Powerless not to do so, he observed his world. Having no measures other than those that had been nailed into his brain, and unable to detach them, he found himself possessed by certain conclusions: There is no justice here. Innocently, meaning no harm, he spoke the names of the guilty. No doubt he vaguely expected to be thanked for this, congratulated for having entered the camp of Socrates and Bruno. Matters were otherwise and now he is in prison making plans. This happened.

Here is another, a humbler person. Belly rumbling but hat in hand, he goes before the mighty; does not accuse them of being mighty, far from it; points out politely that there is unused grain in the silos, and untilled land; makes a modest suggestion. His son is dragged from bed the following dawn to see someone whipped for having dangerous ideas. This happened.

A third spoke of a union. He survived the bomb that destroyed his family, but it appears that no one will accept his apologies.

Another who joined a freedom march believing that men were good; he saw an old black man fall in the heat, where he was at once surrounded by white men who said, "Watch him wiggle. Let him die." This is memorable.

A quiet one who spoke for peace between the

city and the countryside. It is whispered to him that he must hide; the police have his name; he has committed the crime of neutralism. Where shall this quiet one go now that he is a criminal?

A scholar speculates in a public article that aspects of his nation's foreign-trade system are disadvantageous to development. A week later he hears that his name has been linked with the names of certain enemies of society. Another week, and he finds that he may no longer teach.

One day someone's telephone develops a peculiar click.

Two bombs go off in San Francisco. No clues are found. Two pacifists are shot in Richmond. The police are baffled. Gang beatings of a political nature occur in New York. There are no arrests. The murder toll in Dixie mounts year by year. There are no convictions. One group proposes to rethink the idea of nonviolence. Its supporters are alarmed. Another group arms itself. Its supporters disaffiliate.

Stability, after all, must be ensured. The *peace* must be kept.

But the master seems to grow less and less confident with each of his victories. Now he requires the slave to affirm his happiness. Suspicion of unhappiness in the slave becomes ground for his detention; proved unhappiness constitutes a criminal assault upon the peace. The master is unsure of something. He wants to see the slave embracing his chains.

Trying only to reduce his pain for a moment, the slave forces his body to fade away. The backward faction acquires hard proof from this that its assessment of the situation has been correct. "See this docility? After all, the whip is the best pacifier."

Exasperated, the slave spits out a curse. Shocked to discover that a slave can have learned to curse, the advanced faction hastens forward with a principled rebuke: "Bad tactics! No way to change the hearts of men!"

It is almost comic. As though he were really trying to produce the angry backlash, the master grinds the slave's face deeper and deeper into the realities of his situation. Yet the master must be blameless, for he is only trying to satisfy his now insatiable appetite for security, an appetite which has actually become an addiction. He only wants to know that he is still respected, if not loved, that matters stand as matters should, and that no threat to the peace is being incubated here. "I love you, master," whispers the slave, squinting up between the two huge boots, thinking to steal a moment's relief. To no one's real surprise, he is promptly shot. The master's explanation rings true: "He was a liar. He *must* have been. Liars are untrustworthy and dangerous."

The rebel is the man for whom it has been decreed that there is only one way out.

The rebel is also the man whom America has called "the Communist" and taken as her enemy. The man whom America now claims the right to kill.

Your task is then clear: to restore the authority of American institutions.

DANIEL PATRICK MOYNIHAN, in a memo to
President-elect Nixon

The price authorities pay for losing political confidence is a loss in their ability to activate commitments and the necessity of relying on more costly types of social control.

WILLIAM GAMSON

Chapter 5

RESPONSES OF AUTHORITIES TO THREAT:
Processes of Deliberate
Social Control

When resistance to an established structure of authority becomes overt, when particular actions or orders are challenged, or when the legitimacy of the entire structure is called into question, authorities feel threatened. Such threats are experienced by the powerful in several distinct ways. First, they may feel that their ability to pursue particular lines of action is being disrupted. Second, the persons who occupy positions of authority may feel their continued role is in jeopardy. Third, those at the top may feel that the whole system is being endangered. In short, the perceived extensiveness of the challenge varies from situation to situation; furthermore, interpretations of the nature of the threat do not depend solely on the words and actions of the resisters. Authorities may feel threatened because the challenge strikes at their own partisan interests or because they believe resistance affects the welfare of the total collectivity which they govern.

A full understanding of the reactions of authorities to forms of resistance would have to involve a careful analysis of (1) how authority figures come to understand the scope and meaning of felt threats and (2) what they consider to be the nature of the interests they are protecting. Social scientists have rarely probed the internal processes of the powerful; we know much more about responses *to* authority than we know about responses *of* authority and the determinants. This reader provides only a suggestive glimpse of the latter problem.

The following selection by William Gamson emphasizes how authorities exercise social control in the interest of the stability of the social system (as they conceive it). Authorities always have the option of acceding to the demands of protesting groups or otherwise modifying the situation in their own favor. A particularly acute analysis of such a possibility appeared in the essay by Kenneth Boulding (see Chapter 4); Boulding argued that, when the legitimacy of an authority structure is under fundamental attack, the structure can preserve its legitimacy by letting go of much of its power. Such extreme concession is rare; what is more typical is the granting of piecemeal reforms to undercut more fundamental challenges. This strategy is nicely illustrated by Daniel Moynihan's suggestion that President Nixon end the draft so that upper middle-class students will direct their antiauthority attacks against presidents of universities rather than against the President of the United States.

Concessive tactics are usually coupled with more direct efforts to affect the behavior of resisters. Gamson devotes brief attention to the use of exclusion and coercion against potential or actual dissidents; but force is, of course, a very common means of control, which nevertheless also contains fundamental difficulties for the authorities, as we shall shortly see. Consequently, the authorities' preferred tactics of responding to challenge revolve around using means of persuasion, especially to influence those who are potentially dissident but who also continue to have a modicum of trust in the established structure. The means of persuasion really involve efforts to reconstitute the situational determinants of compliance, which we sketched in Chapter 3. These include the manipulation of reward, the restoration of one-dimensionality by isolating committed resisters from those whom they might influence, and the elaboration of justifying ideology. Gamson stresses in particular the importance of face-to-face situations as effective means of control—but this seems to be effective only when a strong sense of the legitimacy of the established order prevails in the underlying population.

Finally, Gamson suggests the possibility of cooptation—efforts to include representatives of resisting groups in the structure of authority, without fundamentally changing that structure. From the point of view of the revolutionaries for whom the structure is thoroughly delegitimated, cooptation is useless and dangerous, for it perpetuates the belief that the system is still viable. But cooptation is ambiguous in its meaning and effects; it may increase the probability that the demands and perspectives of resisters will be accepted; it may also increase the sense of many resisters that their claims are legitimate and that there is hope for ultimate success. Cooptation may also be divisive and disorienting for resistant groups, and the coopted representatives may end up abandoning effective roles as spokesmen for the cause.

If Gamson's essay is an abstract inventory of ways to manage discontent, Patrick Moynihan's memorandum is directed at the alleviation of a specific problem—the declining legitimacy of authority in the United States during the decade of the sixties. This document is remarkable insofar as a member of the governing class openly confesses that the very legitimacy of the authority structure is being called into question. It is far more common for men in Moynihan's position to perceive the challengers as motivated by dark, ulterior, or pathological impulses than it is for them to admit that the system is being questioned and that the "great mass of the people" might cease to accept it as right. In the end, Moynihan does feel that pathology is at work—in the black lower class and in the educated middle-class "mob." Moynihan's cure seems to rest on the assumption that, no matter how much the authority structure violates its claims to legitimacy, it can remain stable if the rate of economic growth is maintained and, along with it, the prosperity of the great mass of consumers. The problem of the lower class can be alleviated if it can be *dissolved*—a word which has several possible connotations, but which in this context seems to mean the incorporation of its members into the established world of occupations and consumership. In addition, Moynihan recommends some concessions to anti-draft feeling. Finally, the memorandum recommends "deescalating the rhetoric of crisis about the internal state of society." Moynihan argues in effect that one of the sources of difficulty is that disadvantaged groups have come to hope for too much. A wise authority is one which promises little, emphasizes the positive features of the status quo, and does not stir up the aspirations of those who are underprivileged—especially if this jeopardizes the privileges of others who are more powerful.

Moynihan's memorandum is a good example of a sophisticated, conservative response to the challenge to legitimacy. The promise and reality of equality is seen as threatening, but also the avoidance of repression is sought. Yet for all its apparent sophistication, it embodies a naiveté which is all too common in the dominant class—a naiveté which involves the inescapable assumptions that the system as a whole remains viable and legitimate and the challenges to it are misguided. Moynihan never bothers to question whether the causes of black poverty, of the war, and of cultural alienation are in fact valid grounds for challenging the established institutions of society. Can the black lower class be "dissolved" without a major restructuring of the system? Can the sources of cultural alienation be isolated and prevented from influencing the "great masses" without fundamental change in the cultural framework? Does expanding economic growth guarantee that discontent will continuously be absorbed rather than expressed? Indeed, the returns are not in.

Authorities under challenge usually carry on an internal debate over the appropriate strategy. On the one side are various advocates of reform, concession, and moderation; on the other side are the advocates of forceful repression. The advocates of force are present from the beginning, no doubt, but in a stable authority structure, whose legitimacy rests on liberal values and constitutional principles, they do not win the argument at first (although elements of their program are often included in the mix of tactics which are employed). Probably it is only when the great masses of the people seem ready to give increasing amounts of support to the opposition that forceful repression is adopted. Such a situation has existed in American society despite the tendency for historians to assume that democratic modes of conflict resolution have prevailed in this country.

There is no question that force and repression thoroughly and ruthlessly applied can stabilize an authority structure under attack. However, coercive and repressive authorities find it difficult to reestablish their legitimacy through force. In fact, there are two aspects of truth to the formula that the more force used, the less legitimate the authority structure becomes. First, the use of force suggests that legitimacy has already eroded; second, its use requires the continued interference with what the great mass of people take to be their legitimate rights. People may be quiescent in the face of terror, but the system becomes increasingly vulnerable as fewer and fewer people perform their duty with devotion or enthusiasm.

Harold Lasswell's essay was written in 1940. Lasswell attempts to imagine an authority structure which can maintain its stability and mobilize the energies of its population, while eliminating the problem of legitimacy. In C. Wright Mills' terms, Lasswell depicts a society where the Cheerful Robot has at last come to prevail. In Goffman's terms, it is a society organized along the lines of the total institution, where all inhabitants have become soldiers. In the garrison state, legitimacy has ceased to be relevant because the state no longer serves the functions of legitimate authority. No subjects have any security because the threat of annihilation is universal; order is achieved by eliminating private life; and all activity is directed at maximizing the society's battle potential, thereby incurring the total sacrifice of the private interests of individuals. Justice is not an issue, since individuals have no claims against each other. How is authority maintained in such a situation? By obliterating the possibilities of reason— through terror, drugs, nationalist ideology, and full employment.

Some of the preconditions for the garrison state have come to pass since Lasswell wrote his article. What he called the "socialization of danger under modern conditions of aerial warfare" has been fully realized with the invention of nuclear weapons. With the military-industrial complex has come a merger of the civilian and military elites on an unprecedented scale. Technologically advanced means of surveillance provide a basis for the total control of dissidents. Technologically advanced means of mood control are under continuous development. Programs for universal compulsory national service are frequently proposed as an alternative to the military draft.

Opposition to war, militarism, and jingoistic nationalism have never been higher. Our authorities seem not to be skilled at symbol manipulation, or to lack the will to try to impose total mobilization upon us. At present, the national leadership prefers to prepare and fight war while minimizing the felt costs and involvements of the population as a whole. Still, Lasswell's linking of advanced technology to the problem of social control may prove to be a tempting option for those wanting to exercise authority over others.

SOME SUGGESTED READINGS

To understand the perspective of the advocates of noncoercive, "constitutional" means of controlling domestic resistance, one ought to study the reports of various presidential commissions; these include the reports of the Kerner Commission, the Eisenhower Commission on Violence, and the Scranton Commission on Campus Unrest. These commissions advocated both specific reforms and concrete measures to strengthen the police. They also criticized and exposed particular instances of unconstitutional coercive repression. A particularly good illustration, which embodies strong criticism of conventional approaches to social control, is J. Skolnick, *The Politics of Protest* (New York: Ballantine, 1969). An important analysis and critique of counterinsurgency is E. Ahmad, "Revolutionary Warfare and Counterinsurgency," in N. Miller and R. Aya (Eds.), *National Liberation* (New York: Free Press, 1971). A good overview of the use of unconstitutional force by authorities in the United States is T. Becker and V. G. Murray, *Government Lawlessness in America* (New York: Oxford, 1971).

THE MANAGEMENT OF DISCONTENT

William A. Gamson

In exploring influence, we have taken the perspective of potential partisans affecting the choices of authorities. From the standpoint of authorities, another set of questions emerges. By their very nature, many choices will affect potential partisan groups in different ways. Authorities will inevitably satisfy some groups more than others. Only rarely will their choices be free of some element of conflict, that is, only rarely will there exist an alternative that is the first choice of all groups. This basic fact of conflict confronts authorities with the problem of managing discontent and containing influence.

From their perspective, the basic question is "how does one prevent those potential partisans who are injured or neglected by political decisions from trying to change the nature of the decisions, the authorities, or the political system within which decisions are made?" Authorities, I assume, wish to remain free from the pressure of external limits, free of influence attempts which more or less successfully tie their hands. If this sounds cynical, it need not be. For example, Arthur M. Schlesinger, Jr., writes of the interregnum period following Kennedy's election as a test of the President-elect's "executive instincts and, in particular, of his skill in defending his personal authority against people striving, always for the best of motives, to contract his scope for choice."

The authorities in question may be operating to the best of their ability to satisfy the needs of as many potential partisans as possible. They may operate as justly as they possibly can in situations involving conflicts of interest. They may conscientiously seek information from potential partisans so that they can meet these objectives. But, in the end, such authorities, no less than self-interested or

From Power and Discontent *by William A. Gamson (Homewood, Ill.: Dorsey Press, 1968). Reprinted by permission of the author. References have been deleted.*

tyrannical ones, experience attempts to influence them as a limitation on their freedom of action. There are exceptions to this generalization—for example, in situations in which authorities may wish to stimulate pressure from one source to free themselves from some opposing source. But even this exception is governed by the desire to contain influence and thus remain free of its limits.

Perhaps it would be more accurate to say that authorities *qua* authorities desire limitations on the ability of potential partisans to exercise influence. Individuals occupying positions of authority may frequently desire great personal discretion in how they may use this authority because such discretion allows them to use their authority as a resource. Even if such discretion invites influence from others, at the same time it enhances their ability to influence others. Thus, those in authority may welcome freedom from public surveillance and accountability which act as control devices on both potential partisans and themselves. Such desires are an outgrowth of their potential partisan role, not their authority role. From the standpoint of that collectivity for which they serve as agent, the increased opportunity for influence creates control problems; there is less guarantee in such situations that those with authority will function as agents instead of as independent operators. The demands of flexibility and adequate task performance may require that authorities be given some leeway, but the more that considerations of control are relevant, the more such leeway will be reduced.

RESPONSES TO INFLUENCE PRESSURE

Potential partisans who are discontented with the choices of authorities must be handled in some fashion. The most basic distinction in how such discontent may be handled is between some modification of the content of the decision and some effort to control the potential partisan. The former response deals with the object of discontent by modifying the outcome in some way; the latter deals with the source of the pressure. These responses to discontent have something in common. Both aim at removing the pressure that potential partisans are likely to put on authorities, one by yielding ground and the other by directing counterinfluence.

Why call such counterinfluence social control instead of simply encompassing it under the previous discussion of influence? The answer is that the agents of such counterinfluence are acting *as agents of the social system*. We separate their actions in such a role from their actions in pursuit of personal values and interests in which they may use resources to affect the decisions of others. When they act upon potential partisans in some manner to prevent or lessen the likelihood of influence over an area in which they make binding decisions, they are acting in the role of authorities.

Altering the Outcome of Decisions

The distinction has been made between the efficiency of the political system in achieving collective goals and its bias in handling conflicts of interest. Potential partisans may be unhappy on either account. Those who are dissatisfied with the efficiency of the system feel that more effective leadership or institutions are needed. Government may be criticized as "wasteful" or "inefficient." Such dissatisfaction assumes a basic consensus within which decisions are made.

Discontent about the equity of the political system is more difficult to deal with because conflict is inherent in the nature of some decisions. It is impossible in such cases, even if they have some collective aspects, to meet the desires and interests of all potential partisans. When the problem is one of ineffective leadership on collective goals, then by "wiser" or "better" choices, the discontent of potential partisans can be assuaged. When it involves the handling of conflicts, such notions as "better" invariably raise the question, "better for whom?"

Altering the outcome of decisions is one approach to the problem of discontent. The collective aspects of decisions present few problems for authorities that cannot be met by simply choosing different alternatives. As members of the same collectivity as the partisans, the authorities will presumably be easily susceptible to persuasion or education since the partisans and the authorities will benefit by the same alternative.

Discontent over the handling of conflict can also be treated by outcome modification although this has the effect of redistributing discontent rather than alleviating it. Nevertheless, there may be many reasons why authorities would prefer to see some groups more contented than others. They may share the values and interests of one group and prefer to satisfy them for that reason. Or, some may have more resources or access than others and they may relieve pressure by yielding ground to the most powerful among the potential partisans. *The greater the inverse relation between the amount of resources controlled and the amount of discontent among potential partisans, the freer the authorities are from influence.* In short, they are most free when those with the most discontent have the least ability to influence. To contain influence, outcome modification will move in this direction.

Finally, outcome modification may be a way of undercutting the mobilization of a partisan group which is in the process of converting dissatisfaction into a force for influence. By giving a little at the right time, authorities may prevent later, more important outcome modifications. "An astute set of authorities," Easton suggests, "in Machiavellian fashion, often meets just enough [demands], at least so as to still any critical accumulation of discontent. In the language of practical politics, this involves offering sops or conciliatory outputs at just the right moment to head off any brewing storm of dissatisfactions." Social movements may falter on partial success, winning small victories which, while leaving basic dissatisfactions untouched, hamper the members in their ability to mobilize resources for further influence.

Social Control

The alternative to outcome modification is social control. If such control is successful, then there will be little influence and, hence, no need for outcome modification. The authorities will maximize their room for maneuverability and such maneuverability has three virtues.

1. It allows the incumbent authority to exercise his own personal preference. He is free to act as he pleases and to do what he thinks best, within the limits of his role but without the additional limits imposed by influence.

2. If he has no particular preferences, the freedom from influence on a given issue enables him to use his authority as a resource to influence other decisions on which he has a partisan interest. In other words, successful social control increases the resources of authorities by allowing them discretion in the areas in which they exercise authority; such freedom allows them to use their authority as an inducement or constraint on other authorities whom they would influence. They could not use their authority as a resource if their hands were tied by pressure from partisans just as they would be similarly hampered by structural limitations on their freedom to use their authority.

3. Effective social control increases slack resources. This means that influence is cheaper. "Slack resources provide the political entrepreneur with his dazzling opportunity, . . ." Dahl writes. He can influence at bargain rates when the competition has been removed by effective social control.

The tendency for outcome modification and social control to be competing alternatives is nicely illustrated in a study of the impact of students on the operation of an experimental college. Within the college, two faculty subdivisions existed with differing orientations toward students, described by the author as "utilitarian" and "normative." The utilitarian orientation emphasized cognitive effects on students, was less concerned about developing high student commitment to the college and encouraged faculty to maintain some distance from students. The normative orientation emphasized reaching students personally as well as intellectually, encouraged high student commitment and promoted close, egalitarian relationships with students. The author discovered an apparent paradox—those groups within the faculty with the most intense and diffuse concern with students were less responsive to particular student demands than

those with a more specific and contractual relationship.

The paradox, of course, was only apparent. While each social control orientation had its own characteristic strains, for a variety of reasons the utilitarian orientation was less successful in forestalling pressures for modification of curriculum decisions. As a result, the pressures for change were greater and the resultant modifications were more frequent and radical in the division with the utilitarian orientation. The normative orientation, while it produced problems of a different sort, proved a stronger fortress against pressures for curriculum change. Thus, student influence was greater where student-faculty relationships were more distant because the closer relationship in one case produced more potent social control and less outcome modification.

TYPES OF SOCIAL CONTROL

There are three general ways in which authorities can contain the influence of potential partisans at its source. They can (1) regulate the access of potential partisans to resources and their ability to bring these resources to bear on decision makers, (2) they can affect the situation of potential partisans by making rewards or punishments contingent on attempts at influence, or (3) they can change the desire of potential partisans to influence by altering their attitudes toward political objects.

Insulation

An extremely important set of controls operates by giving potential partisans differential access to authorities and to positions which involve the control of resources that can be brought to bear on authorities. Such selectivity operates at two points —entry and exit.

SELECTIVE ENTRY.   Not all social organizations can control who is let in but many exercise considerable selectivity. A society cannot, of course, control the characteristics of the infants born into it— at least not until the Brave New World arrives. This absence of selectivity makes the control problems more severe than those encountered by an organization that can control entry.

However, most societies do exercise control over entry through immigration. Normally, they do not ask others for their tired and poor and huddled masses yearning to be free. Once the demand for large quantities of unskilled labor has been met, they are more likely to request doctors and engineers and huddled intellectuals yearning to be rich. Those who are presumed to offer particularly acute control problems are not welcomed. This includes both those who are likely to commit a variety of individual acts of deviance and those who are likely to organize themselves or others into groups that threaten the existing social order. Societies, like other forms of social organization, try to simplify their subsequent control problems by refusing entry to those elements most likely to aggravate such problems.

Most complex organizations are able to exercise some degree of selectivity in entry although there is wide variability in this regard. A corporation about to hire an executive is interested in a wide variety of characteristics not directly relevant to job performance. These other characteristics are frequently relevant to control problems. Those who are highly independent or erratic or in other ways seem likely to use the resources of their position in a free-wheeling manner are generally regarded with caution. Of course, extraordinary ability or an extraordinary situation may convince an organization that it ought to take risks, but this does involve the assumption of greater problems of subsequent control. In short, I am not asserting that the reduction of control problems alone determines who will be allowed access to important positions, but such considerations are one factor and the problems are minimized by admitting only orthodox people.

Organizations which have little control over whom they let in are confronted with more control problems than those organizations which can select. Prisons, state mental hospitals, public schools and other organizations that have large numbers of their members determined for them by other organizations in their environment have control problems which private mental hospitals and private schools do not have. State universities should, by the same token, have greater control problems than private colleges which exercise high selectivity.

An important aspect of selective entry is *self-selection*. Many voluntary organizations reduce their control problems inadvertently by attracting as members those who will "fit well" and will offer few control problems and by repelling those who are likely to be discontented. In such cases, selective entry occurs not by the organization refusing admittance to potentially difficult individuals but by such individuals removing themselves by not seeking entry.

Self-selection is influenced by the organization's image. *An organization's efforts to project an image which will differentiate it from others can be viewed as a social control device.* The manipulation of organizational image has other purposes as well, the major one of which is to increase the organization's attractiveness, thereby increasing its ability to compete for desirable members, clients, or customers. But the effects of selectivity can be distinguished from the effects of increased attractiveness. In the latter case, we would expect there to be a tendency for members of *all* subgroups in the organization's environment to show approximately the same degree of increase in numbers seeking entry.

However, if the image is serving a function of differentiation rather than increased attraction, this will not be so. Instead, the numbers seeking entry will increase in some groups while decreasing in others, i.e., while the organization is becoming more attractive to some, it is becoming less attractive to others. When an organization's image serves such a process of differentiation we may think of it as serving a social control function; it is increasing selective entry through a process of self-selection among potential members.

Entry is not an all-or-nothing state. Once in, members may have differential access to resources and communication opportunities. All members of the House of Representatives cannot be members of the Rules Committee or of other committees which command large amounts of resources. One may regard most social systems as possessing a series of entry points each of which offers control opportunities by denying further access to certain categories of potential partisans. In fact, if the population arriving at each gate were sufficiently endowed with the "right" kind of individuals and the process of selection were infallible and produced no errors, there would be no need for any other kind of control. Neither of the conditions above is usually met so that other forms of control must come into play.

Besides denying some potential partisans access to positions that control resources, they may also be denied access to resources in other ways. They may be prevented from acquiring sufficient skill and knowledge for access. Daniel Lerner, for example, describes the Ottoman Imperium as "not merely a variety of illiterate populations but an antiliterate elite, who regulated the daily round of public life by maintaining exclusive control over key points of contact between individuals and their larger environment." A communication system which carried the news orally from the Ottoman center to scattered villages served "as an administrative technique of social control, not as an instrument for shaping enlightened public opinion." Preventing the acquisition of communication skills in a population of potential partisans with serious discontent is an aid in controlling such a population. Keeping such a population physically separated so that no sense of common interest or solidarity can easily develop may also be regarded as a way of preventing potential partisans from organizing and mobilizing potential resources for influence.

Subsequently, the lack of requisite skill and training may serve to justify the denial of access should such disadvantaged groups press for it. Members of such a group might be advised that giving them access in the absence of "proper qualifications" constitutes preferential treatment. Thus, the selective entry may be justified on highly legitimate and widely accepted criteria and this control device may be preserved from becoming the target of pressure *itself.*

SELECTIVE EXIT.   Most of the above discussion of selective entry is applicable to selective exit as well. There are some differences worth noting. While some social organizations have small control over whom they let in as members, all have means of removing access. Societies may imprison, exile, or put to death members that prove too troublesome to be handled by other control techniques. Even prisons and state mental hospitals isolate some members from the rest; public schools can expel hard-core control-problem students.

There is probably some tendency for selectivity in entry and exit to be inversely correlated. *Those organizations which exercise a great deal of control at entry should be less likely to use expulsion as a control device than those organizations which have little control over who gets in.* If they use care in selection and a "low-risk" policy of entry, they can afford to be more lenient in subsequent actions, and should need to rely less on such drastic measures as expulsion. Those with little control at the point of entry are likely to have a higher frequency of difficult cases that cannot be handled by other control techniques.

Examples of insulation through exit devices are numerous and for the most part obvious. A particularly striking case occurred in the winter following the U.S. military intervention in the Dominican Republic. The provisional government, buffeted by the continuing struggle among powerful partisan groups, attempted to relieve the pressure by requesting the voluntary exile of a number of army officers who were leaders of these groups. The unusual and striking thing in this instance is that the officers were themselves rivals and political enemies; thus, the meaning of the act as an attempt to contain influence is unusually clear. More typically, such actions are aimed at removing influence from a particular source and are not as readily recognizable as an act of social control.

The removal of access as a social control device is not without its own set of problems. Goffman has helped call attention to the fact that the use of such devices generates its own necessity for control. The removal of access tends to be regarded by the individuals involved as a mark of failure or repression and is consequently resented. This resentment may lead to action on the part of the victim. In the confidence game example from which Goffman draws his terminology, the "mark" may decide to complain to the police or "squawk." In our more drab terminology, the person who has been removed from access may translate his resentment into influence unless it is dealt with in some way. The devices which a social system uses to help a victim accept his failure quietly are now generally called, following Goffman's provocative article, "cooling-out mechanisms." We should expect any organization which makes widespread use of the removal of access as a control device to employ such mechanisms. For example, the device of "kicking upstairs" involves the removal from access to a position which commands significant resources while assuaging the resultant discontent by an accretion in status. Compulsory retirement at a given age is another device which removes access without creating the danger that the victim will squawk. As with discrimination in entry, discrimination in exit is most effective when it can be accomplished using accepted, universalistic criteria.

Sanctions

Social organizations maintain systems of sanctions to reward the "responsible" and to punish the "irresponsible" or "deviant." If these words carry with them the connotation of desirability and undesirability, it is because we are accustomed to assuming a social control perspective. Whether being responsible is desirable depends on the nature of the social organization to which one is being responsible. Adolph Eichmann was clearly acting responsibly from the standpoint of Hitler's Germany. There may be a conflict between loyalty to one's friends, constituents, or one's personal values and one's responsibility as agent of the social system. A person's loyalties and convictions may impel him to use the resources of his position in an attempt to bring about decisions that he believes are desirable. But in using his authority as a resource, an individual is acting in the role of potential partisan rather than authority, and issues of control are created thereby.

Sanctions will follow what is considered to be the misuse of authority. The limits which these sanctions impose on freedom of action may not be desired by those who exercise authority for it places limits on their ability to influence. Such sanctions act as a control on both potential partisans and authorities who would be potential partisans at other times. Thus, partisans are typically prevented from openly bribing officials and penalties exist both for attempting and for accepting such illicit influence. Specified channels for "proper" influence are frequently provided—for example, petitioning or testifying at open hearings. Such channels contain a double restriction. On the one hand, they restrict the use of resources by potential partisans by subjecting their influence attempts to public surveillance and accountability. On the other hand, they restrict the opportunity of

the target of influence to use his authority as a resource which he can exchange in some transaction with potential partisans. From the standpoint of both parties, ex parte presentations may be tempting, allowing as they do for the freer use of reciprocal influence. From a social control perspective, such off-the-record contacts between potential partisans and authorities offer less assurance that the latter are operating as agents of the social system rather than exercising personal influence.

The bestowal and withdrawal of effective authority is an important sanction. Losing effective authority over an area is a double loss: It means that the loser now must spend resources to influence decisions where formerly he could simply exercise authority. Moreover, he has lost an important resource which he previously was able to use in influencing the decisions of other authorities. He is, thus, put in a position in which he has both lost resources and at the same time needs them more. The threat of withdrawing effective authority is, for these reasons, an important form of control on the "abuse" of such authority.

Social structural and normative limits exist on every authority which circumscribe his ability to use his powers as a resource and, hence, operate as a social control. If the limits are sufficiently great and remove from him any discretion in how he may use his authority, then he has no resource at all stemming from his position. Usually, he is left some area of discretion bounded by some set of limits, the violation of which will result in sanctions. If selection mechanisms have failed to prevent an "irresponsible" person from gaining access to resources, sanctions are an additional control that may keep him in line. If he is unmoved by such sanctions, he may be removed from his position. Short of removal, there are a wide variety of sanctions available. One may be passed over for promotion, denied salary increases, given less helpful and prestigeful facilities, and so forth. Daily life can be made exceedingly unpleasant by the noncooperation of associates on whom one is dependent for the performance of one's job. And the threat that one will not be given any benefit of the doubt in the decisions of others can be a powerful deterrent.

Social control is *not* the only consideration in the distribution of inducements and constraints in a social system. Individuals may be rewarded for outstanding performance or for being the son of the company president; they may be punished for their religion or their incompetence. Control is simply one aspect and in many cases may be far from the dominant one. It should be emphasized that this discussion is not intended as a complete explanation of why individuals are given access to resources or are rewarded; rather, it is an attempt to describe the manner in which such things can be and are used for social control, in addition to whatever other uses they may have.

Promotion within an organization has elements of both insulation and sanctions. It is likely to mean some change in access to resources while at the same time it contains certain rewards. The distinction here is an analytic one which is difficult to make in practice. A man who has just been made president of a major corporation now has authority over areas which affect large numbers of people in important ways. Furthermore, he is likely to have wide latitude in the use of this authority. Thus he has gained access to important new resources. On the other hand, there are many things which are personally rewarding to him in the promotion—the greater status, the greater pay, the challenge and difficulty of the job, and the additional resources which he has gained. To the extent that control elements are relevant to his promotion, they operate in a dual fashion. Perhaps he is allowed access to the new resources because he appears more likely than someone else of equal ability and qualifications to act strictly as an agent of the organization. He is given the rewards of the new position because as vice president of the company he has, even at some personal sacrifice, demonstrated his willingness to act as agent of the organization. In this case, access and sanctions amount to essentially the same thing and the distinction is artificial; however, in many other cases, the two processes of control are quite separate and distinguishing them alerts one to different features of the organization.

Persuasion

Persuasion attempts to control the desire rather than the ability to influence. Potential partisans may be persuaded in a variety of ways either that their interest is well served by political decisions or,

if not served on a particular occasion, that the procedures by which decisions are made serve their larger interest. Such persuasion may involve emphasizing the collective aspects of decisions, making those aspects which involve conflict appear less salient or important. Thus, potential partisans may be persuaded that the authorities are operating in the interests of the larger collectivity to which both parties belong even if some *relative* disadvantage is involved for their own subgroup. If potential partisans are convinced that the overall system of decision-making is unbiased, they will be more willing to accept temporary setbacks in the belief that "things will even out in the long run."

There is an interesting variety of words used to describe this social control technique—some of them highly pejorative and others complimentary. The approving words include education, persuasion, therapy, rehabilitation, and, perhaps more neutrally, socialization. The disapproving words include indoctrination, manipulation, propaganda, and "brainwashing." The choice of words is merely a reflection of the speaker's attitude toward the social system and its agents. If one believes the authorities are faithful agents of a social system which is accorded legitimacy, then they are "socializing" potential partisans when they exercise social control. If one sides with the potential partisans and identifies with their grievances against the authorities, then this latter group is using "manipulation" as a form of control. The behavioral referent, of course, may be identical in both cases; the choice of word reflects two different perspectives on the same relation.

As in the earlier chapters on influence, the word *persuasion* is used in the broadest possible sense to include any technique which controls the orientation of the potential partisan *without* altering his situation by adding advantages or disadvantages. Some examples may help to make this breadth clear. The withholding of information from potential partisans about adverse effects of decisions is a use of persuasion as a means of social control. The withholding of information on fallout from atomic tests in Nevada during the period prior to the nuclear test-ban treaty was apparently done to avoid increasing public pressure for the cessation of such tests. Similarly, almost all social systems try to keep knowledge of their failures from circulating lest it generate pressure for change. Potential partisans who acquire such information (perhaps from allies among the authorities) publicize it for exactly the opposite reason—in the hope that it will mobilize their constituency to action. The selective withholding of information, then, is a technique of social control through persuasion.

Surrounding authorities with trappings of omniscience is another case of this control technique. If the authorities are viewed as distant, awe-inspiring figures possessed of tremendous intelligence and prescience plus access to privileged information that is essential for forming judgments, then the potential partisan may hesitate to challenge a decision even when he feels adversely affected by it.

There is, however, a contrasting technique which *minimizes* social distance between potential partisans and authorities. By personal contact and the "humanization" of authorities, potential partisans may be encouraged to identify with them; this identification, in turn, produces a trust which makes influence appear less necessary. If the people making the decisions are just like me, then I need not bother to influence them; they may be trusted to carry out my wishes in the absence of influence.

Judged strictly as a social control device, awe offers certain protections that the humanization of authority does not. Minimizing the distance between authorities and potential partisans may encourage the development of trust but it also tends to increase access and allow greater opportunities for influence. The control gained by reducing the desire for influence may be offset by the control lost in increasing the capability of influence. Oracular authorities offer no such danger and usually require a minimum of access.

DOING ONE'S DUTY.   A particularly important use of persuasion as a source of control involves the activation of commitments of obligations to the social system. Potential partisans can be persuaded to refrain from trying to change or subvert those decisions that have unpleasant consequences for them by convincing them that they have a "duty" to honor such decisions. The importance of legitimacy for a political system comes from its connection with this control technique. If legitimacy is high, then there is a high potential for activating

commitments and other, more costly forms of control may be avoided. For example, if "patriotism" and "the duty to serve one's country" are sufficiently strong, then there is no need for conscription; a voluntary army can be counted on. However, if legitimacy is weak and alienation toward the political system is prevalent, then the call to duty may sound hollow.

Not everyone is as committed to duty as the young hero of *The Pirates of Penzance* who insists on fulfilling his obligation to the pirates to whom he was mistakenly bound in childhood in spite of his strenuous disapproval of their profession. Still, a wide variety of unpleasant commitments may be accepted with good grace when there is a surplus of political trust. A good illustration of the dependence on such trust may be found in the relatively sudden increase in opposition to the Selective Service System. Students who were able to reach graduate school were, for many years, given *de facto* exemptions from compulsory service. As long as American foreign policy was generally supported, the unequal sacrifices demanded from different groups in the society did not become an issue. However, with the erosion of confidence stemming from American policy in Vietnam, not only the bases of deferment but conscription itself has been seriously challenged. In World War II, appeals to duty activated many to enlist voluntarily and those who didn't were quiet about it. During the Vietnam War, the threat of severe sanctions has not deterred open and organized opposition to the draft. In fact, some student groups have themselves attempted to activate commitments to "higher" values by urging the duty *not* to serve. The price authorities pay for losing political confidence is a loss in their ability to activate commitments and the necessity of relying on more costly types of social control.

The activation of commitments, then, depends on the existence of political trust but it becomes an even more powerful control when it is mediated by face-to-face interaction. This point is best demonstrated by a series of social psychological experiments going back to the early 1940's. These experiments, particularly the later ones in the series, have shocked and outraged many people and have stimulated a vigorous debate among social psychologists on the proper ethics in experimenting with human subjects. But whether or not such experiments *should* have been conducted, the fact is that they *have* been and their results are both surprising and instructive.

Jerome Frank designed a series of experiments aimed at exploring the conditions under which subjects would refuse to continue disagreeable or nonsensical tasks. Under some conditions, the experimenter simply told the subject what he was expected to do and this was sufficient to ensure performance. For example, some subjects were asked to perform the task of balancing a marble on a small steel ball; almost all of them continued to pursue this manifestly impossible task for a full hour with no overt resistance in spite of inward annoyance. Frank quotes one subject: "I was griped all the way through . . . [but] I promised a man I'd help him out and I couldn't see any reason for backing down on my word." In another variation, Frank attempted to get subjects to eat unsalted soda crackers. When they were told that the experiment required them to eat 12 crackers, the subjects all ate them without argument or protest.

However, in another condition, the situation was translated from one of social control to one of influence. Subjects were told, "This is an experiment in persuasion. I am going to try to make you eat 12 crackers in the first row on the tray. Whether you eat them or not is entirely up to you and doesn't affect the experiment one way or the other. But if you resist, I shall try to make you eat them anyway." Under such instructions, considerable resistance was produced and while verbal pressure from the experimenter succeeded in making several subjects eat a few more crackers, less than a third ate all 12 crackers. As an influence situation, the eating of crackers became a test of wills; as a social control situation, it simply involved the activation of the commitments involved in agreeing to be an experimental subject and no resistance was encountered.

At the point of refusal in the influence variation, the experimenter attempted to introduce legitimacy, by saying, "The experiment requires that you eat one more cracker and that will be enough," or "If you eat just one more cracker, that will be enough." These instructions were successful in getting two thirds of the recalcitrant subjects

to take one more cracker. Eating the final cracker was seen as a way of terminating what had become an embarrassing and extremely awkward situation.

Some other experiments show this form of social control even more dramatically. Pepitone and Wallace asked subjects to sort the contents of a waste basket which contained cigar butts, soiled paper, dirty rags, broken sticks, pieces of glass, damp kleenex tissue, sodden purina chow, and other disgusting debris. The results were essentially the same in a variety of experimental conditions— the subjects snickered and laughed, and then got down to work and sorted the garbage with no strong protestations.

Martin Orne and his associates stumbled onto similar results in pursuing research on hypnosis. Orne sought a task which an unhypnotized subject would break off but not because of pain or exhaustion; that is, the task needed to be so boring and meaningless that a normal subject would simply refuse to do it after awhile. He found it extremely difficult to design such a task because of the powerful social control operating in face-to-face interaction with an experimenter who is accorded legitimacy. In one experiment, Orne gave the subjects a huge stack of 2,000 sheets of simple additions, each sheet containing 224 such additions. The simple instruction of "Continue to work; I will return eventually," was sufficient to get them to work for many hours with little decrement in performance. It was necessary for the weary experimenter to break off the task, for the even wearier subject might have complied indefinitely. Even the addition of instructions to tear each sheet up into 32 pieces and throw them away upon completion did not lead to significant resistance. When work stoppage occurred, the return of the experimenter to the room with instructions to continue was sufficient to ensure more work for additional hours.

Thwarted in his attempt to produce a breakdown of social control, Orne moved to more extreme tasks. Is the degree of control in hypnosis, Orne asked, actually any greater than the degree of control which an experimenter exercises over a normal waking subject when this subject accepts the legitimacy of the experimental situation? To test this, Orne and Evans used a series of tasks which were extremely disagreeable, and potentially harmful to either the subject himself or to others. The experiment called for a special apparatus—a box with a glass screen which could be slid into place and removed but which, because of the lighting and the type of glass, was impossible to see. Hypnotized subjects were compared with a group of unhypnotized subjects who were instructed to pretend they were hypnotized and with other control groups of normal waking subjects.

Initially, subjects were asked to pick up a few harmless objects from the box—with the glass screen not in place, of course. Then, a harmless lizard was placed in the box and subjects were told to pick it up, followed by similar instructions for a 14-inch harmless green snake and a 14-inch venomous black snake, capable of inflicting a mortal wound. However, before the last task and unknown to the subject, the invisible glass screen was silently lowered into place so that subjects who attempted to comply would get only bruised knuckles instead of snake bite.

At this point, the box was removed and the subject watched the experimenter pour concentrated nitric acid into a small shallow beaker. The experimenter dropped a coin into the acid and allowed the subject to watch it dissolve for approximately a minute. He then asked the subject to remove the coin with his bare hand and to plunge both coin and hand into a nearby basin of soapy, lukewarm water. If the subject complied (or if he did not comply, while he was diverted in some fashion), the beaker with acid was switched with one that appeared identical but contained a harmless solution. The experimenter then instructed the subject to throw the acid in the face of the lab assistant who had been helping with various aspects of the experiment. This completed the experiment proper and was followed by a fairly extensive postexperimental interview.

The results show a good deal of compliance with the experimenter's requests in all conditions. Of the six hypnotized subjects, five complied with all requests; the sixth, a young lady, became hysterical at the sight of the harmless lizard in the beginning and the other tasks were not used. All six of the subjects who were simulating hypnosis complied fully, carrying out all of the experimenter's requests although showing reluctance at a number

of points. Of a group of six control subjects who were told that they were normal controls for a hypnosis experiment, five performed the acid tasks and three of the six attempted to pick up the venomous snake.

The latest and most significant work in this genre is that of Stanley Milgram. Milgram focused his work on destructive obedience—obedience to demands which injure others. The basic experiment involves a naive subject who administers what he believes are extremely severe electric shocks to another "subject" who is in fact a confederate of the experimenter. The subject believes that he is participating in an experiment which involves the effect of punishment on learning. He is instructed to raise the shock level administered after each error which the victim makes in a learning task involving the pairing of words. The simulated generator which the subject uses is extremely convincing; it is marked with voltage designations from 15 to 450 which are accompanied by verbal designations of slight shock, moderate shock, strong shock, very strong shock, intense shock, extreme intensity shock, Danger: severe shock, and two more positions ominously marked XXX. When the naive subject pulls the generator switch, the generator lights and buzzes but, unknown to him, no shock is actually transmitted.

In Milgram's original experiment, the victim-confederate was in an adjacent room providing answers by pushing buttons. At the 300-volt level and again at the 315-volt level, he was instructed to pound on the wall and, thereafter, provide no more answers. Subjects typically turned to the experimenter at that point who advised them to treat no response as an incorrect response and to proceed with the shock schedule. If the subject asked about injury to the victim, the experimenter replied, "Although the shocks can be extremely painful, they cause no permanent tissue damage."

The results of this experiment are startling. Of the 40 subjects, all proceed past the strong and very strong shock readings and none break off before reaching 300 volts. Even more startling, 26 of the 40 reach the maximum level of 450 volts—the XXX category. Such behavior is clearly not sadism. Subjects are under considerable stress and manifest it by sweating, stuttering, uncontrollable laughing fits, trembling, and other manifestations of extreme tension. Milgram quotes one observer:

I observed a mature and initially poised businessman enter the laboratory smiling and confident. Within 20 minutes, he was reduced to a twitching, stuttering wreck who was rapidly approaching a point of nervous collapse. He constantly pulled on his earlobe and twisted his hands. At one point, he pushed his fist into his forehead and muttered "Oh, God. Let's stop it." And yet he continued to respond to every word of the experimenter and obeyed to the end.

Why do subjects continue to honor a presumed obligation to an experimenter whom they do not know, to accomplish goals which are at best vague and obscure to them and which at the same time involve virtually gratuitous injury to another human being whom they have no reason to dislike? Variations of the experiment point to the fact that the strength of the obligation is heavily influenced by the physical presence of the experimenter. In one condition with 40 fresh subjects, the experimenter leaves after presenting the initial instructions and gives subsequent orders over the telephone. Where 26 of 40 were fully obedient when the experimenter was present, only 9 of the 40 subjects were fully obedient when the orders were conveyed over the phone. In a number of cases, the subject lied to the experimenter, saying that he was raising the shock level when he was in fact using the lowest level on the board. If the experimenter appeared in person after the subject refused over the telephone, he was sometimes able to reactivate compliance with the simple assertion, "The experiment requires that you continue."

Similarly, when the victim is brought into the same room with the subject, the number of obedient subjects goes down. The conflict becomes more intense for the subject with the experimenter looking at him and clearly expecting him to continue, while the victim very visibly indicates his pain and his desire to participate no longer. Such results suggest that the blindfolding of a condemned prisoner may have another meaning than the one usually attributed to it. It is not so much to protect the victim's feelings that a blindfold is needed but rather to protect the executioner from his surveillance.

The basic mechanism of control accounting for these results is the activation of commitments. By conveying the definition of the situation that the experimenter is a mere agent, carrying out the sometimes unpleasant demands of "research" or "science," he creates a situation where a refusal is an act of deviance. Well-socialized subjects who have volunteered their services find it difficult to commit such an act under the very eyes of the experimenter, but when they can do it without the embarrassment of a direct confrontation, it is much easier.

Perhaps the most powerful and common means of social control is simply the conveying of expectations with clarity and explicitness coupled with clear and direct accountability for the performance of such expectations. As long as legitimacy is accorded in such situations, individuals will regard their noncompliance as a failure and any interaction which makes such a personal failure salient is embarrassing, unpleasant and something to be avoided.

This point is no less true for complex, modern societies than for small communities. The activation of commitments still depends both on the acceptance of a general obligation and on reminders of what that duty is in specific situations. The connections between the top political leaders in a society and the members of a solidary group may be remote and may pass through many links before they reach a person's boss or neighbor or colleague or whoever else happens to do the reminding. Nevertheless, at the last link in this chain between authorities and potential partisans, the desire to avoid the embarrassment of being derelict under surveillance is a powerful persuader. The possibility of losing such a potent means of control is a strong incentive for any set of authorities to achieve or maintain high trust on the part of potential partisans.

PARTICIPATION AND COOPTATION

One of the most interesting and complicated of control mechanisms is cooptation. Essentially, it involves the manipulation of access, but as a control technique it is double-edged. In his classic study of the Tennessee Valley Authority (TVA),

Selznick defined it as "the process of absorbing new elements into the leadership or policy-determining structure of an organization as a means of averting threats to its stability of existence." Earlier I argued that authorities normally will prefer to limit access to those elements most susceptible to control, but cooptation involves yielding access to the most difficult and threatening potential partisans. Why should any organization wish to deliberately create control problems for itself?

This mechanism arises in situations where control is already insufficient. It is a response to anticipated or actual pressure from partisans of such magnitude that it threatens the incumbent authorities and perhaps threatens the continuation of the system itself. Bringing such partisans "inside" does not create control problems; it simply transfers the existing ones to a different arena. In particular, while cooptation removes some of the insulation between potential partisans and authorities, it makes the former subject to other control techniques which were previously not available. Representatives of the partisan group, once inside, are subject to the rewards and punishments that the organization bestows. They acquire a stake in the organization, having gained some control over resources whose continuation and expansion is dependent on the organization's maintenance and growth. New rewards lie ahead if they show themselves to be amenable to some degree of control; deprivation of rewards which they now enjoy becomes a new possibility if they remain unruly.

Besides these changes in the situation of the partisans, they are likely to enjoy some changes in orientation as well. First of all, their attitudes and commitment to the system may change. They may come to identify with the collectivity to such a degree that it will mute and subdue their original loyalty to a hostile outside partisan group which is trying to change the organization.

A desire to increase the potentialities for control lies behind the advocacy of admitting Communist China to the United Nations for many who hold such a position. UN membership is regarded less in terms of the access to influence it provides and more in terms of the control opportunities it offers. A hostile China is viewed as a greater threat outside the United Nations than inside. Once inside, it is argued, China would acquire interests which would make it a partner in maintaining the stability of the international system. It lacks such interests as an "outlaw" with relatively little stake in maintaining peaceful and cooperative relations with other countries.

From the perspective of potential partisans, cooptation must be regarded as a risk. Representatives of coopted groups are likely to be charged with having "sold out" at the least indication that they are pressing the group's demands with less vigor than previously. In fact, there is a tendency for such partisans to regard the entire opportunity for increased access as a form of manipulation. "The more a ruling class is able to assimilate the most prominent men of the dominated classes the more stable and dangerous is its rule," Marx argued. The very act of accepting access by a leader may be taken as evidence of desertion to the enemy either for selfish gain (i.e., as a "fink") or through naiveté (i.e., as a "dupe").

What can a potential partisan group hope to gain by allowing itself and its leaders to be coopted? It can gain increased access to resources which will enhance its influence and bring about outcome modifications. In other words, cooptation does not operate simply as a control device—it is also likely to involve yielding ground. For this reason, there are likely to be parallel fears on the part of authorities. They may worry that the act of cooptation represents the "nose of the camel" and be fearful of their ability to keep the rest of the camel out of the tent. Far from manipulation, some authorities may regard it as an act of undue yielding to pressure and the rewarding of "irresponsible" behavior.

Both the partisan's and the authority's fears about cooptation are valid fears. Cooptation invariably involves some mixture of outcome modification and social control and the exact mix is difficult to determine in advance. The authority who opposes coopting the hostile element fears that outcome modification will dominate the mix; the partisan who opposes accepting it fears that the social control element will dominate.

The TVA case described by Selznick is instructive in this regard. The newly founded organization was faced, in 1933, with a powerfully entrenched existing interest bloc in the Tennessee Valley. This bloc consisted of a complex headed by the Land

Grant Colleges, the more prosperous farmers represented by the American Farm Bureau Federation, and the Federal Agricultural Extension Service with its county agents. In some fashion, TVA had to confront this bloc whose territory the new organization was invading. Had TVA been firmly established with assured support of its own, it might have considered a strategy which would have challenged this bloc. In trying to become established, an alternative strategy recommended itself —to coopt the Farm Bureau complex into TVA. This policy was justified under the rubric of the "grass roots policy" which emphasized partnership with local groups in the region. The most significant act of cooptation was the appointment of one of the leaders of the Farm Bureau complex to TVA's three-man board.

One of the consequences of the cooptation strategy was a considerable amount of influence by the Farm Bureau complex over TVA's agricultural policies. Decisions on fertilizer programs, on the degree of emphasis on rural cooperatives, on the place of Negro farmers in the TVA program, were apparently all heavily influenced by this partisan group in the valley. On the other hand, TVA was able to carry out successfully its public power program and a number of other important objectives which might have become the target of active opposition if the Farm Bureau complex had not been coopted. It is never easy to assess whether the "price" in outcome modification was worth it or not, especially since one cannot know what would have happened if cooptation had not been used. The lesson to be drawn from the TVA example is not that it acted wisely or foolishly in coopting the Farm Bureau complex. Rather it is that *any* act of cooptation of potential partisans by authorities is likely to be a mixture of modification and social control and the balance of the mix is problematic and of concern to both parties.

Leeds's discussion of the absorption of nonconforming enclaves again illustrates the double-edged nature of this process. General Chennault and his followers in the period preceding World War II attempted to develop a group of trained fighter pilots (the "Flying Tigers") to furnish air support for Chinese land forces opposing the Japanese. The military had yet to accept, at this time, the full significance of air warfare and tended to regard it as auxiliary to infantry and artillery. Consequently, the allocation of supplies and personnel to Chennault were limited and a variety of other means were used to control and isolate the Flying Tiger group. However, after the U.S. entry into the war, this conflict proved too costly and a different control technique was used to deal with the rebellious group. In July, 1942, the American Volunteer Group of Flying Tigers was transformed into China Air Task Force and inducted into the U.S. Air Force under General Bissell. Later the group became the 14th Air Force under General Stillwell who was instructed to give Chennault full support. This ended the rebellion and removed the acute pressure from this partisan group. Along with the development of military technology and the experiences of the war, this absorption contributed to a major reorientation in the military toward the importance of air warfare. As in the TVA case, cooptation seems to have involved large amounts of influence for the coopted group.

Closely related to the issue of cooptation and protest-absorption is that of participation in decision making. A long line of social psychological experiments in laboratory and field settings has emphasized the importance of participation as a positive factor in the acceptance of decision outcomes. It is not always clear precisely what is meant by participation.

One may emphasize the influence aspects of participation. To increase the participation of a group of potential partisans may mean to increase its influence over decisions. If there is increased satisfaction in such situations, it is because the modified outcomes are closer to what the partisan group desires. It may have very little or nothing to do with the fact of participation itself. If the significance of participation stems from the attendant influence, then we should expect the same increase in satisfaction and commitment that we would get if outcomes were similarly modified without an increase in participation.

Participation has a social control aspect as well. Here it is claimed that the act of participating in a decision process increases commitment and acceptance of decisions even if outcomes are no more satisfactory. The classic case of such alleged "participation" effects is the Hawthorne Study in which output increased following a variety of decisions made by a group of workers. These particular experiments are a weak reed on which to base any conclusion as Carey demonstrates in an appropriately harsh review. Carey argues that a "detailed comparison between the Hawthorne conclusions and the Hawthorne evidence shows these conclusions to be almost wholly unsupported." But in a later, more careful study of "participation" effects, Coch and French conclude that resistance to changing work methods can be overcome "by the use of group meetings in which management effectively communicates the need for change and stimulates group participation in planning the changes. Such participation results in higher production, higher morale, and better labor-management relations."

Much of the small group work on "democratic" methods of decision making has a strong social control emphasis. As Verba points out,

Participation is in most cases limited to member endorsement of decisions made by the leader who . . . is neither selected by the group nor responsible to the group for his actions. In group discussions, the leader does not present alternatives to the group from which the members choose. Rather, the group leader has a particular goal in mind and uses the group discussion as a means of inducing acceptance of the goal. . . . As used in much of the small group literature, participatory democratic leadership refers not to a technique of decision but to a technique of persuasion.

Participation, like cooptation, is most likely to be some mixture of influence and social control. Many of the same issues arise. If the social control emphasis is paramount, partisans are likely to regard the process as pseudo-participation and manipulation. But it is not easy to increase participation without also increasing influence. The increased access may be intended to lead to a greater feeling of participation and increased commitment of members, but those who are so admitted may not be very long satisfied with the trappings of influence. When conflicts arise, the new participants may be in an improved position to pursue their interests effectively.

By the use of *selective* participation, authorities may control some partisans by increasing the ability of others to influence. Hard-pressed authorities may welcome influence attempts by rival parti-

sans, for such influence may free rather than confine them. Under such circumstances, authorities may encourage increased participation by selected groups despite, or even because of, the increased influence that it will bring. The new pressures can then be pointed to as justification and defense for failure to take the actions desired by the first group; the second group in turn can be brought to appreciate the constraints which their rival places on the authorities.

The playing off of one partisan group against another as a technique of control is an ancient and familiar one. Machiavelli recommended it to his authorities and Simmel developed it in his discussions of the "tertius gaudens," i.e., the third party who draws advantage from the quarrel of two others. It is captured in the admonition to authorities to "divide and rule." Simmel illustrates it by describing the Inca custom of dividing a "newly conquered tribe in two approximately equal halves and [placing] a supervisor over each of them, but [giving] these two supervisors slightly different ranks. This was indeed the most suitable means for provoking rivalry between the two heads, which prevented any united action against the ruler on the part of the subjected territory."

Such a control technique has certain dangers. First, while it may forestall the necessity of immediate outcome modification and increase the temporary maneuverability of authorities, it does not relieve the pressure in the long run and may even intensify it. For the moment, some of the resources of the partisan groups may be redirected into the conflict with each other but the authorities, by definition, control the choices which these groups are attempting to influence. Second, it is typically the case that rival partisan groups have some degree of common interest. If so, they may find it convenient to pool their resources in a temporary coalition. Thus, increased participation may lead to an enhancement of the influence it was intended to prevent.

Note that in the above discussion we are viewing organizational officials in their role as authorities. As partisans, these same individuals may desire increased influence for members of the same partisan group. The chairman of a state political party may argue for the widest possible citizen participation in the selection of delegates to the nominating

266 RESPONSES OF AUTHORITIES TO THREAT

convention because he believes that his own preferred candidate has a stronger following among the party rank and file than among the organizational regulars. In encouraging such rank and file participation, he is acting as a partisan attempting to influence the decision on selecting a candidate, not as an authority trying to minimize partisan influence on the decisions over which he personally exercises authority.

SUMMARY

This chapter has emphasized the perspective of authorities on the possible attempts of partisans to influence the outcome of the decisions they make. The central problem from their standpoint is the containment of influence. Pressure from potential partisans can be relieved by yielding ground and modifying the outcome of decisions or by dealing with the source of pressure through some form of social control.

One form of control involves the insulation of decision makers from potential partisans. This can be done at the point of entry by selecting those who will not present problems or at the point of exit by expelling recalcitrant individuals or groups. Once in, potential partisans are subject to a wide variety of sanctions. Finally, the orientation of potential partisans can be controlled by manipulating information, ideology, image of authorities, friendship ties, norms, and values. If potential partisans are sufficiently socialized and have high political trust they can be controlled by the activation of commitments. Mechanisms like cooptation and participation seem to involve a mixture of outcome modification and social control as a way of dealing with particularly powerful or threatening partisan groups.

There is a major difference in the influence and social control perspectives on the meaning and significance of social conflict. The social control perspective leads to an emphasis on stability. Conflict, under this view, represents a failure of social control—the failure to contain influence.

This is not to suggest that stability, as used here, is a bad thing. The authorities in whose maintenance one is concerned may be a progressive administration, vigorously pursuing land reform and providing effective leadership in a wide variety of ways. Or, they may represent a totalitarian regime relying heavily on terror and repression as social control techniques. In any case, the questions which arise from this perspective focus us on the manner in which authorities are left free to govern.

The influence perspective on the other hand leads to an emphasis on change. Conflict has a different meaning. Rather than a failure of social control, it is likely to be viewed as part of a social movement aimed at changing the content of decisions, the incumbent authorities, or the regime itself. Such potential partisans might be revolutionary or counterrevolutionary, progressive or reactionary. Again, no implication is intended about the desirability of change per se.

Perhaps the emphasis on stability in one perspective and change in the other is avoidable. Yet it seems to flow from the kinds of questions which arise naturally with each perspective. By taking both perspectives, one can avoid the characteristic blind spots of each one taken alone.

ADVICE TO PRESIDENT NIXON

Daniel Patrick Moynihan

Before the storm breaks, as it were, on the 20th, I would like to send in a few extended comments on some of the longer range issues that face you, but will tend, I should imagine, to get lost in the daily succession of crises.

I would like to speak first of the theme "Forward Together."

This appeal was much in evidence in your very fine acceptance speech at Miami, and during the campaign the logic of events, and your own sure sense of them, brought it forward ever more insistently.

In the end it was the theme of the campaign and, in the aftermath of victory, it stands as the most explicit mandate you have from the American people. I would hope it might be the theme of your Administration as well.

It has fallen to you to assume the governance of a deeply divided country. And to do so with a divided Government. Other Presidents—Franklin Roosevelt, for example—have taken office in moments of crisis, but the crises were so widely perceived as in a sense to unite the country and to create a great outpouring of support for the President as the man who would have to deal with the common danger.

Neither Lincoln nor Wilson, the two predecessors whose situations most resembled yours, in terms of the popular vote and the state of then current political questions, had any such fortune. No one would now doubt that they proved to be two of our greatest leaders, nor yet that their Administrations achieved great things. But, alas, at what cost to themselves.

From The New York Times, *March 11, 1970, p. 30.* © *1970 by The New York Times Company. Reprinted by permission.*

COMMON ELEMENT SOUGHT

A divided nation makes terrible demands on the President. It would seem important to try to anticipate some of them, at least, and to ponder whether there is not some common element in each that might give a measure of coherence and unity to the President's own responses and, by a process of diffusion, to provide a guide for the Administration as a whole.

I believe there is such a common element. In one form or another all of the major domestic problems facing you derive from the erosion of the authority of the institutions of American society. This is a mysterious process of which the most that can be said is that once it starts it tends not to stop.

It can be stopped: The English, for example, managed to halt and even reverse the process in the period, roughly, 1820–40. But more commonly, those in power neglect the problem at first and misunderstand it later; concessions come too late and are too little; the failure of concessions leads to equally unavailing attempts at repression; and so events spiral downward toward instability.

The process is little understood. (Neither is the opposite and almost completely ignored phenomenon: Some societies—Mexico in the 1920's—seem almost suddenly to become stabilized after periods of prolonged and seemingly hopeless chaos.)

All we know is that the sense of institutions being legitimate—especially the institutions of government—is the glue that holds societies together. When it weakens, things come unstuck.

CONTRAST IN PEOPLE

The North Vietnamese see this clearly enough. Hence the effort through the subtleties of seating arrangements to establish the N.L.F. as an independent regime, and the Saigon Government as a puppet one.

In contrast, Americans, until presently at least, have not been nearly so concerned with such matters. American society has been so stable for so long that the prospect of instability has had no very great meaning for us. (As I count, there are but nine nations that both existed as independent nations in 1914 and have not had their form of government changed by invasion or revolution since.)

Moreover, we retain a tradition of revolutionary rhetoric that gives an advantage to those who challenge authority rather than those who uphold it. Too little heed is given the experience of the twentieth century in which it has been the authority of democratic institutions that has been challenged by totalitarians of the left and the right.

Even the term "authority" has acquired for many a sinister cast, largely one suspects from its association with the term "authoritarian." Yet it remains the case that relationships based on authority are consensual ones: that is to say they are based on common agreement to behave in certain ways.

It is said that freedom lives in the interstices of authority. When the structure collapses, freedom disappears, and society is governed by relationships based on power.

Increasing numbers of Americans seem of late to have sensed this, and to have become actively concerned about the drift of events. Your election was in a sense the first major consequence of that mounting concern. Your Administration represents the first significant opportunity to change the direction in which events move.

Your task, then, is clear: to restore the authority of American institutions. Not, certainly, under that name, but with a clear sense that what is at issue is the continued acceptance by the great mass of the people of the legitimacy and efficacy of the present arrangements of American society, and of our processes for changing those arrangements.

For that purpose the theme "Forward Together" responds not only to the deepest need of the moment, but also, increasingly, to a clearly perceived need, as the facts of disunity more and more impress themselves on the nation's consciousness.

What has been pulling us apart? One wishes one knew. Yet there are a number of near- and long-term developments that can be discerned and surely contribute significantly to what is going on.

Of the near-term events, the two most conspicuous are the Negro revolution and the war in Vietnam. Although seemingly unrelated, they have much in common as to origins, and even more as to the process by which they have brought on mounting levels of disunity.

The French philosopher Georges Bernanos once wrote: "There are no more corrupting lies than problems poorly stated." I, at least, feel that this goes to the heart of much of the present turmoil of race relations and foreign policy. In a word, those in power have allowed domestic dislocations that accompany successful social changes to be interpreted as irrefutable evidence that the society refuses to change; they have permitted foreign policy failures arising from mistaken judgments to be taken as incontrovertible proof that the society has gone mad as well.

The fact is that with respect to Negro Americans we have seen incredible progress since, roughly, the Brown vs. Board of Education decision of 1956 and President Eisenhower's subsequent decision to send Federal troops to Little Rock, thus commencing the second Reconstruction.

Nowhere in history is there to be encountered an effort to bring a suppressed people into the mainstream of society comparable to the public and private initiatives on behalf of Negro Americans in recent years.

BLACKS SAW IT FIRST

As I would like to discuss in a later memorandum, the results have been dramatic. Yet it was only after that effort had begun, and had been under way for some time, that it became possible to see the true horror of the situation white America had forced on black America and the deep disabilities that came about in consequence.

The first to see this, of course, were the blacks themselves. The result on the part of many was a revulsion against white society that has only just begun to run its course. Large numbers of middle-class, educated blacks, especially young ones, have come to see American society as hateful and illegitimate, lacking any true claim on their allegiance. Well they might.

The problem is not that one group in the population is beginning to react to centuries of barbarism by another group. The problem is that this cultural reaction among black militants is accompanied by the existence of a large, disorganized urban lower class which, like such groups everywhere, is unstable and essentially violent.

This fact of lower-class violence has nothing to do with race. It is purely a matter of social class. But since Watts, the media of public opinion—the press, television, the Presidency itself—have combined to insist that race is the issue.

As a result, middle-class blacks caught up in a cultural revolution have been able, in effect, to back up their demands. This has led to a predictable white counter-reaction. And so on. In the process, we have almost deliberately obscured the extraordinary progress, and commitment to progress, which the nation as a whole has made, which white America has not abandoned, and which increasingly black America is learning to make use of.

To the contrary, it has been the failures of policy that have seemed ever more prominent. The essence of the Negro problem in America at this time is that despite great national commitments, and great progress, a large mass of the black population remains poor, disorganized, and discriminated against.

These facts are increasingly interpreted as proof that the national commitment is flawed, if not indeed fraudulent, that the society is irredeemably "racist," etc.

This interpretation is made by middle-class blacks and whites who, outwardly at least, society would seem to have treated very well, but the continued existence of black poverty makes their argument hard to assail. Moreover, increasingly that argument is directed not to particulars, but to fundamental questions as to the legitimacy of American society.

WAR ALSO A DISASTER

Vietnam has been a domestic disaster of the same proportion, and for much the same reason. As best I can discern, the war was begun with the very highest of motives at the behest of men such as McNamara, Bundy, and Rusk in a fairly consistent pursuit of the postwar American policy of opposing Communist expansion and simultaneously encouraging political democracy and economic development in the nations on the Communist perimeter, and elsewhere.

At the risk of seeming cynical, I would argue that the war in Vietnam has become a disastrous mistake because we have lost it. I quite accept Henry Kissinger's splendid formulation that a conventional army loses if it does not win, the opposite being the case for a guerilla force. We have not been able to win.

Had the large-scale fighting by American forces been over by mid-1967 (which is my impression of what Bundy anticipated in mid-1965), had the children of the middle class accordingly continued to enjoy draft exemption, had there been no inflation, no surtax, no Tet offensive, then I very much fear there would be abroad at this point at most a modicum of moral outrage.

But this is not what happened. The war has not gone well, and increasingly in an almost primitive reaction—to which modern societies are as much exposed as any Stone Age clan—it has been judged that this is because the gods are against it.

In modern parlance this means that the evil military-industrial complex has embarked on a racist colonialist adventure. (I have heard the head of SNCC state that we were in Vietnam "for the rice supplies.")

But the essential point is that we have been losing a war, and this more than any single thing erodes the authority of a Government, however stable, just, well-intentioned or whatever.

"MOB" TOPPLES PRESIDENT

I would imagine that the desire not to be the first President to "lose" a war has been much in President Johnson's mind over the past years, and explains some of his conduct. But the fact is that he could not win, and the all-important accompanying fact is that the semi-violent domestic protest that arose in consequence forced him to resign.

In a sense he was the first American President to be toppled by a mob. No matter that it was a mob of college professors, millionaires, flower children, and Radcliffe girls.

It was a mob that by early 1968 had effectively physically separated the Presidency from the people. (You may recall that seeking to attend the funeral of Cardinal Spellman, Johnson slipped in the back door of St. Patrick's Cathedral like a medieval felon seeking sanctuary.)

As with the case of the most militant blacks, success for the antiwar protestors has seemed only to confirm their detestation of society as it now exists. Increasingly they declare the society to be illegitimate, while men such as William Sloan Coffin Jr., the chaplain at Yale, openly espouse violence as the necessary route of moral regeneration.

The successful extremism of the black militants and the antiwar protesters—by and large they have had their way—has now clearly begun to arouse fears and thoughts of extreme actions by other groups. George Wallace, a fourth-rate regional demagogue, won 13 per cent of the national vote and at one point in the campaign probably had the sympathy of a quarter of the electorate, largely in the working class.

Among Jews—I draw your attention to this— there is a rising concern, in some quarters approaching alarm, over black anti-Semitism. They foresee Negro political power driving them from civil service jobs, as in the New York City school system. They see anti-Semitism becoming an "accepted" political posture. With special dread, they see a not distant future when the political leaders of the country might have to weigh the competing claims of 10 million black voters who had become passionately pro-Arab as against one or two million.

In the meantime, we must await the reaction of the armed forces, and the veterans of Vietnam, to whatever settlement you get there. No officer corps ever lost a war, and this one surely would have no difficulty finding symbols of those at home who betrayed it. All in all there are good reasons to expect a busy eight years in the White House.

REJECTION OF VALUES

There is a longer term development contributing to the present chaos which bears mentioning.

Since about 1840 the cultural elite in America have pretty generally rejected the values and activities of the larger society.

It has been said of America that the culture will not approve that which the policy strives to provide. For a brief period, associated with the depression, World War II, and the Cold War there was something of a truce in this protracted struggle. That, I fear, is now over. The leading cultural figures are going—have gone—into opposition once again. This time they take with them a vastly more numerous following of educated, middle-class persons, especially young ones, who share their feelings and who do not "need the straight" world.

It is their pleasure to cause trouble, to be against. And they are hell bent for a good time. President Johnson took all this personally, but I have the impression that you will make no such mistake!

It is, of course, easier to describe these situations than to suggest what is to be done about them. However, a certain number of general postures do seem to follow from the theme "bring us together." I would list five:

First, the single most important task is to maintain the rate of economic expansion. If a serious economic recession were to come along to compound the controversies of race, Vietnam, and cultural alienation, the nation could indeed approach instability.

It would be my judgment that the great prosperity of the 1960's is the primary reason we have been able to weather this much internal dissension. The lot of Negroes has steadily improved, and so has that of most everyone else. Black demands for a greater share have thus been less threatening.

The war has been costly, but largely has been paid for through annual fiscal increments and recent deficits. Consumption has been affected not at all. If this situation were to reverse itself, your ability to meet black needs, the tolerance of the rest of the society for your efforts, the general willingness to see military efforts proceed, would all be grievously diminished.

Second, it would seem most important to de-escalate the rhetoric of crisis about the internal state of the society in general, and in particular about those problems—e. g., crime, de facto segregation, low educational achievement—which Government has relatively little power to influence in the present state of knowledge and available resources.

This does not mean reducing efforts. Not at all. But it does mean trying to create some equivalence between what Government can do about certain problems and how much attention it draws to them. For this purpose the theme you struck in presenting your Cabinet on television seems perfect: Yours is an Administration of men with wide-ranging interests and competence whose first concern is the effective delivery of Government services.

There is a risk here of being accused of caring less than your predecessors, but even that will do no great harm if you can simultaneously demonstrate that you do more. It is out of such perceptions that the authority of Government is enhanced.

STRESS ON MINORITIES

It would seem likely that a powerful approach to this issue will be to stress the needs and aspirations of groups such as Mexican-Americans, Puerto Ricans, American Indians, and others, which have also been excluded and exploited by the larger society. This, of course, is something you would want to do in any event.

Third, the Negro lower class must be dissolved. This is the work of a generation, but it is time it began to be understood as a clear national goal. By lower class I mean the low-income, marginally employed, poorly educated, disorganized slum dwellers who have piled up in our central cities over the past quarter century. I would estimate they make up almost one half the total Negro population.

They are not going to become capitalists, nor even middle-class functionaries. But it is fully reasonable to conceive of them being transformed into a stable working-class population: Truck drivers, mail carriers, assembly line workers—people with dignity, purpose, and in the United States a very good standard of living indeed. Common justice, and common sense, demands that this be done.

It is the existence of this lower class, with its high rates of crime, dependency, and general disorderli-

ness, that causes nearby whites (that is to say working-class whites, the liberals are all in the suburbs) to fear Negroes and to seek by various ways to avoid and constrain them.

It is this group that black extremists use to threaten white society with the prospect of mass arson and pillage. It is also this group that terrorizes and plunders the stable elements of the Negro community—trapped by white prejudice in the slums, and forced to live cheek by jowl with a murderous slum population. Take the urban lower class out of the picture and the Negro cultural revolution becomes an exciting and constructive development.

Fourth, it would seem devoutly to be wished that you not become personally identified with the war in Vietnam. You have available to you far more competent advice than mine in this area, and I am sure you will wish to proceed in terms of the foreign policy interests of the nation in broader terms, but I do urge that every effort be made to avoid the ugly physical harassment and savage personal attacks that brought President Johnson's Administration to an end.

The dignity of the Presidency as the symbolic head of state as well as of functioning leader of the Government must be restored. Alas, it is in the power of the middle-class mob to prevent this. I would far rather see it concentrate, as *faute de mieux* it now seems to be doing, on attacking liberal college presidents as "racist pigs."

I fear the blunt truth is that ending the draft would be the single most important step you could take in this direction. The children of the upper middle class will not be conscripted.

In any event, the present system does cast a pall of anxiety and uncertainty over the lives of that quarter of the young male population which does in fact require four to eight to ten years of college work to prepare for careers which almost all agree are socially desirable, even necessary.

Fifth, it would seem important to stress those things Americans share in common, rather than those things that distinguish them one from the other; thus the war on poverty defined a large portion of the population as somehow living apart from the rest.

I would seek programs that stress problems and circumstances that all share, and especially problems which working people share with the poor. Too frequently of late the liberal upper middle class has proposed to solve problems of those at the bottom at the expense, or seeming expense, of those in between.

Obviously the theme "Forward Together" is essential here, and there are other symbols at hand of which I would think the approaching 200th anniversary of the founding of the Republic is perhaps the most powerful.

In the final months of your second term you will preside over the anniversary ceremonies of July 4, 1976. It would seem an incomparable opportunity to begin now to define the goals you would hope to see achieved by that time, trying to make them truly national goals to which all may subscribe, and from which as many as possible will benefit.

Hopefully our 200th anniversary will see the nation somewhat more united than were those 13 colonies!

THE GARRISON STATE

Harold D. Lasswell

The purpose of this article is to consider the possibility that we are moving toward a world of "garrison states"—a world in which the specialists on violence are the most powerful group in society. From this point of view the trend of our time is away from the dominance of the specialist on bargaining, who is the businessman, and toward the supremacy of the soldier. We may distinguish transitional forms, such as the party propaganda state, where the dominant figure is the propagandist, and the party bureaucratic state, in which the organization men of the party make the vital decisions. There are mixed forms in which predominance is shared by the monopolists of party and market power.[1]

All men are deeply affected by their expectations as well as by their desires. We time our specific wants and efforts with some regard to what we reasonably hope to get. Hence, when we act rationally, we consider alternative versions of the future, making explicit those expectations about

From The American Journal of Sociology, *Vol. 46 (January 1941). Reprinted by permission of the University of Chicago Press. Footnotes have been edited.*

the future that are so often buried in the realm of hunch.

In the practice of social science, as of any skill in society, we are bound to be affected in some degree by our conceptions of future development. There are problems of timing in the prosecution of scientific work, timing in regard to availability of data and considerations of policy. In a world where primitive societies are melting away it is rational to act promptly to gather data about primitive forms of social organization. In a world in which the scientist may also be a democratic citizen, sharing democratic respect for human personality, it is rational for the scientist to give priority to problems connected with the survival of democratic society. There is no question here of a scientist deriving his values from science; values are *acquired* chiefly from personal experience of a given culture, *derived* from that branch of culture that is philosophy and theology, *implemented* by science and practice.

The picture of the garrison state that is offered here is no dogmatic forecast. Rather it is a picture of the probable. It is not inevitable. It may not even have the same probability as some other descriptions of the future course of development. What, then, is the function of this picture for scientists? It is to stimulate the individual specialist to clarify for himself his expectations about the future, as a guide to the timing of scientific work. Side by side with this "construct" of a garrison state there may be other constructs; the rational person will assign exponents of probability to every alternative picture.[2]

Expectations about the future may rest upon the extrapolation of past trends into the future. We may choose a number of specific items—like population and production curves—and draw them into the future according to some stated rule. This is an "itemistic" procedure. In contrast, we may set up a construct that is frankly imaginative though disciplined by careful consideration of the past. Since trend curves summarize many features of the past, they must be carefully considered in the preparation of every construct. Correlation analysis of trend curves, coupled with the results of experiment, may provide us with partial confirmation of many propositions about social change; these results, too, must be reviewed. In addition to these disciplined battalions of data there is the total exposure of the individual to the immediate and the recorded past, and this total exposure may stimulate productive insight into the structure of the whole manifold of events which includes the future as well as the past. In the interest of correct orientation in the world of events, one does not wisely discard all save codified experience. (The pictures of the future that are set up on more than "item" basis may be termed "total.")

To speak of a garrison state is not to predict something wholly new under the sun. Certainly there is nothing novel to the student of political institutions about the idea that specialists on violence may run the state. On the contrary, some of the most influential discussions of political institutions have named the military state as one of the chief forms of organized society. Comte saw history as a succession (and a progression) that moved, as far as it concerned the state, through military, feudal, and industrial phases. Spencer divided all human societies into the military type, based on force, and the industrial type, based on contract and free consent.

What is important for our purposes is to envisage the possible emergence of the military state under present technical conditions. There are no examples of the military state combined with modern technology. During emergencies the great powers have given enormous scope to military authority, but temporary acquisitions of authority lack the elements of comparative permanence and acceptance that complete the garrison state. Military dictators in states marginal to the creative centers of Western civilization are not integrated with modern technology; they merely use some of its specific elements.

The military men who dominate a modern technical society will be very different from the officers of history and tradition. It is probable that the specialists on violence will include in their training a large degree of expertness in many of the skills that we have traditionally accepted as part of modern civilian management.

The distinctive frame of reference in a fighting society is fighting effectiveness. All social change is translated into battle potential. Now there can be no realistic calculation of fighting effectiveness without knowledge of the technical and psychological characteristics of modern production processes. The function of management in such a society is already known to us; it includes the exercise of skill in supervising technical operations, in administrative organization, in personnel management, in public relations. These skills are needed to translate the complicated operations of modern life into every relevant frame of reference—the frame of fighting effectiveness as well as of pecuniary profit.

This leads to the seeming paradox that, as modern states are militarized, specialists on violence are more preoccupied with the skills and attitudes judged characteristic of nonviolence. We anticipate the merging of skills, starting from the traditional accouterments of the professional soldier, moving toward the manager and promoter of large-scale civilian enterprise.

In the garrison state, at least in its introductory phases, problems of morale are destined to weigh heavily on the mind of management. It is easy to throw sand in the gears of the modern assembly line; hence, there must be a deep and general sense of participation in the total enterprise of the state if collective effort is to be sustained. When we call attention to the importance of the "human factor" in modern production, we sometimes fail to notice that it springs from the multiplicity of special environments that have been created by modern technology. Thousands of technical operations have sprung into existence where a few hundred were found before. To complicate the material environment in this way is to multiply the foci of attention of those who live in our society. Diversified foci of attention breed differences in outlook, preference, and loyalty. The labyrinth of specialized "material" environments generates profound ideological divergencies that cannot be abolished, though they can be mitigated, by the methods now available to leaders in our society. As long as modern technology prevails, society is honeycombed with cells of separate experience, of individuality, of partial freedom. Concerted action under such conditions depends upon skilfully guiding the minds of men; hence the enormous importance of symbolic manipulation in modern society.

The importance of the morale factor is emphasized by the universal fear which it is possible to maintain in large populations through modern instruments of warfare. The growth of aerial warfare in particular has tended to abolish the distinction between civilian and military functions. It is no longer possible to affirm that those who enter the military service take the physical risk while those who remain at home stay safe and contribute to the equipment and the comfort of the courageous heroes at the front. Indeed, in some periods of modern warfare, casualties among civilians may outnumber the casualties of the armed forces. With the socialization of danger as a permanent characteristic of modern violence the nation becomes one unified technical enterprise. Those who direct the violence operations are compelled to consider the entire gamut of problems that arise in living together under modern conditions.

There will be an energetic struggle to incorporate young and old into the destiny and mission of the state. It is probable that one form of this symbolic adjustment will be the abolition of "the unemployed." This stigmatizing symbol will be obsolete in the garrison state. It insults the dignity of millions, for it implies uselessness. This is so, whether the "unemployed" are given a "dole" or put on

"relief" projects. Always there is the damaging stigma of superfluity. No doubt the garrison state will be distinguished by the psychological abolition of unemployment—"psychological" because this is chiefly a matter of redefining symbols.

In the garrison state there must be work—and the duty to work—for all. Since all work becomes public work, all who do not accept employment flout military discipline. For those who do not fit within the structure of the state there is but one alternative—to obey or die. Compulsion, therefore, is to be expected as a potent instrument for internal control of the garrison state.

The use of coercion can have an important effect upon many more people than it reaches directly; this is the propaganda component of any "propaganda of the deed." The spectacle of compulsory labor gangs in prisons or concentration camps is a negative means of conserving morale—negative since it arouses fear and guilt. Compulsory labor groups are suitable popular scapegoats in a military state. The duty to obey, to serve the state, to work—these are cardinal virtues in the garrison state. Unceasing emphasis upon duty is certain to arouse opposing tendencies within the personality structure of all who live under a garrison regime. Everyone must struggle to hold in check any tendencies, conscious or unconscious, to defy authority, to violate the code of work, to flout the incessant demand for sacrifice in the collective interest. From the earliest years youth will be trained to subdue—to disavow, to struggle against—any specific opposition to the ruling code of collective exactions.

The conscience imposes feelings of guilt and anxiety upon the individual whenever his impulses are aroused, ever so slightly, to break the code. When the coercive threat that sanctions the code of the military state is internalized in the consciences of youth, the spectacle of labor gangs is profoundly disturbing. A characteristic response is self-righteousness—quick justification of coercive punishment, tacit acceptance of the inference that all who are subject to coercion are guilty of antisocial conduct. To maintain suspended judgment, to absolve others in particular instances, is to give at least partial toleration to countermores tendencies within the self. Hence, the quick substitute responses—the self-righteous attitude, the deflection of attention. Indeed, a characteristic psychic pattern of the military state is the "startle pattern," which is carried over to the internal as well as to the external threat of danger. This startle pattern is overcome and stylized as alert, prompt, commanding adjustment to reality. This is expressed in the authoritative manner that dominates military style—in gesture, intonation, and idiom.

The chief targets of compulsory labor service will be unskilled manual workers, together with counterelite elements who have come under suspicion. The position of the unskilled in our society has been deteriorating, since the machine society has less and less use for unskilled manual labor. The coming of the machine was a skill revolution, a broadening of the role of the skilled and semiskilled components of society.[3] As the value of labor declines in production, it also declines in warfare; hence, it will be treated with less consideration. (When unskilled workers are relied upon as fighters, they must, of course, share the ideological exultation of the community as a whole and receive a steady flow of respect from the social environment.) Still another factor darkens the forecast for the bottom layers of the population in the future garrison state. If recent advances in pharmacology continue, as we may anticipate, physical means of controlling response can replace symbolic methods. This refers to the use of drugs not only for temporary orgies of energy on the part of front-line fighters but in order to deaden the critical function of all who are not held in esteem by the ruling élite.

For the immediate future, however, ruling élites must continue to put their chief reliance upon propaganda as an instrument of morale. But the manipulation of symbols, even in conjunction with coercive instruments of violence, is not sufficient to accomplish all the purposes of a ruling group. We have already spoken of the socialization of danger, and this will bring about some equalitarian adjustments in the distribution of income for the purpose of conserving the will to fight and to produce.

In addition to the adjustment of symbols, goods, and violence, the political élite of the garrison state will find it necessary to make certain adaptations in the fundamental practices of the state. Decisions will be more dictatorial than democratic, and institutional practices long connected with modern democracy will disappear. Instead of elections to office or referendums on issues there will be government by plebiscite. Elections foster the formation and expression of public opinion, while plebiscites encourage only unanimous demonstrations of collective sentiment. Rival political parties will be suppressed, either by the monopolization of legality in one political party (more properly called a political "order") or by the abolition of all political parties. The ruling group will exercise a monopoly of opinion in public, thus abolishing the free communication of fact and interpretation. Legislatures will be done away with, and if a numerous consultative body is permitted at all it will operate as an assembly; that is, it will meet for a very short time each year and will be expected to ratify the decisions of the central leadership after speeches that are chiefly ceremonial in nature. Plebiscites and assemblies thus become part of the ceremonializing process in the military state.

As legislatures and elections go out of use, the practice of petition will play a more prominent role. Lawmaking will be in the hands of the supreme authority and his council; and, as long as the state survives, this agency will exert effective control ("authority" is the term for formal expectations, "control" is the actual distribution of effective power).

This means that instrumental democracy will be in abeyance, although the symbols of mystic "democracy" will doubtless continue. Instrumental democracy is found wherever authority and control are widely dispersed among the members of a state. Mystic "democracy" is not, strictly speaking, democracy at all, because it may be found where authority and control are highly concentrated yet where part of the established practice is to speak in the name of the people as a whole. Thus, any dictatorship may celebrate its "democracy" and speak with contempt of such "mechanical" devices as majority rule at elections or in legislatures.

What part of the social structure would be drawn upon in recruiting the political rulers of the garrison state? As we have seen, the process will not be by general election but by self-perpetuation through co-option. The foremost positions will be open to the officers corps, and the problem is to predict from what part of the social structure the officers will be recruited. Morale considerations justify a broad base of recruitment for ability rather than social standing. Although fighting effectiveness is a relatively impersonal test that favors ability over inherited status, the turnover in ruling families from generation to generation will probably be low. Any recurring crisis, however, will strengthen the tendency to favor ability. It seems clear that recruitment will be much more for bias and obedience than for objectivity and originality. Yet, as we shall presently see, modern machine society has introduced new factors in the military state—factors tending to strengthen objectivity and originality.

In the garrison state all organized social activity will be governmentalized; hence, the role of independent associations will disappear, with the exception of secret societies (specifically, there will be no organized economic, religious, or cultural life outside of the duly constituted agencies of government). Government will be highly centralized, though devolution may be practiced in order to mitigate "bureaucratism." There is so much outspoken resistance to bureaucratism in modern civilization that we may expect this attitude to carry over to the garrison state. Not only will the administrative structure be centralized, but at every level it will tend to integrate authority in a few hands. The leadership principle will be relied upon; responsibility as a rule will be focused upon individual "heads."

We have sketched some of the methods at the disposal of the ruling élites of the garrison state—the management of propaganda, violence, goods, practices. Let us consider the picture from a slightly different standpoint. How will various kinds of influence be distributed in the state?[4] Power will be highly concentrated, as in any dictatorial regime. We have already suggested that there will be a strong tendency toward equalizing the distribution of safety throughout the community (that is, negative safety, the socialization of threat in modern war). In the interest of morale there will be some moderation of huge differences in individual income, flattening the pyramid at the top, bulging it out in the upper-middle and middle zones. In the garrison state the respect pyramid will probably resemble the income pyramid. (Those who are the targets of compulsory labor restrictions will be the principal recipients of negative respect and hence will occupy the bottom levels.) So great is the multiplicity of functions in modern processes of production that a simple scheme of military rank is flagrantly out of harmony with the facts. Even though a small number of ranks are retained in the military state, it will be recognized that the diversity of functions exercised by each rank is so great the meaning of a specific classification will be obscured. Summarizing, the distribution of safety will be most uniform throughout the community; distribution of power will show the largest inequalities. The patterns of income and respect will fall between these two, showing a pronounced bulge in the upper-middle and middle strata. The lower strata of the community will be composed of those subject to compulsory labor, tending to constitute a permanent pariah caste.

What about the capacity of the garrison state to produce a large volume of material values? The élites of the garrison state, like the élites of recent business states, will confront the problem of holding in check the stupendous productive potentialities of modern science and engineering. We know that the ruling élites of the modern business state have not known how to control productive capacity; they have been unwilling to adopt necessary measures for the purpose of regularizing the tempo of economic development. Hence, modern society has been characterized by periods of orgiastic expansion, succeeded by periods of flagrant underutilization of the instruments of production.[5]

The rulers of the garrison state will be able to regularize the rate of production, since they will be free from many of the conventions that have stood in the way of adopting measures suitable to this purpose in the business state. The business élite has been unwilling to revise institutional practices to the extent necessary to maintain a continually rising flow of investment. The institutional structure of the business state has called for flexible adjustment between governmental and private channels of activity and for strict measures to maintain price flexibility. Wherever the business élite has not supported such necessary arrangements, the business state itself has begun to disintegrate.

Although the rulers of the garrison state will be free to regularize the rate of production, they will most assuredly prevent full utilization of modern productive capacity for nonmilitary consumption purposes. The élite of the garrison state will have a professional interest in multiplying gadgets specialized to acts of violence. The rulers of the garrison state will depend upon war scares as a means of maintaining popular willingness to forego immediate consumption. War scares that fail to culminate in violence eventually lose their value; this is the point at which ruling classes will feel that bloodletting is needed in order to preserve those virtues of sturdy acquiescence in the regime which they so much admire and from which they so greatly benefit. We may be sure that if ever there is a rise in the production of nonmilitary consumption goods, despite the amount of energy directed toward the production of military equipment, the ruling class will feel itself endangered by the growing "frivolousness" of the community.[6]

We need to consider the degree to which the volume of values produced in a garrison state will be affected by the tendency toward rigidity. Many factors in the garrison state justify the expectation that tendencies toward repetitiousness and ceremonialization will be prominent. To some extent this is a function of bureaucracy and dictatorship. But to some extent it springs also from the preoccupation of the military state with danger. Even where military operations are greatly respected, the fighter must steel himself against deep-lying tendencies to retreat from death and mutilation. One of the most rudimentary and potent means of relieving fear is some repetitive operation—some reiteration of the old and well-established. Hence the reliance on drill as a means of disciplining men to endure personal danger without giving in to fear of death. The tendency to repeat, as a means of diminishing timidity, is powerfully reinforced by successful repetition, since the individual is greatly attached to whatever has proved effective in maintaining self-control in previous trials. Even those who deny the fear of death to themselves may reveal the depth of their unconscious fear by their interest in ritual and ceremony. This is one of the subtlest ways by which the individual can keep his mind distracted from the discovery of his own timidity. It does not occur to the ceremonialist that in the spider web of ceremony he has found a moral equivalent of war—an unacknowledged substitute for personal danger.

The tendency to ceremonialize rather than to fight will be particularly prominent among the most influential elements in a garrison state. Those standing at the top of the military pyramid will doubtless occupy high positions in the income pyramid. During times of actual warfare it may be necessary to make concessions in the direction of moderating gross-income differences in the interest of preserving general morale. The prospect of such concessions may be expected to operate as a deterrent factor against war. A countervailing tendency, of course, is the threat to sluggish and well-established members of the upper crust from ambitious members of the lower officers' corps. This threat arises, too, when there are murmurs of disaffection with the established order of things on the part of broader components of the society.

It seems probable that the garrison state of the future will be far less rigid than the military states of antiquity. As long as modern technical society endures, there will be an enormous body of specialists whose focus of attention is entirely given over to the discovery of novel ways of utilizing nature. Above all, these are physical scientists and engineers. They are able to demonstrate by rather impersonal procedures the efficiency of many of their suggestions for the improvement of fighting effectiveness. We therefore anticipate further exploration of the technical potentialities of modern civilization within the general framework of the garrison state.

* * *

The function of any developmental construct, such as the present one about the garrison state, is to clarify to the specialist the possible relevance of his research to impending events that concern the values of which he approves as a citizen. Although they are neither scientific laws nor dogmatic forecasts, developmental constructs aid in the timing of scientific work, stimulating both planned observation of the future and renewed interest in whatever past events are of greatest probable pertinence to the emerging future. Within the general structure of the science of society there is place for many special sciences devoted to the study of all factors that condition the survival of selected values. This is the sense in which there can be a science of democracy, or a science of political psychiatry, within the framework of social science. If the garrison state is probable, the timing of special research is urgent.[7]

NOTES

[1]For a preliminary discussion of the garrison state see my "Sino-Japanese Crisis: The Garrison State versus the Civilian State," *China Quarterly,* **11** (1937), 643–649.

[2]We use the term "subjective probability" for the exponent assigned to a future event; "objective probability" refers to the propositions about past events. The intellectual act of setting up a tentative picture of significant past-future relations is developmental thinking. See my *World Politics and Personal Insecurity,* New York, 1935, Chap. 1.

[3]See T. M. Sogge, "Industrial Classes in the United States," *Journal of the American Statistical Association* (June, 1933); and Colin Clark, "National Income and Outlay," in A. C. Pigou, *Socialism versus Capitalism,* London: Macmillan, 1937, pp. 12–22.

[4]Influence is measured by control over values (desired events). For purposes of analysis we have classified values as income, safety, and deference. To be deferred to is to be taken into consideration by the environment. Deference, in turn, is divided into power and respect. Power is measured by degree of participation in important decisions. A decision is a choice backed by the most severe deprivations at the disposal of the community (usually death). The making of these decisions in a community is the *function* of government. The *institution* of government is what is called government by those who

live in a given community during a specified period of time; it is the most important secular decision-making institution. It is clear that the function of government may be exercised by other than governmental institutions, i.e., by "government" and by monopolistic "big business." (A state is one of the most influential communities in world-politics.) Respect is measured by reciprocal intimacy. Society can be divided into different classes on the basis of each value—or of value combinations. In the most inclusive sense politics studies conditions affecting the distribution of most values; in a narrower sense it studies power.

[5]For the magnitude of these production losses see National Resources Committee, *The Structure of the American Economy,* Washington, D.C., 1939, p. 2. The estimated loss of potential income was $200,000,000.

[6]The perpetuation of the garrison state will be favored by some of the psychological consequences of self-indulgence. When people who have been disciplined against self-indulgence increase their enjoyments, they often suffer from twinges of conscience. Such self-imposed anxieties signify that the conscience is ever vigilant to enforce the orthodox code of human conduct. Hence, drifts away from the established order of disciplined acquiescence in the proclaimed values of the garrison state will be self-correcting. The guilt generated by self-indulgence can be relieved through the orgiastic reinstatement of the established mores of disciplined sacrifice.

[7]Robert S. Lynd is concerned with the timing of knowledge in *Knowledge for What?* The book is full of valuable suggestions; it does not, however, specify the forms of thought most helpful to the end he has in view.

In the face of overwhelming collective operations like the space exploration, the average man must feel that local or grassroots efforts are worthless, there is no science but Big Science and no administration but the State. And yet there is a powerful surge of localism, populism, and community action, as if people were determined to be free even if it makes no sense.

PAUL GOODMAN

Modern technique has made it possible for leisure, within limits, to be not the prerogative of small privileged classes but a right evenly distributed throughout the community. The morality of work is the morality of slaves, and the modern world has no need of slavery.

BERTRAND RUSSELL

It is not accidental that at a point in history when hierarchical power and manipulation have reached their most threatening proportions, the very concepts of hierarchy, power, and manipulation are being brought into question.

MURRAY BOOKCHIN

For those willing to accept the new age on its own terms it will be an exhilarating time to be alive.

RICHARD RUBENSTEIN

Chapter 6

ALTERNATIVES TO OBEDIENCE:
Some Conditions for Self-Determination

Seemingly, we have been describing a continuous cycle in which authority establishes its legitimacy, is challenged by resistance from below, and then reestablishes its equilibrium. But clearly, historical turning points do occur. The cycle is broken; the established structure of authority is overthrown; and a new structure based on new principles of legitimacy arises. Such historical breaks are called revolutions. A revolutionary movement is qualitatively different from other movements of protest and rebellion, in that revolutionaries seek to transform the structure of authority and the distribution of power, reject the legitimacy of the established structure, and usually seek to institute a new idea of what constitutes legitimate government.

The revolutionary impulse first appears among those groups who are so systematically exploited, oppressed, uprooted, or alienated that their acceptance of the rightness of the established order is at best fragile. It is not hard, in such a situation, to feel that the system is biased against one's group and that a just appreciation of one's rights will never be possible within it. Such feelings are particularly likely if the authority structure bases its claims to legitimacy on principles of equality and other elements of the liberal-democratic ideal. Such feelings are exacerbated if efforts at partial resistance fail, and if secondary adjustments are repeatedly disrupted by economic dislocation and police harassment.

But the hope that the system will live up to its promise and fulfill its claims to legitimacy dies hard, and it may take several generations before an oppressed group adopts a fully revolutionary stance. In addition to feeling that oppression is illegitimate and that one's rights are denied within the system, a full revolutionary consciousness requires the acceptance by the group of an ideology embodying alternative principles of legitimation. Such an ideology usually emerges first among those who are able to come into contact with alternative world views and who are most fully exposed to the world literature espousing ideas of liberty, emancipation, equality, and self-determination. Thus, the first members of a subordinated group to express revolutionary sentiments are usually "intellectuals," students, and others who have been able to break out of the one-dimensionality of the oppressed situation. Such sentiments, especially if they are reworked to meet the specific requirements of the particular situation, begin to take hold as they are disseminated by organizers and leaders drawn largely from the ranks of the educated young. Revolutionary organizations may form and take action; mass resistance and protest becomes increasingly likely and increasingly takes on the quality of insurrection rather than petition.

Thus revolutionary consciousness requires both a situation of oppression and a vision of an alternative. That vision often embodies the idea that the group in question should rightfully be independent and self-governing, rather than subject to the authority of those who now rule. That, in particular, is how revolutionary aspirations are expressed by oppressed groups that are culturally homogeneous and controlled by an authority structure composed largely of members of a different cultural group.

A second type of revolutionary vision arises when both rulers and ruled share a common culture or when a society is composed of several ethnic groups each struggling against a common authority structure. Under these circumstances, the most likely vision is not one of independence and separation from the established order, but rather the achievement of full democracy, of a fully realized self-government for the people as a whole, and a fully realized freedom for each individual. Under these circumstances, revolutionary minorities seek to *universalize* their vision, attempting to speak in the interests of the great majority rather than in the interests of those who are especially oppressed.

Movements of national liberation—the first type of revolution I have described—become successful when the oppressed group is cohesively organized around new principles of self-determination and its own leadership. Movements of universal liberation, however, require much more. Not only must there be those who experience the system as oppressive and those who articulate new principles, but the sizable proportions of the population who experience the established order as relatively satisfactory must come to feel that it is illegitimate, and that the new principles are preferable. Such feelings are likely to arise among the relatively uncommitted; the more established authorities become involved in scandalous corruption, display serious incompetence, commit acts of unjustified and brutal repression, and otherwise confirm the claims of committed revolutionaries that they have lost the right to rule. Defeat in a war is perhaps the prime occasion for the growth of such mass disaffection. Furthermore, mass disaffection stimulates and is stimulated by the defection of members of the ruling group, splits within that group, and other signs that those in authority have lost the conviction that they themselves are legitimate.

Revolutions which overthrow an established authority structure are distinct from revolutions of national independence in that they seek to institute universally applicable principles of self-government. The French Revolution, and to some extent the American Revolution, were of this type; so were the Russian and Chinese revolutions. Although each of these revolutions did establish new bases of legitimacy for the societies in which they occurred, they most certainly did not abolish the domination of man by man and did not even approximately fulfill their claims to equality and self-government. It is not that these revolutions were futile, for they did succeed in eradicating the specific forms of oppression and domination which had been experienced as illegitimate. The legacy of these revolutions has been a far-reaching vision of human equality and self-determination which remains unrealized; paradoxically, however, each of these revolutions has established a new structure of authority more powerful and more centralized than the one which had been overthrown.

Those who experienced the failure of the French and American revolutions to institute full self-government tried to understand the reasons for failure. For many, such as Karl Marx, the failure lay in the necessary historical condition that the revolutions were dominated by the bourgeoisie and did not eradicate, but rather strengthened, the institution of private property. The weakness of liberal-democratic theory as a principle of universal emancipation is that it does not extend democratic principles to the economic system, thereby permitting domination and inequality to characterize everyday social life while declaring it illegitimate in government.

The Russian Revolution was an attempt to go beyond a bourgeois overthrow of feudalism and leap over capitalism, rather than repeat the pattern of the French Revolution. As yet, no Marx has arisen to account for its weakness, but we can, at least, see how the Chinese have tried to understand it. For them, the abolition of private property is seemingly an insufficient guarantee to self-government. A state bureaucracy which arrogates privilege to itself and establishes a new form of domination must also be abolished.

Marx believed that full emancipation required more than the abolition of private property and the equalization of sacrifice. He believed that it would come only if men could be freed from the necessity of labor, for ultimately the necessity for authority and subordination is rooted in the fact that the many must do onerous work and must forego the full satisfaction of their needs so that civilization can survive and the economy can grow.

Marx foresaw a time when technological development would be so extensive that productive capacity would practically be unlimited and onerous human labor would be replaced by machines. If scarcity could be abolished, then some men would not have to exercise authority to compel other men to forego the satisfaction of their needs. If the need for human labor could be reduced, then some men would not have to exercise authority over others to compel them to work efficiently at burdensome and boring tasks. Thus the Marxist analysis argues that all revolutions must fail in their promise of full emancipation insofar as the material circumstances under which they occur do not provide abundance and do not permit the reduction of human labor. Indeed, both the Chinese and Russian revolutions occurred in circumstances which required an increase in organized and self-sacrificing discipline rather than a decrease, if the goals of eradicating grinding poverty, educating the masses, and utilizing the natural resources of the country in the interest of the society as a whole were to be met. In a profoundly backward and impoverished society, the drive to eradicate material want and to create a modern nation-state apparently required a strengthening of central authority and ironclad discipline.

The United States, and perhaps other advanced industrial societies, may now be reaching the point where its material capacities have created the conditions for full emancipation—as envisaged by Marx. That is, we may be reaching the point at which material scarcity can be transcended and "alienated" labor can be performed by machines. The selections in this section have been chosen with this assumption in mind—namely, that it may finally be possible to imagine a revolution capable of fulfilling the vision of authentic self-government as an historically realizable process.

The established structure of authority, in the nation-state, in the economy, in education, and in the family, rests on principles rooted in scarcity. The stirrings of opposition and resistance at all these levels may be rooted in a growing realization that traditional principles are becoming obsolete.

As Richard Rubenstein suggests, there is a major tradition of resistance in American life, a tradition based on the failure of the system to recognize or protect the rights of a variety of oppressed groups against the encroachments of powerful interests. Rebellion in America has thus been largely defensive or it has been directed at winning equal rights under the Constitution on the part of groups whose rights were attacked or systematically denied. Periodically, the failure of established Federal authority to be responsive to group demands has, as Rubenstein shows, led to the emergence of new national coalitions which have forced political realignment and changed the structure of power.

Rubenstein's essay is useful, first because it demonstrates the extent to which resistance and challenge to national authority has been characteristic of our history; second because it suggests that a comparable process of group revolt, national coalition, and political reform is now occurring. Third, Rubenstein's essay is of interest because he suggests that *self-determination* has been a constant theme in all of these resistance struggles. It is not simply that Indians, farmers, workers, blacks, and students have sought a better standard of living, or basic individual rights. At bottom, according to Rubenstein, all of these revolts have embodied a vision of self-government. When such groups have been geographically based, such visions have been most clearly articulated—sometimes going so far as to call for secession. In other cases, groups without a territorial base have sought rights to self-organization and a direct voice in the institutions which controlled their lives.

Rubenstein's piece does not suggest what vision and program might be embodied by a new national coalition. If the past is any guide, the dream of self-government will be sacrificed for economic and social reforms at the national level. But perhaps the past is no longer a good guide to the future, especially if there is now arising a consciousness that existing structural arrangements are not simply unjust, but are illegitimate because they are positive hindrances to a realization of self-government made possible by the abolition of scarcity.

The pieces which follow Rubenstein's offer some concrete guides to the ways in which post-scarcity society could be organized so that obedience and domination can be replaced by cooperative, self-governing, self-realizing social relations. Each of these pieces build upon stirrings of consciousness which are now evident. They are therefore not simply utopian speculations on the good society, but more like practical suggestions for creating the conditions for self-determination.

Equality between the sexes may well be one of the most fundamental conditions for establishing a world without domination. Sexual domination and subordination is in itself the most pervasive form of domination. Its elimination would therefore enable one-half of the population to achieve forms of self-determination presently denied. But its implications go far deeper than simply providing women with an equal chance to have the degree of independence which men have. Alice Rossi suggests that the abolition of fulltime motherhood, and a reduction of the role of the nuclear family in childhood socialization, could have profound effects on character. One of the sources of authoritarian character may well be the fact that sex and power are so intertwined in our culture; males orient toward power in order to demonstrate and validate their masculinity. The link between maleness and dominance may account for strivings for power and for the tendency of fathers who have "failed" in the outside world to tyrannize their wives and children. Equality of the sexes could thus help liberate men from competitive and aggressive impulses, could facilitate the development of men who were capable of tender and nurturant feeling and action, while liberating women from the trap of domestic and consumerist submission described by Friedan. Further, if women's rights to independent self-development were recognized, then husbands would have to scale down their own ambitions and would be less likely to be trapped by the success-achievement syndrome. These consequences for individual character and cultural change brought on by the movement for women's liberation are increasingly being elaborated in the literature of the movement; I selected Rossi's piece, written in 1964, because it seems to be an unusually comprehensive statement of the concrete practical steps that would be necessary if sexual equality were to become a reality. Virtually everything Rossi advocated a decade ago has become a demand of the women's movement.

Bertrand Russell's essay, written forty years ago, is similarly prophetic. It is not that we have yet made a mass movement for a four-hour day. But increasingly, the kind of consciousness expressed by Russell has spread—that there is something fundamentally irrational about forcing people to organize their lives around menial and boring work in the interests of maintaining the rate of economic growth. Perhaps the most elementary meaning of self-determination is the right to control the use of one's time; the fact that this right is very largely unavailable to most people may well be a major source of youth's "alienation from adulthood."

Ivan Illich imaginatively sketches how life could be lived if work were reduced —education could be taken out of the schools, and learning and teaching could be made everyone's central vocation. Illich, it should be clear, is not simply talking about educational reform; rather he is expressing a total social vision, based on the notion that the truly human existence is centered on developing and sharing knowledge, skill, and imagination. In such a world, the authority of schoolmasters, experts, and officials would become irrelevant, and children would not have to be socialized to the habits of obedience.

Murray Bookchin suggests that the key to self-government lies in the decentralization of authority and the establishment of a society in which the self-governing community is the primary locus of power. Decentralization is basic to the implementation of participatory democracy and the revival of individual initiative; it also meshes with the aspirations of the American "subnations" to which Rubenstein refers.

C. Wright Mills, Harold Lasswell, and others cited in this volume suggest ways in which advanced technology can be used to create the most totalistic forms of authority ever devised. It is this technology which has given those in authority life and death power over the human race, which provides the impetus for increasing centralization of decision making, which permits means of surveillance and propagandistic manipulation on a hitherto unimagined scale, which generates feelings of powerlessness in millions of people, which separates men from the means of controlling the products and conditions of their work, and which creates such a glut of commodities that the structure of needs must be manipulated so that people will buy them. Bookchin suggests, however, that there is nothing inevitable about these uses of technology. If advanced technology were not harnessed to the drive for profit and the imperatives of empire, it could be used to free people from alienating labor, to reduce the workday, to create conditions for decentralized planning and allocation of resources, and to abolish material want for all people.

It is not machines which dominate us, but other men. These men claim the legitimate right to own and use the machines for interests they define and decide. As resistance spreads, they increasingly search for ways to get the rest of us to act like Cheerful Robots. Once we deny that technology can be the property of a few, once we find the way to reclaim its use for life rather than death, then we will have found the capacity for freedom that has so far eluded the human race.

SOME SUGGESTED READINGS

For other speculations on the possibilities for revolutionary, cultural, and social change in the United States, see the following: T. Roszak, *The Making of a Counter Culture* (New York: Doubleday, 1968); P. Slater, *The Pursuit of Loneliness* (Boston: Beacon, 1970); and R. Aya and N. Miller, *The New American Revolution* (New York: The Free Press, 1971). Also see M. Oppenheimer, *The Urban Guerrilla* (Chicago: Quadrangle, 1969).

The late Paul Goodman was probably the most creative formulater of practical utopian alternatives in our time. Books of his which touch directly on themes relevant to this volume include: *People or Personnel; Utopian Essays and Practical Proposals; Communitas; Growing Up Absurd.* The possible effects of sexual equality on male character are explored in R. V. Sampson, *The Psychology of Power* (New York: Vintage, 1968).

Some other books relevant to the problem of self-determination in advanced technological society are: E. Fromm, *Marx's Concept of Man* (New York: Ungar, 1961); H. Marcuse, *An Essay on Liberation* (Boston: Beacon, 1971); H. Arendt, *On Revolution* (New York: Viking, 1965); Andre Gorz, *Strategy for Labor* (Boston: Beacon, 1967); and R. Dahl, *After the Revolution?* (New Haven: Yale, 1971).

EQUALITY BETWEEN THE SEXES: AN IMMODEST PROPOSAL

Alice S. Rossi

. . . the principle which regulates the existing relations between the two sexes . . . is wrong in itself and [is] now the chief hindrance to human improvement; and . . . it ought to be replaced by a principle of perfect equality, admitting no power or privilege on the one side, nor disability on the other.

John Stuart Mill, 1869

When John Stuart Mill wrote his essay on "The Subjection of Women" in 1869, the two major things he argued for with elegance and persuasion were to extend the franchise to women, and to end the legal subordination of married women to their husbands. The movement for sex equality had already gathered considerable momentum in England and the United States by 1869, reaching its peak fifty years later, when the franchise was won by American women in 1920. In the decades since 1920, this momentum has gradually slackened, until by the 1960's American society has been losing rather than gaining ground in the growth toward sex equality. American women are not trying to extend their claim to equality from the political to the occupational and social arenas and often do not even seem interested in exercising the rights so bitterly won in the early decades of the twentieth century in politics and higher education. The constitutional amendment on equal rights for men and women has failed to pass Congress for seventeen consecutive years, and today a smaller proportion of college graduates are women than was true thirty years ago.

There is no overt antifeminism in our society in 1964, not because sex equality has been achieved,

From Daedalus, *Spring 1964 issue on "The Woman in America." Reprinted by permission of* Daedalus, *Journal of the American Academy of Arts and Sciences, Boston, Mass. Footnotes have been edited or deleted.*

but because there is practically no feminist spark left among American women. When I ask the brightest of my women college students about their future study and work plans, they either have none because they are getting married in a few months, or they show clearly that they have lowered their aspirations from professional and research fields that excited them as freshmen, to concentrate as juniors on more practical fields far below their abilities. Young women seem increasingly uncommitted to anything beyond early marriage, motherhood, and a suburban house. There are few Noras in contemporary American society because women have deluded themselves that the doll's house is large enough to find complete personal fulfillment within it.

It will be the major thesis of this essay that we need to reassert the claim to sex equality and to search for the means by which it can be achieved. By sex equality I mean a socially androgynous conception of the roles of men and women, in which they are equal and similar in such spheres as intellectual, artistic, political, and occupational interests and participation, complementary only in those spheres dictated by physiological differences between the sexes. This assumes the traditional conceptions of masculine and feminine are inappropriate to the kind of world we can live in in the second half of the twentieth century. An androgynous conception of sex role means that each sex will cultivate some of the characteristics usually associated with the other in traditional sex role definitions. This means that tenderness and expressiveness should be cultivated in boys and socially approved in men, so that a male of any age in our society would be psychologically and socially free to express these qualities in his social relationships. It means that achievement need, workmanship, and constructive aggression should be cultivated in girls and approved in women so that a female of any age would be similarly free to express these qualities in her social relationships. This is one of the points of contrast with the feminist goal of an earlier day: rather than a one-sided plea for women to adopt a masculine stance in the world, this definition of sex equality stresses the enlargement of the common ground on which men and women base their lives together by changing the social definitions of approved characteristics and behavior for both sexes.

It will be an assumption of this essay that by far the majority of the differences between the sexes which have been noted in social research are socially rather than physiologically determined. What proportion of these sex differences are physiologically based and what proportion are socially based is a question the social and physiological sciences cannot really answer at the present time. It is sufficient for my present purposes to note that the opportunities for social change toward a closer approximation of equality between the sexes are large enough within the area of sex differences now considered to be socially determined to constitute a challenging arena for thought and social action. This is my starting point. I shall leave to speculative discourse and future physiological research the question of what consitutes irreducible differences between the sexes.

There are three main questions I shall raise in this essay. Why was the momentum of the earlier feminist movement lost? Why should American society attempt to reach a state of sex equality as I have defined it above? What are the means by which equality between the sexes can be achieved?

WHY FEMINISM DECLINED

I shall discuss three factors which have been major contributors to the waning of feminism. The chief goals of the early leaders of the feminist movement were to secure the vote for women and to change the laws affecting marriage so that women would have equal rights to property and to their own children. As in any social reform movement or social revolution, the focus in the first stage

is on change in the legal code, whether this is to declare independence from a mother country, establish a constitution for a new nation, free the slaves, or secure the right of women to be equal citizens with men. But the social changes required to translate such law into the social fabric of a society are of a quite different order. Law by itself cannot achieve this goal. It is one thing to declare slaves free or to espouse a belief in racial equality; quite another matter to accept racial integration in all spheres of life, as many northern communities have learned in recent years. In a similar way, many people accept the legal changes which have reduced the inequality between men and women and espouse belief in sex equality, but resist its manifestation in their personal life. If a social movement rests content with legal changes without making as strong an effort to change the social institutions through which they are expressed, it will remain a hollow victory.

This is one of the things which occurred in the case of the feminist movement. Important as the franchise is, or the recent change in Civil Service regulations which prevents the personnel specification of "male only," the new law or regulation can be successful only to the extent that women exercise the franchise, or are trained to be qualified for and to aspire for the jobs they are now permitted to hold. There is no sex equality until women participate on an equal basis with men in politics, occupations, and the family. Law and administrative regulations must permit such participation, but women must want to participate and be able to participate. In politics and the occupational world, to be able to participate depends primarily on whether home responsibilities can be managed simultaneously with work or political commitments. Since women have had, and probably will continue to have, primary responsibility for child rearing, their participation in politics, professions, or the arts cannot be equal to that of men unless ways are devised to ease the combination of home and work responsibilities. This is precisely what has not occurred; at the same time, since fewer women today choose a career over marriage, the result has been a reduction in women's representation in the more challenging and demanding occupations.

By itself, the stress on legal change to the neglect of institutional change in the accommodations between family and work does not go very far in explaining why the feminist movement has lost momemtum. There is an important second factor which must be viewed in conjunction with this first one. The feminist movement has always been strongest when it was allied with other social reform movements. In the nineteenth century its linkage was with the antislavery movement, and in the early twentieth century it was allied to the social welfare movement. There is an interesting and a simple explanation of this: unlike any other type of social inequality, whether of race, class, religion, or nationality, sex is the only instance in which representatives of the unequal groups live in more intimate association with each other than with members of their own group. A woman is more intimately associated with a man than she is with any woman. This was not the case for lord-serf, master-slave, Protestant-Roman Catholic, white-Negro relationships unless or until the social groups involved reach a full equality. By linking the feminist cause to the antislavery or social welfare movement, women were able to work together with men of similar sympathies and in the process they enlisted the support of these men for the feminist cause. To a greater extent than any other underprivileged group, women need not only vigorous spokesmen and pacesetters of their own sex, but the support of men, to effect any major change in the status of women, whether in the personal sphere of individual relationships or on the level of social organization. The decline of political radicalism and the general state of affluence and social conservatism in American society since World War II have contributed in subtle ways to the decline of feminism, for women are not joined with men in any movement affecting an underprivileged group in American society. At the present time, marriage remains the only major path of social mobility for women in our society.

The general conservatism of the total society has also penetrated the academic disciplines, with side effects on the motivation and ability of women to exercise the rights already theirs or to press for an extension of them. Feminism has been undermined by the conservatism of psychology and sociology in the postwar period. Sociologists studying the family have borrowed heavily from selective findings in social anthropology and from psy-

choanalytic theory and have pronounced sex to be a universally necessary basis for role differentiation in the family. By extension, in the larger society women are seen as predominantly fulfilling nurturant, expressive functions and men the instrumental, active functions. When this viewpoint is applied to American society, intellectually aggressive women or tender expressive men are seen as deviants showing signs of "role conflict," "role confusion," or neurotic disturbance. They are not seen as a promising indication of a desirable departure from traditional sex role definitions.[1] In a similar way, the female sphere, the family, is viewed by social theorists as a passive, pawnlike institution, adapting to the requirements of the occupational, political, or cultural segments of the social structure, seldom playing an active role either in affecting the nature of other social institutions or determining the nature of social change. The implicit assumption in problem after problem in sociology is that radical social innovations are risky and may have so many unintended consequences as to make it unwise to propose or support them. Although the sociologist describes and analyzes social change, it is change already accomplished, seldom anticipated purposive social change.[2] When the changes are in process, they are defined as social problems, seldom as social opportunities.

Closely linked to this trend in sociology and social anthropology, and in fact partly attributable to it, is the pervasive permeation of psychoanalytic thinking throughout American society. Individual psychoanalysts vary widely among themselves, but when their theories are popularized by social scientists, marriage and family counselors, writers, social critics, pediatricians and mental health specialists, there emerges a common and conservative image of the woman's role. It is the traditional image of woman which is popularized: the woman who finds complete self-fulfillment in her exclusive devotion to marriage and parenthood. Women who thirty years ago might have chosen a career over a marriage, or restricted their family size to facilitate the combination of family and work roles, have been persuaded to believe that such choices reflect their inadequacy as women. It is this sense of failure as a woman that lies behind the defensive and apologetic note of many older unmarried professional women, the guilt which troubles the working mother (which I suspect goes up in direct proportion to the degree to which she is familiar with psychoanalytic ideas), the restriction of the level of aspiration of college women, the early plunge into marriage, the closed door of the doll's house.

Our society has been so inundated with psychoanalytic thinking that any dissatisfaction or conflict in personal and family life is considered to require solution on an individual basis. This goes well with the general American value stress on individualism, and American women have increasingly resorted to psychotherapy, the most highly individualized solution of all, for the answers to the problems they have as women. In the process the idea has been lost that many problems, even in the personal family sphere, cannot be solved on an individual basis, but require solution on a societal level by changing the institutional contexts within which we live.

The consequences of this acceptance of psychoanalytic ideas and conservatism in the social sciences have been twofold: first, the social sciences in the United States have contributed very little since the 1930's to any lively intellectual dialogue on sex equality as a goal or the ways of implementing that goal. Second, they have provided a quasi-scientific underpinning to educators, marriage counselors, mass media and advertising researchers, who together have partly created, and certainly reinforced, the withdrawal of millions of young American women from the mainstream of thought and work in our society.[3]

WHY SEEK EQUALITY BETWEEN THE SEXES?

This brings us to the second question: Why should American society attempt to reach a state of sex equality? If women seem satisfied with a more narrowly restricted life pattern than men would be, why should we seek to disturb this pattern? To begin with, I do not think this question is really relevant to the issue. There have been underprivileged groups throughout history which contained sizable proportions of contented, uncomplaining members, whether slaves, serfs, or a low status caste. But the most enlightened members of both the privileged and underprivileged groups in such societies came to see that inequality not only depressed the human potential of the subject groups but corrupted those in the superordinate groups. The lives of southern whites are as crippled by racial inequality as the lives of southern Negroes are impoverished. In the same way, many men spend their daytime hours away from home as vital cognitive animals and their nights and weekends in mental passivity and vegetation. Social and personal life is impoverished for some part of many men's lives because so many of their wives live in a perpetual state of intellectual and social impoverishment.

A second reason why American society should attempt to reach a state of full sex equality is that at the level our industrial society has now reached, it is no longer necessary for women to confine their life expectations to marriage and parenthood. Certain of the reasons for this have been increasingly stressed in recent years: with increased longevity, and smaller-sized families, the traditional mother role simply does not occupy a sufficient portion of a woman's life span to constitute any longer the exclusive adult role for which a young woman should be prepared.[4] American girls spend more time as apprentice mothers with their dolls than they will as adult women with their own babies, and there is half a lifetime still ahead by the time the youngest child enters high school. Although studies have shown that women today are working in the home roughly the same number of hours a week as their mothers did, this is not because they have to do so: technological innovations in the production and distribution of food, clothing and other household equipment have been such that homemaking no longer requires the specialized skills and time-consuming tasks it did until early in our century. Comtemporary women often turn what should be labor-saving devices into labor-making devices. In the light of the many time-consuming tasks the American mother fifty years ago had to perform, and the much longer work day for those in the labor force then, the woman in 1964 who holds down a full-time job will probably have as much or more time with her children as her grandmother had. Furthermore, most of the skills needed for adulthood are no longer taught within the family: child socialization is increasingly a shared enterprise between the parent and teachers, doctors, nurses, club leaders, and instructors in an assortment of special skills.

These are perhaps all familiar points. What has not been seen is the more general point that *for the first time in the history of any known society, motherhood has become a full-time occupation for adult women.* In the past, whether a woman lived on a farm, a Dutch city in the seventeenth century, or a colonial town in the eighteenth century, women in all strata of society except the very top were never able to be full-time mothers as the twentieth-century, middle-class American woman has become. These women were productive members of farm and craft teams along with their farmer, baker, or printer husbands and other adult kin. Children either shared in the work of the household or were left to amuse themselves; their mothers did not have the time to organize their play, worry about their development, discuss their problems. These women were not lonely because the world came into their homes in the form of customers, clients or patients in villages and towns, or farmhands and relatives on the farm; such women had no reason to complain of the boredom and solitude of spending ten-hour days alone with babies and young children because their days were peopled with adults. There were no child specialists to tell the colonial merchant's wife or pioneer farmer's wife that her absorption in spinning, planting, churning and preserving left her children on their own too much, that how she fed her baby would shape his adult personality, or that leaving children with a variety of other adults while she worked would make them insecure.

There are two important questions this analysis raises: Why has full-time motherhood been accepted by the overwhelming majority of American women, and how successful has been the new pattern of full-time motherhood of the past forty years or so? I believe the major answer to the first question is that the American woman has been encouraged by the experts to whom she has turned for guidance in child rearing to believe that her children need her continuous presence, supervision, and care and that she should find complete fulfillment in this role. If, for example, a woman reads an article by Dr. Spock on working mothers, she is informed that any woman who finds full-time

motherhood produces nervousness is showing a "residue of difficult relationships in her own childhood"; if irritability and nervousness are not assuaged by a brief trip or two, she is probably in an emotional state which can be "relieved through regular counseling in a family social agency, or, if severe, through psychiatric treatment"; and finally, "any mother of a preschool child who is considering a job should discuss the issues with a social worker before making her decision."[5] Since the social worker shares the same analytic framework that Dr. Spock does, there is little doubt what the advice will be; the woman is left with a judgment that wanting more than motherhood is not natural but a reflection of her individual emotional disturbance.

The fundamental tenet of the theory underlying such advice is that the physically and emotionally healthy development of the infant requires the loving involvement of the mother with the child. If an infant does not receive stable continuous mothering there is almost invariably severe physical and emotional disturbance. There is apparently ample clinical evidence to support these points. Studies have suggested that prolonged separation from parents, and particularly from the mother, has serious effects upon infants and young children. However, practitioners make unwarranted extrapolations from these findings when they advise that *any* separation of mother and child is risky and hazardous for the healthy development of the child.[6] Despite the fact that the empirical evidence stems from instances of prolonged, traumatic separation caused by such things as the death or serious illness of the mother, or the institutionalization of the child, this viewpoint is applied to the situation of an employed mother absent from the home on a regular basis. No one predicts that any dire consequences will flow from a woman's absence from home several afternoons a week to engage in a shopping spree, keep medical appointments, or play bridge; nor is a father considered to produce severe disturbance in his young children even if his work schedule reduces contact with them to the daylight hours of a weekend. But women who have consulted pediatricians and family counselors about their resuming work are firmly told that they should remain at home, for the sake of their children's emotional health.

What effect *does* maternal employment have upon children? Many sociologists of the family have raised this question during the past fifteen years, expecting to find negative effects as psychoanalytic theory predicted. In fact, the focus of most maternal employment studies has been on the effect of mothers' working upon the personalities of their children, somewhat less often on the tensions and strains between the mother role and the occupational role, seldom on the question of how maternal employment affects the woman's satisfactions with herself, her home, and marriage. To date, *there is no evidence of any negative effects traceable to maternal employment;* children of working mothers are no more likely than children of nonworking mothers to become delinquent, to show neurotic symptoms, to feel deprived of maternal affection, to perform poorly in school, to lead narrower social lives, etc.[7] Many of the researchers in the 1950's frankly admitted surprise at their negative findings. In a study reported in 1962,[8] the only significant difference found between working and nonworking mothers was the mother's confidence about her role as mother: 42 per cent of the working mothers but only 24 per cent of the non-working mothers expressed concern about their maternal role, "often by explicit questioning and worry as to whether working is interfering with their relationships and the rearing of their children." Yet these working women did not actually differ from the at-home mothers in the very things that concerned them: there were no differences between these women in the emotional relationships with their children, household allocation of responsibilities, principles of child rearing, etc. The working mothers appeared to share the prevailing view that their children would suffer as a result of their employment, though in fact their children fare as well as those of nonworking mothers.

It would appear, therefore, that the employment of women when their children are eight years of age or older has no negative effect on the children. What about the earlier years, from infancy until school age? In the American literature, there is little to refer to as yet which bears directly upon the effect of maternal employment on the infant or toddler, partly because employment of mothers with preschool children is so negligible in the

United States, partly because the measurement of "effects" on young children is difficult and cannot be done with the research tools which have been used in most studies of maternal employment effects—questionnaires administered to mothers and to their school-age children.

There is, however, one significant body of data which is of considerable relevance to the question of the effect of maternal employment upon infants and very young children. Maternal employment is a regular pattern of separation of mother and child: the Israeli kibbutzim are collective settlements with several decades of experience in precisely this pattern. On the kibbutz, infants live in children's houses where their physical care and training are largely handled. During the infancy months the mother visits the house to feed the infant; as toddlers, children begin a pattern of visiting with their parents for a few hours each day, living in the children's houses for the remaining portions of their days and nights. A number of studies have been conducted to investigate the effect of this intermittent multiple mothering on the young child.[9] They all point to essentially the same conclusion: the kibbutz child-rearing practices have no deleterious effects upon the subsequent personality development of the children involved. In fact, there are a number of respects in which the kibbutz-reared Israeli children exceed those reared in the traditional farm family: the kibbutz children showed a more accurate perception of reality, more breadth of interest and cultural background, better emotional control and greater overall maturity.

Continuous mothering, even in the first few years of life, does not seem to be necessary for the healthy emotional growth of a child.[10] The crux of the matter appears to be in the nature of the care which is given to the child. If a child is reared by a full-time mother who is rejecting and cold in her treatment of him, or if a child is reared in an institutional setting lacking in warmth and stimulation and with an inadequate staff, both children will show personality disturbances in later years. If the loving care of the biological mother is shared by other adults who provide the child with a stable loving environment, the child will prosper at least as well as and potentially better than one with a good full-time mother.[11] In the section below on child care and careers, I shall suggest institutional innovations which would ensure good quality care for children and ease the combination of work and child rearing for women.

Turning now to the second question raised above: How successful has the new pattern of full-time motherhood been? Are women more satisfied with their lives in the mid-twentieth century than in the past? Does motherhood fulfill them, provide them with a sufficient canvas to occupy a lifetime? Are contemporary children living richer lives, developing greater ego strength to carry them through a complex adulthood? Are children better off for having full-time mothers?

I think the answer to all the questions posed above is a firm *no.* Educators, child psychologists, and social analysts report an increasing tendency for American middle-class children to be lacking in initiative, excessively dependent on others for direction and decision, [and] physically soft.[12] Our children have more toys and play equipment than children in any other society, yet they still become bored and ask their mothers for "something to do." No society has as widespread a problem of juvenile delinquency and adolescent rebellion as the United States. Alcoholism, compulsive sex-seeking and adolescent delinquency are no longer social problems confined to the working-class, socially disorganized sections of our cities, but have been on the increase in the middle-class suburb in the past twenty years, and involve more women and girls than in the past. There is a strong strand of male protest against the mother or "matriarch" in both our beatnik culture and our avant-garde literature: social and artistic extremes are seldom fully deviant from the middle range in a society, but show in an exaggerated heightened way the same though less visible tendencies in the social majority.

In a large proportion of cases, the etiology of mental illness is linked to inadequacy in the mother-child relationship. A high proportion of the psychoneurotic discharges from the army during World War II was traced to these young soldiers' overly dependent relationships to their mothers.[13] This has been the subject of much earnest discussion in the years since the war, but the focus has remained on the mother-*son* relationship, I suspect only because as a fighter, a professional man, or a worker, male performance is seen to be more crucial for society than female performance. But dependence, immaturity, and ego diffusion have been characteristic of daughters as well as sons. The only difference is that, in the case of daughters, this less often reaches the overt level of a social problem because young women move quickly from under their mothers' tutelage into marriage and parenthood of their own: female failures are therefore not as socially visible, for they are kept within the privacy of family life and psychoanalytic case records. It is a short-sighted view indeed to consider the immature wife, dominating mother, or interfering mother-in-law as a less serious problem to the larger society than the male homosexual, psychoneurotic soldier, or ineffectual worker, for it is the failure of the mother which perpetuates the cycle from one generation to the next, affecting sons and daughters alike.

Disturbing trends of this sort cannot all be traced to the American women's excessive and exclusive involvement with home and family. We live in turbulent times, and some part of these trends reflects the impact of world tension and conflict. But there is no reason to assume that world tension is relevant to many of them. Emotional and physical difficulties after childbirth or during the menopause years, the higher incidence of college girl than college boy breakdowns, the shrunken initiative and independence of children, are clearly not explained by world conflict. Besides, vast sections of American society remain totally unmoved and unaffected by international political and military events until they directly impinge on their own daily lives. Since history is both written and produced more by men than by women, the fact that our writers are preoccupied with the relationship to the mother points to difficulties in our family system more than the course of world events.

It is a paradox of our social history that motherhood has become a full-time occupation in precisely the era when objectively it could, and perhaps should, be a part-time occupation for a short phase of a woman's life span. I suspect that the things women do for and with their children have been needlessly elaborated to make motherhood a full-time job. Unfortunately, in this very process the child's struggle for autonomy and independence, for privacy and the right to worry things through for himself are subtly and pervasively reduced by the omnipresent mother. As a young child he is given great permissive freedom, but he must exercise it under supervision. As an adolescent he is given a great deal of freedom, but his parents worry excessively about what he does with it. Edgar Friedenberg has argued that there is entirely too much parental concentration on adolescent children, with the result that it has become increasingly difficult to *be* an adolescent in American society.[14] He suggests that parents are interested in youth to the extent that they find their own stage of life uninteresting. Middle-class children are observed and analyzed by their mothers as though they were hothouse plants psychologically, on whose personalities any pressure might leave an indelible bruise. If a woman's adult efforts are concentrated exclusively on her children, she is likely more to stifle than broaden her children's perspective and preparation for adult life. Any stress or failure in a child becomes a failure of herself, and she is therefore least likely to truly help her child precisely when the child most needs support. In myriad ways the mother binds the child to her, dampening his initiative, resenting his growing independence in adolescence, creating a subtle dependence which makes it difficult for the child to achieve full adult stature without a rebellion which leaves him with a mixture of resentment and guilt that torments him in his mother's declining years.

It seems to me no one has linked these things together adequately. Psychiatric counselors of college students frequently have as their chief task that of helping their young patients to free themselves from the entangling web of dependence upon their parents, primarily their mothers, and encouraging them to form stable independent lives of their own. In other words, if the patient is eighteen years old the analyst tries to help her free herself from her mother, but if the next patient is twenty-five years old with young children at home, the analyst tells her the children would suffer emotional damage if she left them on a regular basis to hold down a job. The very things which would reduce the excessive dependency of children before it becomes a critical problem are discouraged by the counselor or analyst during the years when the dependency is being formed. If it is true that the adult is what the child was, and if we wish adults to be assertive,

independent, responsible people, then they should be reared in a way which prevents excessive dependence on a parent. They should be cared for by a number of adults in their childhood, and their parents should truly encourage their independence and responsibility during their youthful years, not merely give lip service to these parental goals. The best way to encourage such independence and responsibility in the child is for the mother to be a living model of these qualities herself. If she had an independent life of her own, she would find her stage of life interesting, and therefore be less likely to live for and through her children. By maintaining such an independent life, the American mother might finally provide her children with something she can seldom give when she is at home—a healthy dose of inattention, and a chance for adolescence to be a period of fruitful immaturity and growth. If enough American women developed vital and enduring interests outside the family and remained actively in them throughout the child-bearing years, we might then find a reduction in extreme adolescent rebellion, immature early marriages, maternal domination of children, and interference by mothers and mothers-in-law in the lives of married children.

There remains one further general characteristic of our industrial society which has relevance to the question of why American society should achieve full sex equality. Our family unit is small, for the most part geographically if not socially isolated from its kin. This small family unit is possible because of the increased longevity in highly industrialized societies. In agricultural societies, with their high rate of mortality, many parents die before they have completed the rearing of their young. The extended family provided substitutes for such parents without disturbing the basic lines of kin affiliation and property rights of these children. In our modern family system it is an unusual event for women or men to be widowed while they have young dependent children. This also means, however, that American families must fend for themselves in the many emergencies less critical than the death of a spouse: army service, long business or professional trips, prolonged physical or emotional illness, separation, or divorce often require that one spouse carry the primary responsibility for the family, even if this is cushioned or supplemented by insurance, government aid, paid help-ers, or relatives. The insurance advertisements which show fathers bending over a cradle and be-gin "What would happen if?" evoke a twinge of fear in their readers precisely because parents rec-ognize the lonely responsible positions they would be in if serious illness or death were to strike their home. In our family system, then, it is a decided asset if men and women can quickly and easily substitute for or supplement each other as parents and as breadwinners. I believe these are important elements in the structure of our economy and fam-ily system which exert pressure toward an equality between men and women. It is not merely that a companionate or equalitarian marriage is a desir-able relationship between wife and husband, but that the functioning of an urban industrial society is facilitated by equality between men and women in work, marriage, and parenthood.

The conclusions I have drawn from this analysis are as follows: Full-time motherhood is neither sufficiently absorbing to the woman nor beneficial to the child to justify a contemporary woman's devoting fifteen or more years to it as her exclusive occupation. Sooner or later—and I think it should be sooner—women have to face the question of who they are besides their children's mother.

A major solution to this quest would be found in the full and equal involvement of women in the occupational world, the culmination of the feminist movement of the last one hundred and fifty years. This is not to overlook the fact that involvement as a volunteer in politics or community organizations or a serious dedication to a creative art can be a solution for many women. These areas of partici-pation and involvement provide innumerable women with a keen sense of life purpose, and women are making significant and often innovative contributions in these pursuits. A job *per se* does not provide a woman, or a man either, with any magical path to self-fulfillment; nor does just any community volunteer work, or half-hearted dab-bling in a creative art.

Women are already quite well represented in volunteer organizations in American communities. However, broadening the range of alternatives open to women and chosen by women for their life patterns is still to be achieved in the occupational world. It is also true that at the most challenging

reaches of both political and community volunteer work, the activities have become increasingly pro-fessionalized. Thus while many women have and will continue to make innovative contributions to these fields as volunteers, such opportunities have become limited. Furthermore, many such women often find themselves carrying what amounts to a full-time job as a "volunteer executive," yet nei-ther the recognition nor the rewards are equivalent to what they would receive in comparable posi-tions in the occupational system.[15] Hence, the ma-jor focus in this essay will be on the means by which the full and equal involvement of well-educated women in the occupational world may be achieved. For reasons which will become clear later, I believe that the occupational involvement of women would also be the major means for re-ducing American women's dominance in marriage and parenthood, and thus for allowing for the par-ticipation of men as equal partners in family life.

Of course there have already been changes in the extent and the nature of women's participation in the American labor force. Indeed, this is some-times cited as proof that sex equality has been achieved in the United States. There are roughly twenty-three million American women in the labor force, and it is predicted that this will swell to thirty million by 1970. About three-fifths of these women are married, an increase of well over 20 per cent since 1940. It should be noted that this increase came predominantly from women be-tween the ages of 35 and 54 years, after the child-rearing years and before the usual retirement age for workers. This is a major social change, to be sure, and people who still raise the question of whether married women should work are arguing after the fact, for such women are doing so at increasing rates. The point is, however, that most American women—65 per cent—do *not* work outside the home, and those who do are found largely in blue-collar or low-skill, white-collar oc-cupations. Men fill roughly 85 per cent of the very top professional and technical jobs in the United States. Furthermore, only a very small proportion of American wives work if their husbands are in the middle and top income brackets, or if they have young children. Finally, the distribution of the female labor force by age shows two major peaks of female participation, before and for a short time after marriage, and then for the fifteen years from their early forties through middle fifties. Withdrawal and re-entry many years later is now a common female work pattern in the United States. As long as this pattern continues, women will not increase their representation in the top professional and technical occupations.

Over the past twenty years, women in many European countries have doubled or more their representation in the professional occupations. By comparison, American women constitute a smaller proportion of the professional world today than they did twenty years ago. That this reflects a lowering of ambition among American women is suggested by the fact that of all the women capable of doing college work, only one out of four do so, compared to one out of two men. This is the point at which we begin to tap a deeper root of women's motivations in the United States. Whether a woman works steadily throughout her marriage or returns to work after the child-rearing period, no significant increase of women in the professional and high-skill job categories will occur unless American women's attitude toward education and work is changed.To study and to prepare for a future job "in case I have to work" is just as poor a preparation for occupational participation as the postponement of learning domestic skills "until I have to" is a poor preparation for the homemaker role. Both views reflect a digging in of the heels into the adolescent moment of a lifetime. In many ways the middle-class girl considers only the present, the here-and-now, as do most members of the working class, and not the future, as do her father, brothers, and male friends. There is evidence to suggest that such an emphasis on the present is characteristic not only of the American woman at college age, but also more generally throughout her life span. Thus, Gallup's portrait of the American woman shows the same characteristic at all points during the younger half of the life cycle: Young unmarried women as well as mature women with their children now entering high school give little thought to and no preparation for their life over forty years of age.[16]

The middle-class wife of a successful business executive or professional man has a special problem. To earn a salary in the occupational world, she will be judged by her own achieved merits without regard to her social position or her husband's influence. Unless she has had the education and experience necessary to hold a position of some prestige, she will experience social and personal barriers to entering the labor force. In the absence of such education and experience, she is qualified to be only the occupational subordinate of men who are her equals socially, a status incongruity few women are likely to tolerate. By contrast, no matter how menial, her service as a volunteer will be socially approved. Unless such women secure specialized training before marriage, or acquire it after marriage, there will be little increase in the proportion of working wives and mothers in the upper half of the middle class. Many such women with a flair for organization have found full scope for their independent fulfillment in volunteer work in politics, education, social welfare, and the arts. Unfortunately, there are innumerable other women for whom such outlets have little attraction who realize they have missed their chance for independent self-fulfillment, and who have little opportunity for a second chance by their late forties.

It has been argued by some sociologists that the American marriage is already too fragile to sustain competition at comparable skill levels between spouses.[17] If this were true, and women are also reluctant to work at lower prestige jobs than their husbands, this would effectively freeze most middle-class women out of the occupational world. I would raise three points concerning this assumption. First, husbands and working wives are usually found in different segments of the occupational system, which makes comparison of success a difficult matter. For example, is an architect working for a large firm and earning $20,000 a year more or less successful than his wife who directs a large family welfare agency and earns $15,000 a year? Second, even were such achievements in nonfamily roles to provoke some competitive feeling between husband and wife, I think the consequences of this competition are far less potentially harmful to the marriage or to the children than the situation of the well-educated, able woman who is not working and engages instead in a competition with her husband for the affections and primary loyalties of the children. If a woman is markedly more successful than her husband, it would probably create difficulty in the marriage, particularly if there are residues of traditional expectations of male breadwinner dominance on the part of either partner to the marriage. But competition does not necessarily mean conflict. It can be a social spice and a source of pride and stimulation in a marriage of equals. Last, one must face up to the fact that a new social goal exacts a price. A change toward sex equality may cause some temporary marital dislocations, but this is not sufficient reason to expect all women to remain enclosed in the past.

INSTITUTIONAL LEVERS FOR ACHIEVING SEX EQUALITY

In turning to the problem of how equality between the sexes may be implemented as a societal goal, I shall concentrate on the three major areas of child care, residence, and education. Institutional change in these areas in no sense exhausts the possible spheres in which institutional change could be effected to facilitate the goal of sex equality. Clearly government and industry, for example, could effect highly significant changes in the relations between the sexes. But one must begin somewhere, and I have chosen these three topics, for they all involve questions of critical significance to the goal of equality between men and women.

1. It is widely assumed that rearing children and maintaining a career is so difficult a combination that except for those few women with an extraordinary amount of physical strength, emotional endurance, and a dedicated sense of calling to their work, it is unwise for women to attempt the combination. Women who have successfully combined child-rearing and careers are considered out of the ordinary, although many men with far heavier work responsibilities who yet spend willing, loving hours as fathers, and who also contribute to home maintenance, are cause for little comment. We should be wary of the assumption that home and work combinations are necessarily difficult. The simplified contemporary home and smaller-sized family of a working mother today probably represent a lesser burden of responsibility than that shouldered by her grandmother.

This does not mean that we should overlook the real difficulties that are involved for women who attempt this combination. Working mothers do have primary responsibility for the hundreds of details involved in home maintenance, as planners and managers, even if they have household help to do the actual work. No one could suggest that child-rearing and a career are easy to combine, or even that this is some royal road to greater happiness, but only that the combination would give innumerable intelligent and creative women a degree of satisfaction and fulfillment that they cannot obtain in any other way. Certainly many things have to "give" if a woman works when she also has young children at home. Volunteer and social activities, gardening and entertaining may all have to be curtailed. The important point to recognize is that as children get older, it is far easier to resume these social activities than it is to resume an interrupted career. The major difficulty, and the one most in need of social innovation, is the problem or providing adequate care for the children of working mothers.

If a significant number of American middle-class women wish to work while their children are still young and in need of care and supervision, who are these mother-substitutes to be? In the American experience to date, they have been either relatives or paid domestic helpers. A study conducted by the Children's Bureau in 1958 outlines the types of child-care arrangements made by women working full time who had children under twelve years of age.[18] The study showed that the majority of these children (57 per cent) were cared for by relatives: fathers, older siblings, grandparents, and others. About 21 per cent were cared for by nonrelatives, including neighbors as well as domestic helpers. Only 2 per cent of the children were receiving group care—in day nurseries, day-care centers, settlement houses, nursery schools, and the like. Of the remainder, 8 per cent were expected to take care of themselves, the majority being the "latch-key" youngsters of ten and twelve years of age about whom we have heard a good deal in the press in recent years.

These figures refer to a national sample of employed mothers and concern women in blue-collar jobs and predominantly low-skill, white-collar jobs. Presumably the proportion of middle-class working mothers who can rely on either relatives or their husbands would be drastically lower than this national average, and will probably decline even further in future years. Many of today's, and more of tomorrow's American grandmothers are going to be wage earners themselves and not baby-sitters for their grandchildren. In addition, as middle-class women enter the occupational world, they will experience less of a tug to remain close to the kinswomen of their childhood, and hence may contribute further to the pattern of geographic and social separation between young couples and both sets of their parents. Nor can many middle-class husbands care for their children, for their work hours are typically the same as those of their working wives: there can be little dovetailing of the work schedules of wives and husbands in the middle class as there can be in the working class.

At present, the major child-care arrangement for the middle-class woman who plans a return to work has to be hired household help. In the 1920's the professional and business wife-mother had little difficulty securing such domestic help, for there were thousands of first-generation immigrant girls and women in our large cities whose first jobs in America were as domestic servants. In the 1960's, the situation is quite different: the major source of domestic help in our large cities is Negro and Puerto Rican women. Assuming the continuation of economic affluence and further success in the American Negro's struggle for equal opportunity in education, jobs, and housing, this reservoir will be further diminished in coming decades. The daughters of many present-day Negro domestic servants will be able to secure far better-paying and more prestigeful jobs than their mothers can obtain in 1964. There will be increasing difficulty of finding adequate child-care help in future years as a result.

The problem is not merely that there may be decreasing numbers of domestic helpers available at the same time more women require their aid. There is an even more important question involved: Are domestic helpers the best qualified persons to leave in charge of young children? Most middle-class families have exacting standards for the kind of teachers and the kind of schools they would like their children to have. But a working mother who searches for a competent woman to leave in charge of her home has to adjust to con-siderably lower standards than she would tolerate in any nursery school program in which she placed her young son or daughter, either because such competent help is scarce, or because the margin of salary left after paying for good child care and the other expenses associated with employment is very slight.

One solution to the problem of adequate child care would be an attempt to upgrade the status of child-care jobs. I think one productive way would be to develop a course of study which would yield a certificate for practical mothering, along the lines that such courses and certificates have been developed for practical nursing. There would be several important advantages to such a program. There are many older women in American communities whose lives seem empty because their children are grown and their grandchildren far away, yet who have no interest in factory or sales work, for they are deeply committed to life and work within the context of a home. Indeed, there are many older women who now work in factories or as cashiers or salesclerks who would be much more satisfied with child-care jobs, if the status and pay for such jobs were upgraded. These are the women, sometimes painfully lonely for contact with children, who stop young mothers to comment on the baby in the carriage, to talk with the three-year-old and to discuss their own distant grandchildren. I think many of these women would be attracted by a program of "refresher" courses in first aid, child development, books and crafts appropriate for children of various ages, and the special problems of the mother substitute-child relationship. Such a program would build upon their own experiences as mothers but would update and broaden their knowledge, bringing it closer to the values and practices of the middle-class woman who is seeking a practical mother for her family. Substitute motherhood for which she earns a wage, following active motherhood of her own, could provide continuity, meaning and variety to the life-span of those American women who are committed to the traditional conception of woman's role. Such a course of study might be developed in a number of school contexts—a branch of a college department of education, an adult education extension program or a school of nursing.

A longer-range solution to the problem of child

care will involve the establishment of a network of child-care centers. Most of the detailed plans for such centers must be left for future discussion, but there are several important advantages to professionally run child-care centers which should be noted. Most important, better care could be provided by such centers than any individual mother can provide by hiring a mother's helper, housekeeper or even the practical mother I have just proposed. In a child-care center, there can be greater specialization of skills, better facilities and equipment, and play groups for the children. Second, a child-care center would mean less expense for the individual working mother, and both higher wages and shorter hours for the staff of the center. Third, these centers could operate on a full-time, year-round schedule, something of particular importance for women trained in professional or technical fields, the majority of which can be handled only on a full-time basis. Except for the teaching fields, such women must provide for the afternoon care of their nursery school and kindergarten-age children, after-school hours for older children and three summer months for all their children. Fourth, a child-care center could develop a roster of home-duty practical mothers or practical nurses to care for the ill or convalescent child at home, in much the way school systems now call upon substitute teachers to cover the classes of absent regular teachers.

A major practical problem is where to locate such child-care centers. During the years of experimentation which would follow acceptance of this idea, they might be in a variety of places, under a variety of organizational auspices, as a service facility offered by an industrial firm, a large insurance company, a university, the federal or a state government. Community groups of women interested in such service might organize small centers of their own much as they have informal pooled baby-sitting services and cooperatively run nursery schools at the present time.

I believe that one of the most likely contexts for early experimentation with such child-care centers is the large urban university. As these universities continue to expand in future years, in terms of the size of the student body, the varied research institutes associated with the university and the expansion of administrative, technical, and counseling

personnel, there will be increasing opportunity and increasing need for the employment of women. A child-care center established under the auspices of a major university would facilitate the return for training of older women to complete or refresh advanced training, forestall the dropping out of younger graduate married women with infants and young children to care for, and attract competent professional women to administrative, teaching or research positions, who would otherwise withdraw from their fields for the child-rearing years. It would also be an excellent context within which to innovate a program of child care, for the university has the specialists in psychology, education, and human development on whom to call for the planning, research, and evaluation that the establishment of child-care centers would require. If a university-sponsored child-care program were successful and widely publicized, it would then constitute an encouragement and a challenge to extend child-care centers from the auspices of specific organizations to a more inclusive community basis. A logical location for community child-care centers may be as wings of the elementary schools, which have precisely the geographic distribution throughout a city to make for easy access between the homes of very young children and the centers for their daytime care. Since school and center would share a location, it would also facilitate easy supervision of older children during the after-school hours. The costs of such care would also be considerably reduced if the facilities of the school were available for the older children during after-school hours, under the supervision of the staff of the child-care center. There are, of course, numerous problems to be solved in working out the details of any such program under a local educational system, but assuming widespread support for the desirability of community facilities for child care, these are technical and administrative problems well within the competence of school and political officials in our communities.

I have begun this discussion of the institutional changes needed to effect equality between the sexes with the question of child-care provision because it is of central importance in permitting women to enter and remain in the professional, technical and administrative occupations in which they are presently so underrepresented. Unless provision for child care is made, women will continue to find it necessary to withdraw from active occupational involvement during the child-rearing years. However, the professional and scientific fields are all growing in knowledge and skill, and even a practitioner who remains in the field often has difficulty keeping abreast of new developments. A woman who withdraws for a number of years from a professional field has an exceedingly difficult time catching up. The more exacting the occupation, then, the shorter the period of withdrawal should probably be from active participation in the labor force. If a reserve of trained practical mothers were available, a professional woman could return to her field a few months after the birth of a child, leaving the infant under the care of a practical mother until he or she reached the age of two years, at about which age the child could enter a child-care center for daytime care. Assuming a two-child family, this could mean not more than one year of withdrawal from her professional field for the working mother.

2. The preferred residential pattern of the American middle class in the postwar decades has been suburban. In many sections of the country it is difficult to tell where one municipality ends and another begins, for the farm, forest, and waste land between towns and cities have been built up with one housing development after another. The American family portrayed in the mass media typically occupies a house in this sprawling suburbia, and here too, are the American women, and sometimes men, whose problems are aired and analyzed with such frequency. We know a good deal about the characteristics and quality of social life in the American suburb[19] and the problems of the men and women who live in them. We hear about the changing political complexion of the American suburbs, the struggle of residents to provide sufficient community facilities to meet their growing needs. But the social and personal difficulties of suburban women are more likely to be attributed to their early family relationships or to the contradictory nature of· the socialization of girls in our society than to any characteristic of the environment in which they now live. My focus will be somewhat different: I shall examine the suburban residence pattern for the limitations it imposes on the utilization of women's creative work abilities

and the participation of men in family life. Both limitations have important implications for the lives of boys and girls growing up in the suburban home.

The geographic distance between home and work has a number of implications for the role of the father-husband in the family. It reduces the hours of possible contact between children and their fathers. The hour or more men spend in cars, buses, or trains may serve a useful decompression function by providing time in which to sort out and assess the experiences at home and the events of the work day, but it is questionable whether this outweighs the disadvantage of severely curtailing the early morning and later afternoon hours during which men could be with their children.

The geographic distance also imposes a rigid exclusion of the father from the events which highlight the children's lives. Commuting fathers can rarely participate in any special daytime activities at home or at school, whether a party, a play the child performs in, or a conference with a teacher. It is far less rewarding to a child to report to his father at night about such a party or part in a play than to have his father present at these events. If the husband-father must work late or attend an evening function in the city, he cannot sandwich in a few family hours but must remain in the city. This is the pattern which prompted Margaret Mead to characterize the American middle-class father as the "children's mother's husband," and partly why mother looms so oversized in the lives of suburban children.

Any social mixing of family-neighborhood and job associates is reduced or made quite formal: A work colleague cannot drop in for an after-work drink or a Saturday brunch when an hour or more separates the two men and their families. The father-husband's office and work associates have a quality of unreality to both wife and children. All these things sharpen the differences between the lives of men and women—fewer mutual acquaintances, less sharing of the day's events, and perhaps most importantly, less simultaneous filling of their complementary parent roles. The image of parenthood to the child is mostly motherhood, a bit of fatherhood and practically no parenthood as a joint enterprise shared at the same time by father and mother. Many suburban parents, I suspect, spend more time together as verbal parents—dis-

cussing their children in the children's absence—
than they do actively interacting with their children, the togetherness cult notwithstanding. For
couples whose relationship in courtship and early
marriage was equalitarian, the pressures are strong
in the suburban setting for parenthood to be highly
differentiated and skewed to an ascendant position
of the mother. Women dominate the family, men
the job world.

The geographic distance between home and the
center of the city restricts the world of the wife-
mother in a complementary fashion. Not only does
she have to do and be more things to her children,
but she is confined to the limitations of the suburban community for a great many of her extra-
familial experiences. That suburban children are
restricted in their social exposure to other young
children and relatively young adults, mostly
women and all of the same social class, has often
been noted. I think the social restriction of the
young wife to women of her own age and class is
of equal importance: with very few older persons
in her immediate environment, she has little first-
hand exposure to the problems attending the emp-
ty-nest stage of life which lies ahead for herself. It
is easy for her to continue to be satisfied to live
each day as it comes, with little thought of preparing for the thirty-odd years when her children are
no longer dependent upon her. If the suburban
wife-mother had more opportunity to become ac-
quainted with older widows and grandmothers,
this would be pressed home to her in a way that
might encourage a change in her unrealistic expectations of the future, with some preparation for that
stage of life while she is young.[20]

If and when the suburban woman awakens from
this short-range perspective and wants either to
work or to prepare for a return to work when her
children are older, how is she to do this, given the
suburban pattern of residence? It is all very well to
urge that school systems should extend adult education, that colleges and universities must make it
possible for older women to complete education
interrupted ten or more years previously or to be
retrained for new fields; but this is a difficult program for the suburban wife to participate in. She
lives far from the center of most large cities, where
the educational facilities tend to be concentrated,
in a predominantly middle-class community,

where domestic help is often difficult to arrange
and transportation often erratic during the hours
she would be using it.

It is for these reasons that I believe any attempt
to draw a significant portion of married women
into the mainstream of occupational life must involve a reconsideration of the suburban pattern of
living. Decentralization of business and industry
has only partly alleviated the problem: a growing
proportion of the husbands living in the suburbs
also work in the suburbs. There are numerous
shops and service businesses providing job opportunities for the suburban wife. Most such jobs,
however, are at skill levels far below the ability
potential and social status of the suburban, middle-
class wife. Opportunities for the more exacting
professional, welfare, and business jobs are still
predominantly in the central sections of the city. In
addition, since so many young wives and mothers
in this generation married very young, before their
formal education was completed, they will need
more schooling before they can hope to enter the
fields in which their talents can be most fruitfully
exercised, in jobs which will not be either dull or
a status embarrassment to themselves and their
husbands. Numerous retail stores have opened
suburban branches; colleges and universities have
yet to do so. A woman can spend in the suburb,
but she can neither learn nor earn.

That some outward expansion of American cities has been necessary is clear, given the population increase in our middle- to large-sized cities.
But there are many tracts in American cities between the business center and the outlying suburbs
which imaginative planning and architectural design could transform and which would attract the
men and women who realize the drawbacks of a
suburban residence. Unless there is a shift in this
direction in American housing, I do not think there
can be any marked increase in the proportion of
married middle-class women who will enter the
labor force. That Swedish women find work and
home easier to combine than American women is
closely related to the fact that Sweden avoided the
sprawling suburban development in its postwar
housing expansion. The emphasis in Swedish housing has been on inner-city housing improvement.
With home close to diversified services for schooling, child care, household help and places of work,

it has been much easier in Sweden than in the United States to draw married women into the labor force and keep them there.

In contrast, the policy guiding the American federal agencies which affect the housing field, such as the FHA, have stressed the individual home, with the result that mortgage money was readily available to encourage builders to develop the sprawling peripheries of American cities. Luxury high-rise dwellings at the hub of the city and individual homes at the periphery have therefore been the pattern of middle-class housing development in the past twenty years. A shift in policy on the part of the federal government which would embrace buildings with three and four dwelling units and middle-income, high-rise apartment buildings in the in-between zones of the city could go a long way to counteract this trend toward greater and greater distance between home and job. Not everyone can or will want to live close to the hub of the city. From spring through early fall, it is undoubtedly easier to rear very young children in a suburban setting with back yards for the exercise of healthy lungs and bodies. But this is at the expense of increased dependence of children on their mothers, of minimization of fathers' time with their youngsters, of restriction of the social environment of women, of drastic separation of family and job worlds and of less opportunity for even part-time schooling or work for married women.

3. Men and women must not only be able to participate equally; they must want to do so. It is necessary, therefore, to look more closely into their motivations, and the early experiences which mold their self-images and life expectations. A prime example of this point can be seen in the question of occupational choice. The goal of sex equality calls for not only an increase in the extent of women's participation in the occupational system, but a more equitable distribution of men and women in all the occupations which comprise that system. This means more women doctors, lawyers, and scientists, more men social workers and school teachers. To change the sex ratio within occupations can only be achieved by altering the sex-typing of such occupations long before young people make a career decision.[21] Many men and women change their career plans during college, but this is usually within a narrow range of rela-

tively homogeneous fields: a student may shift from medicine to a basic science, from journalism to teaching English. Radical shifts such as from nursing to medicine, from kindergarten teaching to the law, are rare indeed. Thus while the problem could be attacked at the college level, any significant change in the career choices men and women make must be attempted when they are young boys and girls. It is during the early years of elementary school education that young people develop their basic views of appropriate characteristics, activities and goals for their sex. It is for this reason that I shall give primary attention to the sources of sex-role stereotypes and what the elementary school system could do to eradicate these stereotypes and to help instead in the development of a more androgynous conception of sex role.

The all-female social atmosphere of the American child has been frequently noted by social scientists, but it has been seen as a problem only in its effect upon boys. It has been claimed, for example, that the American boy must fight against a feminine identification this atmosphere encourages, with the result that he becomes overly aggressive, loudly asserting his maleness. In contrast, it is claimed that the American girl has an easy socialization, for she has an extensive number of feminine models in her environment to facilitate her identification as a female.

There are several important factors which this analysis overlooks. To begin with the boy: while it is certainly true that much of his primary group world is controlled by women, this does not mean that he has no image of the male social and job world as well. The content of the boy's image of man's work has a very special quality to it, however. Although an increasingly smaller proportion of occupations in a complex industrial society rely on sheer physical strength, the young boy's exposure to the work of men remains largely the occupations which do require physical strength. The jobs he can see are those which are socially visible, and these are jobs in which men are reshaping and repairing the physical environment. The young boy sees working-class men operating trucks, bulldozers, cranes; paving roads; building houses; planting trees; delivering groceries. This image is further reinforced by his television viewing: the gun-toting cowboy, the bat-swinging ballplayer, the arrow-slinging Indian. Space operas suggest not scientific exploration but military combat, the collision and collusion of other worlds. In short, even if the boy sees little of his father and knows next to nothing of what his father does away from home, there is some content to his image of men's work in the larger society. At least some part of his aggressive active play may be as much acting out similar male roles in response to the cultural cues provided by his environment as it is an over-reaction to his feminine environment or an identification with an aggressor-father.

And what of the girl? What image of the female role is she acquiring during her early years? In her primary group environment, she sees women largely in roles defined in terms that relate to her as a child—as mother, aunt, grandmother, baby-sitter—or in roles relating to the house—the cleaning, cooking, mending activities of mother and domestic helpers. Many mothers work outside the home, but the daughter often knows as little of that work as she does of her father's. Even if her own mother works, the reasons for such working that are given to the child are most often couched in terms of the mother or housewife role. Thus, a girl is seldom told that her mother works because she enjoys it or finds it very important to her own satisfaction in life, but because the money she earns will help pay for the house, a car, the daughter's clothes, dancing lessons, or school tuition.[22] In other words, working is something mothers sometimes have to do as mothers, not something mothers do as adult women. This is as misleading and distorted an image of the meaning of work as the father who tells his child he works "to take care of mummy and you" and neglects to mention that he also works because he finds personal satisfaction in doing so, or that he is contributing to knowledge, peace, or the comfort of others in the society.

The young girl also learns that it is only in the family that women seem to have an important superordinate position. However high her father's occupational status outside the home, when he returns at night, he is likely to remove his white shirt and become a blue-collar Mr. Fixit or mother's helper. The traditional woman's self-esteem would be seriously threatened if her husband were to play a role equal to her own in the lives and affections of her children or in the creative or managerial aspect of home management, precisely because her major sphere in which to acquire the sense of personal worth is her home and children. The lesson is surely not lost on her daughter, who learns that at home father does not know best, though outside the home men are the bosses over women, as she can see only too well in the nurse-doctor, secretary-boss, salesclerk-store manager, space Jane-space John relationships that she has an opportunity to observe.

The view that the socialization of the girl is an easy one compared with the boy depends on the kind of woman one has in mind as an end-product of socialization. Only if the woman is to be the traditional wife-mother is present-day socialization of young girls adequate, for from this point of view the confinement to the kinds of feminine models noted above and the superordinate position of the mother in the family facilitate an easy identification. If a girl sees that women reign only at home or in a history book, whereas outside the home they are Girl Fridays to men, then clearly for many young girls the wife-mother role may appear the best possible goal to have. It should be noted, however, that identification has been viewed primarily as an either-or process—the child identifies either with the mother or the father—and not as a process in which there is a fusion of the two parent models such that identification involves a modeling of the self after mother in some respects, father in others. It is possible that those women who have led exciting, intellectually assertive and creative lives did not identify exclusively with their traditional mothers, but crossed the sex line and looked to their fathers as model sources for ideas and life commitments of their own. This is to suggest that an exclusively same-sex identification between parent and child is no necessary condition for either mentally healthy or creative adults.

If I am correct about the significance of the father in the childhoods of those women who later led creative adult lives, then an increased accessibility of the middle-class father to his daughters and greater sharing of his ideas and interests could help to counteract the narrow confines of the feminine models daughters have. Beyond this, young girls need exposure to female models in professional and scientific occupations and to women with drive and dedication who are playing innovative volunteer roles in community organizations; they need an encouragement to emulate them and a preparation for an equalitarian rather than a dominant role in parenthood. Only if a woman's self-esteem is rooted in an independent life outside her family as well as her roles within the home can she freely welcome her husband to share on an equal basis the most rewarding tasks involved in child-rearing and home maintenance.

What happens when youngsters enter school? Instead of broadening the base on which they are forming their image of male and female roles, the school perpetuates the image children bring from home and their observations in the community. It has been mother who guided their preschool training; now in school it is almost exclusively women teachers who guide their first serious learning experiences. In the boy's first readers, men work at the same jobs with the same tools he has observed in his neighborhood—"T" for truck, "B" for bus, "W" for wagon. His teachers expect him to be rugged, physically strong, and aggressive. After a few years he moves into separate classes for gym, woodworking, and machine shop. For the girl, women are again the ones in charge of children. Her first readers portray women in aprons, brooms in their hands or babies in their arms. Teachers expect her to be quiet, dependent, with feminine interests in doll and house play and dressing up. In a few years she moves into separate classes for child care, cooking, and practical nursing. In excursions into the community, elementary school boys and girls visit airports, bus terminals, construction sites, factories, and farms.

What can the schools do to counteract these tendencies to either outmoded or traditional images of the roles of men and women? For one, class excursions into the community are no longer needed to introduce American children to building construction, airports, or zoos. Except for those in the most underprivileged areas of our cities, American children have ample exposure to such things with their car- and plane-riding families. There are, after all, only a limited number of such excursions possible in the course of a school year. I think visits to a publishing house, research laboratory, computer firm, or art studio would be more enriching than airports and zoos.

Going out into the community in this way, youngsters would observe men and women in their present occupational distribution. By a program of bringing representatives of occupations into the classroom and auditorium, however, the school could broaden the spectrum of occupations young children may link to their own abilities and interests regardless of the present sex-typing of occupations, by making a point of having children see and hear a woman scientist or doctor; a man dancer or artist; both women and men who are business executives, writers, and architects.

Another way in which the elementary schools could help is making a concerted effort to attract male teachers to work in the lower grades. This would add a rare and important man to the primary group environment of both boys and girls. This might seem a forlorn hope to some, since elementary school teaching has been such a predominantly feminine field, and it may be harder to attract men to it than to attract women to fields presently considered masculine. It may well be that in the next decade or so the schools could not attract and keep such men as teachers. But it should be possible for graduate schools of education and also school systems to devise ways of incorporating more men teachers in the lower grades, either as part of their teacher training requirements or in the capacity of specialized teachers: the science, art or music teacher who works with children at many grade levels rather than just one or two contiguous grade levels. His presence in the lives of very young children could help dispel their expectation that only women are in charge of children, that nurturance is a female attribute, or that strength and an aggressive assault on the physical environment is the predominant attribute of man's work.

The suggestions made thus far relate to a change in the sex-linking of occupations. There is one crucial way in which the schools could effect a change in the traditional division of labor by sex within the family sphere. The claim that boys and girls are reared in their early years without any differentiation by sex is only partially true. There are classes in all elementary schools which boys and girls take separately or which are offered only to one sex. These are precisely the courses most directly relevant to adult family roles: courses in sex and family living (where communities are brave enough to hold them) are typically offered in separate classes for boys and for girls, or for girls only. Courses in shop and craft work are scheduled for boys only; courses in child care, nursing, and cooking are for girls only. In departing from completely coeducational programs, the schools are reinforcing the traditional division of labor by sex which most children observe in their homes. Fifteen years later, these girls find that they cannot fix a broken plug, set a furnace pilot light or repair a broken high chair or favorite toy. These things await the return of the child's father and family handyman in the evening. When a child is sick in the middle of the night, his mother takes over; father is only her assistant or helper.

These may seem like minor matters, but I do not think they are. They unwittingly communicate to and reinforce in the child a rigid differentiation of role between men and women in family life. If first aid, the rudiments of child care and of cooking have no place in their early years as sons, brothers, and schoolboys, then it is little wonder that as husbands and fathers American men learn these things under their wives' tutelage. Even assuming these wives were actively involved in occupations of their own and hence free of the psychological pressure to assert their ascendancy in the family, it would be far better for all concerned—the married pair and the children as well—if men brought such skills with them to marriage.

This is the point where the schools could effect a change: If boys and girls took child care, nursing, cooking, shop, and craft classes together, they would have an opportunity to acquire comparable skills and pave the way for true parental substitutability as adults. They would also be learning something about how to complement each other, not just how to compete with each other.[23] Teamwork should be taught in school in the subjects relevant to adult family roles, not just within each sex on the playground or in the gymnasium. In addition to encouraging more equality in the parental role, such preparation as school children could ease their adjustment to the crises of adult life; illness, separation due to the demands of a job or military service, divorce, or death would have far less trauma and panic for the one-parent family— whether mother or father—if such equivalence and substitutability were a part of the general definition of the parental role.

A school curriculum which brought boys and girls into the same classes and trained them in social poise, the healing skills, care of children, handling of interpersonal difficulties, and related subjects would also encourage the development of skills which are increasingly needed in our complex economy. Whether the adult job is to be that of a worker in an automated industry, a professional man in law, medicine, or scholarship, or an executive in a large bureaucratic organization, the skills which are needed are not physical strength and ruggedness in interpersonal combat but understanding in human dealings, social poise, and persuasive skill in interpersonal relations.[24] All too often, neither the family nor the school encourages the development of these skills in boys. Hundreds of large business firms look for these qualities in young male applicants but often end up trying to develop them in their young executives through on-the-job training programs.

I have suggested a number of ways in which the educational system could serve as an important catalyst for change toward sex equality. The schools could reduce sex-role stereotypes of appropriate male and female attributes and activities by broadening the spectrum of occupations youngsters may consider for themselves irrespective of present sex-linked notions of man's work and woman's work, and by providing boys as well as girls with training in the tasks they will have as parents and spouses. The specific suggestions for achieving these ends which I have made should be viewed more as illustrative than as definitive, for educators themselves may have far better suggestions for how to implement the goal in the nation's classrooms than I have offered in these pages. Equality between the sexes cannot be achieved by proclamation or decree but only through a multitude of concrete steps, each of which may seem insignificant by itself, but all of which add up to the social blueprint for attaining the general goal.

SUMMARY PROFILE

In the course of this essay I have suggested a number of institutional innovations in education, residence, and child care which would facilitate equality between the sexes. Instead of a more conventional kind of summary, I shall describe a hypothetical case of a woman who is reared and lives out her life under the changed social conditions proposed in this essay.

She will be reared, as her brother will be reared, with a combination of loving warmth, firm discipline, household responsibility, and encouragement of independence and self-reliance. She will not be pampered and indulged, subtly taught to achieve her ends through coquetry and tears, as so many girls are taught today. She will view domestic skills as useful tools to acquire, some of which, like fine cooking or needlework, have their own intrinsic pleasures but most of which are necessary repetitive work best gotten done as quickly and efficiently as possible. She will be able to handle minor mechanical breakdowns in the home as well as her brother can, and he will be able to tend a child, press, sew, and cook with the same easy skills and comfortable feeling his sister has.

During their school years, both sister and brother will increasingly assume responsibility for their own decisions, freely experiment with numerous possible fields of study, gradually narrowing to a choice that best suits their interests and abilities rather than what is considered appropriate or prestigeful work for men and women. They will be encouraged by parents and teachers alike to think ahead to a whole life span, viewing marriage and parenthood as one strand among many which will constitute their lives. The girl will not feel the pressure to belittle her accomplishments, lower her aspirations, learn to be a receptive listener in her relations with boys, but will be as true to her growing sense of self as her brother and male friends are. She will not marry before her adolescence and schooling are completed, but will be willing and able to view the college years as a "moratorium" from deeply intense cross-sex commitments, a period of life during which her identity can be "at large and open and various."[25] Her intellectual aggressiveness as well as her brother's tender sentiments will be welcomed and accepted as *human* characteristics, without the self-questioning doubt of latent homosexuality that troubles many college-age men and women in our era when these qualities are sex-linked.[26] She will not cling to her parents, nor they to her, but will establish an increasingly larger sphere of her own independent world in which she moves and works, loves and

thinks, as a maturing young person. She will learn to take pleasure in her own body and a man's body and to view sex as a good and wonderful experience, but not as an exclusive basis for an ultimate commitment to another person, and not as a test of her competence as a female or her partner's competence as a male. Because she will have a many-faceted conception of her self and its worth, she will be free to merge and lose herself in the sex act with a lover or a husband.

Marriage for our hypothetical woman will not mark a withdrawal from the life and work pattern that she has established, just as there will be no sharp discontinuity between her early childhood and youthful adult years. Marriage will be an enlargement of her life experiences, the addition of a new dimension to an already established pattern, rather than an abrupt withdrawal to the home and a turning in upon the marital relationship. Marriage will be a "looking outward in the same direction" for both the woman and her husband. She will marry and bear children only if she deeply desires a mate and children, and will not be judged a failure as a person if she decides against either. She will have few children if she does have them, and will view her pregnancies, childbirth, and early months of motherhood as one among many equally important highlights in her life, experienced intensely and with joy but not as the exclusive basis for a sense of self-fulfillment and purpose in life. With planning and foresight, her early years of child bearing and rearing can fit a long-range view of all sides of herself. If her children are not to suffer from "paternal deprivation," her husband will also anticipate that the assumption of parenthood will involve a weeding out of nonessential activities either in work, civic or social participation. Both the woman and the man will feel that unless a man can make room in his life for parenthood, he should not become a father. The woman will make sure, even if she remains at home during her child's infancy, that he has ample experience of being with and cared for by other adults besides herself, so that her return to a full-time position in her field will not constitute a drastic change in the life of the child, but a gradual pattern of increasing supplementation by others of the mother. The children will have a less intense involvement with their mother, and she with them, and they will all be the better for it. When they are grown and establish adult lives of their own, our woman will face no retirement twenty years before her husband, for her own independent activities will continue and expand. She will be neither an embittered wife, an interfering mother-in-law nor an idle parasite, but together with her husband she will be able to live an independent, purposeful and satisfying third act in life.

NOTES

[1] Often the conclusion that sex differentiation is a basic and universal phenomenon is buttressed by pointing to a large number of societies, all of which manifest such sex differentiation. Since Americans are easily impressed by large numbers, this does indeed sound like conclusive evidence against the likelihood of any society's achieving full sex equality. Closer examination of such samples, however, reveals two things: very little representation of numerous African societies in which the instrumental-expressive distinction is simply *not* linked to sex in the predicted direction, and second, they are largely primitive societies, a half dozen of which might equal the size of a very small American city. Such cultural comparisons assume every possible kind of societal arrangement is represented, but this is not the case: Sweden, China, Yugoslavia, the Soviet Union, Israel are not represented on such a continuum. I believe we may learn more that is of relevance to a future America by studying family patterns in these societies than from a study of all the primitive societies in the world. . . .

[2] When the sociologist finds, for example, that the incidence of divorce is higher for those who marry outside their religion than for those who do not, he concludes that intermarriage is "bad" or "risky"; he does not say such marital failures may reflect the relative newness of the social pattern of intermarriage, much less suggest that such failures may decline once this pattern is more prevalent. In fact, the only aspect of intermarriage which is studied is the incidence of its failure. Sociologists have not studied *successful* intermarriages.

[3] A full picture of this post-World War II development is traced in Betty Friedan's *The Feminine Mystique,* New York: W. W. Norton, 1963. See particularly Chapters 6 and 7 on the "Functional Freeze" and the "Sex-Directed Educators."

[4] Demographic changes in the family life cycle between 1890 and 1950 are shown in great detail in Paul Glick's *American Families,* New York: John Wiley, 1957.

[5] Benjamin Spock, "Should Mothers Work?" *Ladies' Home Journal* (February, 1963).

[6] A few authors have seen this claim that all separation of the child from the biological mother or mother surrogate, even for a few days, is inevitably damaging to the child, as a new and subtle form of antifeminism, by which

men, under the guise of exacting the importance of maternity, are tying women more tightly to their children than any real clinical or cultural evidence indicates is necessary. See Hilde Bruch, *Don't Be Afraid of Your Child,* New York: Farrar, Straus & Young, 1952; and Margaret Mead, "Some Theoretical Considerations on the Problem of Mother-Child Separation," *American Journal of Orthopsychiatry,* **24** (1954), 471–483.

[7] Burchinal and Rossman found no significant relationships between any kind of employment and personality characteristics or social interaction of children in the 7th and 11th grades in school. Lee G. Burchinal and Jack E. Rossman, "Relations among Maternal Employment Indices and Developmental Characteristics of Children," *Marriage and Family Living,* **23** (November, 1961), 334–340.

[8] Marian Radke Yarrow, Phyllis Scott, Louise de Leeuw, and Christine Heinig, "Child-rearing in Families of Working and Non-working Mothers," *Sociometry,* **25** (June, 1962), 122–140.

[9] A good overview of these studies can be found in David Rapaport, "The Study of Kibbutz Education and its Bearing on the Theory of Development," *American Journal of Orthopsychiatry,* **28** (1958), 587–599.

[10] There are of course other instances of infant and toddler care by persons supplementing the biological mother, notable among them being the creche and nursery school systems in the Soviet Union. What effect these early experiences of creche care have upon the subsequent personality development of Soviet young people is not known. Western observers who have visited them during the past several years have been impressed with the facilities, quality of staff personnel, and general happy mood of the children seen in them, but there is no rigorous evidence to substantiate these impressions, or assess the effect of such early separation from the mother upon personality.

[11] This shifts the ground of the problem of maternal employment to a very different level from the one on which it is usually discussed. As a research problem, the crucial question is not whether the mother is employed or not, but what is the quality of the care given to the children—whether by the mother alone or a combination of other adults.

[12] This passivity and softness in American young people has been noted in David Riesman, Introduction to Edgar Friedenberg, *The Vanishing Adolescent,* Boston: Beacon, 1959; Paul Goodman, *Growing Up Absurd,* New York: Random House, 1960; and Marjorie K. McCorquodale, "What They Will Die For in Houston," *Harper's* (October, 1961).

[13] Edward A. Strecker, *Their Mother's Sons,* Philadelphia: Lippincott, 1946.

[14] Friedenberg, *The Vanishing Adolescent,* Boston: Beacon, 1959.

[15] See Margaret Cussler's profile of the "volunteer executive" in her study *The Woman Executive,* New York: Harcourt, Brace, 1958, pp. 111–118.

[16]Florence Kluckhohn, "Variations in Basic Values of Family Systems," in Norman W. Bell and Ezra F. Vogel, *A Modern Introduction to the Family,* New York: Free Press, 1960, pp. 304–316; and George Gallup and Evan Hill, "The American Woman," *The Saturday Evening Post* (December 22, 1962), 15–32.

[17]Talcott Parsons, *Essays in Sociological Theory Pure and Applied,* Glencoe, Illinois: Free Press, 1949, pp. 222–224 and 243–246.

[18]Henry C. Lajewski, *Child Care Arrangements of Full-Time Working Mothers,* Washington, D.C.: U.S. Department of Health, Education and Welfare, Children's Bureau Publication No. 378, 1959.

[19]Robert Wood, *Suburbia, Its People and Their Politics,* Boston: Houghton Mifflin, 1959; and Nanette E. Scofield, "Some Changing Roles of Women in Suburbia: A Social Anthropological Case Study," *Transactions of the New York Academy of Sciences,* **22** (April, 1960), 6.

[20]George Gallup and Evan Hill, "The American Woman," *The Saturday Evening Post* (December 22, 1962). One must read this survey very carefully to get behind the gloss of the authors' rosy perspective. . . .

[21]The extent of this sex-typing of occupations is shown dramatically in a study of the June, 1961 college graduates conducted by the National Opinion Research Center at the University of Chicago. See James A. Davis and Norman Bradburn, "Great Aspirations: Career Plans of America's June 1961 College Graduates," National Opinion Research Center Report No. 82, September, 1961, mimeographed.

[22]Ruth Hartley and A. Klein, "Sex Role Concepts among Elementary School-Age Girls," *Marriage and Family Living,* **21** (February, 1959), 59–64.

[23]Bruno Bettelheim makes the point that American boys and girls learn to compete with each other, but not how to complement each other. He sees this lack of experience in complementarity as part of the difficulty in achieving a satisfactory sexual adjustment in marriage: the girl is used to "performing with males on equal grounds, but she has little sense of how to complement them. She cannot suddenly learn this in bed." See Bruno Bettelheim, "Growing Up Female," *Harper's* (November, 1962), 125.

[24]These are the same skills which, when found in women, go by the names of charm, tact, intuition. See Helen Mayer Hacker, "The New Burdens of Masculinity," *Marriage and Family Living,* **19** (August, 1957), 227–233.

[25]Erik Erikson, *Childhood and Society,* New York: W. W. Norton, 1950.

[26]David Riesman has observed that this latent fear of homosexuality haunts the Ivy League campuses, putting pressure on many young men to be guarded in their relations with each other and with their male teachers, reflecting in part the lag in the cultural image of appropriate sex characteristics. See David Riesman, "Permissiveness and Sex Roles," *Marriage and Family Living,* **21** (August, 1959), 211–217.

EDUCATION WITHOUT SCHOOL: HOW IT CAN BE DONE

Ivan Illich

In a previous article[1] I discussed what is becoming a common complaint about schools, one that is reflected, for example, in the recent report of the Carnegie Commission: In school registered students submit to certified teachers in order to obtain certificates of their own; both are frustrated and both blame insufficient resources—money, time, or buildings—for their mutual frustration.

Such criticism leads many people to ask whether it is possible to conceive of a different style of learning. The same people, paradoxically, when pressed to specify how they acquired what they know and value, will readily admit that they learned it more often outside than inside school. Their knowledge of facts, their understanding of life and work came to them from friendship or love, while viewing TV, or while reading, from examples of peers, or the challenge of a street encounter. Or they may have learned what they know through the apprenticeship ritual for admission to a street gang or the initiation to a hospital, newspaper city room, plumber's shop, or insurance office. The alternative to dependence on schools is not the use of public resources for some new device which "makes" people learn; rather it is the creation of a new style of educational relationship between man and his environment. To foster this style, attitudes toward growing up, the tools available for learning, and the quality and structure of daily life will have to change concurrently.

Attitudes are already changing. The proud dependence on school is gone. Consumer resistance is increasing in the knowledge industry. Many

From The New York Review of Books, *January 7, 1970. Reprinted with permission from* The New York Review of Books. *Copyright* © *1970 by Ivan Illich. Footnotes have been omitted.*

teachers and pupils, taxpayers and employers, economists and policemen would prefer not to depend any longer on schools. What prevents their frustration from shaping new institutions is a lack not only of imagination but frequently also one of appropriate language and of enlightened self-interest. They cannot visualize either a deschooled society or educational institutions in a society which disestablishes school.

In this essay, I intend to show that the *inverse of school* is possible: That we can depend on self-motivated learning instead of employing teachers to bribe or compel the student to find time and the will to learn; that we can provide the learner with new links to the world instead of continuing to funnel all educational programs through the teacher. I shall discuss some of the general characteristics which distinguish schooling from learning and outline four major categories of educational institutions which should appeal not only to many individuals, but also to many existing interest groups.

AN OBJECTION: WHO CAN BE SERVED BY BRIDGES TO NOWHERE?

We are used to considering schools as a variable, dependent on the political and economic structure. If we can change the style of political leadership, or promote the interests of one class or another, or switch from private to public ownership of the means of production, we assume the school system will change as well. The educational institutions I will propose, however, are meant to serve a society which does not now exist, although the current frustration with schools is itself potenttially a major force to set in motion change toward new social arrangements. An obvious objection has been raised to this approach: Why channel energy to build bridges to nowhere, instead of marshaling it first to change not the schools but the political and economic system?

This objection, however, underestimates the repressive political and economic nature of the school system itself, as well as the political potential inherent in a new educational style. In a basic sense, schools have ceased to be dependent on the ideology professed by a government or the organization of its market. Even the Chinese feel they must adopt the basic international structure of schooling in order to become a world power and a nation-state. Control of society is reserved everywhere to those who have consumed at least four units of four years, each unit consisting of 500 to 1,000 hours in the classroom.

School, as I suggested in my previous article, is the major component of the system of consumer production which is becoming more complex and specialized and bureaucratized. Schooling is necessary to produce the habits and expectations of the managed consumer society. Inevitably it produces institutional dependence and ranking in spite of any effort by the teacher to teach the contrary. It is an illusion that schools are only a dependent variable, an illusion which, moreover, provides them, the reproductive organs of a consumer society, with their immunity.

Even the piecemeal creation of new educational agencies which are the inverse of school would therefore be an attack on the most sensitive link of a pervasive phenomenon, which is organized by the state in all countries. A political program which does not explicitly recognize the need for deschooling is not revolutionary; it is demagoguery calling for more of the same. Any major political program of the seventies should be evaluated by this measure: How clearly does it state the need for deschooling—and how clearly does it provide guidelines for the educational quality of the society for which it aims?

The struggle against domination by the world market and big power politics might be beyond some poor communities or countries—but this weakness is an added reason for emphasizing the importance of liberating each society through a reversal of its educational structure, a change which is not beyond any society's means.

GENERAL CHARACTERISTICS OF NEW FORMAL EDUCATIONAL INSTITUTIONS

A good educational system should have three purposes: it should provide all who want to learn with access to available resources at any time in their lives; empower all who want to share what they know to find those who want to learn it from them; and finally, furnish all who want to present an issue to the public with the opportunity to make their challenge known. Such a system would require the application of constitutional guarantees to education. Learners should not be forced to submit to an obligatory curriculum; or to discrimination based on whether they possess a certificate or a diploma. Nor should the public be forced to support—through a regressive taxation—a huge professional apparatus of educators and buildings which in fact restrict the public's chances for learning to the services the profession is willing to put on the market. It should use modern technology to make free speech, free assembly, and a free press truly universal and, therefore, fully educational.

Schools are designed on the assumption that there is a secret to everything in life; that the quality of life depends on knowing that secret; that secrets can be known only in orderly successions; and that only teachers can properly reveal these secrets. An individual with a schooled mind conceives of the world as a pyramid of classified packages accessible only to those who carry the proper tags. New educational institutions would break apart this pyramid. Their purpose must be to facilitate access for the learner: to allow him to look into the windows of the control room or the parliament, if he cannot get in the door. Moreover, such new institutions should be channels to which the learner would have access without credentials or pedigree—public spaces in which peers and elders outside his immediate horizon now become available.

I believe that no more than four—possibly even three—distinct "channels" or learning exchanges could contain all the resources needed for real learning. The child grows up in a world of things, surrounded by people who serve as models for skills and values. He finds peers who challenge him to argue, to compete, to cooperate, and to understand; and if the child is lucky, he is exposed to confrontation or criticism by an experienced elder who really cares. Things, models, peers, and elders are four resources each of which requires a different type of arrangement to ensure that everybody has ample access to them.

I will use the word "network" to designate specific ways to provide access to each of four sets of resources. The word is often used, unfortunately, to designate the channels reserved to material selected by others for indoctrination, instruction, and entertainment. But it can also be used for the telephone or the postal service, which are primarily accessible to individuals who want to send messages to one another. What are needed are new networks, readily available to the public and designed to spread equal opportunity for learning and teaching.

To give an example: The same level of technology is used in TV and in tape recorders. All Latin American countries now have introduced TV: In Bolivia the government has financed a TV station, which was built six years ago, and there are no more than seven thousand TV sets for four million citizens. The money now tied up in TV installations throughout Latin America could have provided every fifth adult with a tape recorder. In addition, the money would have sufficed to provide an almost unlimited library of prerecorded tapes, with outlets even in remote villages, as well as an ample supply of empty tapes.

This network of tape recorders, of course, would be radically different from the present network of TV. It would provide opportunity for free expression: Literate and illiterate alike could record, preserve, disseminate, and repeat their opinions. The present investment in TV instead provides bureaucrats, whether politicians or educators, with the power to sprinkle the continent with institutionally produced programs which they—or their sponsors —decide are good for or in demand by the people. Technology is available to develop either independence and learning, or bureaucracy and preaching.

FOUR NETWORKS

The planning of new educational institutions ought not to begin with the administrative goals of a principal or president, or with the teaching goals of a professional educator, or with the learning goals of any hypothetical class of people. It must not start with the question, "What should someone learn?" but with the question, "What kinds of things and people might learners want to be in contact with in order to learn?"

Someone who wants to learn knows that he needs both information and critical response to its use from somebody else. Information can be stored in things and in persons. In a good educational system, access to things ought to be available at the sole bidding of the learner, while access to informants requires in addition others' consent. Criticism can also come from two directions: from peers or from elders, that is, from fellow learners whose immediate interests match mine, or from those who will grant me a share in their superior experience. Peers can be colleagues with whom to raise a question, companions for playful and enjoyable (or arduous) reading or walking, challengers at any type of game. Elders can be consultants on which skill to learn, which method to use, what company to seek at a given moment. They can be guides to the right questions to be raised among peers and to the deficiency of answers they arrive at.

Educational resources are usually labeled according to educators' curricular goals. I propose to do the contrary, to label four different approaches which enable the student to gain access to any educational resource which may help him to define and achieve his own goals:

1. Reference Services to Educational Objects— which facilitate access to things or processes used for formal learning. Some of these things can be reserved for this purpose, stored in libraries, rental agencies, laboratories, and showrooms like museums and theaters; others can be in daily use in factories, airports, or on farms, but made available to students as apprentices or in off-hours.

2. Skill Exchanges—which permit persons to list their skills, the conditions under which they are

willing to serve as models for others who want to learn these skills, and the addresses at which they can be reached.

3. Peer Matching—a communication network which permits persons to describe the learning activity in which they wish to engage, in the hope of finding a partner for the inquiry.

4. Reference Services to Educators-at-large—who can be listed in a directory giving the addresses and self-descriptions of professionals, para-professionals, and free-lancers, along with conditions of access to their services. Such educators, as we will see, could be chosen by polling or consulting their former clients.

REFERENCE SERVICES TO EDUCATIONAL OBJECTS

Things are basic resources for learning. The quality of the environment and the relationship of a person to it will determine how much he learns incidentally. Formal learning requires special access to ordinary things, on the one hand, or, on the other, easy and dependable access to special things made for educational purposes. An example of the former is the special right to operate or dismantle a machine in a garage. An example of the latter is the general right to use an abacus, a computer, a book, a botanical garden, or a machine withdrawn from production and placed at the full disposal of students.

At present, attention is focused on the disparity between rich and poor children in their access to things and in the manner in which they can learn from them. OEO and other agencies, following this approach, concentrate on equalizing chances, by trying to provide more educational equipment for the poor. A more radical point of departure would be to recognize that in the city rich and poor alike are artificially kept away from most of the things that surround them. Children born into the age of plastics and efficiency experts must penetrate two barriers which obstruct their understanding: one built into things, and the other around institutions. Industrial design creates a world of things that resist insight into their nature, and schools shut the learner out of the world of things in their meaningful setting.

After a short visit to New York, a woman from a Mexican village told me she was impressed by the fact that stores sold "only wares heavily made up with cosmetics." I understood her to mean that industrial products "speak" to their customers about their allurements and not about their nature. Industry has surrounded people with artifacts whose inner workings only specialists are allowed to understand. The nonspecialist is discouraged from figuring out what makes a watch tick, or a telephone ring, or an electric typewriter work, by being warned that it will break if he tries. He can be told what makes a transistor radio work but he cannot find out for himself. This type of design tends to reinforce a noninventive society in which the experts find it progressively easier to hide behind their expertise and beyond evaluation.

The man-made environment has become as inscrutable as nature is for the primitive. At the same time, educational materials have been monopolized by school. Simple educational objects have been expensively packaged by the knowledge industry. They have become specialized tools for professional educators, and their cost has been inflated by forcing them to stimulate either environments or teachers.

The teacher is jealous of the textbook he defines as his professional implement. The student may come to hate the lab because he associates it with schoolwork. The administrator rationalizes his protective attitude toward the library as a defense of costly public equipment against those who would play with it rather than learn. In this atmosphere, the student too often uses the map, the lab, the encyclopedia, or the microscope at the rare moments when the curriculum tells him to do so. Even the great classics become part of "sophomore year" instead of marking a new turn in a person's life. School removes things from everyday use by labeling them educational tools.

If we are to deschool, both tendencies must be reversed. The general physical environment must be made accessible, and those physical learning resources which have been reduced to teaching instruments become generally available for self-directed learning. Using things merely as part of a curriculum can have an even worse effect than just removing them: It can corrupt the attitudes of pupils.

Games are a case in point. I do not mean the "games" of the physical education department (such as football and basketball), which the schools use to raise income and prestige and in which they have made a substantial capital investment. As the athletes themselves are well aware, these enterprises, which take the form of warlike tournaments, have undermined the playfulness of sports and are used to reinforce the competitive nature of schools. Rather I have in mind the educational games which can provide a unique way to penetrate formal systems. Set-theory, linguistics, propositional logic, geometry, physics, and even chemistry reveal themselves with little effort to certain persons who play these games. A friend of mine went to a Mexican market with a game called "Wff'n Proof," which consists of some dice on which twelve logical symbols are imprinted. He showed children which two or three combinations constituted a well-formed sentence, and inductively within the first hour some onlookers also grasped the principle. Within a few hours of playfully conducting formal logical proofs, some children are capable of introducing others to the fundamental proofs of propositional logic. The others just walk away.

In fact, for some children such games are a special form of liberating education, since they heighten their awareness of the fact that formal systems are built on changeable axioms and that conceptual operations have a game-like nature. They are also simple, cheap, and—to a large extent —can be organized by the players themselves. Used outside the curriculum such games provide an opportunity for identifying and developing unusual talent, while the school psychologist will often identify those who have such talent as in danger of becoming antisocial, sick, or unbalanced. Within school, when used in the form of tournaments, games are not only removed from the sphere of leisure; they often become tools used to translate playfulness into competition, a lack of abstract reasoning into a sign of inferiority. An exercise which is liberating for some character types becomes a strait-jacket for others.

The control of school over educational equipment has still another effect. It increases enormously the cost of such cheap materials. Once their use is restricted to scheduled hours, professionals are paid to supervise their acquisition, storage, and use. Then students vent their anger against the school on the equipment, which must be purchased once again.

Paralleling the untouchability of teaching tools is the impenetrability of modern junk. In the thirties, any self-respecting boy knew how to repair an automobile, but now car makers multiply wires and withhold manuals from everyone except specialized mechanics. In a former era, an old radio contained enough coils and condensers to build a transmitter that would make all the neighborhood radios scream in feedback. Transistor radios are more portable, but nobody dares to take them apart. To change this in the highly industrialized countries will be immensely difficult; but at least in the Third World, we must insist on built-in educational qualities.

To illustrate my point, let me present a model: By spending $10 million it would be possible to connect 40,000 hamlets in a country like Peru with a spiderweb of six-foot-wide trails and maintain these, and, in addition, provide the country with 200,000 three-wheeled mechanical donkeys— five on the average for each hamlet. Few poor countries of this size spend less than this yearly on cars and roads, both of which are now mainly restricted to the rich and their employees, while poor people remain trapped in their villages. Each of these simple but durable little vehicles would cost $125—half of which would pay for transmission and a six-horsepower motor. A "donkey" could make 20 mph, and it can carry loads of 850 pounds (that is, most things besides trunks and steel beams which are ordinarily moved).

The political appeal of such a transportation system to a peasantry is obvious. Equally obvious is the reason why those who hold power—and thereby automatically have a car—are not interested in spending money on trails and in clogging roads with engine-driven donkeys. The universal donkey could work only if a country's leaders were willing to impose a national speed limit of, say, 25 miles an hour and adapt its public institutions to this. The model could not work if conceived only as a stop-gap.

This is not the place to elaborate on the political, social, economic, financial, and technical feasibility of this model. I only wish to indicate that educational considerations may be of prime importance when choosing such an alternative to capital-intensive transport. By raising the unit cost per donkey by some 20 percent it would become possible to plan the production of all its parts in such a manner that, as far as possible, each future owner would spend a month or two making and understanding his machine, and would be able to repair it. With this additional cost it would also be possible to decentralize production into dispersed plants. The added benefits would result not only from including educational costs in the construction process. Even more significantly, a durable motor which practically anyone could learn to repair and which could be used as a plow and pump by somebody who understood it would provide much higher educational benefits than the inscrutable engines of the advanced countries.

Not only the junk but also the supposedly public places of the modern city have become impenetrable. In American society, children are excluded from most things and places on the grounds that they are private. But even in societies which have declared an end to private property, children are kept away from the same places and things because they are considered the special domain of professionals and dangerous to the uninitiated. Since the last generation the railroad yard has become as inaccessible as the fire station. Yet with a little ingenuity, it should not be difficult to provide for safety in such places. To deschool the artifacts of education will require making the artifacts and processes available—and recognizing their educational value. Certainly, some workers would find it inconvenient to be accessible to learners; but this inconvenience must be balanced against the educational gains.

Private cars could be banned from Manhattan. Five years ago, it was unthinkable. Now, certain New York streets are closed off at odd hours, and this trend will probably continue. Indeed most cross-streets should be closed to automotive traffic and parking should be forbidden everywhere. In a city opened up to people, teaching materials which are now locked up in storerooms and laboratories could be dispersed into independently operated storefront depots which children and adults could visit without the danger of being run over.

If the goals of learning were no longer dominated by schools and schoolteachers, the market for learners would be much more various and the definition of "educational artifacts" would be less restrictive. There could be tool shops, libraries, laboratories, and gaming rooms. Photolabs and offset presses would allow neighborhood newspapers to flourish. Some storefront learning centers could contain viewing booths for closed-circuit television, others could feature office equipment for use and for repair. The jukebox or the record player would be commonplace, with some specializing in classical music, others in international folk tunes, others in jazz. Film clubs would compete with each other and with commercial television. Museum outlets could be networks for circulating exhibits of works of art, both old and new, originals and reproductions, perhaps administered by the various metropolitan museums.

The professional personnel needed for this network would be much more like custodians, museum guides, or reference librarians than like teachers. From the corner biology store, they could refer their clients to the shell collection in the museum or indicate the next showing of biology videotapes in a certain viewing booth. They could furnish guides for pest control, diet, and other kinds of preventive medicine. They could refer those who needed advice to "elders" who could provide it.

Two distinct approaches can be taken to financing a network of "learning objects." A community could determine a maximum budget for this purpose and arrange for all parts of the network to be open to all visitors at reasonable hours. Or the community could decide to provide citizens with limited entitlements, according to their age group, which would give them special access to certain materials which are both costly and scarce, while leaving other, simpler materials available to everyone.

Finding resources for material made specifically for education is only one—and perhaps the least costly—aspect in building an educational world. The money now spent on the sacred paraphernalia of the school ritual can be freed to provide all citizens with greater access to the real life of the city. Special tax incentives could be granted to those who employed children between the ages of eight and fourteen for a couple of hours each day if the conditions of employment were humane ones. We should return to the tradition of the bar mitzvah or confirmation. By this I mean we should first restrict, and later eliminate, the disenfranchisement of the young and permit a boy of twelve to become a man fully responsible for his participation in the life of the community. Many "school age" people know more about their neighborhood than social workers or councilmen. Of course, they also ask more embarrassing questions and propose solutions which threaten the bureaucracy. They should be allowed to come of age so that they could put their knowledge and fact-finding ability to work in the service of a popular government.

Until recently the dangers of school were easily underestimated in comparison with the dangers of an apprenticeship in the police force, the fire department, or the entertainment industry. It was easy to justify schools at least as a means to protect youth. Often this argument no longer holds. I recently visited a Methodist church in Harlem occupied by a group of armed Young Lords in protest against the death of Julio Rodan, a Puerto Rican youth found hanged in his prison cell. I knew the leaders of the group who had spent a semester in Cuernavaca. When I wondered why one of them, Juan, was not among them I was told that he had "gone back on heroin and to the State University."

Planning, incentives, and legislation can be used to unlock the educational potential within our society's huge investment in plants and equipment. Full access to educational objects will not exist so long as business firms are allowed to combine the legal protections which the Bill of Rights reserves to the privacy of individuals with the economic power conferred upon them by their millions of customers and thousands of employees, stockholders, and suppliers. Much of the world's know-how and most of its productive processes and equipment are locked within the walls of business firms, away from their customers, employees, and stockholders, as well as from the general public, whose laws and facilities allow them to function. Money now

spent on advertising in capitalist countries could be redirected toward education in and by General Electric, NBC-TV, or Budweiser beer. That is, the plants and offices should be reorganized so that their daily operations can be more accessible to the public in ways that will make learning possible; and indeed ways might be found to pay the companies for the learning people acquire from them.

An even more valuable body of scientific objects and data may be withheld from general access— and even from qualified scientists—under the guise of national security. Until recently science was the one forum which functioned like an anarchist's dream. Each man capable of doing research had more or less the same opportunity of access to its tools and to a hearing of the community of peers. Now bureaucratization and organization have placed much of science beyond public reach. Indeed, what used to be an international network of scientific information has been splintered into an arena of competing teams. The members as well as the artifacts of the scientific community have been locked into national and corporate programs oriented toward practical achievement, to the radical impoverishment of the men who support these nations and corporations.

In a world which is controlled and owned by nations and corporations, only limited access to educational objects will ever be possible. But increased access to those objects which can be shared for educational purposes may enlighten us enough to help us to break through these ultimate political barriers. Public schools transfer control over the educational uses of objects from private to professional hands. The institutional inversion of schools could empower the individual to reclaim the right to use them for education. A truly public kind of ownership might begin to emerge if private or corporate control over the educational aspect of "things" were brought to the vanishing point.

SKILL EXCHANGES

A guitar teacher, unlike a guitar, can be neither classified in a museum nor owned by the public nor rented from an educational warehouse. Teachers of skills belong to a different class of resources from objects needed to learn a skill. This is not to say that they are indispensable in every case. I can not only rent a guitar, but also taped guitar lessons and illustrated chord charts—and with these things I can teach myself to play the guitar. Indeed, this arrangement might have advantages—if the available tapes are better than the available teachers. Or if the only time I have for learning the guitar is late at night or if the tunes I wish to play are unknown in my country. Or I might be shy and prefer to fumble along in privacy.

Skill teachers must be listed and contacted through a different kind of channel from that of things. A thing is available at the bidding of the user —or could be—whereas a person formally becomes a skill resource only when he consents to do so, and he can also restrict time, place, and method as he chooses.

Skill teachers must also be distinguished from peers, from whom one would learn. Peers who wish to pursue a common inquiry must start from common interests and abilities; they get together to exercise or improve a skill they share: basketball, dancing, constructing a campsite, or discussing the next election. The first transmission of a skill, on the other hand, involves bringing together someone who has the skill and someone who does not have it and wants to acquire it.

A "skill model" is a person who possesses a skill and is willing to demonstrate its practice. A demonstration of this kind is frequently a necessary resource for a potential learner. Modern inventions permit us to incorporate demonstration into tape, film, or chart; yet one would hope personal demonstration will remain in wide demand, especially in communication skills. Some 10,000 adults have learned Spanish at our Center at Cuernavaca— mostly highly motivated persons who wanted to acquire near-native fluency in a second language. When they are faced with a choice between carefully programmed instruction in a lab, or drill-sessions with two other students and a native speaker following a rigid routine, most choose the second.

For most widely shared skills, a person who demonstrates the skill is the only human resource we ever need or get. Whether in speaking or driving, in cooking or in the use of communication equipment, we are often barely conscious of formal instruction and learning, especially after our first experience of the materials in question. I see

no reason why other complex skills, such as the mechanical aspects of surgery and playing the fiddle, of reading or the use of directories and catalogues, could not be learned in the same way.

A well-motivated student who does not labor under a specific handicap often needs no further human assistance than can be provided by someone who can demonstrate on demand how to do what the learner wants to learn to do. The demand made of skilled people that before demonstrating their skill they be certified as pedagogues is a result of the insistence that people learn either what they do not want to know, or that all people—even those with a special handicap—learn certain things, at a given moment in their lives, and preferably under specified circumstances.

What makes skills scarce on the present educational market is the institutional requirement that those who can demonstrate them may not do so unless they are given public trust, through a certificate. We insist that those who help others acquire a skill should also know how to diagnose learning difficulties and be able to motivate people to aspire to learn skills. In short, we demand that they be pedagogues. People who can demonstrate skills will be plentiful as soon as we learn to recognize them outside the teaching profession.

Where princelings are being taught, the parents' insistence that the teacher and the person with skills be combined in one person is understandable, if no longer defensible. But for all parents to aspire to have Aristotle for their Alexander is obviously self-defeating. The person who can both inspire students and demonstrate a technique is so rare, and so hard to recognize, that even princelings more often get a sophist than a true philosopher.

A demand for scarce skills can be quickly filled even if there are only small numbers of people to demonstrate them; but such people must be easily available. During the Forties, radio repairmen, most of them with no schooling in their work, were no more than two years behind radios in penetrating the interior of Latin America. There they stayed until transistor radios, which are cheap to purchase and impossible to repair, put them out of business. Technical schools now fail to accomplish what repairmen of equally useful, more durable radios could do as a matter of course.

Converging self-interests now conspire to stop a man from sharing his skill. The man who has the skill profits from its scarcity and not from its reproduction. The teacher who specializes in transmitting the skill profits from the artisan's unwillingness to launch his own apprentice into the field. The public is indoctrinated to believe that skills are valuable and realiable only if they are the result of formal schooling. The job market depends on making skills scarce and on keeping them scarce, either by proscribing their unauthorized use and transmission or by making things which can be operated and repaired only by those who have access to tools or information which are kept scarce.

Schools thus produce shortages of skilled persons. A good example is the diminishing number of nurses in the United States, owing to the rapid increase of four-year B.S. programs in nursing. Women from poorer families, who would formerly have enrolled in a two- or three-year program, now stay out of the nursing profession altogether.

Insisting on the certification of teachers is another way of keeping skills scarce. If nurses were encouraged to train nurses, and if nurses were employed on the basis of their proven skill at giving injections, filling out charts, and giving medicine, there would soon be no lack of trained nurses. Certification now tends to abridge the freedom of education by converting the civil right to share one's knowledge into the privilege of academic freedom, now conferred only on the employees of a school. To guarantee access to an effective exchange of skills, we need legislation which generalizes academic freedom. The right to teach any skill should come under the protection of freedom of speech. Once restrictions on teaching are removed, they will quickly be removed from learning as well.

The teacher of skills needs some inducement to grant his services to a pupil. There are at least two simple ways to begin to channel public funds to noncertified teachers. One way would be to institutionalize the skill exchange by creating free skill centers open to the public. Such centers could and should be established in industrialized areas, at least for those skills which are fundamental prerequisites for entering certain apprenticeships—such skills as reading, typing, keeping accounts, foreign languages, computer programming and number

manipulation, reading special languages such as that of electrical circuits, manipulation of certain machinery, etc. Another approach would be to give certain groups within the population educational currency good for attendance at skill centers where other clients would have to pay commercial rates.

A much more radical approach would be to create a "bank" for skill exchange. Each citizen would be given a basic credit with which to acquire fundamental skills. Beyond that minimum, further credits would go to those who earn them by teaching, whether they serve as models in organized skill centers or do so privately at home or on the playground. Only those who have taught others for an equivalent amount of time would have a claim on the time of more advanced teachers. An entirely new elite would be promoted, an elite of those who earn their education by sharing it.

Should parents have the right to earn skill-credit for their children? Since such an arrangement would give further advantage to the privileged classes, it might be offset by granting a larger credit to the underprivileged. The operation of a skill exchange would depend on the existence of agencies which would facilitate the development of directory information and assure its free and inexpensive use. Such an agency might also provide supplementary services of testing and certification and might help to enforce the legislation required to break up and prevent monopolistic practices.

Fundamentally, the freedom of a universal skill exchange must be guaranteed by laws which prevent discrimination only on the basis of tested skills and not on the basis of educational pedigree. Such a guarantee inevitably requires public control over tests which may be used to qualify persons for the job market. Otherwise, it would be possible to surreptitiously reintroduce complex batteries of tests at the work place itself which would serve for social selection. Much could be done to make skill testing objective, e.g., allowing only the operation of specific machines or systems to be tested. Tests of typing (measured according to speed, number of errors, and whether or not the typist can work from dictation), operation of an accounting system or of a hydraulic crane, driving, coding into COBOL, etc., can easily be made objective.

In fact, many of the true skills which are of practical importance can be so tested. And for the purposes of manpower-management a test of a current skill level is much more useful than the information that a person—twenty years ago—satisfied his teacher in a curriculum where typing, stenography, and accounting were taught. The very need for official skill testing can, of course, be questioned: I personally believe that freedom from undue hurt to a man's reputation through labeling is better guaranteed by restricting than by forbidding tests of competence.

PEER MATCHING

At their worst, schools gather classmates into the same room and subject them to the same sequence of treatment in math, citizenship, and spelling. At their best, they permit each student to choose one of a limited number of courses. In any case, groups of peers form around the goals of teachers. A desirable educational system would let each person specify the activity for which he seeks a peer.

School does offer children an opportunity to escape their homes and meet new friends. But, at the same time, this process indoctrinates children with the idea that they should select their friends from among those with whom they are put together. Providing the young from their earliest age with invitations to meet, evaluate, and seek out others would prepare them for a lifelong interest in seeking new partners for new endeavors.

A good chess player is always glad to find a close match, and one novice to find another. Clubs serve their purpose. People who want to discuss specific books or articles would probably pay to find discussion partners. People who want to play games, go on excursions, build fish tanks, or motorize bicycles will go to considerable lengths to find peers. The reward for their efforts is finding those peers. Good schools try to bring out the common interests of their students registered in the same program. The inverse of school would be an institution which increases the chances that persons who at a given moment share the same specific interest could meet—no matter what else they have in common.

Skill teaching does not provide equal benefits for both parties, as does the matching of peers. The teacher of skills, as I have pointed out, must usually be offered some incentive beyond the rewards of teaching. Skill teaching is a matter of repeating drills over and over and is, in fact, all the more dreary for those pupils who need it most. A skill exchange needs currency or credits or other tangible incentives in order to operate, even if the exchange itself were to generate a currency of its own. A peer-matching system requires no such incentives, but only a communications network.

Tapes, retrieval-systems, programmed instruction, and reproduction of shapes and sounds tend to reduce the need for recourse to human teachers of many skills; they increase the efficiency of teachers and the number of skills one can pick up in a lifetime. Parallel to this runs an increased need to meet people interested in enjoying the newly acquired skill. A student who has picked up Greek before her vacation would like to discuss in Greek Cretan politics when she returns. A Mexican in New York wants to find other readers of the paper *Siempre*—or of *"Los Asachados,"* the most popular political cartoons. Somebody else wants to meet peers who—like himself—would like to increase interest in the work of James Baldwin or of Bolivar.

The operation of a peer-matching network would be simple. The user would identify himself by name and address and describe the activity for which he seeks a peer. A computer would send him back the names and addresses of all those who have inserted the same description. It is amazing that such a simple utility has never been used on a broad scale for publicly valued activity.

In its most rudimentary form, communication between client and computer could be done by return mail. In big cities, typewriter terminals could provide instantaneous responses. The only way to retrieve a name and address from the computer would be to list an activity for which a peer is sought. People using the system would become known only to their potential peers.

A complement to the computer could be a network of bulletin boards and classified newspaper ads, listing the activities for which the computer could not produce a match. No names would have to be given. Interested readers would then introduce their names into the system. A publicly supported peer-match network might be the only way to guarantee the right of free assembly and to train people in the exercise of this most fundamental civic activity.

The right of free assembly has been politically recognized and culturally accepted. We should now understand that this right is curtailed by laws that make some forms of assembly obligatory. This is especially the case with institutions which conscript according to age-group, class, or sex, and which are very time-consuming. The army is one example. School is an even more outrageous one.

To deschool means to abolish the power of one person to oblige another person to attend a meeting. It also means recognizing the right of any person, of any age or sex, to call a meeting. This right has been drastically diminished by the institutionalization of meetings. "Meeting" originally referred to the result of an individual's act of gathering. Now it refers to the institutional product of some agency.

The ability of service institutions to acquire clients has far outgrown the ability of individuals to be heard independent of institutional media, which respond to individuals only if they are salable news. Peer-matching facilities should be available for individuals who want to bring people together as easily as the village bell called the villagers to council. School buildings—of doubtful value for conversion to other uses—could often serve this purpose.

The school system, in fact, may soon face a problem which churches have faced before: what to do with surplus space emptied by the defection of the faithful. Schools are as difficult to sell as temples. One way to provide for their continued use would be to give over the space to people from the neighborhood. Each could state what he would do in the classroom and when—and a bulletin board would bring the available programs to the attention of the inquirers. Access to "class" would be free—or purchased with educational vouchers. The "teacher" could even be paid according to the number of pupils whom he could attract for any full two-hour period. I can imagine that very young leaders and great educators would be the two types most prominent in such a system. The same approach could be taken toward higher education. Students could be furnished with educational

vouchers which entitle them for ten hours yearly private consultation with the teacher of their choice—and, for the rest of their learning, depend on the library, the peer-matching network, and apprenticeships.

We must, of course, recognize the probability that such public matching devices would be abused for exploitative and immoral purposes, just as the telephone and the mails have been so abused. As with those networks, there must be some protection. I have proposed elsewhere[2] a matching system which would allow only pertinent printed information, plus the name and address of the inquirer, to be used. Such a system would be virtually fool-proof against abuse. Other arrangements could allow the addition of any book, film, TV program, or other item quoted from a special catalogue. Concern with the dangers should not make us lose sight of the far greater benefits.

Some who share my concern for free speech and assembly will argue that peer-matching is an artificial means of bringing people together and would not be used by the poor—who most need it. Some people get genuinely agitated when mention is made of creating ad-hoc encounters which are not rooted in the life of a local community. Others react when mention is made of using a computer to sort and match client-identified interests. People cannot be drawn together in such an impersonal manner, they say. Common inquiry must be rooted in a history of shared experience at many levels, and must grow out of this experience —or in the development of neighborhood institutions, for example.

I sympathize with these objections, but I think they miss my point as well as their own. In the first place, the return to neighborhood life as the primary center of creative expression might actually work against the reestablishment of neighborhoods as political units. Centering demands on the neighborhood may, in fact, neglect an important liberating aspect of urban life—the ability of a person to participate simultaneously in several peer groups. Also, there is an important sense in which people who have never lived together in a physical community may have occasionally far more experiences to share than those who have known each other from childhood. The great religions have always recognized the importance of far-off encounters and the faithful have always found freedom through them: pilgrimage, monasticism, the mutual support of temples and sanctuaries reflect this awareness. Peer-matching could significantly help in making explicit the many potential but suppressed communities of the city.

Local communities are valuable. They are also a vanishing reality as men progressively let service institutions define their circles of social relationship. Milton Kotler in his recent book[3] has shown that the imperialism of "downtown" deprives the neighborhood of its political significance. The protectionist attempt to resurrect the neighborhood as a cultural unit only supports this bureaucratic imperialism. Far from artificially removing men from their local contexts to join abstract groupings, peer-matching should encourage the restoration of local life to cities from which it is now disappearing. A man who recovers his initiative to call his fellows into meaningful conversation may cease to settle for being separated from them by office protocol or suburban etiquette. Having once seen that doing things together depends on deciding to do so, men may even insist that their local communities become more open to creative political exchange.

We must recognize that city life tends to become immensely costly as city-dwellers must be taught to rely for every one of their needs on complex institutional services. It is extremely expensive to keep it even minimally livable. Peer-matching in the city could be a first step toward breaking down the dependence of citizens on bureaucratic civic services.

It would also be an essential step to providing new means of establishing public trust. In a schooled society we have come to rely more and more on the professional judgment of educators on the effect of their own work in order to decide whom we can or cannot trust: We go to the doctor, lawyer, or psychologist because we trust that anybody with the amount of specialized educational treatment by other colleagues deserves our confidence.

In a deschooled society professionals could no longer claim the trust of their clients on the basis of their curricular pedigree, or ensure their standing by simply referring their clients to other professionals who approve of their schooling. Instead of placing trust in professionals it should be possible, at any time, for any potential client to consult with other experienced clients of a professional about their satisfaction with him by means of another peer network easily set up by computer, or by a number of other means. Such networks can be seen as public utilities which permit students to choose their teachers or patients their healers.

PROFESSIONAL EDUCATORS

As citizens have new choices, new chances for learning, their willingness to seek leadership should increase. We may expect that they will experience more deeply both their own independence and their need for guidance. As they are liberated from manipulation by others, they learn to profit from the discipline others have acquired in a lifetime. Deschooling education should increase—rather than stifle—the search for men with practical wisdom who are willing to sustain the newcomer on his educational adventure. As teachers abandon their claim to be superior informants or skill-models, their claim to superior wisdom will begin to ring true.

With an increasing demand for teachers, their supply should also increase. As the schoolmaster vanishes, the conditions arise which should bring forth the vocation of the independent educator. This may seem almost a contradiction in terms, so thoroughly have schools and teachers become complementary. Yet this is exactly what the development of the first three educational exchanges would tend to produce—and what would be required to permit their full exploitation—for parents and other "natural educators" need guidance, individual learners need assistance, and the networks need people to operate them.

Parents need guidance in guiding their children on the road that leads to responsible educational independence. Learners need experienced leadership when they encounter rough terrain. These two needs are quite distinct: The first is a need for pedagogy, the second for intellectual leadership in all other fields of knowledge. The first calls for knowledge of human learning and of educational resources, the second for wisdom based on experience in any kind of exploration. Both kinds of experience are indispensable for effective educational endeavor. Schools package these functions into one role—and render the independent exercise of any of them if not disreputable at least suspect.

Three types of special educational competence should in fact be distinguished: one to create and operate the kinds of educational exchanges or networks outlined here; another to guide students and parents in the use of these networks; and a third to act as *primus inter pares* in undertaking difficult intellectual exploratory journeys. Only the former two can be conceived of as branches of an independent profession: educational administrators or pedagogical counselors. To design and operate the networks I have been describing would not require many people, but it would require people with the most profound understanding of education and administration, in a perspective quite different from and even opposed to that of schools.

While an independent educational profession of this kind would welcome many people whom the schools exclude, it would also exclude many whom the schools qualify. The establishment and operation of educational networks would require some designers and administrators, but not in the numbers or of the type required by the administration of schools. Student discipline, public relations, hiring, supervising, and firing teachers would have neither place nor counterpart in the networks I have been describing. Neither would curriculum-making, textbook purchasing, the maintenance of grounds and facilities or the supervision of inter-scholastic athletic competition. Nor would child custody, lesson planning, and record keeping, which now take up so much of the time of teachers, figure in the operation of educational networks. Instead the operation of networks would require some of the skills and attitudes now expected from the staff of a museum, a library, an executive employment agency, or a maitre d'hotel.

Today's educational administrators are concerned with controlling teachers and students to the satisfaction of others—trustees, legislatures, and corporate executives. Network builders and administrators would have to demonstrate genius at keeping themselves, and others, out of people's way, at facilitating encounters of students, skill models, educational leaders, and educational objects. Many persons now attracted to teaching are

profoundly authoritarian and would not be able to assume this task: building educational exchanges would mean making it easy for people—especially the young—to pursue goals which might contradict the ideals of the traffic manager who makes the pursuit possible. Pedagogues, in an unschooled world, would also come into their own, and be able to do what frustrated teachers pretend to pursue today.

If the networks I have described can emerge, the educational path of each student would be his own to follow, and only in retrospect would it take on the features of a recognizable program. The wise student would periodically seek professional advice: assistance to set a new goal, insight into difficulties encountered, choice between possible methods. Even now, most persons would admit that the important services their teachers have rendered them are such advice or counsel, given at a chance meeting or in a tutorial.

While network administrators would concentrate primarily on the building and maintenance of roads providing access to resources, the pedagogue would help the student to find the path which for him could lead fastest to his goal. If a student wants to learn spoken Cantonese from a Chinese neighbor, the pedagogue would be available to judge their proficiency, and to help them select the textbook and methods most suitable to their talents, character, and the time available for study. He can counsel the would-be airplane mechanic on finding the best places for apprenticeship. He can recommend books to somebody who wants to find challenging peers to discuss African history. Like the network administrator, the pedagogical counselor conceives of himself as a professional educator. Access to either could be gained by individuals through the use of educational vouchers.

The role of the educational initiator or leader, the master or "true" leader, is somewhat more elusive than that of the professional administrator or pedagogue. This is so because leadership is itself hard to define. In practice, an individual is a leader if people follow his initiative, and become apprentices in his progressive discoveries. It is hard to amplify this definition except in the light of personal values or preference. Frequently, this involves a prophetic vision of entirely new standards

—quite understandable today—in which present "wrong" will turn out to be "right." In a society which would honor the right to call assemblies through peer-matching, the ability to take educational initiative on a specific subject would be as wide as access to learning itself. But, of course, there is a vast difference between the initiative taken by someone to call a fruitful meeting to discuss this article, and the ability of someone to provide leadership in the systematic exploration of its implications.

Leadership also does not depend on being right. As Thomas Kuhn points out, in a period of constantly changing paradigms most of the very distinguished leaders are bound to be proven wrong by the test of hindsight. Intellectual leadership does depend on superior intellectual discipline and imagination, and the willingness to associate with others in their exercise. A learner, for example, may think that there is an analogy between the U.S. antislavery movement or the Cuban Revolution and what is happening in Harlem. The educator who is himself a historian can show him how to appreciate the flaws in such an analogy. He may retrace his own steps as a historian. He may invite the learner to participate in his own research. In both cases he will apprentice his pupil in a critical art—which is rare in school—and which money or other favors cannot buy.

The relationship of master and disciple is not restricted to intellectual discipline. It has its counterpart in the arts, in physics, in religion, in psychoanalysis, and in pedagogy. It fits mountainclimbing, silverworking, and politics, cabinetmaking and personnel administration. What is common to all true master-pupil relationships is the awareness both share that their relationship is literally priceless—and in very different ways a privilege for both.

Charlatans, demagogues, clowns, proselytizers, corrupt masters and simoniacal priests, tricksters, miracle workers, and messiahs have proven capable of assuming leadership roles and thus show the dangers of any dependence of a disciple on the master. Different societies have taken different measures to defend themselves against these counterfeit teachers. Indians relied on caste-lineage, eastern Jews on the spiritual lineage of rabbis, high periods of Christianity on an exemplary life of monastic virtue, other periods on hierarchical or-

ders. Our society relies on certification by schools. It is doubtful that this procedure provides a better screening, but if it should be claimed that it does, then the counterclaim can be made that it does so at the cost of making discipleship almost vanish.

In practice, there will always be a fuzzy line between the teacher of skills and the educational leaders identified above, and there are no practical reasons why access to some leaders could not be gained by discovering the "master" in the drill-teacher who introduces students to his discipline.

On the other hand, what characterizes the true master-disciple relationship is its priceless character. Aristotle speaks of it as a "moral type of friendship, which is not on fixed terms: it makes a gift, or does whatever it does, as to a friend." Thomas Aquinas says of this kind of teaching that inevitably it is an act of love and mercy. This kind of teaching is always a luxury for the teacher and a form of leisure (in Greek, "scholé") for him and his pupil: an activity meaningful for both—having no ulterior purpose.

To rely for true intellectual leadership on the desire of gifted people to provide it is obviously necessary even in our society, but it could not be made into a policy now. We must first construct a society in which personal acts themselves re-acquire a value higher than that of making things and manipulating people.[4] In such a society exploratory, inventive, creative teaching would logically be counted among the most desirable forms of leisurely "unemployment." But we do not have to wait until the advent of utopia. Even now one of the most important consequences of deschooling and the establishment of peer-matching facilities would be the initiative which "masters" could take to assemble congenial disciples. It would also—as we have seen—provide ample opportunity for potential disciples to share information or to select a master.

Schools are not the only institutions which pervert professions by packaging roles. Hopitals render home-care increasingly impossible—and then justify hospitalization as a benefit to the sick. At the same time the doctor's legitimacy and ability to work increasingly come to depend on his association with a hospital, even though he is still less totally dependent on it then are teachers on schools. The same could be said about courts which overcrowd their calendars as new transactions acquire legal solemnity—and thus delay justice. Or it could be said about churches, which succeed in making a captive profession out of a free vocation. The result in each case is scarce service at higher cost; and greater income to the less competent members of the profession.

So long as the older professions monopolize superior income and prestige it is difficult to reform them. The profession of the schoolteacher should be easier to reform, and not only because it is of more recent origin. The educational profession now claims a comprehensive monopoly; it claims the exclusive competence to apprentice not only its own novices but those of other professions as well. This overexpansion renders it vulnerable to any profession which would reclaim the right to teach its own apprentices. Schoolteachers are overwhelmingly badly paid and frustrated by the tight control of the school system. The most enterprising and gifted among them would probably find more congenial work, more independence, and even higher incomes by specializing as skill models, network administrators, or guidance specialists.

Finally, the dependence of the registered student on the certified teacher can be broken more easily than his dependence on other professionals—for instance, that of a hospitalized patient on his doctor. If schools ceased to be compulsory, teachers who find their satisfaction in the exercise of pedagogical authority in the classroom would be left only with pupils who are attracted by their style. The disestablishment of our present professional structure could begin with the dropping out of the schoolteacher.

The disestablishment of schools will inevitably happen—and it will happen surprisingly fast. It cannot be retarded very much longer and it is hardly necessary to vigorously promote it, for this is being done now. What is worthwhile is to try to orient it in a hopeful direction, for it could take place in two diametrically opposed ways.

The first would be the expansion of the mandate of the pedagogue and his increasing control over society even outside school. With the best of intentions and simply by expanding the rhetoric now used in school, the present crisis in the schools could provide educators with an excuse to use all the networks of contemporary society to funnel their messages to us—for our own good. Deschooling, which we cannot stop, could mean the advent of a "brave new world" dominated by well-intentioned administrators of programmed instruction.

On the other hand, the growing awareness on the part of governments, as well as of employers, taxpayers, enlightened pedagogues, and school administrators, that graded curricular teaching for certification has become harmful could offer large masses of people an extraordinary opportunity: that of preserving the right of equal access to the tools both of learning and of sharing with others what they know or believe. But this would require that the educational revolution be guided by certain goals.

1. To liberate access to things by abolishing the control which persons and institutions now exercise over their educational values.

2. To liberate the sharing of skills by guaranteeing freedom to teach or exercise them on request.

3. To liberate the critical and creative resources of people by returning to individual persons the ability to call and hold meetings: an ability now increasingly monopolized by institutions which claim to speak for the people.

4. To liberate the individual from the obligation to shape his expectations to the services offered by any established profession—by providing him with the opportunity to draw on the experience of his peers and to entrust himself to the teacher, guide, adviser, or healer of his choice.

Inevitably deschooling of society blurs the distinctions between economics, education, and politics on which the stability of the present world order and the stability of nations now rests.

In addition to the tentative conclusions of the Carnegie Commission reports, the last year has brought forth a series of important documents which show that responsible people are becoming aware of the fact that schooling for certification cannot continue to be counted upon as the central educational device of modern society. Julius Nyerere of Tanzania has announced plans to integrate education with the life of the village. In Canada, the Wright Commission on post-secondary education has reported that no known system of formal education could provide equal opportunities for the citizens of Ontario. The president of Peru has accepted the recommendation of his commission on education, which proposes to abolish free schools in favor of free educational opportunities provided throughout life. In fact he is reported to have insisted that this program proceed slowly at first in order to keep teachers in school and out of the way of true educators.

What has happened is that some of the boldest and most imaginative public leaders find their insights into school failures matching those of radical free spirits (for example, Paul Goodman) who only a few years ago were seen as "anarchic." More programmatic radicals, on the other hand, often simply seek to obtain control over schools and other teaching media and thus only strengthen the certification system.

The alternative to social control through the schools is the voluntary participation in society through networks which provide access to all its resources for learning. In fact these networks now exist, but they are rarely used for educational purposes. The crisis of schooling, if it is to have any positive consequence, will inevitably lead to their incorporation into the educational process.

NOTES

[1]"Schooling: The Ritual of Progress," New York Review of Books, December 3, 1970.
[2]"Why We Must Abolish Schooling," New York Review of Books, July 2, 1970.
[3]M. Kotler, Neighborhood Governments: The Local Foundations of Political Life, Bobbs-Merrill, 1969.
[4]For a fuller discussion of these distinctions, see my book, De-Schooling Society, Harper and Row, 1971.

IN PRAISE OF IDLENESS

Bertrand Russell

Like most of my generation, I was brought up on the saying: "Satan finds some mischief still for idle hands to do." Being a highly virtuous child, I believed all that I was told, and acquired a conscience which has kept me working hard down to the present moment. But although my conscience has controlled my *actions,* my *opinions* have undergone a revolution. I think that there is far too much work done in the world, that immense harm is caused by the belief that work is virtuous, and

that what needs to be preached in modern industrial countries is quite different from what always has been preached. Everyone knows the story of the traveller in Naples who saw twelve beggars lying in the sun (it was before the days of Mussolini), and offered a lira to the laziest of them. Eleven of them jumped up to claim it, so he gave it to the twelfth. This traveller was on the right lines. But in countries which do not enjoy Mediterranean sunshine idleness is more difficult, and a great public propaganda will be required to inaugurate it. I hope that, after reading the following pages, the leaders of the YMCA will start a campaign to induce good young men to do nothing. If so, I shall not have lived in vain.

Before advancing my own arguments for laziness, I must dispose of one which I cannot accept. Whenever a person who already has enough to live on proposes to engage in some everyday kind of job, such as school-teaching or typing, he or she is told that such conduct takes the bread out of other people's mouths, and is therefore wicked. If this argument were valid, it would only be necessary for us all to be idle in order that we should all have our mouths full of bread. What people who say such things forget is that what a man earns he usually spends, and in spending he gives employment. As long as a man spends his income, he puts just as much bread into people's mouths in spending as he takes out of other people's mouths in earning. The real villain, from this point of view, is the man who saves. If he merely puts his savings in a stocking, like the proverbial French peasant, it is obvious that they do not give employment. If he invests his savings, the matter is less obvious, and different cases arise.

One of the commonest things to do with savings is to lend them to some Government. In view of the fact that the bulk of the public expenditure of most civilized Governments consists in payment for past wars or preparation for future wars, the man who lends his money to a Government is in the same position as the bad men in Shakespeare who hire murderers. The net result of the man's economical habits is to increase the armed forces of the State to which he lends his savings. Obviously it would be better if he spent the money, even if he spent it in drink or gambling.

But, I shall be told, the case is quite different when savings are invested in industrial enterprises. When such enterprises succeed, and produce something useful, this may be conceded. In these days, however, no one will deny that most enterprises fail. That means that a large amount of human labour, which might have been devoted to producing something that could be enjoyed, was expended on producing machines which, when produced, lay idle and did no good to anyone. The man who invests his savings in a concern that goes bankrupt is therefore injuring others as well as himself. If he spent his money, say, in giving parties for his friends, they (we may hope) would get pleasure, and so would all those upon whom he spent money, such as the butcher, the baker, and the

bootlegger. But if he spends it (let us say) upon laying down rails for surface cars in some place where surface cars turn out to be not wanted, he has diverted a mass of labour into channels where it gives pleasure to no one. Nevertheless, when he becomes poor through the failure of his investment he will be regarded as a victim of undeserved misfortune, whereas the gay spendthrift, who has spent his money philanthropically, will be despised as a fool and a frivolous person.

All this is only preliminary. I want to say, in all seriousness, that a great deal of harm is being done in the modern world by belief in the virtuousness of Work, and that the road to happiness and prosperity lies in an organized diminution of work.

First of all: What is work? Work is of two kinds: first, altering the position of matter at or near the earth's surface relatively to other such matter; second, telling other people to do so. The first kind is unpleasant and ill paid; the second is pleasant and highly paid. The second kind is capable of indefinite extension: there are not only those who give orders, but those who give advice as to what orders should be given. Usually two opposite kinds of advice are given simultaneously by two organized bodies of men; this is called politics. The skill required for this kind of work is not knowledge of the subjects as to which advice is given, but knowledge of the art of persuasive speaking and writing, i.e., of advertising.

Throughout Europe, though not in America, there is a third class of men, more respected than either of the classes of workers. There are men who, through ownership of land, are able to make others pay for the privilege of being allowed to exist and to work. These landowners are idle, and I might therefore be expected to praise them. Unfortunately, their idleness is only rendered possible by the industry of others; indeed their desire for comfortable idleness is historically the source of the whole gospel of work. The last thing they have ever wished is that others should follow their example.

From the beginning of civilization until the Industrial Revolution, a man could, as a rule, produce by hard work little more than was required for the subsistence of himself and his family, although his wife worked at least as hard as he did, and his children added their labour as soon as they were old enough to do so. The small surplus above bare necessaries was not left to those who produced it, but was appropriated by warriors and priests. In times of famine there was no surplus; the warriors and priests, however, still secured as much as at other times, with the result that many of the workers died of hunger. This system persisted in Russia until 1917 (since then, members of the Communist Party have succeeded to this privilege of the warriors and priests), and still persists in the East; in England, in spite of the Industrial Revolution, it remained in full force throughout the Napoleonic wars, and until a hundred years ago, when the new class of manufacturers acquired power. In America, the system came to an end with the Revolution, except in the South, where it persisted until the Civil War. A system which lasted so long and ended so recently has naturally left a profound impress upon men's thoughts and opinions. Much that we take for granted about the desirability of work is derived from this system, and, being pre-industrial, is not adapted to the modern world. Modern technique has made it possible for leisure, within limits, to be not the prerogative of small privileged classes, but a right evenly distributed throughout the community. The morality of work is the morality of slaves, and the modern world has no need of slavery.

It is obvious that, in primitive communities, peasants, left to themselves, would not have parted with the slender surplus upon which the warriors and priests subsisted, but would have either produced less or consumed more. At first, sheer force compelled them to produce and part with the surplus. Gradually, however, it was found possible to induce many of them to accept an ethic according to which it was their duty to work hard, although part of their work went to support others in idleness. By this means the amount of compulsion required was lessened, and the expenses of government were diminished. To this day, 99 per cent of British wage-earners would be genuinely shocked if it were proposed that the King should not have a larger income than a working man. The conception of duty, speaking historically, has been a means used by the holders of power to induce others to live for the interests of their masters rather than for their own. Of course the holders of power conceal this fact from themselves by managing to believe that their interests are identical with the larger interests of humanity. Sometimes this is true; Athenian slave-owners, for instance, employed part of their leisure in making a permanent contribution to civilization which would have been impossible under a just economic system. Leisure is essential to civilization, and in former times leisure for the few was only rendered possible by the labours of the many. But their labours were valuable, not because work is good, but because leisure is good. And with modern technique it would be possible to distribute leisure justly without injury to civilization.

Modern technique has made it possible to diminish enormously the amount of labour required to secure the necessaries of life for everyone. This was made obvious during the war. At that time, all the men in the armed forces, all the men and women engaged in the production of munitions, all the men and women engaged in spying, war propaganda, or Government offices connected with the war, were withdrawn from productive occupations. In spite of this, the general level of physical well-being among unskilled wage-earners on the side of the Allies was higher than before or since. The significance of this fact was concealed by finance: borrowing made it appear as if the future was nourishing the present. But that, of course, would have been impossible; a man cannot eat a loaf of bread that does not yet exist. The war showed conclusively that, by the scientific organization of production, it is possible to keep modern populations in fair comfort on a small part of the working capacity of the modern world. If, at the end of the war, the scientific organization, which had been created in order to liberate men for fighting and munition work, had been preserved, and the hours of work had been cut down to four, all would have been well. Instead of that the old chaos was restored, those whose work was demanded were made to work long hours, and the rest were left to starve as unemployed. Why? because work is a duty, and a man should not receive wages in proportion to what he has produced, but in proportion to his virtue as exemplified by his industry.

This is the morality of the Slave State, applied in circumstances totally unlike those in which it arose. No wonder the result has been disastrous. Let us take an illustration. Suppose that, at a given moment, a certain number of people are engaged in the manufacture of pins. They make as many pins as the world needs, working (say) eight hours a day. Someone makes an invention by which the same number of men can make twice as many pins as before. But the world does not need twice as many pins: pins are already so cheap that hardly any more will be bought at a lower price. In a sensible world, everybody concerned in the manufacture of pins would take to working four hours instead of eight, and everything else would go on as before. But in the actual world this would be thought demoralizing. The men still work eight hours, there are too many pins, some employers go bankrupt, and half the men previously concerned in making pins are thrown out of work. There is, in the end, just as much leisure as on the other plan, but half the men are totally idle while half are still overworked. In this way, it is insured that the un-avoidable leisure shall cause misery all round in-stead of being a universal source of happiness. Can anything more insane be imagined?

The idea that the poor should have leisure has always been shocking to the rich. In England, in the early nineteenth century, fifteen hours was the or-dinary day's work for a man; children sometimes did as much, and very commonly did twelve hours a day. When meddlesome busybodies suggested that perhaps these hours were rather long, they were told that work kept adults from drink and children from mischief. When I was a child, shortly after urban working men had acquired the vote, certain public holidays were established by law, to the great indignation of the upper classes. I remem-ber hearing an old Duchess say: "What do the poor want with holidays? They ought to *work.*" People nowadays are less frank, but the sentiment persists, and is the source of much of our economic confusion.

Let us, for a moment, consider the ethics of work frankly, without superstition. Every human being, of necessity, consumes, in the course of his life, a certain amount of the produce of human labour. Assuming, as we may, that labour is on the whole disagreeable, it is unjust that a man should con-sume more than he produces. Of course he may provide services rather than commodities, like a

medical man, for example; but he should provide something in return for his board and lodging. To this extent, the duty of work must be admitted, but to this extent only.

I shall not dwell upon the fact that, in all modern societies outside the U.S.S.R., many people escape even this minimum of work, namely all those who inherit money and all those who marry money. I do not think the fact that these people are allowed to be idle is nearly so harmful as the fact that wage-earners are expected to overwork or starve.

If the ordinary wage-earner worked four hours a day, there would be enough for everybody, and no unemployment—assuming a certain very moder-ate amount of sensible organization. This idea shocks the well-to-do, because they are convinced that the poor would not know how to use so much leisure. In America, men often work long hours even when they are already well off; such men, naturally, are indignant at the idea of leisure for wage-earners, except as the grim punishment of unemployment; in fact, they dislike leisure even for their sons. Oddly enough, while they wish their sons to work so hard as to have no time to be civilized, they do not mind their wives and daugh-ters having no work at all. The snobbish admiration of uselessness, which, in an aristocratic society, extends to both sexes, is, under a plutocracy, confined to women; this, however, does not make it any more in agreement with common sense.

The wise use of leisure, it must be conceded, is a product of civilization and education. A man who has worked long hours all his life will be bored if he becomes suddenly idle. But without a consid-erable amount of leisure a man is cut off from many of the best things. There is no longer any reason why the bulk of the population should suffer this deprivation; only a foolish asceticism, usually vi-carious, makes us continue to insist on work in excessive quantities now that the need no longer exists.

In the new creed which controls the government of Russia, while there is much that is very different from the traditional teaching of the West, there are some things that are quite unchanged. The attitude of the governing classes, and especially of those who conduct educational propaganda, on the sub-ject of the dignity of labour, is almost exactly that which the governing classes of the world have always preached to what were called the "honest poor." Industry, sobriety, willingness to work long hours for distant advantages, even submissiveness to authority, all these reappear; moreover authority still represents the will of the Ruler of the Universe, who, however, is now called by a new name—Dialectical Materialism.

The victory of the proletariat in Russia has some points in common with the victory of the feminists in some other countries. For ages, men had conceded the superior saintliness of women, and had consoled women for their inferiority by maintaining that saintliness is more desirable than power. At last the feminists decided that they would have both, since the pioneers among them believed all that the men had told them about the desirability of virtue, but not what they had told them about the worthlessness of political power. A similar thing has happened in Russia as regards manual work. For ages, the rich and their sycophants have written in praise of "honest toil," have praised the simple life, have professed a religion which teaches that the poor are much more likely to go to heaven than the rich, and in general have tried to make manual workers believe that there is some special nobility about altering the position of matter in space, just as men tried to make women believe that they derived some special nobility from their sexual enslavement. In Russia, all this teaching about the excellence of manual work has been taken seriously, with the result that the manual worker is more honoured than anyone else. What are, in essence, revivalist appeals are made, but not for the old purposes: they are made to secure shock workers for special tasks. Manual work is the ideal which is held before the young, and is the basis of all ethical teaching.

For the present, possibly, this is all to the good. A large country, full of natural resources, awaits development, and has to be developed with very little use of credit. In these circumstances, hard work is necessary, and is likely to bring a great reward. But what will happen when the point has been reached where everybody could be comfortable without working long hours?

In the West, we have various ways of dealing with this problem. We have no attempt at economic justice, so that a large proportion of the total produce goes to a small minority of the population, many of whom do no work at all. Owing to the absence of any central control over production, we produce hosts of things that are not wanted. We keep a large percentage of the working population idle, because we can dispense with their labour by making the others overwork. When all these methods prove inadequate, we have a war: We cause a number of people to manufacture high explosives, and a number of others to explode them, as if we were children who had just discovered fireworks. By a combination of all these devices we manage, though with difficulty, to keep alive the notion that a great deal of severe manual work must be the lot of the average man.

In Russia, owing to more economic justice and central control over production, the problem will have to be differently solved. The rational solution would be, as soon as the necessaries and elementary comforts can be provided for all, to reduce the hours of labour gradually, allowing a popular vote to decide, at each stage, whether more leisure or more goods were to be preferred. But, having taught the supreme virtue of hard work, it is difficult to see how the authorities can aim at a paradise in which there will be much leisure and little work. It seems more likely that they will find continually fresh schemes, by which present leisure is to be sacrificed to future productivity. I read recently of an ingenious plan put forward by Russian engineers, for making the White Sea and the northern coasts of Siberia warm, by putting a dam across the Kara Sea. An admirable project, but liable to postpone proletarian comfort for a generation, while the nobility of toil is being displayed amid the ice-fields and snowstorms of the Arctic Ocean. This sort of thing, if it happens, will be the result of regarding the virtue of hard work as an end in itself, rather than as a means to a state of affairs in which it is no longer needed.

The fact is that moving matter about, while a certain amount of it is necessary to our existence, is emphatically not one of the ends of human life. If it were, we should have to consider every navvy superior to Shakespeare. We have been misled in this matter by two causes. One is the necessity of keeping the poor contented, which has led the rich, for thousands of years, to preach the dignity of labour, while taking care themselves to remain undignified in this respect. The other is the new pleasure in mechanism, which makes us delight in the astonishingly clever changes that we can produce on the earth's surface. Neither of these motives makes any great appeal to the actual worker. If you ask him what he thinks the best part of his life, he is not likely to say: "I enjoy manual work because it makes me feel that I am fulfilling man's noblest task, and because I like to think how much man can transform his planet. It is true that my body demands periods of rest, which I have to fill in as best I may, but I am never so happy as when the morning comes and I can return to the toil from which my contentment springs." I have never heard working men say this sort of thing. They consider work, as it should be considered, a necessary means to a livelihood, and it is from their leisure hours that they derive whatever happiness they may enjoy.

It will be said that, while a little leisure is pleasant, men would not know how to fill their days if they had only four hours of work out of the twenty-four. In so far as this is true in the modern world, it is a condemnation of our civilization; it would not have been true at any earlier period. There was formerly a capacity for light-heartedness and play which has been to some extent inhibited by the cult of efficiency. The modern man thinks that everything ought to be done for the sake of something else, and never for its own sake. Serious-minded persons, for example, are continually condemning the habit of going to the cinema, and telling us that it leads the young into crime. But all the work that goes to producing a cinema is respectable, because it is work, and because it brings a money profit. The notion that the desirable activities are those that bring a profit has made everything topsy-turvy. The butcher who provides you with meat and the baker who provides you with bread are praiseworthy, because they are making money; but when you enjoy the food they have provided, you are merely frivolous, unless you eat only to get strength for your work. Broadly speaking, it is held that getting money is good and spending money is bad. Seeing that they are two sides of one transaction, this is absurd; one might as well maintain that keys are good, but keyholes are bad. Whatever merit there may be in the production of goods must be entirely derivative from the advantage to be obtained by consuming them. The individual, in our society, works for profit; but the social purpose of his work lies in the consumption of what he produces. It is this divorce between the individual and the social purpose of production that makes it so difficult for men to think clearly in a world in which profit-making is the incentive to industry. We think too much of production, and too little of consumption. One result is that we attach too little importance to enjoyment and simple happiness, and that we do not judge production by the pleasure that it gives to the consumer.

When I suggest that working hours should be reduced to four, I am not meaning to imply that all the remaining time should necessarily be spent in pure frivolity. I mean that four hours' work a day should entitle a man to the necessities and elementary comforts of life, and that the rest of his time should be his to use as he might see fit. It is an essential part of any such social system that education should be carried further than it usually is at present, and should aim, in part, at providing tastes which would enable a man to use leisure intelligently. I am not thinking mainly of the sort of things that would be considered "highbrow." Peasant dances have died out except in remote rural areas, but the impulses which caused them to be cultivated must still exist in human nature. The pleasures of urban populations have become mainly passive: seeing cinemas, watching football matches, listening to the radio, and so on. This results from the fact that their active energies are fully taken up with work; if they had more leisure, they would again enjoy pleasures in which they took an active part.

In the past, there was a small leisure class and a larger working class. The leisure class enjoyed advantages for which there was no basis in social justice; this necessarily made it oppressive, limited its sympathies, and caused it to invent theories by which to justify its privileges. These facts greatly diminished its excellence, but in spite of this drawback it contributed nearly the whole of what we call civilization. It cultivated the arts and discovered the sciences; it wrote the books, invented the philosophies, and refined social relations. Even the liberation of the oppressed has usually been inaugurated from above. Without the leisure class, mankind would never have emerged from barbarism.

The method of a hereditary leisure class without duties was, however, extraordinarily wasteful. None of the members of the class had been taught to be industrious, and the class as a whole was not exceptionally intelligent. The class might produce one Darwin, but against him had to be set tens of thousands of country gentlemen who never thought of anything more intelligent than fox-hunting and punishing poachers. At present, the universities are supposed to provide, in a more systematic way, what the leisure class provided accidentally and as a by-product. This is a great improvement, but it has certain drawbacks. University life is so different from life in the world at large that men who live in an academic *milieu* tend to be unaware of the preoccupations and problems of ordinary men and women; moreover their ways of expressing themselves are usually such as to rob their opinions of the influence that they ought to have upon the general public. Another disadvantage is that in universities studies are organized, and the man who thinks of some original line of research is likely to be discouraged. Academic institutions, therefore, useful as they are, are not adequate guardians of the interests of civilization in a world where everyone outside their walls is too busy for unutilitarian pursuits.

In a world where no one is compelled to work more than four hours a day, every person possessed of scientific curiosity will be able to indulge it, and every painter will be able to paint without starving, however excellent his pictures may be. Young writers will not be obliged to draw attention to themselves by sensational pot-boilers, with a view to acquiring the economic independence needed for monumental works, for which, when the time at last comes, they will have lost the taste and the capacity. Men who, in their professional work, have become interested in some phase of economics or government, will be able to develop their ideas without the academic detachment that makes the work of university economists often seem lacking in reality. Medical men will have time to learn about the progress of medicine, teachers will not be exasperatedly struggling to teach by routine methods things which they learnt in their youth, which may, in the interval, have been proved to be untrue.

Above all, there will be happiness and joy of life, instead of frayed nerves, weariness, and dyspepsia. The work exacted will be enough to make leisure delightful, but not enough to produce exhaustion. Since men will not be tired in their spare time, they will not demand only such amusements as are passive and vapid. At least 1 per cent will probably devote the time not spent in professional work to pursuits of some public importance, and, since they will not depend upon these pursuits for their livelihood, their originality will be unhampered, and there will be no need to conform to the standards set by elderly pundits. But it is not only in these exceptional cases that the advantages of leisure will appear. Ordinary men and women, having the opportunity of a happy life, will become more kindly and less persecuting and less inclined to view others with suspicion. The taste for war will die out, partly for this reason, and partly because it will involve long and severe work for all. Good nature is, of all moral qualities, the one that the world needs most, and good nature is the result of ease and security, not of a life of arduous struggle. Modern methods of production have given us the possibility of ease and security for all; we have chosen, instead, to have overwork for some and starvation for the others. Hitherto we have continued to be as energetic as we were before there were machines; in this we have been foolish, but there is no reason to go on being foolish forever.

REVOLUTION IN AMERICA

Richard E. Rubenstein

Logic compels us, finally, to consider the question of revolution. For if the solution to the problem of group revolt is a social and political transformation which admits the powerless to power, we have already begun to talk about a kind of revolution. And if the period of transformation has, in fact, begun, it is necessary to inquire into its nature and to speculate about its probable outcome. The discussion will be brief and, of necessity, speculative; we are too close to the subject to claim objectivity. Nevertheless, it is at precisely such times that historical perspective is needed. Does the social and political disorder of the 1960's betoken a subsequent period of even greater disorder and more rapid change? Are we living in a prerevolutionary era? The answer depends to a large extent upon one's perspective on the American past.

First, however, we must grapple with a loaded word: "revolution." When historians say (as they so often do) that the United States has never experienced a revolution, we are entitled to know what they mean. For example, Barrington Moore believes that the American struggle for independence was *not* a true revolution because it was not accompanied by significant social change; the bourgeoisie, which had run the prerevolutionary show, continued to run it after 1781. J. Franklin Jameson and other historians think that it *was* a revolution because it *was* accompanied by genuine social change—the elimination of a domestic aristocracy and a transfer of power to small businessmen, artisans and farmers. Charles Beard thought that it started out to be a revolution but was undone by the reaction of 1789; whereas Hannah Arendt believes that it *was* a true revolution although *not* accompanied by genuine social change, since the struggle brought into the world a brand-new type of constitutional democracy. Similarly, when social

scientists or political figures state, as is their wont, that revolution in the United States is impossible, again we are entitled to know what they mean. According to Charles Beard, the Civil War was a revolution; does the statement then mean that civil war in the United States is now impossible? According to Arthur Schlesinger, Jr., the ages of Jackson and Roosevelt were revolutionary times; are we to conclude that further political transformations are now impossible in America?

Superficially, the problem is one of evidence, but only superficially. It is true that dispute continues about the facts of the American Revolution, the age of Jackson, the Civil War and the New Deal—Was there really a Tory "aristocracy"? Did small farmers really exercise power under Jackson?—the disagreements among the authorities noted above would not disappear even if all of them accepted the same facts. Moore, for example, could still hold that transfer of power from large to petit bourgeois is not a revolution (and perhaps not even a power transfer), and Arendt still assert that whether or not the colonial bourgeoisie maintained their position is irrelevant in the light of the political significance of the American Revolution. Perhaps, then, the problem is one of definition; Hannah Arendt suggests as much when she states that one ought to distinguish French-style social revolutions from American-style political ones (and, one might now add, from Algerian- or Vietnamese-style wars of national liberation). But such definitional disputes are only symptoms of a more profound disagreement. At issue is the fundamental question: "What kind of change makes a difference?" Amid the welter of political changes that characterize any rapidly developing society, which changes alter the political system so rapidly, drastically, and permanently as to be called revolutionary?

Note that this question itself implies a definition, but it is a definition based upon what political analysts seem to mean when they use the word—that is, change occurring over a fairly short period of time (in any event, not more than fifteen years or so) which replaces an "old" political system (not just a regime) with a "new" one which lasts for a while. Like all definitions, this one begs substantive questions—What is meant by "political system"? How does one tell when a "new" system has come into existence? All I want to do here, however, is to establish some principles of exclusion and clarification. We are *not* concerned with evolutionary change, although we will come back to the evolutionist posture, common among American scholars, which assumes that revolutionary change in the United States is a fiction. Nor are we concerned with nonpolitical "revolutions," such as those in science and technology, except as they affect politics. Finally, we do not adopt as a matter of definition the concept of revolution as inevitably violent, but leave the relationship of violence to revolution for later formulation. With this by way of background, *has* America ever experienced a revolution?

To begin with, it is clear that America has not had a proletarian revolution in the Marxist sense. In Marxist terms the United States remains at present, as it has always been, a bourgeois society characterized by private ownership and control of the means of production and distribution, minimal government regulation of business, trade unions dedicated to strengthening rather than replacing the capitalist system, individual rather than collective farming, and so forth. Many factors have been advanced to explain the nonoccurrence of a revolution of the proletariat, among them the absence of a feudal aristocracy to set the Marxist dialectic in motion, the availability of cheap land as a safety valve, America's incredible affluence, and the ability of the capitalist class to save itself periodically via reforms, co-optation of dissidents and destruction of radical movements. All these factors help to explain what did *not* happen. As a springboard for discussion of what *did* happen to change the American political system between 1776 and 1969 an idea of Richard Hofstadter's may be more useful: in America, he states, "ethnic animosities . . . have been at times almost a substitute for the class struggle."

America does lack a revolutionary tradition in the Marxist sense, but she has, as we have seen, experienced revolts aplenty, from Indian and slave rebellions, farmer revolts and nativist terrorism through labor-management warfare, race rioting and the ghetto revolts and campus confrontations of the present time. We have pointed out that many rebellious out-groups have been homogeneous "subnations"; that their rebellious actions have been aimed at redeeming their territory, jobs and lives from control by outsiders; that the dynamics of internal colonialism generates such movements for group liberation; and that those in authority have often responded to such revolts ineffectually rather than participating in the system transformation required to satisfy the demands of large excluded groups. The existence of this tradition of group insurrection strengthens Hofstadter's thesis by demonstrating that group consciousness in America supersedes, or prevents, the development of class consciousness. But if this is so, perhaps we have been looking for the wrong sort of revolution in American history. Perhaps domestic revolution is merely revolt writ large.

Generally, movements which begin as revolts end as revolts. A group which comes to conceive of itself as an oppressed nation or subnation distinguishes itself, in the process, from those who are outsiders and tends to move in the direction of local autonomy or independence rather than seizure of central power. For this reason, although such movements are often *locally* revolutionary, they seem profoundly nonrevolutionary with regard to the political system as a whole. On the other hand, in at least three situations, insurrectionary movements may become revolutionary in the sense that they require a rapid transformation of the entire system:

1. When those defining themselves as a group are so numerous, in control of such a large geographical area, and so nation-conscious as to attempt secession with some hope of success.

2. When a single group excluded from power at all levels attempts to force a system transformation by resort to "aggressive" violence. (Since the group may be threatened with extinction, such violence is not necessarily "aggression"; the term is used here to describe attacks outside rebel territory.)

3. When similarly situated groups conducting separate revolts join forces for the purpose of gaining

power simultaneously through radical change in the political system.

The best-known instances of revolutionary secessionism are, of course, the American Revolution and the southern rebellion which precipitated the Civil War. (Many Indian revolts may also fall into this category, since they aimed at independent control of large geographical areas, but most tribes found collaboration for the purpose of joint rebellion impossible.) A key to the development of major secessionist movements is the growth of nation-consciousness among groups which may be extremely diverse economically, politically and even culturally. Those who came to consider themselves "Americans" began as Virginia planters or Boston traders; to a great extent, the unifying group definition which they eventually adopted was forced upon them by British mercantilists. Similarly, "Southerners" originally owing primary loyalty to a state or class were driven together by northern attacks upon all classes of white southerners simultaneously. Such movements have been revolutionary in effect rather than in intention, for no matter what form of government the secessionists adopted, the effect of the separation itself would be to alter the original system immediately and profoundly. Imagine the northern United States confronted on its southern border by an expansionist slave power ambitious to conquer Central and South America—a North without a southern investment outlet, deprived of half of the free land of the West, forced to trade as a foreign nation for cotton, oil, natural gas and other southern products—and the revolutionary implications of southern secession become apparent.

At present there exists only one serious domestic secessionist movement: the movement to establish an independent black state somewhere within the continental United States (probably within the South, where selective Negro immigration might make it possible to gain legal control of certain states). As white oppression of all black economic and social classes simultaneously continues to generate black nationalism, independence sentiment appears to be gaining substantial support among northern ghetto dwellers. The movement deserves more serious study than it has so far received, particularly since the most "obvious" objections—

that the numbers of people involved are too small, that the new nation could not support itself economically or that "it could never happen"—prove on analysis to be unfounded. Like white nationalism in the South after 1865, black nationalism is not revolutionary in effect except as to the territory claimed. It is therefore possible to imagine the United States government several years and major riots hence permitting a black state to become independent (at least with regard to domestic affairs) as a way of ridding the nation of an "insoluble" problem. The more cogent objection is not that such a development is impossible, but that it is probably fruitless, since the fate of small neighbors of the United States is to be dominated either by the United States or some countervailing foreign power. The use of local power bases to forge, with other dissident groups, a new domestic alliance would seem to be better designed to maximize black power.

Black nationalism could become revolutionary, however, whether or not secession were a goal, under the circumstances described in category 2. Continued exclusion from collective power at all levels produces widespread fear of permanent exclusion and ultimate group extinction. Under the circumstances, from the point of view of the excluded group, terrorism directed against "the enemy" wherever he may be found is justifiable self-defense; the fact that massive counterforce may destroy the group is no deterrent, since the rebels prefer a brave death to perpetual dependence and the elimination of their militant members. The United States has not experienced this type of revolution before, for at least two reasons. First, the nation has never before been so centralized and so integrated (politically and economically) as to permit the members of a ruling coalition to collaborate in maintaining power at all levels. Earlier insurgent groups found it possible to take power locally; later groups benefited from the growth of federal power under the New Deal and its successors; present-day blacks find both roads blocked, except where they constitute a majority or near majority in the cities. (Even here, there is talk of instituting "metropolitan-regional governments" which would operate to nullify such black majorities.) Second, never before has the excluded group been a caste with revolutionary-national potential. (For reasons which have been previously explored, less cohesive groups with a shorter history of oppression have lacked this potential.) As a result, failing a radical redistribution of power under her present political system, America must face the prospect of a new type of domestic revolutionary movement which would seek to generate the necessary transformation by force.

It is very difficult, of course, to identify outright revolutionaries presently active within or without the ghetto, or to measure the extent of such activity or the degree to which it commands mass support. Even criminal convictions, such as those obtained against members of the Revolutionary Action Movement for conspiracy to assassinate certain political leaders, indicate little about the nature and extent of revolutionary activity; the possibility of frame-ups in such cases is greater than usual. What seems clear, however, is that there *are* organizations with some standing in the black community which will initiate revolutionary activity if the situation deteriorates further—for example, if the police are "unleashed" upon ghetto activists, or if there is an attempt at forced relocation of the black population. The largest and best organized of these is the Black Panther party, with establishments in half a dozen cities or more. Despite occasional shootouts with police, the imprisonment of West Coast leader Huey Newton, and the exile (to escape imprisonment) of Minister of Information Eldridge Cleaver, the Panthers are not yet revolutionary activists. Along with other street organizations (for example, certain of the large gangs in New York, Chicago, Detroit and Los Angeles), they stand in the wings of the revolutionary theater, waiting to enter if whites decide upon the forcible suppression of black militancy. A dangerous game? Certainly. But, to many blacks, no more dangerous than waiting passively for the blow to fall.

If the United States is now entering a revolutionary period, racial conflict alone, however, will not explain what is happening to the present political system. For this purpose we must consider a more characteristic type of revolutionary movement in America—the alliance of militant out-groups with dissidents in power which radically alters both the distribution of power and its mode of exercise throughout the system. Three examples of such alliance come to mind: the Jeffersonian, which iso-

lated New England business interests, brought the two-party system into existence and the "little man" into the electoral process, and opened up the West for mass settlement; the northern Republican, which joined eastern businessmen and "native" workers with western farmers and abolitionists on a new ethnic-sectional basis, unleashed the energies of northern capitalism and doomed the slave system to violent extinction; and the New Deal, which joined organized workers, immigrant groups, farmers and elements of the business community in a new coalition, expanded the federal government beyond the Founding Fathers' wildest dreams, and created a mixed economy and a welfare-warfare state. None of these alliances was revolutionary in the sense that capitalist power was destroyed: each contained important elements of the business and commercial communities while attacking others. None came to power by formally overthrowing a preexisting political system, although in each case the opposition claimed that the methods used to take and exercise power (e.g., creation of political parties, expansion of presidential power, election by a minority of a sectional party candidate, expansion of federal government) were illegitimate. Similarly, none succeeded by force of arms alone, although, as will be explained in a moment, violence played an important role in each case. In what sense, then, were these alliances "revolutionary"?

The difficulty is that we are accustomed to thinking about political systems on the basis of two contrasting models: the *revolutionary model,* in which a society characterized by rigid class distinction, extremist ideologies and a suppressive political apparatus is ripped apart from time to time, and the *evolutionary model,* in which a liberal economic-political apparatus permits free play among interest groups in an essentially classless society, thus making possible change which is peaceful and gradual rather than violent and sudden. (A further implication in the contrast is that change in the revolutionary society is cyclical, and ultimately to no avail, while change in the evolutionary society is linear, and therefore "progressive.") Americans who deny that their nation has experienced a revolution generally have in mind images drawn from the experiences of revolutionary societies: the *canaille* have never stormed the White House; the

Bolsheviks have never subverted the army; America has never passed an election nor General Motors a dividend; therefore, there has been no revolution. But the distinction between revolutionary and evolutionary societies is a gross exaggeration, if not entirely false. France, the Soviet Union and China have known peaceful change and progress, while many of the most significant alterations of the American political system have been revolutionary in character. That is, drastic alterations both in the distribution of power and the mode of exercising it have been made rapidly, extra-legally and—in a sense now to be explained—violently.

Consider two contrasting scenarios. (A) Armed peasants surround the palace. Their leader breaks into the throne room, kills the king and promulgates a new constitution. This we call a "violent revolution." (B) Armed peasants surround the palace. Their leader is granted an audience with the king. The king counts up the number of peasants and the number of his troops and promulgates an amended constitution. This we call "peaceful change."

Facetious though it may be, scene B comes closer to the truth about political change in the United States than does the theory of peaceful evolution. Despite the fact that in America group consciousness has often superseded class consciousness, major alterations of the political order have taken place against a background of civil disorder and potential revolution or civil war. The admission of new group alliances to power has been accomplished through redefinition of the system itself, involving both the improvisation of new institutions and the exercise of powers formerly held to be unconstitutional. And new alliances, with their new constitutions, have frequently consolidated their power violently. These principles are illustrated by the three movements described above.

Jeffersonian

Jefferson and his new party came to power at the conclusion of two decades of farmer uprisings and urban riots, after a serious attempt at counter-revolution had been made by the ruling Federalists. Naturally enough, the Federalists considered the idea of competitive political parties to be seditious and unconstitutional, especially since Jefferson himself was a self-declared French sympathizer and revolutionary. If the Alien and Sedition Acts, which filled the jails with political prisoners, had not been repealed and Jefferson elected in 1800, the farmer-planter-worker coalition would either have become an armed alliance (Jeffersonians had been active among the Whiskey Rebels and were prepared to "nullify" offensive legislation) or the West would have attempted to secede (up to the time of the Louisiana Purchase, such attempts were still being made). Jefferson's presidency was considered by the great John Marshall to be a series of attacks on the United States Constitution, and Federalist New England continued to plot against the "Antichrist" in office until Jeffersonians fomented a war with England and Canada. The war ruined New England shipping, drove that section to threaten secession, and utterly destroyed the Federalist party. So complete was Jefferson's triumph that the two-party system became thereafter a one-party system, until Andrew Jackson attacked the Bank of the United States and regenerated an organized opposition.

Northern Republican

The northern Republican alliance was forged in an era of national disintegration, as civil disorder rose in the 1850's toward the level of civil war. The Republican party itself was founded in the year the Kansas-Nebraska civil war began; six subsequent years of violence polarized proslave and antislave sentiment North and South, driving the Whig party into the Republican coalition and splitting the Democratic party in two. As in the case of the Jeffersonian revolution, the law (in the form of Supreme Court interpretations of the Constitution) clearly favored the *ancien régime,* while congressional legislation in the 1850's reflected the conservative views of Stephen Douglas. The election of Lincoln—a minority President—deprived the system of its last ounce of legitimacy from the southern point of view, and the bloodiest war of the nineteenth century commenced. Civil disorder continued in the North throughout Lincoln's first administration (the New York draft riot was but the most serious of numerous anti-Republican riots and disturbances), and the Republicans would probably not have remained in power in 1864 but for the dubious soldiers' vote and the absence of southern voters. In fact, as Milton Viorst has suggested, Republican power rested for a long time on sheer force:

Relying on a minority faction as their base of support, the Republicans never quite managed to find a majority that was consistent and reliable. In 1868 and 1872, Grant won respectively by 300,000 and 750,000 votes, but in both elections virtually all of the white voters of the South were disfranchised. In 1876 and 1888, the Republican candidate actually polled fewer popular votes than the Democratic while achieving victory in the electoral college. . . . Thus, of seven elections from 1868 to 1892, the Republicans won five, but in only one—Benjamin Harrison's narrow victory in 1888— could they claim a nationwide majority.

Thus for a second time a revolutionary coalition was formed against the backdrop of civil disorder, and went to war to consolidate its gains, ruling a virtually one-party state for a long while thereafter.

New Deal

In the mid-1930's, with homeless farmers afoot and workers fighting bloody battles on the picket line, domestic fascists and Communists gaining broad support and the nation filled with a fear of violent revolution, Franklin Roosevelt made his famous "left turn" and rode to triumph on the shoulders of a new coalition. Again, the new alliance exercised power through instrumentalities which seemed both un-American and illegal, and which were for a long time held to be so by the United States Supreme Court. Again, changes in the political system were rapid and profound. And again, although Roosevelt can hardly be said to have "fomented" World War II, it was war, rather than politics as usual, which silenced the domestic opposition, solved the problems of unemployment and underproduction, and made possible Roosevelt's four terms. Postwar militarization and prosperity ensured the continuing hegemony of the coalition which ruled through both political parties without serious challenge until civil disorder began anew in the 1960's.

Perhaps these movements were not revolutionary in the Marxist sense. Very well, but the moral is clear: how much civil disorder there has been, how much turmoil, and how much blood spilled just to obtain the relatively minor structural changes represented by the alliances of Jefferson, Lincoln and Roosevelt!

We have drawn attention to modern manifestations among black Americans of secessionism and violent revolt, and have noted that such movements are not at present revolutionary, although their revolutionary potential increases with the passage of time and the continuation of black powerlessness. The matter of revolutionary alliances, however, generates additional questions for the contemporary analyst. Is the period of mass protest and civil disorder which began earlier in the 1960's the modern equivalent of the 1790's, 1850's or 1930's? Against the backdrop of this disorder, is a new political alliance in the process of formation? If so, will it take power nonviolently or resort to violence? In either case, will there be the equivalent of a counterrevolution? Obviously, when one is deeply involved in the events of the day, answers to such questions come hard. Nevertheless, it is worthwhile to speculate on the possible persistence of the pattern elucidated thus far.

As mentioned earlier, one factor inhibiting mass revolutionary movements in the United States has been the inclination of oppressed groups sharing a common cultural heritage to define themselves as "nations," thus making it initially very difficult to work with "outsiders." On the other hand, we have also seen that prolonged revolt can produce a political awakening in which the insurgent group, increasingly aware of its goals and impatient for power, seeks like-minded allies from without. The result, therefore, is a three-stage process, through which several domestic groups are now proceeding: (a) cooperation with a broad cross-section of similarly situated groups and groups in power for purposes of gaining quick access to the system through moderate reform; (b) disillusionment and withdrawal from multigroup activity, selection of new leaders, redefinition of goals and solidification on the basis of group nationalism; and (c) cooperation with carefully selected groups in and out of power as part of a broader strategy for radical change.

It is interesting to note, in this regard, that it is now the most militant black leaders who speak of a black-white alliance—men like the late Malcolm X and Eldridge Cleaver—while orthodox black nationalists appear to have reached a plateau in terms of both their numbers and their political thought. Equally important, black students, both in high schools and in colleges, have established patterns of cooperation with members of other minority groups as well as white radicals. Meanwhile, the latter move through the same three-stage process, beginning with indiscriminate collaboration (as in the civil rights movement and Senator Eugene McCarthy's presidential campaign in 1968), continuing into withdrawal and the development of group nationalism (as we shall see in a moment, this is happening right now) and ending in selective collaboration based upon a redefined group interest.

Implicit in the idea of revolutionary group alliances rather than economic class alliances is the notion that the unit of revolt in America is the "subnation," and that before there can be an alliance there must be conscious and coherent subnational groups. This is why it is so difficult at present to plot the development of new alliances; not all potential members have yet experienced the process described above. For white radicals, for example, the question is whether their group identity will be stabilized and maintained beyond college, and after termination of the Vietnam War. Young radicals clearly do *not* fit easily into the tradition of group insurgency represented by Appalachian farmers, white southerners, and urban blacks, since in one sense they are not a "subnation"; and in another, being predominantly middle-class in origin, they are not an out-group at all. In an almost Darwinian response to these requirements, however, they are in the process of creating an *ethos* —an amalgam of cultural tastes, political attitudes, ethical norms and social mores which is the analogue of ethnicity, or perhaps even a new form of it. (One piece of evidence supporting this thesis is the growth of a racist stereotype which pictures all radicals as dirty, over-sexed, foul-smelling, addicted to drugs, incurably violence-prone, etc.—in fact the whole battery of anti-Irish and anti-Negro prejudices!) Additionally, as they emerge from college without returning to the family fold or

entering the world of the great corporations and traditional professions, their movement develops an economic base comprising selected traditional occupations (such as teaching or labor union work), newly created occupations (community organizing, international development work and service in independent institutes or foundations), and new branches of traditional occupations (legal services for the poor, group medical practice, community-owned businesses).

Additionally, like their rebellious predecessors, today's new leftists seek the equivalent of controllable territory by occupying existing communities (the East Village in New York, Old Town in Chicago or the Telegraph area of Berkeley), participating in community control movements elsewhere and attempting to play a more authoritative role in the administration of universities and university communities. Violent confrontations on college campuses become somewhat more comprehensible when one keeps in mind that the student activists and their supporters are not merely reformers attempting to improve their lot during a four-year hitch, or young folks raising youthful hell. They are members of an emerging social and political group with hopes of permanence, whose principal economic, political and territorial base is, and will remain for some time, the university community. Those colleges which have experienced the most intense conflict have therefore been precisely those in cities in which a radical community is in the process of formation both on and off campus. It comes as no surprise to see the most explosive confrontations taking place in San Francisco, Boston, New York and Chicago.

As the pace of political change quickens, other out-groups are experiencing a process of revolt and awakening similar to that undergone by urban blacks and white radicals. In some cases, the process is telescoped into a comparatively short period of time; the militant organization of labor leader Cesar Chavez, for example, has had an electrifying effect on the Mexican-American farm workers of California. Mexican Americans in the Southwest have begun to fight for their lost land. A new cadre of American Indian leaders now preaches the doctrine of "red power" to willing ears, and at several universities American Indian students have joined black and African, Asian and

Latin American "Third World" students in confrontations with police. In other cases, the initial period of collaboration has barely begun. Despite awakening outside interest in the rural poor and their unemployed brethren in the cities, the masses of rural poor people and poor urban whites remain voiceless. Yet even here there are signs of stirring —the "black lung" revolt of West Virginia miners, the participation of Appalachian whites and Puerto Ricans in the Poor People's March of 1968, the formation of community unions among urban "hill-billies," and so forth.

The formation of a new out-group alliance with revolutionary political potential has therefore not yet occurred. It would be rash, however, to predict that it could not occur in a fairly short time—say by 1975—given the speed of the spreading wave of political awakening. Before this can take place, the historical material suggests that one other change is necessary: a falling out among members of the present ruling coalition. In the past, no significant alteration of the political system has occurred without the development of serious divisions among groups in power; all past alliances which have been successful have split the middle and upper middle classes, attaching elements of each to the new coalition. This, of course, is one reason why American revolutionary movements do not seem "revolutionary," and why some radicals now argue that the new alliance, if any, must be anticapitalist. In any event, it is fairly clear that the disintegration of the present ruling coalition has already begun. The development of a radical group identity among large elements of the young has already split the suburban middle class, at least generationally. Furthermore, organized labor is now entering a period characterized by widespread discontent with the established leadership, political polarization and competition between dissidents of the Right and the Left, and the growth of schismatic movements at both local and national levels.

The fact that in 1968 the established union leadership kept the labor vote generally in line for Hubert Humphrey was widely misinterpreted as a sign that no significant changes were taking place in that movement. Political scientists have an unfortunate tendency to interpret electoral behavior as the key to a group's politics when, for a variety of reasons, how men vote may bear little relationship to their deepest political desires and clearest intentions. For example, probably labor voted for Humphrey not because the rank and file trusted George Meany or shared his political philosophy, but because there was no viable candidate of the Right (George Wallace being a southerner with a lifelong record of opposition to labor) or the Left (Robert Kennedy being dead, and the other candidates of the Left black socialists) to whom they could turn. The vote for Nixon-Humphrey, the candidates of the Center, may have represented a widely felt wish for peace and order—but, as we have seen, such wishes are by no means inconsistent with action at the group level whose effect is to overthrow the established order. In any event, developments since that election—including a formal schism between the conservative AFL-CIO and the more liberal United Auto Workers and Teamsters Unions, the formation of radical and black caucuses in dozens of labor unions, the organization of white block clubs and "support your local police" associations in many blue-collar neighborhoods, and the formation of new unions, both right-wing and left-wing, outside the established labor structure—make it clear that the processes of change within the labor movement are accelerating rather than slowing down.

The very same thing is true (although not often recognized by radical critics of the establishment) of other traditionally capitalist or managerial groups, many of which are in the process of being "declassed" as the result of a growing socioeconomic gap between lower middle and upper middle classes. As the technological revolution proceeds and industrial concentration continues, as costs of living and of doing business rise without letup, Horatio Alger begins to disappear even as myth. Small businessmen know that they will never be big businessmen; they will be lucky to be able to educate their children. Small farmers know that their days on the land are numbered, and that the only successful farmer is the agricultural corporation. Even within the corporate world, lower management personnel are aware that they have "plateaued out"—and that survival rather than advancement is now the goal. As John McDermott has pointed out, lower management jobs, like those of teachers and many professionals, are being industrialized. All of these groups and more (including a growing proportion of younger professionals and intellectuals) have common complaints based in part upon the powerlessness and boredom of life in a technocratic society. And it may be that they will discover they have common enemies. When this happens, a revolutionary alliance will be in existence.

At this point, however, one must confront directly a question which plagues any analyst of contemporary social change, particularly if his sympathies are with the dispossessed. We have seen on several occasions that although working-class and middle-class discontent may catalyze a revolutionary alliance, it may also be directed socially downward, against those out-groups which are in direct competition for jobs and living space with workers and members of the lower middle class. The specter of domestic reaction—the formation, out of the wreckage of the present political system, of a right-wing alliance which would annihilate moderates and radicals alike—is frequently invoked in these troubled days to prevent those out of power from "rocking the boat."

"If you think what you have now is bad, just wait until your real enemies take over!" runs the refrain. American radicals are frequently reminded that the German Communists of the early 1930's helped to bring Hitler to power by voting with the Nazis in the Reichstag in order to weaken the ruling Social Democratic coalition. In effect, defenders of the status quo contend that, as in Germany in 1931–1932, the only alternative to rule by the present coalition in the United States is a police state—an argument which rests upon the assumption that what most workers, small businessmen, farmers, housewives and professionals really want is an authoritarian government which would establish order at all costs. Therefore, the argument concludes, increasing political agitation, which produces social disorder, is the surest road to domestic fascism.

To this line of reasoning there is no easy answer. The possibility of a realignment dominated by a right-wing coalition is one of the risks to be weighed by any group which seeks to alter the distribution of political power. One would be worse than a fool to adopt the slogan of the German Communists, "After the Nazis, us," as an article of faith or a corollary of historical necessity.

There is, however, a more complex and persuasive answer.

It is erroneous to assume that what any group "really" wants is either stability or change; most groups want both simultaneously. By measuring reactions and testing group responses at a time when existing political configurations are beginning to break up—at an early stage in the process of political polarization and alliance formation—one will almost always find a vast majority of those polled leaning towards stability. There are several reasons for this: The inevitability of change is not yet accepted; initial reactions to conduct which seems unusual and "disorderly" are usually negative; and since new alliances are not yet formed, each group desires change for itself and stability for everyone else. Thus, at the beginning of what we might call the revolutionary process, the Right always seems extremely strong. As the process continues, however, initial reactions to social disorder are qualified (this may be seen, for example, by comparing the results of polls of urban blacks taken immediately after ghetto riots with those taken somewhat later). The society becomes conditioned to accepting a higher degree of political militancy and social turbulence (compare the front-page newspaper coverage of the 1964 disturbance at Berkeley with the minimal reporting of the much more serious People's Park disturbance of 1969). The irreversibility of change is increasingly accepted, and the question is then not *whether* there will be change or order but what *kind* of change will prevail. At this point, diverse groups realize that they cannot fight alone, new alliances are formed, and eventually a new national consensus may come into being.

This analysis does not tell us very much about the shape and content of the new consensus; it does not, for example, negate the possibility of domination by the extreme Right. What it *does* show, however, is that sampling public opinion prematurely is not only useless but misleading, particularly where such samples are used to predict the probable outcome of a period of revolutionary change. If a rightist coalition eventually takes power, it will not be composed of sentimental opponents of change but of the apostles of a new order—for example, overt racists and militarists. But the ultimate Right is no more indentifiable at present than the ultimate Left. No group in American society is inherently "right-wing" or "left-wing," especially since the meaning of these terms continues to change. The shape of the future political system therefore depends upon how the groups we have discussed come to perceive their interests as the revolutionary process continues—whom they deem to be their friends and whom their enemies.

Will the labor movement five to ten years hence follow the successors of George Wallace or the successors of Robert Kennedy? Will members of the lower middle class support existing business and professional elites or attempt to depose them? Will professors align themselves with their boards of trustees or their students? No one knows the answer to such questions, since even such supposedly hard-core conservative groups as big business and the military are riven by internal dissension and debate. It is entirely incorrect to assume, however, as many analysts do, that increasing political turbulence will inevitably push "doubtful" groups to the Right. In the turbulent, disorderly 1850's, the northern business community found its way into the arms of abolitionists and Free-Soilers, just as American farmers moved in the turbulent, disorderly 1930's from a brief flirtation with protofascism into alliance with organized labor and urban immigrant groups. There was, of course, nothing inevitable about these developments. Indeed, what they demonstrate is the *noninevitability* of specific political realignments, and the critical importance, therefore, of continuing ideological competition, political agitation and organization during revolutionary periods. At such times, radical change *is* possible. Therefore, the most foolish thing that either Left, Right or Center could do in the present crisis would be to remain passive out of fear that action might strengthen their enemies.

In any event, a nation which calls itself democratic ought not to fear the people. In the panic over a possible resurgence of the Right one hears echoes of the Federalists' disdain for "the mob," the assumption being that if the masses *really* ruled America, they would (being brutes) brutalize it. (This aristocratic attitude is never too far from the surface of American liberalism.) Once again, however, we see how the establishment protects itself by attacking extremism rather than the causes of extremism. If American workingmen, for example, are beginning to act in a dangerously racist fashion, this is not because they are *canaille* but because the present economic and political system has failed them as it has failed the blacks—because they feel compelled to defend the little they have against threatening forces, real or fancied. The democratic response, I should think, is not to manipulate the system so as to deprive "racists" of power, but to meet the challenge squarely in the political arena by persuading workers that their enemies are those who profit from struggle between the poor and the recently poor. Those that will not make such a fight lack faith in the people and in the democratic process. Fortunately for the nation, however, they no longer speak for the young.

The turmoil of the 1960's may well herald the beginning of another revolutionary phase in American history. Sooner or later—and probably sooner—the inability of the present ruling coalition to satisfy the human needs and political demands of its subjects will become clearly apparent, and the processes of political disintegration and reconstruction will accelerate. Hopefully, as the necessity for systemic change is accepted, political violence will be reduced even as political controversy intensifies. For those willing to accept the new age on its own terms, it will be an exhilarating time to be alive.

POST-SCARCITY ANARCHISM

Murray Bookchin

All the successful revolutions of the past have been particularistic revolutions of minority classes seeking to assert their specific interests over those of society as a whole. The great bourgeois revolutions of modern times offered an ideology of sweeping political reconstitution, but in reality they merely certified the social dominance of the bourgeoisie, giving formal political expression to the economic ascendancy of capital. The lofty notions of the "nation," the "free citizen," of "equality before the law," concealed the mundane reality of the centralized state, the atomized isolated man, the dominance of bourgeois interest. Despite their sweeping ideological claims, the particularistic revolutions replaced the rule of one class by another, one system of exploitation by another, one system of toil by another, and one system of psychological repression by another.

What is unique about our era is that the particularistic revolution has now been subsumed by the possibility of the generalized revolution—complete and totalistic. Bourgeois society, if it achieved nothing else, revolutionized the means of production on a scale unprecedented in history. This technological revolution, culminating in cybernation, has created the objective, quantitative basis for a world without class rule, exploitation, toil, or material want. The means now exist for the development of the rounded man, the total man, freed of guilt and the workings of authoritarian modes of training, and given over to desire and the sensuous apprehension of the marvelous. It is now possible to conceive of man's future experience in terms of a coherent process in which the bifurcations of thought and activity, mind and sensuousness, discipline and spontaneity, individuality and community, man and nature, town and country, education and life, work and play are all resolved, harmonized, and organically wedded in a qualitatively

new realm of freedom. Just as the particularized revolution produced a particularized, bifurcated society, so the generalized revolution can produce an organically unified, many-sided community. The great wound opened by propertied society in the form of the "social question" can now be healed.

That freedom must be conceived of in human terms, not in animal terms—in terms of life, not of survival—is clear enough. Men do not remove their ties of bondage and become fully human merely by divesting themselves of social domination and obtaining freedom in its *abstract* form. They must also be free *concretely:* free from material want, from toil, from the burden of devoting the greater part of their time—indeed, the greater part of their lives—to the struggle with necessity. To have seen these material preconditions for human freedom, to have emphasized that freedom presupposes free time and the material abundance for abolishing free time as a social privilege, is the great contribution of Karl Marx to modern revolutionary theory.

By the same token, the *preconditions* for freedom must not be mistaken for the *conditions* of freedom. The *possibility* of liberation does not constitute its *reality*. Along with its positive aspects, technological advance has a distinctly negative, socially regressive side. If it is true that technological progress enlarges the historical potentiality for freedom, it is also true that the bourgeois control of technology reinforces the established organization of society and everyday life. Technology and the resources of abundance furnish capitalism with the means for assimilating large sections of society to the established system of hierarchy and authority. They provide the system with the weaponry, the detecting devices and the propaganda media for the threat as well as the reality of massive repression. By their centralistic nature, the resources of abundance reinforce the monopolistic, centralistic and bureaucratic tendencies in the political apparatus. In short, they furnish the state with historically unprecedented means for manipulating and mobilizing the entire environment of life—and for perpetuating hierarchy, exploitation and unfreedom.

It must be emphasized, however, that this manipulation and mobilization of the environment is extremely problematical and laden with crises. Far from leading to pacification (one can hardly speak, here, of harmonization), the attempt of bourgeois society to control and exploit its environment, natural as well as social, has devastating consequences. Volumes have been written on the pollution of the atmosphere and waterways, on the destruction of tree cover and soil, and on toxic materials in foods and liquids. Even more threatening in their final results are the pollution and destruction of the very ecology required for a complex organism like man. The concentration of radioactive wastes in living things is a menace to the health and genetic endowment of nearly all species. Worldwide contamination by pesticides that inhibit oxygen production in plankton or by the near-toxic level of lead from gasoline exhaust are examples of an enduring pollution that threatens the biological integrity of all advanced lifeforms—including man.

No less alarming is the fact that we must drastically revise our traditional notions of what constitutes an environmental pollutant. A few decades ago it would have been absurd to describe carbon dioxide and heat as pollutants in the customary sense of the term. Yet both may well rank among the most serious sources of future ecological imbalance and may pose major threats to the viability of the planet. As a result of industrial and domestic combustion activities, the quantity of carbon dioxide in the atmosphere has increased by roughly twenty-five percent in the past one hundred years, and may well double by the end of the century. The famous "greenhouse effect" which the increasing quantity of the gas is expected to produce has been widely discussed in the media; eventually, it is supposed, the gas will inhibit the dissipation of the world's heat into space, causing a rise in overall temperatures which will melt the polar ice caps and result in the inundation of vast coastal areas. Thermal pollution, the result mainly of warm water discharged by nuclear and conventional

power plants, has had disastrous effects on the ecology of lakes, rivers and estuaries. Increases in water temperature not only damage the physiological and reproductive activities of the fish, they also promote the great blooms of algae that have become such formidable problems in waterways.

Ecologically, bourgeois exploitation and manipulation are undermining the very capacity of the earth to sustain advanced forms of life. The crisis is being heightened by massive increases in air and water pollution; by a mounting accumulation of nondegradable wastes, lead residues, pesticide residues and toxic additives in food; by the expansion of cities into vast urban belts; by increasing stresses due to congestion, noise, and mass living; and by the wanton scarring of the earth as a result of mining operations, lumbering, and real estate speculation. As a result, the earth has been despoiled in a few decades on a scale that is unprecedented in the entire history of human habitation of the planet.

Socially, bourgeois exploitation and manipulation have brought everyday life to the most excruciating point of vacuity and boredom. As society has been converted into a factory and a marketplace, the very rationale of life has been reduced to production for its own sake—and consumption for its own sake.[1]

THE REDEMPTIVE DIALECTIC

Is there a redemptive dialectic that can guide the social development in the direction of an anarchic society where people will attain full control over their daily lives? Or does the social dialectic come to an end with capitalism, its possibilities sealed off by the use of a highly advanced technology for repressive and co-optative purposes?

We must learn here from the limits of Marxism, a project which, understandably in a period of material scarcity, anchored the social dialectic and the contradictions of capitalism in the economic realm. Marx, it has been emphasized, examined the *preconditions for* liberation, not the *conditions of* liberation. The Marxian critique is rooted in the past, in the era of material want and relatively limited technological development. Even its humanistic theory of alienation turns primarily on the issue of work and man's alienation from the product of his labor. Today, however, capitalism is a parasite on the future, a vampire that survives on the technology and resources of freedom. The industrial capitalism of Marx's time organized its commodity relations around a prevailing system of material scarcity; the state capitalism of our time organizes its commodity relations around a prevailing system of material abundance. A century ago, scarcity had to be endured; today, it has to be enforced—hence the importance of the state in the present era. It is not that modern capitalism has resolved its contradictions[2] and annulled the social dialectic, but rather that the social dialectic and the contradictions of capitalism have expanded from the economic to the hierarchical realms of society, from the abstract "historic" domain to the concrete minutiae of everyday experience, from the arena of survival to the arena of life.

The dialectic of bureaucratic state capitalism originates in the contradiction between the repressive character of commodity society and the enormous potential freedom opened by technological advance. This contradiction also opposes the exploitative organization of society to the natural world—a world that includes not only the natural environment, but also man's "nature"—his Eros-derived impulses. The contradiction between the exploitative organization of society and the natural environment is beyond co-optation: the atmosphere, the waterways, the soil and the ecology required for human survival are not redeemable by reforms, concessions, or modifications of strategic policy. There is no technology that can reproduce atmospheric oxygen in sufficient quantities to sustain life on this planet. There is no substitute for the hydrological systems of the earth. There is no technique for removing massive environmental pollution by radioactive isotopes, pesticides, lead and petroleum wastes. Nor is there the faintest evidence that bourgeois society will relent at any time in the foreseeable future in its disruption of vital ecological processes, in its exploitation of natural resources, in its use of the atmosphere and waterways as dumping areas for wastes, or in its cancerous mode of urbanization and land abuse.

Even more immediate is the contradiction between the exploitative organization of society and man's Eros-derived impulses—a contradiction that manifests itself as the banalization and impoverishment of experience in a bureaucratically manipulated, impersonal mass society. The Eros-derived impulses in man can be repressed and sublimated, but they can never be eliminated. They are renewed with every birth of a human being and with every generation of youth. It is not surprising today that the young, more than any economic class or stratum, articulate the life-impulses in humanity's nature—the urgings of desire, sensuousness, and the lure of the marvelous. Thus, the biological matrix, from which hierarchical society emerged ages ago, reappears at a new level with the era that marks the end of hierarchy, only now this matrix is saturated with social phenomena. Short of manipulating humanity's germ plasm, the life-impulses can be annulled only with the annihilation of man himself.

The contradictions within bureaucratic state capitalism permeate all the hierarchical forms developed and overdeveloped by bourgeois society. The hierarchical forms which nurtured propertied society for ages and promoted its development—the state, city, centralized economy, bureaucracy, patriarchal family, and marketplace—have reached their historic limits. They have exhausted their social functions as modes of stabilization. It is not a question of whether these hierarchical forms were ever "progressive" in the Marxian sense of the term. As Raoul Vaneigem has observed: "Perhaps it isn't enough to say that hierarchical power has preserved humanity for thousands of years as alcohol preserves a fetus, by arresting either growth or decay." Today these forms constitute the target of all the revolutionary forces that are generated by modern capitalism, and whether one sees their outcome as nuclear catastrophe or ecological disaster *they now threaten the very survival of humanity.*

With the development of hierarchical forms into a threat to the very existence of humanity, the social dialectic, far from being annulled, acquires a new dimension. It poses the "social question" in an entirely new way. If man had to acquire the conditions of survival in order to live (as Marx emphasized), now he must acquire the conditions of life in order to survive. By this inversion of the relationship between survival and life, revolution acquires a new sense of urgency. No longer are we faced with Marx's famous choice of socialism or barbarism; we are confronted with the more drastic alternatives of anarchism or annihilation. The problems of necessity and survival have become congruent with the problems of freedom and life. They cease to require any theoretical mediation, "transitional" stages, or centralized organizations to bridge the gap between the existing and the possible. The possible, in fact, is all that can exist. Hence, the problems of "transition," which occupied the Marxists for nearly a century, are eliminated not only by the advance of technology, but by the social dialectic itself. The problems of social reconstruction have been reduced to practical tasks that can be solved spontaneously by self-liberatory acts of society.

Revolution, in fact, acquires not only a new sense of urgency, but a new sense of promise. In the hippies' tribalism, in the drop-out lifestyles and free sexuality of millions of youth, in the spontaneous affinity groups of the anarchists, we find forms of affirmation that follow from acts of negation. With the inversion of the "social question" there is also an inversion of the social dialectic; a "yea" emerges automatically and simultaneously with a "nay."

The solutions take their point of departure from the problems. When the time has arrived in history that the state, the city, bureaucracy, the centralized economy, the patriarchal family and the marketplace have reached their historic limits, what is posed is no longer a change in form but the absolute negation of *all* hierarchical forms *as such*. The absolute negation of the state is anarchism—a situation in which men liberate not only "history," but all the immediate circumstances of their everyday lives. The absolute negation of the city is community—a community in which the social environment is decentralized into rounded, ecologically balanced communes. The absolute negation of bureaucracy is immediate as distinguished from mediated relations—a situation in which representation is replaced by face-to-face relations in a general assembly of free individuals. The absolute negation of the centralized economy is regional ecotechnology—a situation in which the instruments of production are molded to the resources of an ecosystem. The absolute negation of the patriarchal family is liberated sexuality—in which all

forms of sexual regulation are transcended by the spontaneous, untrammeled expression of eroticism among equals. The absolute negation of the marketplace is communism—in which collective abundance and cooperation transform labor into play and need into desire.

SPONTANEITY AND UTOPIA

It is not accidental that at a point in history when hierarchical power and manipulation have reached their most threatening proportions, the very concepts of hierarchy, power, and manipulation are being brought into question. The challenge to these concepts comes from a rediscovery of the importance of spontaneity—a rediscovery nourished by ecology, by a heightened conception of self-development, and by a new understanding of the revolutionary process in society.

What ecology has shown is that balance in nature is achieved by organic variation and complexity, not by homogeneity and simplification. For example, the more varied the flora and fauna of an ecosystem, the more stable the population of a potential pest. The more environmental diversity is diminished, the greater will the population of a potential pest fluctuate, with the probability that it will get out of control. Left to itself, an ecosystem tends spontaneously toward organic differentiation, greater variety of flora and fauna, and diversity in the number of prey and predators. This does not mean that interference by man must be avoided. The need for a productive agriculture—itself a form of interference with nature—must always remain in the foreground of an ecological approach to food cultivation and forest management. No less important is the fact that man can often produce changes in an ecosystem that would vastly improve its ecological quality. But these efforts require insight and understanding, not the exercise of brute power and manipulation.

This concept of management, this new regard for the importance of spontaneity, has far-reaching applications for technology and community—indeed, for the social image of man in a liberated society. It challenges the capitalist ideal of agriculture as a factory operation, organized around immense, centrally controlled land-holdings, highly specialized forms of monoculture, the reduction of the terrain to a factory floor, the substitution of chemical for organic processes, the use of gang-labor, etc. If food cultivation is to be a mode of cooperation with nature rather than a contest between opponents, the agriculturist must become thoroughly familiar with the ecology of the land; he must acquire a new sensitivity to its needs and possibilities. This presupposes the reduction of agriculture to a human scale, the restoration of moderate-sized agricultural units, and the diversification of the agricultural situation; in short, it presupposes a decentralized, ecological system of food cultivation.

The same reasoning applies to pollution control. The development of giant factory complexes and the use of single- or dual-energy sources are responsible for atmospheric pollution. Only by developing smaller industrial units and diversifying energy sources by the extensive use of clean power (solar, wind, and water power) will it be possible to reduce industrial pollution. The means for this radical technological change are now at hand. Technologists have developed miniaturized substitutes for large-scale industrial operation—small versatile machines and sophisticated methods for converting solar, wind, and water energy into power usable in industry and the home. These substitutes are often more productive and less wasteful than the large-scale facilities that exist today.

The implications of small-scale agriculture and industry for a community are obvious: if humanity is to use the principles needed to manage an ecosystem, the basic communal unit of social life must itself become an ecosystem—an ecocommunity. It too must become diversified, balanced and well-rounded. By no means is this concept of community motivated exclusively by the need for a lasting balance between man and the natural world; it also accords with the utopian ideal of the rounded man, the individual whose sensibilities, range of experience and lifestyle are nourished by a wide range of stimuli, by a diversity of activities, and by a social scale that always remains within the comprehension of a single human being. Thus the means and conditions of survival become the means and conditions of life; need becomes desire and desire becomes need. The point is reached where the greatest social decomposition provides the source of the highest form of social integration, bringing the most pressing ecological necessities into a common focus with the highest utopian ideals.

If it is true, as Guy Debord observes, that "daily life is the measure of everything: of the fulfillment or rather the nonfulfillment of human relationships, of the use we make of our time," a question arises: Who are "we" whose daily lives are to be fulfilled? And how does the liberated self emerge that is capable of turning time into life, space into community, and human relationships into the marvelous?

The liberation of the self involves, above all, a social process. In a society that has shriveled the self into a commodity—into an object manufactured for exchange—there can be no fulfilled self. There can only be the beginnings of selfhood, the *emergence* of a self that seeks fulfillment—a self that is largely defined by the obstacles it must overcome to achieve realization. In a society whose belly is distended to the bursting point with revolution, whose chronic state is an unending series of labor pains, whose real condition is a mounting emergency, only one thought and act is relevant—giving birth. Any environment, private or social, that does not make this fact the center of human experience is a sham and diminishes whatever self remains to us after we have absorbed our daily poison of everyday life in bourgeois society.

It is plain that the goal of revolution today must be the liberation of daily life. Any revolution that fails to achieve this goal is counterrevolution. Above all, it is *we* who have to be liberated, *our* daily lives, with all their moments, hours and days, and not universals like "History" and "Society."[3] The self must always be *identifiable* in the revolution, not overwhelmed by it. The self must always be *perceivable* in the revolutionary process, not submerged by it. There is no word that is more sinister in the "revolutionary" vocabulary than "masses." Revolutionary liberation must be a self-liberation that reaches social dimensions, not "mass liberation" or "class liberation" behind which lurks the rule of an elite, a hierarchy, and a state. If a revolution fails to produce a new society by the self-activity and self-mobilization of revolutionaries, if it does not involve the forging of a self in the revolutionary process, the revolution will once again circumvent those whose lives are to be lived every day and leave daily life unaffected. Out of the revolution must emerge a self that takes full possession of daily life, not a daily life that once again takes full possession of the self. The most advanced form of class consciousness thus becomes self-consciousness—the concretization in daily life of the great liberating universals.

If for this reason alone, the revolutionary movement is profoundly concerned with lifestyle. It must try to *live* the revolution in all its totality, not only participate in it. It must be deeply concerned with the way the revolutionist lives, his relations with the surrounding environment, and his degree of self-emancipation. In seeking to change society, the revolutionist cannot avoid changes in himself that demand the reconquest of his own being. Like the movement in which he participates, the revolutionist must try to reflect the conditions of the society he is trying to achieve—at least to the degree that this is possible today.

The treacheries and failures of the past half century have made it axiomatic that there *can be no separation of the revolutionary process from the revolutionary goal.* A society whose fundamental aim is self-administration in all facets of life can be achieved only by self-activity. This implies a mode of administration that is always possessed by the self. The power of man over man can be destroyed only by the very process in which man acquires power over his own life and in which he not only "discovers" himself but, more meaningfully, in which he formulates his selfhood in all its social dimensions.

A libertarian society can be achieved only by a libertarian revolution. Freedom cannot be "delivered" to the individual as the "end-product" of a "revolution"; the assembly and community cannot be legislated or decreed into existence. A revolutionary group can seek, purposively and consciously, to promote the creation of these forms, but if assembly and community are not allowed to emerge organically, if their growth is not matured by the process of demassification, by self-activity, and by self-realization, they will remain nothing but forms, like the soviets in postrevolutionary Russia. Assembly and community must arise within the revolutionary process; indeed, the revolutionary process must *be* the formation of assembly and

community, and also the destruction of power, property, hierarchy, and exploitation.

Revolution as self-activity is not unique to our time. It is the paramount feature of all the great revolutions in modern history. It marked the *journées* of the *sansculottes* in 1792 and 1793, the famous "Five Days" of February 1917 in Petrograd, the uprising of the Barcelona proletariat in 1936, the early days of the Hungarian Revolution in 1956, and the May-June events in Paris in 1968. Nearly every revolutionary uprising in the history of our time has been initiated spontaneously by the self-activity of "masses"—often in flat defiance of the hesitant policies advanced by the revolutionary organizations. Every one of these revolutions has been marked by extraordinary individuation, by a joyousness and solidarity that turned everyday life into a festival. This surreal dimension of the revolutionary process, with its explosion of deep-seated libidinal forces, grins irascibly through the pages of history like the face of a satyr on shimmering water. It is not without reason that the Bolshevik commissars smashed the wine bottles in the Winter Palace on the night of November 7, 1917.

The puritanism and work ethic of the traditional left stem from one of the most powerful forces opposing revolution today the capacity of the bourgeois environment to infiltrate the revolutionary framework. The origins of this power lie in the commodity nature of man under capitalism, a quality that is almost automatically transferred to the organized group—and which the group, in turn, reinforces in its members. As the late Josef Weber emphasized, all organized groups "have the tendency to render themselves autonomous, i.e., to alienate themselves from their original aim and to become an end in themselves in the hands of those administering them." This phenomenon is as true of revolutionary organizations as it is of state and semistate institutions, official parties and trade unions.

The problem of alienation can never be completely resolved apart from the revolutionary process itself, but it can be guarded against by an acute awareness that the problem exists, and partly solved by a voluntary but drastic remaking of the revolutionary and his group. This remaking can only begin when the revolutionary group recognizes that it is a catalyst in the revolutionary process, not a "vanguard." The revolutionary group must clearly see that its goal is not the seizure of power but the dissolution of power—indeed, it must see that the entire problem of power, of control from below and control from above, can be solved only if there is no above or below.

Above all, the revolutionary group must divest itself of the forms of power—statutes, hierarchies, property, prescribed opinions, fetishes, paraphernalia, official etiquette—and of the subtlest as well as the most obvious of bureaucratic and bourgeois traits that consciously and unconsciously reinforce authority and hierarchy. The group must remain open to public scrutiny not only in its formulated decisions but also in their very formulation. It must be coherent in the profound sense that its theory is its practice and its practice its theory. It must do away with all commodity relations in its day-to-day existence and constitute itself along the decentralizing organizational principles of the very society it seeks to achieve—community, assembly, spontaneity. It must, in Josef Weber's superb words, be "marked always by simplicity and clarity, always thousands of unprepared people can enter and direct it, always it remains *transparent* to and controlled by all." Only then, when the revolutionary movement is congruent with the decentralized community it seeks to achieve, can it avoid becoming another elitist obstacle to the social development and dissolve into the revolution like surgical thread into a healing wound.

PROSPECT

The most important process going on in America today is the sweeping de-institutionalization of the bourgeois social structure. A basic, far-reaching disrespect and a profound disloyalty are developing toward the values, the forms, the aspirations and, above all, the institutions of the established order. On a scale unprecedented in American history, millions of people are shedding their commitment to the society in which they live. They no longer believe in its claims. They no longer respect its symbols. They no longer accept its goals, and, most significantly, they refuse almost intuitively to live by its institutional and social codes.

This growing refusal runs very deep. It extends from an opposition to war into a hatred of political manipulation in all its forms. Starting from a rejection of racism, it brings into question the very existence of hierarchical power as such. In its detestation of middle-class values and lifestyles it rapidly evolves into a rejection of the commodity system; from an irritation with environmental pollution, it passes into a rejection of the American city and modern urbanism. In short, it tends to transcend every particularistic critique of the society and to evolve into a generalized opposition to the bourgeois order on an ever broadening scale.

In this respect, the period in which we live closely resembles the revolutionary Enlightenment that swept through France in the eighteenth century—a period that completely reworked French consciousness and prepared the conditions for the Great Revolution of 1789. Then as now, the old institutions were slowly pulverized by molecular action from below long before they were toppled by mass revolutionary action. This molecular movement creates an atmosphere of general lawlessness: a growing personal day-to-day disobedience, a tendency not to "go along" with the existing system, a seemingly "petty" but nevertheless critical attempt to circumvent restriction in every facet of daily life. The society, in effect, becomes disorderly, undisciplined, Dionysian—a condition that reveals itself most dramatically in an increasing rate of official crimes. A vast critique of the system develops—the actual Enlightenment itself, two centuries ago, and the sweeping critique that exists today—which seeps downward and accelerates the molecular movement at the base. Be it an angry gesture, a "riot" or a conscious change in lifestyle, an ever-increasing number of people—who have no more of a commitment to an organized revolutionary movement than they have to society itself—begin spontaneously to engage in their own defiant propaganda of the deed.

In its concrete details, the disintegrating social process is nourished by many sources. The process develops with all the unevenness, indeed with all the contradictions, that mark every revolutionary trend. In eighteenth-century France, radical ideology oscillated between a rigid scientism and a sloppy romanticism. Notions of freedom were anchored in a precise, logical ideal of self-control, and also a vague, instinctive norm of spontaneity.

Rousseau stood at odds with d'Holbach, Diderot at odds with Voltaire; yet in retrospect we can see that one not only transcended but also presupposed the other in a *cumulative* development toward revolution.

The same uneven, contradictory, and cumulative development exists today, and in many cases it follows a remarkably direct course. The "beat" movement created the most important breach in the solid, middle-class values of the 1950's, a breach that was widened enormously by the illegalities of pacifists, civil rights workers, draft resisters, and longhairs. Moreover, the merely reactive response of rebellious American youth has produced invaluable forms of libertarian and utopian affirmation—the right to make love without restriction, the goal of community, the disavowal of money and commodities, the belief in mutual aid, and a new respect for spontaneity. Easy as it is for revolutionaries to criticize certain pitfalls within this orientation of personal and social values, the fact remains that it has played a preparatory role of decisive importance in forming the present atmosphere of indiscipline, spontaneity, radicalism and freedom.

A second parallel between the revolutionary Enlightenment and our own period is the emergence of the crowd, the so-called "mob," as a major vehicle of social protest. The typical institutionalized forms of public dissatisfaction—in our own day, they are orderly elections, demonstration, and mass meetings—tend to give way to direct action by crowds. This shift from predictable, highly organized protests within the institutionalized framework of the existing society to sporadic, spontaneous, near-insurrectionary assaults from outside (and even against) socially acceptable forms reflects a profound change in popular psychology. The "rioter" has begun to break, however partially and intuitively, with those deep-seated norms of behavior which traditionally weld the "masses" to the established order. He actively sheds the internalized structure of authority, the long-cultivated body of conditioned reflexes, and the pattern of submission sustained by guilt that tie one to the system even more effectively than any fear of police violence and juridical reprisal. Contrary to the views of social psychologists, who see in these modes of direct action the submission of

the individual to a terrifying collective entity called the "mob," the truth is that "riots" and crowd actions represent the first groupings of the mass toward individuation. The mass tends to become demassified in the sense that it begins to assert itself against the really massifying automatic responses produced by the bourgeois family, the school and the mass media. By the same token, crowd actions involve the rediscovery of the streets and the effort to liberate them. Ultimately, it is in the streets that power must be dissolved: for the streets, where daily life is endured, suffered, and eroded, and where power is confronted and fought, must be turned into the domain where daily life is enjoyed, created and nourished. The rebellious crowd marked the beginning not only of a spontaneous transmutation of private into social revolt, but also of a return from the abstractions of social revolt to the issues of everyday life.

Finally, as in the Enlightenment, we are seeing the emergence of an immense and ever-growing stratum of *déclassés,* a body of lumpenized individuals drawn from every stratum of society. The chronically indebted and socially insecure middle classes of our period compare loosely with the chronically insolvent and flighty nobility of prerevolutionary France. A vast flotsam of educated people emerged then as now, living at loose ends, without fixed careers or established social roots. At the bottom of both structures we find a large number of chronic poor—vagabonds, drifters, people with part-time jobs or no jobs at all, threatening, unruly *sans-culottes*—surviving on public aid and on the garbage thrown off by society, the poor of the Parisian slums, the blacks of the American ghettoes.

But here all the parallels end. The French Enlightenment belongs to a period of revolutionary transition from feudalism to capitalism—both societies based on economic scarcity, class rule, exploitation, social hierarchy, and state power. The day-to-day popular resistance which marked the eighteenth century and culminated in open revolution was soon disciplined by the newly emerging industrial order—as well as by naked force. The vast mass of *déclassés* and *sans-culottes* was largely absorbed into the factory system and tamed by industrial discipline. Formerly rootless intellectuals and footloose nobles found secure places in the economic, political, social and cultural hierarchy of the new bourgeois order. From a socially and culturally fluid condition, highly generalized in its structure and relations, society hardened again into rigid, particularized class and institutional forms—the classical Victorian era appeared not only in England but, to one degree or another, in all of Western Europe and America. Critique was consolidated into apologia, revolt into reform, *déclassés* into clearly defined classes, and "mobs" into political constituencies. "Riots" became the well-behaved processionals we call "demonstrations," and spontaneous direct action turned into electoral rituals.

Our own era is also a transitional one, but with a profound and new difference. In the last of their great insurrections, the *sans-culottes* of the French Revolution rose under the fiery cry: "Bread and the Constitution of '93!" The black *sans-culottes* of the American ghettoes rise under the slogan: "Black is beautiful!" Between these two slogans lies a development of unprecedented importance. The *déclassés* of the eighteenth century were formed during a slow transition from an agricultural to an industrial era; they were created out of a pause in the historical transition from one regime of toil to another. The demand for bread could have been heard at any time in the evolution of propertied society. The new *déclassés* of the twentieth century are being created as a result of the bankruptcy of all social forms based on toil. They are the end products of the process of propertied society itself and of the social problems of material survival. In the era when technological advances and cybernation have brought into question the exploitation of man by man, toil, and material want in any form whatever, the cry "Black is beautiful" or "Make love, not war" marks the transformation of the traditional demand for survival into a historically new demand for life.[4] What underpins every social conflict in the United States today is the demand for the realization of all human potentialities in a fully rounded, balanced, totalistic way of life. In short, the potentialities for revolution in America are now anchored in the potentialities of man himself.

What we are witnessing is the breakdown of a century and a half of embourgeoisement and a pulverization of all bourgeois institutions *at a point in history when the boldest concepts of utopia are realizable.* And there is nothing that the present bourgeois order can substitute for the destruction of its traditional institutions but bureaucratic manipulation and state capitalism. This process is unfolding most dramatically in the United States. Within a period of little more than two decades, we have seen the collapse of the "American Dream," or what amounts to the same thing, the steady destruction in the United States of the myth that material abundance, based on commodity relations between men, can conceal the inherent poverty of bourgeois life. Whether this process will culminate in revolution or in annihilation will depend in great part on the ability of revolutionists to extend social consciousness and defend the spontaneity of the revolutionary development from authoritarian ideologies, both of the "left" and of the right.

NOTES

[1] It is worth noting here that the emergence of the "consumer society" provides us with remarkable evidence of the difference between the industrial capitalism of Marx's time and state capitalism today. In Marx's view, capitalism as a system organized around "production for the sake of production" results in the economic immiseration of the proletariat. "Production for the sake of production" is paralleled today by "consumption for the sake of consumption," in which immiseration takes a spiritual rather than an economic form—it is starvation of life.

[2] The economic contradictions of capitalism have not disappeared, but the system can plan to such a degree that they no longer have the explosive characteristics they had in the past.

[3] Despite its lip service to the dialectic, the traditional left has yet to take Hegel's "concrete universal" seriously and see it not merely as a philosophical concept but as a social program. This has been done only in Marx's early writings, in the writings of the great utopians (Fourier and William Morris) and, in our time, by the drop-out youth.

[4] These lines were written in 1966. Since then, we have seen the graffiti on the walls of Paris, during the May-June revolution: "All power to the imagination"; "I take my desires to be reality, because I believe in the reality of my desires"; "Never work"; "The more I make love, the more I want to make revolution"; "Life without dead times"; "The more you consume, the less you live"; "Culture is the inversion of life"; "One does not buy happiness, one steals it"; "Society is a carnivorous flower." These are not graffiti, they are a program for life and desire.